EXAM✓CRAM

CISSP® Exam Cram

Fourth Edition

Michael Gregg

D0169553

CISSP® Exam Cram, Fourth Edition

Copyright © 2017 by Pearson Education, Inc.

All rights reserved. No part of this book shall be reproduced, stored in a retrieval system, or transmitted by any means, electronic, mechanical, photocopying, recording, or otherwise, without written permission from the publisher. No patent liability is assumed with respect to the use of the information contained herein. Although every precaution has been taken in the preparation of this book, the publisher and author assume no responsibility for errors or omissions. Nor is any liability assumed for damages resulting from the use of the information contained herein.

ISBN-13: 978-0-7897-5553-7

ISBN-10: 0-7897-5553-X

Library of Congress Control Number: 2016940474

Printed in the United States of America

1   16

Trademarks

All terms mentioned in this book that are known to be trademarks or service marks have been appropriately capitalized. Pearson cannot attest to the accuracy of this information. Use of a term in this book should not be regarded as affecting the validity of any trademark or service mark.

Warning and Disclaimer

Every effort has been made to make this book as complete and as accurate as possible, but no warranty or fitness is implied. The information provided is on an "as is" basis. The author and the publisher shall have neither liability nor responsibility to any person or entity with respect to any loss or damages arising from the information contained in this book.

Special Sales

For information about buying this title in bulk quantities, or for special sales opportunities (which may include electronic versions; custom cover designs; and content particular to your business, training goals, marketing focus, or branding interests), please contact our corporate sales department at corpsales@pearsoned.com or (800) 382-3419.

For government sales inquiries, please contact

governmentsales@pearsoned.com.

For questions about sales outside the U.S., please contact

intlcs@pearson.com.

Editor-in-Chief
Mark Taub

Product Line Manager
Brett Bartow

Acquisitions Editor
Michelle Newcomb

Development Editor
Ellie C. Bru

Managing Editor
Sandra Schroeder

Project Editor
Mandie Frank

Copy Editor
Larry Sulky

Indexer
Lisa Stumpf

Proofreader
H.S. Rupa

Technical Editors
Chris Crayton
Michael Angelo

Publishing Coordinator
Vanessa Evans

Page Layout
codeMantra

Contents at a Glance

Table of Contents

CHAPTER 11:
Software Development Security **541**

About the Author

As the CEO of Superior Solutions, Inc., a Houston-based IT security consulting and auditing firm, **Michael Gregg** has more than 20 years of experience in information security and risk management. He holds two associate's degrees, a bachelor's degree, and a master's degree. Some of the certifications he holds include CISSP, SSCP, MCSE, CTT+, A+, N+, Security+, CASP, CCNA, GSEC, CEH, CHFI, CEI, CISA, CISM, and CGEIT.

In addition to his experience with performing security audits and assessments, Gregg has authored or coauthored more than 20 books, including *Certified Ethical Hacker Exam Prep* (Que), *CISSP Exam Cram 2* (Que), and *Security Administrator Street Smarts* (Sybex). He has testified before U.S. Congress, his articles have been published on IT websites, and he has been sourced as an industry expert for CBS, ABC, CNN, Fox News and the New York Times. He has created more than 15 security-related courses and training classes for various companies and universities. Although audits and assessments are where he spends the bulk of his time, teaching and contributing to the written body of IT security knowledge are how Michael believes he can give something back to the community that has given him so much.

He is a board member for Habitat for Humanity and when not working, Michael enjoys traveling and restoring muscle cars.

About the Technical Reviewers

Chris Crayton (MCSE) is an author, technical consultant, and trainer. He has worked as a computer technology and networking instructor, information security director, network administrator, network engineer, and PC specialist. Chris has authored several print and online books on PC repair, CompTIA A+, CompTIA Security+, and Microsoft Windows. He has also served as technical editor and content contributor on numerous technical titles for several of the leading publishing companies. He holds numerous industry certifications, has been recognized with many professional teaching awards, and has served as a state-level SkillsUSA competition judge.

Michael Angelo During his tenure in security he was responsible for the secure development, implementation, and deployment of products. This included driving the creation of security solutions, policies and procedures, threat modeling and product analysis exercises, practical encryption techniques, biometric and token access authentication technology, common criteria certifications, and residual risk management scoring methodologies.

Amongst his accomplishments, Michael has 57 U.S. patents, was recognized by the City of Houston as the "2003 Inventor of the Year," and is a former Sigma-Xi distinguished lecturer. In 2011, he was named ISSA Security Professional of the Year and in 2013 was added to the ISSA Hall of Fame.

Dedication

I dedicate this book to my godson, Alexander Bucio.
May his life be filled with success and happiness. Mucho gusto!

Acknowledgments

I would like to thank my wife, Christine, for understanding the long hours such a project entails. Also, thanks to Michelle Newcomb and the entire Pearson crew.

We Want to Hear from You!

As the reader of this book, *you* are our most important critic and commentator. We value your opinion and want to know what we're doing right, what we could do better, what areas you'd like to see us publish in, and any other words of wisdom you're willing to pass our way.

We welcome your comments. You can email or write to let us know what you did or didn't like about this book—as well as what we can do to make our books better.

Please note that we cannot help you with technical problems related to the topic of this book.

When you write, please be sure to include this book's title and author as well as your name and email address. We will carefully review your comments and share them with the author and editors who worked on the book.

Email: feedback@pearsonitcertification.com
Mail: Pearson IT Certification
        ATTN: Reader Feedback
        800 East 96th Street
        Indianapolis, IN 46240 USA

Reader Services

Register your copy of *CISSP Exam Cram* at www.pearsonitcertification.com for convenient access to downloads, updates, and corrections as they become available. To start the registration process, go to www.pearsonitcertification.com/register and log in or create an account*. Enter the product ISBN 9780789755537 and click Submit. When the process is complete, you will find any available bonus content under Registered Products.

*Be sure to check the box that you would like to hear from us to receive exclusive discounts on future editions of this product.

Introduction

Welcome to *CISSP® Exam Cram!* This book covers the CISSP certification exam. Whether this is your first or your fifteenth *Exam Cram*, you'll find information here and in Chapter 1 that will ensure your success as you pursue knowledge, experience, and certification. This introduction explains the ISC^2 certification programs in general and talks about how the *Exam Cram* series can help you prepare for the CISSP exam.

This book is one of the *Exam Cram* series of books and will help by getting you on your way to becoming an ISC^2 Certified Information Systems Security Professional (CISSP).

This introduction discusses the basics of the CISSP exam. Included are sections covering preparation, how to take an exam, a description of this book's contents, how this book is organized, and, finally, author contact information.

Each chapter in this book contains practice questions. There are also two full-length practice exams at the end of the book. Practice exams in this book should provide an accurate assessment of the level of expertise you need to obtain to pass the test. Answers and explanations are included for all test questions. It is best to obtain a level of understanding equivalent to a consistent pass rate of at least 95% on the practice questions and exams in this book before you attempt the real exam.

Let's begin by looking at preparation for the exam.

How to Prepare for the Exam

Preparing for the CISSP exam requires that you obtain and study materials designed to provide comprehensive information about security. The following list of materials will help you study and prepare:

▶ The ISC^2 website at www.isc2.org

▶ The exam outline available at the ISC^2 website

Many people form study groups, attend seminars, and attend training classes to help them study for and master the material needed to pass the CISSP exam.

Practice Tests

You don't need to know much about practice tests, other than that they are a worthwhile expense for three reasons:

▶ They help you diagnose areas of weakness.

▶ They are useful for getting used to the format of questions.

▶ They help you to decide when you are ready to take the exam.

This book contains questions at the end of each chapter and includes two full-length practice tests. However, if you still want more, a related *Exam Cram CISSP Practice Questions* book has more than 500 additional questions. Many other companies provide CISSP certification practice tests, flash cards, and aids as well.

Taking a Certification Exam

When you have prepared for the exam, you must register with ISC^2 to take the exam. The CISSP exam is given at Pearson VUE testing centers. ISC^2 has implemented regional pricing: As an example, as of the publication of this book registration is $599 in the United States. Check the Pearson VUE website at www.pearsonvue.com to get specific details.

After you register, you will receive a confirmation notice. Some locations may have limited test centers available, which means that you should schedule your exam in advance to make sure you can get the specific date and time you would like.

Arriving at the Exam Location

As with any examination, arrive at the testing center early. Be prepared! You will need to bring the confirmation letter and identification, such as a driver's license, green card, or passport. Any photo ID will suffice. Two forms of ID are usually required. The testing center staff requires proof that you are who you say you are and that someone else is not taking the test for you. Arrive early because if you are late, you will be barred from entry and will not receive a refund for the cost of the exam.

ExamAlert

You'll be spending a lot of time in the exam room. The total test time is six hours, so eat a good breakfast. Policies differ from location to location regarding bathroom breaks—check with the testing center before beginning the exam.

In the Testing Center

You will not be allowed to take study materials or anything else into the examination room with you that could raise suspicion that you're cheating. This includes practice test material, books, exam prep guides, or other test aids.

After the Exam

Examination results are available after the exam. If you pass the exam, you will simply receive a passing grade—your exact score will not be provided. Candidates who do not pass will receive a complete breakdown on their score by domain. This allows those individuals to see what areas they are weak in.

Retaking a Test

If you fail the exam, you must wait at least 30 days to take it again. Each of the ten domains will be shown, with your score in each. As an example, you may have received a 95% score in the Communications and Network Security domain and only 12% in Asset Security. Use this feedback to better understand what areas you were weak in and where to spend your time and effort in your studies. Additionally, invest in some practice tests if you have not already done so. There is much to be said for getting used to a testing format.

Tracking Your CISSP Status

When you pass the exam, you still need to attest to the CISSP code of ethics and have an existing CISSP complete an endorsement form for you.

When you pass the exam, you will next be required to complete an endorsement form. The endorsement form must be completed by someone who can attest to your professional experience and who is an active CISSP in good standing. If you don't know anyone who is CISSP-certified, ISC^2 allows endorsements from other professionals who are certified, licensed, or commissioned, and an officer of the corporation where you are employed. You can review complete information on the endorsement form at the ISC^2 website.

About This Book

The ideal reader for an *Exam Cram* book is someone seeking certification. However, it should be noted that an *Exam Cram* book is an easily readable, rapid presentation of facts. Therefore, an *Exam Cram* book is also extremely useful as a quick reference manual.

Most people seeking certification use multiple sources of information. Check out the links at the end of each chapter to get more information about subjects you're weak in. Various security books from retailers also describe the topics in this book in much greater detail. Don't forget that many have described the CISSP exam as being a "mile wide."

This book includes other helpful elements in addition to the actual logical, step-by-step learning progression of the chapters themselves. *Exam Cram* books use elements such as exam alerts, tips, notes, and practice questions to make information easier to read and absorb.

> **Note**
>
> Reading this book from start to finish is not necessary; this book is set up so that you can quickly jump back and forth to find sections you need to study.

Use the *Cram Sheet* to remember last-minute facts immediately before the exam. Use the practice questions to test your knowledge. You can always brush up on specific topics in detail by referring to the table of contents and the index. Even after you achieve certification, you can use this book as a rapid-access reference manual.

The Chapter Elements

Each *Exam Cram* book has chapters that follow a predefined structure. This structure makes *Exam Cram* books easy to read and provides a familiar format for all *Exam Cram* books. The following elements typically are used:

▶ Opening hotlists

▶ Chapter topics

▶ Exam Alerts

▶ Notes

▶ Tips

▶ Sidebars

▶ Cautions

▶ Exam preparation practice questions and answers

▶ A "Need to Know More?" section at the end of each chapter

> **Note**
>
> Bulleted lists, numbered lists, tables, and graphics are also used where appropriate. A picture can paint a thousand words sometimes, and tables can help to associate different elements with each other visually.

Now let's look at each of the elements in detail.

▶ **Opening hotlists**—The start of every chapter contains a list of terms you should understand. A second hotlist identifies all the techniques and skills covered in the chapter.

▶ **Chapter topics**—Each chapter contains details of all subject matter listed in the table of contents for that particular chapter. The objective of an *Exam Cram* book is to cover all the important facts without giving too much detail; it is an exam cram. When examples are required, they are included.

▶ **Exam Alerts**—Exam Alerts address exam-specific, exam-related information. An Exam Alert addresses content that is particularly important, tricky, or likely to appear on the exam. An Exam Alert looks like this:

> **ExamAlert**
>
> Make sure you remember the different ways in which DES can be implemented and that ECB is considered the weakest form of DES.

▶ **Notes**—Notes typically contain useful information that is not directly related to the current topic under consideration. To avoid breaking up the flow of the text, they are set off from the regular text.

> **Note**
>
> This is a note. You have already seen several notes.

▶ **Tips**—Tips often provide shortcuts or better ways to do things.

> **Tip**
>
> A clipping level is the point at which you set a control to distinguish between activity that should be investigated and activity that should not be investigated.

▶ **Sidebars**—Sidebars are longer and run beside the text. They often describe real-world examples or situations.

How Caller ID Can Be Hacked

Sure, we all trust caller ID, but some Voice over IP (VoIP) providers allow users to inject their own call party number (CPN) into the call. Because VoIP is currently outside FCC regulation, these hacks are now possible.

▶ **Cautions**—Cautions apply directly to the use of the technology being discussed in the Exam Cram. For example, a Caution might point out that the CER is one of the most important items to examine when examining biometric devices.

> **Caution**
>
> The crossover error rate (CER) is the point at which Type 1 errors and Type 2 errors intersect. The lower the CER is, the more accurate the device is.

▶ **Exam preparation practice questions**—At the end of every chapter is a list of at least 10 exam practice questions similar to those in the actual exam. Each chapter contains a list of questions relevant to that chapter, including answers and explanations. Test your skills as you read.

▶ **"Need to Know More?" section**—This section at the end of each chapter describes other relevant sources of information. With respect to this chapter, the best place to look for CISSP certification information is at the ISC[2] website, www.ISC2.org.

Other Book Elements

Most of this *Exam Cram* book on CISSP follows the consistent chapter structure already described. However, there are various, important elements that are not part of the standard chapter format. These elements apply to the entire book as a whole.

▶ **Practice exams**—In addition to exam-preparation questions at the end of each chapter, two full practice exams are included at the end of the book.

▶ **Answers and explanations for practice exams**—These follow each practice exam, providing answers and explanations to the questions in the exams.

▶ **Glossary**—The glossary contains a listing of important terms used in this book with explanations.

▶ **Cram Sheet**—The Cram Sheet is a quick-reference, tear-out cardboard sheet of important facts useful for last-minute preparation. Cram Sheets often include a simple summary of facts that are most difficult to remember.

▶ **Companion website**—The companion website contains the Pearson IT Certification Practice Test engine, which provides multiple test modes that you can use for exam preparation. The practice tests are designed to appropriately balance the questions over each technical area (domain) covered by the exam. All concepts from the actual exam are covered thoroughly to ensure you're prepared for the exam.

Chapter Contents

The following list provides an overview of the chapters.

▶ **Chapter 1, "The CISSP Certification Exam"**—This chapter introduces exam strategies and considerations.

▶ **Chapter 2, "Logical Asset Security"**—This chapter discusses logical security and the countermeasures available for protecting an organization's resources. Key topics include CIA, data classification, and control of an organization's assets from creation to destruction.

▶ **Chapter 3, "Physical Asset Security"**—This chapter discusses physical security and the importance of providing physical protection for an organization's resources. Physical security plays a key role in securing an organization's assets. Without effective physical security, there can be no effective security structure at all.

▶ **Chapter 4, "Security and Risk Management"**—This chapter discusses asset management and the protection of critical resources. Quantitative and qualitative risk assessment are two major topics of this chapter. Readers must understand how these concepts are used to assess and measure risk while reducing threats to the organization. Key concepts include the development of policies, procedures, guidelines, and assorted controls.

▶ **Chapter 5, "Security Engineering"**—This chapter discusses key concepts such as computer hardware, operating system design, security models (Biba, Bell-LaPadula, Clark-Wilson, etc.) and documentation used to verify, certify, and accredit systems and networks.

▶ **Chapter 6, "The Application and Use of Cryptography"**—This chapter discusses the methods and systems used to encrypt and protect data. Symmetric, asymmetric, and hashing algorithms are introduced, along with PKI and cryptographic methods of attack.

▶ **Chapter 7, "Communication and Network Security"**—This chapter discusses telecommunication technology. Items such as the OSI model, TCP/IP, network equipment, LAN, MAN, and WAN protocols, and wireless technologies are just a few of the technologies discussed. This is an expansive domain and covers a lot of information for the CISSP candidate to master.

▶ **Chapter 8, "Identity and Access Management"**—This chapter covers the basics of access control. It addresses the three A's: authentication, authorization, and accountability. Items like identification, single sign-on, centralized authentication, and federation are discussed.

▶ **Chapter 9, "Security Assessment and Testing"**—This chapter discusses security assessments, ethical hacking, and vulnerability scanning. It also reviews common types of malware and various attack methodologies.

▶ **Chapter 10, "Security Operations"**—This chapter covers operation controls—that is, the types of controls that the organization can implement. Topics such as background checks, dual controls, mandatory vacations, rotation of duties, and auditing are introduced.

▶ **Chapter 11, "Software Development Security"**—This chapter discusses databases, the system development life cycle, and the importance of building security into applications and systems as early as possible during the development process. Project management is reviewed, as are malicious code, knowledge-based systems, and application issues.

▶ **Chapter 12, "Business Continuity Planning"**—This chapter covers all the aspects of the BCP process. Although some may discount the importance of this domain, storms, floods, hurricanes, earthquakes, and other natural disasters. should demonstrate the criticality of this domain. This chapter addresses key elements of disaster recovery. One important item is that no demonstrated recovery exists until the business continuity plan has been tested. Exam candidates must understand what is needed to prevent, minimize, and recover from disasters.

▶ **Practice Exam I**—This is a full-length practice exam.

▶ **Answers to Practice Exam I**—This element contains the answers and explanations for the first practice exam.

▶ **Practice Exam II**—This is a second full-length practice exam.

▶ **Answers to Practice Exam II**—This element contains the answers and explanations for the second practice exam.

Companion Website

Register this book to get access to the Pearson IT Certification test engine and other study materials, plus additional bonus content. Check this site regularly for new and updated postings written by the author that provide further insight into the more troublesome topics on the exam. Be sure to check the box that you would like to hear from us to receive updates and exclusive discounts on future editions of this product or related products.

To access this companion website, follow the steps below:

1. Go to www.pearsonITcertification.com/register and log in or create a new account.

2. Enter the ISBN: 9780789757142.

3. Answer the challenge question as proof of purchase.

4. Click on the "Access Bonus Content" link in the Registered Products section of your account page, to be taken to the page where your downloadable content is available.

Please note that many of our companion content files can be very large, especially image and video files.

If you are unable to locate the files for this title by following the steps at left, please visit www.pearsonITcertification.com/contact and select the "Site Problems/Comments" option. Our customer service representatives will assist you.

Pearson IT Certification Practice Test Engine and Questions

The companion site includes the Pearson IT Certification Practice Test engine—software that displays and grades a set of exam-realistic multiple-choice questions. Using the Pearson IT Certification Practice Test engine, you can either study by going through the questions in Study Mode, or take a simulated exam that mimics real exam conditions.

The installation process requires two major steps: installing the software and then activating the exam. The website has a recent copy of the Pearson IT Certification Practice Test engine. The practice exam—the database of exam questions—is not on this site.

> **Note**
>
> The cardboard case in the back of this book includes a piece of paper. The paper lists the activation code for the practice exam associated with this book. Do not lose the activation code. Also included on the paper is a unique, one-time use coupon code for the purchase of the Premium Edition eBook and Practice Test.

Install the Software

The Pearson IT Certification Practice Test is a Windows-only desktop application. You can run it on a Mac using a Windows Virtual Machine, but it was built specifically for the Windows platform. The minimum system requirements are:

▶ Windows 10, Windows 8.1, or Windows 7

▶ Microsoft .NET Framework 4.5 Client

▶ Pentium class 1 GHz processor (or equivalent)

▶ 512 MB RAM

▶ 650 MB disc space plus 50 MB for each downloaded practice exam

▶ Access to the Internet to register and download exam databases

The software installation process is pretty routine compared to other software installation processes. If you have already installed the Pearson IT Certification Practice Test software from another Pearson product, there is no need for you to reinstall the software. Simply launch the software on your desktop and proceed to activate the practice exam from this book by using the activation code included in the access code card sleeve in the back of the book.

The following steps outline the installation process:

1. Download the exam practice test engine from the companion site.

2. Respond to Windows prompts as with any typical software installation process.

The installation process will give you the option to activate your exam with the activation code supplied on the paper in the cardboard sleeve. This process requires that you establish a Pearson website login. You will need this login in order to activate the exam, so please do register when prompted. If you already have a Pearson website login, there is no need to register again. Just use your existing login.

Activate and Download the Practice Exam

Once the exam engine is installed, you should then activate the exam associated with this book (if you did not do so during the installation process), as follows:

Step 1: Start the Pearson IT Certification Practice Test software from the Windows **Start** menu or from your desktop shortcut icon.

Step 2: To activate and download the exam associated with this book, from the **My Products** or **Tools** tab, select the **Activate** button.

Step 3: At the next screen, enter the activation code from the paper inside the cardboard holder in the back of the book. Once entered, click the **Activate** button.

Step 4: The activation process will download the practice exam. Click **Next**, and then click **Finish**.

Once the activation process is completed, the **My Products** tab should list your new exam. If you do not see the exam, make sure you have selected the **My Products** tab on the menu. At this point, the software and practice exam are ready to use. Simply select the exam and click the **Open Exam** button.

To update a particular exam that you have already activated and downloaded, simply select the **Tools** tab and select the **Update Products** button. Updating your exams will ensure you have the latest changes and updates to the exam data.

If you wish to check for updates to the Pearson Cert Practice Test exam engine software, simply select the **Tools** tab and select the **Update Application** button. This will ensure you are running the latest version of the software engine.

Activating Other Exams

The exam software installation process, and the registration process, only has to happen once. Then, for each new exam, only a few steps are required. For instance, if you buy another new Pearson IT Certification book, extract the activation code from the cardboard sleeve in the back of that book—you don't even need the exam engine at this point. From there, all you have to do is start the exam engine (if not still up and running), and perform steps 2 through 4 from the previous list.

Contacting the Author

Hopefully, this book provides you with the tools you need to pass the CISSP exam. Feedback is appreciated. You can contact the author at mikeg@thesolutionfirm.com.

Thank you for selecting my book; I have worked to apply the same concepts in this book that I have used in the hundreds of training classes I have taught. Spend your study time wisely and you, too, can become a CISSP. Good luck on the exam!

Self-Assessment

This self-assessment section enables you to evaluate your readiness to take the CISSP certification exam. It should also help you understand what's required to obtain the CISSP certification. Are you ready?

CISSPs in the Real World

Security continues to be on everyone's mind. The CISSP certification continues to be one of the most sought-after security certifications. Increasing numbers of people are studying for and obtaining their CISSP certifications. Congratulations on making the decision to follow in their footsteps. If you are willing to tackle the process seriously and do what it takes to obtain the necessary experience and knowledge, you can pass the exam on the first try.

> **Tip**
>
> You can also assess your CISSP skill set by using the MeasureUp Certification Mode.

The Ideal CISSP Candidate

The CISSP is designed for individuals who are leading, planning, organizing, or controlling the security initiative of an organization. The ideal CISSP candidate is likely to have a 4-year college education and have at least 5–7 years' experience in one or more of the 8 CISSP domains. The most applicable degree is in computer science or perhaps a related field. A degree is not a prerequisite for taking the test. However, exam candidates must have a minimum of 5 years of direct full-time security work experience in 2 or more of the 8 domains. One year of experience can be substituted for a 4-year college degree or an approved certification such as CompTIA Security+ or CASP. The complete list of approved certifications can be found at www.isc2.org/credential_waiver/default.aspx

Don't be lulled into thinking that this is an easy test. Some words of caution might be in order:

- ▶ The CISSP exam requires the candidate to absorb a substantial amount of material. The test is 6 hours long and consists of 225 graded questions. This is longer than typical exams at Microsoft and most other IT vendors.

- ▶ The pass mark is set high, at 700 points. The individual questions are weighted, which means that harder questions are worth more than easier ones.

- ▶ Most of the individuals attempting the exam are familiar with one to three of the domains. This means that studying for the exam can be overwhelming because there is so much material to cover. This book can help by guiding you to the areas in which you are weak or strong.

▶ To be eligible for the CISSP exam, students are required to have five years of experience, or four years of experience and a college degree.

Put Yourself to the Test

In this section, you answer some simple questions. The objective is for you to understand exactly how much work and effort you must invest to pass the CISSP certification exam. The simple answer to this question is this: The experience and education you have will dictate how difficult it will be for you to pass. Be honest in your answers or you will end up wasting around $600 on an exam you were not ready to take. From the beginning, two things should be clear:

▶ Any educational background in computer science will be helpful, as will other IT certifications you have achieved.

▶ Hands-on actual experience is not only essential, but also required to obtain this certification.

Your Educational Background

▶ **Do you have a computer science degree?**

You'll have a good basic knowledge needed for three or more of the eight domains, assuming that you finished your degree and your schooling and have some fairly sophisticated computer skills. Subject areas such as application development, networking, and database design are a great help.

▶ **Did you attend some type of technical school or week-long CISSP course?**

This question applies to low-level or short-term computer courses. Many of these courses are extremely basic or focused in one particular area. Although the CISSP exam is not platform-specific, training classes that focused on networking, security, hacking, or database design will help you pass the exam.

▶ **Have you developed any security policies, performed security audits, performed penetration tests, or developed response plans?**

If yes, you will probably be able to handle about half of the CISSP exam domains.

► **Do you have a photographic memory?**

If yes, you might have a slim chance of passing simply by reading this book, taking some practice exams, and using the Internet to brush up on the subjects you are weak in. However, the goal here is to gain a real understanding of the material. As a CISSP, you might be asked to lead, plan, organize, or control your organization's security operations; if that happens, you'll need a real understanding of how the various technologies and techniques work. Don't cheat yourself or gamble with your career.

Again, the education and requirements given here are by no means absolute. Still, an education can give you a very good grounding in any endeavor—the higher the level of education, the better.

Testing Your Exam Readiness

Whether you attend a training class, form a study group, or study on your own, preparing for the CISSP exam is essential. The exam will cost you about $600, depending on where you are located, so you'll want to do everything you can to make sure you pass on the first try. Reading, studying, and taking practice exams are the best ways to increase your readiness. Practice exams help in two main ways:

► Practice exams highlight weak spots for further study.

► Practice exams give you a general perspective on the question format. Practicing the questions the way they are asked can help enormously on the actual testing day.

Two full-length practice exams are provided with this book. Que also publishes a second book, CISSP Practice Questions Exam, with more than 500 practice CISSP test questions; it is an excellent supplement to this book.

After the Exam

After you have passed the exam, you will need to gain continuing education credits each year to maintain your certification. Your certification will come up for renewal every 3 years, so you'll need to obtain 120 continuing education credits (CPE) or retake the exam. Retaking the exam is not a popular choice. These are some ways to gain CPEs to keep your certification current:

► Write a book.

► Read a book. (Only one per year can be used for credit.) This will give you a couple of credits, but not enough to keep your certification current.

▶ Do volunteer work that is approved by ISC^2. When you are certified, you can log on to the ISC^2 website for more information. A variety of volunteer work is available.

▶ Attend a training class. Just about any type of technology training class is accepted as long as it is tied to one of the domains.

▶ Teach a training class.

▶ Attend a college-level security class.

As you can see, the goal here is to help you stay current. As technology changes, we all must continue to learn to keep up the pace.

Now that we have covered some of the ways in which to assess your exam readiness, let's move on to Chapter 1, "The CISSP Certification Exam," where you will learn more about how the exam is structured and some effective test-taking strategies.

CHAPTER 1

The CISSP Certification Exam

Terms you'll need to understand:

▶ Common body of knowledge (CBK)

▶ Exam strategy

Techniques you'll need to master:

▶ Assessing exam requirements

▶ Determining whether you're ready for the exam

▶ Using practice questions

▶ Using your time wisely

Introduction

Welcome to CISSP Exam Cram! The aim of this chapter is to help you become prepared for the CISSP exam and understand what to expect when you enter the testing area. For most people, exam taking is not something that they eagerly anticipate. The best way to reduce that anxiety is to be fully prepared before you attempt to pass the exam. Taking those extra steps will help you feel more relaxed and confident when you enter the testing area.

Before beginning your studies, take a few minutes to make sure you fully understand the CISSP exam process. This is something that you don't want to wait until the day of the exam to figure out. Reviewing these details now will help you concentrate on the exam so that you aren't worried about how much time you have to answer each question. Finally, mastering a few basic exam-taking skills should help you recognize—and perhaps even overcome—some of the tricks or unusual verbiage you're bound to find on the exam.

In addition to reviewing the exam environment, this chapter describes some proven exam-taking strategies that you can use to your advantage.

Assessing Exam Readiness

Before you rush out and sign up for the CISSP exam, check out the www.ISC2.org website and review the CISSP certification requirements. To be eligible to become a CISSP, you must qualify for and meet two separate requirements:

▶ **Examination**—This portion of the process requires that you submit the examination fee, and assert that you possess a minimum of five years of professional experience in the information security field or four years plus a college degree (this is subject to audit and verification). You must also review and sign the Candidate Agreement stating that you will legally commit to adhere to the CISSP Code of Ethics, and answer several questions regarding criminal history and background.

▶ **Certification**—The second step of the process requires that the candidate pass the exam with a score of 700 points or greater, submit a completed and executed Endorsement Form, and, in some cases, pass a verification audit regarding professional experience.

When you are confident that you meet these requirements, you can continue with your studies. To be fully prepared for the exam, I recommend that you read the entire text, review the practice questions, and review the additional resources identified in each chapter. After you read the book and test yourself with the questions and practice exams, you will have a good idea of whether you are ready to take the real exam.

Be aware that the CISSP exam is difficult and challenging; therefore, this book shouldn't be your only vehicle for CISSP study. Many companies, such as my own (Superior Solutions, Inc., www.thesolutionfirm.com), offer training classes to help you review the material and prepare for the exam. Because of the breadth and depth of knowledge needed to pass the CISSP exam, be sure to use plenty of study materials and use this book to help you gauge your strengths and weaknesses. The ISC^2 website is a good place to find additional study material, and so are the "Need to Know More?" sections at the end of the chapters in this book.

Taking the Exam

When you arrive at the testing center, you need to sign in. You will be asked to show your exam confirmation and photo identification. You cannot take the exam without a photo ID and your exam confirmation number. After you've signed in, find a seat, get comfortable, and wait for the exam to begin.

The exam is completely closed book. In fact, you will not be permitted to take any study materials into the testing area; you will be given scratch paper to use that must be returned at the completion of the exam. The exam is electronic and is very similar to CompTIA exams or those given by Microsoft. ISC^2 allows you to make comments regarding the training environment at the completion of the exam.

During the six-hour time limit, you will need to complete 250 questions. This provides plenty of time to complete the exam and even provides some time to go back and review your answers. The test screen will show a timer to keep you informed of how much time you have left to complete the exam.

All questions on the exam are multiple choice, and the exam contains 250 questions. Twenty-five of the questions are for research purposes, so only 225 questions are actually scored for certification. The research questions do not count against you regardless of your answer. You should attempt all the questions, even if you need to guess the answer. Don't leave any answers blank. The exam questions are developed by an ISC^2 committee and are always being updated and changed. I encourage you to make multiple passes on the test. On the first pass, answer all the questions where you are confident that you know the correct answer and mark the questions you are unsure of. On the second pass, work through the more difficult questions and make sure to underline key words such as "not", "least", and "most". Missing one word on the exam can make a big difference. On the final pass, answer any remaining questions. Remember that it is better to guess at an answer than to leave a question blank.

In the next section, you learn more about how CISSP test questions look and how they must be answered.

Examples of CISSP Test Questions

Here are examples of the different CISSP test question formats. Following each example is a brief summary of each potential answer and why it is either right or wrong.

Multiple-Choice Question Format

These are exam questions that require you to select a single answer from the given choices. To answer this type of question, click the letter or text of one answer. In some cases, more than one answer might appear correct; you must determine which one is most correct.

1. What is the most widely used device to control physical access?

   ○ **A.** Chains

   ○ **B.** Locks

   ○ **C.** Alarms

   ○ **D.** Firewalls

Drag and Drop Question Format

These are exam questions that require you to move one or more correct answers from a pool of possible answers into the correct answers area. To answer this type of question, simply click, drag, and drop the correct answers from the "Possible Answers" section to the "Correct Answers" box.

1. Which of the following are examples of asymmetric encryption?

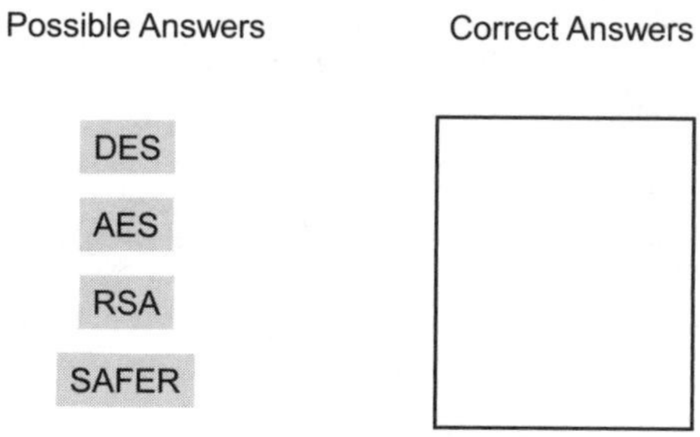

Possible Answers   Correct Answers

DES

AES

RSA

SAFER

FIGURE 1.1   **Drag and Drop Question.**

Hotspot Question Format

These are exam questions that require you to click on the correct area of a diagram—a hotspot—to answer a question.

1. When designing network controls, which would be the proper location for a firewall to protect the DMZ?

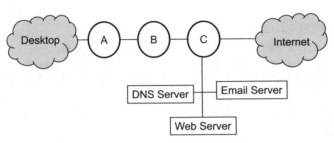

FIGURE 1.2   Location Placement Question.

Answer to Multiple-Choice Question

1. **Answer: B.** Locks are the most commonly used device to control physical access. Locks have been used since the time of the Egyptians. Answer A is incorrect because chains are not the most commonly used devices for physical access control. Answer C is incorrect because alarms don't prevent access; they only inform you that possible unauthorized access has occurred. Answer D is incorrect because a firewall is used to control logical access.

Answer to Drag and Drop Question

1. **Answer: RSA.** RSA is the only example of asymmetric encryption. DES, AES, and SAFER are all examples of symmetric encryption. In this case, you should drag and drop only "RSA" into the "Correct Answers" box.

Answer to Hotspot Question

1. **Answer: C.** To answer the question, hold the mouse cursor over the area on the diagram that you want to choose as your answer. While all available areas will light up (A, B, or C in this example), you must click on the one you believe is correct. In this case, we'd want to deploy a firewall where item C is located between the internal network and the Internet.

Exam Strategy

A well-known principle when taking fixed-length exams is to first read each question, and answer only those questions that you feel absolutely sure of. As you progress through the exam, you might find subsequent questions that clue you into the correct answer on a previous one. Any questions you might have passed you can return to, and at that point you will know exactly how many questions you have left.

As you read each question, if you answer only those you're sure of and mark for review those that you're not sure of, you can keep working through a decreasing list of questions as you answer the trickier ones in order.

> **ExamAlert**
>
> There's at least one potential benefit to reading the exam completely before answering the trickier questions: Sometimes information supplied in later questions sheds more light on earlier questions. At other times, information you read in later questions might jog your memory about earlier questions. Either way, you'll come out ahead if you defer answering those questions about which you're not absolutely sure.

Here are some question-handling strategies that apply to fixed-length and short-form tests. Use these tips whenever you can:

▶ When returning to a question after your initial read-through, read every word again, as if for the first time. Sometimes revisiting a question after turning your attention elsewhere lets you see something you missed, but the strong tendency is to see what you saw before.

▶ If you return to a question more than twice, try to articulate to yourself what you don't understand about the question, why answers don't appear to make sense, or what appears to be missing. If you chew on the subject a while, your subconscious might provide the details you lack or you might notice a "trick" that points to the right answer. If there is more than one good answer, the more general answer that encompasses others will usually take precedence and be the correct answer.

▶ As you work your way through the exam, it's wise to budget your time.

▶ If you're not finished when only five minutes remain, use that time to guess your way through any remaining questions. Remember, guessing is potentially more valuable than not answering because blank answers are always wrong, but a guess might turn out to be right, and there is no penalty for wrong answers. If you don't have a clue about any of the remaining questions, pick answers at random or choose all As, Bs, and so on. The important thing is to submit an exam for scoring that has an answer for every question.

Question-Handling Strategies

Because of the way that multiple choice CISSP exam questions are structured, many times one or two of the answers will be obviously incorrect and two of the answers will be plausible. Take the time to reread the question. Words such as "sometimes", "not", "always", and "best" can make a big difference when choosing the correct answer. Unless the answer leaps out at you, begin the process of answering by eliminating those answers that are most obviously wrong.

Almost always, at least one answer out of the possible choices for a question can be eliminated immediately because it matches one of these conditions:

▶ The answer does not apply to the situation.

▶ The answer describes a nonexistent issue, an invalid option, or an imaginary state.

After you eliminate all answers that are obviously wrong, you can apply your retained knowledge to eliminate further answers. Look for items that sound correct but refer to actions, commands, or features that are not present or not available in the situation that the question describes.

If you're still faced with a blind guess among two or more potentially correct answers, reread the question. Try to picture how each of the possible remaining answers would alter the situation.

Only when you've exhausted your ability to eliminate answers, but remain unclear about which of the remaining possibilities is correct, should you guess at an answer. An unanswered question offers you no points, but guessing gives you at least some chance of getting a question right—just don't be too hasty when making a blind guess!

Mastering the Inner Game

In the final analysis, knowledge breeds confidence and confidence breeds success. If you study the materials in this book carefully and review all the practice questions at the end of each chapter, you should become aware of those areas where additional learning and study are required.

> **ExamAlert**
>
> You will be expected to understand CISSP terminology before attempting the exam. A big part of the exam is not only understanding the terms that might be used, but also applying them in the context provided in the test questions. As an example, the exam might talk about intrusion detection, but a specific question might address physical intrusion detection or logical intrusion detection.

After you've worked your way through this book, take the practice exams at the end of the book. Taking these practice exams will provide a reality check and help you identify areas to study further. Make sure you follow up and review materials related to the questions you missed on the practice exams before taking the real exam. Only when you've covered that ground and feel comfortable with the whole scope of the practice exams should you set an exam appointment. It's advisable to score 90% or better before you attempt the real exam. Otherwise, obtain some additional practice tests and keep trying until you hit that magic number.

> **ExamAlert**
>
> Armed with the information in this book and with the determination to augment your knowledge, you should be able to pass the certification exam. However, you need to work at it or you'll spend the exam fee more than once before you finally pass. If you prepare seriously, you should do well. We are confident that you can do it!

Need to Know More?

CISSP Exam Texting Techniques: searchsecurity.techtarget.com/feature/First-person-Editor-Andrew-Briney-on-how-to-pass-the-CISSP-exam

(ISC)² CISSP Certification Outline: www.isc2.org/cissp/default.aspx

CHAPTER 2
Logical Asset Security

Terms you'll need to understand:

▶ Confidentiality

▶ Integrity

▶ Availability

▶ SANs

▶ Information lifecycle management

▶ Privacy impact assessment

▶ Data classification

▶ Data destruction

▶ Data remanence

Techniques you'll need to master:

▶ Proper methods for destruction of data

▶ Development of documents that can aid in compliance of all local, state, and federal laws

▶ The implementation of encryption and its use for the protection of data

▶ International concerns of data management

Introduction

Asset security addresses the controls needed to protect data throughout its lifecycle. From the point of creation to the end of its life, data protection controls must be implemented to ensure that information is adequately protected during each life cycle phase. This chapter starts by reviewing the basic security principles of confidentiality, integrity, and availability and moves on to data management and governance.

A CISSP must know the importance of data security and how to protect it while it is in transit, in storage, and at rest. A CISSP must understand that protection of data is much more important today than it was ten to fifteen years ago because data is no longer in just a paper form. Today, data can be found on local systems, RAID arrays, or even in the cloud. Regardless of where the data is stored it must have adequate protection and be properly disposed of at the end of its useful life.

Basic Security Principles

Confidentiality, integrity, and availability (CIA) define the basic building blocks of any good security program when defining the goals for network, asset, information, and/or information system security and are commonly referred to collectively as the CIA triad. Although the abbreviation CIA might not be as intriguing as the United States government's spy organization, it is a concept that security professionals must know and understand.

Confidentiality addresses the secrecy and privacy of information and preventing unauthorized persons from viewing sensitive information. There are a number of controls used in the real world to protect the confidentiality of information, such as locked doors, armed guards, and fences. Administrative controls that can enhance confidentiality include the use of information classification systems, such as requiring sensitive data be encrypted. For example, news reports have detailed several large-scale breaches in confidentiality as a result of corporations misplacing or losing laptops, data, and even backup media containing customer account, name, and credit information. The simple act of encrypting this data could have prevented or mitigated the damage. Sending information in an encrypted format denies attackers the opportunity to intercept and sniff clear text information.

Integrity is the second leg in the security triad. Integrity provides accuracy of information, and offers users a higher degree of confidence that the information they are viewing has not been tampered with. Integrity must be protected while in storage, at rest, and in transit. Information in storage can be protected by using access controls and audit controls. Cryptography can enhance this protection through the use of hashing algorithms. Real-life examples of this technology can be seen in programs such as Tripwire, and MD5Sum. Likewise, integrity in transit can be ensured primarily by the use of transport protocols, such as PKI, hashing, and digital signatures.

The concept of *availability* requires that information and systems be available when needed. Although many people think of availability only in electronic terms, availability also applies to physical access. If, at 2 a.m., you need access to backup media stored in a facility that allows access only from 8 a.m. to 5 p.m., you definitely have an availability problem. Availability in the world of electronics can manifest itself in many ways. Access to a backup facility 24 × 7 does little good if there are no updated backups to restore from.

Backups are the simplest way to ensure availability. Backups provide a copy of critical information, should data be destroyed or equipment fail. Failover equipment is another way to ensure availability. Systems such as redundant arrays of independent disks (RAID) and redundant sites (hot, cold, and warm) are two other examples. Disaster recovery is tied closely to availability because it's all about getting critical systems up and running quickly.

Which link in the security triad is considered most important? That depends. In different organizations with different priorities, one link might take the lead over the other two. For example, your local bank might consider integrity the most important; however, an organization responsible for data processing might see availability as the primary concern, whereas an organization such as the NSA might value confidentiality the most. Finally, you should be comfortable seeing the triad in any form. Even though this book refers to it as CIA, others might refer to it as AIC, or as CAIN (where the "N" stands for *nonrepudiation*).

Security management does not stop at CIA. These are but three of the core techniques that apply to asset security. True security requires defense-in-depth. In reality, many techniques are required to protect the assets of an organization; take a moment to look over Figure 2.1.

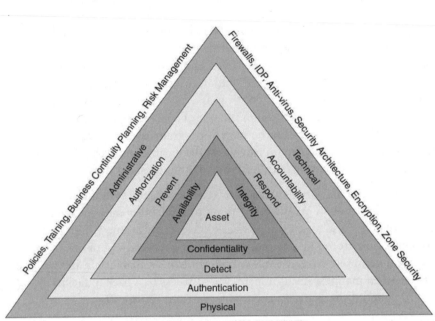

FIGURE 2.1 **Asset protection triad.**

Data Management: Determine and Maintain Ownership

Data management is not easy and has only become more complex over the last ten to fifteen years. Years ago, people only had to be concerned with paper documents and control might have only meant locking a file cabinet. Today, electronic data might be found on thumb drives, SAN storage arrays, laptop hard drives, mobile devices, or might even be stored in a public cloud.

Data Governance Policy

Generally you can think of policies as high-level documents developed by management to transmit the guiding strategy and philosophy of management to employees. A data governance policy is a documented set of specifications for the guarantee of approved management and control of an organization's digital assets and information. Data governance programs generally address the following types of data:

▶ Sets of master data

▶ Metadata

▶ Sensitive data

▶ Acquired data

Such specifications can involve directives for business process management (BPM) and enterprise risk planning (ERP), as well as security, data quality, and privacy. The goal of data governance is:

▶ To establish appropriate responsibility for the management of data

▶ To improve ease of access to data

▶ To ensure that once data are located, users have enough information about the data to interpret them correctly and consistently

▶ To improve the security of data, including confidentiality, integrity, and availability

Issues to consider include:

▶ **Cost**—This can include the cost of providing access to the data as well as the cost to protect it.

▶ **Ownership**—This includes concerns as to who owns the data or who might be a custodian. As an example, you may be the custodian of fifty copies of Microsoft Windows Server 2012 yet the code is owned by Microsoft. This is why users pay for a software license and not the ownership of the software itself, and typically have only the compiled ".exe" file and not the source code itself.

▶ **Liability**—This refers to the financial and legal costs an organization would bear should data be lost, stolen, or hacked.

▶ **Sensitivity**—This includes issues related to the sensitivity of data that should be protected against unwarranted disclosure. As an example, social security numbers, data of birth, medical history, etc.

▶ **Ensuring Law/Legal Compliance**—This includes items related to legal compliance. As examples, you must retain tax records for a minimum number of years, while you may only retain customers' for only the time it takes to process a single transaction.

▶ **Process**—This includes methods and tools used to transmit or modify the data.

Roles and Responsibility

Data security requires responsibility. There must be a clear division of roles and responsibility. This will be a tremendous help when dealing with any security issues. Everyone should be subject to the organization's security policy, including employees, management, consultants, and vendors. The following list describes some general areas of responsibility. Specific roles have unique requirements. Some key players and their responsibilities are as follows:

▶ **Data Owner**—Because senior management is ultimately responsible for data and can be held liable if it is compromised, the data owner is usually a member of senior management, or head of that department. The data owner is responsible for setting the data's security classification. The data owner can delegate some day-to-day responsibility.

▶ **Data Custodian**—Usually a member of the IT department. The data custodian does not decide what controls are needed, but does implement controls on behalf of the data owner. Other responsibilities include the day-to-day management of data, controlling access, adding and removing privileges for individual users, and ensuring that the proper controls have been implemented.

▶ **IS Security Steering Committee**—These are individuals from various levels of management that represent the various departments of the organization. They meet to discuss and make recommendations on security issues.

▶ **Senior Management**—These individuals are ultimately responsible for the security practices of the organization. Senior management might delegate day-to-day responsibility to another party or someone else, but cannot delegate overall responsibility for the security of the organization's data.

▶ **Security Advisory Group**—These individuals are responsible for reviewing security issues with the chief security officer and they are also responsible for reviewing security plans and procedures.

▶ **Chief Security Officer**—The individual responsible for the day-to-day security of the organization and its critical assets.

▶ **Users**—This is a role that most of us are familiar with because this is the end user in an organization. Users do have responsibilities; they must comply with the requirements laid out in policies and procedures.

▶ **Developers**—These individuals develop code and applications for the organization. They are responsible for implementing the proper security controls within the programs they develop.

▶ **Auditor**—This individual is responsible for examining the organization's security procedures and mechanisms. The auditor's job is to provide an independent objective as to the effectiveness of the organization's security controls. How often this process is performed depends on the industry and its related regulations. As an example, the health care industry in the United States is governed by the Health Insurance Portability and Accountability Act (HIPAA) regulations and requires yearly reviews.

ExamAlert

The CISSP candidate might be tested on the concept that data access does not extend indefinitely. It is not uncommon for an employee to gain more and more access over time while moving to different positions within a company. Such poor management can endanger an organization. When employees are terminated, data access should be withdrawn. If unfriendly termination is known in advance, access should be terminated as soon as possible to reduce the threat of potential damage.

Data Ownership

All data objects within an organization must have an owner. Objects without a data owner will be left unprotected. The process of assigning a data owner and set of controls to information is known as information lifecycle management (ILM). ILM is the science of creating and using policies for effective information management. ILM includes every phase of a data object from its creation to its end. This applies to any and all information assets.

ILM is focused on fixed content or static data. While data may not stay in a fixed format throughout its lifecycle there will be times when it is static. As an example consider this book; after it has been published it will stay in a fixed format until the next version is released.

For the purposes of business records, there are five phases identified as being part of the lifecycle process. These include the following:

▶ Creation and Receipt

▶ Distribution

▶ Use

▶ Maintenance

▶ Disposition

Data owners typically have legal rights over the data. The data owner typically is responsible for understanding the intellectual property rights and copyright of their data. Intellectual property is agreed on and enforced worldwide by various organizations, including the United Nations Commission on International Trade Law (UNCITRAL), the European Union (EU), and the World Trade Organization (WTO). International property laws protect trade secrets, trademarks, patents, and copyrights:

▶ **Trade secret**—A *trade secret* is a confidential design, practice, or method that must be proprietary or business related. For a trade secret to remain valid, the owner must take precautions to ensure the data remains secure. Examples include encryption, document marking, and physical security.

▶ **Trademark**—A *trademark* is a symbol, word, name, sound, or thing that identifies the origin of a product or service in a particular trade. The ISC^2 logo is an example of a trademarked logo. The term *service mark* is sometimes used to distinguish a trademark that applies to a service rather than to a product.

▶ **Patent**—A *patent* documents a process or synthesis and grants the owner a legally enforceable right to exclude others from practicing or using the invention's design for a defined period of time.

▶ **Copyright**—A *copyright* is a legal device that provides the creator of a work of authorship the right to control how the work is used and protects that person's expression on a specific subject. This includes the reproduction rights, distribution rights, music, right to create, and right to public display.

Data Custodians

Data custodians are responsible for the safe custody, transport, and storage of data and the implementation of business rules. This can include the practice of due care and the implementation of good practices to protect intellectual assets such as patents or trade secrets. Some common responsibilities for a data custodian include the following:

▶ **Data owner identification**—A data owner must be identified and known for each data set and be formally appointed. Too many times data owners do not know that they are data owners and do not understand the role and its responsibilities. In many organizations the data custodian or IT department by default assumes the role of data owner.

▶ **Data controls**—Access to data is authorized and managed. Adequate controls must be in place to protect the confidentiality, integrity, and availability of the data. This includes administrative, technical, and physical controls.

▶ **Change control**—A change control process must be implemented so that change and access can be audited.

▶ **End-of-life provisions or disposal**—Controls must be in place so that when data is no longer needed or is not accurate it can be destroyed in an approved method.

Data Documentation and Organization

Data that is organized and structured can help ensure that that it is better understood and interpreted by users. Data documentation should detail how data was created, what the context is for the data, the format of the data and its contents, and any changes that have occurred to the data. It's important to document the following:

▶ Data context

▶ Methodology of data collection

▶ Data structure and organization

▶ Validity of data and quality assurance controls

▶ Data manipulations through data analysis from raw data

▶ Data confidentiality, access, and integrity controls

Data Warehousing

A *data warehouse* is a database that contains data from many other databases. This allows for trend analysis and marketing decisions through data analytics (discussed below). Data warehousing is used to enable a strategic view. Because of the amount of data stored in one location, data warehouses are tempting targets for attackers who can comb through and discover sensitive information.

Data Mining

Data mining is the process of analyzing data to find and understand patterns and relationships about the data (see Figure 2.2). There are many things that must be in place for data mining to occur. These include multiple data sources, access, and warehousing. Data becomes information, information becomes knowledge, and knowledge becomes intelligence through a process called data analytics, which is simply examination of the data. *Metadata* is best described as being "data about data". As an example, the number 212 has no meaning by itself. But, when qualifications are added, such as to state the field is an area code, it is then understood the information represents an area code on Manhattan Island. Organizations treasure data and the relationships that can be deduced between individual elements. The relationships discovered can help companies understand their competitors and the usage patterns of their customers, and can result in targeted marketing. As an example, it might not be obvious why the diapers are at the back of the store by the beer case until you learn from data mining that after 10 p.m., more men than women buy diapers, and that they tend to buy beer at the same time.

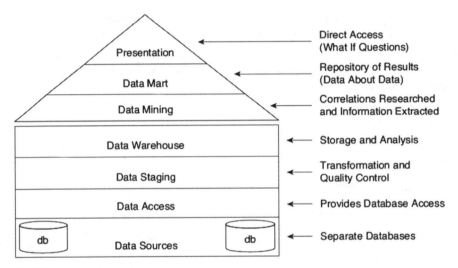

FIGURE 2.2 **Data mining.**

Knowledge Management

Knowledge management seeks to make intelligent use of all the data in an organization by applying wisdom to it. This is called turning data into intelligence through analytics. This skill attempts to tie together databases, document management, business processes, and information systems. The result is a huge store of data that can be mined to extract knowledge using artificial intelligence techniques. These are the three main approaches to knowledge extraction:

▶ **Classification approach**—Used to discover patterns; can be used to reduce large databases to only a few individual records or data marts. Think of data marts as small slices of data from the data warehouse.

> ► **Probabilistic approach**—Used to permit statistical analysis, often in planning and control systems or in applications that involve uncertainty.

> ► **Statistical approach**—A number-crunching approach; rules are constructed that identify generalized patterns in the data.

Data Standards

Data standards provide consistent meaning to data shared among different information systems, programs, and departments throughout the product's life cycle. Data standards are part of any good enterprise architecture. The use of data standards makes data much easier to use. As an example, say you get a new 850-lumen flashlight that uses two AA batteries. You don't need to worry about what brand of battery you buy as all AA batteries are manufactured to the same size and voltage.

> **Tip**
>
> If you would like to see an example of a data standard check out Texas Education Agency. It requires all Texas school districts to submit data to the PEIMS data standard. Learn more at: tea.texas.gov/Reports_and_Data/Data_Submission/PEIMS/ PEIMS_Data_Standards/PEIMS_Data_Standards/

Data Lifecycle Control

Data lifecycle control is a policy-based approach to managing the flow of an information system's data throughout its life cycle from the point of creation to the point at which it is out of date and is destroyed or archived.

Data Audit

After all the previous tasks discussed in this chapter have been performed, the organization's security-management practices will need to be evaluated periodically. This is accomplished by means of an *audit process*. The audit process can be used to verify that each individual's responsibility is clearly defined. Employees should know their accountability and their assigned duties. Most audits follow a code or set of documentation. As an example, financial audits can be performed using Committee of Sponsoring Organizations of the Treadway Commission (COSO). IT audits typically follow the Information Systems Audit and Control Association (ISACA) Control Objectives for

Information and related Technology (COBIT) framework. COBIT is designed around four domains:

▶ Plan and organize

▶ Acquire and implement

▶ Deliver and support

▶ Monitor and evaluate

Although the CISSP exam will not expect you to understand the inner workings of COBIT, you should understand that it is a framework to help provide governance and assurance. COBIT was designed for performance management and IT management. It is considered a system of best practices. COBIT was created by the Information Systems Audit and Control Association (ISACA), and the IT Governance Institute (ITGI) in 1992.

Although auditors can use COBIT, it is also useful for IT users and managers designing controls and optimizing processes. It is designed around 34 key controls that address:

▶ Performance concerns

▶ IT control profiling

▶ Awareness

▶ Benchmarking

Audits are the only way to verify that the controls put in place are working, that the policies that were written are being followed, and that the training provided to the employees actually works. To learn more about COBIT, check out www.isaca.org/cobit/. Another set of documents that can be used to bench-mark the infrastructure is the family of ISO 27000 standards.

Data Storage and Archiving

Organizations have a never-ending need for increased storage. My first 10-megabyte thumb drive is rather puny by today's standards. Data storage can include:

▶ Network attached storage (NAS)

▶ Storage area network (SAN)

▶ Cloud

Organizations should fully define their security requirements for data storage before a technology is deployed. For example, NAS devices are small, easy to use, and can be implemented quickly, but physical security is a real concern, as is implementing strong controls over the data. A SAN can be implemented with much greater security than a NAS. Cloud-based storage offers yet another option but also presents concerns such as:

- ▶ Is it a private or public cloud?
- ▶ Does it use physical or virtual servers?
- ▶ How are the servers provisioned and decommissioned?
- ▶ Is the data encrypted and if so what kind of encryption is used?
- ▶ Where is the data actually stored?
- ▶ How is the data transferred (data flow)?
- ▶ Where are the encryption keys kept?
- ▶ Are there co-tenants?

Keep in mind that storage integration also includes securing virtual environments, services, applications, appliances, and equipment that provide storage.

SAN

The Storage Network Industry Association (SNIA) defines a SAN as "a data storage system consisting of various storage elements, storage devices, computer systems, and/or appliances, plus all the control software, all communicating in efficient harmony over a network." A SAN appears to the client OS as a local disk or volume that is available to be formatted and used locally as needed.

- ▶ **Virtual SAN**—A virtual SAN (VSAN) is a SAN that offers isolation among devices that are physically connected to the same SAN fabric. A VSAN is sometimes called fabric virtualization. VSANs were developed to support independent virtual fabrics on a single switch. VSANs improve consolidation and simplify management by allowing for more efficient SAN utilization. A VSAN will allow a resource on any individual VSAN to be shared by other users on a different VSAN without merging the SAN fabrics.

- ▶ **Internet Small Computer System Interface (iSCSI)**—iSCSI is a SAN standard used for connecting data storage facilities and allowing remote SCSI devices to communicate. Many see it as a replacement for fiber channel, because it does not require any special infrastructure and can run over existing IP LAN, MAN, or WAN networks.

▶ **Fiber Channel over Ethernet (FCoE)**—FCoE is another transport protocol that is similar to iSCSI. FCoE can operate at speeds of 10 GB per second and rides on top of the Ethernet protocol. While it is fast, it has a disadvantage in that it is non-routable. iSCSI is, by contrast, routable because it operates higher up the stack, on top of the TCP and UDP protocols.

▶ **Host Bus Adapter (HBA) Allocation**—The host bus adapter is used to connect a host system to an enterprise storage device. HBAs can be allocated by either soft zoning or by persistent binding. Soft zoning is more permissive, whereas persistent binding decreases address space and increases network complexity.

▶ **LUN Masking**—LUN masking is implemented primarily at the HBA level. It is a number system that makes LUN numbers available to some but not to others. LUN masking implemented at this level is vulnerable to any attack that compromises the local adapter.

▶ **Redundancy (Location)**—Location redundancy is the idea that content should be accessible from more than one location. An extra measure of redundancy can be provided by means of a replication service so that data is available even if the main storage backup system fails.

▶ **Secure Storage Management and Replication**—Secure storage management and replication systems are designed to allow an organization to manage and handle all its data in a secure manner with a focus on the confidentiality, integrity, and availability of the data. The replication service allows the data to be duplicated in real time so that additional fault tolerance is achieved.

▶ **Multipath Solutions**—Enterprise storage multipath solutions reduce the risk of data loss or lack of availability by setting up multiple routes between a server and its drives. The multipath software maintains a listing of all requests, passes them through the best possible path, and reroutes communication if a path fails.

▶ **SAN Snapshots**—SAN snapshot software is typically sold with SAN solutions and offers a way to bypass typical backup operations. The snapshot software has the ability to temporarily stop writing to physical disk and then make a point-in-time backup copy. Snapshot software is typically fast and makes a copy quickly, regardless of the drive size.

▶ **Data De-Duplication (DDP)**—Data de-duplication is the process of removing redundant data to improve enterprise storage utilization. Redundant data is not copied. It is replaced with a pointer to the one unique copy of the data. Only one instance of redundant data is retained on the enterprise storage media, such as disk or tape.

Data Security, Protection, Sharing, and Dissemination

Data security is the protection of data from unauthorized activity by authorized users and from access by unauthorized users. Although laws differ depending on which country an organization is operating in, organizations must make the protection of personal information in particular a priority. To understand the level of importance, consider that according to the Privacy Rights Clearing-house (www.privacyrights.org), the total number of records containing sensitive personal information accumulated from security breaches in the United States between January 2005 and December 2015 is 895,531,860.

From a global standpoint the international standard ISO/IEC 17799 covers data security. ISO 17799 makes clear the fact that all data should have a data owner and data custodian so that it is clear whose responsibility it is to secure and protect access to that data.

An example of a proprietary international information security standard is the Payment Card Industry Data Security Standard. PCI-DSS sets standards for any entity that handles cardholder information for credit cards, prepaid cards, and POS cards. PCI DSS version is comprised of six control objectives that contain one or more requirements:

1. Build and Maintain a Secure Network

   Requirement 1: Install and maintain a firewall configuration to protect cardholder data

   Requirement 2: Do not use vendor-supplied defaults for system passwords and other security parameters

2. Protect Cardholder Data

   Requirement 3: Protect stored cardholder data

   Requirement 4: Encrypt transmission of cardholder data across open, public networks

3. Maintain a Vulnerability Management Program

   Requirement 5: Use and regularly update anti-virus software

   Requirement 6: Develop and maintain secure systems and applications

4. Implement Strong Access Control Measures

   Requirement 7: Restrict access to cardholder data by business need-to-know

   Requirement 8: Assign a unique ID to each person with computer access

   Requirement 9: Restrict physical access to cardholder data

5. Regularly Monitor and Test Networks

   Requirement 10: Track and monitor all access to network resources and cardholder data

   Requirement 11: Regularly test security systems and processes

6. Maintain an Information Security Policy

   Requirement 12: Maintain a policy that addresses information security

Privacy Impact Assessment

Another approach for organizations seeking to improve their protection of personal information is to develop an organization-wide policy based on a *privacy impact analysis* (PIA). A PIA should determine the risks and effects of collecting, maintaining, and distributing personal information in electronic-based systems. The PIA should be used to evaluate privacy risks and ensure that appropriate privacy controls exist. Existing data controls should be examined to verify that accountability is present and that compliance is built-in every time new projects or processes are planned to come online. The PIA must include a review of the following items as they adversely affect the CIA of privacy records:

▶ **Technology**—Any time new systems are added or modifications are made, reviews are needed.

▶ **Processes**—Business processes change, and even though a company might have a good change policy, the change management system might be overlooking personal information privacy.

▶ **People**—Companies change employees and others with whom they do business. Any time business partners, vendors, or service providers change, the impact of the change on privacy needs to be reexamined.

Privacy controls tend to be overlooked for the same reason many security controls are. Management might have a preconceived idea that security controls will reduce the efficiency or speed of business processes. To overcome these types of barriers, senior management must make a strong commitment to protection of personal information and demonstrate its support. Risk-assessment activities aid in the process by informing stakeholders of the actual costs for the loss of personal information of clients and customers. These costs can include fines, lawsuits, lost customers, reputation, and the company going out of business.

Information Handling Requirements

Organizations handle large amounts of information and should have policies and procedures in place that detail how information is to be stored. Think of policies as high level documents, whereas procedures offer step-by-step instructions. Many organizations are within industries that fall under regulatory standards that detail how and how long information must be retained.

One key concern with storage is to ensure that media is appropriately labeled. Media should be labeled so that the data librarian or individual in charge of media management can identify the media owner, when the content was created, the classification level, and when the content is to be destroyed. Figure 2.3 shows an example of appropriate media labeling.

Date: Oct 31, 2016
Author: Christine Gregg
Classification: Top Secret
Retention Period: 3 Years
Title and Description: Project X

FIGURE 2.3   Data labeling.

Data Retention and Destruction

All data has a lifetime. Eventually it should either be purged, released, or unclassified. As an example, consider the JFK Records Act. The JFK Records Act was put in place to eventually declassify all records dealing with the assassination of President John F. Kennedy. The JFK Records Act states that all assassination records must finally be made public by 2017. This is an example of declassification, but sometimes data in an organization will never be released and will need to be destroyed.

If the media is held on hard drives, magnetic media, or thumb drives, it must be sanitized. *Sanitization* is the process of clearing all identified content, such that no data remnants can be recovered. Some of the methods used for sanitization are as follows:

▶ **Drive wiping**—This is the act of overwriting all information on the drive. As an example, DoD.5200.28-STD (7) specifies overwriting the drive with a special digital pattern through seven passes. Drive wiping allows the drive to be reused.

▶ **Zeroization**—This process is usually associated with cryptographic processes. The term was originally used with mechanical cryptographic devices. These devices would be reset to 0 to prevent anyone from recovering the key. In the electronic realm, *zeroization* involves overwriting the data with zeros. Zeroization is defined as a standard in ANSI X9.17.

▶ **Degaussing**—This process is used to permanently destroy the contents of a hard drive or magnetic media. Degaussing works by means of a powerful magnet whose field strength penetrates the media and reverses the polarity of the magnetic particles on the tape or hard disk. After media has been degaussed, it cannot be reused. The only method more secure than degaussing is physical destruction.

Data Disposal is a Big Problem

While hard drive size and performance has continued to grow at a rapid pace most hard drive and thumb drives are still shipped without encryption enabled. What this means is that you can take a hard drive from a computer you bought at an auction that will not boot up, plug the drive into another computer, and possibly have access to the data on the drive. While many of us have used a shredder, few have probably ever sanitized a hard drive. Whether your organization is planning to sell old hard drives, give them to charity, or just throw them away, you need to make sure the data on the drive is impossible to recover.

If you are thinking that most organizations already do this, consider the following. Two researchers from MIT bought 158 used hard drives from eBay. Out of the 158 hard drives, 129 had data that the researchers were able to copy. Some of the data on these drives included personal information, company HR records, medical information, a pharmacies database, and another database with 3,700 credit card numbers.

Physical media should be protected with a level of control equal to electronic media. These issues are covered in much greater detail in Chapter 3, "Physical Asset Security."

With the discussion of controls concluded, the next section focuses on auditing and monitoring. It is time to review some of the ways organizations can maintain accountability.

> **Note**
>
> Unless you're a 1960s car enthusiast like I am, it might have been a while since you have seen a working 8-track player. The point is that technology changes and the requirement to be able to read and access old media is something to consider. Be it 8-tracks, laser discs, Zip drives, or floppy disks, stored media must be readable to be useful.

Data Remanence and Decommissioning

Object reuse is important because of the remaining information that may reside on a hard disk or any other type of media. Even when data has been sanitized there may be some remaining information. This is known as data remanence. Data remanence is the residual data that remains after data has been erased. Most objects that may be reused will have some remaining amount of information left on media after it has been erased. If the media is not going to be destroyed outright, best practice is to overwrite it with a minimum of seven passes of random ones and zeros.

When information is deemed too sensitive assets such as hard drive, media, and other storage devices may not be reused and the decision may be made for asset disposal. Asset disposal must be handled in an approved manner and part of the system development life cycle. As an example, media that has been used to store sensitive or secret information should be physically destroyed. Before systems or data are decommissioned or disposed of, you must understand any existing legal requirements pertaining to records retention. When archiving information, you must consider the method for retrieving the information.

Classifying Information and Supporting Assets

Organizational information that is proprietary or confidential in nature must be protected. Data classification is a useful way to rank an organization's informational assets. A well-planned data classification system makes it easy to store and access data. It also makes it easier for users of data to understand its importance. As an example, if an organization has a clean desk policy and mandates that company documents, memos, and electronic media not be left on desks, it can change people's attitudes about the value of that information. However, whatever data classification system is used, it should be simple enough that all employees can understand it and execute it properly. Two common data classification plans are discussed next.

Data Classification

The two most common data-classification schemes are military and public. Organizations store and process so much electronic information about their customers and employees that it's critical for them to take appropriate precautions to protect this information. The responsibility for the classification of data lies with the data owner. Both military and private data classification systems accomplish this task by placing information into categories and applying labels to data and clearances to people that access the data.

The first step of this process is to assess the value of the information. When the value is known, it becomes much easier to decide the amount of resources that should be used to protect the data. It would make no sense to spend more on protecting something with a lesser value. By using this system, not all data is treated equally; data that requires more protection gets it, and funds are not wasted protecting data that does not need it.

Each level of classification established should have specific requirements and procedures. The military and commercial data-classification models have predefined labels and levels. When an organization decides which model to use, it can evaluate data placement by using criteria such as the following:

- Data value
- Data age
- Laws pertaining to data

▶ Regulations pertaining to disclosure

▶ Replacement cost

Regardless of which model is used, the following questions will help determine the proper placement of the information:

▶ Who owns the asset or data?

▶ Who controls access rights and privileges?

▶ Who approves access rights and privileges?

▶ What level of access is granted to the asset or data?

▶ Who currently has access to the asset or data?

Classification of data requires several steps:

1. Identify the data custodian.

2. Determine the criteria used for data classification.

3. Task the owner with classifying and labeling the information.

4. Identify any exceptions to the data classification policy.

5. Determine security controls to be applied to protect each category of information.

6. Specify sunset policy or end of life policy and detail in a step-by-step manner how data will be reclassified or declassified. Reviews specifying rentention and end of life should occur at specific periods of time.

7. Develop awareness program.

Military Data Classification

The military data-classification system is mandatory within the U.S. Department of Defense. This system has five levels of classification:

▶ **Top Secret**—Grave damage if exposed.

▶ **Secret**—Serious damage if exposed.

▶ **Confidential**—Disclosure could cause damage.

▶ **Sensitive but Unclassified or Restricted**—Disclosure should be avoided.

▶ **Unclassified or Official**—If released, no damage should result.

Each classification represents a level of sensitivity. *Sensitivity* is the desired degree of secrecy that the information should maintain. If you hold a confidential clearance, it means that you could access unclassified, sensitive, or confidential information for which you have a need to know. Your need to know would not extend to the secret or top secret levels. The concept of need-to-know is similar to the principle of least privilege in that employees should have access only to information that they need to know to complete their assigned duties.

Public/Private Data Classification

The public or commercial data classification is also built on a four-level model:

▶ **Confidential**—This is the highest level of sensitivity and disclosure could cause extreme damage to the organization.

▶ **Private**—This information is for organization use only and its disclosure would damage the organization.

▶ **Sensitive**—This information requires a greater level of protection to prevent loss of confidentiality.

▶ **Public**—This information might not need to be disclosed, but if it is, it shouldn't cause any damage.

Table 2.1 provides details about the military and public/private data-classification models.

TABLE 2.1 **Commercial and Military Data Classifications**

Commercial Business Classifications	Military Classifications
Confidential	Top secret
Private	Secret
Sensitive	Confidential
Public	Sensitive (BU)
	Unclassified

Caution

Information has a useful life. Data classification systems need to build in mechanisms to monitor whether information has become obsolete. Obsolete information should be declassified or destroyed.

Asset Management and Governance

The job of asset management and governance is to align the goals of IT to the business functions of the organization, to track assets throughout their life-cycle, and to protect the assets of the organization. Asset management can be defined as any system that inventories, monitors, and maintains items of value. Assets can be both tangible and intangible. Assets can include the following:

▶ Hardware

▶ Software

▶ Employees

▶ Services

▶ Reputation

▶ Documentation

You can think of asset management as a structured approach of deploying, operating, maintaining, upgrading, and disposing of assets cost-effectively. Asset management is required for proper risk assessment. Before you can start to place a value on an asset you must know what it is and what it is worth. Its value can be assessed either quantitatively or qualitative. A quantitative approach requires:

1. Estimation of potential losses and determination of single loss expectancy (SLE)

2. Completion of a threat frequency analysis and calculation of the annual rate of occurrence (ARO)

3. Determination of the annual loss expectancy (ALE)

A qualitative approach does not place a dollar value on the asset and ranks it as high, medium, or low concern. The downside of performing qualitative evaluations is that you are not working with dollar values, so it is sometimes harder to communicate the results of the assessment to management.

One key asset is software. CISSP candidates should understand common issues related to software licensing. Because software vendors usually license their software rather than sell it, and license it for a number of users on a number of systems, software licenses must be accounted for by the purchasing organization. If users or systems exceed the licensed number, the organization can be held legally liable.

As we move into an age where software is being delivered over the Internet and not with media (CD), software asset management is an important concern.

Software Licensing

Intellectual property rights issues have always been hard to enforce. Just consider the uproar that Napster caused years ago as the courts tried to work out issues of intellectual property and the rights of individuals to share music and files. The software industry has long dealt with this same issue. From the early days of computing, some individuals have been swapping, sharing, and illegally copying computer software. The unauthorized copying and sharing of software is considered software piracy, which is illegal. Many don't think that the copy of that computer game you gave a friend is hurting anyone. But software piracy is big business, and accumulated loss to the property's owners is staggering. According to a 2008 report on intellectual property to the United States Congress, in just one raid in June 2007, the FBI recovered more than two billion dollars worth of illegal Microsoft and Symantec software. Internationally, losses from illegal software are estimated to be in excess of $200 billion.

Microsoft and other companies are actively fighting to protect their property rights. Some organizations have formed the Software Protection Association, which is one of the primary bodies that work to enforce licensing agreements. The Business Software Alliance (BSA) and the Federation Against Software Theft are international groups targeting software piracy. These associations target organizations of all sizes from small, two-person companies to large multinationals.

Software companies are making clear in their licenses what a user can and cannot do with their software. As an example, Microsoft Windows XP allowed multiple transfers of licenses whereas Windows 8 and 10 have different transfer rules. As an example, Windows 8 allows only one transfer. The user license states, "The first user of the software may reassign the license to another device one time." Some vendors even place limits on virtualization. License agreements can actually be distributed in several different ways, including the following:

▶ **Click-wrap license agreements**—Found in many software products, these agreements require you to click through and agree to terms to install the software product. These are often called *contracts of adhesion*; they are "take it or leave it" propositions.

▶ **Master license agreements**—Used by large companies that develop specific software solutions that specify how the customer can use the product.

▶ **Shrink-wrap license agreements**—Created when software started to be sold commercially and named for the fact that breaking the shrink wrap signifies your acceptance of the license.

Even with licensing and increased policing activities by organizations such as the BSA, improved technologies make it increasingly easy to pirate software, music, books, and other types of intellectual property. These factors and the need to comply with two World Trade Organization (WTO) treaties led to the passage of the 1998 Digital Millennium Copyright Act (DMCA). Here are some salient highlights:

▶ The DMCA makes it a crime to bypass or circumvent antipiracy measures built into commercial software products.

▶ The DMCA outlaws the manufacture, sale, or distribution of any equipment or device that can be used for code-cracking or illegally copying software.

▶ The DMCA provides exemptions from anti-circumvention provisions for libraries and educational institutions under certain circumstances; however, for those not covered by such exceptions, the act provides penalties up to $1,000,000 and 10 years in prison.

▶ The DMCA provides Internet service providers exceptions from copyright infringement liability enabling transmission of information across the Internet.

Equipment Lifecycle

The equipment lifecycle begins at the time equipment is requested to the end of its useful life or when it is discarded. The equipment lifecycle typically consist of four phases:

▶ Defining requirements

▶ Acquisition and implementation

▶ Operation and maintenance

▶ Disposal and decommission

While some may think that much of the work is done once equipment has been acquired, that is far from the truth. There will need to be some established support functions. Routine maintenance is one important item.

Without routine maintenance equipment will fail, and those costs can be calculated. Items to consider include:

▶ Lost productivity

▶ Delayed or canceled orders

▶ Cost of repair

▶ Cost of rental equipment

▶ Cost of emergency services

▶ Cost to replace equipment or reload data

▶ Cost to pay personnel to maintain the equipment

Technical support is another consideration. The longer a piece of equipment has been in use the more issues it may have. As an example, if you did a search for exploits for Windows 7 or Windows 10 which do you think would return more results? Most likely Windows 7. This all points to the need for more support the longer the resource has been in use.

Determine Data Security Controls

Any discussion on logical asset security must at some point discuss encryption. While there is certainly more to protecting data than just encrypting it, encryption is one of the primary controls used to protect data. Just consider all the cases of lost hard drives, laptops, and thumb drives that have made the news because they contained data that was not encrypted. In many cases encryption is not just a good idea; it is also mandated by law. CISSP candidates must ensure that corporate policies addressing where and how encryption will be used are well defined and being followed by all employees.

Let's examine the two areas at which encryption can be used to protect data at a high level. These topics will be expanded on in Chapter 6, "The Application and Use of Cryptography."

Data at Rest

Data at rest is information stored on some form of media that is not traversing a network or residing in temporary memory. Failure to properly protect data at rest can lead to attacks such as the following:

▶ Pod slurping, a technique for illicitly downloading or copying data from a computer. Typically used for data exfiltration.

▶ Various forms of USB (Universal Serial Bus) malware, including but not limited to USB Switchblade and Hacksaw.

▶ Other forms of malicious software, including but not limited to viruses, worms, Trojans, and various types of key loggers.

Data at rest can be protected via different technical and physical hardware or software controls that should be defined in your security policy. Some hardware offers the ability to build in encryption. A relatively new hardware security device for computers is called the *trusted platform module* (TPM) chip. The TPM is a "slow" cryptographic hardware processor which can be used to provide a greater level of security than software encryption. A TPM chip installed on the motherboard of a client computer can also be used for system state authentication. The TPM can also be used to store the encryption keys.

The TPM measures the system and stores the measurements as it traverses through the boot sequence. When queried, the TPM will return these values signed by a local private key. These values can be used to discover the status of a platform. The recognition of the state and validation of these values is referred to as *attestation*. Phrased differently, attestation allows one to confirm, authenticate, or prove a system to be in a specific state. Data can also be encrypted using these values. This process is referred to as *sealing a configuration*. In short, the TPM is also a tamper-resistant cryptographic module that can provide a means to report the system configuration to a policy enforcer or "health monitor."

The TPM also provides the ability to encrypt information to a specific platform configuration by calculating hashed values based on items such as the system's firmware, configuration details, and core components of the operating system as it boots. These values, along with a secret key stored in the TPM, can be used to encrypt information and only allow it to become usable in a specific machine configuration. This process is called *sealing*.

The TPM is now addressed by ISO 11889-1:2009. It can also be used with other forms of data and system protection to provide a layered approach, referred to as defense in depth. For example, the TPM can help protect the actual system, while another set of encryption keys can be stored on a user's common access card or smart card to decrypt and access the data set.

Another potential option that builds on this technology is self-encrypting hard drives (SEDs). These pieces of hardware offer many advantages over non-encrypted drives:

▶ Compliance—SEDs have the ability to offer built-in encryption. This can help with compliance laws that many organizations must adhere to.

▶ Strong security—SEDs make use of strong encryption. The contents of an SED are always encrypted and the encryption keys are themselves encrypted and protected in hardware.

▶ Ease of use—Users only have to authenticate to the drive when the device boots up or when they change passwords/credentials. The encryption is not visible to the user.

▶ Performance—As SEDs are not visible to the user and are integrated into hardware, the system operates at full performance with no impact on user productivity.

Software encryption is another protection mechanism for data at rest. There are many options available, such as EFS, BitLocker, and PGP. Software encryption can be used on specific files, databases, or even entire RAID arrays that store sensitive data. What is most important about any potential software option is that not only must the encrypted data remain secure and remain inaccessible when access controls, such as usernames and passwords, are incorrect; the encryption keys themselves must be protected, and should therefore be updated on a regular basis.

> **Caution**
>
> Encryption keys should be stored separately from the data.

Data in Transit

Any time data is being processed or moved from one location to the next, it requires proper controls. The basic problem is that many protocols and applications send information via clear text. Services such as email, web, and FTP were not designed with security in mind and send information with few security controls and no encryption. Examples of insecure protocols include:

▶ FTP—Clear-text username and password

▶ Telnet—Clear-text username and password

▶ HTTP—Clear text

▶ SMTP—All data is passed in the clear

For data in transit that is not being protected by some form of encryption, there are many dangers, which include the following:

▶ Eavesdropping

▶ Sniffing

▶ Hijacking

▶ Data alteration

Today, many people connect to corporate networks from many different locations. Employees may connect via free Wi-Fi from coffee shops, restaurants, airports, or even hotels.

One way to protect this type of data in transit is by means of a Virtual Private Network (VPN). VPNs are used to connect devices through the public Internet. Three protocols are used to provide a tunneling mechanism in support of VPNs: Point-to-Point Tunneling Protocol (PPTP), Layer 2 Tunneling Protocol (L2TP), and IP Security (IPSec). When an appropriate protocol is defined, the VPN traffic will be encrypted. Microsoft supplies Microsoft Point-to-Point Encryption (MPPE), with PPTP, native to the Microsoft operating systems. L2TP offers no encryption, and as such is usually used with IPSec in ESP mode to protect data in transit. IPSec can provide both tunneling and encryption.

Two types of tunnels can be implemented:

▶ **LAN-to-LAN tunnels**—Users can tunnel transparently to each other on separate LANS.

▶ **Host-to-LAN tunnels**—Mobile users can connect to the corporate LAN.

Having an encrypted tunnel is just one part of protecting data in transit. Another important concept is that of authentication. Almost all VPNs use digital certificates as the primary means of authentication. X.509 v3 is the de facto standard. X.509 specifies certificate requirements and their contents. Much like that of a state driver's license office, the Certificate Authority (CA) guarantees the authenticity of the certificate and its contents. These certificates act as an approval mechanism.

Just as with other services, organizations need to develop policies to define who will have access to the VPN and what encryption mechanisms will be used. It's important that VPN policies be designed to map to the organization's security policy. As senior management is ultimately responsible, they must approve and support this policy.

Standard email is also very insecure and can be exposed while in transit. Standard email protocols such as SMTP, POP3, and IMAP all send data via clear text. To protect email in transit you must use encryption. Email protection mechanisms include PGP, Secure Multipurpose Internet Mail Extensions (S/MIME), and Privacy Enhanced Mail (PEM). Regardless of what is being protected periodic auditing of sensitive data should be part of policy and should occur on a regular schedule.

Data in transit will also require a discussion of how the encryption will be applied. Encryption can be performed at different locations with different amounts of protection applied.

▶ **Link encryption**—The data is encrypted through the entire communication path. Because all header information is encrypted each node must decrypt and encrypt the routing information. Source and destination address cannot be seen to someone sniffing traffic.

▶ **End to end encryption**—Generally performed by the end user and as such can pass through each node without further processing. However, source and destination addresses are passed in clear text, so they can be seen to someone sniffing traffic.

Endpoint Security

No review of logical asset security would be complete without a discussion of endpoint security. Endpoint security consists of the controls placed on client or end user systems, such as control of USB and CD/DVD, antivirus, anti-malware, anti-spyware, and so on. The controls placed on a client system are very important.

▶ Removable media—A common vector for malware propagation is via USB thumb drive. Malware such as Stuxnet, Conficker, and Flame all had the capability to spread by thumb drives. Removable drives should be restricted and turned off when possible.

▶ Disk encryption—Disk encryption software such as EFS and BitLocker can be used to encrypt the contents of desktop and laptop hard drives. Also, corporate smartphones and tablets should have encryption enabled.

▶ Application whitelisting—This approach only allows known good applications and software to be installed, updated, and used. Whitelisting techniques can include code signing, digital certificates, known good cryptographic hashes, or trusted full paths and names. Blacklisting, alternatively, blocks known bad software from being downloaded and installed.

▶ Host-based firewalls—Defense in depth dictates that the company should consider not just enterprise firewalls but also host-based firewalls.

▶ Configuration lockdown—Not just anyone should have the ability to make changes to equipment or hardware. Configurations controls can be used to prevent unauthorized changes.

▶ Antivirus—This is the most commonly deployed endpoint security product. While it is a needed component, antivirus has become much less effective over the last several years.

One basic starting point is to implement the principle of least privilege. This concept can also be applied to each logical asset: each computer, system component or process should have the least authority necessary to perform its duties.

Baselines

A baseline can be described as a standard of security. Baselines are usually mapped to industry standards. As an example, an organization might specify that all computer systems be certified by Common Criteria to an Evaluation Assurance Level (EAL) 3. Another example of baselining can be seen in NIST 800-53. NIST 800-53 describes a tailored baseline as a starting point for determining the needed level of security as seen in Figure 2.4.

▶ IT structure analysis (survey)—Includes analysis of technical, operation, and physical aspects of the organization, division, or group.

▶ Assessment of protection needs—Determination of the needed level of protection. This activity can be quantitative or qualitative.

▶ Selection of actions—Determination of what specific controls need to be implemented.

▶ Running comparison of nominal and actual—Periodic review of activities and actions to measure the change between what was previously occurring and what is currently occurring.

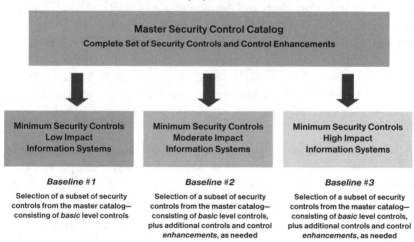

FIGURE 2.4   NIST 800-53 Scoping and Baselining Controls.

NIST 800-53 specifies scoping or tailoring activities and categorizes information based on impact.

- ▶ Low impact
- ▶ Moderate impact
- ▶ High impact

Scoping or tailoring is the act of adding or removing controls as needed to get the right level of protection. Obviously, adding controls will increase cost and generally increase system security, whereas removing controls reduces costs but can expose the system to unnecessary threats. Therefore due care must be used to determine the proper level of controls. Scoping and tailoring activities should be well documented with appropriate justification. In some cases, information and information systems must be protected regardless of the cost, because of laws that may govern certain industries.

Laws, Standards, Mandates and Resources

The following laws, standards, and mandates have an impact on information security and can affect the risk profile of an organization. Regardless of the laws and mandates, organizations should be proactive when it comes to corporate governance. Several laws and mandates are described here:

- ▶ Health Insurance Portability and Accountability Act (HIPAA)—HIPAA was signed into law in 1996. It has two areas. Title I of the HIPAA of 1996 protects health insurance coverage for workers and their families when they change or lose their jobs. Title II requires the U.S. Department of Health and Human Services (DHHS) to establish national standards for electronic health care transactions and national identifiers for providers, health plans, and employers.

Under HIPAA, the U.S. DHHS was required to publish a set of rules regarding privacy. The Privacy Rule dictates controls that organizations must put in place to protect personal information. The privacy rule defines three major purposes:

- ▶ "To protect and enhance the rights of consumers by providing them access to their health information and controlling the inappropriate use of that information."

► "To improve the quality of health care in the United States by restoring trust in the health care system among consumers, health care professionals, and the multitude of organizations and individuals committed to the delivery of care."

► "To improve the efficiency and effectiveness of health care delivery by creating a national framework for health privacy protection that builds on efforts by states, health systems, and individual organizations and individuals."

Gramm-Leach-Bliley Act (GLBA)—GLBA was signed into law in 1999 and resulted in the most sweeping overhaul of financial services regulation in the United States.

Title V of GLBA addresses financial institution privacy with two subtitles. Subtitle A requires financial institutions to make certain disclosures about their privacy policies and to give individuals an opt-out capability. Subtitle B criminalizes the practice known as pretexting, which can be described as the practice of obtaining personal information under false pretenses.

Under GLBA, financial institutions are required to protect the confidentiality of individual privacy information. As specified in GLBA, financial institutions are required to develop, implement, and maintain a comprehensive information security program with appropriate administrative, technical, and physical safeguards. Administrative controls include items such as background checks and separation of duties. Technical controls can be hardware or software, such as encryption or an IDS. Physical controls include gates, guards, and fences. The controls specified in the information security program must include:

► The assignment of a designated program manager for the organization's information security program

► A periodic risk and vulnerability assessment and audit

► A program of regular testing and monitoring

► The development of policies and procedures for control of sensitive information and PII

Federal Information Security Management Act (FISMA)—FISMA was signed into law in 2002. One of the big changes that FISMA brought about was a set of clear guidelines for information security designed for the protection of federal government IT infrastructure and data assets. FISMA requirements specify the following responsibilities:

▶ Develop and maintain an information assurance (IA) program with an entire IT security architecture and framework.

▶ Ensure that information security training is conducted to keep IAT and IAM personnel properly trained and certified in accordance with DoD. 8570.

▶ Implement accountability for personnel with significant responsibilities for information security.

FISMA also requires periodic risk assessments, risk assessment policies and procedures, periodic (at least annual) testing and evaluation, and proper training and awareness to senior management so that proper security awareness programs can be deployed.

Sarbanes-Oxley Act (SOX)—SOX was signed into law in 2002. This act mandated a number of reforms to enhance corporate responsibility, enhance financial disclosures, and combat corporate and accounting fraud. Sections 302 and 404 are the two sections that address IT infrastructures and information security. Section 302 requires the CEO and CFO to personally certify that the organization has the proper internal controls. It also mandates that the CEO and CFO report on effectiveness of internal controls around financial reporting.

Section 404 sets requirements on management's structure, control objectives, and control procedures. Staying compliant with Section 404 requires companies to establish an infrastructure that is designed to archive records and data and protect them from destruction, loss, unauthorized alteration, or other misuse. It requires that a set of comprehensive controls be put in place and holds CEOs and CFOs accountable.

United States Resources

NIST started as the National Bureau of Standards and changed its name in 1989 to the National Institute of Standards and Technology. Some of the NIST documents a CISSP should have knowledge of are:

▶ NIST 800-37—Guide for applying risk management.

▶ NIST 800-53—Government publication that provides guidelines for selecting and specifying security controls for information systems supporting the executive agencies of the federal government. Many organizations in private industry use NIST SP 800-53 as a guide for their own security management.

▶ NIST 800-60—Guide for Mapping Types of Information and Information.

Federal Information Processing Standards (FIPS) are publicly announced standards developed by the United States federal government for use in computer systems by non-military government agencies and government contractors.

▶ FIPS 199—Establishes security categories of information systems used by the federal government.

▶ FIPS 200—Mandatory security standards for government systems.

International Resources

Our first item is the information technology infrastructure library (ITIL). ITIL provides a framework for identifying, planning, delivering, and supporting IT services for business.

The IT Governance Institute has developed a process that begins with setting objectives for the enterprise's IT, providing the initial direction and then evolving into a continuous loop.

ITIL presents a service lifecycle that includes

▶ Continual service improvement

▶ Service strategy

▶ Service design

▶ Service transition

▶ Service operation

Next up are some of the standards from the International Organization for Standardization that a CISSP should be familiar with:

▶ ISO **27001**—This standard describes requirements on how to establish, implement, operate, monitor, review, and maintain an information security management system (ISMS); it is based on British Standard 7799.

▶ ISO **27002**—This standard is considered a code of practice that describes ways to develop a security program within the organization.

▶ ISO **27003**—This standard focuses on implementation.

▶ ISO **27004**—This standard is a standard for information security measurements.

▶ ISO **27005**—This standard describes how to implement solutions based on risk management.

▶ ISO **27799**—This standard describes how to protect personal health information.

ISO 9001 is a quality management standard that has widespread support and attention. ISO 9001 describes how production processes are to be managed and reviewed. It is not a standard of quality; it is about how well a system or process is documented. Companies that wish to obtain 9001 certification will need to perform a gap analysis to determine areas that need improvement. ISO 9001 is actually six documents that specify:

▶ Control of Documents

▶ Control of Records

▶ Control of Non-conforming Product

▶ Corrective Action

▶ Preventive Action

▶ Internal Audits

> **Tip**
>
> **Achieving ISO 9001:2000 Certification**—ISO 9001 certification requires an organization to perform a gap analysis. This allows the company to identify shortcomings that need to be addressed in order to obtain certification.

Being ISO-certified means that the organization has the capability to provide products that meet specific requirements, and includes a process for continual improvement. It may also have a direct bearing on an audit as it places strong controls on documented procedures. Another ISO standard that the auditor should be aware of is ISO 17799. 17799 provides the best practice guidance on information security management. It is divided into 12 main sections:

▶ Risk assessment and treatment

▶ Security policy

► Organization of information security

► Asset management

► Human Resources security

► Physical and environmental security

► Communications and operations management

► Access control

► Information systems acquisition, development, and maintenance

► Information security incident management

► Business continuity management

► Compliance

> **Tip**
>
> CISSP exam candidates should have a basic understanding of ISO standards and their purpose; however, the exam does not cover U.S. laws.

Finally, let's review a couple of European documents:

► 10 Steps to Cyber Security—Detailed cyber-security information and advice across 10 critical technical and procedural areas. Created by CESG, the information security arm of GCHQ, and the National Technical Authority for Information Assurance within the United Kingdom.

► Cybersecurity Strategy of the European Union—This document was developed by the European Union; it describes their approach to preventing and responding to cyber-security attacks.

Exam Prep Questions

1. Which of the following levels best represents the military classification system?

   ○ **A.** Confidential, private, sensitive, and public

   ○ **B.** Top secret, secret, private, sensitive, and public

   ○ **C.** Top secret, confidential, private, sensitive, and unclassified

   ○ **D.** Top secret, secret, confidential, sensitive, and unclassified

2. Which of the following standards describes how well a system or process is documented?

   ○ **A.** ISO 27001

   ○ **B.** ISO 9001

   ○ **C.** ISO 27002

   ○ **D.** ISO 17799

3. Which of the following endpoint security controls could have been used to potentially prevent malware such as Stuxnet, Conficker, and Flame?

   ○ **A.** Implementing disk encryption

   ○ **B.** Hardening edge devices

   ○ **C.** Blocking removable media

   ○ **D.** Enforcing application whitelisting

4. Place the following in their proper order:

   ○ **A.** Determine SLE, ARO, and ALE, then asset value.

   ○ **B.** Determine asset value, then ARO, SLE, and ALE.

   ○ **C.** Determine asset value, then SLE, ALE, and SLE.

   ○ **D.** Determine asset value, then SLE, ARO, and ALE.

5. The downside of performing this type of assessment is that you are not working with dollar values, so it is sometimes harder to communicate the results of the assessment to management. Which of the following assessment types does this describe?

   ○ **A.** Qualitative

   ○ **B.** Quantitative

   ○ **C.** Numeric mitigation

   ○ **D.** Red team

6. Which of the following categories of control can include the logical mechanisms used to control access and authenticate users?

   ○ **A.** Administrative

   ○ **B.** Clerical

   ○ **C.** Technical

   ○ **D.** Physical

7. Which of the following is incorrect when describing an SED?

   ○ **A.** Eases compliance

   ○ **B.** Slow performance

   ○ **C.** Ease of use

   ○ **D.** Strong security

8. Which of the following is the top level of protection for commercial business classification?

   ○ **A.** Secret

   ○ **B.** Confidential

   ○ **C.** Top secret

   ○ **D.** Private

9. Which of the following is the most specific of security documents?

   ○ **A.** Procedures

   ○ **B.** Standards

   ○ **C.** Policies

   ○ **D.** Baselines

10. The last thing you want in an organization is that everyone is accountable but no one is responsible. Therefore, the data owner should be in which of the following groups?

   ○ **A.** End users

   ○ **B.** Technical managers

   ○ **C.** Senior management

   ○ **D.** Everyone is responsible; therefore, all groups are owners

11. Which term best describes a symbol, word, name, sound, or thing that uniquely identifies a product or service?

- ○ **A.** Trade secret
- ○ **B.** Copyright
- ○ **C.** Patent
- ○ **D.** Trademark

12. After opening a new branch in the Midwest your company is analyzing buying patterns to determine the relationship between various items purchased. Which of the following best describes this situation?

- ○ **A.** Data mining
- ○ **B.** Knowledge management
- ○ **C.** Data warehouse
- ○ **D.** Data standards

13. Which ISO document is used for a standard for information security management?

- ○ **A.** ISO 27001
- ○ **B.** ISO 27002
- ○ **C.** ISO 27004
- ○ **D.** ISO 27799

14. Which of the following SAN solutions is fast, rides on top of Ethernet, yet is non-routable?

- ○ **A.** SCSI
- ○ **B.** iSCSI
- ○ **C.** HBA
- ○ **D.** FCoE

15. Who is ultimately responsible for the security of an asset?

- ○ **A.** Asset owner
- ○ **B.** Auditor
- ○ **C.** Custodian
- ○ **D.** Risk assessment team

Answers to Exam Prep Questions

1. **D.** The military data classification system is widely used within the Department of Defense. This system has five levels of classification: unclassified, sensitive, confidential, secret, and top secret. Each level represents an increasing level of sensitivity.

2. **B.** ISO 9001 describes how production processes are to be managed and reviewed. It is not a standard of quality; it is about how well a system or process is documented. Answers A, C, and D are incorrect: ISO 27001 describes requirements on how to establish, implement, operate, monitor, review, and maintain an information security management system; ISO 27002 is considered a code of practice that describes ways to develop a security program within the organization; ISO 17799 provides best practice guidance on information security management.

3. **C.** Restricting removable media may have helped prevent infection from malware that is known to spread via thumb drive or removable media. Answer A is incorrect because encryption of media would not have helped. Answer B is incorrect because edge devices were not specifically targeted. Answer D is incorrect because enforcing application whitelisting would not have prevented advanced persistent threats from executing on local systems.

4. **D.** The proper order is to determine the asset value, then SLE, ARO, and ALE. Answers A, B, and C are incorrect; they are not in the proper order.

5. **A.** Qualitative assessment is scenario-driven and does not attempt to assign dollar values to components of the risk analysis. Quantitative assessment is based on dollar amounts; both numeric mitigation and red team are distractors.

6. **C.** Technical controls can be hardware or software. They are the logical mechanisms used to control access and authenticate users, identify unusual activity, and restrict unauthorized access. Clerical is a nonexistent category and all other answers are incorrect: administrative controls are procedural and physical controls include locks, guards, gates, and alarms.

7. **B.** Self-encrypting hard drives offer many advantages, such as easing compliance issues with items like PII. They are easy to use and offer strong encryption. Answer B is correct because SEDs do not slow down performance; they are actually integrated into the hardware and operate at full performance with no impact on user productivity.

8. **B.** Confidential is the top level of data classification for commercial business classification. Answers A, C, and D are incorrect because secret and top secret are both part of the military classification, while private is a lower level of commercial business classification.

9. **A.** A procedure is a detailed, in-depth, step-by-step document that lays out exactly what is to be done. It's tied to specific technologies and devices. Standards are tactical documents; policies are high-level documents; and baselines are minimum levels of security that a system, network, or device must adhere to.

10. **C.** Senior management is the ultimate owner because these individuals are responsible for the asset and must answer if data is compromised. Although answer C is the best possible choice, it is important to realize that, in most cases, the data owner will be a member of management but might not be the most senior executive within the organization. For example, the CFO would be the data owner for all financial data, the director of human resources would be the data owner for all HR data, and so on. All other answers are incorrect because end users, technical managers, and other employees are not typically the data owners.

11. **D.** A trademark is a symbol, word, name, sound, or thing that identifies the origin of a product or service in a particular trade. Answers A, B, and C are incorrect as they do not properly describe a trademark.

12. **A.** Data mining. It is the process of analyzing data to find and understand patterns and relationships about the data. Answers B, C, and D are incorrect. Knowledge management seeks to make intelligent use of all the knowledge in an organization. A data warehouse is a database that contains data from many different databases. Data standards provide consistent meaning to data shared among different information systems.

13. **C.** ISO 27004 is the standard for security management. ISO 27001 is focused on requirements. ISO 27002 was developed from BS 7799, and ISO 27799 is focused on health.

14. **D.** Fiber Channel over Ethernet (FCoE) can operate at speeds of 10 GB per second and rides on top of the Ethernet protocol. While it is fast, it has a disadvantage in that it is non-routable. Answers A, B, and C are incorrect. SCSI is used for local devices only. iSCSI is a SAN standard used for connecting data storage facilities and allowing remote SCSI devices to communicate. HBAs are used to connect a host system to an enterprise storage device.

15. **A.** Some day-to-day responsibility may be passed down to the custodian; however, ultimately the owner is responsible.

Need to Know More?

Data valuation: www.cio.com/article/2375569/cio-role/why-cios-must-own-data-valuation.html

Understanding FIPS guidelines: www.sans.org/reading-room/whitepapers/standards/securing-sensitive-data-understanding-federal-information-processing-standards-fips-549

ISO27002 overview: en.wikipedia.org/wiki/ISO/IEC_27002

Site security: www.faqs.org/rfcs/rfc2196.html

IT asset management: searchcio.techtarget.com/definition/IT-asset-management-information-technology-asset-management

Building effective security policies: www.sans.org/security-resources/policies/

IT security baselines: www.securestate.com/services/minimum-security-baselines

Building effective policy: csrc.nist.gov/nissc/1997/panels/isptg/pescatore/html/

Hard drive disposal: www.semshred.com/contentmgr/showdetails.php/id/2480

CHAPTER 3

Physical Asset Security

Terms you'll need to understand:

▶ CPTED

▶ Perimeter intrusion and detection assessment system

▶ Bollards

▶ CCTV

▶ Annunciator

▶ Piggyback

▶ Intrusion detection

▶ Tamper protection

▶ Halon

Topics you'll need to master:

▶ Physical barrier design

▶ Fence height and grade specification

▶ Lock mechanisms and strengths identification

▶ Fire safety design

▶ Fire suppression methods

▶ Fire detection systems identification

▶ Light placement and design

▶ Specifying requirements for new facilities

Introduction

Physical security is a key element of asset security. Many of us might underestimate the importance of physical controls. Yet these controls represent one of the three key areas (along with administrative and logical controls) into which all controls are categorized. Each control can be measured against the basic requirements of availability, confidentiality, and integrity. After all, if attackers can walk off with a portable hard drive, tablet, or smartphone, they have (at the least) denied you availability. If a co-worker throws away a DVD containing propri-etary information that a criminal could recover, confidential information can be disclosed to unauthorized persons. If a disgruntled employee can physically access a server on which a key database resides as opposed to remotely accessing the database and change amounts, values, or data integrity can be compromised.

Implementations of physical security surround us. For example, you might have a sticker on your car that permits you to park in the company parking garage. Perhaps company policy requires you to get a new photo taken each year for your company ID badge. Access to the equipment room might be limited to those employees that have been assigned keys. You deal with physical security every day.

CISSP candidates must also have a good understanding of what is involved in securing a site. The goals of overall physical security are to deter, delay, detect, assess, and respond. Physical security controls are like all other controls, and must be designed in layers. Candidates must understand the benefits of layered protections, also referred to as *defense in breadth*, such as fences, locks, physical access control, and closed-circuit television (CCTV) to protect employees and critical infrastructures. Defense in breadth is achieved when several layers of security within one control are applied. *Defense in depth*, by contrast, is achieved by applying several security layers using more than one control; that is, technical, administrative, and physical.

Physical Security Risks

Threats to physical security have existed for as long as humans have inhabited Earth. Consider the Incan city, Machu Picchu, built high on a mountain more than 7,000 feet above sea level. This ancient city was surrounded by thick stone walls and many natural exterior defenses that made it difficult to attack. Careful and even ingenious planning is still evident in the design of this city's defense.

In the modern world, our multinational organizations might not be headquar-tered on remote mountain peaks, but security is still evident, because a variety of threats to physical security still exist. These threats can be divided into broad categories, such as natural disasters, man-made threats, and technical problems. The sections that follow delve into these threats in greater detail.

Natural Disasters

Natural disasters come in many forms. Although natural disasters are not something that you can prevent, you can have a disaster recovery plan to mitigate the impact. A recovery and corrective plan can be implemented for facilities, information, and information systems that could be affected that will detail how you will respond when confronted with disasters. As an example, organizations planning to establish a facility in New Orleans, Louisiana, might have minimal earthquake concerns; however, hurricanes would be considered an imminent threat. Understanding a region and its associated weather-related issues are important in planning physical security. Natural disasters that organizations should consider include:

▶ **Hurricanes, typhoons, and tropical cyclones**—These natural products of the tropical ocean and atmosphere are powered by heat from the sea. They grow in strength and velocity as they progress across the ocean and spawn tornadoes and cause high winds and floods when they come ashore.

▶ **Tidal waves/tsunamis**—The word tsunami is based on a Japanese word meaning "harbor wave." This natural phenomenon consists of a series of huge and widely dispersed waves that cause massive damage when they crash on shore.

▶ **Floods**—Floods can result when the soil has poor retention properties or when the amount of rainfall exceeds the ground's capability to absorb water. Floods are also caused when creeks and rivers overflow their banks.

▶ **Earthquakes**—These are caused from movement of the earth along fault lines. One example is the Nepal earthquake of 2015 that killed over 8,000 people and injured more than 21,000. Areas in the United States, such as California and Alaska, are especially vulnerable because they are on top of major active fault lines.

▶ **Tornadoes**—Tornadoes are violent storms that descend to the ground as violent rotating columns of air. Tornadoes leave a path of destruction that may be quite narrow or extremely broad—up to about a mile wide.

▶ **Fire**—This disaster can be man-made (intentional or accidental) or natural, and is the most common cause of damage to property and loss of life. According to statistics at fema.gov, there were some 3,005 deaths due to fire in the United States in 2011. That's a great loss of life. Wildfires can also cause massive damage.

Man-Made Threats

Man-made threats are another major concern when planning your organization's physical security. Natural threats such as floods, hurricanes, or tornadoes must be planned for, knowing that they cannot be prevented. However, man-made threats require controls that minimize (or eliminate) opportunity of occurrence, and provide for quick response in the event of any occurrence. Consider the man-made threats in the list that follows:

▶ **Terrorism**—As demonstrated in events such as the Paris attacks in November 2015 and the San Bernardino, California, attack in December 2015, and as painfully understood by victims worldwide, terrorists act with calculated inhumane tactics to force their goals on society. Terrorists often claim vindication in religious or political extremism. By doing a risk analysis and threat modeling, organizations can determine what aspects of their business make them a possible target for terrorism—that is, a "soft" target. This could drive the need for physical security controls. Organizations that have a higher volume of human traffic along with sensitive information to protect are increasingly becoming targets for acts of traditional terrorism and cyber-terrorism.

▶ **Vandalism**—Since the Vandals sacked Rome in 455 A.D., the term *vandalism* has been synonymous with the willful destruction of another's property.

▶ **Theft**—Theft of company assets can range from an annoyance to legal liability. Sure, the company laptop, tablet, or smartphone can be replaced, but what about the data on the device? For example, Sophos. com reported that the average cost of a stolen laptop is upwards of $49,000. If you are curious to know how much of a problem this is, take a moment to review blogs.sophos.com/2013/09/12/how-much-does-a-lost-laptop-cost-your-business/.

▶ **Destruction**—Physical and logical assets are vulnerable to destruction by current employees, former employees, and/or outsiders. Consider that in 2012, the Shamoon malware is believed to have destroyed 30,000 Saudi Aramco workstations.

▶ **Criminal activities**—This category is a catch-all for other malicious behaviors that threaten your employees or your infrastructure. Maybe your company thought it was getting a real tax break by moving into a lower-income area. Now, employees don't feel safe walking to their cars at night. Or, maybe the company's web administrator is running his own music and movie download site on the company network. After all, it's just for fun and a little added pocket money.

Technical Problems

Unlike natural disasters or man-made threats, technical problems are the events that just seem to happen, often at highly inopportune times. These events can range from inconvenient glitches to potential large-scale disasters. Emergency situations can include the following:

▶ **Communication loss**—Voice and data communication systems play a critical role in today's organizations. Communication loss can be the outage of voice communication systems or data networks. As more organizations use convergence technologies such as network-controlled door locks, Internet Protocol (IP) video cameras, and VoIP (Voice over IP), a network failure means that not only the data connection fails, but also the voice communication.

▶ **Utility loss**—Utilities include water, gas, communication systems, and electrical power. The loss of utilities can bring business to a standstill. Generators and backups can prevent these problems if they are used.

▶ **Equipment failure**—Equipment will fail over time. This is why maintenance is so important. With insufficient planning, you might experience a business outage. A Fortune 1,000 study found that 65% of all businesses that fail to resume operations within one week never recover at all and permanently cease operation.

Caution

Service-level agreements (SLAs) are one good way to plan for equipment failure. With an SLA in place, the vendor agrees to repair or replace the covered equipment within a given time. Just keep in mind that while an SLA covers replacement of materials or repair time, it still doesn't cover the cost incurred by the downtime or loss of credibility.

Facility Concerns and Requirements

Whether you are charged with assessing an existing facility, moving into a new facility, or planning to construct a new facility, physical security must be a high priority. It's important to consider all the threats that have been discussed, as well as additional threats that might be unique to your operations. The last thing you want is to build a facility in an area where your employees fear for their personal safety. At the same time, you don't want the facility to feel like a bank vault or be designed like a prison. You need a facility in which employees can be comfortable, productive, and feel safe.

CPTED

A key component of achieving this balance is Crime Prevention Through Environmental Design (CPTED). The benefits of CPTED include the following:

▶ Natural access control

▶ Natural surveillance

▶ Territorial reinforcement

CPTED is unique in that it considers the factors that facilitate crime and seeks to use the proper design of a facility to reduce the fear and incidence of crime. At the core of CPTED is the belief that physical environments can be structured to reduce crime. Let's look at a few examples. Maybe you have noticed limited entrance and exit points into and out of mall parking lots. This is an example of *natural access control*. Another example is the organization that decides to place the employee parking lot in an area visible from the employee's workspace. This enables employees to look out their windows in the office and see their parked cars. Even if this company employs a single guard, the facility's design allows increased surveillance by all the employees.

The effect of CPTED is that it causes the criminal to feel an increase in the threat of being discovered and provides *natural surveillance that can serve as a physical deterrent control*. The concept of CPTED can also be applied to CCTV. CCTV should be mounted so that potential criminals can easily see the cameras and know there is a much higher risk of getting caught. A CCTV can serve as a physical deterrent control and a detective control as well. Criminals may be deterred from entering property by the presence of a warning sign that alerts intruders that the property is under surveillance. Police can refer back to video, along with log books and other technical logs, to make a human judgment of who, how, when, and where a crime was committed; therefore, a CCTV is a great physical detective control. CCTV is also a great tool for detecting and deterring the insider threat.

Every facet of facility design should be reviewed with a focus on CPTED. Even items such as hedges are important, as an aid in natural surveillance; they should not be higher than 2.5 feet. Overgrown hedges obstruct visibility.

The third benefit of CPTED is territorial reinforcement. Strategic use of walls, windows, fences, barriers, landscaping, and so on define areas and create a sense of ownership with employees. Use fences, lighting, sidewalks, and designated parking areas on the outside of the facility and move critical assets toward the center of the facility.

Area Concerns

Finding the right location is your first concern when planning a new facility. Key points to consider include:

▶ **Accessibility**—An organization's facility needs to be in a location that people can access. Depending on your business and individual needs, requirements will vary, but aspects such as roads, freeways, local traffic patterns, public transportation, and convenience to regional airports need to be considered.

▶ **Climatology and natural disasters**—Mother Nature affects all of us. If you're building in Phoenix, Arizona, you will not have the same weather concerns as someone building a facility in Anchorage, Alaska. Events such as hurricanes, earthquakes, floods, snowstorms, dust storms, and tornadoes should be discussed and planned before starting construction.

▶ **Local considerations**—Issues such as freight lines, flight paths of airlines, toxic waste dumps, and insurance costs all play into the picture of where you should build a facility. Although cheap land for a new facility might seem like a bargain, the discovery that it is next to a railway used to haul toxic chemicals could change your opinion.

▶ **Utilities**—You should check that water, gas, and electric lines are adequate for the organization's needs. This might seem like a nonissue, but California found out otherwise in the California energy crisis of 2000 and 2001, which left many without power and caused periods of rolling blackouts.

▶ **Visibility**—Area population, terrain, and types of neighbors are also concerns. Depending on the type of business, you might want a facility that blends into the neighborhood. You might design individual buildings that cloak activities taking place there. Some organizations might even place an earthen dike or barrier around the facility grounds to obstruct the view of those that pass by. A good example of obscuring the location of a facility can be seen in the design of Skype's London office (see tinyurl.com/5lzbcx).

Location

The location of the facility is an important issue. Before construction begins, an organization should consider how the location fits with the organization's overall tasks and goals. A good example is the NSA museum outside Baltimore. It's the kind of place every cryptographic geek dreams of going. It's actually behind the main NSA facility in what used to be a hotel. (Rumor has it that this was a favorite hangout of the KGB before the NSA bought the hotel.) Although having facilities nearby for visitors and guests is seen as a good idea, the placement of the hotel so close to a critical agency might be a problem as it allows for spying.

Keep in mind that the acquisition of a new corporate site involves more than just the cost of the property. Cheap property doesn't necessarily mean a good deal. If your company manufactures rockets for satellites, you might want to be near fire stations and hospitals in case there's an accident.

Construction

After you have chosen a location, your next big task is to determine how the facility will be constructed. In many ways, this is driven by what the facility will be used for and by federal, state, and local laws. Buildings used to store the groundskeeper's equipment have different requirements than those used as a clean room for the manufacturer of microchips. In other words, you'll need to know how various parts of the facility will be used. I once saw a facilities crew trying to install an electromagnetic interference (EMI) chamber on the third floor of a building. EMI chambers require the placement of many heavy tiles and copper shielding used to block radio signals. This would have placed a huge load on the floor of this building, but no one had checked to verify the load-bearing limit of the floor. Remember to make sure that the facility is built to support whatever equipment you plan to put in it.

> **Tip**
>
> The load is how much weight the walls, floor, and ceiling is being asked to support.

Doors, Walls, Windows, and Ceilings

Have you ever wondered why most doors on homes open inward, whereas almost all doors on businesses open outward? This design is rooted in security. The door on your home is hinged to the inside. This makes it harder for thieves to remove your door to break in, but it also gives you an easy way to remove the door to bring in that big new leather couch. Years ago, the individuals who designed business facilities had the same thought. The problem is that open-in designs don't work well when people panic. It's a sad fact that the United States has a long and tragic history of workplace fires. In 1911, nearly 150 women and young girls died when they couldn't exit the Triangle Shirtwaist factory they were working in when it caught fire. The emergency exit doors were locked! Because of this and other tragic losses of life, modern businesses are required to maintain exits that are accessible, unlocked, and open out. These doors are more expensive because they are harder to install and remove. Special care must be taken to protect the hinges so that they cannot be easily removed. Many doors include a panic bar that permit quick exit: just push and you're out. In emergencies or situations in which a crowd is exiting the building quickly, panic bars help keep people moving away from danger.

Maybe you have heard the phrase "security starts at the front door." It is of the utmost importance to keep unauthorized individuals out of the facility or areas where they do not belong. Doors must be as secure as the surrounding walls, floor, and ceiling. If the door is protecting a critical area such as a data center or an onsite server room, the door needs to have the hinges on the inside of the door so that hinge pins cannot be removed. The structural components around the door must also be strengthened. The lock, hinges, strike plate, and the doorframe must all have enough strength to prevent someone from attempting to kick, pry, pick, or knock it down.

The construction of a door can vary. Critical infrastructure should be protected with solid core doors. The core material is the material within the door used to fill space, provide rigidity, and increase security. Hollow core doors simply have a lattice or honeycomb made of corrugated cardboard or thin wooden slats. Unlike a hollow core door, a solid core door is hard to penetrate. Solid core doors consist of low-density particle board, ridged foam, solid hardwood, or even steel that completely fills the space within the door. Solid core flush doors have much greater strength. The outer portion of the door is the skin, which can be wood, steel, or other materials such as polymers. Commercial steel doors are classified by ANSI/SDI A250.8-2014 into various categories that include standard duty, heavy duty, extra-heavy duty, and maximum duty. Selection of a steel door should be based on usage, degree of abuse, and required protection factor.

Many companies use electrically powered doors to control access. As an example, an employee might have to insert an ID card to gain access to the facility. The card reader then actuates an electric relay that allows the door to open. A CISSP should know the state of these door relays in the event of a power loss. An unlocked (or disengaged) state allows employees to ingress or egress and without being locked in. If a door lock defaults to open during a power disruption, this is referred to as fail-safe. If the lock defaults to locked during a power disruption this is referred to as fail-secure. In this situation, a panic bar or release must be provided so employees are not trapped inside the facility. For high-security doors, it is also important to consider delay alarms. A *delay alarm* is used to alert security that a security door has been open for a long time. A fail-safe option may be the best option and/or may be a regulatory requirement (fire code) when there are people employed within the facility verses an unmanned data warehouse.

> **Caution**
>
> Fail-safe locks protect employees in case of power loss because they allow employees to exit the facility.

> **ExamAlert**
>
> The terms *fail-safe* and *fail-secure* have very different meanings when discussed in physical security versus logical security. During the exam, read the questions carefully to determine the context in which the terms are being used.

Doors aren't the only factor you need to consider. Data centers typically should have raised floors. These need to be constructed in such a way that they are grounded against static electricity. Cables and wiring should be in conduit, not loose nor above the raised floor such that a trip hazard exists. Walls must be designed to slow the spread of fires, and emergency lighting should be in place to light the way for anyone trying to escape in case of emergency. Other considerations include the following:

▶ **Walls**—These need to be floor-to-ceiling for critical areas and where they separate key departments. Walls should have an adequate fire rating, and have reinforcement to keep unauthorized personnel from accessing secure areas, such as data centers or server rooms. Anyone who works in a cubicle environment understands the deficiency of short walls. A loud noise of excitement leads other employees to "prairie dog" and look over the wall of the cube to see what is happening.

▶ **Ceilings**—These need to be waterproof above the plenum space, have an adequate fire rating, and be reinforced to keep unauthorized personnel from accessing secure areas, such as server rooms.

▶ **Electrical and HVAC**—Plan for adequate power. Rooms that have servers or other heat-producing equipment need additional cooling to protect contained equipment. Heating, ventilating, and air conditioning (HVAC) systems should be controllable by fire-suppression equipment; otherwise, HVAC systems can inadvertently provide oxygen and help feed a fire.

Caution

Air intakes should be properly designed to protect people from breathing toxins that might be introduced into an environment. The anthrax threat of 2001 drove home this critical concern. (see www.cdc.gov/anthrax/bioterrorism/threat.html)

▶ **Windows**—Windows are a common point of entry for thieves, burglars, and others seeking access. Windows are usually designed with aesthetics in mind, not security. Interior or exterior windows need to be fixed in place and should at a minimum be shatterproof on the first and second floors. Depending on placement, the windows might need to be either opaque or translucent. Windows can be standard glass, tempered, laminated, acrylic, or be embedded with wire mesh that can help prevent the glass from shattering. Alarms or sensors might also be needed.

▶ **Fire escapes**—These are critical because they provide a point of egress and allow personnel to exit in case of a fire. It is critical that fire drills be performed to practice evacuation plans and determine real exit times. After the first attack on the World Trade Center towers in 1993, it was discovered that it took people two to three times longer to exit the facility than had been planned. Increased drills would have reduced evacuation time.

▶ **Fire detectors**—Smoke detectors should be installed to warn employees of danger. Sprinklers and detectors should be used to reduce the spread of fire. Placement of smoke detectors can include under raised floors, above suspended ceilings, in the plenum space, and within air ducts.

Tip

Human safety should always be your first concern.

Asset Placement

Security management includes the appropriate placement of high-value assets, such as servers and data centers. Well-placed data centers should not be above the second floor of a facility because a fire might make them inaccessible. Likewise, you wouldn't want the data center located in the basement because it could be subjected to flooding. I once saw a data center that was located outside the company break room. You had to literally walk through the server room to get to the break room. Another unfortunate placement I witnessed was underneath restrooms. Plumbing issues led to a flood in the server room. Although the situation was anything but humorous, I did ask the CTO if this meant the organization was "all washed up." Unsurprisingly, she was not amused.

It's not a good idea to have a data center with uncontrolled access or in an area where people will congregate or mill around. Even placing the data center off a main hallway is not a good idea. I often tell students that the location of the server room should be like Talkeetna, Alaska. If you are going there, you cannot be going anywhere else because that is where the road ends.

A well-placed data center should have limited accessibility and typically no more than two doors. A first-floor interior room is a good location for a data center. The ceilings should extend all the way up past the drop ceiling, access to the room should be controlled, and doors should be solid-core with hinges to the inside. The goal in your design should be to make it as hard as possible for unauthorized personnel to gain access to the data center. Server rooms should not have exterior windows or walls. Placing them inside of the facility protects against potential destruction from storms, and makes it more difficult for thieves or vandals to target them. If individuals can gain physical access to your servers, you have no security.

Physical Port Controls

After an attacker gains physical access to a system, there is no limit to the damage that can occur. One common means of accessing a system is via the ports. A computer system can have many different types of ports, such as FireWire, Thunderbolt, and USB. USB is a common form factor. USB ports can be physically blocked, unplugged or blocked via software. Microsoft Windows also allow for ports to be locked by means of an Active Directory Group Policy, which is an example of an OS being able to restrict usage of items that may not be needed.

Perimeter Controls

Many types of perimeter control mechanisms can be deployed. The overall concept is to provide *defense in depth*. With this approach, layers of defensive mechanisms, using different types of controls, are created. Physical security controls are your first line of defense and should be designed so that the breach of any one will not compromise the physical security of the organization. CCTV cameras, gates, lighting, guards, dogs, and locks are but a few of the layers of physical security that can be added to build a defense-in-depth strategy. Let's work from the outside in.

Fences

Consider the Berlin Wall. This monument to the Cold War was quite effective at preventing East Germans from escaping to the West. Before its fall in 1989, most people that escaped to the west did so by hiding in trunks of cars or by bribing guards. The wall worked as both a strong physical and psychological barrier. The amount of control provided by a fence depends on the type you build. A 3-to-4-foot fence will deter only a casual trespasser, but an 8-foot fence will keep out a determined intruder. Adding three strands of razor wire topping is an additional effective security measure. If you are trying to keep individuals inside an area, you should point the razor wire in, and if you are trying to keep individuals out, you should point the razor wire out. Table 3.1 provides more details. If you are really concerned about who's hanging around the perimeter of your facility, you might consider installing a perimeter intrusion and detection assessment system (PIDAS). This special fencing system has sensors to detect intruders. The downside is that a stray deer or other wildlife might also trigger an alarm.

TABLE 3.1 **Fence Heights**

Height	Purpose
3–4 feet high	Will deter only casual trespassers.
6–7 feet high	Considered too tall to easily climb.
8 feet high	Should deter a determined intruder. A topping of three strands of razor wire should be pointed out, in, or in both directions at a 45° angle. Pointed inward toward the facility typically is a security measure to keep people in; pointed outward is a security measure to keep people out.

Fencing can be made from a range of components, such as steel, wood, brick, or concrete. Chain link, wire, and steel mesh fences are used at many facilities and can be ranked from high- to low-security. The gauge of the wire and the size of the mesh help determine the security of these fences. The gauge is the measurement of the diameter of the wire. Keep in mind that the higher the gauge number, the smaller the wire diameter. Table 3.2 lists the common wire gauges and diameters.

TABLE 3.2 **Gauge and Diameter**

Gauge	Diameter
6 gauge	.192 inch
9 gauge	.148 inch
11 gauge	.120 inch
11 1/2 gauge	.113 inch
12 gauge	.106 inch
12 1/2 gauge	.099 inch

The American Society for Testing and Materials (ASTM) defines fence standards and certifies vendors' fencing. ASTM has established standards for residential, commercial, and high-security products. The distance between the two wires in the fence is the *mesh size*. Table 3.3 lists common fence mesh sizes and their corresponding security ratings. To visualize: a high fence with small holes is difficult for an intruder to climb, whereas a high fence with large holes can be easily climbed.

TABLE 3.3 **Fence Mesh Size**

Mesh	Rating
2 inch	Normal usage
1 inch	Higher security
3/8 inch	Extremely high security

Gates

Whereas a fence acts as a barrier, a gate is a choke point and controls ingress and egress of pedestrian and vehicle traffic. A gate must be of the same level of security as the fence to act as an effective deterrent. Gates are covered by UL Standard 325 and ASTM-F2200. Gates can be designed as swing gates, rolling gates, and cantilever gates. There are four classes of gates, as shown in Table 3.4.

TABLE 3.4 **Gate Classes**

Class	Rating
Class I	Residential
Class II	Commercial
Class III	Industrial
Class IV	Restricted access, high security

Other flow control mechanisms include turnstiles and mantraps. A *turnstile* is a form of gate that prevents more than one person at a time from gaining access to a controlled area. Turnstiles usually only rotate in one direction, restricting flow. You see turnstiles at sporting events, in the subway, and so on.

A *mantrap* is a set of two doors. The idea behind a mantrap is that one or more people must enter the mantrap and shut the outer door before the inner door will open. Some mantraps lock both the inner and outer door if authentication fails so that the individual cannot leave until a guard arrives to verify the person's identity. Mantraps can be used to control the flow of individuals into and out of sensitive areas. Mantraps can help prevent *piggybacking*. Piggybacking is commonly attempted at controlled-entry points where authentication is required. Although some individuals use terms *piggybacking* and *tailgating* synonymously, tailgating is also associated with the practice of attempted unauthorized access at vehicle access points and gates. Some gates might open long enough that a second car can attempt to pass through.

> **ExamAlert**
>
> A mantrap is used to prevent piggybacking and additional layers of defense can be obtained by using guards and CCTV.

Bollards

Bollards are another means of perimeter control. Made of concrete or steel, they block vehicular traffic or protect areas where pedestrians might be entering or leaving buildings. After 9/11, these barriers have advanced far beyond the standard steel poles of the past. Companies now make bollards with electronic sensors to notify building inhabitants that someone has rammed or breached the bollards. Although fences act as a first line of defense, bollards are a close second because they can deter individuals from ramming a facility with a car or truck. Figure 3.1 shows an example of a bollard.

FIGURE 3.1 **Bollards.**
Source: www.deltascientific.com/bollards2.htm

Perimeter controls need not look like concrete and steel. Have you ever noticed majestic ponds located next to many corporate headquarters? Don't be lulled into believing they were placed there merely as a community beautification project. They are another form of a barricade or barrier. They are also useful in case of fire because they can serve as an additional water source. Access controls are a critical piece of premises security that can be either natural, such as a body of water, or structural, such as a fence.

What else can be done? Warning signs or notices should be posted to deter trespassing. A final review of the grounds area should be conducted to make sure that nothing has been missed. This includes any opening that is around 96 square inches or larger and 18 feet or less above the ground, such as manholes/tunnels, gates leading to the basement, elevator shafts, ventilation openings, and skylights. Even the roof, basement, and walls of a building might contain points vulnerable to entry and should be assessed.

After the premises of the facility have been secured, a CISSP should move on to an analysis of other perimeter control mechanisms (such as CCTV, card keys, radio frequency ID [RFID] tags, lighting, guards, dogs, locks, and biometric access controls). Just as networks use chokepoints and multiple layers of defenses, so should physical security controls. Each of these is explained in more depth in the sections that follow.

CCTV Cameras

CCTVs can be used as monitoring devices or as physical detective controls to assess and identify intruders. They also serve as a great deterrent. Before the first camera is installed, several important questions must be answered: Will the video feed be monitored in real-time? How long will recordings be stored? What type of area will be monitored? The CCTV by itself cannot prevent anything. If the CCTV system is to be used in a real-time, it must be used with human intervention by way of monitoring to serve as a preventative control. A guard or other individual is needed to watch as events occur. If the CCTV system is being used after the fact, it is functioning as a detection control. Different environments require different systems.

If a CCTV system is to be used outside, the amount of illumination is important. Illumination is controlled by an iris that regulates the amount of light that enters the CCTV camera. An auto iris lens is designed to be used outside where the amount of light varies between night and day; a manual iris lens is used for cameras to be used indoors. CCTV cameras can even be equipped with built-in LEDs or configured for infrared recording.

The focal length of the lens controls the camera's depth of field, which determines how much of the visual environment is in focus on the CCTV monitor. The depth of field is critical if there is not a human being monitoring the system to make adjustments to the focus. Although some systems have fixed focal lengths, others offer the capability to pan, tilt, and zoom (*PTZ*), allowing the operator to zoom in or adjust the camera as needed. Older CCTV cameras are analog, whereas most modern cameras are digital, capturing enhanced detail quickly by the use of *charged coupled devices* (CCDs). A CCD is similar to the technology found in a fax machine or a photocopier.

A CCTV system can be wired or wireless and comprises many components including cameras, transmitters, receivers, recorders, monitors, and controllers. CCTV systems provide effective surveillance of entrances and critical access points. If employees are not available to monitor in real time, activity can be recorded and reviewed later. An *annunciator* can be used to reduce the burden of the individual monitoring the alarm. An annunciator can detect intrusions or other types of noise and trip an alarm so that a guard does not have to constantly watch a monitor. If you are considering CCTV systems, remember to provide for the rights of worker privacy or notification of the absence of privacy, and consider the existence of potential blind spots.

Lighting

Lighting is a common type of perimeter protection. Some studies have found that up to 80% of criminal acts at businesses and shopping centers happen at night in adjacent parking lots, so companies need to practice due care when installing exterior lights. Failure to provide adequate lighting in parking lots and other high-traffic areas could lead to lawsuits if an employee or visitor is attacked. Outside lighting discourages prowlers and thieves. Some common types of exterior lights are:

▶ Floodlights

▶ Streetlights

▶ Searchlights

Terms used for the measurement of light include *lumen*, *lux*, and *foot-candle*. One lux is one lumen per square meter and one foot-candle is one lumen per square foot. The National Institute of Standards and Technologies (NIST) states that for effective perimeter control, buildings should be illuminated with 2 foot-candles of light in a projection that is 8 feet high.

Take a moment to look at how the lights are configured the next time you visit a mall or department store. You will see rows of lights placed evenly around the facility. That is an example of *continuous lighting*. Areas such as exits, stairways, and building evacuation routes are equipped with *standby lighting*. Standby lighting activates only in the event of power outages or during emergencies; however, standby lighting is more commonly used with homes and/or businesses that are set to turn on after at a certain time after normal operating hours late at night to give the appearance that the home or business is occupied, thus deterring intruders and trespassers.

As with all security, the provision of lighting takes planning. Effective lighting requires more than the placement of a light bulb atop a pole. Security professionals need to consider what areas need to be illuminated, which direction that light should be directed, and how bright the light will be. Some lights make use of a *Fresnel lens*. These lenses are designed to focus light in a specific direction and were originally found in theaters and lighthouses.

Security checkpoints are another location where you will see careful design of the illumination. Here, lights are aimed away from the guard post so that anyone approaching the checkpoint can easily be seen and guards are not exposed in the light. This is an example of *glare protection*. If lights are used for perimeter detection, they are typically mounted above the fence. Doing so blinds intruders to the surrounding view and allows intruders to be more easily seen by the guard force.

Just as too little light can be a problem, too much light can lead to a less secure environment. Glare and over-lighting can cause problems by creating very dark areas just outside the range of the lighted area. In addition, neighboring businesses or homes might not appreciate residing in such a brightly lit area. Therefore, exterior lighting involves the balance of too little versus too much light. Exterior lights should each cover their own zone but still allow for some overlap between zones.

Guards and Dogs

Guards can offer the best and worst in the world of protection. Although our increased need for security has driven the demand for more guards, they are only human and their abilities vary. Technology has also driven our need for security guards. As we get more premises control equipment, intrusion detection systems, and computerized devices, additional guards are required to control these systems.

Unlike computerized systems, guards have the ability to make judgment calls and think through how they should handle specific situations. This is called *discernment*. Guards can also be used in multiple roles so that they can monitor, greet, sign in, and escort visitors. Just by having them in a facility or guarding a site, an organization has provided a visual deterrence. Before you go out and hire your own personal bodyguard, you should also be aware that guards do have some disadvantages. Guards are expensive, make mistakes, can be poorly trained, make policy exceptions for people they like or trust, can be manipulated, might sleep on the job, steal company property, or even injure someone.

Dogs, much like guards, have also been used to secure property throughout time. Breeds such as Chows, Dobermans, and German Shepherds were bred specifically for guard duty. Although dogs can be trained, loyal, obedient, and steadfast, they are sometimes unpredictable and could bite or harm the wrong person. Because of these factors, dogs are usually restricted to exterior premises control and should be used with caution.

Locks

Locks come in many types, sizes, and shapes, and are both one of the oldest forms of theft-deterrent mechanisms and the most commonly used deterrent. Locks have the highest return on investment. Locks have been around since their use in 2000 B.C. by the Egyptians.

It's important to select the appropriate lock for your designated area. Different types of locks provide different levels of protection. Locks are designed to various strengths and levels of security. The grade of the lock specifies its level of construction. Table 3.5 lists the three basic grades of locks and their common usage.

TABLE 3.5 **Lock Strengths**

Grade	Usage
Grade 3	Residential and consumer usage
Grade 2	Light-duty commercial and heavy-duty residential locks
Grade 1	High-security commercial and industrial-use locks

ANSI standards define the strength and durability of locks. As an example, a grade 3 lock is designed to function for 200,000 cycles, whereas a grade 2 lock must function for 400,000 cycles, and a grade 1 lock must function for 800,000 cycles. Some common lock types include combination locks, mechanical locks, cipher locks, and device locks.

A basic *combination lock* requires the owner to input a correct combination of numbers to unlock it, and usually has a series of wheels inside. The longer the length of the combination, the more secure the lock is. Figure 3.2 shows an example of a three- and four-digit combination lock. Even with a four-digit lock that would only be 10,000 combinations to choose from, so basic locks are more of a deterrent than a preventive control.

Three-Digit Lock

Four-Digit Lock

FIGURE 3.2 **Combination locks.**

Mechanical locks have been used for hundreds of years to secure items of importance. Early locks were made of wood and attempts to improve the lock designs increased throughout the 1700s. Mechanical locks include warded locks and pin-and-tumbler locks. The modern tumbler lock was patented by Linus Yale in 1848.

A *warded lock* is a basic padlock that uses a key with a spring loaded bolt. Warded locks use a series of wards, or blockages, that a key must match up to. It is the cheapest type of mechanical lock and is also the easiest to pick. It can be picked by inserting a stiff piece of wire or thin strip of metal; a simple warded lock is one that can be opened with a skeleton key. Warded locks do not provide a high level of security. *Tumbler locks* are somewhat more complex than a warded lock. Instead of wards, they use tumblers, which increases the difficulty of using the wrong key to open a lock. When the right key is inserted into the cylinder of a tumbler lock, the pins are lifted to the right height so that the lock can open or close. Figure 3.3 illustrates a basic tumbler lock design.

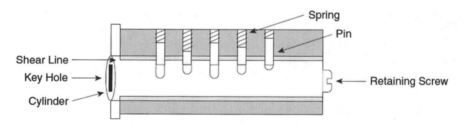

FIGURE 3.3 **Tumbler lock design.**

In a tumbler lock, the correct key has the notches and raised areas to shift the pins into the proper position. The pins are spring-loaded so that when the key is removed, the pins return to the locked position. Tumbler locks can be designed as pin tumblers, wafer tumblers, lever tumblers, or tubular locks. Tubular locks are also known as *ace locks* and are considered to be of higher security. These are used for computers, vending machines, and other high-security devices.

These are not the only types of locks. There is also the category of locks known as cipher locks or *programmable locks*. These require the user to enter a preset or programmed sequence. Cipher locks are designed to use keypads or ciphers to control access into restricted areas. One shortcoming with a keypad device is that bystanders can "shoulder-surf" and steal passcodes. Or someone that knows the code props the door open so others can easily enter. That's why door delay alarms should be considered. To increase security and safety, visibility shields should be used to prevent bystanders from viewing the passcodes that are entered. Door delay alarms may also be used to alert if someone props the door open. One main advantage to cipher locks is that some systems, referred to as smart locks, allow for granular roles and rules-based access control of physical security along with user access auditing. This makes it very easy to revoke user access quickly to a secure area by deleting the access code and not having to collect a "key or access card." It is also a detective control and allows for effective auditing to account for who accessed secured areas.

Locks can also be used to secure a wide range of devices. Device locks can be used to secure ports and laptops. Employees who are issued laptops should be given a laptop-locking device. Although data security is important, the security of the device should also be considered; it takes only a moment for someone to take a laptop or other mobile device. Device locks can help protect physical assets and signal to employees your concern that devices issued to them should be protected.

Caution

Although locks are important to use to secure laptops, it's also important to use encryption because the data is most likely worth more than the hardware.

Many organizations don't change locks frequently. Others fail to require terminated employees to return keys. Some locks even have master keys. This option allows a supervisor or housekeeper to bypass use of the normally required key and gain entry. Finally, there is the issue of lock picking. Although locks can be used to deter and delay, all locks are subject to attack.

Keep in mind that a lock is a deterrent and not a preventive control. Most locks keep out honest people and should work as a layer of security in your overall security solution. Even high-end Simplex locks have been bypassed with strong magnets.

Lock Picking

Lock picking is one way to bypass the security intended by a lock. Although not the fastest way to break in, it does offer a stealthy way to bypass the locks, and might mask from the victim that a security violation has occurred. If you have any doubts whether lock picking is a common hacker skill, check out any of the large hacking conferences such as DEF CON. This yearly hacker conference usually has presentations and contests devoted to lock picking. Deviant Ollam has a list of lock picking resources at deviating.net/lockpicking/.

Lock-picking is basically the manipulation of a lock's components to open it without a key. The basic components used to pick locks are:

▶ **Tension wrenches**—These are not much more than a small angled flathead screwdriver. They come in various thicknesses and sizes.

▶ **Picks**—Just as the name implies, these are similar to a dentist's pick. They are small, angled, and pointed.

Together, these tools can be used to pick a lock. One basic technique is *scrubbing* or *raking*. *Scrubbing* is the act of scraping the pins quickly with a pick while the tension wrench is used to place a small amount of force on the lock. Some of the pins will be placed in a mechanical bind and will be stuck in the unlocked position. With practice, this can be done quickly so that all the pins stick and the lock disengages. *Key-bumping* is another lock-picking technique that has gained notoriety. Key-bumping is performed by using a key for a specific brand of lock that has been cut to the number nine position. This is the lowest possible cut for the key, as shown in Figure 3.4. Notice how the inner 4 ridges are lower than what is normal.

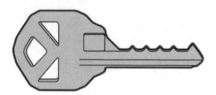

FIGURE 3.4   **Key-bumping key.**

The key is inserted into the lock and slight pressure is applied while the key is tapped (bumped). A search of YouTube will return many videos if you would like to learn more about key-bumping. This transference of force causes the pins to jump inside of the cylinder so that the lock is disengaged.

Other tools to bypass locks include:

▶ **Lock pick sets**—These vary in price and design, and might contain anything from a couple of tools to more than two dozen various picks and tension wrenches.

▶ **Electric lock pick guns**—These devices attempt to speed up manual lock picking by working somewhat like an electric toothbrush or an electric knife.

▶ **Tubular picks**—These are designed to pick tubular locks. These locks are the same kind as used on Kryptonite bicycle locks, which were thought to be highly secure until 2004, when someone demonstrated that the lock could be opened with a Bic pen. The same issue exists with Kensington-style laptop locks. These are sometime refered to as ACE locks.

▶ **Lock shims**—Formed pieces of thin, stiff metal that can be inserted into the latch of a padlock and used to push back the locking mechanism.

Employee Access Control

Where employees go and what they do is of importance to the organization. Such information is critical not only for monitoring access control, but also for reconstructing events following an intrusion, theft, or attack.

> **Caution**
>
> It is unfortunate but true that cleaning crews are sometimes overlooked as potential security threats. They are typically around after everyone else leaves and they have full access to the facility. Unlocked computers can make a tempting and easy target. One of the editors of this book shared the story of how the cleaning crew of his former employer shared badges and often had friends or relatives fill in for them for a day or two using the same badge.

Badges, Tokens, and Cards

Tokens, cards, and keys are another means of physical access control. Chapter 8, "Identity and Access Management," covers these issues in much more depth, but the physical characteristics and use of these controls are discussed here.

Table 3.6 details common types of access cards and badges.

TABLE 3.6 **Card Key Types**

Type of Card	Attribute
Photo card	Contains a facial photograph of the card holder
Active electronic	Can transmit electronic data
Magnetic stripe	Has a stripe of magnetic material
Magnetic strip	Contains rows of copper strips
Optical coded	Contains a laser-burned pattern of encoded dots or 3D barcodes
Smart card	Has an electronic circuit and processor embedded
RFID card	Has a small radio-frequency identification (RFID) circuit embedded

Physical access control cards can be separated into two broad categories: *dumb cards* and *smart cards*. Dumb cards are those that contain no electronics and are used at many different organizations. These cards often include an individual's photo to verify a person's right to be in a particular area. These photo ID cards are really just a form of identity badge. Photo badges are effective only if inspected by guards and controls are put in place to ensure that they are inspected at key points in and around a facility.

The second type of access control is a smart card. European countries widely use smart card technology in credit cards, whereas the United States just started to implement them in late 2015. Smart cards are much more versatile than photo cards. Smart cards can make entry decisions electronically. These devices can be configured in several different ways. Some require only that the user get close to the access-control device. These proximity readers don't require the user to physically insert the card. Some identification technologies use RFID. Others require user activation, such as requiring the user to input a key code. One example of a deployed smart card is the Common Access Card (CAC) used by the U.S. Department of Defense. CACs are considered to be dual-factor—also known as multi-factor or strong authentication—and are also used with a public key infrastructure (PKI).

Some organizations provide card users with two key codes. One key code is used for normal access, whereas the second is used as a *silent hostage alarm or duress alarm*. The silent hostage alarm code allows an employee to gain access, but also silently alerts the authorities of a hostage situation.

Caution

High-security facilities have a history of mandating that employees make sure their badges are not visible after leaving the workplace to go home or out to lunch. This is an effective control for any organization that uses badges to reduce social engineering or targeting of specific vehicles, briefcases, laptops, tablets, smartphones, etc.

RFID Tags

RFID tags are another emerging trend in the field of physical access control. RFID tags are extremely small electronic devices composed of a microchip and an antenna. These devices transmit small amounts of information. RFID tags can be designed in different ways:

▶ **Active**—Active tags have a battery or power source used to power the microchip and constantly transmit a weak signal.

▶ **Passive**—These devices have no battery. They are powered by an RFID reader/transponder, which generates an electromagnetic wave that induces a current in the RFID tag.

▶ **Semipassive**—These hybrid devices have a battery to power the microchip, but still transmit data by harnessing energy from the reader.

RFID tags are manufactured in various sizes, down to dust particle size—their placement possibilities are endless. The United States military has conducted trials to test the possibilities of using RFID tags to control vehicle traffic at military locations. Some states are considering embedding RFID tags in license and automobile registrations so that passing police cars can be alerted about out-of-date registrations. Many countries are starting to use RFID tags in passports. The U.S. Federal Drug Administration (FDA) has approved an RFID tag that will be used to prevent the possibility of wrong-site, wrong-procedure, and wrong-patient surgeries. Government officials have advocated that these devices become standard issue for firefighters, police officers, and emergency rescue individuals because their jobs place them in situations in which their identification could be lost or destroyed.

Attacks against these devices are on the rise. To learn more, see rfidiot.org. Expect to see continued usage and exploitation of these devices in the coming years.

Biometric Access Controls

Biometric controls are discussed extensively in Chapter 8. Because they are used for premises control, they should be mentioned here. The fascinating thing about biometric controls is that they are based on a physiological attribute or behavioral characteristic of an individual. As an example, one consulting job I had was with a government agency that took security seriously. This agency implemented two-factor authentication by means of an access card and biometric sensor. As if these two were not enough, I was also weighed while in the mantrap before being allowed access to the data center. These are some of the primary types of biometric systems: All biometric data collected from humans is turned into binary data, formatted, then hashed and stored in a reference file. When a user goes to authenticate, the user's biometric sample is collected again, hashed using the same algorithm, and compared to the reference filed; a match to a certain degree is required for access.

▶ **Fingerprint scan**—Widely used for access control to facilities and or items, such as laptops, smartphones and some tablets. This control works by distinguishing up to 40 details about the peaks, valleys, and ridges of the user's fingerprint. Most systems only attempt to match between six and a dozen points because the more points that are used the more chance of a false rejection; however, the lower the number of points the more chance of a false acceptance.

▶ **Palm scan**—Analyzes characteristics associated with the user's palm, such as the creases, grooves, and ridges. A palm scan also includes the fingerprint of the fingers on the hand being scanned. If a match is found, the individual is allowed access.

▶ **Hand geometry**—Another biometric system that uses the unique geometry of a user's hand to determine the user's identity. Looks specifically at the shape, length, and width of the hand, knuckles, and fingers.

▶ **Iris scan**—An eye-recognition system that is very accurate because it has over 400 points of reference. Looks at the color of the eye surrounding the pupil. Iris scanning examines the crypts, furrows, ridges, striations, ligaments, and collarette. This is considered to be the most accurate form of biometric.

▶ **Retina scan**—Another eye-recognition system that is considered accurate for identification. However, these blood vessels can change with diseases, such as glaucoma.

▶ **Facial scan**—Uses points of comparison like hand geometry and performs a mathematical comparison with the face prints it holds in a database to allow or block access.

Regardless of what biometric method is used, each follows a similar usage pattern:

1. **Users must first enroll in the system**—Enrollment is not much more than a process of allowing the system to take one or more samples for later comparison.

2. **A user requests to be authenticated**—Statistics collected during enrollment are used to compare to data scanned during the user's authentication request.

3. **A decision is reached**—A match allows the user access, whereas a discrepancy between causes the user to be denied access.

Environmental Controls

Heat can be damaging to computer equipment. This is why most data centers are kept at temperatures of around 70°F. Higher and lower temperatures can reduce the useful life of electronic devices. But temperature should not be your only concern. High humidity can cause electronics to corrode and low humidity increases the risk of static electricity. What might feel like only a small shock to human touch can totally destroy electronic components. Grounding devices such as antistatic wrist bands and antistatic flooring can be used to reduce the possibility of damage.

Heating, Ventilating, and Air Conditioning

Do you know what can be hotter than Houston in the summer? A room full of computers without sufficient HVAC. Data centers, or any areas that are full of computer or electrical equipment, are going to generate heat. Modern electronic equipment is very sensitive to heat and can tolerate temperatures of only 110°F to 115°F degrees without permanent damage to circuits.

Data centers should have HVAC systems separate from the HVAC of the rest of the facility. The HVAC should maintain positive pressurization and ventilation. This controls contamination by pushing air outside. This is especially important in case of fire because it ensures that smoke will be pushed out of the facility instead of being pulled in.

Security management should know who is in charge of the HVAC system and how they can be contacted. Intake vents should be protected so that contaminates cannot be easily spread. These systems must be controlled to protect organizations and their occupants from chemical and biological threats. HVAC systems generate water; this can be as a gas (affecting humidity) or as a liquid (encouraging growth of mold, structural damage, and decay). As previously mentioned, high humidity causes rust and corrosion. Low humidity can increase the risk of static electricity. The ideal humidity for a data center is between 35% and 45%.

> **Caution**
>
> The American Society of Heating, Refrigerating, and Air-conditioning Engineers (ASHRAE) has expanded the allowable temperatures for data centers in an effort to promote green environmental practices and to provide a wider range of allowed temperatures.

The Importance of HVAC

HVAC is like any other critical system and needs to be protected. During a security assessment in 2007, I encountered a page at the client's website that requested authentication. What surprised me is that it appeared to be a control for HVAC. A quick review of the vendor's site provided me with a default username and password. Because I was approved to perform the assessment, I entered the username and password and was taken to a web page that had all the organization's HVAC controls online. Although my task was simply to report the problem, what might a malicious hacker have done? Maybe apply a little heat to the CEO's office, or play a game of freeze-out with accounting?

Electrical Power

Electrical power, like HVAC, is a resource that most of us take for granted. Residents of the United States are lucky, but large portions of the world live without dependable electrical power. Even areas that have dependable power can be subject to line noise or might suffer from *electromagnetic interference* (EMI). Electrical motors and other electronic devices can cause EMI. You might have noticed that fluorescent lights can also cause electrical problems; this phenomenon is known as *radio frequency interference* (RFI). Table 3.7 lists some other power anomalies.

TABLE 3.7 **Power Faults and Descriptions**

Fault	Description
Blackout	Prolonged loss of power
Brownout	Power degradation; less than normal power available
Sag	Momentary low voltage
Fault	Momentary loss of power
Spike	Momentary high voltage
Surge	Prolonged high voltage
Noise	Interference superimposed onto the power line
Transient	Electrical noise of a short duration
Inrush	Initial surge of power at startup

Luckily, power conditioners, surge protectors, and uninterruptible power supplies can provide clean power. Although most of the time we seek this clean power, there are other times when we need to kill electricity quickly. This is especially true if someone is electrocuted, or if there is a danger of water coming into direct contact with power sources. National fire protection codes require that you have an *emergency power off* (EPO) switch located near server room exit doors to kill power quickly if needed. These switches are easy to recognize because they are in the form of a big red button.

> ### Caution
>
> The EPO switch should have a plastic cover installed to prevent anyone from accidentally pressing it.

Uninterruptible Power Supply

Because computers have become an essential piece of technology, downtime of any significant duration can be devastating to an organization. Power outages can happen and businesses must be prepared to deal with the situation. Uninterruptible power supplies (UPS) are one of the primary means of meeting this challenge. Two categories of UPS exist:

▶ **Online system**—An online system uses AC power to charge a bank of DC batteries. These batteries are held in reserve until power fails. At that time, a power inverter converts the DC voltage back to AC for the computer systems to use. These systems are good for short-term power outages. Many have a software component that can perform a graceful shutdown.

▶ **Standby system**—This type of system monitors a power line for a failure. When a failure is sensed, backup power is switched on. This system relies on generators or power subsystems to keep computers running for longer power outages.

Most standby generators run on diesel fuel or natural gas:

▶ **Diesel fuel**—Should maintain at least 12 hours of fuel.

▶ **Natural gas**—Suitable for areas that have a good supply of natural gas and are geologically stable.

Equipment Life Cycle

Even when you have done all the right things, performed preventative maintenance, kept equipment at the right operating temperature, and used surge protectors, equipment will eventually cease to function. This is why many companies choose to maintain service-level agreements (SLA).

> **ExamAlert**
>
> An SLA is a contract with a hardware vendor that provides a certain level of protection. For a fee, the vendor agrees to repair or replace the equipment within the contracted time.

You need to know two important statistics when purchasing equipment or when attempting to calculate how long the equipment will last. First is the *mean time between failure* (MTBF), which is used to calculate the expected lifetime of a device. The higher the MTBF is, the better. The second value is the *mean time to repair* (MTTR). The MTTR is an estimate of how long it takes to repair the equipment and get it back into use. For MTTR, lower numbers are better.

Fire Prevention, Detection, and Suppression

A fire needs three things: oxygen, heat, and fuel. When all three items are present, a fire can ignite and present a lethal threat, as shown in the fire tetrahedron in Figure 3.5. Fires can be devastating to people and facilities. Saving human lives should always be your first priority. As a CISSP candidate, it's important to understand that proper precautions, preparation, and training must be performed to help save lives and limit potential damage.

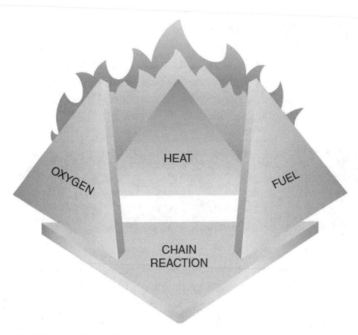

FIGURE 3.5 **Fire tetrahedron.**

Fire prevention is one of the key items that must be addressed to have an effective proactive defense against fires. A big part of prevention is making sure people are trained and know how to prevent potential fire hazards. Corporate policy must define how employees will be trained to deal with fires.

Fire drills are another important part of building a good security policy. Fire drills should be periodic, yet random. Employees should have a designated area to go to in a safe zone outside the facility. Supervisors or others should be in charge of the safe zones, and responsible for performing an employee head count to ensure that everyone is present and accounted for. After the drill, employees should be badged in on the way back into the facility to deter social engineering and piggyback attacks.

Fire-Detection Equipment

Having plans and procedures to carry out in case of a fire is only part of the overall fire-prevention program. Companies should make sure they have appropriate and functioning fire-detection equipment so that employees can be alerted to possible danger. Fire detectors can work in different ways and can be activated by the following:

▶ **Heat**—A heat-activated sensor is triggered when a predetermined temperature is reached or when the temperature rises quickly within a specified time period. The rate-of-rise type of sensor produces more false positives.

▶ **Smoke**—A smoke-activated sensor can be powered by a photoelectric optical detector or by a radioactive smoke-detection device.

▶ **Flame**—A flame-activated sensor is the most expensive of the three types discussed. It functions by sensing either the infrared energy associated with flame or the pulsation of flame.

Fire Suppression

Just being alerted to a fire is not enough. Employees need to know what to do and how to handle different types of fires. A fire can be suppressed by removing heat, fuel, or oxygen. Fires are rated according to the types of materials burning. Although it might be acceptable to throw some water on smoldering paper, it would not be a good idea to throw water on a combustible metal fire; water on a metal fire can actually make the fire spread. Table 3.8 lists fire classes and their corresponding suppression methods.

TABLE 3.8 **Fire Suppression Methods**

Class	Suppression Method
Class A	Paper or wood fires should be suppressed with water or soda acid.
Class B	Gasoline or oil fires should be suppressed by using CO_2, soda acid, or halon.
Class C	Electronic or computer fires should be suppressed by using CO_2, or halon replacement such as FM-200.
Class D	Fires caused by combustible metals should be suppressed by applying dry powder or using special techniques.
Class K	Commercial kitchen fires should be suppressed with *saponifying* agents that blanket the fire.

Tip

Hint on ABCD—think of them in the order of frequency of occurrence. Paper more than liquid, liquid more than electric, electric more than metal.

The two primary methods of corporate fire suppression include *water sprinklers* and *gas discharge systems*. Water is easy to work with, widely available, and nontoxic. Gas discharge systems are better suited for areas where humans are not present. Both suppression systems are discussed next.

Water Sprinklers

Water sprinklers are an effective means of extinguishing Class A fires. The disadvantage of using sprinkler systems is that water is damaging to electronics. Four variants of sprinkler systems are available:

▶ **Dry pipe**—As the name implies, this sprinkler system contains no standing water. The line contains compressed air. When the system is triggered the clapper valve opens, air flows out of the system, and water flows in (see Figure 3.6). The benefit of this type of system is that it reduces the risk of accidental flooding and gives some time to cover or turn off electrical equipment. These systems are also great for cold-weather areas, unmanned warehouses, and other locations where freezing temperatures could freeze any water standing in the system.

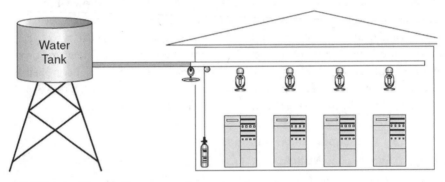

FIGURE 3.6 **Dry pipe fire suppression system.**

▶ **Wet pipe**—Wet pipe systems are widely used and are ready for activation. This system is charged and full of water. When triggered, only the affected sprinklers activate. Wet pipe systems are not triggered by smoke, and they are more prone to leaks and accidental discharge. The next time you are staying in a hotel, take a look around and you'll probably see this type of system. Wet pipe systems typically use some type of fusible link that allows discharge after the link breaks or melts.

▶ **Pre-action**—This is a combination system. Pipes are initially dry and do not fill with water until air pressure is reduced. Even then, the system will not activate until a secondary mechanism triggers. The secondary mechanism might be some type of fusible link similar to what is used in a wet pipe system. The advantage of pre-action systems is that the design provides an extra level of control that reduces the chance of accidental triggering.

▶ **Deluge**—This is similar to a dry pipe system, except that after the system is triggered, there is no holding back the water. A large volume of water will cover a large area quickly. If your company builds booster rockets for supplies being shuttled to the International Space Station, this might be a preferred suppression system.

Halon

Sometimes we become smug in our belief that the products we create can do no harm. During the industrial revolution, asbestos was hailed as a miracle fiber. By the 1920s, it was discovered that it caused major health problems. Halon has a similar history. Originally used in computer rooms for fire suppression, halon was considered the perfect fire suppression method. Halon mixes easily with air, doesn't harm computer equipment, and once dissipated, halon leaves no solid or liquid residue. Halon is unique in that it does not remove or reduce any of the three necessary components of a fire; instead, halon interferes with the fire's chemical reaction. There are two types of halon:

▶ **Halon 1211**—This type is found in portable extinguishers and is stored as a liquid.

▶ **Halon 1301**—This version is used in fixed flooding systems and is stored as a gaseous agent.

The Montreal Protocol of 1987 designated halon as an ozone-depleting substance. Halon is 3–10 times more damaging to the ozone layer than CFCs. Other issues with halon exist. If it is deployed in concentrations of greater than 10% and in temperatures of 900°F or more, it degrades into hydrogen fluoride, hydrogen bromide, and bromine. This toxic brew is not something that people should be breathing.

If you currently have a halon fire-suppression system, you can leave it in place, but there are strict regulations on reporting discharges. Laws also govern the removal and disposal of halon fire-suppression systems. Some of the more ecological and less toxic EPA-approved replacements for halon include:

▶ FM-200

▶ CEA-410

▶ NAF-S-III

▶ FE-13

▶ Argon

▶ Low-pressure water mist

▶ Argonite

Alarm Systems

Although this chapter is focused on physical security, there is a range of technical controls that can be used to enhance physical security. Alarm systems are one such control.

An alarm system is made up of many components, including an intrusion detection system, control panel, arming systems, and annunciators. Every time there is an alarm, someone must respond and determine whether the event is real.

Intrusion Detection Systems

This section discusses physical intrusion detection systems (IDS), which are used for detecting unauthorized physical access. You might have seen IDS sensors around windows or attached to doors and not even realized what they were. These sensors can detect the breakage of glass or the opening of doors. Overall, these systems are effective in detecting changes in the environment. Some common types of IDS sensors include:

▶ **Audio detection or acoustical detection**—These sensors use microphones and listen for changes in the ambient noise level. They are susceptible to false positives.

▶ **Dry contact switches**—These sensors detect when a door or window is opened.

▶ **Electro-mechanical**—These sensors trigger on a break in the circuit.

▶ **Motion detectors**—You have probably seen this type of sensor on one of the many security lights sold commercially. Motion detectors can be triggered from audio, radio wave pattern, or capacitance.

▶ **Vibration sensors**—These sensors use piezoelectric technology to detect vibration and trigger on movement.

▶ **Pressure sensitive**—These sensors are sensitive to weight. Most measure a change in resistance to trigger the device. Pressure mats are an example of this type of technology.

▶ **Photoelectric**—These sensors use infrared light and are laid out as a grid over an area. If the grid is disturbed, the sensor will detect a change.

▶ **Passive infrared**—These sensors can sense changes in heat generated by humans.

> **ExamAlert**
>
> When you encounter intrusion detection questions on the actual exam, note whether the question is referencing a *physical* intrusion detection system or a *logical* intrusion detection system.

Sometimes organizations choose not to use IDS solutions because they can produce false positives. A false positive result indicates that a condition is present when it actually is not. Before these systems are deployed, a risk assessment should be performed to determine the true value of these devices to the organization. IDS solutions often are a layer of security used as monitoring tools that alert a security guard for further human inspection to determine further preventative measures to be taken.

Monitoring and Detection

Alarm systems must be monitored and controlled. Either an in-house guard or a third-party company will need to be assigned the task of monitoring the alarm system. Alarm systems use one of four basic designs, as shown in Table 3.9.

TABLE 3.9 **Alarm Systems**

Alarm System	Description
Local alarms	The alarm triggers an audio and visual alert locally. A guard is required to respond.
Central stations	Operated by private third-party organizations that can respond at the customers' premises within 10 to 15 minutes.
Proprietary systems	An in-house system that is much like a central station except that it is owned and operated by the company.
Auxiliary systems	A subcategory of the preceding three systems that is unique in that it has dialup capabilities. Such a system can dial the police or fire department when a triggering event occurs.

Ever notice how movies show the criminal disconnecting the alarm system or maybe even cutting the red wire to disable it? In reality, this doesn't work. Alarm systems have built-in *tamper protection*. Any attempt to compromise detection devices, controllers, annunciators, or other alarm components initiates a tamper alarm. Even if power is cut, the alarm will still sound because modern alarm systems are backed up by battery power. Many systems also provide cellular phone backup. The National Fire Protection Association (NFPA) Fire Code 72 standard specifies that a local alarm system must provide 60 hours of battery backup, whereas a central station signaling system is required to provide only 24 hours of backup. In any situation in which the annunciator signals an alarm, Fire Code Standard 72 states that the audible alert should be at least 105 dB and have a visual component for the deaf or hearing-impaired.

Exam Prep Questions

1. You are a security consultant and your client would like you to recommend some commonly used control mechanisms. Which of the following control mechanisms work by means of supplying secret information (such as a key-code or password)?

   ○ **A.** Guards

   ○ **B.** Fences

   ○ **C.** Locks

   ○ **D.** Cameras

2. You are a security officer and your client has asked you for your recommendation for a physical deterrent mechanism that will discourage casual trespassers. His facility is near a highly populated residential area with many family homes and children. What is the BEST recommendation you can give them from the following options?

   ○ **A.** Recommend installing an 8' fence with 3 strands of razor-wire

   ○ **B.** Recommend a 3' to 4' fence

   ○ **C.** Recommend a 6' to 7' fence

   ○ **D.** Recommend an 8' fence with a sign that says "No Trespassing"

3. What is the first priority after determining that there is a fire?

   ○ **A.** Removing valuable assets

   ○ **B.** Calling the fire department

   ○ **C.** Alerting employees to evacuate the building

   ○ **D.** Informing senior management

4. Doors with electric locks should default to which of the following in case of a power outage?

   ○ **A.** Engaged

   ○ **B.** Locked

   ○ **C.** Energized

   ○ **D.** Fail-safe

5. Halon was replaced by which of the following?

   ○ **A.** AM-100

   ○ **B.** AM-200

   ○ **C.** FM-100

   ○ **D.** FM-200

6. You have been asked to illuminate an area of critical importance. What is the correct amount of light to use for this area?

   ○ **A.** 4 feet high, with 1 foot-candle

   ○ **B.** 6 feet high, with 2 foot-candles

   ○ **C.** 8 feet high, with 2 foot-candles

   ○ **D.** 8 feet high, with 4 foot-candles

7. Gasoline or oil fires should be suppressed by which of the following?

   ○ **A.** Water

   ○ **B.** Soda acid

   ○ **C.** Dry powder

   ○ **D.** Cleaning fluid

8. Which of the following water sprinkler systems will not activate until triggered by a secondary mechanism?

   ○ **A.** Dry pipe

   ○ **B.** Wet pipe

   ○ **C.** Preaction

   ○ **D.** Deluge

9. Which of the following is a cipher lock?

   ○ **A.** Latches

   ○ **B.** Keypads

   ○ **C.** Cylinders

   ○ **D.** Deadbolts

10. You are a security consultant and your client has complained to you that he keeps experiencing extended periods of low voltage following a blackout that they recently experienced. He has already replaced the power line conditioner devices. What is the *most* likely event that is occurring?

    ○ **A.** Fault

    ○ **B.** Blackout

    ○ **C.** Brownout

    ○ **D.** Static electricity

11. Which is not a component of CPTED?

    ○ **A.** Natural access control

    ○ **B.** Natural reinforcement

    ○ **C.** Natural surveillance

    ○ **D.** Territorial reinforcement

12. The method of fire suppression used depends on the type of fire that needs to be extinguished. Which of the following fire suppression methods does not suppress any of the fire's three key elements, and led to the creation of the fire tetrahedron?

- ○ **A.** CO_2
- ○ **B.** Halon
- ○ **C.** Water
- ○ **D.** A dry pipe system

13. A differential latching clapper valve is most closely associated with which of the following?

- ○ **A.** Mantrap
- ○ **B.** Wet pipe fire suppression
- ○ **C.** Shim locks
- ○ **D.** Dry pipe fire suppression

14. Common access cards make use of which of the following?

- ○ **A.** RFID
- ○ **B.** Smart card
- ○ **C.** Magnetic strip
- ○ **D.** Copper strip

15. What is the *best* answer that correctly describes the difference between MTBF and MTTR?

- ○ **A.** The MTBF is the estimated time that a piece of hardware, device, or system will operate before it is fails. The MTTR is an estimate of how long it takes to repair the equipment and get it back into use.
- ○ **B.** MTBF is time that would be required to correct or repair a device in the event it fails and the MTTR is the estimated time that a piece of hardware, device, or system will operate before it fails.
- ○ **C.** The MTBF is a value that can be used to compare devices to one another and also to determine the need for an SLA for a device.
- ○ **D.** There is no need for a company to determine MTBF and the MTTR for assets if they do not live in an area where natural disasters such as hurricanes are not common.

Answers to Exam Prep Questions

1. **C.** Locks are one of the most effective and widely used theft deterrents. Locks work by means of supplying secret information, such as a key-code or password. All other answers are incorrect because locks are the most widely used and offer the greatest return on initial investment.

2. **B.** B is the correct answer as the question asks how to deter casual trespassers. A is not the *best* answer; while it does meet the intent of your client, it exceeds his expectations for security. Moreover, the razor wire would certainly harm anyone who attempts to climb the fence. Answers C and D are incorrect because while these may keep out an intruder they do not meet the requirements of the client. An 8-foot fence would exceed the requirements of the client.

3. **C.** The safety of employees should always be your first concern. All other answers are incorrect: Protecting assets (answer A), calling the fire department (answer B), and informing senior management (answer D) should be done only after ensuring the safety of the employees.

4. **D.** Fail-safe locks are designed to protect employees in case of power loss because they allow employees to exit the facility. If doors are electrically powered, an unlocked (or disengaged) state allows employees to exit and not be locked in. All other answers are incorrect because they would result in employees being locked in. This could have tragic results.

5. **D.** Halon is a gas that is an effective fire suppressant. It was widely used because it did not leave liquid or solid residue and did not damage computer equipment. The Montreal Protocol of 1987 worked to ban halon in certain countries because it was known to damage the ozone layer. New installations of suppression equipment must deploy alternative fire-suppression methods. FM-200 is the most popular of its replacements.

6. **C.** The National Institute of Standards and Technologies (NIST) states that for effective perimeter control, buildings should be illuminated 8 feet high, with 2 foot-candles of illumination.

7. **B.** Gasoline or oil fires should be suppressed by using CO_2, soda acid, or halon replacement such as FM-200. Water (answer A) is used for paper or wood fires, dry powder (answer C) is used for metal fires, and cleaning fluid (answer D) is flammable and should not be used on any fire.

8. **C.** A pre-action fire sprinkler system is a combination system. Pipes are initially dry and do not fill with water until a predetermined temperature is reached. Even then, the system will not activate until a secondary mechanism triggers. Answers A, B, and D are incorrect because they do not require a secondary mechanism to trigger.

9. **B.** Cipher locks use keypads. All the other answers list preset key locks.

10. **C.** A brownout is an extended period of low voltage. Answer A is incorrect; a fault is a short period of power loss. Answer B is incorrect; a blackout is a complete loss of power. Answer D is incorrect; static electricity is caused by low humidity.

11. **B.** Natural reinforcement is not a component of CPTED. CPTED comprises natural access control (answer A), natural surveillance (answer C), and territorial reinforcement (answer D). CPTED is unique in that it considers the factors that facilitate crime and seeks to use the proper design of a facility to reduce the fear and incidence of crime. At the core of CPTED is the belief that physical environments can be structured in such a way as to reduce crime.

12. **B.** Halon is unique in that it does not work in the same way as most fire suppression agents. Halon interferes with the chemical reaction of the fire and is one reason the fire tetrahedron was created. The other answers are incorrect because water (answer C) removes one of the needed items for a fire, as does carbon dioxide (answer A). A dry pipe system (answer D) is a water suppression system design, and does not hold water continuously.

13. **D.** A clapper valve is found in fire suppression systems, such as a dry pipe system. It is a simple valve technology that controls the flow of water. It is not found in mantraps or locks.

14. **B.** A Common Access Card is an example of smart card technology. This means of access control allows for cryptographic signing and PKI, and establishes identity. Answers A, C, and D are incorrect because a CAC does not make use of RFID, magnetic strip, or copper strip technology.

15. **A.** The MTBF is the lifetime of a device. The MTTR is the time that would be required to correct or repair a device in the event that it fails. Answers B, C, and D are incorrect. Answer B is not the correct description. Answer C describes only part of the correct answer, as it is only an estimate of the failure rate. Answer D is not correct as these values are not affected by natural disasters one way or the other.

Suggested Reading and Resources

Fire safety and equipment information: www.nfpa.org/safety-information/for-consumers/fire-and-safety-equipment

Bollards and other premises-security controls: en.wikipedia.org/wiki/Bollard

Halon alternatives: www.halcyon.com/NAFED/HTML/Halonalt.html

Biometric systems used by U.S. Homeland Security: www.biometrics.gov/ReferenceRoom/FederalPrograms.aspx

Alarm annunciator systems: www.dartelectronicsinc.com/viewtopic.php?f=2&t=6

Perimeter fence design: www.doityourself.com/stry/chainlinkfaq

Fence standards: www.astm.org/Standards/F1553.htm

Gate specifications: www.astm.org/Standards/F2200.htm

Information on RFID technology: www.rfidjournal.com

Lock picking: www.digitaltrash.org/defcon/

Fire suppression methods: www.nbcert.org/firesuppression.htm

Alarm specifications: www.sdmmag.com/
articles/85224-horns-strobes-clarifying-code-requirements

CPTED Specifications: www.cptedsecurity.com/cpted_design_guidelines.htm

CHAPTER 4

Security and Risk Management

Terms you'll need to understand:

▶ Security governance principles

▶ Compliance

▶ Regulation

▶ Trans-border data flow

▶ Laws that address software licensing and intellectual property

▶ Professional ethics

▶ Threat

▶ Vulnerability

▶ Security and risk management

▶ Single loss expectancy (SLE)

▶ Annual rate of occurrence (ARO)

▶ Residual risk

▶ Annual loss expectancy (ALE)

Topics you'll need to master:

▶ Calculations used for risk management

▶ Approved approaches to good security management

▶ How to perform qualitative risk analysis

▶ How to perform quantitative risk analysis

▶ How to perform hybrid risk analysis

▶ Good resource protection

▶ The role of security policies, procedures, guidelines, and baselines

▶ Proper data classification

▶ Proper implementation of security roles

▶ How to perform risk calculations

Introduction

The security and risk management domain identifies data classification and evaluation. This domain also introduces security governance and protection of intellectual property. Each of these is driven by documents that include policies, procedures, and guidelines. These documents are of great importance because they spell out how the organization manages its security practices and details what is most important to the organization. These documents are a roadmap, demonstrating the level and amount of governance an organization has. These documents are not developed in a void. Senior management must lead by driving this process. Senior management has the vision, knows the overall goals of the organization, and knows the mission of the organization.

This chapter goes into more depth in discussing the two techniques used to calculate risk: qualitative and quantitative. The key to mastering this domain is understanding these two processes. Is one method better than the other? No, both quantitative and qualitative risk assessment methods have advantages and disadvantages. It is important that the CISSP candidate understand the differences, and how each can be used to address threats, assess risk potential, and evaluate the organization's vulnerabilities.

Finally, it's important not to forget the employees. Employees play a key part in this process. They are tasked with carrying out the policies implemented by management. Although the workers of the organization will want to do the right thing and help the company succeed, they must be trained. This training can be on a wide range of topics, from ethics, to acceptable use, to social engineering. Training helps employees know what the proper actions are and understand the security practices of the organization. The overall goal of this domain, like the others you have studied, is to ensure confidentiality, integrity, and availability of an organization's assets and information.

Security Governance

Security management has changed throughout the years. In the 1970s, the focus was on computer security, whereas in the 1980s and 1990s, the focus shifted to data and information security systems. Only during the last few years have more organizations begun to look at security more holistically.

Today, there is a focus on governance, which encompasses all of security. Good governance requires total enterprise protection, often referred to as a holistic enterprise security program, which includes physical, logical, and administrative components. Luckily for security management, there are many guidance documents available to help build an effective security management program. Some examples of these include:

▶ **Government recommendations**—NIST SP 800-30, NIST SP 800-55, and NIST SP 800-100

▶ **Security configuration recommendations**—The NSA Security Configuration Guides and RFC 2196, The Site Security Handbook

▶ **Standards**—ISO 17799, Trusted Computer System Evaluation Criteria (TCSEC), Information Technology Security Evaluation Criteria (ITSEC), and Common Criteria (CC) regulations such as United States Health Insurance Portability and Accountability Act (HIPAA) and Sarbanes-Oxley (SOX)

Risk management is the ultimate requirement in support of all information security activities. One of the key documents that can be used to achieve this goal is ISO/IEC 27002. It is considered a code of practice for information security. ISO 27002 provides the best practice guidance on information security management. It is divided into 12 main sections:

▶ Risk assessment and treatment

▶ Security policy

▶ Organization of information security

▶ Asset management

▶ Human Resources security

▶ Physical and environmental security

▶ Communications and operations management

▶ Access control

▶ Information systems acquisition, development, and maintenance

▶ Information security incident management

▶ Business continuity management

▶ Compliance

ISO 27002 is written for the individuals responsible for initiating, implementing, and/or maintaining information security management systems. Its goal is to provide a template for protectors, provide technical guidance, and to help train those tasked with protecting the organization's assets.

Third-Party Governance

Governance is not just about managing in-house processes; it is also about managing external entities. Third-party governance must verify compliance with all stated security objectives, requirements, regulations, and contractual obligations that have been agreed upon. As reliance on third parties continues to grow so does the need to manage these relationships. Some of the documents used for third-party governance are listed here:

▶ Interconnection Security Agreement (ISA)—A security document that specifies the requirements for establishing, maintaining, and operating an interconnection between systems or networks. The document lists the requirements for connecting the systems and networks, and details what security controls are to be used to protect the systems and sensitive data. An ISA typically maintains a drawing of the network topology and details how specific systems and networks are connected.

▶ Interoperability Agreement (IA)—A document that specifies any and all requirements for creating and maintaining requirements for companies to be able to exchange data. As an example, United Airlines may code-share flights with Hawaiian Airlines, so both need access to a common data set.

▶ Memorandum of Understanding (MOU)—This documents specifies terms and conditions for outsourcing partner organizations that must share data and information resources. To be legally binding, the MOU must be signed by a representative from each organization that has the legal authority to sign. Such documents are typically secured, as they are considered confidential.

▶ Authorization to Operate (ATO)—A formal statement that authorizes operation and agrees to accept any and all risks.

▶ Continuity of Operations (COOP)—Things will go wrong and when they do the COOP specifies the processes and procedures that organizations must put in place to ensure that businesses can continue to operate.

▶ Service Level Agreement (SLA)—Sometimes used in conjunction with an ISA or MOU. If the outsourcing provider with which you have signed an MOU is going to provide a time-sensitive service, an SLA is one way to obtain guarantees of the level of service the partner is agreeing to provide. The SLA should specify the uptime, response time, and maximum outage time that the provider is agreeing to. For a service fee, the provider agrees to repair or replace the equipment within the contracted time.

▶ Operating Level Agreement (OLA)—Functions in conjunction with SLAs in that it supports the SLA process. The OLA defines the responsibilities of each partner's internal support group. For example, the SLA may promise no more than five minutes of downtime, while the OLA will define which group and resources will be used to meet that downtime goal.

▶ Uptime Agreement (UA)—Details the agreed amount of uptime, usually as a percentage. For example, UAs can be used for network services, such as a WAN link, or equipment, such as a server. It's common to see uptimes like 99.999%, which is equal to about five minutes' downtime per year.

▶ Nondisclosure Agreement (NDA)—Used to protect confidential information. For example, before taking the CISSP exam, you will be asked to sign an NDA stating that you will not reveal exam questions to others.

▶ Business Partnership Agreement (BPA)—A legally binding document that is designed to provide safeguards and compel certain actions among business partners in relation to specific security-related activities. The BPA is a written agreement created by lawyers along with input from the partners; it contains standard clauses related to security and cooperation.

> **Note**
>
> One item that should be reviewed when dealing with business partners is the Statement of Auditing Standards 70 (SAS 70). The SAS 70 report verifies compliance and that the outsourcing or business partner has had its control objectives and activities examined by an independent accounting and auditing firm.

Organization Processes

Risk management requires an understanding of the organization and its time-sensitive business requirements. It's also a fact that nothing stays static in business. Organizational units change, products and services are added and removed, and portions of a business may be spun off or divested. Let's discuss some of the common types of events that a security professional may have to deal with.

First, there are mergers and acquisitions. A *merger* can be defined as the combination of two or more commercial entities into a single surviving entity. From the standpoint of risk, there are many things that can go wrong.

Businesses typically look for synergy, but some businesses just don't fit together. Regardless of the situation, some questions must be asked before the merger. Is the merger a win for both companies? Is the purpose of the merger to siphon off resources, such as talent and intellectual property, and then spin off a much weaker company later?

Sometimes companies enter a merger–acquisition phase without an adequate plan of action. This can potentially lead to security exposures and increased expenditures.

Lastly, many people don't like change. Once a company culture is established and people become set in their ways, attitudes can be hard to change. Mergers are all about change, and that goes against the grain of what many employees expect.

For the security professional it's common to be asked to quickly establish connectivity with the proposed business partner. While there is a need for connectivity, security should remain a driving concern. You need to understand the proposed merger partner's security policies and what controls they are enforcing. The last thing you would want to allow is an attacker's entry into your network through the merging company's network.

There will always be security concerns when it comes to merging diverse companies You should also be concerned with items such as the following:

▶ Rules—What is or is not allowed by each individual company.

▶ Policies—High-level documents that outline the security goals and objectives of the company.

▶ Regulations—Diverse entities may very well be governed by different regulatory entities or regulations, such as PCI or HIPAA.

▶ Geography—A company that is located in London, England will be operating on different standards than one that is based in San Jose, California.

▶ Demerger/divestiture—Any time businesses break apart you have many of the same types of issues to deal with.

▶ Trust or clearance level—The level of access or control of any current or new employees accessing information.

▶ Skill set, training, and awareness—Level of users and employee training with access to company information systems.

Protection of Intellectual Properly

Although the laws discussed in the following list are specific to the United States, intellectual property is agreed on and enforced worldwide by various organizations, including the United Nations Commission on International Trade Law (UNCITRAL), the European Union (EU), and the World Trade Organization (WTO). International property laws protect copyrights, patents trademarks, and trade secrets. These were discussed in some detail in Chapter 2.

The length of a copyright in the United States and the European Union is life plus 70 years.

Privacy Laws and Protection of Personal Information

Privacy laws are of critical importance because technology has simplified the process of accumulating large amounts of data about individuals. Commercial and government databases contain tremendous amounts of data that can be used to infringe on people's sense of privacy and anonymity. The misuse of these databases can lead to targeted advertising and disclosure of personal preferences that some individuals believe is intrusive. Privacy is increasingly being recognized as a fundamental right in many countries and organizations that hold personal information are being required to protect it.

The European Union has been on the forefront in developing laws that protect individual privacy. The European Union deals with privacy on the federal level and has a department called the *Data Protection Authority*. This authority has the power to enforce privacy directives. E.U. privacy guidelines enacted in 1998 state the following:

- ▶ Data is to be used only for the purposes for which it was collected and within a reasonable time.

- ▶ If requested, individuals are entitled to receive a report on data about them.

- ▶ An individual's personal data cannot be disclosed to third parties unless authorized by statute or consent of the individual.

- ▶ Persons have a right to make corrections to their personal data.

- ▶ Transmission to locations where equivalent personal data protection cannot be assured is prohibited.

The European Union has also implemented a concept known as the *right to be forgotten*. It has been in practice in the European Union and Argentina since 2006. On request, information that is irrelevant, private, or no longer relevant should be removed from Internet searches.

In the United States, the federal government reacts only to obvious abuses when they are reported. Privacy laws are driven by government actions.

The Fourth Amendment of the United States Constitution is the basis of privacy law in the United States. Two laws worth noting are the Privacy Act of 1974 and the Identity Theft and Assumption Deterrence Act of 1998. The Privacy Act of 1974 limits the personal information a federal agency can collect, maintain, and disclose. The Identity Theft and Assumption Deterrence Act of 1998 raises the penalties for identity theft and establishes that the person whose identity was stolen is a true victim. Before passage of this act, only a credit grantor who suffered monetary losses was considered a victim.

Even with these laws in place, there is still a large amount of information that can be obtained about individuals in the United States. To get a better idea about what types of information are available, take a moment to review Table 4.1. Although most of these sites will give you some information for free, for just a few dollars you can get much more. This is just a short list; there are many more sites from which to gather personal information.

TABLE 4.1 **Personal Information Websites**

Resource	Usage	URL
Location of individual	Used to find location, address, age, and other information	www.zabasearch.com
Informants	Used to identify informants	www.whosarat.com
Social networking search	Used to find individuals that post to social networking sites	www.pipl.com

Note

Although the United States and the European Union take a different approach to privacy, U.S. companies handling information from customers based in the European Union must be aware of the European Commission's 1998 Directive on Data Protection (Safe Harbor), and provide a standard for privacy protection equal to what would be provided in the European Union.

Relevant Laws and Regulations

Security professionals should be aware of the laws that pertain to them locally and understand terms such as *due care* and *due diligence*. Due care is taking reasonable care to protect the assets of an organization. For example, think of it as information gathering. Doing the right thing over a period of time—implementation—is considered due diligence.

The CISSP exam does not test you on country-specific laws, but you should have an understanding of laws in your region of the world. The following laws are mentioned briefly:

▶ **Computer Fraud and Abuse Act (CFAA) of 1986**—Amended in 1996, it now makes distribution of malware illegal. It deals with computers used by the federal government, but can include others.

▶ **Federal Sentencing Guidelines of 1991**—Provides guidelines to judges so that sentences are handed down in a more uniform manner for crimes dealing with computers.

▶ **Economic Espionage Act of 1996**—Defines strict penalties for those accused of espionage.

▶ **U.S. Child Pornography Prevention Act of 1996**—Enacted to combat and reduce the use of computer technology to produce and distribute child pornography.

▶ **U.S. Patriot Act of 2001**—Strengthens computer crime laws to expand law enforcement's capability to fight terrorism; has been the subject of some controversy.

United States Legal System and Laws

The U.S. legal system can trace its roots to the United Kingdom. The United States, United Kingdom, and Canada all use a *common law* system. Common law is based on previous rulings and principles such as *stare decisis*—the concept that court cases that are similar should be decided in a consistent manner. Common law also recognizes the rule of reasonable doubt and that a defendant is innocent until proven guilty. Categories of common law include:

▶ **Criminal law**—*Criminal law* exists to punish someone who violates the government's laws and is therefore considered to have committed crimes against society. Cases are brought forth by the state or federal government. Punishment can include financial penalties, imprisonment, or both. Broadly speaking, felonies are more serious crimes that can result in large fines and more than one year of imprisonment, while misdemeanors are less serious crimes that result in smaller fines and no more than one year of imprisonment. Penalties for both are designed to punish criminals and deter criminal activity.

▶ **Civil law**—*Civil law* has no ability to prescribe prison time. Cases are brought forth by victims or those individuals who believe they have been wronged. Victims are compensated by means of financial awards of punitive, compensatory, or statutory damages if the defendant is found guilty. Punitive damages are determined by a jury. Compensatory damages are payments based on actual damage, whereas statutory damages are awarded based on law and preset limits.

▶ **Administrative (regulatory) law**—*Administrative law* establishes standards of performance and conduct that governmental agencies expect from industries, organizations, officials, and officers. Individuals and organizations that violate these laws can be punished by financial penalties and/or imprisonment. These laws typically apply to industries such as health care, financial, industrial, petrochemical, and pharmaceutical.

International Legal Systems and Laws

Legal systems vary throughout the world regarding the rights of the accused, the role of the judge, the nature of evidence, and other essential legal concepts. Claims and cases can be handled quite differently; Figure 4.1 shows an example of where some of these various systems are used in the world.

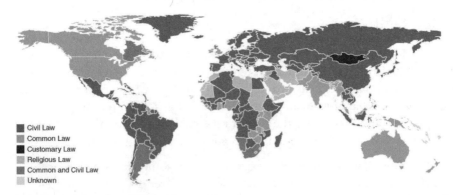

FIGURE 4.1 **Legal systems of the world.**

Much of Europe is based on civil (code) law, also known as *Napoleonic law*. Civil law evolved in Europe from around the time of the Roman Empire. The Romans used *Corpus Juris Civilis*, which featured a comprehensive system of written rules of law that serves as the basis of civil law used today. The major difference between civil law and common law is that civil law uses legislation as the main source of legal rulings in court cases.

Religious law is based on religious tenets. Examples include *halakha* in Judaism and *sharia* in Islam. The Islamic system is an autonomous legal system based on religious tenets and references items found in the Qur'an. China and some African countries use *customary law*, which is based on the concept of what is considered customary and normal conduct.

If two or more of these legal systems are combined, the result is a *mixed law* system. Mixed law systems are noted for their inclusion of more than one type of legal framework and might feature components of two or more basic types. As an example, Louisiana has features of both civil law and common law, whereas parts of the Middle East mix customary law with religious law.

This international patchwork of legal systems is superimposed on international property laws that affect data handling, so although the CISSP exam will most likely focus on common law, it is important that the CISSP candidate understand the differences between the various legal systems used around the world.

Computer Crime and Hackers

Hackers are one of the threats that CISSPs must be prepared to deal with. It's commonly thought that only one tenth or so of all the computer crimes committed are detected. How could this be true? It is difficult to develop accurate numbers regarding the detection and reporting of computer crime. Many crimes go undetected and others are detected but never reported to law-enforcement agencies or the general public. Some companies are worried about a possible negative reputation and the loss of customers; others are afraid that it might make them appear vulnerable. One good source of information about computer crime and data breaches is at www.informationisbeautiful.net/, which has a list of the top data breaches for each year, as shown in Figure 4.2.

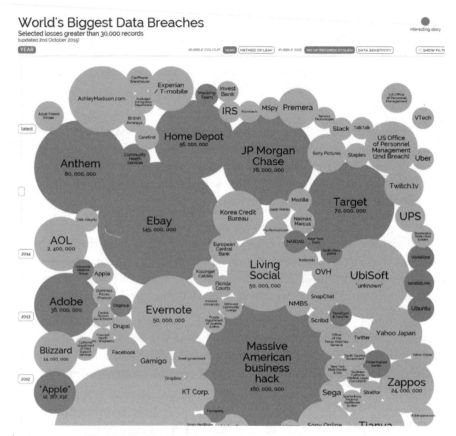

FIGURE 4.2 **World's Biggest Data Breaches.**

There are multiple attack vectors for computer crime:

▶ **Physical security attack**—Physically accessing systems

▶ **Personnel security attack**—Harassing, extorting, or threatening employees

▶ **Communications attack**—Eavesdropping on wired, wireless, or satellite communications

▶ **Logical attack**—Logically accessing systems

▶ **Social engineering attack**—Tricking employees or others into providing access or information

No discussion of computer crime would be complete without a review of the criminals. Most security professionals think of computer criminals as hackers. Originally, the term *hacker* was used for a computer enthusiast who enjoyed understanding the internal workings of a system, computer, and computer network. Over time, the popular press began to describe hackers as individuals who broke into computers with malicious intent. The industry responded by developing the term cracker, which is short for *criminal hacker*. The term was meant to describe individuals who seek to compromise the security of a system without permission from an authorized party; however, the public continues to use the term *hacker* to describe the computer criminal. There are actually many other terms that can be used to identify the criminal and to categorize criminal activities, including the following:

- ▶ **Phreakers**—The original hackers. These individuals hacked telecommunication and PBX systems to explore their capabilities and make free phone calls.

- ▶ **Script kiddies**—A term used to describe younger attackers that use widely available, freeware vulnerability assessment tools and hacking tools that are designed for attacking purposes only. These attackers typically have very limited programming or hacking skills and depend on tools written by others.

- ▶ **Disgruntled employees**—Employees who have lost respect for the employer and act accordingly. These individuals might or might not have more skills than script kiddies. Insiders or former insiders are a real risk because of the knowledge they have or the access they might possess.

- ▶ **Cyberterrorists/cybercriminals**—Individuals or groups who are typically funded to conduct clandestine or espionage activities on governments, organizations, and people in an unlawful manner. These individuals are typically engaged in sponsored acts of defacement, DoS/DDoS (Denial of Service/Distributed Denial of Service) attacks, identity theft, financial theft; they may also compromise critical infrastructure, such as nuclear power plants, electric plants, water treatment plants, and so on.

- ▶ **Corporate spy/government spy**—Elite hackers who have specific expertise in attacking vulnerabilities of systems and networks. These attackers can be differentiated by their level of skill. These individuals know what they want and will go to great lengths to get it. They have no interest in making a public name for themselves, which sets them apart from hackers of years ago who were motivated by notoriety.

> **Tip**
>
> If you want to learn more about hacking and all the players in the security realm, such as hackers, security professionals, and law enforcement, consider local options such as ISSA and INFRAGARD or security conferences such as Black Hat or DEF CON. Conferences are one of the ways you can gain ISC^2 continuing professional education (CPE) credits and learn more about current security trends and exposures.

Sexual Harassment

United States law requires companies to provide a safe workplace where employees are free from sexual harassment and offensive behavior. Therefore, companies that fail to enforce acceptable use policies (AUPs) could find themselves in legal jeopardy.

Risk Management Concepts

Risk management is the systematic ongoing approach to analyzing risk, identifying threats, and implementing controls to mitigate risk. With any new topic, the terminology and semantics used within the context of the technology can be confusing, misused, and misrepresented. Risk management should be driven by senior management, who appoint someone to lead the risk assessment process.

When senior management is driving the process, a company has top-down support for a security program; this is the preferred method. Sometimes senior management might not see the value of a structured risk assessment process. In these situations, a bottom-up process might still be able to drive the risk assessment process.

It is imperative that individuals driving the risk assessment gain the support of senior management. One common technique to secure senior management commitment and support is by educating them using a formal presentation. Presentations can communicate key aspects of the overall risk management program and remind senior management that they are ultimately responsible.

A major part of risk management includes developing the risk-management team, identifying threats and vulnerabilities, placing a value on the organization's assets, and determining how you will deal with the risk you uncover.

After senior management is on board, the risk management process can begin. The goal of this process is that the organization build the controls necessary to protect the organization's staff and assets, while meeting stakeholder expectations.

Risk Management Frameworks

The risk management framework supports the risk management process. As an example, British Standard BS 31100 provides guidance on the objectives, mandate, and commitment to manage risk. Another example is NIST Special Publication 800-37, "Guide for Applying the Risk Management Framework to Federal Information Systems", which details a six-step risk management framework (RMF). These steps are listed below and are shown in Figure 4.3:

▶ Categorize

▶ Select

▶ Implement

▶ Assess

▶ Authorize

▶ Monitor

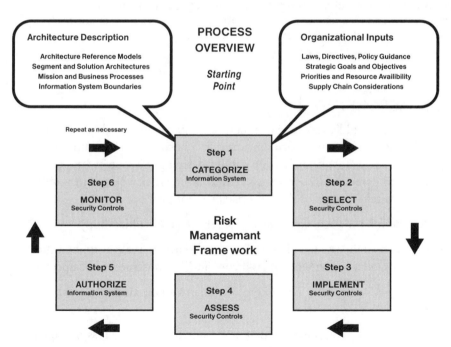

FIGURE 4.3 **NIST risk framework.**

Some of the other approaches to risk management and assessment that have been developed include:

▶ Factor analysis of information risk (FAIR)—An approach to risk management that develops baselines of probabilities for the frequency and magnitude of loss events. It's considered an add-on to existing risk frameworks.

▶ Risk factor analysis—Another approach to risk analysis that uses a six-step methodology to identify factors that drive the behavior of the project schedule, cost, and technical performance.

▶ Probabilistic risk assessment—Designed for use with large-scale complex projects where risk is defined as a feasible detrimental outcome of an activity or action. The results are expressed numerically.

> **Note**
>
> A risk register is one of the tools that can be used to act as a repository of identified risk and the nature of each risk. You can see an example of one here: www.slideshare.net/KashifMastan/risk-register-34631122

Risk Assessment

A *risk assessment*, unlike risk management, has a start and stop date. It is the process of identifying and prioritizing risks to a business. Completion of this assessment is crucial. Without it, you cannot design good security policies or procedures to defend your company's critical assets. Risk assessment requires individuals to take charge of the risk-management process.

First, let's define the basic concepts of risk, threat, and vulnerability.

Risk is the probability or likelihood of an occurrence or realization of a threat. There are three basic elements of risk from an IT infrastructure perspective:

▶ **Asset**—A component or an item of value to an organization, such as data assets.

▶ **Threat**—Any circumstance that could potentially cause loss or damage to an asset.

▶ **Vulnerability**—A weakness in infrastructure, design, or components that might be exploited by a threat to destroy, damage, or compromise an asset.

A *threat* is any agent, condition, or circumstance that could potentially cause harm, loss, damage, or compromise to an asset. From an IT perspective, threats can be categorized as circumstances that can affect the confidentiality, integrity, or availability of an asset. Threats can be natural, man-made, or technical. Threats can result in destruction, disclosure, modification, or corruption of corporate resources, or can cause a denial of service.

A *vulnerability* is a weakness in the design of a product, a weakness in the implementation of a product, or a weakness in how the product's software or code was developed. Vulnerabilities can be reduced or even possibly eliminated by the implementation of safeguards, controls, and security countermeasures.

> **Note**
>
> Controls are mechanisms used to restrain, regulate, or reduce vulnerabilities. Controls can be corrective, detective, preventive, or deterrent.

Before you start to fret over how one person could ever accomplish this task alone, understand that risk management is a big job. You'll need co-workers and employees from other departments to help. To do an effective job of risk management analysis, you must involve individuals from all the different departments of the company. Otherwise, you run the risk of not seeing the big picture.

It's hard for any one person to understand the inner workings of all departments. Sure, as an IT or security administrator, you understand the logical risks the IT infrastructure faces, but do you really have a grasp of the problems HR might have? These might include employee controls, effective termination practices, and control of confidentiality information. Bringing in key employees from other functional areas is required if you expect the risk management process to be successful. Consider including employees from each of the following groups in a risk management team:

- ▶ Information system security
- ▶ IT and operations management
- ▶ System and network administration
- ▶ Internal audit
- ▶ Physical security
- ▶ Business process and information owners
- ▶ Human Resources

▶ Legal

▶ Physical safety

Asset owners should also be represented on the team. Because the asset owners are responsible for assets, they should have a voice in the types of controls that are implemented. Having asset owners on the team ensures the team is aware of, and can address, the many threats it will need to examine.

The team must also be kept informed and guided by personnel knowledge-able about the legal and regulatory requirements of the organization. As an example, some teams are established specifically to examine ways to decrease insurance costs, reduce attacks against the company's technical infrastructure, or even to verify compliance with government standards such as GLBA, SOX, or HIPAA.

After the risk management team has been established, their tasks are to

1. Perform asset valuation

2. Perform threat analysis

3. Perform quantitative or qualitative risk assessment

4. Choose remedial measures

5. Reduce, assign, or accept the risk

The key security management practices necessary to assess risk have been broken into six broad steps shown here and in Figure 4.4:

1. Asset identification

2. Risk assessment

3. Policy development

4. Implementation

5. Training and education

6. Auditing the security infrastructure

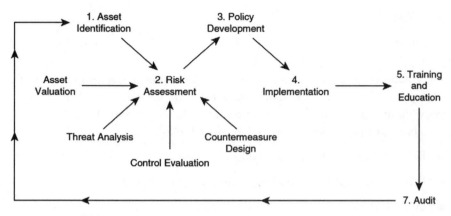

FIGURE 4.4 **Risk management strategy.**

Now that we have created a risk management team that has the support of senior management, let's examine the methods used to place a value on assets.

Asset Identification and Valuation

The next step is to list the value of organization's assets. A proper *asset valuation* enables the organization's risk management team to start making business decisions regarding deployment of security controls and security countermeasures.

One of the most important steps for securing an organization's assets is to identify and inventory all of those assets. For example, imagine you work for a bank that is in charge of protecting a customer database containing names, Social Security numbers, and addresses. You would want to place a much higher level of control over these assets than you would another database that contained locations, manager names, and phone numbers of all your bank's local branches. Yet you would not know the level of protection if you were unaware of the database asset. Without a complete and accurate inventory of all assets, an asset valuation cannot be performed.

When recording information about the organization's assets, you should record the following information:

- ► Identification
- ► Location
- ► Risk
- ► Protection

▶ Group

▶ Owner

Assets can be both tangible and intangible. One final important aspect offered by documented asset management is demonstrated due care. To valuate an asset properly, appreciate that the value is often based on more than just the cost to create or purchase that item. Consider the following:

▶ What did the asset cost to acquire or create?

▶ What is the liability should the asset be compromised?

▶ What is the production cost should the asset be made unavailable?

▶ What is the value of the asset to competitors and foreign governments?

▶ How critical is the asset, and how would its loss affect the company?

▶ What skill sets and how many hours per day, week, or month are required to maintain this asset?

▶ What are the subsystems, applications, hardware, or software that this asset is dependent on?

After listing the values of assets, the team can consider the organization's most critical systems, resources, applications, and data. This information provides the ability to prioritize investments for security controls and security counter-measures. Controls are not cost-free and require expenditure of limited funds. Most organizations must justify the investment needed for proper security controls and security countermeasures.

Without an asset valuation, it is difficult to understand a control's return on investment (ROI), or the cost-benefit analysis pertaining to the investment in security countermeasures. Knowing the value of assets that you are trying to protect is also important because it would be foolish to exceed the value of the asset by spending more on the countermeasure than what the asset is worth, or spending more on a control than you stand to lose if a threat targets a vulner-ability. A common problem is failing to take into account how the secondary and tertiary systems affect value assigned to key assets.

You can't protect everything. When defining your scope, organizations have only limited funds and resources, so countermeasures must be strategically deployed to guard what has been deemed most critical. Focus is first given to protect assets that face high levels of risk as the consequence of events that result in high impact. An example of this can be seen in Figure 4.5.

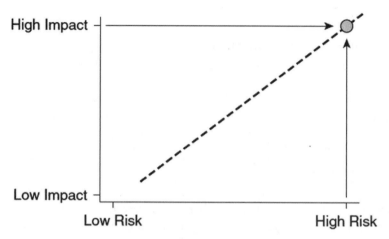

FIGURE 4.5 **High risk, high impact assets.**

Asset identification and evaluation is also needed for insurance purposes. An organization might determine that some risks should be transferred to third parties. As such, asset valuation offers the organization the capability to accurately assess its business insurance requirements. Starting around the year 2000, some companies actually started offering technical and cyber risk coverage, more popularly known as *hacker insurance.*

Threats Analysis

Earlier, we discussed how threats can have negative impacts on the organization. Now, let's look at where these threats might originate. Threats can occur because of technical failures, natural factors, or be caused by humans, maliciously or accidentally. Identifying all potential threats is a huge responsibility. Instead of random brainstorming on potential threats, a somewhat easier approach is to categorize common types of threats (after all, why list a tornado if you live in Alaska):

▶ Natural catastrophes

▶ Physical threat/theft

▶ Human error/insider threat

▶ Application error/buffer overflow

▶ Equipment malfunction

▶ Environmental hazards

▶ Malicious software/covert channels

- ▶ Hacker attacks

- ▶ Disclosure of confidential information

- ▶ Stolen, lost, damaged, or modified data

- ▶ Unauthorized access

- ▶ Terrorism

- ▶ Viruses, worms, and malware

- ▶ Denial of service

A threat coupled with a vulnerability and a threat agent can lead to a loss. Think of the threat agent as the individual or group that can manifest the threat. As mentioned earlier, vulnerabilities are flaws or weaknesses in security systems, software, or procedures. An example of a vulnerability is lack of employee training. This vulnerability might permit an improperly trained help desk employee to unknowingly give a password to a potential hacker. This could result in a loss. Examples of losses or impacts include:

- ▶ Financial loss

- ▶ Loss of reputation

- ▶ Endangerment or injury of staff, clients, or customers

- ▶ Loss of business opportunity

- ▶ Breach of confidence or violation of law

Losses might have immediate or delayed impact. A delayed loss has a negative effect on an organization well after the period of loss. This could perhaps be a few days, a few months, or even a few years. For example, an organization could have its website hacked and thus suffer an immediate loss. No e-commerce transactions can occur until technical support is brought in to rebuild the web server; all normal processing is halted. But these immediate losses might not be the only effects the company feels. Later, when the local news channel reports the company was hacked and that personal information was lost, the company could suffer from poor reputation and lose future customers. State laws vary, but some, such as California, might require the company to report the breach. Customers might remember this event for years to come, and now choose to use a competitor. These are examples of delayed loss.

Take a moment to review Figure 4.6, which displays the relationship among threats, vulnerabilities, and controls. Notice that a threat by itself does not represent a danger, and is not sufficient for a successful attack. A threat agent can be described as the actual circumstance or event that does cause harm to information assets through destruction, disclosure, or modification. Figure 4.6 uses a sample threat of a web application being hacked. The threat is the possibility that someone might hack the web application. The threat agent is the skilled hacker that will perform that attack. The vulnerability is the unpatched buffer overflow on the web application; and the risk is a measure of how probable it is that this attack will be successful.

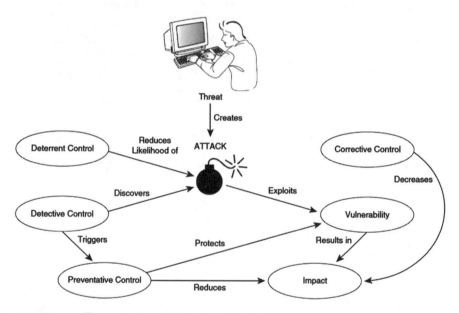

FIGURE 4.6   Threats, vulnerabilities, and controls.

Identifying threats, vulnerabilities, and controls is just part of the risk management process. Without placing dollar values or using some other metric to assess these variables, how can you start to analyze the threats and vulnerabilities that an organization faces? One approach is to develop a table such as the one shown in Table 4.2. This helps demonstrate the relationship among threats, vulnerabilities, and risks. For example, an intruder can represent a threat that might expose the organization to the theft of equipment because there is the vulnerability of no security guard or controlled entrance. We will look at dollar costs a little later in the chapter, but for now consider the relationship between these items.

TABLE 4.2 **Threat, Vulnerability, and Risk**

Threat Type	Threat	Exploit/Vulnerability	Exposed Risk
Human factor internal threat	Intruder	No security guard or controlled entrance	Theft
Human factor external threat	Hacker	Misconfigured firewall	Stolen credit card information
Human factor internal threat	Current employee	Poor accountability; no audit policy	Loss of integrity; altered data
Natural	Fire	Insufficient fire prevention	Damage or loss of life
Natural	Hurricane	Insufficient preparation	Damage or loss of life
Malicious external threat	Virus	Out-of-date antivirus software	Virus infection and loss of productivity
Technical internal threat	Hard drive failure	No data backup	Data loss and unrecoverable downtime

The risk management team must gather input from a range of sources in order to identify threats. Sources that might be consulted or considered to help identify current and emerging threats include:

▶ Asset owners

▶ Network administrators

▶ Security administrators

▶ Operations group

▶ Facility records

▶ Government records and watchdog groups, such as CERT and Bugtraq

▶ Private organizations, such as SANS

Risk management can examine assets and their associated risks by dollar or non-dollar methods. Quantitative assessments assign a cost (monetary value) to assets and anticipated exposures caused by a threat identified in the risk analysis. Qualitative assessment methods use scenarios to drive a prioritized list of critical concerns, and do not focus on dollar amounts. Qualitative and quantitative assessment techniques are described more in the following two sections.

> **Note**
>
> Quantitative and qualitative risk assessment can be combined for a hybrid risk assessment approach, which is more comprehensive.

Quantitative Assessment

Quantitative assessments deal with numbers and dollar amounts. The goal is to assign a cost or a numeric value to the elements of risk assessment and to the assets and threats of a risk analysis.

> **ExamAlert**
>
> When you hear the word quantitative, just remember "quantity." This will help you remember that it's numbers-based for the exam.

To fully complete a quantitative risk assessment, all elements of the process (asset value, impact, threat frequency, safeguard effectiveness, safeguard costs, uncertainty, and probability) are quantified. And that's the problem with purely quantitative risk assessment: It is difficult, if not impossible, to assign dollar values to all elements. Therefore, some qualitative types of measurements often augment quantitative elements. A quantitative assessment requires substantial time and personnel resources. The quantitative assessment process involves:

1. **Single Loss Expectancy (SLE)**—This step involves determining the single amount of loss you could lose on an asset if a threat becomes realized. SLE is calculated as follows:

   Single loss expectancy = Asset value × Exposure factor

   Items to consider when calculating the SLE include the physical destruction or theft of assets, the loss of data, the theft of information, and threats that might cause a delay in processing. The exposure factor is the measure or percent of damage that a realized threat would have on a specific asset.

2. **Annual Rate of Occurrence (ARO)**—The purpose of an ARO is to determine the likelihood that an unwanted event will occur annually. Simply stated, how many times is this expected to happen in one year?

3. **Determine annual loss expectancy (ALE)**—This third and final step of the quantitative assessment seeks to combine the potential loss and

rate per year to determine the magnitude of the risk. This is expressed as annual loss expectancy (ALE). ALE is calculated as follows:

Annualized loss expectancy (ALE) = Single loss expectancy (SLE) × Annualized rate of occurrence (ARO)

When performing the calculations discussed in this section, you should include all associated costs such as these and ensure that they are considered during SLE calculation:

▶ Lost productivity

▶ Cost of repair

▶ Value of the damaged equipment or lost data

▶ Cost to replace the equipment or reload the data

> **Caution**
>
> What makes quantitative assessment difficult is that it is hard to place a dollar amount on every possible event and to extrapolate all the costs associated with that event.

When these costs are accumulated and specific threats are determined, the annualized loss expectancy can be calculated. This builds a complete picture of the organization's risk and allows the organization to plan an effective strategy.

Review Table 4.3; we can work through the virus risk example given. First, calculate the SLE. The SLE requires that you multiply the asset value by the exposure factor:

$$\$9,450 \times 0.17 = \$1,650$$

The asset value is the value you have determined the asset to be worth. The exposure factor is the amount of damage that the risk poses to the asset. For example, the risk-management team might consult with its experts and determine that 17% of Word documents and data could be destroyed from a virus.

Next, the ARO is calculated. The ARO is the frequency at which this event is expected to happen within a given period. For example, the experts might have determined that there is a 90% chance of this event occurring within a one-year period. These numbers are not always easy to determine because insurance and historical records, although helpful, do not always provide a complete picture. This is still a scientific guess with a degree of uncertainty.

Finally, the ALE is calculated. The ALE is the SLE multiplied by the ARO:

$1,650 × 0.90 = $1,485

This third and final step of the quantitative assessment seeks to combine the potential loss with the rate per year to determine the magnitude of the risk. You can interpret this figure to mean that the business should expect to lose an average of $1,485 each year due to computer viruses.

TABLE 4.3 **How SLE, ARO, and ALE Are Used**

Asset	Risk	Asset Value	Exposure Factor	SLE	Annualized Frequency	ALE
Customer database	Hacked	$432,000	0.74	$320,000	0.25	$80,000
Word documents and data files	Ransom-ware	$9,450	0.17	$1,650	0.90	$1,485
Domain controller	Server failure	$82,500	0.88	$72,500	0.25	$18,125
E-commerce website	DDoS	$250,000	0.44	$110,000	0.45	$49,500

Automated tools that minimize the effort of the manual process are available. These programs enable users to rerun the analysis with different parameters to answer "what-ifs." They perform calculations quickly and can be used to estimate future expected losses more easily than performing the calculations manually. Some individuals swear by these programs, whereas others are more comfortable verifying their results.

Using Quantitative Formulas

In real life, quantitative assessment requires many different variables to be determined. Although these issues are beyond the scope of the test, it is important to see the big picture of risk assessment. As an example, let's say Superior Solutions, Inc. has an SQL database that is valued at $850,000. The asset value was derived from the IT systems, resources, applications, and hardware. This would also include the profit potential from the customer database for projected revenue and profitability.

If the SQL database has a potential threat from a critical software bug that Microsoft has just identified, the potential for a threat being realized is real. Because of this critical security defect, the vendor releases a security bulletin advising customers of the problem. Because of this known vulnerability, the risk assessment team assigns an exposure factor of 35%. There is a 35% probability that this known vulnerability could be exploited by an attacker. The calculated SLE would be:

SLE = $850,000 (Asset Value) × 0.35 (Exposure Factor)

SLE = $297,500

If this database also has a threat from malicious code or malicious software and the server that the customer database resides in does not have antivirus or other security controls, this could result in a significantly higher exposure factor. The assessment team might provide an 80% probability that a virus, worm, or Trojan may attack the production server and customer database. The calculated SLE would be:

SLE = $850,000 (Asset Value) × 0.80 (Exposure Factor)

SLE = $680,000

What is most important is defining a consistent and standard method for probability of occurrence. This will allow for consistent and standard SLE calculations so that a ranking and prioritization of IT assets' SLE values can be accomplished. In reality, many sources are used to gather this information. Most teams will rely heavily on tools and software to aid in evaluating risk. Although not required for the test, listed here are some of the companies that offer tools to aid in the risk assessment process and help with the project management aspects of such tasks:

▶ Method123: www.method123.com

▶ Palisade: www.palisade.com

▶ cyWren Systems: www.cywrensystems.com

▶ ProjectManagement.com: www.projectmanagement.com

ExamAlert

Math is a big component of quantitative assessment; the CISSP exam might require you to use basic formulas on the exam such as SLE, ALE, and ARO. Memorizing and understanding these formulas will help you be fully prepared for the exam.

Qualitative Assessment

Maybe you are thinking that there has to be another way to perform an assessment. If so, you are right. *Qualitative assessment* is scenario-driven and does not attempt to assign dollar values to components of the risk analysis. Purely quantitative risk assessment is hard to achieve because some items are difficult to tie to fixed dollar amounts. Absolute qualitative risk analysis is possible because it ranks the seriousness of threats and sensitivity of assets into grades or classes such as low, medium, and high. Table 4.4 provides a sample qualitative scale.

TABLE 4.4 **Qualitative Assessment Impact Scale**

Score	Damage	Trigger Time	Potential Impact
High	Critical	Minutes to hours	Loss of life, failure of business, civil or criminal charges
Medium	Disruptive	Hours to days	Bad PR, loss of customers, loss of prestige, loss of income
Low	Moderate	Days to weeks	Requires workaround, reduces output, might result in a reduction in profit
Insignificant	Minor	Up to one month	Inconvenience

It's important to assign a consistent and subjective assessment of the risk to specific IT assets. This typically involves a group or team of members participating in the assessment. Asset owners responsible for maintaining the confidentiality, integrity, and availability of the IT asset should have a voice in the process. The basic steps for a qualitative assessment are:

1. List all the organization's critical IT assets in a spreadsheet.

2. Specify the critical threats and vulnerabilities for each IT asset in the spreadsheet. There might be more than one critical threat or vulnerability for a given IT asset.

3. Develop a consistent exposure severity scale to measure impact. A value from the scale should be assigned according to the IT asset and the specific threat that can be exploited.

4. Organize and prioritize the risk assessment results from the most critical to the least. This will immediately bring to the top of the list those assets that have the greatest risk to exploitation from a threat or vulnerability.

5. Prioritize funds for security controls and security countermeasures for those IT assets that have the greatest importance to the organization, and have the greatest exposure to risk.

6. Ensure that the organization's critical IT assets achieve the appropriate confidentiality, integrity, and availability controls according to the threat and security policy.

The result of the qualitative assessment process is this prioritized list, and might look something like the information provided in Table 4.5. Notice how facility power is identified as a critical concern.

TABLE 4.5 **Qualitative Assessment Results**

Asset	Threat	Exposure
Facility power	Loss of power	High
Customer database	Software vulnerability	Medium
Email server	Virus attack	Medium
File server	Loss of data	Low
File server	Hard drive failure	Low

A disadvantage of performing a qualitative assessment is that you are not working with dollar values, so it is harder to communicate the results of the assessment to management personnel, who are used to working with dollar amounts. However, qualitative assessments can be completed quickly.

Qualitative assessment is subjective, based on opinions from the team or experts in the company, but not always an exact assessment that senior management will want to receive from you. For example, when predicting the possibility for a natural disaster or even man-made incidents, one can never establish exact numeric certainty.

The *Delphi technique* is one approach to qualitative risk assessment. The Delphi technique uses a group approach designed to allow individuals to contribute anonymous opinions. The idea is to avoid being swayed by pushy people, to find synergy, and to allow participants to be honest.

Facilitated Risk Assessment Process (FRAP) is another subjective process that obtains results by asking questions. It is designed to be completed in a matter of hours, making it a quick process to perform. Qualitative assessments can use many techniques such as brainstorming, surveys, questionnaires, checklists, one-on-one meetings with asset owners, and interviews.

The NSA Information Assurance Methodology

The NSA developed the Information Assurance Methodology (IAM) in 1998 in response to Presidential Decision Directive (PDD)-63. PDD-63 mandated that all federal computer systems be assessed to determine their overall security. The purpose of the IAM is to review an organization's InfoSec posture, identify potential vulnerabilities, and provide recommendations on their elimination or mitigation. It uses the security triad (confidentiality, integrity, and availability) as a basis of assessment. You can learn more about the IAM at www.isatrp.org.

NIST provides another resource for qualitative risk assessment methodologies. NIST 800-53 defines confidentiality, integrity, and availability as categories of loss and then ranks each loss based on a scale of low, medium, and high. The ranking is subjective:

▶ **Low**—Minor inconvenience that could be tolerated for a short period of time.

▶ **Medium**—Could result in damage to the organization or cost a moderate amount of money to repair.

▶ **High**—Would result in loss of goodwill between the company and clients or employees. Could result in a legal action or fine or cause the company to lose revenue or earnings.

Table 4.6 displays an example of how this assessment is performed. As you can see, no dollar amounts are used. Potential loss is only ranked as high, medium, or low.

TABLE 4.5 **Performing a Qualitative Assessment**

Asset	Loss of Confidentiality	Loss of Integrity	Loss of Availability
Customer database	High	High	Medium
Internal documents	Medium	Medium	Low
Advertising literature	Low	Medium	Low
HR records	High	High	Medium

Regardless of the method used, quantitative or qualitative, the results of the risk assessment process provide the team with the information needed to make a decision as to how to handle risk. Before moving on to that step, Table 4.7 summarizes the differences between quantitative and qualitative risk assessments.

TABLE 4.7 **Quantitative and Qualitative Risk Assessment**

Property	Quantitative	Qualitative
Provides dollar values	✓	–
Can be automated	✓	–
Very little guesswork	✓	–
No complex math	–	✓
Is user objective	–	✓

(Continued)

TABLE 4.7 **Continued**

Property	Quantitative	Qualitative
Low volume of info	–	✓
Short preparation time	–	✓
Easy to communicate to management	✓	–

> **Note**
>
> There are many ways to perform a qualitative risk assessment. As an example, in New Zealand they use the ANZ 4360 standard for qualitative risk assessment.

Countermeasure Selection

After you have identified potential risk and estimated its impact, the team is tasked with determining how to compensate for the potential risk. There are three acceptable ways in which the team can respond:

▶ **Risk acceptance** addresses risk by accepting the potential cost of the loss if the risk occurs. This option can be chosen when no other options are available or the potential loss is small when compared to the project's benefits. If this is the chosen path, it is important to prepare contingency plans to make sure you will be able to deal with the risk if it occurs. As an example, if your daughter was planning a wedding you might decide that because your daughter has her heart set on a summer wedding on the beach in the Bahamas, it might be best just to go along. After all, is it really wise to go against the wishes of your wife and your daughter? Although what she doesn't know is that the hotel has agreed to allow you to hold the event indoors should the weather turn bad. Just knowing there is a contingency plan can make everyone feel a little better.

> **Note**
>
> Some sources list risk avoidance as an option. This simply means that you avoid the activity to avoid the risk. Depending on the situation, this may not be possible.

▶ **Risk transference** is another valid approach. Insurance is an example of *risk transference*. Insurance can be used to transfer a portion or all of the potential cost of a loss to a third party. To transfer the risk, you will move ownership of the risk to a third party. The third party assumes the risk but the organization is saddled with the cost of the insurance. Back to the example of the wedding, you could transfer some of the risk by buying hurricane, travel and hotel insurance. It should be understood in the real world risk transfer may be a viable option for a continuity of operations (COOP) plan to replace tangible items such as furniture, hardware, buildings, etc. for recovery operations following a disaster; however, it is a fallacy that this method for risk option will work for data protection and reputation. The best option for data protection is encryption and backups.

▶ **Risk mitigation** could mean implementing a countermeasure to alter or reduce the risk. Examples of risk reduction include firewalls and encryption, increased frequency of patch management, and/or stronger authentication. Consider again the example of your daughter's wedding. To reduce the risk, you might have asked her to postpone the wedding until next spring to reduce the possible ill effects of a major storm.

What approach is the right cost? That depends on the cost of the countermeasure, the value of the asset, and the amount by which risk-reduction techniques reduce the total risk to a value that is acceptable. *Acceptable risk* or *risk tolerance* is the minimum acceptable risk that an organization is willing to tolerate. When assessing safeguards, it's important to look at the total cost of ownership (TCO). The TCO includes purchase price, maintenance fees, updates, insurance, etc. All costs are included. The risk assessment team must try to find a solution that provides the greatest risk reduction while maintaining the lowest annual cost. These concepts are expressed numerically by the following formula:

Threat × Vulnerability × Asset value = Total risk

No organization can ever be 100% secure. There will always be some risk left over. This is known as *residual risk*, the amount of risk left after safeguards and controls have been put in place. The formula for this concept is

(Threats × Vulnerability × Asset value) × Controls gap = Residual risk

The objective is to balance the cost of control against the value of the asset and potential for loss, and not to spend more on the control than the cost of the asset itself, as illustrated in Figure 4.7.

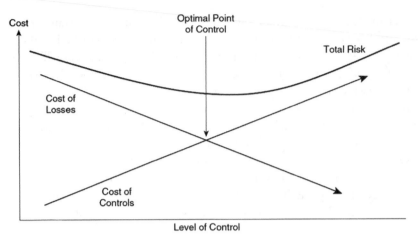

FIGURE 4.7   **Cost of risk versus level of control.**

> **Note**
>
> Any risk involving human life is extremely high and should be given the highest priority.

At the completion of the risk-handling step, the risk assessment team will produce a final report that presents all the findings, information, assessments, and recommendations for the organization. The final assessment report becomes the instrument used by management to make sound business decisions pertaining to the organization's overall risk and vulnerability assessment, and is the basis for how that organization will mitigate the identified risks, threats, and vulnerabilities.

> **Note**
>
> What's cost-benefit analysis? The cost-benefit analysis of a safeguard or protection measure is measured as the control gap:
>
> ALE before the safeguard – ALE after the safeguard = control gap (value of the safeguard to the organization).
>
> This formula can be used to evaluate the cost-effectiveness of a safeguard or to compare various safeguards to determine which are most effective. The higher the resulting value is, the more cost-effective the safeguard is. Most organizations should avoid spending more funds on a control than the actual cost of the asset itself, but not always—private organizations and government agencies have different priorities. As an example, federal, state, and local government may sometimes provide controls to protect critical systems regardless of the cost of the controls. Often, it is not easy to measure the potential for damage with a numeric value as discussed previously.

ExamAlert

Some organizations use a risk analysis matrix. A risk matrix looks at likelihood and impact. One example can be seen in MITRE's Risk Matrix Users Guide.

Develop and Implement Security Policy

Security is truly a multilayered process. After an assessment is completed, administrative controls should be reviewed. Policies can be created or modified based on the results of the risk assessment. The assessment should help drive policy creation on items such as the following:

▶ Passwords

▶ Patch management

▶ Employee hiring and termination practices

Note

Low-level checks refer to checks completed for employees starting at low-level jobs. Before they move to a higher-level position, additional checks should be performed. Some companies are even moving to rolling and continuous background checks.

▶ Backup practices and storage requirements

▶ Security awareness training

▶ Antivirus

▶ System setup and configuration

▶ System hardening

For security to be effective, it must start at the top of an organization and permeate every level of the hierarchy. Senior management must make decisions on what should be protected, how it should be protected, and to what extent it should be protected. These findings should be crafted into written documents.

Before these documents are locked in as policies, they must be researched to verify that they will be compliant with all federal, state, and local laws. These documents should also clearly state what is expected from employees and how the company will deal with policy violations.

Security Policy

Policies are high-level documents developed by senior management to transmit the guiding strategy and philosophy of management to employees. Management and business process owners are responsible for the organization, and for designing policies that will guide it toward success. Policies apply a strong emphasis to words spoken by management. They define, detail, and specify what is expected from employees and how management intends to meet the needs of customers, employees, and stakeholders. Policies are high-level documents that provide a general statement about the organization's assets and what level of protection they should have. Well-written policies should spell out who's responsible for security, what needs to be protected, and what is an acceptable level of risk. They are much like a strategic plan because they outline what should be done but don't specifically dictate how to implement the stated goals. Security policies can be written to meet advisory, informative, and regulatory needs. Each has a unique role or function. Table 4.8 shows the relationship of policies to strategic, tactical, and operational control.

TABLE 4.8 **Documentation/Level of Control**

Level/Document	Policy	Standard	Procedure
Strategic	✓		
Tactical		✓	
Operational			✓

One specific type of policy is the organization's *security policy*. A security policy dictates management's commitment to the use, operation, and security of information systems. It specifies the role security plays within the organization. A security policy should be driven by business objectives and should meet all applicable laws and regulations. It should also be used as a basis to integrate security into all business functions. It serves as a high-level guide to develop lower-level documentation such as procedures (see Figure 4.8). A security policy must be balanced in the sense that all organizations are looking for ways to implement adequate security without hindering productivity.

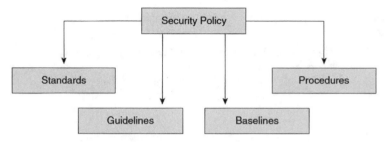

FIGURE 4.8 **Policy structure.**

> **Caution**
>
> The key element of a policy is that it should state management's intention toward security.

Policies can come in many forms. Policies can be advisory, informative, or regulatory. These are reviewed next and should help you understand how policies can be designed to meet a variety of goals.

Advisory Policy

The job of an advisory policy is to ensure that all employees know the consequences of certain behavior and actions. Here's an example advisory policy:

> Illegal copying: Employees should never download or install any commercial software, shareware, or freeware onto any network drives or disks unless they have written permission from the network administrator. Be prepared to be held accountable for your actions including the loss of network privileges, written reprimand, probation, or employment termination if the Rules of Appropriate Use are violated.

Informative Policy

This type of policy isn't designed with enforcement in mind; it is developed for education to inform and enlighten employees. The following is an example informative policy:

> In partnership with Human Resources, the employee ombudsman's job is to serve as an advocate for all employees providing mediation between employees and management. This job is to help investigate complaints and mediate fair settlements when a third party is requested.

> **Caution**
>
> Good policy strikes a balance and is both relevant and understandable. If a policy is too generic, no one will care what it says because it doesn't apply to the company. If a policy is too complex, no one will read it—or understand it if they did.

Regulatory Policy

These policies are used to make certain that the organization complies with local, state, and federal laws. Regulatory policy reinforces applicable laws to include applicable administrative laws, such as HIPAA, FERPA, and SOX; it also explains the applicable parts of specific laws in a way that the employees can understand. This is an area in which the CISSP should work closely with the HR and legal departments. A sample regulatory policy might state:

> Because of recent changes to Texas State law, the Company will now retain records of employee inventions and patents for 10 years; all email messages and any backup of such email associated with patents and inventions will also be stored for 10 years.

Standards

Standards are much more specific than policies. Standards are tactical documents because they lay out specific steps or processes required to meet a certain requirement. As an example, a standard might set a mandatory requirement that all email communication be encrypted. Although the standard does specify encryption, it doesn't spell out how it will be accomplished; this is left for the procedure.

Baselines

A *baseline* is a minimum level of security that a system, network, or device must adhere to. Baselines are usually mapped to industry standards. As an example, an organization might specify that all computer systems comply with a minimum Trusted Computer System Evaluation Criteria (TCSEC) C2 standard. TCSEC standards are discussed in detail in Chapter 5, "Security Engineering." Your security policy might also address the minimum baseline standard for encryption requirements for sensitive data.

Guidelines

A guideline points to a statement in a policy or procedure by which to determine a course of action. It's a recommendation or suggestion of how things should be done. It is meant to be flexible so that it can be customized for individual situations.

> **Caution**
>
> Don't confuse guidelines with best practices. Whereas guidelines are used to determine a recommended course of action, best practices are used to gauge liability. Best practices state what other competent security professionals would have done in the same or similar situation.

Procedures

A procedure is the most specific of security documents. A *procedure* is a detailed, in-depth, step-by-step document that details exactly what is to be done. As an analogy, when my mom sent my wife the secret recipe for a German chocolate cake, it described step-by-step what needed to be done and how. It even specified a convection oven, which was listed as an absolute requirement.

Procedures are detailed documents that are tied to specific technologies and devices. You should expect to see procedures change as equipment changes. As an example, imagine that your company replaced its Check Point border device such as a firewall, VPN, or IDS with a Cisco border device. Although the policies and standards dictating the device's role in your organization probably will not change, the procedure for configuration of the firewall will.

It's unfortunate that sometimes instead of the donkey leading the cart, the cart leads the donkey. By this, I mean that sometimes policies and procedures are developed because of a negative event or an audit. The audit or policy shouldn't be driving the process; the risk assessment should be. The assessment's purpose is to give management the tools needed to examine all currently identified concerns. From this, management can prioritize the level of exposure they are comfortable with and select an appropriate level of control. This level of control should then be locked into policy.

Types of Controls

One of the main reasons to have a variety of control types is to provide the organization with true defense in depth. Each control type provides a different level of protection, and because each level can be tweaked to meet the needs of the organization, the security administrator has a very granular level of control over the security mechanisms. Security mechanisms can serve many purposes, although they are primarily used to prevent, detect, or recover from problems. The best approach is for the organization to focus the bulk of its controls on prevention because this allows the organization to stop problems before they start. The three access control types include administrative, technical, and physical controls.

Administrative Controls

Administrative controls are the policies and procedures implemented by the organization. Preventive administrative controls can include security awareness training, strong password policies, HR practices, and robust pre-employment checks.

The Need for Robust HR Practices

On February 20, 2006, Dave Edmondson, resigned his position as CEO of Radio Shack. What would cause a CEO to step down?

Mr. Edmondson had come under increasing pressure to explain errors noted in his educational background. Although company records indicated that Edmondson had received a degree, the listed college could report no record of the supposed degree. Radio Shack downplayed the incident by stating that, at the time Edmondson was hired in 1994, the company did not perform educational checks on employees even if they were hired into senior management positions (content.time.com/time/specials/packages/article/0,28804,2009445_2009447_2009493,00.html).

Although it would be nice to think that this is an isolated incident, in May of 2012, the CEO of Yahoo! stepped down after a misrepresentation over his resume and errors in the listing of his degrees. Although many of us might see good HR practices as a nonissue, the truth is that it plays a key role in ensuring that the right person is hired for the specific job (articles.latimes.com/2012/may/14/business/la-fi-yahoo-thompson-resigns-20120514).

> **Note**
>
> Does your company enforce acceptable use policies (AUPs)? AUPs are considered one of the best methods to deter unacceptable activity.

Technical Controls

Technical controls are the logical controls you have put in place to protect the IT infrastructure. Technical controls include strong authentication (biometrics or two factor), encryption, network segmentation, DMZs, and antivirus controls.

Physical Controls

Physical controls are the ones you can most likely see. These controls protect against theft, loss, and unauthorized access. Examples of physical access controls include guards, gates, locks, guard dogs, closed-circuit television (CCTV), and alarms.

Access Control Categories

Access controls can be used with different levels of granularity to provide more effective levels of control. The access control categories (as seen in Table 4.9) are as follows:

▶ **Deterrent**—Used to deter a security violation.

▶ **Preventive**—Prevents the incident. An example of this control could be the use of encryption.

▶ **Detective**—Alerts and aids in identification after the incident.

▶ **Corrective**—Repairs damage and restores systems after the incident. An example might be applying patches.

▶ **Recovery**—Restores normal operations. An example might be the deployment of backups.

▶ **Compensating**—Blunts the damage or acts to contain the event or incident.

> ### Note
> Some items can fit in more than one category. Consider locks, which can be a delaying mechanism but can also be a deterrent.

TABLE 4.9 **Access Control Types and Examples**

Attribute	Deterrent	Preventive	Detective	Corrective	Recovery	Compensating
Administrative	AUP	User registration	Audit policy	Reassignment or termination	Incident response plan	Supervision and monitoring
Technical	Warning banner	ACLs	Anti-virus	Reboot or restart	Hot site	Redundant server
Physical	Electric fence sign	8-foot fence	Motion detector	Fire extinguisher	Restoration of backups	Defense in depth (layers)

ExamAlert

Be sure you understand the three types of controls that can be used to limit access—administrative, technical, and physical—and what is contained within each set. This is required knowledge for the CISSP exam. The controls vary from domain to domain. On the actual exam be sure to read each question carefully.

Implement Personnel Security

An organization's personnel security process should begin before the employee is ever hired. During the recruitment process, a prospective employee's background needs to be reviewed to make sure the right person is hired for the job. Some items to review include:

▶ Background check

▶ Reference check

▶ Educational verification/certification check

▶ Criminal, financial, and credit checks

▶ Driving record or other types of verification depending on the specific job

Performing these tasks up front can save the company time and money in the recruitment process and help prevent time and effort lost by hiring the wrong person for a job.

Social Networking's Role on Background Checks

The Internet has changed the way background checks are performed. No longer must a company spend hundreds of dollars trying to assess a candidate. Many online tools will allow an organization to scour the Web searching for public data about an individual.

One of the first places many employers now start their search is at popular social networking sites such as Facebook, Instagram, and Twitter. Social networking sites allow employers to see anything that a candidate has made public. This includes lifestyle, sexual orientation, and even after-work activities. As an example, if a candidate likes to skydive and race performance motorcycles they may be seen as a high insurance risk. Even if the candidate's social networking site doesn't have anything objectionable, links placed there by friends or acquaintances might point to sites or materials others might find offensive. Maybe your college roommate was photographed in front of a poster that stated, "Bong hits for Jesus."

Even more business-oriented sites such as LinkedIn can be used to dig up background and associate information. Employers must use caution as it's always possible that someone may have set up a fake social networking profile that's not a true identity. Companies must also make sure that mistakes are not made when people have similar names. Although not typically the default, users of such sites should consider making all their information private and should control who can view that information.

New-Hire Agreements and Policies

One great way to make sure your employees know what is expected of them is to perform a new-hire orientation. This is the time to discuss issues such as *nondisclosure agreements* (NDAs), good security practices, and AUPs. The goal of this training is to teach your employees your established security policies and procedures. The training should include the employee agreeing to and signing the AUP. Organizations benefit when each employee actively participates in the security of the organization.

Practices that keep employees focused on security include handing out pens, notepads, or other items that outline a few of the organization's security policies. Companies should hold semiannual reviews that refresh employee's knowledge of current policies and require updated signatures. Posters can help reinforce good security practices. Another idea is to send out periodic security-awareness emails or newsletters that reinforce the practices of good security.

Separation of Duties

Separation of duties describes the process of dividing duties so that one person cannot perform a critical task alone. This can mean having dual controls in place, which require more than one person to complete a critical task. This concept closely ties to the principle of least privilege, meaning you only give someone the minimum level of access or rights that are needed. As an example, some banks divide the safe combination numbers between two employees. Each employee has three of the six numbers needed to unlock the safe. Without some form of collusion, there is no way one person can obtain access to the safe's contents.

Organizations that have titles, roles, and duties clearly defined by policy are able to better highlight conflicts of interest and develop a separation of duties matrix. Separation of duties usually falls into four areas of control:

- **Authorization**—Verifying cash, approving purchases, and approving changes

- **Custody**—Accessing cash, merchandise, or inventories

- **Record keeping**—Preparing receipts, maintaining records, and posting payments

- **Reconciliation**—Comparing dollar amounts, counts, reports, and payroll summaries

Job Rotation

Although it's always nice to have cross-trained employees, job rotation is about more than redundancy and control. Its primary benefit is that it allows an organization to maintain backup personnel to more easily identify fraudulent activities. For example, if John is stealing money from the company and Steve is rotated into John's position and discovers such activities, only a deep friendship would keep Steve from telling the boss that John is a thief.

Least Privilege

The principle of *least privilege* is another important concept that can go a long way toward an organization achieving its security goals. Least privilege means that individuals have just enough resources to accomplish their required tasks.

As an example, imagine that your company has just added computer terminals to several of the conference rooms. These terminals have been placed where attendees of meetings, consultants, and sales representatives can access product information. Proper design dictates that these computers be allowed limited Internet access, but that all other Web activities be blocked. In other words, services such as network browsing, email, File Transfer Protocol (FTP), and Telnet are not available. This design reduces the opportunity for resource misuse.

Over time, even the principle of least privilege can result in authorization creep, which means that employees moving from job to job keep picking up more rights and access. Rights and access that are no longer needed should be removed.

> **Tip**
>
> Least privilege is not a concept strictly for individuals. In fact, it is extremely important to apply to sensitive systems, facilities, and applications. All applications and processes should run with the minimum amount of privilege necessary to avoid further exploitation in case they are ever compromised. A great example of this was Internet Information Services IIS. It used to operate with system permissions; this was way too much privilege for a web server. This issue has been corrected since Windows Server 2003 and IIS 6.0.

Mandatory Vacations

Even though everyone thinks it's great that Jane hasn't taken a vacation in 10 years, the fact that the accountant is always at work might be a problem. Jane appears to be a dedicated employee but might not have taken a vacation because she is performing fraudulent activities. By remaining on the job, she is able and available to provide cover for her scheme. Fraudulent activities are much easier to uncover when employees are required to take their vacations. Mandatory vacations provide time for audits and for illicit activities to be discovered.

Termination

Employees will eventually leave organizations for one reason or another. Employees might leave of their own free will or they might leave because they are terminated. *Termination* sometimes is necessary, but many surveys show that it is one of the most disliked tasks managers are required to do. To protect the organization, managers should use standardized termination procedures. This structured process helps ensure that everyone is treated equally and that employees don't have the opportunity to destroy or damage company property. Some prudent steps to incorporate into this procedure include:

1. Disabling computer and facility access immediately at the time of notification.

2. Monitoring the employee while he or she packs belongings.

3. Ensuring that at no time is the employee left alone after the termination process has started.

4. Verifying that the employee returns company identifications and other company property, including access tokens, smart phones, and laptops.

5. Escorting the employee from the building.

What is most important is to avoid making this an adversarial process. Such situations only give employees more reasons to retaliate.

Security Education, Training, and Awareness

Employees look to their employers to provide training. Without proper training, employees are generally unaware of how their actions or activities can affect the security of the organization. One of the weakest links in security is the people who work for the company. Social engineering attacks prey on the fact that users are uneducated in good security practices; therefore, the greatest defense against these types of attacks is training, education, and security awareness (see Figure 4.9).

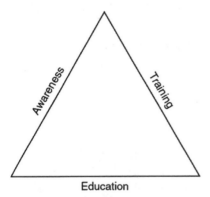

FIGURE 4.9 **Training and education triad.**

Besides security awareness, you might find that your staff needs more in-depth training in matters of organizational security. This might consist of in-house training programs that teach new employees needed security skills, or the decision to send the security staff offsite for a CISSP education program.

> **Tip**
>
> Employee-awareness programs work best when they are run for short periods and changed frequently.

Regardless of which program your company decides it needs, seven steps can help identify what type of security training is appropriate:

1. Establish organizational technology objectives.

2. Conduct a needs assessment.

3. Find a training program that meets these needs.

4. Select the training methods and mode.

5. Choose a means of evaluating.

6. Administer training.

7. Evaluate the training.

Types of training include the following:

▶ In-house training

▶ Web-based training

▶ Classroom training

▶ Vendor training

▶ On-the-job training

▶ Apprenticeship programs

▶ Degreed programs

▶ Continuing education programs

> **Caution**
>
> Training and education are not the same. Training programs are of short duration and usually teach individuals a specific skill. Education is broader-based and longer-term. Degree programs are examples of education.

Security Awareness

Awareness programs can be effective in increasing employee understanding of security. *Security awareness* training helps employees understand how their behavior affects the organization. Security awareness also outlines what is expected of employees. Awareness training must be developed differently for the various groups of employees that make up the organization. Not only will the training vary, but the topics and types of questions you'll receive from the participants will also vary.

Successful employee awareness programs tailor the message to fit the audience. These are three of the primary groups that security awareness training should be targeted to:

▶ **Senior management**—Don't try presenting an in-depth technical analysis to this group; its members are typically interested in the bigger picture. They want to know the costs, benefits, and ramifications if good security practices are not followed.

▶ **Data custodians**—This group requires a more structured presentation on how good security practices should be implemented, who is responsible, and what the individual and departmental cost is for noncompliance.

▶ **Users**—Training for this group must align with employees' daily tasks and map to the users' specific job functions.

> **Note**
>
> The goal of security awareness is to increase management's ability to hold employees accountable for their actions and to modify employee behavior toward security.

Social Engineering

Social engineering is the art of tricking someone into giving you something they should not. Those skilled in the art of social engineering can use their skills to gain access or information that they should not have. As organizations develop better physical and technical controls, attackers are always going to look for the easiest path to gain access. This very well could be the manipulation of people. An organization can have the best firewalls, IDS, network design, authentication system, or access controls and still be successfully attacked by a social engineer.

To gain a better understanding of how social engineering works, let's look at the different approaches these attacks use. In his book, *The Science and Practice of Persuasion*, Robert Cialdini describes the following six types of behaviors for positive response to social engineering:

▶ **Scarcity**—Works on the belief that something (such as time) is in short supply. As an example, "I need the password now because my work is past due and the boss is waiting. Can you please help me this one time?"

▶ **Authority**—Work on the premise of power. As an example, "Hi, is this the Help Desk? I work for the senior VP and he needs his password reset to access important email!"

- ► **Liking**—Works because we tend to do more for people we like than people we don't. As an example, "Come on, we are friends, you know I would not misuse your password."

- ► **Consistency**—People like to be consistent. As an example, "Why should I badge in when everyone else just walks in once someone opens the door?"

- ► **Social validation**—Based on the idea that if one person does it, others will too.

- ► **Reciprocation**—If someone gives you a token or small gift, you feel pressured to give something in return. As an example, "You have already won a free gift. All you must do is take a few minutes to answer a few questions for our survey about your current security infrastructure."

Realize these attacks can be launched person-to-person or computer-to-person. Knowing the various techniques that social engineers use can go a long way toward defeating their potential scams. The primary defense against social engineering is training and awareness. A good resource for more information on social engineering is *The Art of Deception: Controlling the Human Element of Security*, by Kevin D. Mitnick and William L. Simon (Wiley, 2002).

Professional Ethics Training and Awareness

This section reviews some of the ethical standards and codes that a CISSP should be aware of. *Ethics* is a set of principles for right conduct. Ethical standards are sometimes different than legal standards: Laws define what we *must* do, whereas ethics define what we *should* do. With that being said, you must remember that not everyone will always act ethically.

CISSPs should uphold high ethical standards and promote high ethical standards in others. Some of the ways CISSPs can help promote proper ethical behavior include making sure that organizations have guidelines on computer ethics, ensuring that ethical issues are included in employee handbooks, promoting computer ethics training, and helping to develop ethical policies on issues such as email and other privacy-related topics. There are several ethical standards that the CISSP should be aware of to help point the way toward proper behavior. Some of these include the following:

- ► ISC^2 Code of Ethics (www.isc2.org)

- ► Ten Commandments of Computer Ethics (computerethicsinstitute.org/publications/tencommandments.html)

▶ RFC 1087 (www.ietf.org/rfc/rfc1087.txt)

▶ NIST 800-14 (csrc.nist.gov/publications/nistpubs/800-14/800-14.pdf)

ISC^2 Code of Ethics

It's a requirement for CISSP candidates to subscribe to and support the ISC^2 Code of Ethics, which states that a CISSP should

▶ Protect society, the commonwealth, and the infrastructure

▶ Act honorably, honestly, justly, responsibly, and legally

▶ Provide diligent and competent service to principals

▶ Advance and protect the profession

Dan Farmer: The Ethics of Vulnerability Assessment

In 1995, some wondered whether Dan Farmer had sold his soul to the devil. While working with Wietse Venema, Mr. Farmer released the program Security Administrator Tool for Analyzing Networks (SATAN). SATAN was the first vulnerability assessment software created.

Although Mr. Farmer saw a great need for such software, his employer at the time did not and fired him. Some individuals also did not like the name of the software and found it offensive. To address this issue, Mr. Farmer actually created an add-on for the tool that renamed the program SANTA. By running the add-on package before running the tool, all the occurrences of the word *Satan* were changed to *Santa* and all images were converted from a graphic image to a picture of Santa Claus.

Regardless of the name, the need for the tool was apparent. At the time of its release, nearly two thirds of websites that were scanned were insecure. So, although some worried that such a tool could be used by attackers to target vulnerable networks, the need was real.

Today, many other tools have been created to perform network assessments, such as SAINT, SARA, Nessus, and Retina. Each owes its existence to SATAN, the first vulnerability assessment tool ever created.

ExamAlert

Exam candidates must read the full Code of Ethics because the exam may include one or two questions related to the code. You can find this document by searching for "Code of Ethics" at www.isc2.org.

Computer Ethics Institute

The Computer Ethics Institute is a group that focuses specifically on ethics in the technology industry. Its website, www.computerethicsinstitute.org, lists the following Ten Commandments of Computer Ethics:

1. Thou shalt not use a computer to harm other people.

2. Thou shalt not interfere with other people's computer work.

3. Thou shalt not snoop around in other people's computer files.

4. Thou shalt not use a computer to steal.

5. Thou shalt not use a computer to bear false witness.

6. Thou shalt not copy or use proprietary software for which you have not paid.

7. Thou shalt not use other people's computer resources without authorization or proper compensation.

8. Thou shalt not appropriate other people's intellectual output.

9. Thou shalt think about the social consequences of the program you are writing or the system you are designing.

10. Thou shalt always use a computer in ways that ensure consideration and respect for your fellow humans.

> **ExamAlert**
>
> Exam candidates are advised to read the Ten Commandments of Computer Ethics and be able to differentiate it from the ISC^2 Code of Ethics.

Internet Architecture Board

The Internet Architecture Board (IAB) is an advisory body of the Internet Society (ISOC). Figure 4.10 shows the layout of the ISOC. The Internet Engineering Steering Group (IESG) is responsible for technical management of IETF activities and the overall Internet standards process. The IAB is responsible for the Internet Standards Process and the Request for Comments (RFC) editor. The actual development of new standards and protocols for the Internet is carried out by working groups chartered by the IETF.

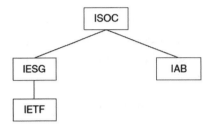

FIGURE 4.10 **ISOC and the IAB.**

An RFC is an engineering white paper that describes the operation of a proto-col, application, behavior, or design of an Internet-connected system. The IAB also has responsibility for architectural oversight of Internet Engineering Task Force (IETF) activities. One RFC that a CISSP should have knowledge of is RFC 1087. The goal of RFC 1087, published by the IAB in January 1987, is to characterize unethical and unacceptable behavior. It states that the following activities are unethical:

▶ Seeking to gain unauthorized access to the resources of the Internet

▶ Disrupting the intended use of the Internet

▶ Wasting resources (people, capacity, computer) through such actions

▶ Destroying the integrity of computer-based information

▶ Compromising the privacy of users

> **ExamAlert**
>
> Print and review RFC 1087 before you attempt the CISSP exam. It is available at www.faqs.org/rfcs/rfc1087.html.

NIST SP 800-14

Not only do individuals have responsibilities but so do organizations. NIST SP 800-14 (Generally Accepted System Security Principles) was created to outline the responsibilities of organizations that use electronic systems. The more significant points made in NIST SP 800-14 are:

▶ Security supports the mission of the organization.

▶ Security is an integral element of sound management.

- ▶ Security should be cost-effective.

- ▶ Systems owners have security responsibilities outside their own organizations.

- ▶ Security responsibilities and accountability should be made explicit.

- ▶ Security requires a comprehensive and integrated approach.

- ▶ Security should be periodically reassessed.

- ▶ Security is constrained by societal factors.

Common Computer Ethics Fallacies

Most hackers profess to having ethical standards and many even state that their actions are not ethically wrong. When interviewed, many hackers state that they have their own set of ethical standards. Some of the reasons often used to rationalize their illegal behavior include the following common ethical fallacies:

- ▶ **Computer game**—If they don't protect it, it's fair game to attack.

- ▶ **Law-abiding citizen**—It's not physical theft, so it's not illegal.

- ▶ **Shatterproof**—If I don't do damage, or it can be repaired, what's the problem?

- ▶ **Candy-from-a-baby**—If it is that easy, how could it be wrong?

- ▶ **Hackers**—If I learn from this, it will benefit society and me.

- ▶ **Free information**—All information should be free.

Tip

While it is true that writing a computer virus is not illegal, distributing it for malicious purposes is illegal according to the CFAA. As an example, Robert T. Morris was not charged with writing the first Internet worm; he was charged and prosecuted for using the code for malicious purposes.

Regulatory Requirements for Ethics Programs

As previously discussed, not everyone sees ethics in the same way. Therefore, there are regulatory requirements in some countries to address ethics and to address proper behaviors and attitudes. In the United States the Federal

Sentencing Guidelines for Organizations (FSGO) outlines ethical requirements and may impose different sentences depending on the ethics programs
and culture of the organization. Several examples of these are listed here:

▶ The Foreign Corrupt Practices Act (FCPA)—Imposes civil and criminal
penalties if publicly held organizations fail to maintain sufficient controls
over their information systems and data. FCPA requires these companies
to have adequate systems of internal accounting controls.

▶ Sarbanes-Oxley Act—This U.S. financial and accounting disclosure and
accountability legislation has requirements for ethics. Section 406 of
the Sarbanes-Oxley Act outlines code of ethics requirements for senior
financial officers.

▶ Committee for Sponsoring Organizations of the Treadway Commission
(COSO)—An internal control framework used by auditors and others,
including expected standards of conduct and ethics.

Note

Although questions dealing with laws specific to any one country are not common
on the CISSP exam, it is still important to have a good understanding of the
applicable laws under which your organization does business.

Tip

Ethics are not the only item to consider when discussing hackers. Another item
of concern is motivation. Hackers are motivated by many different things, ranging
from money to the desire to have fun. Some hackers claim that they carry out their
activities simply for a cause. Hacking for a cause is known as hacktivism. As an
example, in 2015 the hacker group known as Anonymous declared cyberwar
against the Islamic State in retaliation for the 2015 Paris terrorist attacks.

Exam Prep Questions

1. The following statement can be found in which standard?

   "Systems Owners Have Security Responsibilities Outside Their Own Organization."

   ○ **A.** Ethics and the Internet

   ○ **B.** RFC 1087

   ○ **C.** ISC2 Code of Ethics

   ○ **D.** NIST 800-14

2. Which of the following methods of handling risk works by using a third party to absorb a portion of the risk?

   ○ **A.** Risk reduction

   ○ **B.** Risk transference

   ○ **C.** Risk acceptance

   ○ **D.** Risk rejection

3. You have been asked to calculate the annualized loss expectancy (ALE) for the following variables:

   Single loss expectancy = $25

   Exposure factor = 0.90

   Annualized rate of occurrence = 0.40

   Residual risk = $30

   Which of the following is the resulting ALE?

   ○ **A.** $9.00

   ○ **B.** $22.50

   ○ **C.** $10.00

   ○ **D.** $14.27

4. Place the following formulas in their proper order:

   ○ **A.** ALE, residual risk, SLE, ARO

   ○ **B.** ALE, ARO, SLE, residual risk

   ○ **C.** ARO, SLE, ALE, residual risk

   ○ **D.** SLE, ARO, ALE, residual risk

5. Which of the following is the formula for residual risk?

- ○ **A.** (Threats × Vulnerability × Asset value) × Controls gap = Residual risk
- ○ **B.** (Threats × Vulnerability × Asset value) = Residual risk
- ○ **C.** (Threats / Vulnerability × Asset value) × Control = Residual risk
- ○ **D.** (Risk × Vulnerability × Asset value) × Controls gap = Residual risk

6. Which of the following is the length of time for copyright in the United States and the European Union?

- ○ **A.** Life plus 20 years
- ○ **B.** Life plus 30 years
- ○ **C.** Life plus 70 years
- ○ **D.** Life plus 100 years

7. Which of the following formulas represents total risk?

- ○ **A.** Risk × Vulnerability × Asset value = Total risk
- ○ **B.** Threat × Vulnerability × Asset value = Total risk
- ○ **C.** Risk × Value/Countermeasure = Total risk
- ○ **D.** Threat - Vulnerability/Asset value = Total risk

8. Which of the following is a flaw, loophole, oversight, or error that makes an organization susceptible to attack or damage?

- ○ **A.** Risk
- ○ **B.** Vulnerability
- ○ **C.** Threat
- ○ **D.** Exploit

9. Which of the following is the most general of security documents?

- ○ **A.** Procedures
- ○ **B.** Standards
- ○ **C.** Policies
- ○ **D.** Baselines

10. Which of the following groups is responsible for the actual development of new standards and protocols such as RFC 1087?

- ○ **A.** IESG
- ○ **B.** ISOC
- ○ **C.** IAB
- ○ **D.** IETF

11. Which organizational role is tasked with assigning sensitivity labels?

    ○ **A.** Management

    ○ **B.** The auditor

    ○ **C.** The user

    ○ **D.** The owner

12. When the cost of the countermeasure outweighs the value of the asset, which of the following is the best approach?

    ○ **A.** Take no action

    ○ **B.** Transference the risk

    ○ **C.** Mitigate the risk

    ○ **D.** Increase the cost of exposure

13. Which ISO document is used for a standard for information security management?

    ○ **A.** ISO 27001

    ○ **B.** ISO 27002

    ○ **C.** ISO 27004

    ○ **D.** ISO 27799

14. TCO does not include which of the following?

    ○ **A.** Software updates

    ○ **B.** Subscription costs

    ○ **C.** Maintenance costs

    ○ **D.** Cost of not implementing a control

15. It is important that the CISSP candidate understand the differences between the various legal systems used around the world. One early system was *Corpus Juris Civilis*, which featured a comprehensive system of written rules of law that serves as the basis for which legal system today?

    ○ **A.** Civil law

    ○ **B.** Religious law

    ○ **C.** Common law

    ○ **D.** Customary law

Answers to Exam Prep Questions

1. **D.** NIST 800-14 states that responsibilities exceed the network you are in charge of. Answers A and C both point to RFC 1087 Ethics and the Internet. This statement is also not in the ISC^2 Code of Ethics.

2. **B.** The purchase of insurance to transfer a portion or all of the potential cost of a loss to third party is known as risk transference. All other answers are incorrect: Risk reduction implements a countermeasure, risk acceptance deals with risk by accepting the potential cost, and risk rejection pretends it doesn't exist.

3. **C.** $25 × 0.40 = $10, or Single loss expectancy (SLE) × Annualized rate of occurrence (ARO) = Annualized loss expectancy (ALE).

4. **D.** The quantitative assessment process involves the following steps: Estimate potential losses (SLE), conduct a threat analysis (ARO), determine annual loss expectancy (ALE), and determine the residual risk after a countermeasure has been applied.

5. **A.** The formula for residual risk is: (Threats × Vulnerability × Asset value) × Controls gap = Residual risk

6. **C.** Life plus 70 years is the length of time of a copyright in the United States and the European Union. But keep in mind that copyright terms can vary depending on the country and time they were granted.

7. **B.** Risk is expressed numerically as follows:

   Threat × Vulnerability × Asset value = Total risk

   All other answers do not properly define the formula for total risk.

8. **B.** Vulnerability is a flaw, loophole, oversight, or error that makes the organization susceptible to attack or damage. All other answers are incorrect: A risk can be defined as the potential harm that can arise from some present process or from some future event; the event is the action of the threat agent that can result in harm to an asset or service; and an exploit takes advantage of a bug, glitch, or vulnerability.

9. **C.** Policies are high-level documents. A procedure is a detailed, in-depth, step-by-step document that lays out exactly what is to be done. It's a detailed document that is tied to specific technologies and devices. Standards are tactical documents. Baselines are minimum levels of security that a system, network, or device must adhere to.

10. **D.** The actual development of new standards and protocols for the Internet is carried out by working groups chartered by the IETF. Answers A, B, and C are incorrect.

11. **D.** The owner. Data classification should be performed by the owner. When a data item or object is identified, the owner is the one responsible for assigning a security label. If the military data-classification system is used, that label might be top secret, secret, sensitive, or unclassified. It is not the responsibility of the auditor, management, or the user to assign a label to the data.

12. **A.** When the cost of the countermeasure outweighs the value of the asset, the best approach is to take no action. This means the asset would cost more to protect than what it is worth. Answers B, C, and D are incorrect because there would be a loss of value in transferring the risk. In such cases, there would be no reason to mitigate the risk because the cost would be prohibitive. This violated good security practices.

13. **C.** ISO 27004 is the standard for security management. 27001 is focused on requirements. ISO 27002 was developed for BS 7799, and ISO 27799 is focused on health.

14. **D.** TCO includes all costs including software, updates, and maintenance. The only thing that is not included is the cost of not implementing the control.

15. **A.** Much of Europe is based on civil (code) law, also known as Napoleonic law. The Romans used Corpus Juris Civilis, which featured a comprehensive system of written rules of law that serves as the basis of civil law used today. Answer B, C, and D are incorrect as the major difference between civil law and common law is that civil law uses legislation as the main source of laws. Religious law is based on religious tenets. China and some African countries use customary law, which may be combined with other legal systems and is based on the concept of what is customary and considered normal conduct. It is important that the CISSP candidate understand the differences between the various legal systems used around the world.

Need to Know More?

Keeping pre-employment checks legal: www.eeoc.gov/laws/practices/

ISO27002 overview: en.wikipedia.org/wiki/ISO/IEC_27002

Security configuration guides: support.microsoft.com/en-us/kb/885409

The site security handbook: www.faqs.org/rfcs/rfc2196.html

Self-audits of employment practices: library.findlaw.com/2000/Aug/1/127767.html

Building effective security policies: www.crcpress.com/Building-an-Effective-Information-Security-Policy-Architecture/Bacik/p/book/9781420059052

Building effective policy: csrc.nist.gov/nissc/1997/panels/isptg/pescatore/html/

Policy templates and information: www.sans.org/security-resources/policies/

Threat analysis: www.linuxjournal.com/article/5567

CHAPTER 5

Security Engineering

Terms you'll need to understand:

▶ Buffer overflows

▶ Security models

▶ Rings of protection

▶ Trusted Computer System Evaluation Criteria (TCSEC)

▶ Information Technology System Evaluation Criteria (ITSEC)

▶ Common Criteria

▶ Reference monitor

▶ Trusted computing base

▶ Open and closed systems

▶ Emanations

▶ Mobile system vulnerabilities

Topics you'll need to master:

▶ Engineering processes using secure design principles

▶ Understanding confidentiality models such as Bell-LaPadula

▶ Identifying integrity models such as Biba and Clark-Wilson

▶ Understanding common flaws and security issues associated with security architecture designs

▶ Distinguishing between certification and accreditation

Introduction

The security engineering domain deals with hardware, software, security controls, and documentation. When hardware is designed, it needs to be built to specific standards that should provide mechanisms to protect the confidentiality, integrity, and availability of the data. The operating systems (OS) that will run on the hardware must also be designed in such a way as to ensure security.

Building secure hardware and operating systems is just a start. Both vendors and customers need to have a way to verify that hardware and software perform as stated, to rate these systems, and to have some level of assurance that such systems will function in a known manner. This is the purpose of evaluation criteria. They allow the parties involved to have a level of assurance.

This chapter introduces the trusted computer base and the ways in which systems can be evaluated to assess the level of security. To pass the CISSP exam, you need to understand system hardware and software models and how models of security can be used to secure systems. Standards such as Common Criteria Information Technology System Evaluation Criteria (ITSEC) and Trusted Computer System Evaluation Criteria (TCSEC) are covered on the exam.

Fundamental Concepts of Security Models

Modern computer systems are comprised of hardware. These physical components interact with the software in the form of the OS, applications, and firmware to do the things we need done. At the core of every computer system is the central processing unit (CPU) and the hardware that makes it run. The CPU is just one of the items that you can find on the motherboard. The motherboard serves as the base for most crucial system components. Let's start at the heart of the system and work our way out.

Central Processing Unit

The CPU is the heart of the computer system and serves as the brain of the computer. The CPU consists of the following:

▶ An *arithmetic logic unit* (ALU) that performs arithmetic and logical operations. This is the brain of the CPU;

▶ A *control unit* manages the instructions it receives from memory. It decodes and executes the requested instructions and determines what instructions have priority for processing; and

▶ Memory, which is used to hold instructions and data to be processed. This is not your typical memory—it is much faster than non-CPU memory.

The CPU is capable of executing a series of basic operations, including fetch, decode, execute, and write. Pipelining combines multiple steps into one process. The CPU has the capability to fetch instructions and then process them. The CPU can operate in one of four states:

▶ **Supervisor state**—Program can access entire system

▶ **Problem state**—Only non-privileged instructions can be executed

▶ **Ready state**—Program is ready to resume processing

▶ **Wait state**—Program is waiting for an event to complete

Because CPUs have very specific designs, the operating system as well as applications must be developed to work with the CPU. CPUs also have different types of registers to hold data and instructions. The base register contains the beginning address assigned to a process, whereas the limit address marks the end of the memory segment. Together, the components are responsible for the recall and execution of programs. CPUs have made great strides, as Table 5.1 documents. As the size of transistors has decreased, the number of transistors that can be placed on a CPU has increased. By increasing the total number of transistors and ramping up clock speed, the power of CPUs has increased exponentially. As an example, a 3.06 GHz Intel Core i7 can perform about 18 million instructions per second (MIPS).

TABLE 5.1 **CPU Advancements**

CPU	Date	Transistors	Clock Speed
8080	1974	6,000	2 MHz
80386	1986	275,000	12.5 MHz
Pentium	1993	3,100,000	60 MHz
Intel Core 2	2006	291,000,000	2.66 GHz
Intel Core i7	2009	731,000,000	4.00 GHz
Intel Core M	2014	1,300,000,000	2.6 GHz

> **Note**
>
> Processor speed is measured in MIPS (millions of instructions per second). This standard is used to indicate how fast a CPU can work.

Two basic designs of CPUs are manufactured for modern computer systems:

▶ **Reduced Instruction Set Computing (RISC)**—Uses simple instructions that require a reduced number of clock cycles.

▶ **Complex Instruction Set Computing (CISC)**—Performs multiple operations for a single instruction.

The CPU requires two inputs to accomplish its duties: instructions and data. The data is passed to the CPU for manipulation where it is typically worked on in either the problem or the supervisor state. In the *problem state*, the CPU works on the data with non-privileged instructions. In the *supervisor state*, the CPU executes privileged instructions.

> **ExamAlert**
>
> A superscalar processor is one that can execute multiple instructions at the same time, whereas a scalar processor can execute only one instruction at a time. You will need to know this distinction for the exam.

The CPU can be classified in one of several categories depending on its functionality. When the computer's CPU, motherboard, and operating system all support the functionality, the computer system is also categorized according to the following:

▶ **Multiprogramming**—Can interleave two or more programs for execution at any one time.

▶ **Multitasking**—Can perform one or more tasks or subtasks at a time.

▶ **Multiprocessor**—Supports one or more CPUs. Windows 7 does not support multiprocessors, whereas Windows Server 2012 does.

A multiprocessor system can work in symmetric or asymmetric mode. With *symmetric mode* all processors are equal and can handle any tasks equally with all devices (peripherals being equally accessible) or no specialized path is required for resources. With *asymmetric mode* one CPU schedules and coordinates tasks between other processes and resources. The data that CPUs work with is usually part of an application or program. These programs are tracked by a process ID (PID). Anyone who has ever looked at Task Manager in Windows or executed a **ps** command on a Linux machine has probably seen a PID number. You can manipulate the priority of these task as well as start and stop them. Fortunately, most programs do much more than the first C code you wrote that probably just said, "Hello World." Each line of code or piece of functionality that a program has is known as a *thread*.

A program that has the capability to carry out more than one thread at a time is known as multi-threaded. You can see an example of this in Figure 5.1.

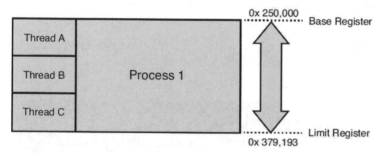

FIGURE 5.1 **Processes and threads.**

Process activity uses process isolation to separate processes. These techniques are needed to ensure that each application receives adequate processor time to operate properly. The four process isolation techniques used are:

▶ **Encapsulation of process or objects**—Other processes do not interact with the application.

▶ **Virtual mapping**—The application is written in such a way that it believes it is the only application running.

▶ **Time multiplexing**—This allows the application or process to share the computer's resources.

▶ **Naming distinctions**—Processes are assigned their own unique name.

ExamAlert

To get a good look at naming distinctions, run **ps -aux** from the terminal of a Linux system and note the unique process ID (PID) values.

An interrupt is another key piece of a computer system. An *interrupt* is an electrical connection between a device and the CPU. The device can put an electrical signal on this line to get the attention of the CPU. The following are common interrupt methods:

▶ **Programmed I/O**—Used to transfer data between a CPU and peripheral device.

▶ **Interrupt-driven I/O**—A more efficient input/output method, but which requires complex hardware.

▶ **I/O using DMA**—I/O based on direct memory access; can bypass the processor and write the information directly into main memory.

▶ **Memory-mapped I/O**—Requires the CPU to reserve space for I/O functions and to make use of the address for both memory and I/O devices.

▶ **Port-mapped I/O**—Uses a special class of instruction that can read and write a single byte to an I/O device.

ExamAlert

Interrupts can be maskable and non-maskable. Maskable interrupts can be ignored by the application or the system, whereas non-maskable interrupts cannot be ignored by the system. An example of a non-maskable interrupt can be seen in Windows when you enter Ctrl-Alt-Delete.

There is a natural hierarchy to memory and, as such, there must be a way to manage memory and ensure that it does not become corrupted. That is the job of the memory management system. Memory management systems on multitasking operating systems are responsible for:

▶ **Relocation**—Maintains the ability to copy memory contents from memory to secondary storage as needed.

▶ **Protection**—Provides control to memory segments and restricts what process can write to memory.

▶ **Sharing**—Allows sharing of information based on a user's security level of access control; for instance, Mike can read the object, whereas Shawn can read and write to the object.

▶ **Logical organization**—Provides for the sharing and support for dynamic link libraries.

▶ **Physical organization**—Provides for the physical organization of memory.

Let's now look at storage media.

Storage Media

A computer is not just a CPU; memory is also an important component. The CPU uses memory to store instructions and data. Therefore, memory is an important type of storage media. The CPU is the only component that can directly access memory. Systems are designed that way because the CPU has a high level of system trust. The CPU can use different types of addressing schemes to communicate with memory, which includes *absolute addressing* and *relative addressing*. Memory can be addressed either physically or logically. *Physical addressing* refers to the hard-coded address assigned to the memory. Applications and programmers writing code use *logical addresses*. *Relative addresses* use a known address with an offset applied. Not only can memory be addressed in different ways, but there are also different types of memory. Memory can be either *nonvolatile* or *volatile*. The sections that follow provide examples of both.

> **Tip**
>
> Two important security concepts associated with storage are protected memory and memory addressing. For the exam, you should understand that protected memory prevents other programs or processes from gaining access or modifying the contents of address space that has previously been assigned to another active program. Memory can be addressed either physically or logically. *Memory addressing* describes the method used by the CPU to access the contents of memory. This is especially important for understanding the root cause for buffer overflow attacks.

RAM

Random access memory (RAM) is volatile memory. If power is lost, the data is destroyed. Types of RAM include *static RAM*, which uses circuit latches to represent binary data, and *dynamic RAM*, which must be refreshed every few milliseconds. RAM can be configured as *Dynamic Random Access Memory* (DRAM) or *Static Random Access Memory* (SRAM).

SRAM doesn't require a refresh signal as DRAM does. The chips are more complex and are thus more expensive. However, they are faster. DRAM access times come in at 60 nanoseconds (ns) or more; SRAM has access times as fast as 10 ns. SRAM is often used for cache memory.

DRAM chips are cheap to manufacture. Dynamic refers to the memory chips' need for a constant update signal (also called a *refresh signal*) to retain the information that is written there. Currently, there are five popular implementations of DRAM:

- **Synchronous DRAM (SDRAM)**—Shares a common clock signal with the transmitter of the data. The computer's system bus clock provides the common signal that all SDRAM components use for each step to be performed.

- **Double Data Rate (DDR)**—Supports a double transfer rate of ordinary SDRAM.

- **DDR2**—Splits each clock pulse in two, doubling the number of operations it can perform.

- **DDR3**—A DRAM interface specification that offers the ability to transfer data at twice the rate (eight times the speed of its internal memory arrays), enabling higher bandwidth or peak data rates.

- **DDR4**—Offers higher speed than DDR2 or DDR3 and is one of the latest variants of dynamic random-access memory (DRAM). It is not compatible with any earlier type of random access memory (RAM).

ExamAlert

Memory leaks occur when programs use RAM but cannot release it. Programs that suffer from memory leaks will eventually use up all available memory and can cause the system to halt or crash.

ROM

Read-only memory (ROM) is nonvolatile memory that retains information even if power is removed. ROM is typically used to load and store firmware. Firmware is embedded software much like BIOS or UEFI.

Tip

Most answer systems use Unified Extensible Firmware Interface (UEFI) instead of BIOS. It offers several advantages over BIOS, including support for remote diagnostics and repair of systems even if no OS is installed.

Some common types of ROM include:

- Erasable Programmable Read-Only Memory (EPROM)
- Electrically Erasable Programmable Read-Only Memory (EEPROM)
- Flash Memory
- Programmable Logic Devices (PLD)

Secondary Storage

Although memory plays an important role in the world of storage, other long-term types of storage are also needed. One of these is *sequential storage*. Anyone who has owned an IBM PC with a tape drive knows what sequential storage is. Tape drives are a type of sequential storage that must be read sequentially from beginning to end. Another well-known type of secondary storage is *direct-access storage*. Direct-access storage devices do not have to be read sequentially; the system can identify the location of the information and go directly to it to read the data. A hard drive is an example of a direct-access storage device: A hard drive has a series of platters, read/write heads, motors, and drive electronics contained within a case designed to prevent contamination. Hard drives are used to hold data and software. *Software* is the operating system or an application that you've installed on a computer system.

Compact discs (CDs) are a type of *optical media*. They use a laser/opto-electronic sensor combination to read or write data. A CD can be read-only, write-once, or rewriteable. CDs can hold up to around 800MB on a single disk. A CD is manufactured by applying a thin layer of aluminum to what is primarily hard clear plastic. During manufacturing or whenever a CD/R is burned, small bumps or pits are placed in the surface of the disc. These bumps or pits are converted into binary ones or zeros. Unlike the tracks and sectors of a floppy, a CD comprises one long spiral track that begins at the inside of the disc and continues toward the outer edge.

Digital video discs (DVDs) are very similar to CDs because both are optical media—DVDs just hold more data. The current version of optical storage is the Blu-ray disc. These optical disks can hold 50GB or more of data. More and more systems today are moving to solid-state drives (SSDs) and flash memory storage. Sizes up to 1 TB can now be found.

I/O Bus Standards

The data that the CPU is working with must have a way to move from the storage media to the CPU. This is accomplished by means of a bus. The *bus* is nothing more than lines of conductors that transmit data between the CPU, storage media, and other hardware devices. From the point of view of the CPU, the various adaptors plugged into the computer are external devices. These connectors and the bus architecture used to move data to the devices has changed over time. Some bus architectures are listed here:

▶ **ISA**—The Industry Standard Architecture (ISA) bus started as an 8-bit bus designed for IBM PCs. It is now obsolete.

▶ **PCI**—The Peripheral Component Interconnect (PCI) bus was developed by Intel and served as a replacement for ISA and other bus standards. PCI express is now the current standard.

▶ **PCIe**—The Peripheral Component Interface Express (PCIe) bus was developed as an upgrade to PCI. It offers several advantages such as greater bus throughput, smaller physical footprint, better performance, and better error detection and reporting.

▶ **SATA**—The Serial ATA (SATA) standard is the current standard for connecting hard drives and solid state drives to computers. It uses a serial design, smaller cable, greater speeds, and better airflow inside the computer case.

▶ **SCSI**—The Small Computer Systems Interface (SCSI) bus allows a variety of devices to be daisy-chained off of a single controller. Many servers use the SCSI bus for their preferred hard drive solution.

Two serial bus standards, Universal Serial Bus (USB) and FireWire, have also gained wide market share. USB overcame the limitations of traditional serial interfaces. USB 2.0 devices can communicate at speeds up to 480 Mbps or 60 MBps, whereas USB 3.0 devices have a maximum bandwidth rate of 5 Gbps or 640 MBps. Devices can be chained together so that up to 127 devices can be connected to one USB slot of one hub in a "daisy chain" mode, eliminating the need for expansion slots on the motherboard. The newest USB standard is 3.1. The biggest improvement for the USB 3.1 standard is a boost in data transfer bandwidth of up to 10 gigabits per second.

USB is used for flash memory, cameras, printers, external hard drives, and even phones. Two of the fundamental advantages of USB are that it has broad product support and that many devices are immediately recognized when connected. Many Apple computers make use of the Thunderbolt interface, and some FireWire (IEEE 1394) interfaces are still found on digital audio and video equipment.

Virtual Memory and Virtual Machines

Modern computer systems have developed other ways in which to store and access information. One of these is *virtual memory*. Virtual memory is the combination of the computer's primary memory (RAM) and secondary storage (the hard drive or SSD). By combining these two technologies, the OS can make the CPU believe that it has much more memory than it actually does. Examples of virtual memory include:

▶ Page file

▶ Swap space

▶ Swap partition

These virtual memory types are user-defined in terms of size, location, and so on. When RAM is nearly depleted, the CPU begins saving data onto the computer's hard drive. This process is called paging. Paging takes a part of a program out of memory and uses the page file to save those parts of the program. If the system requires more RAM than paging will provide, it will *write* an entire process out to the swap space. This process uses a paging file/swap file so that the data can be moved back and forth between the hard drive and RAM as needed. A specific drive can even be configured to hold such data and as such is called a *swap partition*. Individuals who have used a computer's hibernation function or who have ever opened more programs on their computers than they've had enough memory to support are probably familiar with the operation of virtual memory.

Closely related to virtual memory are virtual machines, such as VMware Workstation, and Oracle VM VirtualBox. VMware is one of the leading products in the machine virtualization market. A virtual machine enables the user to run a second OS within a virtual host. For example, a virtual machine will let you run another Windows OS, Linux x86, or any other OS that runs on x86 processor and supports standard BIOS/UEFI booting. Virtual systems make use of a hypervisor to manage the virtualized hardware resources to run a guest operating system. A Type 1 hypervisor runs directly on the hardware with VM resources provided by the hypervisor, whereas a Type 2 hypervisor runs on a host operating system above the hardware. Virtual machines are a huge trend and can be used for development and system administration, production, and to reduce the number of physical devices needed. The hypervisor is also being used to design virtual switches, routers, and firewalls.

Tip

Virtualization is not the only thing that is changing in the workplace; cloud computing enables employees to work from many different locations. Because the applications and data can reside in the cloud, a user can access this content from any location that has connectivity. The potential disadvantage of cloud computer is security-related. Something to consider is who owns the cloud. Is it a private cloud (owned by company) or a public cloud (owned by someone else)? In addition, what is the physical location of the cloud, who has access to the cloud, and is it shared (co-tenancy)? Each of these items are critical to consider before placing any corporate assets in a cloud.

Computer Configurations

The following is a list of some of the most commonly used computer and device configurations:

▶ **Print server**—Print servers are usually located close to printers and allow many users to access the same printer and share its resources.

▶ **File server**—File servers allow users to have a centralized site to store files. This provides an easy way to perform backups because it can be done on one server rather than on all the client computers. It also allows for group collaboration and multi-user access.

▶ **Application server**—This service allows users to run applications not installed on the end users' system. It is a very popular concept in thin client environments. Thin clients depend on a central server for processing power. Licensing is an important consideration.

▶ **Web server**—Web servers provide web services to internal and external users via web pages. A sample web address or URL (uniform resource locator) is www.thesolutionfirm.com.

▶ **Database server**—Database servers store and access data. This includes information such as product inventory, price lists, customer lists, and employee data. Because databases hold sensitive information, they require well-designed security controls. They typically sit in front of a database and broker the request, acting as middleware between the untrusted users and the database holding the data.

▶ **Laptops and tablets**—Mobile devices that are easily lost or stolen. Mobile devices have become much more powerful and must be properly secured.

▶ **Smartphones**—Gone are the cell phones of the past that simply placed calls and sent SMS texts. Today's smartphones are more like computers and have a large amount of processing capability; they can take photos and have onboard storage, Internet connectivity, and the ability to run applications. These devices are of particular concern as more companies start to support *bring your own device* (BYOD). Such devices can easily fall outside of company policies and controls.

▶ **Embedded Devices**—Include ATM machines, point-of-sale terminals, and even smart watches. More and more technology has embedded technology, such as smart refrigerators and Bluetooth-enabled toilets. The security of embedded devices is a growing concern as these devices may not be patched or updated on a regular basis.

> ### Note
>
> Expect more and more devices to have embedded technology as the Internet of Things (IoT) grows. Several companies even sell toilets with Bluetooth and SD card technology built in, and like any other device they are not immune to hacking: www.extremetech.com/extreme/163119-smart-toilets-bidet-hacked-via-bluetooth-gives-new-meaning-to-backdoor-vulnerability.

Security Architecture

Although a robust functional architecture is a good start, real security requires that you have a security architecture in place to control processes and applications. Concepts related to security architecture include the following:

- ▶ Protection rings
- ▶ Trusted computer base (TCB)
- ▶ Open and closed systems
- ▶ Security modes of operation
- ▶ Operating states
- ▶ Recovery procedures
- ▶ Process isolation

Protection Rings

The operating system knows who and what to trust by relying on *protection rings*. Protection rings work much like your network of family, friends, co-workers, and acquaintances. The people who are closest to you, such as your spouse and family, have the highest level of trust. Those who are distant acquaintances or are unknown to you probably have a lower level of trust. It's much like the guy you see in New York City on Canal Street trying to sell new Rolex watches for $100; you should have little trust in him and his relationship with the Rolex company!

In reality, protection rings are conceptual. Figure 5.2 shows an illustration of the protection ring schema. The first implementation of such a system was in MIT's Multics time-shared operating system.

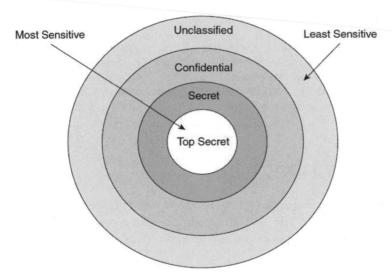

Most Sensitive

Least Sensitive

FIGURE 5.2 **Protection rings.**

The protection ring model provides the operating system with various levels at which to execute code or to restrict that code's access. The idea is to use engineering design to build in layers of control using secure design principles. The rings provide much greater granularity than a system that just operates in user and privileged modes. As code moves toward the outer bounds of the model, the layer number increases and the level of trust decreases.

- ▶ **Layer 0**—The most trusted level. The operating system kernel resides at this level. Any process running at layer 0 is said to be operating in *privileged mode*.

- ▶ **Layer 1**—Contains non-privileged portions of the operating system.

- ▶ **Layer 2**—Where I/O drivers, low-level operations, and utilities reside.

- ▶ **Layer 3**—Where applications and processes operate. This is the level at which individuals usually interact with the operating system. Applications operating here are said to be working in *user mode*. User mode is often referred to as *problem mode*, because this is where the less-trusted applications run; therefore, the most problems occur here.

Not all systems use all rings. Most systems that are used today operate in two modes: *user mode* and *supervisor* (privileged) mode.

Items that need high security, such as the operating system security kernel, are located at the center ring. This ring is unique because it has access rights to all domains in that system. Protection rings are part of the trusted computing base concept.

Trusted Computer Base

The *trusted computer base* (TCB) is the sum of all the protection mechanisms within a computer and is responsible for enforcing the security policy. This includes hardware, software, controls, and processes. The TCB is responsible for confidentiality and integrity. The TCB is the only portion of a system that operates at a high level of trust. It monitors four basic functions:

▶ **Input/output operations**—I/O operations are a security concern because operations from the outermost rings might need to interface with rings of greater protection. These cross-domain communications must be monitored.

▶ **Execution domain switching**—Applications running in one domain or level of protection often invoke applications or services in other domains. If these requests are to obtain more sensitive data or service, their activity must be controlled.

▶ **Memory protection**—To truly be secure, the TCB must monitor memory references to verify confidentiality and integrity in storage.

▶ **Process activation**—Registers, process status information, and file access lists are vulnerable to loss of confidentiality in a multiprogramming environment. This type of potentially sensitive information must be protected.

ExamAlert

For the exam, you should understand not only that the TCB is tasked with enforcing security policy but also that the TCB is the sum of all protection mechanisms within a computer system that have also been evaluated for security assurance. This includes hardware, firmware, and software within the TCB.

Those components that have not been evaluated are said to fall outside the security perimeter.

The TCB monitors the functions in the preceding list to ensure that the system operates correctly and adheres to security policy. The TCB follows the *reference monitor* concept. The reference monitor is an abstract machine that is used to implement security. The reference monitor's job is to validate access to objects by authorized subjects. The reference monitor operates at the boundary between the trusted and untrusted realm. The reference monitor has three properties:

▶ Cannot be bypassed and controls all access, must be invoked for every access attempt

▶ Cannot be altered and is protected from modification or change

▶ Must be small enough to be verified and tested correctly

ExamAlert

For the exam, you should understand that the reference monitor enforces the security requirement for the security kernel.

The reference monitor is much like the bouncer at a club because it stands between each subject and object. Its role is to verify that the subject meets the minimum requirements for access to an object, as illustrated in Figure 5.3.

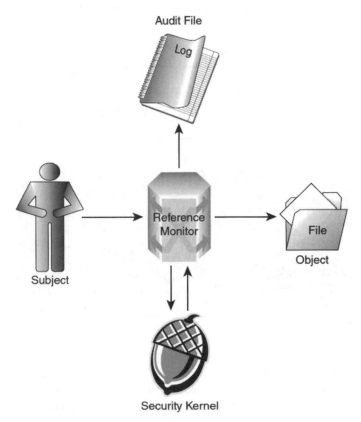

FIGURE 5.3 **Reference monitor.**

> **Note**
>
> *Subjects* are active entities such as people, processes, or devices.

> **Note**
>
> *Objects* are passive entities that are designed to contain or receive information. Objects can be processes, software, or hardware.

The reference monitor can be designed to use tokens, capability lists, or labels.

- ▶ **Tokens**—Communicate security attributes before requesting access

- ▶ **Capability lists**—Offer faster lookup than security tokens but are not as flexible

- ▶ **Security labels**—Used by high-security systems because labels offer permanence. This is provided only by security labels.

> **Note**
>
> Note that each time the term *security labels* is listed, it is used to denote high-security MAC-based systems.

At the heart of the system is the *security kernel*. The security kernel handles all user/application requests for access to system resources. A small security kernel is easy to verify, test, and validate as secure. However, in real life, the security kernel might be bloated with some unnecessary code because processes located inside can function faster and have privileged access. Vendors have taken different approaches in how they develop operating systems. As an example, DOS used a monolithic kernel. Several of these designs are shown in Figure 5.4 and are described here:

- ▶ Monolithic architecture: All of the OS processes work in kernel mode

- ▶ Layered OS design: Separates system functionality into different layers

- ▶ Microkernel: Smaller kernel that only supports critical processes

- ▶ Hybrid microkernel: The kernel structure is similar to a microkernel, but implemented in terms of a monolithic design

Although the reference monitor is conceptual, the security kernel can be found at the heart of every system. The security kernel is responsible for running the required controls used to enforce functionality and resist known attacks. As mentioned previously, the reference monitor operates at the *security perimeter*—the boundary between the trusted and untrusted realm. Components outside the security perimeter are not trusted. All trusted access control mechanisms are inside the security perimeter.

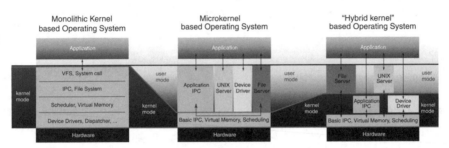

FIGURE 5.4 **Operating System Architecture.**
Source: http://upload.wikimedia.org/wikipedia/commons/d/d0/OS-structure2.svg

Open and Closed Systems

Open systems accept input from other vendors and are based on standards and practices that allow connection to different devices and interfaces. The goal is to promote full interoperability whereby the system can be fully utilized.

Closed systems are proprietary. They use devices that are not based on open standards and that are generally locked. They lack standard interfaces to allow connection to other devices and interfaces.

An example of this can be seen in the United States cell phone industry. AT&T and T-Mobile cell phones are based on the worldwide Global System for Mobile Communications (GSM) standard and can be used overseas easily on other networks by simply changing the subscriber identity module (SIM). These are open-system phones. Phones that are used on the Sprint network use Code Division Multiple Access (CDMA), which does not have worldwide support.

> **Note**
>
> The concept of open and closed can apply to more than just hardware. Open and closed software is about whether others can view and/or alter your source code. As an example, the Galaxy Nexus phone running Android is open source, whereas the Apple iPhone is closed source code.

Security Modes of Operation

Several security modes of operation are based on Department of Defense (DoD 5220.22-M) classification levels. According to the DoD, information being processed on a system, and the clearance level of authorized users, have been defined as one of four modes (see Table 5.2):

▶ **Dedicated**—A need-to-know is required to access all information stored or processed. Every user requires formal access with clearance and approval, and has executed a signed nondisclosure agreement for all the information stored and/or processed. This mode must also support enforced system access procedures. All hardcopy output and media removed will be handled at the level for which the system is accredited until reviewed by a knowledgeable individual. All users can access all data.

▶ **System High**—All users have a security clearance; however, a need-to-know is only required for some of the information contained within the system. Every user requires access approval, and needs to have signed nondisclosure agreements for all the information stored and/or processed. Access to an object by users not already possessing access permission must only be assigned by authorized users of the object. This mode must be capable of providing an audit trail that records time, date, user ID, terminal ID (if applicable), and file name. All users can access some data based on their need to know.

▶ **Compartmented**—Valid need-to-know is required for some of the information on the system. Every user has formal access approval for all information they will access on the system, and requires proper clearance for the highest level of data classification on the system. All users have signed NDAs for all information they will access on the system. All users can access some data based on their need to know and formal access approval.

▶ **Multi-level**—Every user has a valid need-to-know for some of the information that is on the system, and more than one classification level can be processed at the same time. Users have formal access approval and have signed NDAs for all information they will access on the system. Mandatory access controls provide a means of restricting access to files based on their sensitivity label. All users can access some data based on their need to know, clearance, and formal access approval.

TABLE 5.2 **Security Modes of Operation**

Mode	Dedicated	System High	Compartmented	Multi-Level
Signed NDA	All	All	All	All
Clearance	All	All	All	Some
Approval	All	All	Some	Some
Need to Know	All	Some	Some	Some

Operating States

When systems are used to process and store sensitive information, there must be some agreed-on methods for how this will work. Generally, these concepts were developed to meet the requirements of handling sensitive government information with categories such as "sensitive," "secret," and "top secret." The burden of handling this task can be placed on either administration or the system itself.

Generally there are two designs that are used. These include single-state and multistate systems.

Single-state systems are designed and implemented to handle one category of information. The burden of management falls on the administrator who must develop the policy and procedures to manage this system. The administrator must also determine who has access and what type of access the users have. These systems are dedicated to one mode of operation, so they are sometimes referred to as *dedicated systems*.

Multistate systems depend not on the administrator, but on the system itself. They are capable of having more than one person log in to the system and access various types of data depending upon the level of clearance. As you would probably expect, these systems are not inexpensive. The XTS-400 that runs the Secure Trusted Operating Program (STOP) OS from BAE Systems is an example of a multilevel state system. Multistate systems can operate as a compartmentalized system. This means that Mike can log into the system with a secret clearance and access secret-level data, whereas Dwayne can log in with top-secret-level access and access a different level of data. These systems are compartmentalized and can segment data on a need-to-know basis.

> **Tip**
>
> Security-Enhanced Linux and TrustedBSD are freely available implementations of operating systems with limited multistate capabilities. Security evaluation is a problem for these free MLS implementations because of the expense and time it would take to fully qualify these systems.

Recovery Procedures

Unfortunately, things don't always operate normally; they sometimes go wrong and a system failure can occur. A system failure could potentially compromise the system by corrupting integrity, opening security holes, or causing corruption. Efficient designs have built-in recovery procedures to recover from potential problems:

▶ **Fail safe**—If a failure is detected, the system is protected from compromise by termination of services.

▶ **Fail soft**—A detected failure terminates the noncritical process. Systems in fail soft mode are still able to provide partial operational capability.

It is important to be able to recover when an issue arises. This requires taking a proactive approach and backing up all critical files on a regular schedule. The goal of recovery is to recover to a known state. Common issues that require recovery include:

▶ **System Reboot**—An unexpected/unscheduled event.

▶ **System Restart**—Automatically occurs when the system goes down and forces an immediate reboot.

▶ **System Cold Start**—Results from a major failure or component replacement.

▶ **System Compromise**—Caused by an attack or breach of security.

Process Isolation

Process isolation is required to maintain a high level of system trust. To be certified as a multilevel security system, process isolation must be supported. Without process isolation, there would be no way to prevent one process from spilling over into another process's memory space, corrupting data, or possibly making the whole system unstable. *Process isolation* is performed by the operating system; its job is to enforce memory boundaries. Separation of processes is an important topic—otherwise the system could be designed in such a way that one flaw in the design or configuration could cause an entire system to stop operating. This is known as a *single point of failure* (SPOF).

For a system to be secure, the operating system must prevent unauthorized users from accessing areas of the system to which they should not have access, be robust, and have no single point of failure. Sometimes this is accomplished by means of a virtual machine. A virtual machine allows users to believe that they have the use of the entire system, but in reality, processes are completely isolated. To take this concept a step further, some systems that require truly robust security also implement hardware isolation. This means that the processes are segmented not only logically but also physically.

> **Note**
>
> Java uses a form of virtual machine because it uses a sandbox to contain code and allows it to function only in a controlled manner.

Common Formal Security Models

Security models are used to determine how security will be implemented, what subjects can access the system, and what objects they will have access to. Simply stated, they are a way to formalize security policy. Security models of control are typically implemented by enforcing integrity, confidentiality, or other controls. Keep in mind that each of these models lays out broad guidelines and is not specific in nature. It is up to the developer to decide how these models will be used and integrated into specific designs, as shown in Figure 5.5.

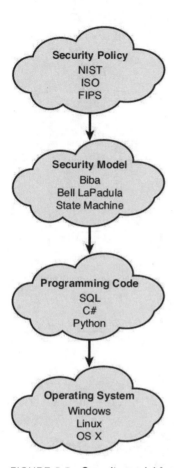

FIGURE 5.5   Security model fundamental concepts used in the design of an OS.

The sections that follow discuss the different security models of control in greater detail. The first three models discussed are considered lower-level models.

State Machine Model

The *state machine model* is based on a finite state machine, as shown in Figure 5.6. State machines are used to model complex systems and deal with acceptors, recognizers, state variables, and transaction functions. The state machine defines the behavior of a finite number of states, the transitions between those states, and actions that can occur.

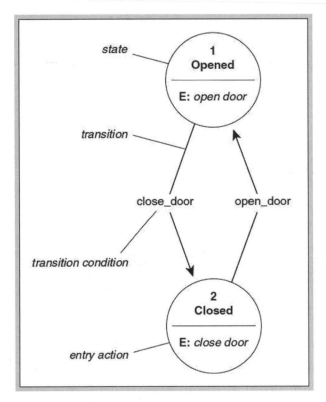

FIGURE 5.6   Finite state model.

The most common representation of a state machine is through a state machine table. For example, as Table 5.3 illustrates, if the state machine is at the current state of (B) and condition (2), the next state would be (C) and condition (3) as we progress through the options.

TABLE 5.3   **State Machine Table**

State Transaction	State A	State B	State C
Condition 1	...	...	...
Condition 2	...	Current State	...
Condition 3	...	...	...

A state machine model monitors the status of the system to prevent it from slipping into an insecure state. Systems that support the state machine model must have all their possible states examined to verify that all processes are controlled in accordance with the system security policy. The state machine concept serves as the basis of many security models. The model is valued for knowing in what state the system will reside. As an example, if the system boots up in a secure state, and every transaction that occurs is secure, it must always be in a secure state and not fail open. (To fail open means that all traffic or actions would be allowed, not denied.)

Information Flow Model

The *information flow model* is an extension of the state machine concept and serves as the basis of design for both the Biba and Bell-LaPadula models, which are discussed in the sections that follow. The information flow model consists of objects, state transitions, and lattice (flow policy) states. The real goal of the information flow model is to prevent unauthorized, insecure information flow in any direction. This model and others can make use of *guards*. Guards allow the exchange of data between various systems.

Noninterference Model

The *Noninterference model* as defined by Goguen and Meseguer was designed to make sure that objects and subjects of different levels don't interfere with the objects and subjects of other levels. The model uses inputs and outputs of either low or high sensitivity. Each data access attempt is independent of all others and data cannot cross security boundaries.

Confidentiality

Although the preceding models serve as a basis for many security models that were developed later, one major concern is confidentiality. Government entities such as the DoD are concerned about the confidentiality of information. The DoD divides information into categories to ease the burden of managing who has access to what levels of information. DoD information classifications are "sensitive but unclassified" (SBU), "confidential," "secret," and "top secret." One of the first models to address the needs of the DoD was the Bell-LaPadula model.

Bell-LaPadula

The *Bell-LaPadula* state machine model enforces confidentiality. This model uses mandatory access control to enforce the DoD multilevel security policy. For subjects to access information, they must have a clear need to know, and must meet or exceed the information's classification level.

The Bell-LaPadula model is defined by the following properties:

▶ **Simple security property (ss property)**—This property states that a subject at one level of confidentiality is not allowed to read information at a higher level of confidentiality. This is sometimes referred to as "no read up." An example is shown in Figure 5.7.

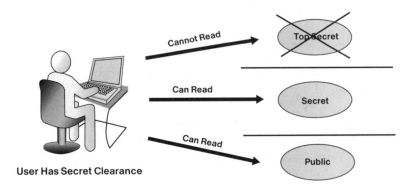

Bell-LaPadula
Simple Security Property

FIGURE 5.7   Bell-LaPadula Simple Security Model.

▶ **Star * security property**—This property states that a subject at one level of confidentiality is not allowed to write information to a lower level of confidentiality. This is also known as "no write down." An example is shown in Figure 5.8.

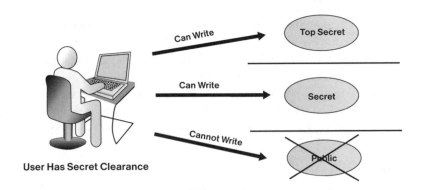

Bell-LaPadula
Star * Property

FIGURE 5.8   Bell-LaPadula Star * Property.

▶ **Strong star * property**—This property states that a subject cannot read or write to an object of higher or lower sensitivity. An example is shown in Figure 5.9.

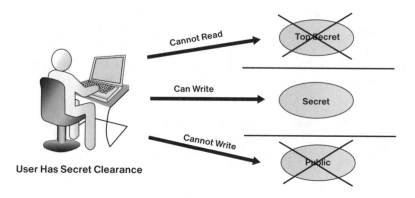

**Bell-LaPadula
Strong Star * Property**

FIGURE 5.9 **Bell-LaPadula Strong Star Property.**

ExamAlert

Review the Bell-LaPadula simple security and Star * security models closely; they are easy to confuse with Biba's two defining properties.

Tip

A fourth but rarely implemented property called the *discretionary security property* allows users to grant access to other users at the same clearance level by means of an access matrix.

Although the Bell-LaPadula model did go a long way in defining the operation of secure systems, the model is not perfect. It did not address security issues such as covert channels. It was designed in an era when mainframes were the dominant platform. It was designed for multilevel security and takes only confidentiality into account.

Tip

Know that the Bell-LaPadula model deals with confidentiality. As such, reading information at a higher level than what is allowed would endanger confidentiality.

Integrity

Integrity is a good thing. It is one of the basic elements of the security triad, along with confidentiality and availability. Integrity plays an important role in security because it can verify that unauthorized users are not modifying data, authorized users don't make unauthorized changes, and that databases balance and data remains internally and externally consistent. Although governmental entities are typically very concerned with confidentiality, other organizations might be more focused on the integrity of information. In general, integrity has four goals:

1. Prevent data modification by unauthorized parties

2. Prevent unauthorized data modification by authorized parties

3. Reflect the real world

4. Maintain internal and external consistency

> **Note**
>
> Some sources list only three goals of security by combining 3 and 4, i.e., must maintain internal and external consistency and the data must reflect the real world.

Two security models that address secure systems integrity include Biba and Clark-Wilson. These models are addressed next. The Biba model only addresses the first integrity goal and the Clark-Wilson addresses all goals.

Biba

The *Biba model* was the first model developed to address the concerns of integrity. Originally published in 1977, this lattice-based model has the following defining properties:

▶ **Simple integrity property**—This property states that a subject at one level of integrity is not permitted to read an object of lower integrity.

▶ **Star * integrity property**—This property states that an object at one level of integrity is not permitted to write to an object of higher integrity.

▶ **Invocation property**—This property prohibits a subject at one level of integrity from invoking a subject at a higher level of integrity.

> **Tip**
>
> One easy way to help you remember these rules is to note that the Star property in both Biba and Bell-LaPadula deal with write. Just remember, "It's written in the stars!"

Biba addresses only the first goal of integrity—protecting the system from access by unauthorized users. Other types of concerns such as confidentiality are not examined. It also assumes that internal threats are being protected by good coding practices, and therefore focuses on external threats.

> **Tip**
>
> To remember the purpose of the Biba model, just keep in mind that the "i" in Biba stands for integrity.

Tibetan Monks and the Biba Model

When teaching this domain in the classroom, security models are one of the areas where students are eager to find something to relate to the material. I typically use the well-known story of Tibetan monks.

After a long journey on your search for Shangri-La and true security awareness, you arrive at a Tibetan monastery. You discover the monks are huge fans of the Biba model and like you have studied for the CISSP exam. As such, they have defined certain rules that you, the commoner, must abide by.

1. A Tibetan monk may write a prayer book that can be read by commoners, but not one to be read by a high priest.
2. A Tibetan monk may read a book written by the high priest, but may not read down to a pamphlet written by a commoner.

Consider this story when you are trying to conceptualize the Biba model and it might make the task a little easier. A final tip is to look at the star * property for both the Bell-LaPadula model and the Biba model. Notice how both star properties deal with write. If this property is applied to *Bell-LaPadula*, a confidentiality model, the result is *no write down*. If the star property is applied to the *Biba* model, the result is *no write up*. Just by knowing one, you can easily solve the other.

> **Tip**
>
> Remember that the Biba model deals with integrity and as such, writing to an object of a higher level might endanger the integrity of the system.

Clark-Wilson

The *Clark-Wilson model* was created in 1987. It differs from previous models because it was developed to be used for commercial activities. This model addresses all the goals of integrity. Clark-Wilson dictates that the separation of duties must be enforced, subjects must access data through an application, and auditing is required. Some terms associated with Clark-Wilson include:

▶ User

▶ Transformation procedure

▶ Unconstrained data item

▶ Constrained data item

▶ Integrity verification procedure

Clark-Wilson features an access control triple, where subjects must access programs before accessing objects (subject-program-object). The access control triple is composed of the user, transformational procedure, and the constrained data item. It was designed to protect integrity and prevent fraud. Authorized users cannot change data in an inappropriate way. The Clark-Wilson model checks three attributes: tampered, logged, and consistent, or "TLC."

It also differs from the Biba model in that subjects are restricted. This means that a subject at one level of access can read one set of data, whereas a subject at another level has access to a different set of data. Clark-Wilson controls the way in which subjects access objects so that the internal consistency of the system can be ensured, and that data can be manipulated only in ways that protect consistency. Integrity verification procedures (IVPs) ensure that a data item is in a valid state. Data cannot be tampered with while being changed and the integrity of the data must be consistent. Clark-Wilson requires that all changes must be logged. Clark-Wilson is made up of transformation procedures (TP). Constrained data items (CDI) are data for which integrity must be preserved. Items not covered under the model are considered unconstrained data items (UDIs).

> **Tip**
>
> Remember that the Clark-Wilson model requires that users be authorized to access and modify data, and that it deals with three key terms: tampered, logged, and consistent, or "TLC."

Take-Grant Model

The *Take-Grant model* is another confidentiality-based model that supports four basic operations: take, grant, create, and revoke. This model allows subjects with the take right to remove take rights from other subjects. Subjects possessing the grant right can grant this right to other subjects. The create and revoke operations work in the same manner: someone with the create right can give the create right to others and those with the revoke right can remove that right from others.

Brewer and Nash Model

The *Brewer and Nash model* is similar to the Bell-LaPadula model and is also sometimes referred to as the *Chinese Wall model*. It was developed to prevent conflict of interest (COI) problems. As an example, imagine that your security firm does security work for many large firms. If one of your employees could access information about all the firms that your company has worked for, that person might be able to use this data in an unauthorized way. Therefore, the Brewer and Nash model is more context-oriented in that it prevents a worker consulting for one firm from accessing data belonging to another, thereby preventing any COI.

Other Models

A security model defines and describes what protection mechanisms are to be used and what these controls are designed to achieve. Although the previous section covered some of the more heavily tested models, you should have a basic understanding of a few more. These security models include:

▶ **Graham Denning model**—This model uses a formal set of eight protection rules for which each object has an owner and a controller. These rules define what you can create, delete, read, grant, or transfer.

▶ **Harrison-Ruzzo-Ullman model**—This model is similar to the Graham Denning model and details how subjects and objects can be created, deleted, accessed, or changed.

▶ **Lipner**—This model combines elements of both Bell-LaPadula and Biba to guard both confidentiality and integrity.

▶ **Lattice model**—This model is associated with MAC. Controls are applied to objects and the model uses security levels that are represented by a lattice structure. This structure governs information flow. Subjects of the lattice model are allowed to access an object only if the security level of the subject is equal to or greater than that of the object. Overall access limits are set by having a least upper bound and a greatest lower bound for each "security level."

ExamAlert

Spend some time reviewing all the models discussed in this section. Make sure you know which models are integrity-based, which are confidentiality-based, and the properties of each; you will need to know this distinction for the exam.

Tip

Although the security models listed in this section are the ones the exam will most likely focus on, there are many other models, such as the Sutherland, Boebert and Kain, Karger, Gong, and Jueneman. Even though many security professionals may have never heard of these, those that develop systems most likely learned of them in college.

Product Security Evaluation Models

A set of evaluation standards will be needed when evaluating the security capabilities of information systems. The following documents and guidelines were developed to help evaluate and establish system assurance. These items are important to the CISSP candidate because they provide a level of trust and assurance that these systems will operate in a given and predictable manner. A trusted system has undergone testing and validation to a specific standard. Assurance is the freedom from doubt and a level of confidence that a system will perform as required every time it is used.

Think of product evaluation models as being similar to EPA gas mileage ratings. These give the buyer and seller a way to evaluate different automotive brands and models. In the world of product security, such systems can be used by developers when preparing to sell a system. The same evaluation models can be used by the buyer when preparing to make a purchase, as they provide a way to measure the system's effectiveness and benchmark its abilities. The following documents and guidelines facilitate these needs.

The Rainbow Series

The Rainbow Series is aptly named because each book in the series has a label of a different color. This 6-foot-tall stack of books was developed by the National Computer Security Center (NCSC), an organization that is part of the National Security Agency (NSA). These guidelines were developed for the Trusted Product Evaluation Program (TPEP), which tests commercial products against a comprehensive set of security-related criteria. The first of these books was released in 1983 and is known as *Trusted Computer System Evaluation Criteria* (TCSEC) or the Orange Book. Many similar guides were also known by the color of the cover instead of their name, such as the Purple Book and the Brown Book. These guidelines have all been replaced with Common Criteria, discussed below. While no longer commercially used, understanding TCSEC will help you understand how product security evaluation models have evolved into what is used today. Because it addresses only standalone systems, other volumes were developed to increase the level of system assurance.

The Orange Book: Trusted Computer System Evaluation Criteria

The Orange Book's official name is the *Trusted Computer System Evaluation Criteria* and was developed to evaluate standalone systems. Its basis of measurement is confidentiality, so it is similar to the Bell-LaPadula model. It is designed to rate systems and place them into one of four categories:

- ▶ **A**—Verified protection. An A-rated system is the highest security category.

- ▶ **B**—Mandatory security. A B-rated system has mandatory protection of the TCB.

- ▶ **C**—Discretionary protection. A C-rated system provides discretionary protection of the TCB.

- ▶ **D**—Minimal protection. A D-rated system fails to meet any of the standards of A, B, or C and basically has no security controls.

> **Note**
>
> The Canadians had their own version of the Orange Book known as *The Canadian Trusted Computer Product Evaluation Criteria* (CTCPEC). It is seen as a more flexible version of TCSEC.

The Orange Book not only rates systems into one of four categories, but each category is also broken down further. For each of these categories, a higher number indicates a more secure system, as noted in the following:

▶ A is the highest security division. An A1 rating means that the system has verified protection and supports mandatory access control (MAC).

    ▶ A1 is the highest supported rating. Systems rated as such must adhere to formal methods and provide formal proof of integrity of the TCB. An A1 system must not only be developed under strict guidelines, but also must be installed and delivered securely. Examples of A1 systems include the Gemini Trusted Network Processor and the Honeywell SCOMP. The true nature of A rating deals with the level of scrutiny the system receives during evaluation.

▶ B is considered a mandatory protection design. Just as with an A-rated system, those that obtain a B rating must support MAC.

    ▶ B1 (labeled security protection) systems require sensitivity labels for all subjects and storage objects. Examples of B1-rated systems include the Cray Research Trusted Unicos 8.0 and the Digital SEVMS.

    ▶ For a B2 (structured protection) rating, the system must meet the requirements of B1 and support hierarchical device labels, trusted path communications between user and system, and covert storage analysis. An example of a B2 system is the Honeywell Multics.

    ▶ Systems rated as B3 (security domains) must meet B2 standards and support trusted path access and authentication, automatic security analysis, and trusted recovery. B3 systems must address covert timing vulnerabilities. A B3 system must not only support security controls during operation but also be secure during startup. An example of a B3-rated system is the Federal XTS-300.

▶ C is considered a discretionary protection rating. C-rated systems support discretionary access control (DAC).

    ▶ Systems rated at C1 (discretionary security protection) don't need to distinguish between individual users and types of access.

    ▶ C2 (controlled access protection) systems must meet C1 requirements and they must distinguish between individual users and types of access by means of strict login controls. C2 systems must also support object reuse protection. A C2 rating is common; products such as Windows NT and Novell NetWare 4.11 have a C2 rating.

▶ Any system that does not comply with any of the other categories or that fails to receive a higher classification is rated as a D-level (minimal protection) system. MS-DOS is a D-rated system.

> ### ExamAlert
>
> The CISSP exam will not expect you to know what systems meet the various Orange Book ratings. These are provided only as examples; however, the test will expect you to know which levels are MAC and DAC certified.

Although the Orange Book is no longer considered current, it was one of the first standards. It is reasonable to expect that the exam might ask you about Orange Book levels and functions at each level. Listed in Table 5.4 are important notes to keep in mind about Orange Book levels.

TABLE 5.4 **Orange Book Levels**

Level	Items to Remember
A1	Built, installed, and delivered in a secure manner
B1	Security labels (MAC)
B2	Security labels and verification of no covert channels (MAC)
B3	Security labels, verification of no covert channels, and must stay secure during startup (MAC)
C1	Weak protection mechanisms (DAC)
C2	Strict login procedures (DAC)
D1	Failed or was not tested

The Red Book: Trusted Network Interpretation

The Red Book's official name is the *Trusted Network Interpretation* (TNI). The purpose of the TNI is to examine security for network and network components. Whereas the Orange Book addresses only confidentiality, the Red Book examines integrity and availability. It also is tasked with examining the operation of networked devices. Three areas of reviews of the Red Book include:

▶ **DoS prevention**—Management and continuity of operations.

▶ **Compromise protection**—Data and traffic confidentiality, selective routing.

▶ **Communications integrity**—Authentication, integrity, and nonrepudiation.

Information Technology Security Evaluation Criteria

ITSEC is a European standard developed in the 1980s to evaluate confidentiality, integrity, and availability of an entire system. ITSEC was unique in that it was the first standard to unify markets and bring all of Europe under one set of guidelines. ITSEC designates the target system as the Target of Evaluation (TOE). The evaluation is actually divided into two parts: One part evaluates functionality and the other evaluates assurance. There are 10 functionality (F) classes and 7 assurance (E) classes. Assurance classes rate the effectiveness and correctness of a system. Table 5.5 shows these ratings and how they correspond to the TCSEC ratings.

TABLE 5.5 **ITSEC Functionality Ratings and Comparison to TCSEC**

(F) Class	(E) Class	TCSEC Rating
NA	E0	D
F1	E1	C1
F2	E2	C2
F3	E3	B1
F4	E4	B2
F5	E5	B3
F5	E6	A1
F6	–	TOEs with high integrity requirements
F7	–	TOEs with high availability requirements
F8	–	TOEs with high integrity requirements during data communications
F9	–	TOEs with high confidentiality requirements during data communications
F10	–	Networks with high confidentiality and integrity requirements

Common Criteria

With all the standards we have discussed, it is easy to see how someone might have a hard time determining which one is the right choice. The International Standards Organization (ISO) had these same thoughts; therefore, it decided that because of the various standards and ratings that existed, there should be a single global standard. Figure 5.10 illustrates the development of Common Criteria.

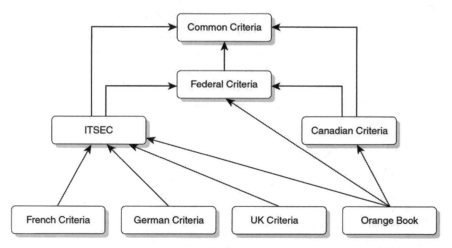

FIGURE 5.10   **Common Criteria development.**

In 1997, the ISO released the *Common Criteria* (ISO 15408), which is an amalgamated version of TCSEC, ITSEC, and the CTCPEC. Common Criteria is designed around TCB entities. These entities include physical and logical controls, startup and recovery, reference mediation, and privileged states. Common Criteria categorizes assurance into one of seven increasingly strict levels of assurance. These are referred to as *Evaluation Assurance Levels* (EALs). EALs provide a specific level of confidence in the security functions of the system being analyzed. A description of each of the seven levels of assurance follows:

▶ **EAL 1**—Functionality tested

▶ **EAL 2**—Structurally tested

▶ **EAL 3**—Methodically checked and tested

▶ **EAL 4**—Methodically designed, tested, and reviewed

▶ **EAL 5**—Semi-formally designed and tested

▶ **EAL 6**—Semi-formally verified, designed, and tested

▶ **EAL 7**—Formally verified, designed, and tested

ExamAlert

If you are looking for an example of a high level, EAL 6 operating system, look no further than Integrity 178B by Green Hills software. This secure OS is used in jet fighters and other critical devices. See www.informationweek.com/news/software/bi/229208909 for more details.

Like ITSEC, Common Criteria defines two types of security requirements: *functional* and *assurance*. Functional requirements define what a product or system does. They also define the security capabilities of a product. The assurance requirements and specifications to be used as the basis for evaluation are known as the *Security Target* (ST). A protection profile defines the system and its controls. The protection profile is divided into the following five sections:

▶ Rationale

▶ Evaluation assurance requirements

▶ Descriptive elements

▶ Functional requirements

▶ Development assurance requirements

A Security Target consists of the following seven sections:

▶ Introduction

▶ Conformance Claims

▶ Security Problem Definition

▶ Security Objectives

▶ Extended Components Definition

▶ Security Requirements

▶ TOE Security Specifications

A Common Criteria certification will either contain a Protection Profile (PP) or a Security Target (ST).

Assurance requirements define how well a product is built. Assurance requirements give confidence in the product and show the correctness of its implementation.

ExamAlert

Common Criteria's seven levels of assurance and its two security requirements are required test knowledge.

System Validation

No system or architecture will ever be completely secure; there will always be a certain level of risk. Security professionals must understand this risk and be comfortable with it, mitigate it, or offset it to a third party. All the documentation and guidelines already discussed dealt with ways to measure and assess risk. These can be a big help in ensuring that the implemented systems meet our requirements. However, before we begin to use the systems, we must complete the two additional steps of certification and accreditation.

U.S. federal agencies are required by law to have their IT systems and infrastructures certified and accredited. Although you shouldn't expect to see this information on the exam, it is worth knowing if you plan to interact with any agencies that require their use. These methodologies look at much more than your standard penetration test. In reality, they are more like an audit. They must validate that the systems are implemented, configured, and operating as expected and meet all security policies and procedures.

Certification and Accreditation

Certification is the process of validating that implemented systems are configured and operating as expected. It also validates that the systems are connected to and communicate with other systems in a secure and controlled manner, and that they handle data in a secure and approved manner. The certification process is a technical evaluation of the system that can be carried out by independent security teams or by the existing staff. Its goal is to uncover any vulnerabilities or weaknesses in the implementation.

The results of the certification process are reported to the organization's management for mediation and approval. If management agrees with the findings of the certification, the report is formally approved. The formal approval of the certification is the *accreditation process*. Management usually issues accreditation as a formal, written approval that the certified system is approved for use as specified in the certification documentation. If changes are made to the system or in the environment in which the system is used, a recertification and accreditation process must be repeated. The entire process is periodically repeated in intervals depending on the industry and the regulations they must comply with. As an example, Section 404 of Sarbanes-Oxley requires an annual evaluation of internal systems that deal with financial controls and reporting systems.

ExamAlert

For the exam, you might want to remember that certification is seen as the technical aspect of validation, whereas accreditation is management's approval.

Note

Nothing lasts forever—and that includes certification. The certification process should be repeated when systems change, items are modified, or on a periodic basis.

Security Guidelines and Governance

The Internet and global connectivity extend the company's network far beyond its traditional border. This places new demands on information security and its governance. Attacks can originate not just from inside the organization, but anywhere in the world.

Information security governance requires more than certification and accreditation. *Governance* should focus on the availability of services, integrity of information, and protection of data confidentiality. Failure to adequately address this important concern can have serious consequences. This has led to the growth of governance frameworks such as the IT Infrastructure Library (ITIL). ITIL specifies a set of processes, procedures, and tasks that can be integrated with the organization's strategy, delivering value and maintaining a minimum level of competency. ITIL can be used to create a baseline from which the organization can plan, implement, and measure its governance progress.

Security and governance can be enhanced by implementing an *enterprise architecture* (EA) plan. The EA is the practice within information technology of organizing and documenting a company's IT assets to enhance planning, management, and expansion. The primary purpose of using EA is to ensure that business strategy and IT investments are aligned. The benefit of EA is that it provides a means of traceability that extends from the highest level of business strategy down to the fundamental technology. EA has grown since first developed it in the 1980s; companies such as Intel, BP, and the United States government now use this methodology. One early EA model is the Zachman

Framework. It was designed to allow companies to structure policy documents for information systems so they focus on who, what, where, when, why, and how, as shown in Figure 5.11.

Enterprise Architecture

Federal law requires government agencies to set up EAs and a structure for its governance. This process is guided by the Federal Enterprise Architecture (FEA) reference model. The FEA is designed to use five models:

▶ **Performance reference model**—A framework used to measure performance of major IT investments.

▶ **Business reference model**—A framework used to provide an organized, hierarchical model for day-to-day business operations.

▶ **Service component reference model**—A framework used to classify service components with respect to how they support business or performance objectives.

▶ **Technical reference model**—A framework used to categorize the standards, specifications, and technologies that support and enable the delivery of service components and capabilities.

▶ **Data reference model**—A framework used to provide a standard means by which data can be described, categorized, and shared.

An independently designed, but later integrated, subset of the Zachman Framework is the *Sherwood Applied Business Security Architecture* (SABSA). Like the Zachman Framework, this model and methodology was developed for risk-driven enterprise information security architectures. It asks what, why, how, and where. More information on the SABSA model is at www.sabsa-institute.org.

	Why	How	What	Who	Where	When
Contextual	Goal List	Process List	Material List	Organizational Unit and Role List	Geographical Locations List	Event List
Conceptual	Goal Relationship	Process Model	Entity Relationship Model	Organizational Unit and Role Relationship Model	Locations Model	Event Model
Logical	Rules Diagram	Process Diagram	Data Model Diagram	Role Relationship Diagram	Locations Diagram	Event Diagram
Physical	Rules Specification	Process Function Speculation	Data Entity Specification	Role Specification	Location Specification	Event Specification
Detailed	Rules Details	Process Details	Data Details	Role Details	Location Details	Event Details

FIGURE 5.11   **Zachman model.**

The British Standard (BS) 7799 was developed in England to be used as a standard method to measure risk. Because the document found such a wide audience and was adopted by businesses and organizations, it evolved into ISO 17799 and then later was used in the development of ISO 27005.

ISO 17799 is a code of practice for information security. ISO 17799 is written for individuals responsible for initiating, implementing, or maintaining information security management systems. Its goal is to help protect confidentiality, integrity, and availability. Compliance with 17799 is an involved task and is far from trivial for even the most security-conscious organizations. ISO 17799 provides best-practice guidance on information security management and is divided into 12 main sections:

▶ Risk assessment and treatment

▶ Security policy

▶ Organization of information security

▶ Asset management

▶ Human resources security

▶ Physical and environmental security

▶ Communications and operations management

▶ Access control

▶ Information systems acquisition, development, and maintenance

▶ Information security incident management

▶ Business continuity management

▶ Compliance

The ISO 27000 series is part of a family of standards that can trace its origins back to BS 7799. Organizations can become ISO 27000 certified by verifying their compliance to an accredited testing entity. Some of the core ISO standards include the following:

▶ **27001**—This document describes requirements on how to establish, implement, operate, monitor, review, and maintain an information security management system (ISMS). It follows a Plan-Do-Check-Act model.

▶ **27002**—This document was originally the BS 7799 standard, then was republished as an ISO 17799 standard. It also describes ways to develop a security program within the organization.

▶ **27003**—This document focuses on implementation.

▶ **27004**—This document describes the ways to measure the effectiveness of the information security program.

▶ **27005**—This document describes the code of practice of information security.

One final item worth mentioning is the information technology infrastructure library (ITIL). ITIL provides a framework for identifying, planning, delivering, and supporting IT services for the business. ITIL presents a service lifecycle that includes:

▶ Continual service improvement

▶ Service strategy

▶ Service design

▶ Service transition

▶ Service operation

True security is a layered process. Each of the items discussed in this section can be used to build a more secure organization.

Regulatory Compliance and Process Control

One area of concern for the CISSP is protection of sensitive information and the security of financial data. One such item is Payment Card Industry Data Security Standard (PCI DSS). This multinational standard was first released in 2004, and was created to enforce strict standards of control for the protection of credit card, debit card, ATM card, and gift card numbers by mandating policies, security devices, controls, and network monitoring. PCI also sets standards for the protection of personally identifiable information that is associated with the cardholder of the account. Participating vendors include American Express, MasterCard, Visa, and Discover.

While PCI is used to protect financial data, Control Objectives for Information and Related Technology (COBIT) was developed to meet the requirements of business and IT processes. It is a standard used for auditors worldwide and was developed by the Information Systems Audit and Control Association (ISACA). COBIT is divided into four control areas:

▶ Planning and Organization

▶ Acquisition and Implementation

▶ Delivery and Support

▶ Monitoring

Vulnerabilities of Security Architectures

Just as in most other chapters of this book, this one also reviews potential threats and vulnerabilities. Any time a security professional makes the case for stronger security, there will be those that ask why such funds should be spent. It's important to point out not only the benefits of good security, but also the potential risks of not implementing good practices and procedures.

We live in a world of risk. As security professionals, we need to be aware of these threats to security and understand how the various protection mechanisms discussed throughout this chapter can be used to raise the level of security.

Buffer Overflow

Buffer overflows occur because of poor coding techniques. A *buffer* is a temporary storage area that has been coded to hold a certain amount of data. If additional data is fed to the buffer, it can spill over or overflow to adjacent buffers. This can corrupt those buffers and cause the application to crash or possibly allow an attacker to execute his own code that he has loaded onto the stack. Ideally, programs should be written to check that you cannot type 32 characters into a 24-character buffer; however, this type of error checking does not always occur. Error checking is really nothing more than making sure that buffers receive the correct type and amount of information required. Here is an example buffer overflow:

```
#include <stdio.h>
#include <stdlib.h>
#include <string.h>
int abc()
{
 char buffer[8];
 strcpy(buffer, "AAAAAAAAAA";
 return 0;
}
```

For example, in 2010, the Aurora Exploit was developed to cause a buffer overflow against Windows XP systems running Internet Explorer. As a result of the attack, attackers could take control of the client system and execute commands remotely. Due diligence is required to prevent buffer overflows. The programmer's work should always be checked for good security practices.

OS vendors are also working to make buffer overflow attacks harder by using techniques such as data execution prevention (DEP) and address space layout randomization (ASLR). Buffer overflows are possible in part because attackers can determine what memory space should be used to load their malicious code onto the stack. DEP marks some areas of memory as either executable or non-executable. DEP can help avert some attacks by preventing the writing of malicious commands designed to be stored in memory. ALSR randomly rearranges address space positions of data. Think of the shell game where a small pea is placed under one of the three shells and is then moved around. To win the game you must guess which shell the pea is under. To defeat randomization, attackers must successfully guess the positions of all areas they wish to attack. Increasing the memory space and entropy makes it harder for attackers to guess all possible positions. Most modern OS's such as Android, Windows, and FreeBSD make use of ALSR.

Other defenses for buffer overflows include code reviews, using safe programming languages, and applying patches and updates in a timely manner. You should also consider the human element; continuous coder training can aid programmers in keeping abreast of ongoing threats and a changing landscape. Finally, since all data should be suspect by default, data being input, processed, or output should be checked to make sure that it matches the correct parameters.

Back Doors

Back doors are another potential threat to the security of systems and software. *Back doors*, which are also sometimes referred to as *maintenance hooks*, are used by programmers during development to allow easy access to a piece of software. Often these back doors are undocumented. A back door can be used when software is developed in sections and developers want a means of accessing certain parts of the program without having to run through all the code. If back doors are not removed before the release of the software, they can allow an attacker to bypass security mechanisms and access the program.

State Attacks

State attacks are a form of attack that typically targets timing. The objective is to exploit the delay between the time of check (TOC) and the time of use (TOU). These attacks are sometimes called *asynchronous attacks* or *race conditions* because the attacker races to make a change to the object after it has been changed but before the system uses it.

As an example, if a program creates a date file to hold the amount a customer owes and the attacker can race to replace this value before the program reads it, he can successfully manipulate the program. In reality, it can be difficult to exploit a race condition because a hacker might have to attempt to exploit the race condition many times before succeeding.

Covert Channels

Covert channels are a means of moving information in a manner in which it was not intended. Covert channels are a favorite of attackers because they know that you cannot deny what you must permit. The term was originally used in

TCSEC documentation to refer to ways of transferring information from a higher classification to a lower classification. Covert channel attacks can be broadly separated into two types:

▶ **Covert timing channel attacks**—Timing attacks are difficult to detect. They function by altering a component or by modifying resource timing.

▶ **Covert storage channel attacks**—These attacks use one process to write data to a storage area and another process to read the data.

Here is an example of how covert channel attacks happen in real life. Your organization has decided to allow ping (Internet Control Message Protocol [ICMP]) traffic into and out of your network. Based on this knowledge, an attacker has planted the Loki program on your network. Loki uses the payload portion of the ping packet to move data into and out of your network. Therefore, the network administrator sees nothing but normal ping traffic and is not alerted, even though the attacker is busy stealing company secrets. Sadly, many programs can perform this type of attack.

ExamAlert

The CISSP exam expects you to understand the two types of covert channel attacks.

Incremental Attacks

The goal of an incremental attack is to make a change slowly over time. By making such a small change over such a long period, an attacker hopes to remain undetected. Two primary incremental attacks include *data diddling*, which is possible if the attacker has access to the system and can make small incremental changes to data or files, and a *salami attack*, which is similar to data diddling but involves making small changes to financial accounts or records, often referred to as "cooking the books."

Getting Rich a Few Cents at a Time

While many readers may have heard stories about salami attacks, some individuals actually practice these techniques in an attempt to get rich. One such attack took place in 2008 by a California hacker.

According to news reports, his get-rich scheme involved a salami attack that worked by opening accounts at many different online services, businesses, and brokers.

A common practice of these services is to send a tiny payment of a few cents to verify the account actually exists. The attacker used this knowledge to open thousands of different online accounts collecting only a few cents from each.

His only problem was that his local bank became suspicious when it found thousands of these small transactions. By the time the authorities were alerted, the attacker had collected more than $50,000. The individual was charged under various bank and wire fraud laws because he had used different names, addresses, and Social Security numbers to open each of the accounts. Complete details are listed at tinyurl.com/3e5v9q.

ExamAlert

The attacks discussed are items that you can expect to see on the exam.

Emanations

Anyone who has seen movies such as *Enemy of the State* or *The Conversation* knows something about surveillance technologies and conspiracy theories. If you ever thought that it was just fringe elements that were worried about such things, guess again. This might sound like science fiction, but the United States government was concerned enough about the possibility of emanation that the Department of Defense started a program to study emanation leakage.

Research actually began in the 1950s with the result being TEMPEST technology. The fear was that attackers might try to sniff the stray electrical signals that emanate from electronic devices. Devices that have been built to TEMPEST standards, such as cathode ray tube (CRT) monitors, have had TEMPEST-grade copper mesh, known as a *Faraday cage*, embedded in the case to prevent signal leakage. This costly technology is found only in very high-security environments.

TEMPEST is now considered somewhat dated; newer technologies such as white noise and control zones are now used to control emanation security. White noise uses special devices that send out a stream of frequencies that makes it impossible for an attacker to distinguish the real information. *Control zones* are facilities whose walls, floors, and ceilings are designed to block electrical signals from leaving the zone.

Another term associated with this category of technology is *Van Eck phreaking*. That is the name given to eavesdropping on the contents of a CRT by emanation leakage. Although you might be wondering if all this is really true, it's worth noting that Cambridge University successfully demonstrated the technique against an LCD monitor in 2004.

> **ExamAlert**
>
> A CISSP candidate is expected to know the technologies and techniques implemented to prevent intruders from capturing and decoding information emanated through the airwaves. TEMPEST, white noise, and control zones are the three primary controls.

Web-based Vulnerabilities

Some attacks can occur on a client. As an example, an input validation attack occurs when client-side input is not properly validated. Application developers should never assume that users will input the correct data. A user bent on malicious activity will attempt to stretch the protocol or an application in an attempt to find possible vulnerabilities. Parameter problems are best solved by implementing pre-validation and post-validation controls. Pre-validation is implemented in the client but can be bypassed by using proxies and other injection techniques. Post-validation is performed to ensure the program's output is correct. Other security issues directly related to a lack of input validation include the following:

- ▶ **Cross-site scripting (XSS)**—An attack that exploits trust so that an attacker uses a web application to send malicious code to a web or application server.

- ▶ **Cross-site request forgery (CSRF)**—An attack that works by third-party redirection of static content so that unauthorized commands are transmitted from a user that the website trusts.

- ▶ **Direct OS commands**—The unauthorized execution of OS commands.

- ▶ **Directory traversal attack**—A technique that allows an attacker to move from one directory to another.

- ▶ **Unicode encoding**—Used to bypass security filters. One famous example used the Unicode string "%c0%af..%c0%af..".

- ▶ **URL encoding**—Used by an attacker to hide or execute an invalid application command via an HTTP request. As an example, www.knowthetrade.com%2fmalicious.js%22%3e%3c%2fscript%3e.

> **Tip**
>
> XSS and CSRF are sometimes confused, so just keep in mind that one key difference is that XSS executes code in a trusted context.

One of the things that makes a programmer's life difficult is that there is no such thing as trusted input. All input is potentially bad and must be verified. While the buffer overflow is the classic example of a poor input validation, these attacks have become much more complex: attackers have learned to insert malicious code within the buffer, instead of just throwing "garbage" (typing random gibberish) at an application to cause a buffer to overflow, which is just messy. There are also many tools available to launch these attacks, an example of which is illustrated in Figure 5.12.

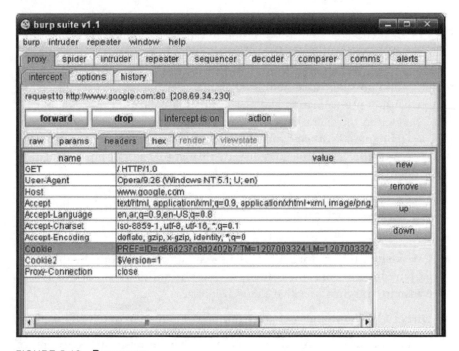

FIGURE 5.12   **Burp proxy.**

Some of the other techniques attackers use to exploit poor input validation:

▶ XML injection

▶ LDAP injection

▶ SQL injection

All of these are the same type of attack; they just target different platforms.

Databases are another common target of malformed input. An attacker can attempt to insert database or SQL commands to disrupt the normal operation of the database. This could cause the database to become unstable and leak information. This type of attack is known as *SQL injection*. The attacker searches for web pages in which to insert SQL commands. Attackers use logic such as ' (a single quote) to test the database for vulnerabilities. Responses such as the one shown in the following code give the attacker the feedback needed to know that the database is vulnerable to attack:

```
Microsoft OLE DB Provider for ODBC Drivers error '80040e07'
[Microsoft][ODBC SQL Server Driver][SQL Server]Syntax error converting
the nvarchar value 'sa login' to a column of data type int.
/index.asp, line 5
```

Although knowing the syntax and response used for a database attack is not required exam knowledge, they are useful to know as you attempt to secure your infrastructure.

> **Caution**
>
> SQL injection attacks are among the top attack vectors and responsible for a large number of attacks. CISSP candidates should understand their potential threat.

Injection attacks, such as SQL, LDAP, and others, can occur in many different programs and applications and share a common problem in that no separation exists between the application code and the input data. This makes it possible for attackers to run their code on the victim's system. Injection attacks require the following:

▶ **Footprinting**—Determining the technology that the web application is running.

▶ **Identifying**—User input points must be identified.

▶ **Testing**—User input that is susceptible to the attack must be tested.

▶ **Exploiting**—Placing extra bits of code into the input to execute commands on the victim's computer.

Mobile System Vulnerabilities

Mobile devices have increased in power, and now have the ability to handle many tasks that previously only desktops and laptops could perform. More and more employees are bringing their own mobile devices to work and using them on the corporate network. Some of the concerns the organization might have include:

- ▶ Eavesdropping on voice calls

- ▶ Mobile viruses and malware

- ▶ Plaintext storage on mobile device

- ▶ Ease of loss and theft of mobile device

- ▶ Camera phones' ability to photograph sensitive information

- ▶ Large storage ability, which can lead to data theft or exfiltration

- ▶ Software that exposes local device data such as names, email addresses, or phone numbers.

Bring your own technology (BYOT), a.k.a. bring your own device (BYOD), requires the organization to build in administrative and technical controls to govern how the devices can be used at work. Some of these basic controls might include:

- ▶ Only allowing managed devices to access to company resources

- ▶ User profiles and policies

- ▶ Mobile device management (MDM)

- ▶ Mobile application management (MAM)

- ▶ Remote wipe

- ▶ Encryption

- ▶ Password protection enforcement

- ▶ Limited password attempts

- ▶ Expanding endpoint security to mobile devices

- ▶ Malware detection and mitigation technology

Exam Prep Questions

1. Which of the following best describes a superscalar processor?

   ○ **A.** A superscalar processor can execute only one instruction at a time.

   ○ **B.** A superscalar processor has two large caches that are used as input and output buffers.

   ○ **C.** A superscalar processor can execute multiple instructions at the same time.

   ○ **D.** A superscalar processor has two large caches that are used as output buffers.

2. Which of the following are developed by programmers and used to allow the bypassing of normal processes during development, but are left in the software when it ships to the customer?

   ○ **A.** Back doors

   ○ **B.** Traps

   ○ **C.** Buffer overflows

   ○ **D.** Covert channels

3. Carl has noticed a high level of TCP traffic in and out of the network. After running a packet sniffer, he discovered malformed TCP ACK packets with unauthorized data. What has Carl discovered?

   ○ **A.** Buffer overflow attack

   ○ **B.** Asynchronous attack

   ○ **C.** Covert channel attack

   ○ **D.** DoS attack

4. You have been promoted to CISO and have instructed the security staff to harden user systems. You are concerned about employee web browsing activity and active web pages they may visit. You have instructed the staff that browsers should be patched and updated, cookie control options should be set, the execution of active code should be controlled, security protocols such as HTTPS, TLS, SSL3, and so on should be used, and to control what can be executed locally. You have informed the CIO that functionality must be sacrificed. What type of attack are you attempting to prevent?

   ○ **A.** SYN flood attack

   ○ **B.** Buffer overflow attack

   ○ **C.** TOC/TOU attack

   ○ **D.** Client side attack

5. Which of the following standards evaluates functionality and assurance separately?

   ○ **A.** TCSEC

   ○ **B.** TNI

   ○ **C.** ITSEC

   ○ **D.** CTCPEC

6. Which of the following was the first model developed that was based on confidentiality?

   ○ **A.** Bell-LaPadula

   ○ **B.** Biba

   ○ **C.** Clark-Wilson

   ○ **D.** Take-Grant

7. Which of the following models is integrity-based and was developed for commercial applications?

   ○ **A.** Information Flow

   ○ **B.** Clark-Wilson

   ○ **C.** Bell-LaPadula

   ○ **D.** Brewer-Nash

8. Which of the following does the Biba model address?

   ○ **A.** Focuses on internal threats

   ○ **B.** Focuses on external threats

   ○ **C.** Addresses confidentiality

   ○ **D.** Addresses availability

9. Which model is also known as the Chinese Wall model?

   ○ **A.** Biba

   ○ **B.** Take-Grant

   ○ **C.** Harrison-Ruzzo-Ullman

   ○ **D.** Brewer-Nash

10. Which of the following examines integrity and availability?

   ○ **A.** Orange Book

   ○ **B.** Brown Book

   ○ **C.** Red Book

   ○ **D.** Purple Book

11. What is the purpose of the * property in the Bell-LaPadula model?

- ○ **A.** No read up
- ○ **B.** No write up
- ○ **C.** No read down
- ○ **D.** No write down

12. What is the purpose of the simple integrity property of the Biba model?

- ○ **A.** No read up
- ○ **B.** No write up
- ○ **C.** No read down
- ○ **D.** No write down

13. Which of the following can be used to connect different MAC systems together?

- ○ **A.** Labels
- ○ **B.** Reference monitor
- ○ **C.** Controls
- ○ **D.** Guards

14. Which of the following security modes of operation best describes when a user has a valid need to know all data?

- ○ **A.** Dedicated
- ○ **B.** System High
- ○ **C.** Compartmented
- ○ **D.** Multilevel

15. Which of the following security models makes use of the TLC concept?

- ○ **A.** Biba
- ○ **B.** Clark-Wilson
- ○ **C.** Bell-LaPadula
- ○ **D.** Brewer Nash

Answers to Exam Prep Questions

1. **C.** A superscalar processor can execute multiple instructions at the same time. Answer A describes a scalar processor; it can execute only one instruction at a time. Answer B does not describe a superscalar processor because it does not have two large caches that are used as input and output buffers. Answer D is incorrect because a superscalar processor does not have two large caches that are used as output buffers.

2. **A.** Back doors, also referred to as *maintenance hooks*, are used by programmers during development to give them easy access into a piece of software. Answer B is incorrect because a trap is a message used by the Simple Network Management Protocol (SNMP) to report a serious condition to a management station. Answer C is incorrect because a buffer overflow occurs due to poor programming. Answer D is incorrect because a covert channel is a means of moving information in a manner in which it was not intended.

3. **C.** A covert channel is a means of moving information in a manner in which it was not intended. A buffer overflow occurs because of poor programming and usually results in program failure or the attacker's ability to execute his code; thus, answer A is incorrect. An asynchronous attack deals with performing an operation between the TOC and the TOU, so answer B is incorrect; whereas a DoS attack affects availability, not confidentiality, making answer D incorrect.

4. **D.** A client side attack is any attack carried out on the client device such as XSS. A is not correct because a SYN flood is when the three-way handshake is exploited; Answer B is incorrect as a buffer overflow is specifically where more data is placed into the buffer than what it can hold; and Answer C is not correct because a TOC/TOU is a timing attack.

5. **C.** ITSEC is a European standard that evaluates functionality and assurance separately. All other answers are incorrect because they do not separate the evaluation criteria. TCSEC is also known as the Orange Book, TNI is known as the Red Book, and CTCPEC is a Canadian assurance standard; therefore, answers A, B, and D are incorrect.

6. **A.** Bell-LaPadula was the first model developed that is based on confidentiality. Answers B, C, and D are incorrect: Biba and Clark-Wilson both deal with integrity, whereas the Take-Grant model is based on four basic operations.

7. **B.** Clark-Wilson was developed for commercial activities. This model dictates that the separation of duties must be enforced, subjects must access data through an application, and auditing is required. Answers A, C, and D are incorrect. The Information Flow model addresses the flow of information and can be used to protect integrity or confidentiality. Bell-LaPadula is an integrity model, and Brewer-Nash was developed to prevent conflict of interest.

8. **B.** The Biba model assumes that internal threats are being protected by good coding practices and, therefore, focuses on external threats. Answers A, C, and D are incorrect. Biba addresses only integrity, not availability or confidentiality.

9. **D.** The Brewer-Nash model is also known as the Chinese Wall model and was specifically developed to prevent conflicts of interest. Answers A, B, and C are incorrect because they do not fit the description. Biba is integrity-based,

Take-Grant is based on four modes, and Harrison-Ruzzo-Ullman defines how access rights can be changed, created, or deleted.

10. **C.** The Red Book examines integrity and availability of networked components. Answer A is incorrect because the Orange Book deals with confidentiality. Answer B is incorrect because the Brown Book is a guide to understanding trusted facility management. Answer D is incorrect because the Purple Book deals with database management.

11. **D.** The * property enforces "no write down" and is used to prevent someone with high clearance from writing data to a lower classification. Answers A, B, and C do not properly describe the Bell-LaPadula model's star property.

12. **C.** The purpose of the simple integrity property of the Biba model is to prevent someone from reading an object of lower integrity. This helps protect the integrity of sensitive information.

13. **D.** A guard is used to connect various MAC systems together and allow for communication between these systems. Answer A is incorrect because labels are associated with MAC systems but are not used to connect them together. Answer B is incorrect because the reference monitor is associated with the TCB. Answer C is incorrect because the term *controls* here is simply a distracter.

14. **A.** Out of the four modes listed, only the dedicated mode supports a valid need to know for all information on the system. Therefore, answers B, C, and D are incorrect.

15. **B.** The Clark-Wilson model was designed to support the goals of integrity and is focused on TLC, which stands for tampered, logged, and consistent. Answers A, C, and D are incorrect; Biba, Bell-LaPadula, and Brewer Nash are not associated with TLC.

Need to Know More?

Protection rings: duartes.org/gustavo/blog/post/cpu-rings-privilege-and-protection/

Common Criteria: www.niap-ccevs.org/cc-scheme/

Smashing the stack for fun and profit: insecure.org/stf/smashstack.html

Covert-timing-channel attacks: www.owasp.org/index.php/Covert_timing_channel

Java security: java.sun.com/javase/technologies/security/

How Windows measures up to TCSEC standards: technet.microsoft.com/en-us/library/cc767092.aspx

The Rainbow Series: csrc.nist.gov/publications/secpubs/rainbow/std001.txt

The Bell-LaPadula model: csrc.nist.gov/publications/secpubs/rainbow/std001.txt

ISO 17799: iso-17799.safemode.org/

CHAPTER 6

The Application and Use of Cryptography

Terms you'll need to understand:

▶ Symmetric encryption

▶ Asymmetric encryption

▶ Algorithm

▶ Key

▶ Encrypt

▶ Decrypt

▶ One-time pad

▶ Hashing

▶ Message digests

▶ Public key infrastructure (PKI)

▶ Zero knowledge proof

▶ Steganography

▶ IPSec

▶ Link encryption

▶ End-to-end encryption

Topics you'll need to master:

▶ Identify cryptographic attacks

▶ Describe the advantages and disadvantages of symmetric and asymmetric systems

▶ Define the structure of public key infrastructure

▶ Detail the components of IPSec

▶ Define the concept of nonrepudiation

▶ Know the importance of key security

▶ Be able to define the different modes of DES

▶ Know the Advanced Encryption Standard (AES)

▶ Determine the difference between block and stream ciphers

Introduction

To make things easier, the cryptographic topics covered in the Security Engineering, Asset Security, and Communications and Network Security domains are all in this one chapter. Before you start to sweat at the thought of learning how to create and decipher complex cryptographic systems, just keep in mind that the CISSP exam is a mile wide and an inch deep. CISSP test candidates won't need to know the complete inner workings of every cryptographic system ever designed.

The exam expects you to understand the application of cryptographic systems, their functions, and their strengths and weaknesses. The CISSP candidate is expected to know basic information about cryptographic systems such as symmetric algorithms, asymmetric algorithms, public key infrastructure, message digests, key management techniques, and alternatives to traditional cryptography, such as steganography.

Test candidates will need to know that cryptography is the science and study of secret writing. *Cryptography* is concerned with the ways in which information can be encoded or encrypted to prevent disclosure. It is tied closely to three basic pillars of security: integrity, nonrepudiation, and confidentiality. Cryptography offers its users the capability to protect the confidentiality of information in spite of eavesdropping or other interception techniques. Cryptography protects integrity by ensuring that only the individuals who have been authenticated and authorized can access and view the data. Cryptography provides integrity services by detecting the modification to, addition to, or deletion of data while in transit or in storage. Cryptography offers assurance that the true source of information can be determined and that nonrepudiation can be insured.

Cryptographic Basics

Cryptography is the process of transforming data so that it appears to be gibberish, except to those who know the key. Today, cryptographic systems are mandatory to protect email, corporate data, personal information, and electronic transactions.

To have a good understanding of cryptography, you should review how it relates to the foundations of security: privacy, authentication, integrity, and nonrepudiation.

> **Tip**
>
> One easy way to remember these foundations is to think of their initials: "PAIN."
> Not pain in the physical sense but "PAIN" in the sense of the four primary goals of
> cryptography: privacy, authentication, integrity, and nonrepudiation.

Confidentiality, or privacy, is the ability to guarantee that private information stays private. Cryptography provides confidentiality by transforming data. This transformation is called encryption. Encryption can protect confidentiality of information in storage or in transit. Just think about the CEO's laptop. If it is lost or stolen, what is really worth more: the laptop or information regarding next year's hot new product line? Information assets can be worth much more than the equipment on which they are stored. Hard disk encryption offers an easy way to protect information should equipment be lost, stolen, or accessed by unauthorized individuals.

Authentication has several roles. First, authentication is usually associated with message encryption. Authentication provides a way to ensure that data or programs have not been modified and really come from the source that you believe it to have come from. Authentication is also used to confirm a user's identity, and is part of the identification and authentication process. The most common implementation of identification and authentication is username and password. Most passwords are encrypted, but they do not have to be. Without encryption, the authentication process is very weak. FTP and Telnet are examples of weak authentication. With these protocols, usernames and passwords are passed in unencrypted or in the clear, and anyone with access to the communication stream can intercept and capture these cleartext passwords. VPNs (virtual private networks) also use authentication, but instead of a cleartext username and password, they normally use digital certificates and digital signatures to more accurately identify the user, and to protect the authentication process from spoofing.

Integrity is the assurance that information remains unaltered from the point it was created until it is received. If you're selling widgets on the Internet for $100 each, you will likely go broke if a criminal can change the posted price to $1 at checkout. Integrity is critical for the exchange of information, be it engaging in e-commerce, maintaining trade secrets, or supplying accurate military communications.

Nonrepudiation is the capability to verify proof of identity. Nonrepudiation is used to ensure that a sender of data is provided with proof of delivery, and that the recipient is assured of the sender's identity. Neither party should be able to deny having sent or received the data at a later date. In the days of face-to-face transactions, nonrepudiation was not as hard to prove. Today, the Internet makes many transactions faceless. You might never see the people that you deal with; therefore, nonrepudiation becomes all the more critical. Nonrepudiation is achieved through digital signatures, digital certificates, and message authentication codes (MACs).

To help make this chapter a little easier to digest, review the following basic terms that will be used throughout this chapter:

▶ **Plaintext / cleartext**—Text that is directly readable.

▶ **Encryption**—The transformation of cleartext into ciphertext

▶ **Ciphertext**—Text that has been rendered unreadable by encryption.

▶ **Cryptographic algorithm**—A set of mathematical procedures used to encrypt and decrypt data in a cryptographic system. As an example, a simple algorithm like Caesar's cipher might simply shift characters forward or backward three characters in the alphabet.

▶ **Cryptographic key**—A piece of information, also called a cryptovariable, that controls how a cryptographic algorithm functions. It can be used to control the transformation of plaintext to ciphertext, or ciphertext to plaintext. As an example, an algorithm that shifts characters might use a key of "+3" to shift characters forward by three positions. The word "cat" would be encrypted as "fdw" using this algorithm and key.

▶ **Symmetric cryptography**—Cryptography that uses a single key for both encryption and decryption.

▶ **Asymmetric cryptography**—Cryptography that uses a public key for encryption and a separate, private key for decryption. What the public key does, the private key can undo.

▶ **Cryptanalysis**—the art and science of breaking a cryptography system or obtaining the plaintext from ciphertext without a cryptographic key. It is used by governments, the military, enterprises, and malicious hackers to find weaknesses and crack cryptographic systems.

▶ **Message digest** or **Hash**—A fixed-length hex string used to uniquely identify a variable anount of data.

▶ **Digital signature**—A hash value that is encrypted with a sender's private key. It is used for authentication and integrity.

When symmetric encryption is used to convert plaintext into ciphertext, the transformation can be accomplished in two ways:

▶ **Block ciphers**—Ciphers that separate the message into blocks for encryption and decryption.

▶ **Stream ciphers**—Ciphers that divide the message into bits for encryption and decryption.

History of Encryption

Encryption dates back through the ages. The truth is that as long as there have been people, there have been secrets. One early system that was used by the ancient Greeks and the Spartans is called *scytale*. This system functioned by wrapping a strip of papyrus around a rod of fixed diameter on which a message was written. The recipient used a rod of the same diameter on which he wrapped the paper to read the message. If anyone intercepted the paper, it appeared as a meaningless letters.

Even Julius Caesar encrypted messages sent between himself and his trusted advisors. Although many might not consider it a robust method of encryption, Caesar's cipher worked by means of a simple substitution cipher. In *Caesar's cipher*, there was a plaintext alphabet and a ciphertext alphabet. The alphabets were arranged as shown in Figure 6.1.

Plain	A	B	C	D	E	F	G	H	I	J	K	L	M	N	O	P	Q	R	S	T	U	V	W	X	Y	Z
Cipher	D	E	F	G	H	I	J	K	L	M	N	O	P	Q	R	S	T	U	V	W	X	Y	Z	A	B	C

FIGURE 6.1   **Caesar's cipher.**

When Caesar was ready to send a message, it was encrypted by moving the text forward according to the key. If the key was 3 characters, for example, then the word "cat" would encrypt to "fdw". You can try this yourself by referring to Figure 6.1. Just look up each of the message's letters in the top row and write down the corresponding letter from the bottom row. Caesar's cipher is also known as a rotation cipher, and a key of three is called ROT3.

Ancient Hebrews used a similar cryptographic system called ATBASH that worked by replacing each letter used with another letter the same distance away from the end of the alphabet; *A* was sent as a *Z*, and *B* was sent as a *Y*, as illustrated in Figure 6.2.

```
A   B   C   D   E   F   G   H   I ...
|   |   |   |   |   |   |   |   |
Z   Y   X   W   T   S   R   Q   P ...
```

FIGURE 6.2 **ATBASH.**

More complicated substitution ciphers were developed through the Middle Ages as individuals became better at breaking simple encryption systems. In the ninth century, Abu al-Kindi published what is considered to be the first paper that discusses how to break cryptographic systems titled, "A Manuscript on Deciphering Cryptographic Messages." It deals with using frequency analysis to break cryptographic codes. *Frequency analysis* is the study of how frequent letters or groups of letters appear in ciphertext. Uncovered patterns can aid individuals in determining patterns and breaking the ciphertext.

As these early ciphers all had weaknesses, people worked to improve them. A *polyalphabetic cipher* makes use of more than one arrangement of the alphabet. The alphabetic cipher, also known as the Vigenère cipher, uses a single encryption/decryption chart shown here:

```
A B C D E F G H I J K L M N O P Q R S T U V W X Y Z
B C D E F G H I J K L M N O P Q R S T U V W X Y Z A
C D E F G H I J K L M N O P Q R S T U V W X Y Z A B
D E F G H I J K L M N O P Q R S T U V W X Y Z A B C
E F G H I J K L M N O P Q R S T U V W X Y Z A B C D
F G H I J K L M N O P Q R S T U V W X Y Z A B C D E
G H I J K L M N O P Q R S T U V W X Y Z A B C D E F
H I J K L M N O P Q R S T U V W X Y Z A B C D E F G
I J K L M N O P Q R S T U V W X Y Z A B C D E F G H
J K L M N O P Q R S T U V W X Y Z A B C D E F G H I
K L M N O P Q R S T U V W X Y Z A B C D E F G H I J
L M N O P Q R S T U V W X Y Z A B C D E F G H I J K
M N O P Q R S T U V W X Y Z A B C D E F G H I J K L
N O P Q R S T U V W X Y Z A B C D E F G H I J K L M
O P Q R S T U V W X Y Z A B C D E F G H I J K L M N
P Q R S T U V W X Y Z A B C D E F G H I J K L M N O
Q R S T U V W X Y Z A B C D E F G H I J K L M N O P
R S T U V W X Y Z A B C D E F G H I J K L M N O P Q
S T U V W X Y Z A B C D E F G H I J K L M N O P Q R
```

T U V W X Y Z A B C D E F G H I J K L M N O P Q R S

U V W X Y Z A B C D E F G H I J K L M N O P Q R S T

V W X Y Z A B C D E F G H I J K L M N O P Q R S T U

W X Y Z A B C D E F G H I J K L M N O P Q R S T U V

X Y Z A B C D E F G H I J K L M N O P Q R S T U V W

Y Z A B C D E F G H I J K L M N O P Q R S T U V W X

Z A B C D E F G H I J K L M N O P Q R S T U V W X Y

The chart is simply the alphabet written repeatedly for a total of 26 times. Each new line shifts the alphabet by one letter. You need a key to use the Vigenère system. Table 6.1 shows an example of a plaintext, key, and ciphertext using this method of encryption.

TABLE 6.1 **Vigenère Cipher**

Item	Value
Plaintext	Cryptorocks
Key	QUEEXAMCRAM
Ciphertext	Slctqocqtke

How does Vigenère encryption work? Note that the first letter of the plaintext is "C", and the first letter of the key is "Q". Compare the natural alphabet to the alphabet arrangement above that begins with "Q":

A B **C** D E F G H I J K L M N O P Q R S T U V W X Y Z

Q R **S** T U V W X Y Z A B C D E F G H I J K L M N O P

You can see that a plaintext "C" correlates to a ciphertext "S". Next, encrypt the second plaintext letter, "R", according to the alphabet that starts with the second letter of the key, "U":

A B C D E F G H I J K L M N O P Q **R** S T U V W X Y Z

U V W X Y Z A B C D E F G H I J K **L** M N O P Q R S T

Plaintext "R" becomes ciphertext "L". This process continues until the entire plaintext is encrypted. If the key is shorter than the plaintext (as it usually is), you start at the beginning of the key again.

Note that using a different key with the same algorithm would result in a completely different ciphertext.

> **Tip**
>
> The Caesar, ATBASH, and Vigenère ciphers are considered symmetric substitution ciphers that operate by replacing bits, bytes, or characters with alternative bits, bytes, or characters. Substitution ciphers are vulnerable to frequency analysis and are not considered secure.

Substitution ciphers use an encryption method to replace each character or bit of the plaintext message with a different character. The Caesar cipher is a basic example of a substitution cipher. Ciphers can also use transposition, which was the basis of the scytale cipher. Transposition ciphers use algorithms to rearrange the letters of a plaintext message. The result is a ciphertext message. The process of decryption reverses the encryption process to retrieve the original message. The transposition cipher is different in that the letters of the original message remain the same, but their positions are scrambled in an ordered way.

An example of this can be demonstrated in a simple column array transposition. The letters of the message are written in a rectangular array by rows and then read out by columns. Our message is CRYPTO IS MY FAVORITE SUBJECT. The message is written here in a 5 × 5 array as follows:

CRYPT

OISMY

FAVOR

ITESU

BJECT

To encrypt the message, each column is processed:

COFIB RIATJ YSVEE PMOSC TYRUT

The result is the ciphertext. Although it appears complex, a transposition cipher can easily be broken given enough time and resources.

> **Tip**
>
> Modern cryptographic systems no longer use simple substitutions or transpositions. However, these substitutions and transpositions are mixed together with other Boolean math operations to create sophisticated algorithms that result in the block and stream ciphers we use today. A block cipher such as Data Encryption Standard (DES) operates on fixed-length groups of bits. A stream cipher inputs and encrypts one bit at a time.

History offers many other examples of systems developed to act as codes and ciphers. One such example is the *concealment cipher*, which hides the message inside another message. One concealment cipher works by burying the intended message a word at a time inside an innocuous message. The intended message might be found as every third word in a sentence. An example can be seen in the letter received by Sir John Trevanion in the 1600s. Sir John was awaiting execution during the English civil war and was eager to escape his captors. The letter stated:

> Worthie Sir John: Hope, that is ye beste comfort of ye afflicted, cannot much, I fear me, help you now. That I would say to you, is this only: if ever I may be able to requite that I do owe you, stand not upon asking me. 'Tis not much that I can do: but what I can do, bee ye verie sure I wille. I knowe that, if dethe comes, if ordinary men fear it, it frights not you, accounting it for a high honor, to have such a rewarde of your loyalty. Pray yet that you may be spared this soe bitter, cup. I fear not that you will grudge any sufferings; only if bie submission you can turn them away, 'tis the part of a wise man. Tell me, an if you can, to do for you anythinge that you wolde have done. The general goes back on Wednesday. Restinge your servant to command. —R.T.

When the message is divided up and every third letter after a punctuation mark is read, it says:

Panel at east end of chapel slides

A somewhat similar technique is a book or running key cipher that uses references to pages, paragraphs, or works in a book. The running key cipher is a form of symmetric substitution cipher in which a text, typically from a book, is used to provide a very long key stream. Usually, the book or text would need to be agreed to ahead of time. These ciphers don't actually encrypt the message using modern mathematical operations, or even scramble the message with yesterday's techniques; however, they do hide the message from the unintended recipient. (A variation of this used to be seen in some computer games. To start the game, you had to input a certain word from a specific page of the game's printed manual. Without the manual, the game could not be started.)

Are any ciphers or codes unbreakable? The only known system unbreakable by brute force is a one-time pad called a Vernam cipher. (Think of a brute force attack as an exhaustive search of all possible keys that could be used in an algorithm, in an attempt to decrypt the message.) The one-time pad was created in 1917 while Gilbert Vernam was investigating methods to potentially improve the polyalphabetic cipher. The one-time pad is a plaintext combined with a random key. This cryptographic system relies on several mechanisms to work correctly. These include:

▶ The message and the key must be stored securely, and the key must be the same length or longer than the message.

▶ The key can only be used once.

▶ The key must be random.

▶ The key must be distributed by an out-of-band mechanism. *Out-of-band* means that communications are outside a previously established method of communication.

Tip

Another cryptographic advancement of the 20th century is the Feistel Network. A German-born cryptographer, Horst Feistel, is the creator of this cryptofunction, and it is the foundation of many symmetric key block ciphers, including DES, 3DES, CAST, and Skipjack. A key feature of the Feistel Network is that it uses the well-known round function.

The early twentieth century was dominated by mechanical encryption devices. Some examples include the German *Enigma machine*, which used a series of internal rotors to perform the encryption, and the *Japanese Purple Machine*. Such devices were developed in an attempt to counter the weaknesses of early substitution ciphers. Both systems were eventually broken. Today, the military, government, industry, and individuals use cryptographic systems. Cryptography is used by the movie industry for DVD and Blu-ray encryption, by Pretty Good Privacy (PGP) for email and file security, by Internet Protocol Security (IPSec) for data transfers, and so on.

In the United States, the National Security Agency (NSA) is responsible for cryptology and the creation and breaking of codes. Cryptography continues to advance; today new implementations are being created that are based on light. This is known as *quantum cryptography*. Quantum cryptography operates by securing optic communications by properties and phenomena of quantum physics.

Longest Running Suppressed Patent Application

Although many people are happy just to know enough about cryptographic processes to perform jobs and pass the CISSP exam, William Friedman always wanted to learn more. He made a career out of cryptography. He is considered one of the best cryptologists of all time. Friedman holds the record for longest running suppressed patent—originally requested in 1933 and finally granted in 2001. Friedman did a huge service to the United States by leading the team that broke the Japanese Purple Machine.

Friedman's role in cracking the encryption scheme used by the Japanese Purple Machine helped save lives and aided the Allies in winning WWII. Although Friedman never actually saw one of these devices, he was still able to lead his team in understanding how the device worked. This gave the United States the capability to decrypt many of the messages being sent by the Japanese. Many of his inventions and cryptographic systems were never patented because they were considered so significant that the release of any information about them might aid an enemy. Much of his work remains secret to this day. Before his death in the 1960s, the NSA went to his house to retrieve many of his personal writings. After his death, his remaining journals and writings were confiscated by the NSA on grounds of national secrecy.

Steganography

Steganography is an art of secret writing that dates back to the time of ancient Greece; the word derives from the Greek words for "covered" and "writing". The mechanism of modern steganography is to hide information by embedding it in a carrier file. Steganography took a big leap forward with the invention of computers, which made it possible for many different types of media to be used to hide information. The carrier file can be a graphic, an audio file, a document, or even a video.

Computer graphics such as bitmaps or image files are commonly used. To the viewer of the image, the picture remains the same, but in reality, information has been hidden in it. The hidden information can be plaintext, ciphertext, or other types of data.

> ### Note
>
> Hackers, terrorists, and others use steganography to move information from one location to another without detection. *USA Today* reported after 9/11 that governmental agencies believed that Al Qaeda operatives used steganography to hide illicit communications.

With steganography, someone could be looking right at some type of covert message and never even realize it! And if the data is encrypted, this dual level of protection vastly increases the security of the hidden object; even if someone discovers the existence of the hidden message, the encryption method to view the contents must be overcome. An example of steganography can be seen in Figure 6.3. I have used an image of one of my prized 8-track players to demonstrate the concept.

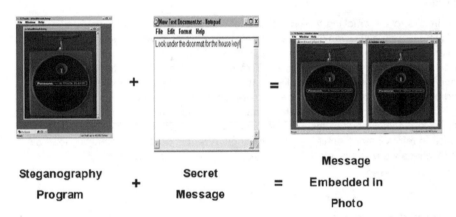

Steganography Program + **Secret Message** = **Message Embedded in Photo**

FIGURE 6.3 **Steganography in action.**

Steganography Operation

There are three basic components used in steganography.

▶ The payload—The data or information that is to be hidden and transmitted.

▶ The carrier or cover—The file or container, such as an image, audio file, document, or video file, that is to contain the hidden payload.

▶ The stegomedium—The final file that contains the hidden payload.

To hide information in an image using steganography you will need to alter the image only slightly. Computer-based images are composed of many dots, called pixels. Each pixel has a color encoded as a set of three brightness values: one for red light, one for green, and one for blue. These brightness values can range from a minimum of 0 to a maximum of 255. These values can be altered slightly to hold information in a way that is undetectable to humans.

As an example, let's say an image has a pixel with brightness values of 38, 74, 130. These correspond to binary values as shown:

38	74	130
00100110	01001010	10000010

To hide the decimal value 7 (binary 111) here, you could simply change the least significant bit of each byte to equal the binary digits 111:

00100111	01001011	10000011
39	75	131

Could a viewer recognize the difference? Most likely not because the actual image file has changed very little. Most monitors offer at least 32-bit color, which equals about four billion color shades. The human eye is not capable of detecting tiny changes from one shade to the next. The size of the payload that can be successfully hidden depends on the size of the carrier.

Steganography in a sound file works in a similar fashion because sound is also represented digitally.

In reality, steganography algorithms can be much more complex, and to further protect the hidden content, you could encrypt the data before encoding it into an image file. Such a technique could be used to make it much harder for a third party to uncover the encrypted data.

Digital Watermark

The most common commercial application of steganography is the use of digital *watermark*. A digital watermark acts as a type of digital fingerprint and can verify proof of source. It's a way to identify the copyright owner, the creator of the work, authorized consumers, and so on. Steganography is perfectly suited for this purpose because a digital watermark should be invisible and permanently embedded into digital data for copyright protection. The importance of digital watermarks cannot be overstated because the Internet makes it so easy for someone to steal and reproduce protected assets; violations occur at an alarming rate. Proprietary information is copied, recopied, and duplicated with amazing speed.

Digital watermarks can be used in cases of intellectual property theft to show proof of ownership. Adobe Photoshop actually includes the capability to add a watermark. Its technology is called Digimarc. It is designed to help artists determine whether their art was stolen. Other applications include marking files such as music when they are prereleased. This allows the identification of the individuals that violate their nondisclosure agreements by releasing the work, using peer-to-peer networks, or other unauthorized sources.

> **Note**
>
> For a good example of watermarking, look no further than the Academy Awards. Individuals that vote on movies for the awards are sent high-quality Blu-ray/DVDs as a convenience so that voters can watch the required movies at home before filling out their ballots. In recent years, screeners have been issued with watermarks to track which screeners release films or provide illegal copies to others. www.afterdawn.com/news/archive/8757.cfm.

Algorithms

An *algorithm* is a set of rules used to encrypt and decrypt data. It's the set of instructions that will be used with the cryptographic key to encrypt plaintext data. Plaintext data encrypted with different keys or with dissimilar algorithms will produce different ciphertext.

Not all cryptosystems are of the same strength. For example, Caesar might have thought his system of encryption was quite strong, but it would be seen as insecure today. How strong should an encryption be? The strength of a cryptosystem relies on the strength of the algorithm itself because a flawed algorithm can be broken.

But the strength of the encryption also rests on the size and complexity of the key. As an example, imagine that you're contemplating buying a combination lock. One lock has three digits, whereas the other has four. Which would you choose? Consider that there are 1,000 possible combinations for the three-digit lock, but 10,000 possible combinations for the four-digit lock. As you can see, just a one-digit increase can create a significant difference. The more possible keys or combinations there are, the longer it takes an attacker to guess the right key.

The size of the key, be it four possible numbers, seven possible numbers, or even sixty-four possible numbers, is known as the key space. In the world of cryptography, key spaces are defined by the number of bits. So, a 64-bit key has a key space of 2 to the power of 64, or 18,446,744,073,709,551,616.

Keys must remain secret. You could buy a seven-digit combination lock, but it would do you little good if everyone knew the combination was your phone number.

> **Note**
>
> DES uses a 64-bit key with every 8th bit being a parity bit. With all three keys being different, 3DES (also called Triple-DES) has a key strength of 168 bits and is the last official version.

The final consideration in the choice of a cryptosystem is the value of the data. Highly valued data requires more protection than data that has little value. Therefore, more valuable information needs stronger algorithms, larger keys, and more frequent key exchange to protect against attacks.

Cryptographic systems might make use of a *nonce*. A nonce is a number generated as randomly as possible and used once. These *pseudorandom* numbers are different each time one is generated. An *initialization vector* (IV) is an example of a nonce. An IV can be added to a key and used to force creation of unique ciphertext even when encrypting the same message with the same cipher and the same key.

Modern cryptographic systems use two types of algorithms for encrypting and decrypting data:

▶ *Symmetric algorithms* use the same key to encrypt and decrypt data.

▶ *Asymmetric algorithms* use different keys, one for encryption and the other for decryption.

Before examining each of these in more detail, review Table 6.2, which highlights some of the key advantages and disadvantages of each style of algorithm.

TABLE 6.2 **Symmetric and Asymmetric Algorithms**

Encryption Type	Advantage	Disadvantage
Symmetric	Faster than asymmetric	Key distribution
		Provides only confidentiality
Asymmetric	Easy key exchange can provide confidentiality, authentication, and nonrepudiation	Slower than symmetric
		Requires larger keys

ExamAlert

Make sure you know the differences between symmetric and asymmetric encryption for the exam.

Cipher Types and Methods

Symmetric encryption methods includes block and stream ciphers. *Block ciphers* operate on blocks or fixed-size chunks of data. The transposition cipher previously discussed is an example of a block cipher. The data was written into a column and then divided into five-character blocks. Most modern encryption algorithms implement some type of block cipher and 64-bit blocks are a commonly used size. Block ciphers are widely used in software products. During the encryption and decryption process, the message is divided into blocks of bits. These blocks are then put through Boolean mathematical functions resulting in the following:

▶ **Confusion**—Occurs from substitution type operations that create a complicated relationship between the plain text and the key so that an attacker can't alter the ciphertext to determine the key.

▶ **Diffusion**—Occurs from transposition type operations that shift pieces of the plain text multiple times. The result is that changes are spread throughout the ciphertext.

The *substitution box* (s-box) performs a series of substitutions, transpositions, and exclusive-or (XOR) operations to obscure the relationship between the plaintext and the ciphertext. When properly implemented, s-boxes are designed to defeat cryptanalysis. An s-box takes a number of input bits (m) and transforms them into some number of output bits (n). S-boxes are implemented as a type of lookup table and used with symmetric encryption systems such as Data Encryption Standard (DES).

A *stream cipher* encrypts a stream of data one bit at a time. To accomplish this, a one-time pad is created from the encryption engine. This one-time pad is a key-stream, and it is XORed with the plaintext data stream (one bit at a time) to result in ciphertext. Stream ciphers differ from each other in the engine they use to create the one-time pad; the engine receives the symmetric key as input to cause the creation of a unique key stream. The XOR operation is a Boolean math function that says when two bits are combined, if either one or the other is a value of one, a one will result; but if both of the bits are the same, a zero will result. Refer to Table 6.3 for a list of commonly used Boolean operators:

TABLE 6.3 **Boolean Operators**

Inputs	AND	OR	NAND	NOR	XOR
0 0	0	0	1	1	0
0 1	0	1	1	0	1
1 0	0	1	1	0	1
1 1	1	1	0	0	0

Stream ciphers operate at a higher speed than block ciphers and, in theory, are well suited for hardware implementation.

Symmetric Encryption

In *symmetric encryption*, a single shared secret key is used for both the encryption and the decryption, as shown in Figure 6.4. The key is referred to as a dual-use key because it is used to lock and unlock data. Symmetric encryption is the oldest form of encryption; scytale and Caesar's cipher are examples of it. Symmetric encryption provides confidentiality by keeping individuals who do not have the key from knowing the true contents of the message.

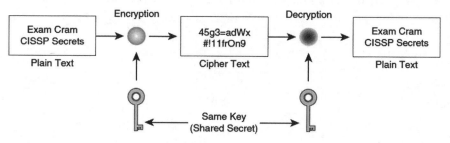

FIGURE 6.4 **Symmetric encryption.**

The simple diagram in Figure 6.4 shows the symmetric encryption process. Plaintext is encrypted with the single shared key resulting in ciphertext; the ciphertext is then transmitted to the message's recipient, who reverses the process to decrypt the message. Symmetric encryption and decryption are fast, and symmetric encryption is very hard to break if a large key is used. However, it has three significant disadvantages:

▶ Distribution of the symmetric key

▶ Key management

▶ Provides only for confidentiality

Distribution of the symmetric key is the most serious deficiency with symmetric encryption. For symmetric encryption to be effective, there must be a secure method in which to transfer keys. In our modern world, there needs to be some type of out-of-band transmission. Just think about it: If Bob wants to send Alice a secret message but is afraid that Eavesdropper Eve can monitor their communication, how can he send the message? If the key is sent in cleartext, Eve can intercept it. Bob could deliver the key in person, mail it, or even send a courier. All these methods are highly impractical in our world of e-commerce and electronic communication.

In addition to the problem of key exchange, there is also a key management problem. If, for example, you had 10 people who all needed to communicate with each other in complete confidentiality, you would require 45 keys for them. That's right, 45 keys! The formula used to calculate the number of keys needed in symmetric encryption is:

$$N(N-1)/2 = 10(10-1)/2 = 45 \text{ keys}$$

Table 6.4 shows how the number of keys climbs as users increase.

TABLE 6.4 **Symmetric and Asymmetric Systems Compared**

Users	Number of Keys
5	10
10	45
100	4,950
1000	499,500

The third and final problem with symmetric encryption is that it provides only for confidentiality. The ultimate goal within cryptography is to supply confidentiality, integrity, authenticity, and nonrepudiation.

You might be thinking that I have offered you nothing but bad news about symmetric encryption, but recall, it does have excellent features that make it the perfect choice for providing confidentiality. SP800-131A specifies encryption key lengths. Some examples of symmetric algorithms include:

▶ **DES**—Data Encryption Standard was once the most commonly used symmetric algorithm. It has been officially retired by NIST. 3DES is still allowed for use while all other DES implementations are no longer allowed.

▶ **Blowfish**—A general-purpose symmetric algorithm intended as a replacement for DES. Blowfish has a variable block size and a key size of 32 bits up to 448 bits.

▶ **Twofish**—A block cipher that operates on 128-bit blocks of data and is capable of using cryptographic keys up to 256 bits in length.

▶ **IDEA**—International Data Encryption Algorithm is a block cipher that uses a 128-bit key to encrypt 64-bit blocks of plaintext. It is patented, but free for noncommercial use, and is used by PGP.

▶ **Rijndael**—This is a block cipher adopted as the Advanced Encryption Standard (AES) by the United States government to replace DES. Although Rijndael supports multiple block sizes, as AES, the block size is fixed at 128 bits. There are three approved key lengths—128, 192, and 256.

▶ **RC4**—Rivest Cipher 4 is a stream-based cipher. Stream ciphers treat the data as a stream of bits.

▶ **RC5**—RC5, or Rivest Cipher 5, is a fast block cipher. It is different from other symmetric algorithms in that it supports a variable block size, a variable key size, and a variable number of rounds. Allowable choices for the block size are 32, 64, and 128 bits. The number of rounds can range from 0 to 255 and the key can range up to 2,040 bits.

▶ **SAFER**—Secure and Fast Encryption Routine is a block-based cipher that processes data in blocks of 64 and 128 bits.

▶ **MARS**—A candidate for AES that was developed by IBM. MARS is a block cipher that has a 128-bit block size and a key length between 128 and 448 bits.

▶ **CAST**—Carlisle Adams/Stafford Tavares is a 128- or 256-bit block cipher that was a candidate for AES.

▶ **Skipjack**—Promoted by the NSA. Skipjack uses an 80-bit key, supports the same four modes of operation as DES, and operates on 64-bit blocks of text. Skipjack faced public opposition because it was developed so that the government could maintain information enabling legal authorities (with a search warrant or approval of the court) to reconstruct a Skipjack access key and decrypt private communications between affected parties.

ExamAlert

Be sure to take your time to review the various encryption types, block sizes, and key lengths; you can expect to see these items on the exam. You will be expected to know some of these algorithms that are discussed in detail in the following section. Others may simply be used as distractors on the exam.

To provide authentication from cryptography, you must turn to asymmetric encryption. But, before discussing asymmetric encryption, the sections that follow complete the discussion of DES and a couple of other popular symmetric encryption methods.

Data Encryption Standard

DES grew out of an early 1970s project originally developed by IBM. IBM and NIST modified IBM's original encryption standard, known as Lucifer, to use a 56-bit key. This revised standard was endorsed by the NSA, named DES, and published in 1977. It was released as an American National Standards Institute (ANSI) standard in 1981.

DES uses a 64-bit block to process 64 bits of plaintext at a time, and outputs 64-bit blocks of ciphertext. As mentioned, DES uses a 64-bit key (with every 8th bit being ignored) and has the following modes of operation:

▶ Electronic Codebook (ECB) mode

▶ Cipher Block Chaining (CBC) mode

▶ Cipher Feedback (CFB) mode

▶ Output Feedback (OFB) mode

▶ Counter (CTR) mode

ExamAlert

These modes of operation can be applied to any symmetric key block cipher, such as DES, 3DES, and AES. You will need to know these for the exam.

The written standard reports the DES key to be 64 bits, but 8 bits are actually used for parity to ensure the integrity of the remaining 56 bits. Therefore, in terms of encryption strength, the key is really only 56 bits long. Each 64-bit plaintext block is separated into two 32-bit blocks, and then processed by this 56-bit key. The processing submits the plaintext to 16 rounds of transpositions and substitutions.

ExamAlert

Keep in mind that while DES operates on 64-bit blocks, the key has an effective length of only 56 bits.

Electronic Codebook Mode

ECB is the native encryption mode of DES. As with all modes, if the last block is not full, padding is added to make the cleartext a full block. Although ECB produces the highest throughput, it is also the easiest form of DES encryption to break. If used with large amounts of data, it can be easily attacked because identical plaintext, when encrypted with the same key, will always produce the same ciphertext. ECB mode is appropriate only when used on small amounts of data. Figure 6.5 illustrates an example of ECB.

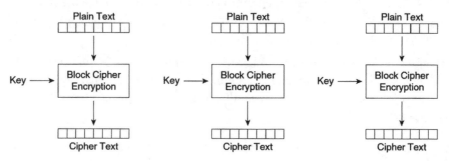

FIGURE 6.5   **DES ECB encryption.**

> **Tip**
>
> When using ECB, a given block of plaintext encrypted with a given key will always give the same ciphertext. ECB is the weakest form of DES.

Cipher Block Chaining Mode

The CBC mode of DES is widely used and is similar to ECB. CBC processes 64-bit blocks of data but inserts some of the ciphertext created from each block into the next block. This process is called *chaining*, and is accomplished by using the XOR operation. This mode of DES makes the ciphertext more secure and less susceptible to cracking. CBC mode will experience a slight risk of propagating transmission errors upon reception. Any error experienced will be propagated into the decryption of the subsequent block of receipt. This can make it impossible to decrypt that block and the following blocks as well.

Cipher Feedback Mode

CFB is implemented using a small block size (of one bit to one byte) so that streaming data can be encrypted without waiting for 64 bits to accrue. The resulting effect is that CFB behaves as a stream cipher. It is similar to CBC in that previously generated ciphertext is added to subsequent blocks. And, as with CBC, errors and corruption during transmission can propagate through the decryption process on the receiving side.

Output Feedback Mode

OFB also emulates a stream cipher. Unlike CFB, however, OFB feeds the plaintext of the data stream back into the next block to be encrypted. Therefore, transmission errors do not propagate throughout the decryption process. An initialization vector is used to create the seed value for the first encrypted block. DES XORs the plaintext with a seed value to be applied with subsequent data.

There is a derivative mode of OFB known as counter mode. *Counter mode* implements DES as a stream cipher and produces a ciphertext that does not repeat for long periods. Figure 6.6 illustrates an example of DES OFB encryption.

> **Tip**
>
> Although DES remained secure for many years, in 1998 the Electronic Frontier Foundation (EFF) was able to crack DES by brute force in about 23 hours. When DES was officially retired, it was recommended that Triple-DES (3DES) be used to ensure security. Triple-DES has since been replaced by AES.

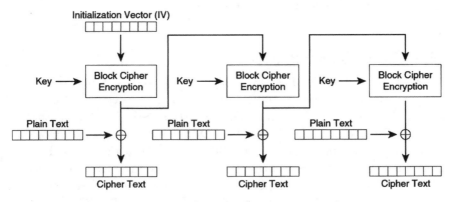

FIGURE 6.6 **DES OFB encryption.**

Counter Mode

Counter mode also implements a block cipher into a stream cipher and adds a counter to the process. The counter is a function which produces a sequence which will not repeat for a long time. The counter value gets combined with an initialization vector to produce the input into the symmetric key block cipher. This value is then encrypted through the block cipher using the symmetric key. Counter mode is designed for operation on a multi-processor machine where blocks can be encrypted in parallel, as shown in Figure 6.7.

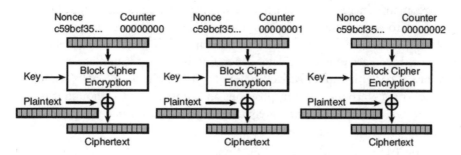

Counter (CTR) mode encryption

FIGURE 6.7   Counter mode encryption.

Triple-DES

Before jumping into the details of Triple-DES, some of you must be wondering why Triple-DES was even invented. DES was adopted with a five-year certification, and needed to be recertified every five years. While initially passing without any problems, DES begin to encounter problems during the 1987 recertification. By 1993, NIST stated that DES was beginning to outlive its usefulness and began looking for candidates to replace it. The new standard was to be referred to as the Advanced Encryption Standard (AES). Why the change? Well, DES had become the victim of increased computing power. Just as Moore's Law had predicted, the number of transistors per square inch doubled every 18 to 24 months, and so did processing power. The result of this is that an encryption standard that originally required years to brute force was becoming dramatically easier to attack. The final demise of DES came in 1998, when the Electronic Frontier Foundation (EFF) was able to crack DES by brute force in about 23 hours. The actual attack used distributed computing involving over 100,000 computers. Although DES had been resistant to cracking for many years, the EFF project demonstrated the need for stronger algorithms.

Although AES was to be the long-term replacement, the government had not chosen a cipher to put behind the label of AES. Another temporary solution was needed to fill the gap before AES could be deployed. Some thought that

Double-DES might be used. After all, Double-DES could have a 112-bit key! However, cryptanalysis proved that Double-DES was no more secure than DES; it requires the same work factor to crack as DES. Double-DES is also susceptible to a meet-in-the-middle attack.

But a geometric increase in performance was provided by using Triple-DES. Therefore, to extend the usefulness of the DES encryption standard, Triple-DES was seen as a stopgap solution. Triple-DES (3DES) can make use of two or three keys to encrypt data, depending on how it is implemented; therefore, it has either an effective key length of 112 bits or 168 bits. Triple-DES performs 48 rounds of transpositions and substitutions. Although it is much more secure, it is approximately three times as slow as 56-bit DES. 3DES can be implemented in several ways:

▶ **DES EEE2 uses two keys**—The first key is reused during the third round of encryption. The encryption process is performed three times (encrypt, encrypt, encrypt).

▶ **DES EDE2 uses two keys**—Again, the first key is reused during the third round of encryption. Unlike DES EEE2, DES EDE2 encrypts, decrypts, and then encrypts.

▶ **DES EEE3 uses three keys and performs the encryption process three times, each time encrypting**—Sometimes, you might see the specifics of these ciphers mathematically summarized. For example, when discussing DES-EEE3 using E(K,P), where E refers to the encryption of plaintext P with key K, the process is summarized as E(K3,E(K2,E(K1,P))).

▶ **DES EDE3 uses three keys but operates by encrypting, decrypting, and then encrypting the data**—Figure 6.8 illustrates an example of EDE3.

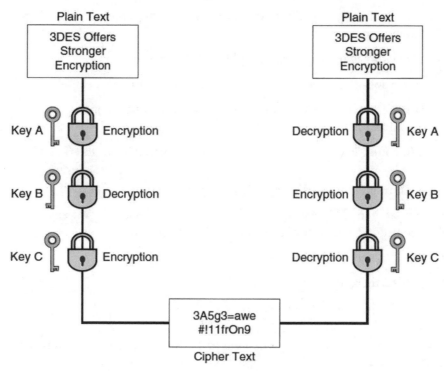

FIGURE 6.8 **3DES EDE3.**

Advanced Encryption Standard (AES)

In 2002, NIST decided on the replacement for DES, to be known as AES. Several algorithms were examined. *Rijndael* (which sounds like "rain doll") was the chosen algorithm. Its name derives from its two developers: Vincent Rijmen and Joan Daemen. It is considered a fast, simple, robust encryption mechanism. AES is likely the most important symmetric encryption standard today. It is widely used and commonly found in wireless access points and other products. Rijndael is also known to stand up well to various types of attacks. The Rijndael algorithm uses three layers of transformations to encrypt/decrypt blocks of message text:

▶ Linear mix transform

▶ Nonlinear transform

▶ Key addition transform

It also uses a four-step, parallel series of rounds. The steps performed during each round are

▶ **Byte sub**—Each byte is replaced by an S-box substitution.

▶ **Shift row**—Bytes are arranged in a rectangular matrix and shifted.

▶ **Mix column**—Matrix multiplication is performed based on the arranged rectangle.

▶ **Add round key**—Each byte of the state is combined with the round key.

On the last round, the fourth step is bypassed and the first is repeated.

Rijndael is an iterated block cipher, and as developed, it supports variable key and block lengths of 128, 192, or 256 bits. If both key and block size are

▶ 128-bit, there are 10 rounds.

▶ 192-bit, there are 12 rounds.

▶ 256-bit, there are 14 rounds.

As specified in the standard for becoming AES, Rijndael is now fixed in block size of 128 but can still deploy multiple key lengths.

International Data Encryption Algorithm

IDEA is a 64-bit block cipher that uses a 128-bit key. Although it has been patented by a Swiss company, it is freely available for noncommercial use. It is considered a secure encryption standard and there have been no known attacks against it. It operates in four distinct modes similar to DES. At one time, it was thought that IDEA would replace DES, but patent fees prevented that from happening.

Rivest Cipher Algorithms

Rivest cipher is a general term for the family of ciphers all designed by Ron Rivest. These include RC2, RC4, RC5, and RC6. Ron Rivest is one of the creators of RSA. RC1 was never released, and RC3 was broken by cryptanalysis before its release.

RC2 is an early algorithm in the series. It features a variable key-size, 64-bit block cipher that can be used as a drop-in substitute for DES.

RC4 is a fast stream cipher, faster than block mode ciphers, and was widely used. It was especially suitable for low power devices. The 40-bit version is used in Wi-Fi's Wired Equivalent Privacy (WEP). Although only 40-bit keys (together with a 24-bit IV, creating 64-bit WEP) were specified by the 802.11 standard, many vendors tried to strengthen the encryption by a de facto deployment of a 104-bit key (with the 24-bit IV, making 128-bit WEP).

RC5 is a block-based cipher in which the number of rounds can range from 0 to 255 and the key can range from 0 bits to 2,048 bits. RC6 is similar; it uses a variable key size and key rounds. RC6 added two features (integer multiplication and four 4-bit working registers) not found in RC5.

Asymmetric Encryption

Asymmetric encryption, known as *public* or *private key cryptography*, is unlike symmetric encryption in that it uses two unique keys, as shown in Figure 6.9. What one key encrypts requires the other key to decrypt. One of the greatest benefits offered by asymmetric encryption is that it overcomes one of the big barriers of symmetric encryption: key distribution.

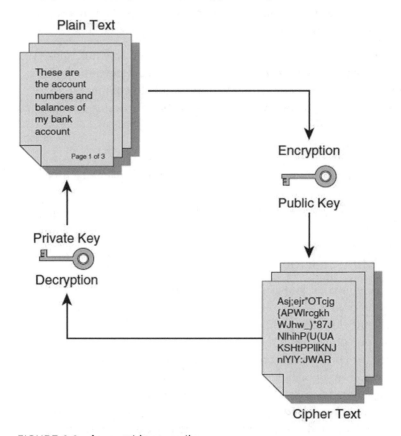

FIGURE 6.9 **Asymmetric encryption.**

Here's how asymmetric encryptions functions: Imagine that you want to send a client a message. You use your client's public key to encrypt the message. When your client receives the message, he uses his private key to decrypt it. The important concepts here are that if the message is encrypted with the public key, only the matching private key will decrypt it. The private key, by definition, is generally kept secret, whereas the public key can be given to anyone. If properly designed, it should not be possible for someone to easily deduce a key pair's private key from the public key.

Cryptographic systems can also make use of *zero knowledge proof*. This concept allows you to prove your knowledge without revealing the fact to a third party. For example, if someone encrypts with the private key it can be decrypted with the public key. This would permit a perfect check of authenticity. Asymmetric encryption provided the mechanism for accomplishing this concept. It is possible for the holder of a private key to prove they hold that key without ever disclosing the contents to anyone. Dr. W. Diffie and Dr. M. E. Hellman (discussed next) used this concept to permit creation of a trusted session key while communicating across an untrusted communication path. And, presto, key distribution was solved.

Public key cryptography is made possible by the use of one-way functions. A one-way function, known as a *trap door*, is a mathematical calculation that is easy to compute in one direction, yet next to impossible to compute in the other. Depending on the type of asymmetric encryption used, this calculation involves one of the following:

▶ Manipulating discrete logarithms

▶ Factoring large composite numbers into their original prime factors

As an example of the trap door function, consider an implementation that uses factoring. If you are given two large prime numbers such as 387 and 283, it is easy to multiply them together and get 109,521. However, if you are given only the product 109,521, it will take a while to find the factors.

As you can see, anyone that knows the trap door can perform the function easily in both directions, but anyone lacking the trap door can perform the function in only one direction. Trap door functions are used in their forward direction when someone is using the public key function; the forward direction is used for encryption, verification of digital signatures, and receipt of symmetric keys. Trap door functions are used in the inverse direction when someone is using the private key function; the inverse direction is used for decryption, generation of digital signatures, and transmission of symmetric keys. Properly implemented, anyone with a private key can generate its public pair, but no one with a public key can easily derive its private pair. We have Dr. W. Diffie and Dr. M. E. Hellman to thank for helping develop public key encryption; they released the first key-exchange protocol in 1976.

Diffie-Hellman

Diffie-Hellman was the first public key-exchange algorithm. It was developed only for key exchange, not for data encryption, or digital signatures. The Diffie-Hellman protocol allows two users to exchange a secret key over an insecure medium without any prior secrets.

Although in-depth knowledge of Diffie-Hellman's operation is not necessary for the CISSP exam, its operation is classic and worth review for anyone interested in the working of cryptographic systems. Diffie-Hellman has two system parameters: p and g. Both parameters are public and can be used by all the system's users. Parameter p is a prime number and parameter g, which is usually called a *generator*, is an integer less than p that has the following property: For every number n between 1 and $p-1$ inclusive, there is a power k of g such that $g^k = n \bmod p$. For example, when given the following public parameters:

p = Prime number

g = Generator

These values are used to generate the function $y = g^x \bmod p$. With this function, Alice and Bob can securely exchange a previously unshared secret (symmetric) key as follows:

Alice can use a private value a, which only she holds, to calculate

$$y^a = g^a \bmod p$$

Bob can use a private value b, which only he holds, to calculate

$$y^b = g^b \bmod p$$

Alice can now send y^a (as Alice's nonce, or A-nonce) to Bob, and Bob can send y^b (as Bob's nonce, or B-nonce) to Alice. Again, starting with Alice, she can again use her private value A on the B-nonce. Her result will be $(y^b)^a$ or

$$g^{ba} \bmod p$$

Similarly, with his private value, b, Bob can calculate $(y^a)^b$ from the received A-nonce:

$$g^{ab} \bmod p$$

But guess what: Mathematically, $g^{ba} \bmod p$ and $g^{ab} \bmod p$ are equivalent. So, in fact, Bob and Alice have just, securely, exchanged a new secret key.

Diffie-Hellman is vulnerable to man-in-the-middle attacks because the key exchange does not authenticate the participants. To prove authenticity, digital signatures and digital certificates by accepting someone's public key in advance, sometimes within a PKI, should be used. Diffie-Hellman is used in conjunction with several authentication methods including the Internet Key Exchange (IKE) component of IPSec. The following list provides some information you should know about Diffie-Hellman:

▶ First asymmetric algorithm

▶ Provides key exchange services

▶ Considered a key agreement protocol

▶ Operates by means of discrete logarithms

RSA

RSA was developed in 1977 by Ron Rivest, Adi Shamir, and Len Adleman at MIT. The cipher's name is based on their initials. Although RSA is much slower than symmetric encryption cryptosystems, it offers symmetric key exchange and is considered very secure. RSA is based on factoring prime numbers, but to be secure, has to use prime numbers whose product is much larger that 129 digits. Decimal numbers less than 130 digits have been factored using a number field sieve algorithm. RSA public and private key generation will also not be required knowledge for the CISSP exam.

Typically, the plaintext will be broken into equal-length blocks, each with fewer digits than n, and each block will be encrypted and decrypted. Cryptanalysts or anyone attempting to crack RSA would be left with the difficult challenge of factoring a large integer into its two factors. Cracking the key would require an extraordinary amount of computer processing power and time. RSA supports a key size up to 2,048 bits.

The RSA algorithm has become the de facto standard for industrial-strength encryption, especially since the patent expired in 2000. It has been built into many protocols, firmware, and software products such as Microsoft's Internet Explorer, Edge, Google Chrome, and Mozilla's Firefox.

> **Note**
>
> LUC is an alternative to RSA. Although not widely used, it was invented in 1991 and uses Lucas functions.

> **Note**
>
> XTR is a public key cryptosystem developed by Arjen Lenstra and Eric Verheul that is also based on finite fields and discrete logs, and is seen as a generic superset function for all discrete log functions.

El Gamal

El Gamal is an extension of the Diffie-Hellman key exchange. It can be used for digital signatures, key exchange, and encryption. El Gamal consists of three discrete components including a key generator, an encryption algorithm, and a decryption algorithm. It was released in 1985 and its security rests in part on the difficulty of solving the discrete logarithm problems.

Elliptical Curve Cryptosystem

ECC is considered more secure because elliptic curve systems are harder to crack than those based on discrete log problems. Elliptic curves are usually defined over finite fields such as real and rational numbers and implemented analogously to the discrete logarithm problem. An elliptic curve is defined by the following equation:

$y^2 = x^3 + ax + b$, along with a single point O, the point at infinity

The space of the elliptic curve has properties where

▶ Addition is the counterpart of modular multiplication.

▶ Multiplication is the counterpart of modular exponentiation.

Thus, given two points, P and R, on an elliptic curve where P = KR, finding K is known as the *elliptic curve discrete logarithm problem*. ECC is fast. According to RFC 4492, a 163-bit key used in ECC has similar cryptographic strength to a 1,024-bit key used in the RSA algorithm and, as such, is being implemented in smaller, less-powerful devices such as smart phones, tablets, smartcards, and other handheld devices.

Merkle-Hellman Knapsack

Merkle-Hellman Knapsack (Knapsack) is an asymmetric algorithm based on fixed weights. Although this system was popular for a while, it has fallen from favor because it was broken in 1982.

ExamAlert

Before attempting the exam, it is prudent that you know which categories each of the asymmetric algorithms discussed fit into. Take some time to review the differences. The following shows how each functions:

▶ Functions by using a discrete logarithm in a finite field: Diffie-Hellman; El Gamal

▶ Functions by the product of large prime numbers: RSA

▶ Functions by means of fixed weights: Merkle-Hellman Knapsack

▶ Functions by means of elliptic curve: Elliptic curve cryptosystem

Review of Symmetric and Asymmetric Cryptographic Systems

To help ensure your success on the CISSP exam, symmetric and asymmetric cryptographic systems are compared in Table 6.5.

TABLE 6.5 **Symmetric and Asymmetric Systems Compared**

Symmetric	Asymmetric
Confidentiality	Confidentiality, integrity, authentication, and nonrepudiation
One single shared key	Two keys: public and private
Require an out-of-band exchange	Useful for in-band exchange
Not scalable, too many keys needed	Scalable, works for ecommerce
Small key size and fast	Larger key size required and slower to process
Useful for bulk encryption	Digital signatures, digital envelopes, digital certificates, and small amounts of data

Hybrid Encryption

Up to this point, we have discussed symmetric and asymmetric ciphers individually, and as noted in Table 6.2 each has advantages and disadvantages. Although symmetric is fast, key distribution is a problem. Asymmetric offers easy key distribution but is not suited for large amounts of data. Hybrid encryption uses the advantages of each approach and combines them together into a truly powerful system. The public-key cryptosystem is used as a key encapsulation scheme and the private key cryptosystem is used as a data encapsulation scheme.

The system works as follows. If Michael wants to send a message to his editor, Betsy, the following would occur, as illustrated in Figure 6.10.

1. Michael generates a random private key for the data encapsulation scheme. We will call this the *session key*.

2. Michael encrypts the message with the data encapsulation scheme using the session key that was generated in step 1.

3. Michael encrypts the session key using Betsy's public key.

4. Michael sends both of these items, the encrypted message and the encrypted key, to Betsy.

5. Betsy uses her private key to decrypt the session key and then uses the session key to decrypt the message.

Nearly all modern cryptosystems work this way because you get the speed of secret key cryptosystems and the "key-exchange-ability" of public key cryptosystems. Hybrid cryptographic systems include IPSec, PGP, SSH, SET, SSL, WPA2-Enterprise, and TLS. Each of these systems will be discussed in detail later in the chapter.

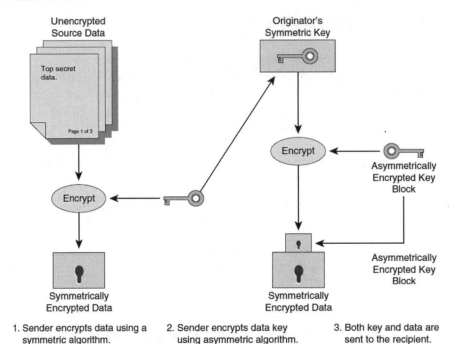

1. Sender encrypts data using a symmetric algorithm.
2. Sender encrypts data key using asymmetric algorithm.
3. Both key and data are sent to the recipient.

FIGURE 6.10 **Hybrid encryption.**

Integrity and Authentication

As mentioned previously, one of the things cryptography offers to its users is the capability to verify integrity and authentication. Integrity assures a recipient that the information remained unchanged and is in its true original form. Authentication provides the capability to ensure that messages are sent from who you believed sent them, and that messages are received by the intended recipient. To help ensure your success on the CISSP exam, review the integrity methods listed in Table 6.6

TABLE 6.6 **Integrity Verification**

Method	Description
Parity	Simple error detection code for networking
Hashing	Integrity
Digital signature	Integrity, authentication, and nonrepudiation
Hashed MAC	Integrity and data origin authentication
CBC MAC	Integrity and data origin authentication
Checksum	Redundancy check, weak integrity

Hashing and Message Digests

Hashing algorithms function by taking a variable amount of data and compressing it into a fixed length value referred to as a *hash value*. Hashing provides a fingerprint or message digest of the data. Strong hashing algorithms are hard to break and will not produce the same hash value for two or more messages. Hashing can be used to meet the goals of integrity and/or nonrepudiation depending on how the algorithms are used. Hashes can help verify that information has remained unchanged. Figure 6.11 gives an overview of the hashing process.

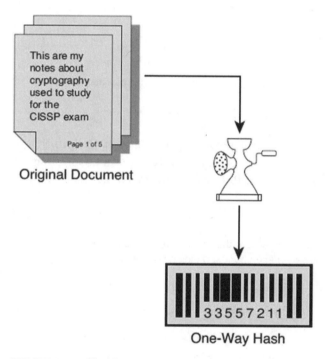

FIGURE 6.11   **Hashing.**

Hashing algorithms are not intended to be reversed to reproduce the data. The purpose of the message digest is to verify the integrity of data and messages. In a well-designed message digest if there is even a slight change in an input string the output hash value should change drastically. This is known as the avalanche effect. As an example, Knoppix STD version 0.1 (s-t-d. org/md5.html) has an MD5 hash value of de03204ea5777d0e5fd6eb97b43034cb. This means if you were to download the distribution, or get it from a friend, the file you receive should produce this saved hash value if you recalculate the MD5 hash. Any other value would indicate the file has been altered or corrupted. Programs such as Tripwire, MD5sum, and Windows System File Verification all rely on hashing. Some common hashing algorithms include:

▶ Message DIGEST Algorithm (MD5) series

▶ Secure Hash Algorithm (SHA) series

▶ HAVAL

▶ RIPEMD

▶ Whirlpool

▶ Tiger

> **Note**
>
> While there are many hashing algorithms, two of the most common are SHA and the MD series.

The biggest problem for hashing is the possibility of collisions. Collisions result when two or more different inputs create the same output. Collisions can be reduced by moving to an algorithm that produces a larger hash.

> **Note**
>
> When considering hash values, remember that close does not count! If the hashes being compared differ in any way, even by just a single bit, the data being digested is not the same.

MD Series

All of the MD algorithms were developed by Ron Rivest. They have progressed through a series of versions over the years as technology has advanced. The original was MD2, which was optimized for 8-bit computers and is somewhat outdated. It has also fallen out of favor because MD2 has been found to suffer from collisions. MD4 was the next algorithm to be developed. The message is processed in 512-bit blocks plus a 64-bit binary representation of the original length of the message, which is concatenated to the message. As with MD2, MD4 was found to be vulnerable to possible attacks. This is why MD5 was developed; it could be considered as an MD4 with additional safety mechanisms. MD5 processes a variable-size input and produces a fixed 128-bit output. As with MD4, it processes the data in blocks of 512 bits.

> **Tip**
>
> Collisions occur when two different messages are passed through a hash and produce the same message digest value. This is undesirable because it can mask the fact that someone might have changed the contents of a file or message. MD5 and SHA-0 have been shown to be vulnerable to forced collisions.

SHA-1/2

SHA-1 is a *secure hashing algorithm* (SHA) that is similar to MD5. It is considered the successor to MD5 and produces a 160-bit message digest. SHA-1 processes messages in 512-bit blocks and adds padding, if needed, to get the data to add up to the right number of bits. Out of the 160 bits, SHA-1 has only 111-bit effectiveness. SHA-1 is one of a series of SHA algorithms including SHA-0, SHA-1, and SHA-2. SHA-0 is no longer considered secure and SHA-1 is no longer recommended. SHA-2 is actually a family of functions and is a safe replacement for SHA-1. The SHA-2 family includes SHA-224, SHA-256, SHA-386, and SHA-512.

SHA-3

SHA-3 is the newest family of hashing algorithms and was designed to replace SHA-1 and SHA-2.

HAVAL

HAVAL is another one-way hashing algorithm that is similar to MD5. Unlike MD5, HAVAL is not tied to a fixed message-digest value. HAVAL-3-128 makes three passes and produces a 128-bit fingerprint and HAVAL-4-256 makes four passes and produces a 256-bit fingerprint.

Message Authentication Code

A MAC is like a poor man's version of a digital signature and is somewhat similar to a digital signature except that it uses symmetric encryption. MACs are created and verified with the same secret (symmetric) key. Four types of MACs exist: unconditionally secure, hash function-based, stream cipher-based, and block cipher-based.

HMAC

The *Hashed Message Authentication Code* (HMAC) was designed to be immune to the multi-collision attack. This immunity was added by including a shared secret key. In simple terms, HMAC functions by using a hashing algorithm such as MD5 or SHA-1 and altering the initial state of the file to be processed by adding a password. Even if someone can intercept and modify the data, it's of little use if that person does not possess the secret key. There is no easy way for the person to re-create the hashed value without it. For HMACS to be used successfully, the recipient would have to have acquired a copy of the symmetric key through some secure out-of-band mechanism.

CBC-Message Authentication Code

A cipher block chaining MAC uses the CBC mode of a symmetric algorithm such as DES to create a MAC. CBC-MACs differ from HMACs in that CBC-MACs use one algorithm, whereas HMACs use two. These two components include a hashing algorithm and a symmetric block cipher. The last block of the message is used as the MAC authentication portion and is appended to the actual message.

Cipher-Based Message Authentication (CMAC)

CMAC addresses some of the security deficiencies of CBC-MACs. CMACs have more complex logic and use mathematical functions that make use of AES for increased security. You can use a CMAC to verify both the integrity and authenticity of a message.

Digital Signatures

Digital signatures are based on public key cryptography and are used to verify the authenticity and integrity of a message. Digital signatures are created by passing a message's contents through a hashing algorithm and encrypting it with a sender's private key once the message is received, the recipient decrypts the encrypted hash and then recalculates the received message's hash. These values should match to ensure the validity of the message and to prove that the message was sent by the party believed to have sent it (because only that party has access to the private key). Let's break this process out step by step with an example to help detail the operation:

1. Bill produces a message digest by passing a message through a hashing algorithm.

2. The message digest is then encrypted using Bill's private key.

3. The message is forwarded to the recipient, Alice.

4. Alice creates a message digest from the message with the same hashing algorithm that Bill used. Alice then decrypts Bill's signature digest by using his public key.

5. Finally, Alice compares the two message digests, the one originally created by Bill and the other that she created. If the two values match, Alice can rest assured that the message is unaltered.

Figure 6.12 illustrates this process and demonstrates how the hashing function ensures integrity, and the signing of the hash value provides authentication and nonrepudiation.

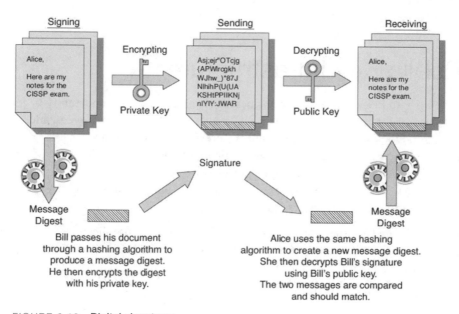

FIGURE 6.12   **Digital signatures.**

Digital Signature Algorithm

Things are much easier when we have standards and that is what the DSA was designed for. The DSA standards were proposed by NIST in 1991 to standardize Digital Signature Standards (DSS). The DSA digital signature algorithm involves key generation, signature generation, and signature verification. It uses SHA-1 in conjunction with public key encryption to create a 160-bit hash. Signing speeds are equivalent to RSA signing, but signature verification is much slower. The DSA digital signature is a pair of large numbers represented as binary digits.

Cryptographic System Review

As a recap and to help ensure your success on the CISSP exam, well-known cryptographic systems are reviewed in Table 6.7.

TABLE 6.7 **Algorithms and Their Functions**

Category	Algorithm
Symmetric	DES, 3DES, Blowfish, Twofish, IDEA, CAST, SAFER, Skipjack, and RC (series)
Asymmetric	RSA, ECC, Diffie-Hellman, Knapsack, LUC, and El Gamal
Hashing	MD (series) SHA (series), HAVAL, Tiger, Whirlpool, and RIPEMD
Digital signature	DSA

Public Key Infrastructure

Dealing with bricks-and-mortar businesses gives us plenty of opportunity to develop trust with a vendor. We can see the store, talk to the employees, and get a good look at how they do business. Internet transactions are far less transparent. We can't see who we are dealing with, don't know what type of operation they really run, and might not be sure we can trust them. The *public key infrastructure* (PKI) was made to address these concerns and bring trust, integrity, and security to electronic transactions.

PKI is a framework that consists of hardware, software, and policies that exist to manage, create, store, and distribute keys and digital certificates. The components of this framework include the following:

▶ The Certificate Authority (CA)

▶ The Registration Authority (RA)

▶ The Certificate Revocation List (CRL)

▶ Digital certificates

▶ A certificate distribution system

Certificate Authority

A good analogy of a CA is that of the Department of Motor Vehicles (DMV). This is the state entity that is responsible for issuing a driver's license, the known standard for physical identification. If you cash a check, go to a night club, or catch a plane, your driver's license is one document that is widely accepted at these locations to prove your identity. CAs are like DMVs: They vouch for your identity in a digital world. VeriSign, Thawte, and Entrust are some of the companies that perform public CA services.

A CA doesn't have to be an external third party; many companies decide to tackle these responsibilities by themselves. Regardless of who performs the services, the following steps must be performed:

1. The CA verifies the request for certificate with the help of the RA.

2. The individual's identification is validated.

3. A certificate is created by the CA, which certifies that the person matches the public key that is being offered.

Registration Authority

The RA is like a middleman: it's positioned between the client and the CA. Although the RA cannot generate a certificate, it can accept requests, verify a person's identity, and pass along the information to the CA for certificate generation.

RAs play a key role when certificate services expand to cover large geographic areas. One central CA can delegate its responsibilities to regional RAs around the world.

ExamAlert

Expect to see exam questions that deal with the workings of PKI. It's important to understand that the RA cannot issue certificates.

Certificate Revocation List

Just as with driver's licenses, digital certificates might not always remain valid. (I had a great aunt that drove with an expired license for years. In her case, she was afraid that at 95 years old, she might not pass the eye exam.) In corporate life, certificates might become invalid because someone leaves the company, information might change, or a private key might become compromised. For these reasons, the CRL must be maintained.

The CRL is maintained by the CA, which signs the list to maintain its accuracy. Whenever problems are reported with digital certificates, they are considered invalid and the CA has the serial number added to the CRL.

Anyone requesting a digital certificate can check the CRL to verify the certificate's integrity. The replacement for CRLs is the Online Certificate Status Protocol (OCSP); it has a client–server design that scales better. When a user requests access to a server, OCSP sends a request for certificate status information. The server sends back a response of current, expired, or unknown. Regardless of which method is used, problems with certificates are nothing new; Dell had such a problem in 2015. You can read more about it at www.infoworld.com/article/3008422/security/what-you-need-to-know-about-dells-root-certificate-security-debacle.html.

Digital Certificates

Digital certificates are at the heart of the PKI system. A digital certificate serves two roles:

▶ It ensures the integrity of the public key and makes sure that the key remains unchanged and in a valid state.

▶ It validates that the public key is tied to the stated owner and that all associated information is true and correct.

The information needed to accomplish these goals is added into the digital certificate. Digital certificates are formatted to the X.509 standard. The most current version of X.509 is version 3. One of the key developments in version 3 was the addition of extensions. Version 3 includes the flexibility to support other topologies. It can operate as a web of trust much like PGP. An X.509 certificate includes the following elements, and examples showing some of these elements are displayed in Figure 6.13:

▶ Version

▶ Serial number

▶ Algorithm ID

▶ Issuer

▶ Validity

    ▶ Not Before (a specified date)

    ▶ Not After (a specified date)

▶ Subject

▶ Subject public key information

    ▶ Public key algorithm

    ▶ Subject public key

▶ Issuer-unique identifier (optional)

▶ Subject-unique identifier (optional)

▶ Extensions (optional)

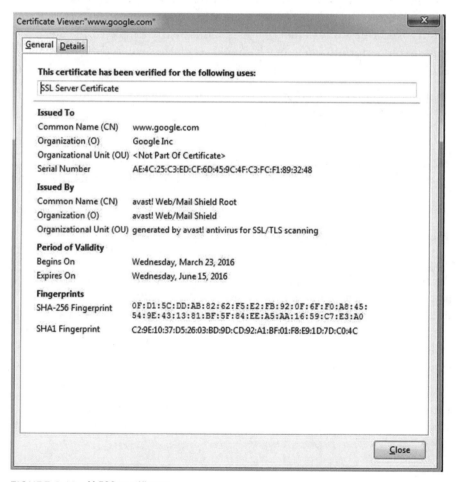

FIGURE 6.13   **X.509 certificate.**

Digital certificates play a vital role in the chain of trust. Public key encryption works well when we are dealing with people we know because it's easy for us to send each other a public key. But what about communicating with people we don't know?

> **Note**
>
> Digital certificates are used to prove your identity when performing electronic transactions.

Although you might want to use an external certificate authority, it is not mandatory. You could decide to have your own organization act as a certificate authority. Regardless of whether you have a third party handle certificate duties or you perform them yourself, digital certificates will typically contain the following critical pieces of information:

▶ Identification information that includes username, serial number, and validity dates of the certificates.

▶ The public key of the certificate holder.

▶ The digital signature of the signature authority. This piece is critical because it certifies and validates the integrity of the entire package.

The Client's Role in PKI

It might seem that up to this point, all the work falls on the shoulders of the CAs; this is not entirely true. Clients are responsible for requesting digital certificates and for maintaining the security of their private keys. Loss or compromise of the private key would be devastating; it would mean that communications were no longer be secure. If you are dealing with credit card numbers or other pieces of user identity, this type of loss of security could lead to identity theft.

Protecting the private key is an important issue because it's easier for an attacker to target the key than to try to crack the certificate service. Organizations should concern themselves with seven key management issues:

▶ Generation

▶ Distribution

▶ Installation

▶ Storage

▶ Key change

▶ Key control

▶ Key disposal

Key recovery and control is an important issue that must be addressed. One basic recovery and control method is the M of N Control method of access. This method is designed to ensure that no one person can have total control and is closely related to dual control. Therefore, if N number of administrators have the ability to perform a process, M number of those administrators must authenticate for access to occur. *M of N Control* should require physical presence for access. Here is an example: Suppose that a typical M of N Control method requires that four people have access to the archive server and at least two of them must be present to accomplish access. In this situation, M = 2 and N = 4. This would ensure that no one person could compromise the security system or gain access.

> ### Note
>
> Many organizations use Hardware Security Modules (HSM) to securely store and securely retrieve these escrowed keys. These HSM systems protect keys and can detect and prevent tampering by destroying the key material if unauthorized access is detected.

Email Protection Mechanisms

Secure email solutions are important because email is one of the most widely used Internet applications. Email is susceptible to several threats including spoofing, spamming, forging, and so on. Standard email uses the Simple Mail Transfer Protocol (SMTP) TCP port 25 to accept messages from clients, and Internet Message Access Protocol (IMAP4) TCP port 143 or Post Office Protocol (POP3) version 3 TCP port 110 to retrieve email from server-based inboxes. Sending an email is much like sending a postcard through the postal service: Anyone along the way can easily read the note you wrote to your mom while visiting Niagara Falls. Fortunately, several digital services enable you to seal your mail in an envelope. Several applications and protocols are available to help secure email.

Pretty Good Privacy

PGP was developed in 1991 by Phil Zimmermann to provide privacy and authentication. Over time, it evolved into an open standard known as OpenPGP, but now can be purchased for enterprise use by Symantec's for endpoint, file and folder and email encryption as well. PGP is unlike PKI in that there is no CA. PGP builds a web of trust that develops as users sign and issue their own keys. Users must determine what level of trust they are willing to place in other parties. The goal of PGP was for it to become the "everyman's encryption." No longer would encryption be available only to companies and corporations. Popular programs and providers such as Hushmail and Veridis are based on PGP.

Other Email Security Applications

PGP is not the only game in town for those looking to secure email. Other options include S/MIME, PEM, MSP, and MOSS. Each is discussed now.

▶ **Secure Multipurpose Internet Mail Extensions (S/MIME)**—By default, MIME does not provide any protection. To overcome this problem, S/MIME was developed by RSA. S/MIME has been built into virtually every email system to encrypt and digitally sign the attachments of protected email messages. S/MIME adds two valuable components to standard email: digital signatures and public key encryption. S/MIME supports X.509 digital certificates and RSA encryption.

▶ **Privacy Enhanced Mail (PEM)**—PEM is an older standard that has not been widely implemented but was developed to provide authentication and confidentiality. PEM public key management is hierarchical. PEM uses MD2/MD5 and RSA for integrity and authentication.

▶ **Message Security Protocol (MSP)**—MSP is the military's answer to PEM. Because it was developed by the NSA, it has not been open to public scrutiny and is not widely used. It is part of the DoD's Defense Messaging System and provides authentication, integrity, and nonrepudiation. The military has its own security network referred to as SIPERNET.

▶ **MIME Object Security Services (MOSS)**—MOSS extended the functionality of PEM and is not widely used. MOSS was eclipsed by S/MIME and by PGP. MOSS is the only email standard that gives users an out-of-the-box mechanism for signing the recipient-list.

Securing TCP/IP with Cryptographic Solutions

Did you ever really consider that security is like a cake? Although it might not taste as good as a cake, it is best to have the option of security in all the layers. Cryptography can be layered to help build a true *defense in depth*. This is not to say that cryptographic controls should be applied at every layer, just that defense in depth should be the target. Just as too much cake might not be good for you, too many layers of cryptography will slow down a system or process. Users might look for ways to bypass some of these controls. Many types of cryptographic solutions are available from the application layer all the way down to the physical frame. Your job as a CISSP is to understand these potential solutions and be able to determine which should be used to meet the goals of the organization.

Because security wasn't one of the driving forces when the TCP/IP protocols were developed, the cryptographic solutions discussed here can go a long way toward protecting the security of an organization. Although in reality encryption at any layer is accomplished on the payload of the next higher layer, most CISSP questions will focus on basic knowledge of encryption processes and the layer at which they are found. Figure 6.14 shows some common cryptographic solutions and their corresponding layers. Chapter 7, "Communications and Network Security," discusses many of these protocols in greater depth. Let's start at the top of the stack and work down through the layers.

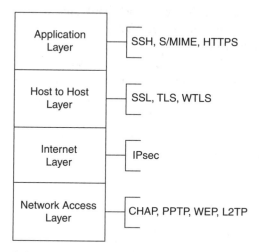

FIGURE 6.14 **Layered security controls.**

Application/Process Layer Controls

The following application-layer protocols can be used to add confidentiality, integrity, or nonrepudiation:

▶ **Secure Shell (SSH)**—SSH is an Internet application that provides secure remote access. It is considered a replacement for FTP, Telnet, and the Berkley "r" utilities. SSH defaults to TCP port 22. SSH version 1 has been found to contain vulnerabilities, so it is advisable to use SSH V2.

▶ **Secure FTP (SFTP)**—SFTP uses an SSH connection, and then tunnels the FTP protocol through the secure shell. The latest version of SSH is v2.0 and typically runs on TCP port 22. The FTP client software must support the SFTP protocol.

▶ **FTP Secure (FTPS)**—FTPS establishes an SSL secure channel, and then runs the FTP session through SSL. IANA assigned ports 989 (data) and 990 (control) for FTPS, but vendors are free to use custom port numbers and often do.

▶ **Secure Hypertext Transfer Protocol (S-HTTP)**—S-HTTP is a superset of HTTP that was developed to provide secure communication with a web server. S-HTTP is a connectionless protocol designed to send individual messages securely.

▶ **Secure Electronic Transaction (SET)**—Visa and MasterCard wanted to alleviate fears of using credit cards over the Internet, so they developed SET. This specification uses a combination of digital certificates and digital signatures among the buyer, merchant, and the bank so that privacy and confidentiality are ensured. While this sounds like a great idea, one of the problems with SET was that the banks wanted to charge for this service, and required hardware and software changes. Many vendors fought these fees and so SET is not widely used. Out of the ashes of SET came the Payment Card Industry Data Security Standard (PCI-DSS). This requires all vendors who accept credit cards to meet and guarantee specific information system security standards designed to protect the credit card data.

Host to Host Layer Controls

The host to host layer of the TCP/IP stack can also be used to add cryptographic solutions to data communications. Some common examples follow:

▶ **Secure Sockets Layer (SSL)**—SSL was developed by Netscape for transmitting private documents over the Internet. Unlike S-HTTP, SSL is application-independent. One of the advantages of SSL is its cryptographic independence. The protocol itself is merely a framework for communicating certificates, encrypted keys, and data. The most current version of SSL is SSLv3, which provides for mutual authentication and compression. Figure 6.15 illustrates the transactions in an SSL session. As of 2014 SSLv3 is considered insecure and is vulnerable to the POODLE exploit. If attackers successfully exploit this vulnerability, they only need to make about 256 SSL 3.0 requests to break the encryption. TLS 1.2 is the current standard for HTTP encryption.

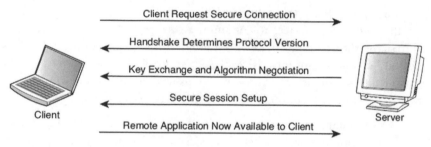

FIGURE 6.15 **Secure Sockets Layer (SSL).**

▶ **Transport Layer Security (TLS)**—TLS encrypts the communication between a host and a client. TLS typically makes use of an X.509 digital certificate for server authentication. This mechanism provides strong authentication of the server to the client, so the client can trust that it is connected to the correct remote system. TLS consists of two layers: the TLS Record Protocol and the TLS Handshake Protocol. One of the most common implementations of TLS is HTTPS, which is simply HTTP over TLS.

▶ **Secure Socket Tunneling Protocol (SSTP)**—SSTP is a form of VPN tunnel that was released in 2008 and provides a mechanism to transport PPP or L2TP traffic through an SSL 3.0 connection. SSTP requires a digital certificate on the server side and establishes an SSL tunnel that encrypts all traffic over TCP port 443. Because it uses the same port used by HTTPS, this facilitates its use through corporate firewalls.

▶ **Wireless Transport Layer Security (WTLS)**—WTLS is a security protocol developed for cellular technology. In an attempt to minimize upper-layer support code, the cellular industry developed its own Wireless Access Protocol (WAP) stack. WTLS encrypts the communication between the cellular wireless client and the ISP tower that the cell phone is connecting to. At the tower, the WTLS packet is decrypted, then re-encrypted with standard TLS and routed on to the Internet. This means that for a moment, customer data exists unencrypted. This is a security vulnerability that has become known as the *gap in WAP*. The cellular industry has since released WAPv2, which incorporates industry standard TLS (minimized as possible), so that decryption is no longer necessary.

Internet Layer Controls

Internet Protocol Security (IPSec) resides at the Internet layer and is a well-known cryptographic solution. IPSec is an end-to-end security technology that allows two devices to communicate securely. IPSec was developed to address the shortcomings of IPv4. Although it is an add-on for IPv4, it was created for, and is built into, IPv6. IPSec can be used to protect just the data or the data and the original IP header. This level of protection can be for integrity and/or encryption. The components of IPSec include:

▶ **Encapsulated secure payload (ESP)**—ESP provides confidentiality by encrypting the data packet. The encrypted data is hidden from prying eyes, so its confidentiality is ensured.

▶ **Authentication header (AH)**—The AH provides integrity and authentication. The AH uses a hashing algorithm and symmetric key to calculate a message authentication code. This message-authentication code is known as the integrity check value (ICV). When the AH is received, an ICV value is calculated and checked against the received value to verify integrity.

▶ **Security Association (SA)**—For AH and ESP to work, there must be some negotiations regarding the rules of conduct for exchanging information between the client and server. These negotiations include the type of symmetric and asymmetric algorithms that will be used, as well as state-specific information in support of the secure channel. The results of these negotiations are stored in an SA. The SA identifies the details of each one-way connection. Two-way communication channels will have two SAs; each distinguished by its *Security Parameter Index* (SPI). If both AH and ESP are used, four SAs are required. IPSec uses a symmetric shared key to encrypt bulk communications. The Diffie-Hellman algorithm is used to generate this shared key.

▶ **IPSec Internet Key Exchange (IKE)**—IPSec must have a procedure to exchange key information between clients, and the *Internet Key Exchange* (IKE) is the default standard. IKE is responsible for creating IPSec's SA and is considered a hybrid protocol because it combines the functions of two other protocols: the Internet Association and Key Management Protocol (ISAKMP) and the OAKLEY protocol.

▶ **The Internet Association and Key Management Protocol (ISAKMP)**—This subset of IKE sets up the framework for performing the negotiations during the client/server handshake process. This could include items such as algorithm types and key sizes.

▶ **OAKLEY Protocol**—This portion of the IKE is responsible for carrying out the negotiations. This protocol is like the errand guy!

▶ **Transport and tunnel modes**—AH and ESP can work in one of two modes: transport mode or tunnel mode. These modes define how the encryption or integrity functions will be applied to the data stream. Transport mode encrypts the payload received from the host-to-host layer. Tunnel mode encapsulates the payload received from the host-to-host layer and the original IP header that was to encapsulate that payload. A new IPv4 header is added for routing between the tunnel endpoints. Tunnel mode is designed to be used by VPNs.

Other lesser-known cryptographic solutions found at the Internet layer include:

▶ **Simple Key Management for Internet Protocol (SKIP)**—SKIP was developed by the IETF. SKIP is rarely used and requires no prior communication; it is similar to SSL. SKIP was evaluated as a key exchange mechanism for IPsec before the adoption of IKE in 1998.

▶ **Software IP Encryption (SwIPe)**—SwIPe was an early attempt to develop an open standard for VPNs. Although freely available, it was available only for SunOS and is not widely used.

Network Access Layer Controls

At the TCP/IP network access layer or OSI Layer 2, we find several cryptographic solutions:

▶ **Point-to-Point Tunneling Protocol (PPTP)**—PPTP was developed by a group of vendors. It consists of two components: the transport, which maintains the virtual connection, and the encryption, which ensures confidentiality. It can operate at a 40-bit or 128-bit key length.

▶ **Layer 2 Tunneling Protocol (L2TP)**—L2TP was created by Cisco and Microsoft to replace L2F and PPTP. L2TP merged the capabilities of both L2F and PPTP into one tunneling protocol. By itself, it provides no encryption; but it is deployed with IPSec as a VPN solution.

> **Note**
>
> L2F does not provide encryption or confidentiality by itself; it relies on the protocol being tunneled to provide privacy

▶ **WPA2-Enterprise**—This is a Wi-Fi Alliance certification that identifies equipment capable of establishing a secure channel of communication at TCP/IP layer 1 / OSI Layer 2 using EAP for authentication, and AES-CTR-CBC-MAC for encryption. Cisco LEAP can be used with WPA and WPA2 networks.

> **Note**
>
> Extensible Authentication Protocol (EAP) is an authentication protocol that is widely used in point-to-point and wireless connections. It is discussed in detail in Chapter 7, "Communications and Network Security."

Link and End-to-End Encryption

As the various protocols have shown, there are many ways to encrypt and secure data. One final decision that must be considered is how information is to be moved between clients. In reality, encryption can happen at any one of many different layers. The question the CISSP must ask is, what is actually getting encrypted? The layer you choose to encrypt at forces encryption of all layers above your chosen layer.

End-to-end encryption encrypts the message and the data packet. Header information, IP addresses, and routing data are left in cleartext. Although this means that a malicious individual can intercept packets and learn the source and target destination, the data itself is secure. The advantage of this type of encryption is speed. No time or processing power is needed to decode address information at any intermediate points. The disadvantage is that even with the data encrypted, an attacker might be able to make an *inference attack*.

Sending information by means of end-to-end encryption prevents the attacker from sniffing host-to-host or application data, but it does not mean the attacker cannot understand something about the actual communication. This is known as inference.

Inference can occur any time an attacker notices a change in activity at a client. As an example, some news agencies allegedly monitor the White House for pizza deliveries. The belief is that a spike in pizza deliveries indicates that officials are working overtime and that there is a pending event of importance. A similar spike in encrypted email traffic could allow similar inferences.

Traffic padding can be used to defeat an inference attack. As an example, a military agency could have a connection between the United States and Afghanistan. Although third parties might be able to see that traffic is flowing, the amount transmitted stays at a constant flow and thereby prevents attackers from performing an inference attack.

Your choice for encryption at the physical layer is link-to-link encryption. *Link-to-link encryption* encrypts all the data sent from a specific communication device to another specific device. This includes the headers, addresses, and routing information. Its primary strength is that it provides added protection against sniffers and eavesdropping. Its disadvantage is that all intermediate devices must have the necessary keys, software, and algorithms to encrypt and decrypt the encrypted packets at each hop along the trip. This adds complexity, consumes time, and requires additional processing power.

Cryptographic Attacks

Attacks on cryptographic systems are nothing new. Whenever someone has information to hide, there is usually someone who would like to reveal it. The name for such activities is cryptanalysis. *Cryptanalysis* is the study of analyzing cryptography and can best be defined by the root meaning of the word, *crypt* = secret, hidden and *analysis* = loosen, dissolve. The ultimate goal of cryptanalysis is to determine the key value, and these types of activities go on every day at organizations like the NSA and at locations where hackers and security specialists are working. Depending on which key is cracked, an attacker could gain access to confidential information or pretend to be someone else and attempt some sort of masquerade attack.

Because cryptography can be such a powerful tool and the ability to break many algorithms is limited, the Coordinating Committee for Multilateral Export Controls (CoCOM) was established to deal with the control of cryptographic systems. CoCOM ended in 1994 and was replaced by the *Wassenaar Arrangement* on Export Controls for Conventional Arms and Dual-Use Goods and Technologies. The Wassenaar Arrangement had wide support; that more than 30 countries have come together to control the export of cryptography.

Methods the United States Government Can Use to Defeat Encryption

The United States government must battle many individuals and organizations that use encryption, such as terrorists and organized crime. Documents made public by whistleblower Edward Snowden have disclosed some of the cryptanalysis techniques that the NSA uses to break cryptographic systems.

These techniques include exerting control over setting of international encryption standards, using supercomputers to brute-force algorithms, and even collaboration with technology companies and Internet service providers to insert backdoors or trapdoors into commercial encryption software.

The NSA has even been rumored to work with major antivirus companies, to developed software that will not be detected by antivirus software. Read more about these techniques: www.spiegel.de/international/germany/inside-the-nsa-s-war-on-internet-security-a-1010361.html.

One issue to consider before launching a cryptographic attack is what is known about the algorithm. Is it public or private? Auguste Kerckhoff is credited with creating, in the nineteenth century, *Kerckhoff's Principle*, which states that a cryptographic system should not require secrecy. Everything should be public except the key. An example of this debate can be seen in the development and crack of *Content Scrambling System* (CSS). This method of encryption was developed by the DVD Copy Control Association (DVD CCA). Because the algorithm was proprietary, it was not made public. CSS was designed to allow only authorized DVD players to decode scrambled content stored on the original DVD discs. This was until Jon Lech Johansen and others got together and cracked CSS, posting a utility called DeCSS to the Internet in late October 1999. So, whereas some argue that algorithms should be secret, others continue to believe that open standards and systems allow for more robust, secure systems.

When attempting a cryptographic attack, the work factor is something that must be considered. The *work factor* can be measured as the time and effort needed to perform a brute-force attack against an encryption system. As an example, the CSS algorithm reduced the effective key length to only around 16 bits. This small key size meant the work factor was low and that CSS could be brute-forced by a 1GHz processor in less than a minute. An example of a distributed cryptographic attack can be seen with www.distributed.net. The program functions by downloading a client utility. Anyone can join in as long as they do not mind sharing some of the local system's CPU cycles. This project was started in 1997 and, on July 14, 2002, was able to crack the RSA Labs 64-bit secret-key for one message.

With the basic concepts of cryptanalysis completed, let's review some common attacks that might target a cryptographic system:

▶ **Known plaintext attack**—This attack requires the attacker to have the plaintext and ciphertext of one or more messages. Encrypted file archives such as ZIP are prone to this attack.

▶ **Ciphertext-only attack**—This attack requires the attacker to obtain several encrypted messages that have been encrypted using the same encryption algorithm. The attacker does not have the associated plaintext; he attempts to crack the code by looking for patterns and using statistical analysis.

▶ **Chosen ciphertext**—If the attacker can decrypt portions of the ciphertext message, the decrypted portion can then be used to discover the key.

▶ **Chosen plaintext**—The attacker has the plaintext messages encrypted and then can analyze the ciphertext output.

▶ **Differential cryptanalysis**—Generally used to target block ciphers, it works by looking for the difference between related plaintexts that are encrypted, and the difference between their resultant ciphertexts.

▶ **Linear cryptanalysis**—Along with differential cryptanalysis, one of the two most widely used attacks on block ciphers. Linear cryptanalysis uses functions to identify the highest probability a specific key was used during the encryption process. The key pairs are then studied to derive information about the key used to create them.

▶ **Birthday attack**—The birthday attack gets its name from the birthday paradox, which states that within a group of people, the chances that two or more will share birthdays is unexpectedly high. This same logic is applied to calculate collisions in hash functions. A message digest can be susceptible to birthday attacks if the output of the hash function is not large enough to avoid collisions.

▶ **Key clustering**—This is a vulnerability that can occur when two different keys produce the same ciphertext from the same message. This can sometimes be the result of having a small key space or might be a characteristic of some cryptosystems. Key clustering is a real problem as it means that two or more different keys could also decrypt the secure content. A strong cryptosystem should have a low frequency of key clustering occurrences. If not, this is yet another way that a cryptosystem might be targeted for attack.

▶ **Replay attack**—This method of attack occurs when the attacker can intercept cryptographic keys and reuse them later to either encrypt or decrypt messages.

▶ **Man-in-the middle attack**—This attack is carried out when attackers place themselves in the communications path between two users. From this position, the possibility exists that they can intercept and modify communications.

▶ **Side channel attack**—These attacks are based on side channel information such as timing, sound, or electromagnetic leaks. Here is a link that provides a good example of a channel attack by analyzing the power consumption of the CPU: .../wiki/Side-channel_attack

> ### ExamAlert
>
> When comparing cryptogra... ...to keep in mind that the larger the work factor, the ... ...ptographers develop systems with high work facto... ...be foolproof. All systems can be cracked with en... ...cker. Sometimes attackers simply look for vulnera... ...cly discovered. These are known as zero-day v...

▶ **Rubber hose attack**—When an ... ...ls, this method might be used to extract a key value or other information. This type of attack might include threats, violence, extortion, or blackmail, because humans are the biggest weakness, not the cryptosystem.

> ### ExamAlert
>
> On the exam, be careful to distinguish a meet-in-the-middle attack from a man-in-the-middle attack. Although the names are similar, they are completely different.

Exam Prep Questions

1. You are security manager for a bank that has 100 employees. They are all required to encrypt data before they send it. While they examined both symmetric and asymmetric encryption, management has decided to use DES encryption. How many keys will they require for all employees??

    ○ **A.** 4950

    ○ **B.** 49.5

    ○ **C.** 99

    ○ **D.** 4900

2. Which of the following best describes obtaining plaintext from ciphertext without a key?

    ○ **A.** Frequency analysis

    ○ **B.** Cryptanalysis

    ○ **C.** Decryption

    ○ **D.** Hacking

3. Which of the following attacks occurs when an attacker can intercept session keys and reuse them at a later date?

    ○ **A.** Known plaintext attack

    ○ **B.** Ciphertext-only attack

    ○ **C.** Man-in-the-middle attack

    ○ **D.** Replay attack

4. Which of the following is a disadvantage of symmetric encryption?

    ○ **A.** Key size

    ○ **B.** Speed

    ○ **C.** Key management

    ○ **D.** Key strength

5. Which of the following is *not* an example of a symmetric algorithm?

    ○ **A.** DES

    ○ **B.** RC5

    ○ **C.** AES

    ○ **D.** RSA

6. Which of the following forms of DES is considered the most vulnerable to attack?

   ○ **A.** CBC

   ○ **B.** ECB

   ○ **C.** CFB

   ○ **D.** OFB

7. DES uses which of the following for a key size?

   ○ **A.** 56 bits

   ○ **B.** 64 bits

   ○ **C.** 96 bits

   ○ **D.** 128 bits

8. Which implementation of Triple-DES uses the same key for the first and third iterations?

   ○ **A.** DES-EEE3

   ○ **B.** HAVAL

   ○ **C.** DES-EEE2

   ○ **D.** DES-X

9. Which of the following algorithms is used for key distribution, not encryption or digital signatures?

   ○ **A.** El Gamal

   ○ **B.** HAVAL

   ○ **C.** Diffie-Hellman

   ○ **D.** ECC

10. Which hashing algorithm produces a 160-bit output?

   ○ **A.** MD2

   ○ **B.** MD4

   ○ **C.** SHA-1

   ○ **D.** El Gamal

11. What is another name for a one-time pad?

   ○ **A.** ATBASH cipher

   ○ **B.** Vigenère cipher

   ○ **C.** Caesar cipher

   ○ **D.** Vernam cipher

12. Which of the following is also known as a ROT3 cipher?

   ○ **A.** ATBASH cipher

   ○ **B.** Vigenère cipher

   ○ **C.** Caesar cipher

   ○ **D.** Vernam cipher

13. Which of the following did the Wassenaar Arrangement replace?

   ○ **A.** IETF

   ○ **B.** ComCo

   ○ **C.** The group of five

   ○ **D.** CoCom

14. Which of the following is not a hashing algorithm?

   ○ **A.** Whirlpool

   ○ **B.** RipeMD

   ○ **C.** Tiger

   ○ **D.** Mars

15. While working with a file integrity program, Tripwire, you have been asked to review some recent issues with a cryptographic program. What is it called when two different keys generate the same ciphertext for the same message?

   ○ **A.** Hashing

   ○ **B.** A collision

   ○ **C.** Key clustering

   ○ **D.** Output verification

Answers to Exam Prep Questions

1. **A.** The formula for computing the number of keys in symmetric cryptography is $n(n-1)/2$. In this question $n = 100$, so the answer is $100(100-1)/2 = 4950$. B, C, and D are all incorrect.

2. **B.** Cryptanalysis is the study and act of breaking encryption systems. Although it can mean obtaining the plaintext from the ciphertext without a key, it can also mean that the cryptosystem was cracked because someone found a weakness in the cryptosystem's implementation. Such was the case with wired equivalent privacy (WEP). Answer A is incorrect because although the cryptanalyst can use frequency analysis to aid in cracking, it is not a valid answer. Answer C is incorrect because decryption is the act of unencrypting data. Answer D is incorrect because *hacking* is a term used to describe the actions of criminal hackers.

3. **D.** A reply attack occurs when the attacker can intercept session keys and reuse them at a later date. Answer A is incorrect because a known plaintext attack requires the attacker to have the plaintext and ciphertext of one or more messages. Answer B is incorrect because a ciphertext-only attack requires the attacker to obtain several messages encrypted using the same encryption algorithm. Answer C is incorrect because a man-in-the middle attack is carried out when attackers place themselves in the communications path between two users.

4. **C.** Key management is a primary disadvantage of symmetric encryption. Answers A, B, and D are incorrect because encryption speed, key size, and key strength are not disadvantages of symmetric encryption.

5. **D.** RSA is an asymmetric algorithm. Answers A, B, and C are incorrect because DES, RC5, and AES are examples of symmetric algorithms.

6. **B.** Electronic Code Book is susceptible to known plaintext attacks because the same cleartext always produces the same ciphertext. Answers A, C, and D are incorrect. Because CBC, CFB, and OFB all use some form of feedback, which helps randomize the encrypted data, they do not suffer from this deficiency and are considered more secure.

7. **A.** Each 64-bit plaintext block is separated into two 32-bit blocks and then processed by the 56-bit key. Total key size is 64 bits but 8 bits are used for parity, thereby making 64, 96, and 128 bits incorrect.

8. **C.** DES-EEE2 performs the first and third encryption passes using the same key. Answers A, B, and D are incorrect: DES-EEE3 uses three different keys for encryption; HAVAL is used for hashing and DES does not use it; DES-X is a variant of DES with only a 56-bit key size, which was designed for DES, not 3DES.

9. **C.** Diffie-Hellman is used for key distribution, but not encryption or digital signatures. Answer A is incorrect because El Gamal is used for digital signatures, data encryption, and key exchange. Answer B is incorrect because HAVAL is

used for hashing. Answer D is incorrect because ECC is used for digital signatures, data encryption, and key exchange.

10. **C.** SHA-1 produces a 160-bit message digest. Answers A, B, and D are incorrect because MD2 and MD4 both create a 128-bit message digest and El Gamal is not a hashing algorithm.

11. **D.** Gilbert Vernam is the creator of the one-time pad. A one-time pad (key) is a keystream that can be used only once and is considered unbreakable if properly implemented. The one-time pad (Vernam cipher) consists of a pad of the same length as the message to which it's applied. The one-time pad is very effective for short messages and is typically implemented as stream ciphers. Therefore, answers A, B, and C are incorrect.

12. **C.** Caesar's cipher is also known as a ROT3 cipher as each character is rotated by three spaces. ATBASH used two separate alphabets that were reversed. The Vigenère cipher is an example of a polyalphabetic cipher, and Gilbert Vernam is the creator of the one-time pad.

13. **D.** CoCom is an acronym for Coordinating Committee for Multilateral Export Controls and was established by Western block powers after the end of World War II. The Wassenaar Arrangement replaced it. Answers A, B, and C are therefore incorrect.

14. **D.** Mars is an example of a symmetric encryption algorithm, whereas Whirlpool, RipeMD, and Tiger are all examples of hashing algorithms.

15. **C.** Key clustering is said to occur when two different keys produce the same ciphertext for the same message. A good algorithm, using different keys on the same plaintext, should generate a different ciphertext. Answers A, B, and D are incorrect: hashing is used for integrity verification; a collision occurs when two different messages are hashed and output the same message digest; and output verification is simply a distractor.

Need to Know More?

History of cryptography: en.wikipedia.org/wiki/History_of_cryptography

IETF PKI Working Group: datatracker.ietf.org/wg/pkix/charter/

Possible Backdoor to ECC: blog.cloudflare.com/how-the-nsa-may-have-put-a-backdoor-in-rsas-cryptography-a-technical-primer/

Concealment ciphers: math.ucdenver.edu/~wcherowi/courses/m5410/m5410cc.html

Historical ciphers: www.cs.trincoll.edu/~crypto/historical/

RFC 3280 information on PKI: www.ietf.org/rfc/rfc3280.txt

Steganography in real life: threatpost.com/attackers-embracing-steganography-to-hide-communication/115394/

Enigma: www.codesandciphers.org.uk/enigma/index.htm

Digital signature algorithm: www.rfc-base.org/rfc-5485.html

Steganography: www.garykessler.net/library/steganography.html

Password hashing: phpsec.org/articles/2005/password-hashing.html

CHAPTER 7

Communications and Network Security

Terms you'll need to understand:

▶ Address Resolution Protocol (ARP)

▶ Domain Name Service (DNS)

▶ Firewall

▶ Network Address Translation (NAT)

▶ IP Security (IPSec)

▶ The Open Systems Interconnect (OSI) model

▶ Transmission Control Protocol/Internet Protocol (TCP/IP)

▶ Local area network (LAN)

▶ Wide area network (WAN)

▶ Cloud computing

Topics you'll need to master:

▶ Secure Network Design

▶ Understand the differences between LAN and WAN topologies

▶ Describe and define the OSI model and its layers

▶ Describe the four layers of the TCP/IP stack

▶ Understand convergence protocols

Introduction

The communications and network security domain addresses communications and network security. This is one of the larger domains, and you can expect a sizable number of questions on this topic. After all, this area covers many of the core concepts a CISSP is required to know. Mastery of this domain requires you to fully understand networking, TCP/IP, LAN, WAN, telecommunications equipment, wireless networking, and related security controls. Being adept in network security requires that you understand the techniques used for preventing network-based attacks.

If you have spent some time working in the network security domain, you might need only a quick review of the material. If your work has led you to concentrate in other domains, you will want to spend adequate time here, reviewing the material to make sure you have the essential knowledge needed for the exam.

Secure Network Design

To be fully prepared for the exam, you need to understand the data communication process and how it relates to network security. Also, knowledge of remote access, use of firewalls, network equipment, and network protocols is required. Just as in other domains, this includes the concept of defense-in-depth—to build layer after layer of control. As an example, before ransomware can be executed by an end host, it must be passed by a firewall, screened by an email server, verified as non-malicious by anti-virus software, and scanned by an intrusion detection system (IDS). The idea is that the failure of any one device should not lead to compromise of the system, and that we have built in layers of defense to protect our assets.

Before we can begin to build these layers of defense, we need to start by understanding the basic building blocks of the network and discussing network models and standards like the Open Systems Interconnect (OSI) and TCP/IP network standards.

Network Models and Standards

Network models and standards play an important role in the telecommunications industry. These standards and protocols set up rules of operation. Protocols describe how requests, messages, and other signals are formatted and transmitted over the network. The network can only function as long as all computers are consistent in following the same set of rules for communication. Protocols like TCP/UDP and TCP/IP are two examples of network standards. These standards have helped build the Internet and the worldwide data networks we have today. The goal of any set of network standards is to provide the following:

▶ Interoperability

▶ Availability

▶ Flexibility

▶ Maintainability

Many groups have been working toward meeting this challenge, including the following organizations:

▶ International Organization for Standardization (ISO)

▶ Institute of Electrical and Electronics Engineers (IEEE)

▶ Internet Engineering Task Force (IETF)

▶ International Telecommunication Union—Telecommunications Standardization Sector (ITU-T)

The next section discusses the ISO model in detail.

OSI Model

The International Standards Organization developed the Open Systems Interconnection model (OSI) model in 1984. The model is based on a specific hierarchy in which each layer encapsulates the output of each adjacent layer. It is described in ISO 7498. Today, it is widely used as a guide in describing the operation of a networking environment. What was considered the universal communications standard now serves as a teaching model for all other protocols.

The OSI model is designed so that network communication is passed down the stack, from layer to layer. Information to be transmitted is put into the application layer, and ends at the physical layer. Then, it is transmitted over the medium (wire, coaxial, optical, or wireless) toward the target device, where it travels back up the stack to the application. Starting at the bottom of the stack and working up the seven layers of the OSI model are the physical, data link, network, transport, session, presentation, and application. Most people remember this order by using one of the many acronyms that have been thought up over the years. My favorite one is "Please Do Not Throw Sausage Pizza Away":

▶ Please (physical—Layer 1)

▶ Do (data link—Layer 2)

▶ Not (network—Layer 3)

▶ Throw (transport—Layer 4)

▶ Sausage (session—Layer 5)

▶ Pizza (presentation—Layer 6)

▶ Away (application—Layer 7)

For a better understanding of how the OSI model works, we'll start at the bottom of the stack and work our way up. Figure 7.1 illustrates the OSI model.

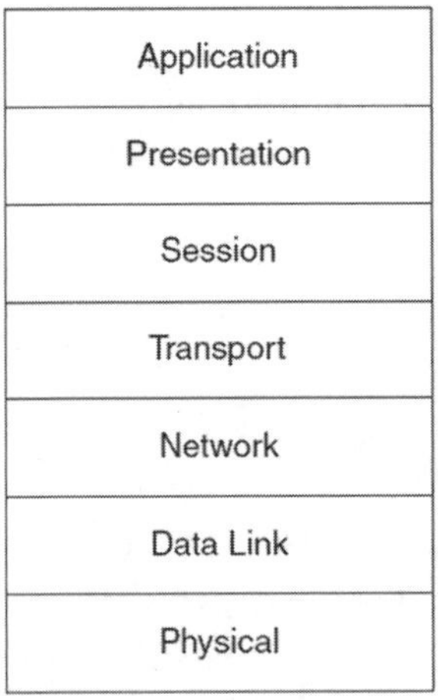

| Application |
| Presentation |
| Session |
| Transport |
| Network |
| Data Link |
| Physical |

FIGURE 7.1 **OSI model.**

ExamAlert

CISSP candidates need to know the seven layers of the OSI model. These include (from Layer 1 to Layer 7): physical, data link, network, transport, session, presentation, and application layer.

Physical Layer

Layer 1 is the *physical layer*. The physical layer accepts data that has been formatted as a frame from the data link layer and converts it to an electrical signal. Physical layer components include the following:

▶ Copper cabling

▶ Fiber cabling

▶ Wireless system components

▶ Wall jacks and connectors

▶ Ethernet hubs and repeaters

At Layer 1, bit-level communication takes place. The bits have no defined meaning on the wire, but the physical layer defines how long each bit lasts and how it is transmitted and received. Standards and specifications found at the physical layer include

▶ High-Speed Serial Interface (HSSI)

▶ V.24 and V.35

▶ EIA/TIA-232 and EIA/TIA-449 (where *EIA/TIA* stands for Electronic Industries Alliance/Telecommunications Industry Association)

▶ X.21

Data Link Layer

Layer 2 is the *data link layer*. It focuses on traffic within a single LAN. The data link layer is responsible for receiving data from the physical layer. The data link layer formats and organizes data. The data link layer components include the following:

▶ Bridges

▶ Switches

▶ NICs (network interface cards)

▶ MAC (Media Access Control) addresses

The data link layer organizes the data into frames. A frame is a logical structure in which data can be placed. The data link layer is responsible for stripping off the header of the data frame, leaving a data packet, which passes up to the network layer. Some of the protocols found at the data link layer include the following:

▶ Layer 2 Forwarding (L2F)

▶ Layer 2 Tunneling Protocol (L2TP)

▶ Fiber Distributed Data Interface (FDDI)

▶ Integrated Services Digital Network (ISDN)

▶ Serial Line Internet Protocol (SLIP)

▶ Point-to-Point Protocol (PPP)

Network Layer

Layer 3 is the *network layer*. Whereas the bottom two layers of the OSI model are associated with hardware, the network layer is tied to software. This layer is concerned with how data moves from network A to network B; ensuring that frames from the data link layer reach the correct network. The network layer is the home of the Internet Protocol, which acts as a postman in determining the best route from the source to the target network. Network layer protocols include the following:

▶ Internet Protocol (IP) (IPv4, IPv6, IPsec)

▶ Internetwork Packet Exchange (IPX)

▶ Internet Control Message Protocol (ICMP)

▶ Open Shortest Path First (OSPF)

▶ Border Gateway Protocol (BGP)

▶ Internet Group Management Protocol (IGMP)

Transport Layer

Layer 4 is the *transport layer*. Whereas the network layer routes information to its destination, the transport layer ensures completeness by handling end-to-end error recovery and flow control, and establishes a logical connection between two devices. Transport layer protocols include the following:

▶ Transmission Control Protocol (TCP), a connection-oriented protocol that provides reliable communication using handshaking, acknowledgments, error detection, and session teardown.

▶ User Datagram Protocol (UDP), a connectionless protocol that offers speed and low overhead as its primary advantage. Applications that use UDP must provide their own forms of error recovery because the protocol does not have this feature built in.

Session Layer

Layer 5 is the *session layer*. The purpose of the session layer is to allow two applications on different computers to establish and coordinate a session. A *session* is simply a name for a connection between two computers. When a data transfer is complete, the session layer is responsible for tearing down the session. Session layer protocols include the following:

▶ Remote Procedure Call (RPC)

▶ Structured Query Language (SQL)

▶ Secure Sockets Layer (SSL)

▶ Network File System (NFS)

Presentation Layer

Layer 6 is the *presentation layer*. The presentation layer performs a job similar to that of a waiter in a restaurant: Its main purpose is to deliver and present data to the application layer. In performing its job, the data must be formatted in a way that the application layer can understand and interpret the data. The presentation layer is skilled in translation because its duties include encrypting data, changing or converting the character set, and handling format conversion. Some standards and protocols found at the presentation layer include the following:

▶ American Standard Code for Information Interchange (ASCII)

▶ Extended Binary-Coded Decimal Interchange Code (EBCDIC)

▶ Joint Photographic Experts Group (JPEG)

▶ Musical Instrument Digital Interface (MIDI)

▶ Tagged Image File Format (TIFF)

ExamAlert

Where's encryption? The presentation layer is the natural home of encryption in the OSI model encryption. Modern systems can implement encryption at other layers, such as data link, network, or even the application layer. An example of this is IPv6.

Note

Encapsulation is the process of adding headers to user data as it is handed from each layer to the next lower layer.

Application Layer

Layer 7 is the *application layer*. Recognized as the top layer of the OSI model, this layer serves as the window for application services—it is the layer that applications talk to. You probably send email or surf the Web, and usually never think about all the underlying processes that make it possible. Layer 7 is not the application itself, but rather the channel through which applications communicate. Examples of protocols operating at the application layer include

- ▶ File Transfer Protocol (FTP)
- ▶ Line Print Daemon (LPD)
- ▶ Telnet
- ▶ Simple Mail Transfer Protocol (SMTP)
- ▶ Trivial File Transfer Protocol (TFTP)
- ▶ Hypertext Transfer Protocol (HTTP)
- ▶ Post Office Protocol version 3 (POP3)
- ▶ Internet Message Access Protocol (IMAP)
- ▶ Simple Network Management Protocol (SNMP)
- ▶ Electronic Data Interchange (EDI)

OSI Summary

Table 7.1 summarizes each of the seven layers and the equipment and protocols that work at each layer as described throughout this chapter.

TABLE 7.1 **OSI Model and Protocols**

Layer	Equipment	Protocols
Application	Application proxy firewall	FTP, DNS, HTTP, SNMP, RIP
Presentation		ASCII, TIFF, JPEG, GIF, MIDI, MPEG
Session		NetBIOS, NFS, SQL, RPC, SMB
Transport	Circuit-level proxy firewall	TCP, UDP, SPX, SSL, TLS
Network	Router	IP, ICMP, IGMP, OSPF, IPX
Data link	Switch, bridge	SLIP, PPP, L2F, L2TP, FDDI, ARP, RARP
Physical	Hub	EIA/TIA-232, HSSI, X.21

ExamAlert

CISSP candidates need to know where various protocols can be found in the OSI model. Make sure you can specify the placement of well-known protocols at each of the seven layers: physical, data link, network, transport, session, presentation, and application layer.

Note

In real life, not all protocols fit cleanly into the OSI layered model. Although SSL is typically shown at the transport layer, it actually provides functionality between Layer 4 (transport) and Layer 7 (application). SSL sits between these layers to provide security services to many modern Internet applications.

Encapsulation/De-encapsulation

Encapsulation is a key concept in networking. Encapsulation is the process of adding headers to the data as it is passed down the stack. Consider the following example:

1. A message is created at the application layer.

2. The message or protocol data unit (PDU) is passed to the presentation layer. Information and a checksum, known as a *header*, are added.

3. The information is passed down to the session layer and the process is repeated. This continues until the data reaches the data link layer.

4. At the data link layer, a header and trailer are added. Now the data is said to be a *frame*. When Ethernet is used for this process, the trailer is a cyclic redundancy check (CRC).

5. The frame is passed to the physical layer and converted to signals appropriate for the transmission medium.

The *de-encapsulation* process starts when the message reaches the recipient. The headers at each layer are stripped off as the data moves back up the stack. The only layer that physically communicates is the physical layer. Processes running at higher layers, say Layer 7, communicate logically as if they were directly connected at Layer 1, even though they are not. Figure 7.2 shows an example of this.

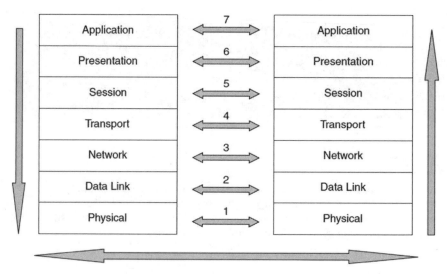

FIGURE 7.2 **OSI communication.**

> **Note**
>
> PDU is just one of the terms used in networking. Don't be surprised to also see such terms as *frame*, *packet*, and *datagram*.

TCP/IP

TCP/IP is the foundation of the Internet as we know it today. Its roots can be traced back to standards adopted by the U.S. government's Department of Defense (DoD) in 1982. *TCP/IP* is similar to the OSI model, but it consists of only four layers: the network access layer, the Internet layer, the host-to-host (transport) layer, and the application layer.

It is of critical importance to remember that the TCP/IP model was originally developed as a flexible, fault-tolerant network. Security was not a driving concern. The network was designed to specifications that could withstand a nuclear strike destroying key routing nodes. The designers of this original network never envisioned the Internet we use today. Therefore, many of the original TCP/IP protocols seem dated and insecure now. Protocols like FTP, Telnet, and RIP (Routing Information Protocol) all suffer from security problems. As an example, Telnet's security was designed to mask the screen display of passwords the user typed because the designers didn't want shoulder surfers stealing passwords; however, the passwords themselves are then sent in clear text on the wire. Little concern was given to the fact that an untrusted party might have access to the wire and be able to sniff the clear text password. FTP is also a clear text protocol; it uses both ports TCP/20 and TCP/21 for data and control. Many of the security mechanisms used in IPv4, such as IPSec, are add-ons to the original protocol suite.

Network Access Layer

The network access layer loosely corresponds to Layers 1 and 2 of the OSI model. Some literature separates this single layer into two and refers to them as *physical access* and *data link*. Whether viewed as one layer or two, this portion of the TCP/IP network model is responsible for the physical delivery of IP packets via frames.

Ethernet is the most commonly used LAN frame type. Ethernet uses Carrier Sense Multiple Access Collision Detection (CSMA/CD). Ethernet frames are addressed with MAC addresses that identify the source and destination devices. MAC addresses are 6 bytes long and are intended to be unique to the NIC in which they are burned. The first three bytes, known as the organizational unique identifier (OUI) are unique to the manufacturer. As an example, Cisco owns OUI 00-00-0C. Any NIC with a MAC address that begins with 00:00:0C is a Cisco NIC. Cisco can then assign this portion of the address until all possible values have been exhausted, at which point a new OUI is needed. Occasionally, though, vendors repeat addresses as they cycle through series.

Sometimes vendors also provide features in the NIC driver to change the MAC address to a unique locally administered address. Third-party programs are available that allow attackers to spoof MAC addresses. Network layer security standards:

▶ 802.1AE (MACsec) defines a security standard designed to provide confidentiality, integrity, and data origin authentication. MACsec frame formats are similar to the Ethernet frame but include Security Tags, Message authentication codes (ICV), Secure Connectivity Associations, and default cipher suites (Galois/Counter Mode of Advanced Encryption Standard cipher with 128-bit key).

▶ 802.1AR ensures the identity of the trusted network components. This standard uses unique per-device identifiers (DevID) along with the cryptography to bind a specific device to a unique identifiers.

> **Note**
>
> Where's Address Resolution Protocol (ARP)? ARP can be discussed at either the TCP/IP Network or Internet layer. The ARP table and NICs are at TCP/IP Layer 1, whereas logical addresses are at Layer 2. The ARP process takes a Layer 2 logical address and resolves it to an unknown Layer 1 physical address.

Internet Layer

The Internet layer maps to OSI Layer 3. Two primary protocol groups found at this layer include routable and routing protocols. IP is an example of a routable protocols. Protocols related to routing include OSPF and IGRP (Internet Gateway Routing Protocol). The Internet layer also contains ICMP, the interface to ARP, and the IGMP. ICMP is usually noted for its support of ping, but can also be used for services like IP support, error, and diagnostic protocols. ICMP can handle problems, such as delivering error messages. IGMP is used for multicast messages. ARP is used to resolve known IP addresses to unknown MAC addresses.

Internet Protocol

IP is a routable protocol whose job is to make the best effort at delivery. The IPv4 header is normally 20 bytes long, but can be as long as 60 bytes with options added. Currently, most organizations use IPv4. IPv6 is the planned replacement. It has better security and increases support for IP addresses from the current 32 bits to 128 bits. IPv4 uses a logical address scheme for IP addresses. Whereas MAC addresses are considered a physical address, an IP address is considered a logical address.

Although an in-depth knowledge of the header is not needed for the test, complete details can be found in Request for Comments (RFC) 791. Examination of the structure of IP packets might not be the most exciting part of security work, but a basic understanding is extremely helpful in recognizing the many attacks based on manipulation of these packets. For example, in a teardrop attack, the Total Length field and Fragmentation fields are modified so that fragments are incorrectly overlapped. Fragmentation and source routing are two potential security issues with IPv4.

If IP needs to transmit a datagram larger than the network access layer allows, the datagram must be divided into smaller packets. Not all network topologies are capable of handling the same datagram size; therefore, *fragmentation* is an important function of IP. And as IP packets pass through routers, the needs of the upcoming network access layer may change again. IP is responsible for reading the acceptable size for the network access layer. If the existing datagram is too large, IP performs fragmentation and divides the datagram into two or more packets. Each fragmented packet is labeled with the following bits:

▶ **Length**—The length specified is the total length of the fragment.

▶ **Offset**—Specifies the distance from the first byte of the original datagram.

▶ **More**—Indicates whether this fragment has more fragments following it or is the last in the series of fragments.

Loose source routing and *strict source routing* are other options that IP supports. These options allow a pseudo-routing path to be specified between the source and the target. Although potentially useful in certain situations, attackers can use this functionality to set up a man-in-the-middle attack.

> **Note**
>
> IP addresses are required because physical addressees are tied to the physical topology used. Some LANs use Ethernet but other LANs are connected to ATM (asynchronous transfer mode) or token ring networks. Because no common format or structure exists, the IP protocol is used to bind these dissimilar networks together.
>
> The newest version of IP is IPv6. IPv6 got a big boost in April of 2011 because that is when APNIC officially ran out of IPv4 addresses. Although the depletion of IPv4 addresses has been a concern for many years, the fact that IPv4 address space has reached exhaustion means we have reached the tipping point of adoption of the IPv6 protocol.

> **Note**
>
> The newest version of IP is IPv6. IPv6 has been supported by more and more operating systems since 2000. Although it might not be used in many places in the United States yet, it is used extensively in Europe and Asia. In addition to offering better security features, it also uses 128-bit addressing, which will allow for the growing need of IP addresses for many years.

Internet Protocol version 6 (IPv6) is the newest version of IP and is the designated replacement for IPv4, as shown in Figure 7.3. IPv6 brings many improvements to modern networks. One of these is that the address space moves from 32 bits to 128 bits. Also, IPv4 uses an option field. IPv6 does not support broadcast traffic; instead, IPv6 uses a link-local scope as an all-nodes multicast address. IPv6 can use multiple addresses, including a global and a local-link. A global (routable) address is used for communication beyond the local network. IPv6 relies on IPv6 routing advertisements to assign the global address. The link-local address is used for local network communication only. IPv6-enabled devices create a link-local address independently. There is no need for an IPv6 router advertisement for the creation of a local-link address.

IPv6 offers built-in support for IPsec so that greater protection exists for data during transmission, and it offers end-to-end data authentication and privacy. With the move to IPv6, Network addess transulation (NAT) will no longer be needed. However, with so many IPv4 networks in place, there is a need for transition mechanisms for migrating from IPv4 to IPv6. Two of these mechanisms are:

▶ 6to4—an Internet transition mechanism for migrating from IPv4 to IPv6 that allows IPv6 packets to be transmitted over an IPv4 network.

▶ Teredo—another transition technology that can be used for IPv6-capable hosts that are on the IPv4 Internet and that have no native connection to an IPv6 network.

When IPv6 is fully deployed, one protocol that will no longer be needed is ARP. IPv6 does not support ARP, and instead uses Network Discovery Protocol (NDP). DHCP is also not required with IPv6. It can be used but has been replaced with stateless autoconfiguration. Common routing protocols to be used with IPv6 include RIPng, OSPFv3, IS-ISv2, and EIGRPv6. To date, Asia has a higher adoption rate of IPv6 compared to the United States.

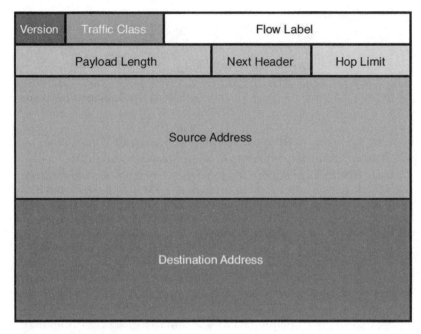

FIGURE 7.3 **IPv6 header.**

Internet Control Message Protocol

One of the protocols residing at the Internet layer is *ICMP*. Its purpose is to provide diagnostic feedback or to report logical errors. Because ICMP resides at the Internet layer, it is a separate protocol and is distinctly different from IP.

All ICMP messages follow the same basic format. The first byte of an ICMP header indicates the type of ICMP message. The following byte contains the code for each particular type of ICMP. Table 7.2 lists the eight most common ICMP types. A complete list of all ICMP parameters is at www.iana.org/assignments/icmp-parameters.

TABLE 7.2 **ICMP Types and Codes**

Type	Code	Function
0/8	0	Echo Response/Request (Ping)
3	0–15	Destination Unreachable
4	0	Source Quench
5	0–3	Redirect
11	0–1	Time Exceeded

(Continued)

TABLE 7.2 **(Continued)**

Type	Code	Function
12	0	Parameter Fault
13/14	0	Time Stamp Request/Response
17/18	0	Subnet Mask Request/Response

One of the most common ICMP types is a ping. Although ICMP can be very helpful, it is also valued by attackers because it can be manipulated and used for a variety of attacks including ping of death, Smurf, timestamp query, netmask query, and redirects.

Address Resolution Protocol

ARP's purpose is to resolve addressing between the network access layer and Internet layer of the TCP/IP model. ARP is a two-step resolution process performed by first sending a broadcast message requesting a target's physical address. If the device with the requested logical address hears the request, it issues a unicast ARP reply containing its MAC address to the original sender. The MAC address is then placed in the requester's ARP cache and used to address subsequent frames. *Reverse ARP* (RARP) is used to resolve known physical addresses to unknown IP addresses.

Attackers can manipulate ARP because it is a trusting protocol. Two well-known attacks include ARP poisoning and ARP flooding. ARP poisoning is possible as a host will accept bogus ARP responses as valid because it cannot tell the difference between a bogus and valid reply. Such attacks can be used to intercept traffic bound for the gateway or can be used to facilitate an attack against a targeted host. ARP poisoning allows attackers to redirect traffic on a switched network. ARP attacks play a role in a variety of man-in-the middle attacks, spoofing, and session-hijacking attacks.

> **Caution**
>
> Remember that ARP is unauthenticated; therefore, an attacker can send unsolicited ARP replies, poison the ARP table, and spoof another host.

Internet Group Management Protocol

IGMP is a Layer 2 protocol that is responsible for managing IP multicast groups. IP multicasts can send messages or packets to a specified group of hosts or routers. This is different from a broadcast, which all users in a network receive. IGMP transmissions are sent to a group of systems.

Host-to-Host (Transport) Layer

The host-to-host layer is responsible for reliable and efficient communication between endpoints. The endpoints referred to are programs or services. This exchange can be peer-to-peer, such as an instant messaging application, or it might be a client/server interaction, such as a web browser sending a request to a web server. The host-to-host layer loosely corresponds to OSI Layer 4 but provides end-to-end delivery. The two primary protocols located at the host-to-host layer are the Transmission Control Protocol (TCP) and the User Datagram Protocol (UDP). Figure 7.4 illustrates the packet header for TCP and UDP.

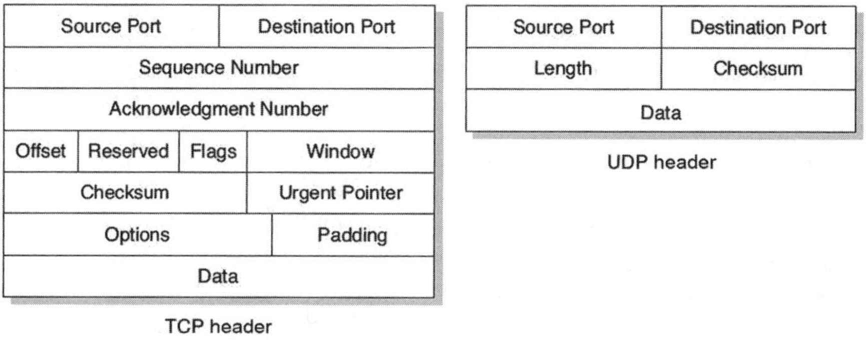

Source Port		Destination Port
Sequence Number		
Acknowledgment Number		
Offset	Reserved	Flags	Window
Checksum		Urgent Pointer
Options		Padding
Data		

TCP header

Source Port	Destination Port
Length	Checksum
Data	

UDP header

FIGURE 7.4 **TCP and UDP header.**

Each of these protocols has its pros and cons, and developers select one or the other depending on what they are trying to accomplish via the network. Generally, trivial and ad-hoc exchanges across the network are done in a connectionless manner (UDP). More persistent network relationships are largely handled with connection-oriented solutions (TCP), especially when a substantial amount of data is being transferred.

At the host-to-host layer, you will find the capability for error checking and retransmission. This ensures that all connection-oriented messages sent will arrive intact at the receiving end. A checksum or similar mechanism is generally used to ensure message integrity. Retransmission strategies vary; for example, in the case of TCP, data not positively acknowledged by the recipient in a timely way is retransmitted.

TCP

TCP enables two hosts to establish a connection and exchange data reliably. TCP has a nominal 20-byte packet size that contains fields to support flow control, reliable communication, and to ensure that missing data is re-sent. At the heart of TCP is a 1-byte flag field. The most common flags are summarized in Table 7.3. These flags help control the TCP communication.

TABLE 7.3 **TCP Flags**

Flag	Name	Function
URG	Urgent	Urgent data
ACK	Acknowledgment	Acknowledge data
PSH	Push	Push buffered data
RST	Reset	Reset TCP connection
SYN	Synchronize	Start session
FIN	Finish	Close session

Although there are actually 8 fields (bits) in the 1 byte reserved for flags, the upper two were not defined until 2001 and are not widely used. These include the CWR (Congestion Window Reduced) and ECN (Explicit Congestion Notification Echo) flags.

TCP provides reliable communication by performing formal startup and shutdown handshakes. The TCP three-step handshake occurs before any data is sent. Figure 7.5 illustrates the three-step startup and four-step shutdown.

FIGURE 7.5 **TCP operation.**

The flags used to manage three-step startup are SYN and ACK, whereas RST and FIN are used to tear down a connection. FIN is used during a normal four-step shutdown, whereas RST is used to signal the end of an abnormal session. Between the startup and shutdown, TCP guarantees delivery of data by using sequence and acknowledgment numbers. Vulnerabilities that exist at this layer include the TCP sequence number attack that results in session hijacking, and the port-based attack of SYN flooding.

UDP

UDP does not perform any handshaking processes. So although this makes it considerably less reliable than TCP, it does offer the benefit of speed. The UDP header is only 8 bytes in length. There are four 2-byte fields in the header. There are no variations on this. The length is fixed. Figure 7.6 illustrates the operation of UDP.

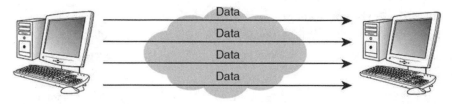

FIGURE 7.6   **UDP operation.**

UDP can be used for services like IPTV (Internet Protocol Television), video multicast, and Voice over IP (VoIP). UDP in VoIP is primarily used for the voice connection portion of the call, and TCP is used for the setup and call control for the actual call. UDP is ideally suited for such applications that require fast delivery. UDP does not use sequence and acknowledgment numbers.

Comparing/Contrasting UDP and TCP

Table 7.4 illustrates the differences between UDP and TCP.

TABLE 7.4   **UDP and TCP Differences**

Service	UDP	TCP
Speed	✓	
Low overhead	✓	
Connectionless	✓	
Reliable		✓
Maintains state		✓
Controls congestion		✓
Uses flow control		✓

Application Layer

The application or process layer sits at the top of the protocol stack and maps loosely to OSI Layers 6 and 7. This layer is responsible for application support. Applications are typically mapped not by name, but by their corresponding port. Ports are placed into TCP and UDP packets so that the correct application can be passed to the required protocols. Although applications can be made to operate on nonstandard ports, the established port numbers serve as the de facto standard. There are 65,535 ports separated into three ranges, as shown in Table 7.5.

TABLE 7.5 **Ports and Ranges**

Range	Usage	Attribute
0–1023	Well known	System services
1024–49151	Registered	Software services
49152–65535	Random	Client programs

A complete list of ports is at www.iana.org/assignments/port-numbers. Some of the more common well-known applications and their associated ports are as follows:

▶ **File Transfer Protocol**—FTP is a TCP service and operates on ports 20 and 21. This application moves files from one computer to another. Port 20 is used for the data stream and transfers the data between the client and the server. Port 21 is the control stream and is used to pass commands between the client and the FTP server. Attacks on FTP commonly target clear-text passwords that can be sniffed. FTP is one of the most commonly targeted services.

▶ **Telnet**—Telnet is a TCP service that operates on port 23. Telnet enables a client at one site to establish a remote session with a host at another site. The program passes the information typed at the client's keyboard to the host computer system. Telnet can be configured to allow anonymous connections, but should be configured to require usernames and passwords. Unfortunately, even then, Telnet sends them in clear text. When a user is logged in, he or she can perform any task allowed by their user permissions. Applications like Secure Shell version 2 (SSHv2) should be considered as a replacement.

▶ **Simple Mail Transfer Protocol**—This TCP service operates on port 25. It is designed for the exchange of electronic mail between networked systems. Messages sent through SMTP have two parts: an address header and the message text. All types of computers can exchange messages with

SMTP. Spoofing, spamming, and open/misconfigured mail relays are several of the vulnerabilities associated with SMTP.

▶ **Domain Name Service**—This application operates on port 53 and performs address translation. DNS converts fully qualified domain names (FQDNs) into numeric IP addresses or IP addresses into FQDNs. This system works in a similar way to a phone directory that enables users to remember domain names (such as examcram2.com) instead of IP addresses (such as 114.112.18.23). On some small networks, *Network Information Service* (NIS) can be used in place of DNS to provide nameserver information and distribute system configuration information. DNS uses UDP for DNS queries and TCP for zone transfers. DNS is subject to poisoning and, if misconfigured, can be solicited to perform a full zone transfer. Security DNS (DNSSEC) is an alternative to DNS. With DNSSEC, the DNS server provides a signature and digitally signs every response. For DNSSEC to function properly, authentication keys have to be distributed before use. Otherwise, DNSSEC is of little use if the client has no means to validate the authentication. You can read more about DNSSEC at www.dnssec.net.

Caution

You should be aware that DNSSEC does not provide confidentiality of data, and it does not protect against DDoS attacks.

▶ **Bootstrap Protocol (BootP)**—BootP is used to download operating parameters to thin clients and is the forerunner to the Dynamic Host Configuration Protocol (DHCP). Both protocols are found on UDP ports 67 and 68.

▶ **Trivial File Transfer Protocol (TFTP)**—TFTP operates on port 69. It is considered a down-and-dirty version of FTP because it uses UDP to cut down on overhead, and is intended for very small files. It not only copies files without the session management offered by TCP, but it also requires no authentication, which could pose a big security risk. It is typically used to transfer router configuration files and to configure cable modems for cable companies.

▶ **Hypertext Transfer Protocol**—HTTP is a TCP service that operates on port 80, and is one of the most well-known protocols that reside at the application layer. HTTP has helped make the Web the popular protocol it is today. The HTTP connection model is known as a *stateless* connection. HTTP uses a request-response protocol in which a client sends a request and a server sends a response. Attacks that exploit HTTP can target a server, a browser, or scripts that run on the browser. Nimda is an example of code that targets a web server.

▶ **Internet Message Authentication Protocol**—IMAPv4 is an alternative to POP3 that operates on port 143. IMAPv4 offers advantages over POP3, such as enhanced functionality in manipulating a user's inbox, the capability to better manage mail folders, and optimized online performance. With IMAPv4, email is stored on the mail server and can be accessed from any IMAPv4 email client on the network. With POP3 email is downloaded to the mail client where it is accessed.

▶ **Simple Network Management Protocol**—SNMP is a UDP service that operates on ports 161 and 162. It was envisioned to be an efficient and inexpensive way to monitor and remotely configure networks. The SNMP protocol allows agents to gather information, including network statistics, and report back to their management stations. Most large corporations have implemented some type of SNMP management. Some of the security problems that plague versions 1 and 2 of SNMP are caused by the fact that community access strings are passed as clear text and the default community strings (public/private) are well known. SNMP version 3 is the most current form and offers encryption for more robust security.

▶ **Secure Sockets Layer**—SSL operates on port 443 and is a secure protocol used to connect to an untrusted network. SSL uses a two-part process to establish communications, and is based on hybrid cryptography. It is the encryption used in HTTPS. Attacks against SSL can be launched if a targeted system supports weak ciphers. In such a situation, an attacker might be able to manipulate the system so that encrypted data is downgraded or even deciphered to achieve access to sensitive data.

▶ **Line Printer Daemon**—LPD operates on TCP port 515 and is a network protocol used to spool and deliver print jobs to printers.

▶ **Lightweight Directory Access Protocol**—LDAP operates on TCP. LDAP was created as a means to access X.500 directory services. X.500 is a series of computer networking standards covering electronic directory services. LDAP had no data encryption method in versions 1 and 2, whereas version 3 has a much greater security model built in and is supported by TLS.

▶ **Routing Information Protocol**—RIP operates on port 520 and allows routing information to be exchanged between routers on an IP network.

Even though RIP is usually listed as part of Layer 3, as are the other routing protocols, it is an application. RIP uses UDP ports to send and receive routing information. The original version of RIP has no security and bogus RIP updates can be used to launch DoS attacks.

▶ **Pretty Good Privacy (PGP)**—PGP was developed in 1991 as a free email security application. PGP v5 uses port 11371. PGP was designed to offer military grade encryption, and works well at securing email. Unlike public key infrastructure (PKI), PGP works by using a web of trust. Users distribute and sign their own public keys. Unlike the PKI certificate authority, this web of trust requires users to determine how much they trust the party they are about to exchange keys with. PGP is a hybrid cryptosystem in that it uses both public and private encryption. Sample algorithms PGP can use include Triple DES and Twofish for symmetric encryption, and RSA for asymmetric encryption.

Although there are hundreds of ports and corresponding applications, in practice only a few hundred are in common use. CISSP exam questions on ports will most likely be focused on common ports like these shown in Table 7.6.

TABLE 7.6 **Common Port Numbers**

Port	Service	Protocol
21	FTP	TCP
22	SSH	TCP
23	Telnet	TCP
25	SMTP	TCP
53	DNS	TCP/UDP
67/68	DHCP	UDP
69	TFTP	UDP
80	HTTP	TCP
88	Kerberos	UDP
110	POP3	TCP
111	SUNRPC	TCP/UDP
143	IMAP	TCP
161	SNMP	UDP
162	SNMP Trap	UDP
389	LDAP	TCP
443	SSL/TLS	TCP

LANs and Their Components

A *local area network* is a critical component of a modern data network. A LAN comprises two or more computers, a communication protocol, a network topology, and cabling or wireless connectivity. A LAN is best defined as computers or other devices that communicate over a small geographical area, such as the following:

▶ A section of a one-story building

▶ The whole floor of a small building

▶ Several buildings on a small campus

LAN Communication Protocols

More than 80% of all LANs use the Ethernet protocol as a means of communication. The Ethernet specification describes how data can be sent between computers in physical proximity. The Digital, Intel, and Xerox (DIX) group first released Ethernet in 1975. Since its introduction, the IEEE Standards Committee has introduced several variations of the Ethernet II protocol, including the following:

▶ IEEE 802.3

▶ IEEE 802.3 with Logical Link Control (LLC)

▶ IEEE 802.3 with Subnetwork Access Protocol (SNAP)

Although the CISSP exam will not delve very far into the specifics of Ethernet, it is helpful to know the size and structure of these frames. Not including the preamble, an Ethernet frame ranges from 64 to 1,518 bytes. The Ethernet frame uses 18 bytes for control information; therefore, the data in an Ethernet frame can be between 46 and 1,500 bytes long. Figure 7.7 illustrates an 802.3 Ethernet frame.

6 Bytes	6 Bytes	2 Bytes	46 to 1500 Bytes	4 Bytes
Destination Address	Source Address	Type Field	Payload	CRC

FIGURE 7.7 **Ethernet frame.**

An older LAN wired networking protocol is token ring, which functions by arranging all the systems in a circle. A special packet, known as a *token*, travels around the circle. If any device needs to send information, it must capture the token, attach a message to it, and then let it continue to travel around the network.

Network Topologies

The design layout of a network is its *topology*. Before a network can be installed, a topology must be chosen to match the network's needs and intended use. Common topologies include bus, star, ring, mesh and fully connected. The sections that follow discuss these topologies in greater detail.

Bus Topology

A bus topology consists of a single cable with multiple computers or devices attached to it. The cable is terminated on each end. In large environments, this is impractical because the medium has physical limitations. Problems range from low speeds to complete network outages; one break can bring down the entire network (see Figure 7.8).

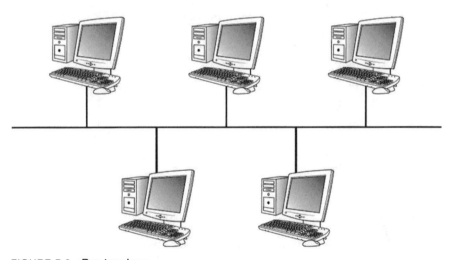

FIGURE 7.8 **Bus topology.**

Star Topology

A star topology is the oldest of the three primary network topologies, and was originally used in telephone systems. The star design consists of multiple computers or devices attached to a central switch. Wires radiate outward from the hub in a star-like pattern. Although this scheme uses the most cable, a break will normally affect only one computer. This is the most widely used LAN topology (see Figure 7.9).

FIGURE 7.9 **Star topology.**

Ring Topology

The ring topology is characterized by the fact that there are no endpoints or terminators. It is laid out as a continuous loop of cable, in which all networked computers are attached. Token Ring Copper Distributed Data Interface (CDDI) and FDDI networks use a ring topology (see Figure 7.10). Some ring technologies use Carrier Sense Multiple Access with Collision Avoidance (CSMA/CA). CSMA/CA is a deterministic protocol, whereas CSMA/CD is contention based.

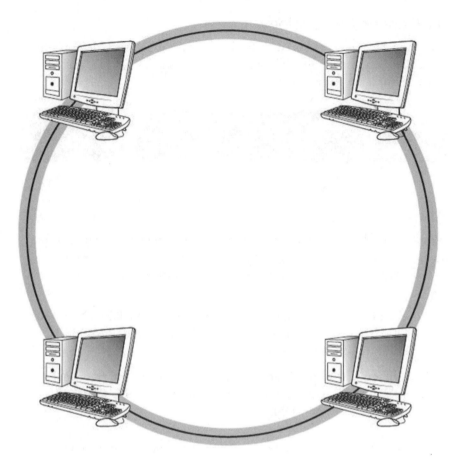

FIGURE 7.10 **Ring topology.**

ExamAlert

CISSP test candidates should make sure to understand how CSMA/CD works because it is Ethernet's media access method. Each device has equal priority when accessing and transmitting data on the wire. Ethernet devices must sense the wire before transmitting. If two devices attempt to transmit simultaneously, a collision occurs. When this happens, the devices retransmit their frames after waiting a random period and sensing the wire again.

Mesh Topology

A mesh network topology is one in which each node relays data for the network. Mesh networks can use either flooding or routing to relay communications.

Fully Connected Topology

A fully connected network connects to all nodes. Although such designs offer great redundancy, the number of connections grows quickly, which makes it impractical for large networks.

> **ExamAlert**
>
> Modern networks commonly implement combinations of network topologies.

LAN Cabling

Even with a defined topology, it is necessary to determine what type of cable will connect the various devices. Cables act as a medium to carry electrical signals between the networked devices. One of two transmission methods can be used:

- ▶ **Baseband**—Baseband transmissions use the entire medium to transport a single channel of communication. Ethernet is an example of this baseband transmission scheme.

- ▶ **Broadband**—Broadband can support many channels and frequencies on its backbone. Two good examples of broadband are cable television and digital subscriber lines (DSL).

Many types of cables can be used for network communications including the following:

- ▶ **Coaxial cable**—Coax cable consists of a single solid-copper wire core to carry data signals. This wire is insulated with a Teflon or plastic material, called a *dielectric*, which is covered with braided shielding used as the signal ground. The entire cable is then coated with plastic (see Figure 7.11). Common types include RG-6 and RG-59. Connectors are typically either BNC or F-connector. Although it was widely used in the early days of networking, its usage has waned.

- ▶ **Twisted pair**—If you're in an office, you will probably notice that twisted-pair wiring is being used to connect your computer to a wall jack located nearby. The most common connector terminating this wiring is the RJ-45. Twisted pair can be purchased in a many varieties, one of which is unshielded twisted pair (UTP). UTP is unshielded copper wires, twisted around each other, and insulated in plastic. Not only is it easy to work with, but it is also generally inexpensive. Shielded twisted pair (STP) cable comprises individually insulated twisted wire pairs, as with

UTP, but has an additional shielding made of a metallic substance, such as foil. This additional shielding offers support against electromagnetic interference. The primary drawbacks to copper cabling are that it is vulnerable to being tapped and it emanates electrical energy that could possibly be intercepted. The most common types of cabling include: CAT3, CAT5, CAT5e, CAT6, CAT6a, and CAT7. Wiring standards include T568A and T568B. Table 7.7 specifies many table types, lengths, and topologies.

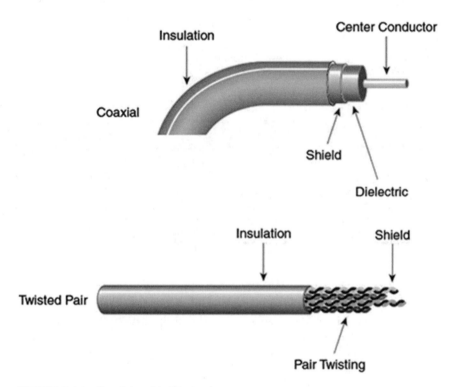

FIGURE 7.11   Coaxial and twisted pair.

TABLE 7.7   **Cable Specification**

Ethernet Name	Cable Specifications	Distance Supported	Topology
10BASE-5	50 ohm, thick coaxial (Thicknet)	500 meters	Bus
10BASE-2	50 ohm, RG-58 A/U (Thinnet)	185 meters	Bus

(Continued)

TABLE 7.7 *(Continued)*

Ethernet Name	Cable Specifications	Distance Supported	Topology
10BASE-T	Cat3 UDP (or better)	100 meters	Star
10BASE-FL	Multimode fiber optic	2,000 meters	Star
100BASE-TX	Cat5 UTP	100 meters	Star
10,000BASE-TX	Cat6/Cat7 UTP	100 meters	Star
100BASE-T4	Cat3 UTP (or better)	100 meters	Star
100BASE-FX multimode fiber optic	Multiple-fiber connections	136 meters	Star
100BASE-FX multimode fiber optic	One-fiber connection	160 meters	Star

ExamAlert

For the exam, you will want to know that plenum-grade cable is coated with a fire-retardant and is designed to be used in plenum spaces, such as crawlspaces, false ceilings, and below the raised floors in a building. This special coating is fluoropolymers instead of polyethylene vinyl chloride used in nonplenum cables. It is designed to not give off toxic gases or smoke as it burns to help ensure the safety of occupants in case of a fire.

▶ **Fiber-optic cable**—Whereas twisted pair cable and coax cable rely on copper wire for data transmissions, fiber uses glass. These strands of glass carry light waves encoded to signal the data being transmitted. Common connector types include SC, ST, and LC. Fiber has several advantages, including greater bandwidth, and is somewhat more secure from physical tapping. Basically, two types of fiber cables are in use. They are constructed differently to handle different types of light:

  ▶ **Multimode fiber**—Typically used in LANs and powered by light-emitting diodes (LEDs).

  ▶ **Single-mode fiber**—Typically used in WANs and powered by laser light.

Caution

You will want to remember that fiber is more secure than copper cable because it does not radiate signals and requires specialized equipment to tap.

Network Types

Networks of computers can range from small to large. On a very small scale there are *personal area networks* (PAN). PANs allow a variety of personal and handheld electronic devices to communicate over a short range. The most common type is a wireless PAN (WPAN). Bluetooth is one technology used in support of WPANs.

Although it is nice to know two computers can communicate locally via a local area network (LAN), most need the capability to communicate over a larger geographical region. To communicate between neighboring buildings, a *campus area network* (CAN) can be used. For those that need to communicate on a citywide level, the *metropolitan area network* (MAN) was created. A MAN is a network that interconnects a region larger than that covered by a LAN. It can include a city, geographic region, or large area.

If you work for a company that owns several buildings located in different states or countries, that network is part of a *wide area network*. A WAN spans a geographic distance that is too large for LANs and MANs. WANs are connected by routers. When two LANs are connected together over a distance, they form a WAN.

You might think that just about covers the different network types, but there is one more worth mentioning. *Global Area Networks* (GANs) offer the interconnection of terminals that do not have a geographical limitation. A GAN can connect computers from various countries or localities from around the world.

Network Storage

Storage area networks (SANs) are networks of storage disks and devices. SANs connect multiple servers to a centralized pool of disk storage. SANs improve system administration by allowing centralized storage instead of having to manage hundreds of servers, each with their own disks. SANs are similar to Network Attached Storage (NAS). One of the big differences is that a NAS appears to the client as a file server or standalone system. A SAN appears to the client as a local disk or volume that is available to be formatted and used locally as needed. SANs are growing in use because of increased server virtualization. SANs can use various types of technologies for connectivity. Several are listed here:

> ▶ Internet Small Computer System Interface (iSCSI)—A SAN standard used for connecting data storage facilities and allowing remote SCSI devices to communicate. It does not require any special infrastructure and can run over existing IP LAN, MAN, or WAN networks.

▶ Fiber Channel over Ethernet (FCoE)—Another transport protocol that is similar to iSCSI. FCoE can operate at speeds of 10 GB per second and rides on top of the Ethernet protocol. Although it is fast, it has a disadvantage in that it is non-routable.

▶ Host Bus Adapter (HBA) Allocation—Used to connect a host system to an enterprise storage device. HBAs can be allocated by either soft zoning or by persistent binding. Soft zoning is the most permissive, whereas persistent binding decreases address space and increases network complexity.

▶ LUN Masking—Implemented primarily at the HBA level. It is a number system that makes LUN numbers available to some but not to others. LUN masking implemented at this level is vulnerable to any attack that compromises the local adapter.

Several issues related to SANs include redundancy, replication, snapshots, and duplication. Location redundancy is the concept that data should be accessible from more than one location as a backup. An extra measure of redundancy can be provided by means of a replication service so that data is available even if the main storage backup system fails. Another issue with SANs is the protection of the data. Secure storage management and replication systems are designed to allow a company to manage and handle all corporate data in a secure manner with a focus on the confidentiality, integrity, and availability of the information. The replication service allows for the data to be duplicated and secured so that confidentiality and fault tolerance are achieved. For better fault tolerance, multipath solutions can be used to reduce the risk of data loss or lack of availability by setting up multiple routes between a server and its drives. The multipathing software maintains a listing of all requests, passes them through the best possible path, and reroutes communication if one of the paths dies.

SAN snapshots provide the capability to temporarily stop writing to physical disk to make a point-in-time backup copy. Snapshot software is typically fast and makes a copy quickly, regardless of the drive size.

Finally, am I the only one that ends up with seven different versions of a file? This common problem can be addressed in SANs by means of data de-duplication. It's simply the process of removing redundant data to improve enterprise storage utilization. Redundant data is not copied. It is replaced with a pointer to the one unique copy of the data. Only one instance of redundant data is retained on the enterprise storage media, such as disk or tape.

Communication Standards

The baseband and broadband communications discussed earlier need to be signaled across the cabling you chose. This signaling can take place in one of three methods:

▶ **Simplex**—Communication occurs in one direction.

▶ **Half duplex**—Communication can occur in both directions, but only one system can send information at a time.

▶ **Full duplex**—Communication occurs in both directions and both computers can send information at the same time.

Something to consider when choosing cabling is how far you need to propagate the signal. Although each communication approach has specific advantages, they share some common disadvantages. These include attenuation and crosstalk. Attenuation is the reduction of signal. As the signal travels farther away from the transmitting device, the signal becomes weaker in intensity and strength. Therefore, all signals need periodic reamplification and regeneration. Figure 7.12 illustrates an example of attenuation.

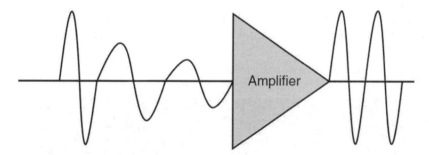

FIGURE 7.12 **Attenuation.**

Your basic choices for signaling are analog or digital transmissions. Both analog and digital signals vary a carrier wave in frequency and amplitude. Analog signals, however, are harder to clean of noise and to determine where the signal ends and where noise begins.

Network Equipment

Telecommunications equipment refers to all the hardware used to move data between networked devices. This includes equipment for LANs and WANs. This is important to know, not only from a networking standpoint, but also to better implement security solutions and pass the CISSP exam.

Repeaters

Repeaters, concentrators, and amplifiers are used to strengthen the communication signal and overcome the problems with attenuation. These devices all operate at OSI Layer 1.

Hubs

Hubs are one of the most basic multiport networking devices. A hub allows all the connected devices to communicate with one another. A hub is logically nothing more than a common wire to which all computers have shared access. Hubs operate at OSI Layer 1. Systems on a hub all share the same broadcast and collision domain.

Hubs have fallen out of favor because of their low maximum throughput. Whenever two or more systems attempt to send packets at the same time on the same hub, there is a collision. As utilization increases, the number of collisions skyrockets and the overall average throughput decreases.

> **ExamAlert**
>
> Don't spend too much time worrying about repeaters and hubs; just know their basic purpose and that they've been replaced by Layer 2 switches.

Bridges

Another somewhat outdated piece of equipment is a wired bridge. Bridges are semi-intelligent pieces of equipment that have the capability to separate collision domains. Bridges examine frames and look up the corresponding MAC address. If the device tied to that MAC address is determined to be local, the bridge blocks the traffic. One big problem with bridges is that, by default, they pass broadcast traffic. Too much broadcast traffic can effectively flood the network and cause a broadcast storm. Almost the only bridges seen today are the wireless bridges used in 802.11x networks.

> **ExamAlert**
>
> Old technology? Although items like bridges are rarely seen in the workplace today, exams are notorious for lagging behind the real world. It is also important to understand from a historical perspective how we got to where we are today and to understand corporate security documentation that describes pre-existing technologies.

Switches

A switch performs in much the same way as a hub; however, switches are considered intelligent devices. Switches segment traffic by observing the source and destination MAC address of each data frame. In the classical sense, switches are OSI Layer 2 devices. Modern switches can operate at higher layers. Switches that work at higher levels have the capability to work with different headers.

A sample technology that bridges Layer 2 and Layer 3 is known as *Multiprotocol Label Switching* (MPLS). MPLS is an OSI Layer 2 protocol. MPLS works with high-speed switches. Commercial switches also offer *virtual LAN* (VLAN) capabilities. Such switches can operate at OSI Layer 3. VLANs allow a group of devices on different physical LAN segments to communicate with each other as if they were all on the same logical LAN.

> **Note**
>
> The basic difference in Layer 2 switches and those that work at higher layers is the way they deal with addresses and tags.

Switches operate by storing the MAC addresses in a lookup table that is located in *random access memory* (RAM). This lookup table is also referred to as *content addressable memory* (CAM). This lookup table contains the information needed to match each MAC address to the corresponding port it is connected to. When the data frame enters the switch, it finds the target MAC address in the lookup table and matches it to the switch port the computer is attached to. The frame is forwarded to only that switch port; therefore, computers on all other ports never see the traffic. Some advantages of a switch are:

▶ Provides higher throughput than a hub

▶ Provides VLAN capability

▶ Can be configured for full duplex

▶ Can be configured to span a port to support IDS/IPS (intrusion detection system/intrusion prevention system), network feed, or for monitoring

Not all switches are made the same. Switches can process an incoming frame in three ways:

▶ **Store-and-forward**—After the frame is completely input into the switch, the destination MAC is analyzed to block or forward the frame.

▶ **Cut-through**—This faster design is similar to the store-and-forward switch, but it examines only the first six bytes before forwarding the packet to its rightful owner.

▶ **Fragment Free**—This is a Cisco Systems design that has a lower error rate.

> **Note**
>
> Originally, switches were Layer 2 devices; today, switches can be found at OSI Layer 3 and can work up to OSI Layer 7. Higher-layer switches are known as *content switches, content-services switches,* or *application switches*.

Mirrored Ports and Network Taps

Monitoring devices have a harder time examining traffic on switched networks than non-switched networks. To overcome this problem, port mirroring is used. Different vendors use different names for this technology.

▶ Cisco Systems: Switched Port Analyzer (SPAN)

▶ 3Com: Roving Analysis Port (RAP)

Port mirroring is used to send a copy of network packets seen on one switch port to a network monitoring connection on another switch port. Therefore, if you are using a managed switch, you can configure port mirroring and easily capture and analyze traffic. Although this works well in corporate environments and in situations where you have control of the managed switch, what about situations where the switch is unmanaged or where someone does not have access to the switch? That is when network taps can be used.

A network tap provides another way to monitor the network and see all traffic, much like what you would see if you were using a hub. This functionality acts as a point to intercept traffic. One handy tool to meet this need is with a Throwing Star LAN Tap. This simple little device allows anyone to easily monitor Ethernet communications. You can find out more at greatscottgadgets.com/throwingstar/.

VLANs

Virtual LANs (VLANs) are used to segment network traffic and result in smaller broadcast domains. VLANs reduce network congestion and increase bandwidth, and do not need to be isolated to a single switch. VLANs can span many switches throughout an organization. Extending VLANs is done by means of a trunking protocol.

A trunking protocol propagates the definition of a VLAN to the entire local area network. Trunking protocols work by encapsulating the Ethernet frame. Two common trunking protocols include the 802.1Q standard and Cisco's proprietary Inter-Switch Link (ISL) trunking protocol. The 802.1Q standard places information inside the Ethernet frame, whereas ISL wraps the Ethernet frame.

> **Note**
>
> Spanning Tree Protocol (STP) is another protocol that can be used within a VLAN. STP is used to prevent networking loops, build active paths, and provide for backup paths if an active path or link fails. The newest version is Rapid Spanning Tree Protocol (RSTP). It is backward-compatible with STP and provides significantly faster spanning tree convergence.

Trunking security is an important concern in regards to VLANs. A trunk is simply a link between two switches that carries more than one VLAN's data. A CISSP should be aware that if an attacker can get access to the trunked connection, he can potentially jump from one VLAN to another. This is called *VLAN hopping*. Making sure that trunked connections are secure so that malicious activity cannot occur is very important.

> **ExamAlert**
>
> VLAN hopping is a hacking technique that enables attackers to send packets outside of their VLAN. These attacks are generally launched by tagging the traffic with a VLAN ID that is outside the attacker's VLAN.

Routers

Routers reside at Layer 3 of the OSI model. Routers are usually associated with the IP protocol, which sends blocks of data that have been formatted into packets. IP is considered a "best effort" delivery protocol, and IP packets are examined and processed by routers. Routers can connect networks that have the same or different medium types. A router's primary purpose is to forward IP packets toward their destination through a process known as *routing*. Whereas bridges and switches examine the physical frame, routers focus on the information found in the IP header. One important item in the IP header is the IP address. As mentioned, an IP address is a logical address; it is laid out in dotted-decimal notation format. The IPv4 address format is four decimal numbers separated by decimal points. Each of these decimal numbers is one byte in length, supporting values from 0 to 255. IPv4 addresses are separated into the following classes:

▶ **Class A networks**—Consist of up to 16,777,214 client devices. Their address range can extend from 1 to 126.

▶ **Class B networks**—Host up to 65,534 client devices. Their address range can extend from 128 to 191.

▶ **Class C networks**—Can have 245 devices. Their address range can extend from 192 to 223.

▶ **Class D networks**—Reserved for multicasting. Their address range can extend from 224 to 239.

▶ **Class E networks**—Reserved for experimental purposes. Their addresses range from 240 to 254.

ExamAlert

You may have noticed that the 127.0.0.0 address range is missing from the preceding text. Although officially part of the Class Address range, it is used for loopback. Such details may be asked about in the CISSP exam.

Not all the addresses shown can be used on the Internet. Some addresses have been reserved for private use and are considered nonroutable. These private addresses include the following:

▶ **Class A**—10.0.0.0

▶ **Class B**—172.16.0.0 to 172.31.0.0

▶ **Class C**—192.168.0.0 to 192.168.255.0

Routers can also be used to improve performance by limiting physical broadcast domains. They act as a limited type of firewall with *access control lists* (ACLs) filtering, and they ease network management by segmenting devices into smaller subnets instead of one large network. The security of a network's router is paramount. A compromised router can have devastating consequences, especially if it is used as an endpoint for other services, such as IPSec, a VPN, or a firewall.

> **ExamAlert**
>
> Blocking unauthorized traffic via routers and firewalls is sometimes referred to as bogon filtering. Bogons are simply IP packets that are spoofed and appear to be from an area of the IP address space that is reserved, but not yet allocated or delegated by the Internet Assigned Numbers Authority (IANA) or a delegated Regional Internet Registry (RIR).

Gateways

A *gateway* connects networks that use dissimilar protocols by converting one software protocol into another. Gateways can be referred to as *protocol translators*. A gateway can be software-based or a standalone hardware device. Gateways function at OSI Layer 7.

Routing

Routing protocols are a key component of modern networks. Confusion often exists over the terms *routed protocol* and *routing protocol*. Both reside at Layer 3. Routed protocols can be forwarded from one router to another. A good example of a routed protocol is IP. A very basic definition of IP is that it acts as the postman of the Internet. Its job is to organize data into a packet, and then address the packet for delivery. IP must place target and source addresses on the packet. This is similar to addressing a package before delivering it to the post office. And please don't forget the postage: In the world of IP, the postage is a TTL (Time-to-Live). The TTL keeps packets from traversing the network forever, and decrements every time a router is passed. If the recipient cannot be found before the TTL reaches one, the packet will be discarded.

A routing protocol also has a specific role. A routing protocol sends and receives routing information to and from other routers. A routing protocol's job is that of the large mechanized mail sort machine. Whereas routed protocols, such as IP, build and address a packet, the routing protocol must decide how to best deliver the packet. In real life, there are many ways to get from point A to point B. Likewise, on the Internet, there are many paths to the target network.

Routing protocols can be placed into several basic categories:

▶ Static routing

▶ Dynamic routing

▶ Default routes

Static, or fixed, routing algorithms are not algorithms at all. They rely on a simple table developed by a network administrator mapping one network to another. Static routing works best when a network is small and the traffic is predicable. The big problem with static routing is that it cannot react to network changes. As networks grow, management of these tables can become difficult. Although this makes static routing unsuitable for use on the Internet or large networks, it can be used in special circumstances where normal routing protocols don't function well.

Dynamic routing uses metrics to determine which path a router should use to send a packet toward its destination. Dynamic routing protocols include RIP, BGP, IGRP, and OSPF. Dynamic routing takes time as all routers must learn about all possible paths. *Convergence* is reached when all routers on a network agree on the state of routing.

Default routes are similar to static routes. When default routes are used, the designated route becomes the default path the router uses to transmit packets when the router knows no other route to use.

Each time a router receives packets, it must examine them and determine the proper interface to forward the packets to. Not all routing protocols that routers work with function in the same manner. Dynamic routing protocols can be divided into two broad categories:

▶ Algorithms based on distance-vector protocols

▶ Algorithms based on link-state protocols

Distance-vector protocols are based on Bellman-Ford algorithms, and try to find the best route by determining the shortest path. The shortest path is commonly calculated by hops. Distance-vector routing is also called *routing by rumor*.

RIP is probably the most common distance-vector protocol currently in use. It is a legacy UDP-based routing protocol that does not use authentication, and determines path by hop count. RIP has a 15-hop count maximum and uses broadcast routing updates to all devices. Later versions of RIP provide authentication in clear text. Although RIP works in small networks, it does not operate successfully in large network environments. RIP makes use of *split horizon* and *poison reverse*. Split horizon is a route advertisement that prevents routing loops in distance-vector routing protocols by prohibiting a router from advertising a route back onto the router interface from which it was discovered. Poison reverse is a way in which a gateway node tells its neighbor gateways that you can't get there from here. It basically means that one of the gateways is no longer connected. Poison reverse sets the number of hops to the unconnected gateway to a number that indicates "infinite": 16 hops.

One major shortcoming of distance-vector protocols is that the path with the lowest number of hops might not be the optimal route. The path with the lowest hop count could have considerably less bandwidth than a route with a higher hop count.

> **Caution**
>
> Distance-vector protocols like RIP can be spoofed and are subject to redirection. It is also easy for attackers to sniff RIP updates. RIP routers update each other by sending out complete routing tables every 30 seconds.

Link-state protocols are based on Dijkstra algorithms. Unlike distance-vector protocols, link-state protocols determine the best path with metrics like delay or bandwidth. When this path is determined, the router informs other routers of its findings. This is how reliable routing tables are developed and routing tables reach convergence. Link-state routing is considered more robust than distance-vector routing protocols. OSPF is probably the most common link-state routing protocol; it is often used as a replacement for RIP.

OSPF is an improved link-state routing protocol that offers authentication. It is an implementation of a link-state-based routing protocol developed in the mid-1980s to overcome the problems associated with RIP. OSPF has several built-in advantages over RIP that include the use of IP multicasts to send out router updates, no limitation on hop count (as with RIP), better support for load balancing, and fast convergence.

Routing protocols can be further divided and defined as interior or exterior routing protocols. RIP, OSPF, and IS-IS are three examples of interior routing protocols. Interior routing protocols are those used within an organization.

Exterior gateway protocols are used by routers connecting different *autonomous systems* (AS's). An example of an exterior routing protocol is BGP. BGP is the core routing protocol used by the Internet. It is based on TCP and is used to connect autonomous systems.

> **Note**
>
> An early exterior routing protocol was Exterior Gateway Protocol (EGP). This term is sometimes used synonymously to describe all exterior routing protocols.

WANs and Their Components

WANs are considerably different from LANs. Organizations usually own their own LANs, but WAN services are typically leased; it's not feasible to have your network guy run a cable from New York to Dallas. WANs are concerned with the long-haul transmission of data and connect remote devices. The Internet is a good example of a WAN. WAN data transmissions typically incur higher costs than LAN transmissions. WAN technologies can be divided into two broad categories: *packet switching* and *circuit switching*.

Packet Switching

Packet-switched networks share bandwidth with other devices. Packet-switched networks divide data into packets and frames. These packets are individually routed among various network nodes at the provider's discretion. They are considered more resilient than circuit-switched networks and work well for on-demand connections with "bursty" traffic. Each packet takes the most expedient route, which means the packets might not arrive in order or at the same time. Packet switching is a form of connectionless networking. A large portion of long-haul data communication is done via fiber. *Synchronous optical networking* (SONET) is one of the leading technologies that makes this possible. SONET uses light to send multiple digital data streams over the same fiber optical cable.

X.25

X.25 is one of the original packet-switching technologies. Although it is not fast, with speeds up to 56 Kbps, it is reliable and works over analog phone lines.

Frame Relay

Frame Relay is a virtual circuit-switched network. It is a kind of streamlined version of X.25. Frame Relay controls bandwidth use with a *committed information rate* (CIR). The CIR specifies the maximum guaranteed bandwidth that the customer is promised. The customer can send more data than specified in the CIR if additional bandwidth is available. If there is additional bandwidth, the data will pass; otherwise, the data is marked discard eligible (DE) and is discarded. Frame Relay can use *permanent virtual circuits* (PVCs) or *switched virtual circuit* (SVCs). A PVC is used to provide a dedicated connection between two locations. An SVC works much like a phone call in that the connection is set up on a per-call basis, and is disconnected when the call is complete. Switched virtual circuits are good when data transmission is sporadic, and for teleconferencing and phone calls.

Asynchronous Transfer Mode

ATM is a cell-switching-based physical layer protocol. It supports high-bandwidth data needs and works well for time-sensitive applications. Because the switching process occurs in hardware, delays are minimized. ATM uses a fixed cell size of 53 bytes. ATM can be implemented on LANs or WANs.

ATM is being surpassed by newer technologies, such as MPLS, which was mentioned earlier. MPLS designers recognized that data didn't need to be converted into 53-byte cells. MPLS packets can be much larger than ATM cells. MPLS can provide traffic engineering, and enables the creation of VPNs without end-user applications. MPLS can carry many types of traffic, handles addresses via labels, and does not encapsulate header data.

> **Note**
>
> For the exam, keep in mind that MPLS uses labels to simplify WAN routing and can carry voice and data.

Circuit Switching

Circuit switching comes in either analog or digital configurations. At the heart of circuit level switching is multiplexing. *Multiplexing* is a technique used to combine multiple channels of data over a single set of wires or transmission path. Today the most common form of circuit switching is the Plain Old Telephone Service (POTS), but ISDN, T-carriers, and digital subscriber line (DSL) are also options. The sections that follow describe these circuit switching options in more detail.

Plain Old Telephone Service

POTS is a voice-grade analog telephone service used for voice calls and for connecting to the Internet and other locations via modem. Modem speeds can vary from 9600 bps to 56 Kbps. Although the POTS service is relatively inexpensive and widely available, it offers only low data speeds.

Integrated Services Digital Network

ISDN is a communication protocol that operates similarly to POTS, except that all-digital signaling is used. Although originally planned as a replacement for POTS, ISDN was not hugely successful. ISDN uses separate frequencies called *channels* on a special digital connection. It consists of B channels used for voice, data, video, and fax services, and a D channel used for signaling by the service provider and user equipment. Keeping the D signaling data separate makes it harder for attackers to manipulate the service. The D channel operates at a low 16 Kbps; the B channels operate at speeds up to 64 Kbps. By binding the B channels together, ISDN can achieve higher speeds. ISDN is available in two levels: Basic Rate Interface (BRI) at up to 128 Kbps and Primary Rate Interface (PRI) at up to 1.544 Mbps. Basic Rate Interface comprises 2B channels and 1 D channel, and Primary Rate Interface comprises of 23 B channels and 1 D channel.

T-Carriers

T-carrier service is used for leased lines. A leased line is locked between two locations. It is very secure, and users pay a fixed monthly fee for this service, regardless of use. The most common T-carrier is a T1. A T1 uses time-division multiplexing and consists of 24 digital signal 0 (DS0) channels. Each DS0 channel is capable of transmitting 64 Kbps of data; therefore, a T1 can provide a composite rate of 1.544 Mbps. T3s are the next available choice. A T3 is made up of 672 DS0s and has a composite data rate of 45 Mbps. For those who don't need a full T1 or a full T3, fractional service is available. A fractional T-line is just a portion of the entire carrier. Table 7.8 details common T-carrier specifications and contrasts them with POTS, ISDN, and DSL.

TABLE 7.8 **T-Carrier Specifications**

Service	Characteristics	Maximum Speed
POTS dialup service	Switch line; widely used	56 Kbps
ISDN BRI digital	Requires a terminal adaptor; can be costly	128 Kbps
ISDN PRI digital	Requires a terminal adaptor; can be costly	1.54 Mbps
DSL	Typically asymmetric; downloads faster than uploads	Up to 52 Mbps
T1	Dedicated leased line; 24 bundled phone lines	1.54 Mbps
T3	Dedicated leased line; 28 bundled T1s	44.736 Mbps

> **Note**
>
> Although T1s are the standard in the United States, Europe uses an E Carrier system. An E1 carries 30 channels; an E3 is 16 E1s. E1s are dedicated 2.048-megabit circuits, and E3 are dedicated 34.368-megabit circuits.

Digital Subscriber Line

DSL is another circuit-switching connectivity option. Most DSLs are asymmetric, which means that the download speed is much faster than the upload speed. The theory is that you usually download more than you upload.

DSL modems are always connected to the Internet; therefore, you do not have to dial in to make a connection. As long as your computer is powered on, it is connected to the Internet and is ready to transmit and receive data. This is the primary security concern of DSL. Unlike the usual lengthy connection time used for dialup service, no waiting time is involved. An advantage of DSL is that it maintains a more fixed speed than cable modems typically do. Table 7.9 details the different DSL types.

TABLE 7.9 **DSL Types and Speeds**

Name	Data Rate	Mode	Distance
IDSL (Internet digital subscriber line)	160 Kbps	Duplex	18,000 ft., 24 AWG
HDSL (High data rate digital subscriber line)	1.544 Mbps	Duplex	12,000 ft., 24 AWG
	2.048 Mbps	Duplex	
SDSL (Symmetric digital subscriber line)	1.544 Mbps	Duplex	10,000 ft., 24 AWG
	2.048 Mbps	Duplex	
ADSL (Asymmetric digital subscriber line)	1.5–9 Mbps	Down	9,000–18,000 ft., 24 AWG
	16–640 kbps	Up	
VDSL (Very high data rate digital subscriber line)	13–52 Mbps	Down	1,000–4,500 ft., 24 AWG
	1.5–2.3 Mbps	Up	

Cable Modems

Cable Internet access refers to the delivery of Internet access over the cable television infrastructure. The Internet connection is made through the same coaxial cable that delivers the television signal to your home. The coaxial cable connects to a special cable modem that demultiplexes the TCP/IP traffic. This always-on Internet connection is a big security issue if no firewall is used. One of the weaknesses of cable Internet access is that there is a shared amount of bandwidth among many users. Cable companies control the maximum data rate of each subscriber by capping the maximum data rate. Some unscrupulous individuals attempt to uncap their line to obtain higher speeds. Uncappers can be caught and prosecuted because cable Internet providers routinely check for this illegal action.

> **Note**
>
> Although uncapping a cable connection might lead only to a disconnection of your service, service providers might push for criminal charges. That's what happened to Brandon Wirtz and other Buckeye Cable customers when their homes were searched by the FBI and they were charged with fifth-degree felonies.

Problems with cable modems continue to be discovered. Some cable modems can be hijacked by nothing more than visiting a vulnerable website, as seen here: www.gnucitizen.org/blog/bt-home-flub-pwnin-the-bt-home-hub/. Another lingering concern is that of the loss of confidentiality. Individuals have worried about the possibility of sniffing attacks. Most cable companies have addressed this issue by implementing the Data Over Cable Service Interface

Specification (DOCSIS) standard. The DOCSIS standard specifies encryption and other security mechanisms that prevent sniffing and protect privacy. DOCSIS is currently at version 3.1.

Other WAN Technologies

When systems communicate with each other remotely, a variety of protocols and standards are needed. Some of these include

- ▶ **Switched Multimegabit Data Service (SMDS)**—A high-speed, packet-switched service used for MANs and WANs.

- ▶ **Synchronous Data Link Control (SDLC)**—Developed by IBM in the 1970s and used to develop HDLC. SDLC is a Layer 2 communication protocol designed for use with mainframes.

- ▶ **High-Level Data Link Control (HDLC)**—Uses a frame format to transmit data between network nodes. It supports full duplex communication and is used in SNA (Systems Network Architecture) network architecture.

- ▶ **High-Speed Serial Interface**—A connection standard used to connect routers and switches to high-speed networks.

Cloud Computing

Cloud computing is an Internet-based approach that provides computing and storage capacity as a service, as illustrated in Figure 7.13. Cloud computing can be broken down into several basic models, including the following:

- ▶ **Infrastructure-as-a-Service (IaaS)**—IaaS describes a cloud solution where you are buying infrastructure. You purchase virtual power to execute your software as needed. This is much like running a virtual server on your own equipment, except you are now running a virtual server on a virtual disk. This model is similar to a utility company model because you pay for what you use.

- ▶ **Software-as-a-Service (SaaS)**—SaaS is designed to provide a complete packaged solution. The software is rented out to the user. The service is usually provided through some type of front-end or web portal. Although the end user is free to use the service from anywhere, the company pays a per-use fee.

▶ **Platform-as-a-Service (PaaS)**—PaaS provides a platform for your use. Services provided by this model include all phases of the system development life cycle (SDLC) and can use application program interfaces (APIs), website portals, or gateway software. These solutions tend to be proprietary, which can cause problems if the customer moves away from the provider's platform.

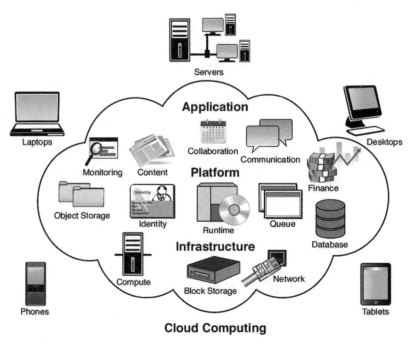

FIGURE 7.13 **Cloud computing.**

Voice Communications and Wireless Communications

Technologies like VoIP and wireless capture more attention and use each year. Some studies report that there are more cell phones in China than there are people in the United States. The following sections will look at these technologies.

Voice over IP

In the old days of networking, before the year 2000, multimedia services, such as voice and video, were deployed on stable circuit-switched networks. This guaranteed the bandwidth and the allowed latency could be controlled. Today, many networks use packet-switching technologies. VoIP is the process of using a data network to transmit voice communication. Voice over IP is not a traditional packet-switching protocol, but VoIP is carried on packet-switched networks in IP packets. Networks configured to carry VoIP treat voice communications as just another form of data. This is one of the big changes in networking that has occurred over the last few years. *Network convergence* refers to the provision of telephone (VoIP), streaming video, and network data communication services, all within a single network. Basically, one pipe is used to transport all forms of communication services. This makes quality of service (QoS) a real concern when discussing VoIP traffic. QoS is used to avoid interruption of phone calls. After all, who wants only a portion of a phone call? QoS can be defined as the capability of the network to provide the following:

▶ Dedicated bandwidth

▶ Control of jitter and latency

These are important goals so that real-time traffic like voice and video can coexist with bursty traffic like HTTP. VoIP has replaced most of the circuit-switched POTS phone service that was common years ago. There is a good chance that if you still have a home phone that it's actually a VoIP connection. Here are some basic characteristics of VoIP:

▶ SIP-based signaling

▶ User-agent client

▶ User-agent server

▶ Three-way handshake

▶ Voice stream carried by RTP

Voice over IP Vulnerabilities

Companies are moving to VoIP because of major cost savings. However, using VoIP is not without risks. As a network service, it is vulnerable in some of the same ways as other data traffic. Attackers can intercept the traffic, hack the VoIP server, or launch a DoS attack against the VoIP server and cause network outages. Attacks against IP phones are also a problem, as are LAN hopping and TFTP alteration for phone firmware image loading. Another consideration is that the vulnerabilities of the operating system the VoIP application is running on are inherited.

One key concern of VoIP is sniffing because protocols like SIP provide little security by default. Without the proper security controls, sniffing a VoIP call can be as easy as using a tool like Wireshark, a common network sniffer. Security issues related to VoIP include the loss of the data network, which can disable VoIP. Other VoIP vulnerabilities include:

▶ **Open network**—After the VoIP packets leave the organization's network, the network is not in charge of where they are routed or who might have access to them.

▶ **DoS attacks**—Because VoIP uses UDP for portions of the communication process, it is extremely susceptible to disruption or denial of service. VoIP uses an isochronous process in which data must be delivered within strict timelines.

▶ **Eavesdropping**—Because VoIP relies on UDP and Session Initiation Protocol (SIP), it is an open service and communications can potentially be sniffed and replayed. Other protocols used by various vendors of VoIP products include IAX, IAX2, SCCP, and UNISTIM.

▶ **Unauthorized phone use**—Services like Skype, GoogleTalk, and so on open the corporate network to exposure to attack and can be a potential policy violation. Such tools can even result in a violation of regulation depending on the industry or how they are used.

▶ **Spam over Internet Telephony (SPIT)**—SPIT is bulk unsolicited SPAM delivered using the Voice over Internet Protocol.

> **Note**
>
> You can use secure real-time transport protocol (SRTP) to secure VoIP. SRTP uses AES for confidentiality and SHA-1 for integrity.

Cell Phones

Cell phones are another technology that has matured over the years. Cell phone technology can be broadly categorized into the following groups:

▶ **1G**—This generation of phones enabled users to place analog calls on their cell phones and continue their conversations as they moved seamlessly from cell to cell around an area or region.

▶ **2G**—The second generation changed analog mechanisms to digital cell phones. Deployed in the 1990s, these phones were based on technologies like GSM (Global System for Mobile Communications) and CDMA (Code Division Multiple Access).

▶ **3G**—The third generation changed the phone into a mobile computer, with fast access to the Internet and additional services. Downstream speeds range from 400 Kbps to several megabits per second.

▶ **4G**—The fourth generation of cell phones were designed to support TV in real time as well as video downloads at much higher speeds. 4G test systems that have been rolled out in South Korea have been demonstrated to support speeds up to a gigabyte of data per second. However, depending on the environment, some indoor or fringe environments can be as low as 100 Mbps. Two of the most widely deployed standards include Mobile WiMAX and Long Term Evolution (LTE).

Today, most cell phones are 4G. The mobile communication scenario throughout the world is growing at an incredible rate and after the Internet, some might argue that mobile phones are the second most important invention in globalizing the world. Table 7.10 shows common cell phone technologies and their generational level.

TABLE 7.10 **Cell Phone Technologies**

Technology	Generation
AMPS	1G
TACS	1G
GSM	2G
CDMA	2G
GPRS	2.5G
EDGE	3G
WWRF	4G

One can easily believe the statistic that Americans now spend more time talking on their cell phones than they do on landlines. Mobile phones have revolutionized connectivity; however, they also have given rise to security concerns for organizations because more companies must consider what controls to place on these devices. With so many cell phones in use, there are numerous ways in which attackers can try to exploit their vulnerabilities. One is through the practice of *cloning*. Cell phones have an electronic serial number (ESN) and an International Mobile Station Equipment Identity (IMEI). Attackers can use specialized equipment to capture and decode these numbers from your phone and install them in another. The attacker then can sell or use this cloned phone. *Tumbling* is another technique used to attack cell phones. Specially modified phones tumble and shift to a different pair of ESN/IMEI numbers after each call. This technique makes the attacker's phone appear to be a legitimate roaming cell phone. First-generation cell phones were vulnerable to this attack. GSM phones also make use of an International Mobile Subscriber Identity (IMSI) to identify the user of a cellular network, and is a unique identification associated with all cellular networks. As an example, a IMSI starting with 310 identifies a user in the United States whereas a IMSI starting with 460 identifies the user is from China. People that attack phone systems are called *phreakers*.

> **Note**
>
> Phone systems can also be the target of Caller ID spoofing and SMShing. Getting a call or text from 867-5309 doesn't mean that Jenny is waiting to talk to you. You can find a good example of this at www.cbsnews.com/news/cell-phones-easy-id-theft-targets/.
>
> It's not just cell phones that the security professional has to worry about: Cordless phones also have security issues. Even though cordless phones have moved into the gigahertz range and now use dozens of channels, they are still vulnerable to eavesdropping if someone has the right equipment.

802.11 Wireless Networks and Standards

The 802.11 family of protocols, or *802.11x* as it is sometimes called, covers a broad group of wireless standards governed by IEEE. Most of these wireless devices broadcast by using *spread-spectrum technology*. This method of transmission transmits data over a wide range of radio frequencies. Spread-spectrum technologies include frequency-hopping spread spectrum, an older technology, and sequence spread spectrum. Spread spectrum technology lessens noise interference and allows data rates to speed up or slow down, depending on the quality of the signal. Obstructions like walls, doors, and other solid objects tend to block or reduce signal strength.

Three common methods include the following:

▶ **Orthogonal frequency division multiplexing (OFDM)**—Splits the signal into smaller subsignals that use a frequency division multiplexing technique to send different pieces of the data to the receiver on different frequencies simultaneously.

▶ **Direct-sequence spread spectrum (DSSS)**—A spread-spectrum technology that uses a spreading code to simultaneously transmit the signal on a small (22 MHz-wide) range of radio frequencies. The wider the spreading code, the more resistant the signal is to interference, but with the cost of a smaller data rate.

▶ **Frequency-hopping spread spectrum (FHSS)**—FHSS works somewhat differently from OFDM and DSSS in that it works by taking a broad slice of the bandwidth spectrum, which is divided into smaller subchannels of about 1 MHz. The transmitter then hops between subchannels. Each subchannel is used to send out short bursts of data for a short period. This period is the *dwell time*. For devices to communicate, each must know the proper dwell time and be synchronized to the proper hopping pattern.

Table 7.11 summarizes the primary standards for wireless LANs (WLANs).

TABLE 7.11 **WLAN Standards and Details**

Service	Frequency	Transmission Scheme
802.11a	5 GHz	OFDM
802.11b	2.4 GHz	DSSS
802.11g	2.4 GHz	OFDM/DSSS
802.11n	2.4 GHz or 5 GHz	MIMO-OFDM
802.11ac	2.4 GHz or 5 GHz	MIMO-OFDM

ExamAlert

CISSP exam candidates will be expected to know WLAN standards, speeds, and transmission schemes.

It's not just wireless access points and equipment that could be a threat to the organization. All wireless devices should have enforced security and strong policies dictating their use. Camera phones allow users to take photos in otherwise secure areas. Smartphones, tablets, and BlackBerrys can be easily lost or stolen. Many forensic tools are available to extract data from these types of wireless devices. Portable wireless devices can also support onboard removable storage that can be lost or removed. It's unfortunate, but these devices usually lack the level of security of wired devices. Corporate security officers must understand that the default wiping options for many modern devices do not remove all stored data.

> **Note**
>
> Camera phones, tablets, and BlackBerrys have more value than just the cost of the device. These small wireless devices can hold tons of data. The McCain campaign found this out the hard way when, after the 2008 presidential campaign, the campaign started selling off computers, laptops, and BlackBerrys. The problem was that much of this equipment had not been wiped. One such BlackBerry was reported by the buyer to contain many phone numbers of people connected to the campaign, memos, messages, and hundreds of emails that spanned from September 2006 until a few days following the November 4, 2008 election (www.theregister.co.uk/2008/12/12/mccain_blackberry/).

Wireless Topologies

Wireless networks can operate in either ad-hoc mode or infrastructure mode. *Adhoc mode*, or *peer-to-peer*, doesn't need any equipment except wireless network adaptors. Ad-hoc mode allows a point-to-point type of communication that works well for the temporary exchange of information. *Infrastructure mode* centers around a wireless access point (AP). A wireless AP is a centralized wireless device that controls the traffic in the wireless medium. Wireless devices use CSMA/CA so that they can communicate efficiently. 802.11 wireless NICs can operate in four modes: managed, master, ad-hoc, and monitor mode.

▶ Managed mode is the most generic wireless option. Clients communicate only with the access point and do not directly communicate with other clients.

▶ Master mode is used by wireless access points to communicate with connected clients in managed mode.

▶ Ad-hoc mode is a peer-to-peer mode with no central access point.

▶ Monitor mode is a read-only mode used for sniffing WLANs. Wireless sniffing tools like Kismet use monitor mode to sniff 802.11 wireless frames.

Wireless Standards

The standard for WLANs is IEEE 802.11, commonly called *Wi-Fi*. Some of the important amendments to this standard include the following:

▶ **802.11a**—This amendment defined physical access that could operate in the 5 GHz frequency range and support speeds up to 54 Mbps at a range of 60 feet.

▶ **802.11b**—Operates in the 2.4 GHz frequency range and can reach speeds of up to 11 Mbps and ranges of 300 feet.

▶ **802.11g**—This popular amendment operates in the 2.4 GHz frequency range and can support speeds up to 54 Mbps.

▶ **802.11i**—This amendment provided for secure authentication and encryption that would be a permanent replacement for the deficient Wired Equivalent Privacy (WEP) mechanism. 802.11i also makes use of Robust Security Network (RSN). RSN uses pluggable authentication modules. This allows for changes to cryptographic ciphers as new vulnerabilities are discovered.

▶ **802.11ac**—IEEE 802.11ac is a wireless networking standard in the 802.11 family that includes multi-station WLAN throughput of at least 1 gigabit per second and a single link throughput of at least 500 Mbps per second.

▶ **802.11n**—This version operates in the 2.4 GHz frequency. To enjoy benefits offered by the vendors, purchasers need to stay with one vendor. Resulting data rates can exceed 200 Mbps.

▶ **802.16**—This broadband wireless access standard is also known as WiMAX and was designed to deliver last mile connectivity to broadband users at speeds of up to 75 Mbs. WiMAX is designed to provide wireless broadband access to Internet users in much the same way that cell phones revolutionized wired phone communication.

Table 7.12 summarizes the primary standards for wireless LANs (WLANs).

TABLE 7.12 **Some Common WLAN Speeds and Frequencies**

Type	Top Speed (Mbps)	Frequency (GHz)
802.11	2	2.4
802.11a	54	5
802.11b	11	2.4
802.11g	54	2.4
802.11n	144 +	2.4 and/or 5

IEEE has written standards in support of our other wireless technologies as well. Bluetooth and RFID (radio frequency identification) are defined by 802.15, written for wireless PANs (WPANs).

Bluetooth

Bluetooth technology is designed for short-range wireless communication between mobile and handheld devices. Bluetooth started to grow in popularity in the mid-to-late 1990s. Versions include, 1.2, 2, 3, and 4. Bluetooth technology has facilitated the growth of a variety of personal and handheld electronic devices. For example, in a WPAN, a smart phone could communicate with a tablet and a laptop. Bluetooth allows these devices to communicate as they come in range of each other or are activated. The classifications of Bluetooth are as follows:

▶ **Class 1**—This classification has the longest range (up to 100 m) and has 100 mW of power.

▶ **Class 2**—Although this classification is not the most popular, it allows transmission of up to 20 m and has 2.5 mW of power.

▶ **Class 3**—This is the most widely implemented classification. It supports a transmission distance of 10 m and has 1 mW of power.

▶ **Class 4**—This classification supports a transmission distance of .5 m and has .5 mW of power.

> **Note**
>
> Although you have most likely heard of Bluetooth, you might not have heard of ZigBee. It's another wireless standard that is designed for low data rates, can operate for many years, and is well-suited for applications like controlling a light, transferring data from an electrical power meter, or sending temperature data to a thermostat.

Although Bluetooth does have some built-in security features, it has been shown to be vulnerable to attack. At a recent DEF CON security conference, security professionals demonstrated ways to sniff Bluetooth transmissions from up to a kilometer away.

Bluetooth is part of the IEEE 802.15 family of protocols designed for WPANs. Although Bluetooth is extremely popular, competing 802.15 technologies, such as wireless USB and infrared, diversify the market.

> **Note**
>
> *Bluejacking* involves the unsolicited delivery of data to a Bluetooth user. *Bluesnarfing* is the actual theft of data or information from a user.

Wireless LAN Components

Wireless system components include

- ▶ **Service Set ID (SSID)**—For a computer to communicate or use the WLAN, it must be configured to use the WLAN's SSID. The SSID distinguishes one wireless network from another.

- ▶ **Wireless access point**—A wireless access point is a centralized wireless device that controls the traffic in the wireless medium and can be used to connect wireless devices to a wired network.

- ▶ **Wireless networking cards**—Used to connect devices to the wireless network.

- ▶ **Encryption**—802.11 encryption was originally provided by the aging WEP protocol, which was intended to provide the same level of privacy as a user might have on a wired network. WEP used RC4 symmetric encryption, but it was a flawed implementation. The amendment offering a secure replacement for WEP is 802.11i, which has become popularized by the Wi-Fi Alliance as Wi-Fi Protected Access (WPA, still using RC4) and WPA2 (uses Advanced Encryption Standard (AES)). These encryption mechanisms are discussed in detail in the next section.

In North America, 802.11 supports bandwidth at 2.4 GHz for 11 channels, three of which (1, 6, and 11) can be used simultaneously as non-overlapping. The channel designates the frequency on which the network will operate. European units support 13 channels (up to 4 non-overlapping) and Japanese units support 14 channels. There are 24 non-overlapping channels at 5 GHz. Worldwide, frequency availability changes according to the pertinent licensing authority. Equipment adjusts to these demands by asking what country the installation is occurring in, and either adjusting the frequencies to the local authority, or terminating transmissions (according to the licenses that the vendor is granted). The 802.11d amendment enables client equipment to ask what country it finds itself in and dynamically adjust its frequencies.

> **Note**
>
> Two very basic wireless security precautions include MAC address filtering and Service Set Identifier (SSID) filtering. Both provide only limited security as MAC address are transmitted in the clear, and thus can be easily sniffed. Setting SSIDs to non-broadcast is also a poor security strategy because wireless sniffers, such as Kismet, can detect the non-broadcast SSID used by clients to bypass this weak control.

Wireless Protection Mechanisms

The original technology used to protect wireless was WEP. WEP is implemented at the data link layer and encrypts data with the RC4 encryption algorithm. The key was limited to 40 bits because of export rules that existed during the late 1990s when the 802.11 protocol was developed. Forty bits is considered a very weak key today.

WEP is based on the RC4 algorithm that used either a 64-bit (IEEE standard) or a 128-bit (commercial enhancement) key. However, the keys can't use that many bits because a 24-bit initialization vector (IV) was used to provide randomness. The "real key" is actually 40 or 104 bits long. Many people are reluctant to learn about such an old and broken technology as WEP; however, it is important to appreciate that WEP is still with us. Credit card information has been stolen from vendors because of the use of WEP. The PCI Security Standards Council has revised its rules on credit card transactions to prohibit the use of WEP, and this equipment was phased out in 2010.

WEP is known as *static WEP* because everyone has the same key. Two of the first weaknesses realized about WEP are that this static encryption key was the same key being used for the shared key authentication (SKA), and that the authentication used a challenge-handshake mechanism that was dictionary-crackable. The immediate solution was to throw away SKA, and use only open system authentication (OSA) and the WEP encryption key. Everyone could connect, but no one could communicate without the encryption key.

One way the industry responded to these potential issues was by incorporating 802.1X (port-based access) into many wireless devices. When used in conjunction with extensible authentication protocol (EAP), it can be used to authenticate devices that attempt to connect to a specific LAN port. Although this was an improvement over WEP, 802.1x has been shown to be vulnerable.

To better understand the WEP process, you need to understand how the exclusive-or (XOR) function works in Boolean logic. Specifically, XORing means exclusively or, never both. XORing is just a simple binary comparison between two bits that produces another bit as the result. When the two bits are compared, XORing looks to see whether they are different. If the answer is yes, the resulting output is a 1. If the two bits are the same, the result is a 0. Let's look at the seven steps of encrypting a message:

1. The transmitting and receiving stations are initialized with the secret key. This secret key must be distributed using an out-of-band mechanism like email, posting it on a website, or giving it to you on a piece of paper the way many hotels do.

2. The transmitting station produces a seed, which is obtained by appending the 40-bit secret key to the 24-bit IV, for input into a Pseudo-Random Number Generator (PRNG).

3. The transmitting station uses the secret key and a 24-bit IV as input into the WEP PRNG to generate a key stream of random bits.

4. The key stream is XORed with plain text to obtain the cipher text.

5. The transmitting station appends the cipher text to a copy of the IV for the receiver to use, and sets a bit in the header to indicate that the packet is WEP-encrypted, and the WEP frame is transmitted. Because WEP encrypts at OSI Layer 2, the Layer 2 header and trailer are sent in clear text.

6. The receiving station checks to see whether the encrypted bit of the frame it received is set. If so, the receiving station extracts the IV from the frame and inputs it and the secret key into its WEP PRNG.

7. The receiver generates the same key stream used by the transmitting station, and XORs it with the cipher text to obtain the sent plain text.

WEP's immediate successor was a stop-gap measure that was popularized as *Wi-Fi Protected Access* (WPA). This name was born out of hardware certification testing by the Wi-Fi Alliance. WPA certification meant that a piece of hardware was compliant with a snapshot of the 802.11i amendment; the amendment itself was still under design. One of the jobs of the 802.11i task group was to reverse-engineer WEP, and develop a software-only upgrade for wireless users that would deploy Temporal Key Integrity Protocol (TKIP) for encryption. TKIP scrambles the user key with network state information using a mixing algorithm, and adds an integrity-checking feature that was much stronger than WEP had to verify the frames haven't been tampered with. WPA certification tested equipment for the implementation of TKIP.

In 2004, IEEE completed the 802.11i amendment, and released Counter Mode with Cipher Block Chaining Message Authentication Code Protocol (CCMP), an AES solution, as a complete replacement for the outdated RC4 mechanism used in WEP and TKIP. CCMP is also tested for and certified by the Wi-Fi Alliance, and is recognized as *WPA2*. Don't be surprised to see key sizes of up to 256 bits, which is a vast improvement over the original 40-bit encryption WEP used. Just keep in mind that in the IT security field, nothing remains static. Additional tools and techniques continue to be developed to attack newer security mechanisms like WPA. coWPAtty is one such tool.

> **Note**
>
> *War driving* is the practice of driving around, finding, mapping, and possibly connecting to open wireless networks. Tools like NetStumbler, Kismet, and AirSnort are typical tools that might be used to aid the war driver.
>
> *War chalking* is the practice of marking the location and status of wireless networks. The practice can be traced to symbols used by hobos during the depression to mark the location of food and work.

Other Wireless Technologies

As technology continues to change, other standards are emerging. One example is *i-Mode*. i-Mode is the packet-based service for mobile phones used in Japan. Another is Digital Enhanced Cordless Communication (DECT). This technology is widely used for cordless phone technology outside the U.S. DECT is the standard for cordless phones and allows different handsets and base units to work together from different manufacturers.

Still another standard you should know is Wireless Application Protocol (WAP). WAP is an open standard to help cell phone users get the same types of content available to desktop and laptop users. A WAP-enabled device customizes the content of a website to work with the small screen size of a mobile phone. A key component of this technology is wireless markup language (WML). Security issues in WAPv1 have been fixed by WAPv2. Anyone considering the use of WAP for sensitive information exchange should understand these issues. WAP was created by the WAP Forum, and was an attempt to rewrite the upper layers of the OSI to minimize the overhead of a mini-browser inside the cell phone. The Forum created its own encryption protocol called WTLS, which was a rewrite of transport layer security (TLS). When a client's signal reached the ISP's gateway, the WTLS packet had to be decrypted from WTLS to re-encapsulate it as a TLS signal and then to send it onto the Internet. This was a vulnerable moment, where data was fully decrypted, and it became known as the *GAP in WAP* (see Figure 7.14). WAP2 has been rewritten as an abbreviated form of TLS instead of WTLS, and the packet no longer needs to be decrypted.

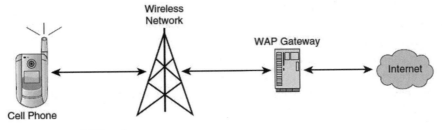

FIGURE 7.14   **WAP gateway.**

Network Access Control Devices

Security should be implemented in layers to erect several barriers against attackers. One good example of a network access control is a firewall. The firewall can act as a choke point to control traffic as it ingresses and egresses the network. Another network access control is the DMZ (demilitarized zone), which establishes a safe zone for internal and external users to work. The sections that follow describe these network security devices and techniques in more detail.

Firewalls

The term *firewall* has been used since the 1990s and describes a device that guards the entrance to a private network. Firewalls were developed to keep unauthorized traffic out. Firewalls have undergone generations of improvements so that today several different types of firewalls exist. These include the packet filter, application proxy, circuit proxy, and stateful inspection. It's a sad fact that we need firewalls. Just as in the real world, some individuals enjoy destroying other people's property. A firewall is a computer, router, or software component implemented to control access to a protected network. It enables organizations to protect their network and control traffic. Remember that models addressed here, such as stateful inspection and proxies, are theoretical, so most vendor products will not match one design perfectly.

Packet Filters

Packet filters are devices that filter traffic based on IP addresses. Savvy hackers use spoofing tools and other programs that are easily available on the Internet to bypass packet filters. The first firewalls ever implemented were packet filters. These devices inspect the TCP/IP headers and make a decision based on a set of predefined rules. Packet filters simply drop packets that do not conform to the predefined rule set. These devices are considered stateless. Packet filters are configured by compiling an access control list. ACLs can deny or permit packet transmission based on IP addresses, protocol types, TCP ports, and UDP ports.

Stateful Firewalls

Stateful firewalls keep track of every communication channel by means of a state table. Because of this, they are considered intelligent firewalls. They're part of the third generation of firewall design. Packet filters do not have this capability.

Proxy Servers

By definition, the word *proxy* means "to stand in place of." Therefore, an Internet proxy is a hardware or software device that can perform address translation and that communicates with the Internet on behalf of the network. The real IP address of the user remains hidden behind the proxy server. The proxy server can also be configured to filter higher-layer traffic to determine whether the traffic is allowed to pass. Proxy servers offer increased security because they don't allow untrusted systems to have a direct connection to internal computers. Proxy servers function as follows:

1. Accept packets from the external network.

2. Copy the packets.

3. Inspect them for irregularities.

4. Change the addresses to the correct internal device.

5. Put them back on the wire to the destination device.

Other types of proxies include the following:

▶ **Application-level proxy**—Not all proxies are made the same. Application-level proxies inspect the entire packet and then make a decision based on what was discovered while inspecting the contents. This method is very thorough and slow. For an application-level proxy to work correctly, it must understand the protocols and applications it is working with.

▶ **Circuit-level proxy**—A circuit-level proxy closely resembles a packet-filtering device in that it makes decisions based on addresses, ports, and protocols. It does not care about higher-layer applications, so it works for a wider range of protocols but doesn't provide the depth of security that an application-level proxy does. SQUID is an example of an open-source proxy. Table 7.13 summarizes the primary differences between application- and circuit-level proxies.

TABLE 7.13 **Application- and Circuit-level proxies**

Application-level proxy	Circuit-level proxy
Each protocol must have a unique proxy	Does not require a proxy for every protocol
Slower than a circuit-level proxy	Faster than an application-level proxy
Requires more processing per packet	Does not provide deep packet inspection
Provides more protection	Acceptable for a wide range of protocols

Caution

An application-level proxy provides a high level of security and offers a very granular level of control. Its disadvantages include the possibility that it could break some applications and that it can be a performance bottleneck.

▶ **SOCKS**—SOCKS takes the proxy servers concept to the next level. SOCKS must be deployed as a client and server solution. It provides a secure channel between the two devices. It examines individual applications to determine whether they are allowed access. Common SOCKS applications include:

   ▶ **FTP**—Blocks or allows files to be transferred into or out of the network

   ▶ **HTTP**—Blocks or allows Internet access

   ▶ **SMTP**—Blocks or allows email

Demilitarized Zone

In the computer world, the DMZ prevents outsiders from getting direct access to internal services. DMZs are typically set up to allow external users access to services within the DMZ. Basically, shared services like Internet, email, and DNS might be placed within a DMZ. The DMZ provides no other access to services located within the internal network. If an attacker is able to penetrate and hack computers within the DMZ, no internal computers should be accessible (as long as no internal machines trust these DMZ computers). Usually the computers placed in the DMZ are *bastion hosts*. A bastion host is a computer that has had all unnecessary services and applications removed; it has been hardened against attack. To add security to the devices in the DMZ, a *screened host* is sometimes used. A screened host is a firewall partially shielded by a router acting as a packet filter. This furthers exemplifies the concept of defense in depth.

NAT

Network Address Translation (NAT) was originally developed because of the explosive growth of the Internet and the increase in home and business networks; the number of available public IP addresses is insufficient to support everyone. NAT allows a single device, such as a router, to act as an agent between the Internet and the local network. This device or router provides a pool of addresses for use by your local network. Only a single, unique IP address is required to represent this entire group of computers. The outside world is unaware of this division and thinks that only one computer is connected. NAT can provide a limited amount of security because it can hide internal addresses from external systems. When private addressing is used, NAT is a requirement because packets with private IP addresses cannot be routed to external IP addresses, and external traffic cannot be routed into the NATed network. RFC 1918 defines the three ranges of private addresses on the 10.0.0.0-10.255.255.255, 172.16.0.0-172-31.255.255, and 192.168.0.0-192.168.255.255 network ranges. Common types of NAT include the following:

- ▶ **Static NAT**—Uses a one-to-one mapping between public and private IP addresses.

- ▶ **Dynamic NAT**—Uses a pool of public addresses. When internal devices need Internet connectivity, they are mapped to the next available public address. When the communication session is complete, the public address is returned to the pool.

- ▶ **Port Address Translation (PAT)**—Most home networks using DSL or cable modems use this type of NAT. It is designed to provide many internal users Internet access through one external address.

Firewall Design

Firewall designs include packet filtering, dual-homed gateway, screened host, and screened subnet. A single tier *packet-filter* design has one packet-filtering router installed between the trusted and untrusted network, usually the Internet and the corporation's network. A *dual-homed gateway* is an improvement over the basic packet-filtering router because it comprises a bastion host that has two network interfaces. One important item is that IP forwarding is disabled on the host. Additional protection can be provided by adding a packet-filtering router in front of the dual-homed host. The *screened host firewall* adds a router and screened host (see Figure 7.15).

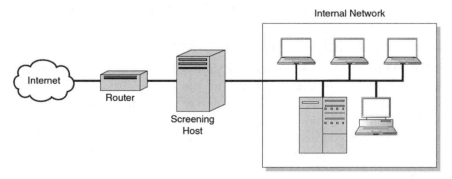

FIGURE 7.15   **Screened host.**

The router is typically configured to see only one host computer on the intranet network. Users on the intranet have to connect to the Internet through this host computer, and external users cannot directly access other computers on the intranet. In this configuration, only one network interface card is needed for the application gateway or the screening host. The screened subnet sets up a DMZ.

Remote Access

Well-designed networks will always require authentication and access control. You might be internal to the organization, or in a hotel on the road. Being outside the organization raises other concerns besides proper authentication, such as confidentiality and privacy. This section discusses an array of topics, including the Password Authentication Protocol (PAP), the Challenge Handshake Authentication Protocol (CHAP), VPNs, and IPSec.

Point-to-Point Protocol

Point-to-Point Protocol (PPP) is the most commonly used protocols for dialup connections. It can run on a line of any speed, from POTS to T1. Developed in 1994 by the IETF, PPP is a replacement to Serial Line IP (SLIP). SLIP is capable of carrying only IP and had no error detection, whereas PPP supports many types of authentication, including PAP, CHAP, and EAP.

Password Authentication Protocol

PAP uses a two-way handshake to authenticate a client to a server when a link is initially established. PAP is vulnerable because it sends the password in clear text, which makes it highly vulnerable to sniffing attacks.

Challenge Handshake Authentication Protocol

CHAP is an improved version of the PAP protocol. It uses a four-way hand-shake to authenticate the client. CHAPv2 provides for mutual authentication. When a client requests authentication, the server sends the client a challenge. The client hashes the challenge with its password and returns it to the server. This hashed value is compared on the server with a hash that the server created. Although no plain text ever crosses the network, anyone knowledgeable of the hashing functions and who captures the exchange can use a dictionary attack in an attempt to defeat the mechanism. CHAP was specifically created to defeat replay attacks because the challenge would vary with each client request, and reauthentications could be periodically demanded by the server.

Extensible Authentication Protocol

EAP makes PPP more robust by adding the capability to implement a variety of authentication mechanisms, including digital certificates, token cards, and MD5-Challenge. EAP is used with 802.1X, and implemented in amendments, such as those of 802.11i, WPA-enterprise, and WPA2-enterprise. When used by wireless devices to authenticate end users or devices, the client (supplicant) initiates the EAP request to the wireless access point (authenticator) that is responsible for keeping the network port closed until the authentication process completes successfully. The authenticator becomes a proxy, forward-ing requests and replies between the supplicant in the authenticating server (RADIUS [Remote Authentication Dial-in User Service], TACACS+, and so on). During this protected series of frames, usually inside an encrypted tunnel, a *pair-wise master key* (PMK) is developed between the supplicant and the authenticating server. If the authentication exchange is successful, the authenticating server delivers this PMK to the access point. The PMK is used to develop transient AES or TKIP encryption keys for the duration of the client's session. Table 7.14 summarizes some of the different types of EAP.

TABLE 7.14 **EAP Types**

EAP Type	Security Status	Description
EAP-LEAP	Weak	LEAP (Lightweight Extensible Authentication Protocol) is a Cisco-proprietary protocol released before 802.1X was finalized. LEAP has significant security flaws, and should not be used.
EAP-MD5	Weak	Weak form of EAP. It offers client to server authentication only and is vulnerable to man-in-the-middle attacks and password-cracking attacks.
EAP-PEAP	Better	Protected EAP (PEAP) was developed by Cisco Systems, Microsoft, and RSA Security, and is similar to EAP-TTLS. It does not require client-side certificates.
EAP-TTLS	Better	EAP-Tunneled Transport Layer Security(EAP-TTLS), offers a simplified EAP-TLS. EAP-TTLS does not use the client-side certificate, allowing other authentication methods (such as password) for client-side authentication. EAP-TTLS is thus easier to deploy than EAP-TLS, but less secure when omitting the client-side certificate.
EAP-SIM	Better	EAP-Subscriber Identity Module (EAP-SIM) is used for authentication and session key distribution for mobile phones using the Global System for Mobile Communications (GSM).
EAP-FAST	Better	EAP-Flexible Authentication via Secure Tunneling (FAST) was designed by Cisco to replace LEAP. It uses a Protected Access Credential (PAC), which acts as a pre-shared key.

ExamAlert

Although EAP-TLS is one of the most secure and most costly, EAP can be implemented in many different ways. Some methods including EAP-MD5, EAP-TLS, EAP-SIM, LEAP, and EAP-TTLS. Although EAP-MD5 is not appropriate for use by itself (a simple hash), and LEAP is dictionary-crackable; the other EAP types are robust. The goal is not for you to memorize each one these in detail, but to understand that as a CISSP, you must be able to select the appropriate protocol, depending on the policy established for authentication strength.

Remote Authentication Dial-in User Service

RADIUS was designed to support dialup users and originally used a modem pool to connect to the organization's network. Because of the features RADIUS offers, it is now used for more than just dialup users. Enterasys uses it for secure network products, and 802.1X/EAP also uses it widely. A RADIUS server contains usernames, passwords, and other information to validate the user (supplicant). *Supplicant* refers to the client machine that wants to gain access to the network. RADIUS is a well-known UDP-based authentication and accountability protocol. Information is passed to the NAS, which is the RADIUS client. The RADIUS client then forwards the information to the RADIUS server to be authenticated. Traffic from the RADIUS client to RADIUS server typically protects the password by means of a shared secret. RADIUS has improved with the IETF's approval of Diameter, and continues to be the most widely deployed AAA (Authentication, Authorization, and Accounting) server.

Terminal Access Controller Access Control System

TACACS is an access-control protocol used to authenticate a user logging onto a network. TACACS is a UDP-based protocol that provides authentication, authorization, and accountability. It was originally used in Cisco devices. TACACS is very similar to RADIUS. When TACACS receives an authentication request, it forwards the received username and password to a central database. This database verifies the information received and returns it to TACACS to allow or deny access based on the results. The fundamental reason TACACS did not become popular is because TACACS is a proprietary solution from Cisco, and its use would require the payment of royalties. TACACS+ is a completely new rewrite of the protocol and separates authentication and authorization. TACACS+ is not compatible with TACACS. TACACS+ is TCP-based and offers extended two-factor authentication. When most people today say "TACACS," they mean TACACS+.

IPsec

IPSec was developed to provide security for IP packets. Without IPSec, someone could capture, read, or change the contents of data packets and then send them back to the unsuspecting target. The current version of IP, IPv4, supports

IPSec as an add-on; IPv6 has IPSec built in. IPSec offers its users several levels of cryptographic security:

▶ **Authentication header (AH)**—Protects data against modification; does not provide privacy.

▶ **Encapsulating security payload (ESP)**—Provides privacy and protects against malicious modification.

▶ **Internet key exchange (IKE)**—Allows secret keys to be exchanged securely before communications begin.

Key exchange is something that must be handled securely. IPSec uses Internet Security Association and Key Management Protocol (ISAKMP). It is defined by RFC 2408 and is used for establishing Security Associations (SA) and cryptographic keys in an Internet environment. Basically, it defines procedures and formats to establish, negotiate, modify, and delete SAs, and defines payloads for exchanging key generation and authentication data. Each has an IP protocol number; ESP is protocol 50, and AH is protocol 51. Because IPSec is applied at OSI Layer 3, any layer above Layer 3 can use it transparently. Other Internet security systems in widespread use, such as Transport Layer Security (TLS) and Secure Shell (SSH), operate in the upper layers at the OSI model. IPSec has two modes of operation:

▶ **Transport mode**—Protects just the payload.

▶ **Tunnel mode**—Protects the payload and the header. In this configuration, IPSec acts as a gateway; traffic for any number of client computers can be carried. IPSec in tunnel mode provides link encryption and is compatible with IPv6. It can be used to encrypt any traffic supported by IP.

See Figure 7.16 to better understand the differences between the two modes.

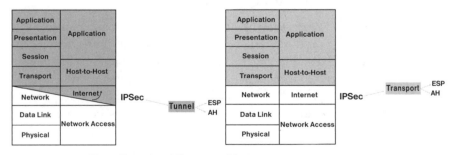

FIGURE 7.16 **IPsec Tunnel and Transport Modes.**

Three different implementation architectures are defined for IPsec in RFC 2401. These include host to gateway, gateway-to-gateway, and host-to-host.

▶ Host to gateway—Used to connect one system that runs IPsec client software to an IPsec gateway.

▶ Gateway-to-gateway—Connects two IPsec gateways to form an IPsec connection that acts as a shared routable network connection.

▶ Host-to-host—Connects two systems to each other via IPsec.

Message Privacy and Multimedia Collaboration

New technologies make it possible to monitor all types of information that one individual might send to another. *Bullrun* is one example of such a program. This controversial program was developed by the National Security Agency (NSA) to give the U.S. government the means to defeat the encryption used in specific network communication technologies. Its full capability is unknown.

Some Internet applications have little or no built-in security. *Instant messaging* (IM) is a good example. Many corporations allow or use IM, but it was built for chatting, not security. Most IM applications lack encryption capabilities, have insecure password management, and have features that actively work to bypass firewalls. IM can be vulnerable to sniffing attacks, can be used to spread viruses and worms, and can be targeted for buffer overflow attacks. If these programs are going to be used, security controls like the Pidgin encryption plug-ins and SSL-based chat should be considered. Although IM is not as popular as it once was, IM products are all highly vulnerable to malware, such as worm viruses, backdoor Trojan horses, hijacking, impersonation, and denial of service. IM can also be used to exfiltrate sensitive information.

Web conferencing is a low-cost method that allows people in different locations to communicate over the Internet. Though useful, web conferencing can potentially be sniffed and intercepted by an attacker. Common solutions include Adobe Connect, GoToMeeting, and Microsoft Office Live Meeting. These technologies usually include displaying PowerPoint slides, sharing audio or video, or even sharing documents. Some solutions allow users to remotely control another connected PC.

Remote meeting and web conferencing software is typically designed tunnel outbound SSL or TLS traffic. These technologies often pass outside the corporate network and as such should be understood, controlled, and made compliant with all applicable policy as they offer attackers and others the ability to exfiltrate data.

Finally, there is email. It's another common network application and in its native state can be very insecure. Sending an email message is much like your parents sending a postcard about their vacation to you through the U.S. mail. Anyone who happens to see the card during transit can read the message they sent you from their trip to Kathmandu. If you need a little privacy, you must use encryption. Using encryption is the equivalent of sending a coded letter in a sealed envelope: Even if someone opens the sealed envelope, the coded letter will prevent anyone from learning about your parents' trip to Kathmandu to see Mount Everest. Email protection mechanisms include PGP, Secure Multipurpose Internet Mail Extensions (S/MIME), and Privacy Enhanced Mail (PEM).

Exam Prep Questions

1. You are a security consultant for a new company that is going to sell products online. Customers will be expected to pay for their products on the company website. It is necessary to establish a secure connection between two TCP-based machines to ensure web communications for financial transactions. You have been asked to suggest some type of extensible authentication protocol to help secure this traffic. Which version would you consider the most secure but also the most costly?

   ○ **A.** EAP-LEAP

   ○ **B.** EAP-MD5

   ○ **C.** EAP-TLS

   ○ **D.** EAP-SIM

2. You just overheard two people discussing ways to steal electronic serial numbers (ESNs). What type of attack are they discussing?

   ○ **A.** Bank card hacking

   ○ **B.** Modem hacking

   ○ **C.** PBX hacking

   ○ **D.** Cell phone hacking

3. You are a security consultant for a company that has a location in Houston, Texas, New York City, and Dallas, Texas. Your client requires link-to-link communications from the LAN to the WAN for data/traffic encryption supported by IP that includes encryption and authentication. They will be using L2TP at L3 of the OSI model. The CIO for the company plans to migrate to IPv6 over the next year so he needs something that will be compatible with IPv6. What is the BEST protocol to use for your client?

   ○ **A.** IPSec Transport mode

   ○ **B.** IPSec Tunnel model

   ○ **C.** PPTP

   ○ **D.** L2F

4. Which of the following is a mechanism for converting internal IP addresses found in IP headers into public addresses for transmission over the Internet?

   ○ **A.** ARP

   ○ **B.** DNS

   ○ **C.** DHCP

   ○ **D.** NAT

5. Samuel has been asked to start the implementation of IPv6 on an existing IPv4 network. The current system has no native connection to an IPv6 network. It has about 130 hosts. The internal routing protocol is OSPF. Which technology would you recommend that Samuel use?

   ○ **A.** VRRP

   ○ **B.** Teredo

   ○ **C.** 802.1AE

   ○ **D.** 6to4

6. You have been brought on as a consultant to a small non-profit where they are using a routing protocol that is based on Bellman-Ford algorithms. Although the network has reached convergence, one path is no longer available and shows an infinite hop count. What is the proper term to describe this situation?

   ○ **A.** Loopback

   ○ **B.** Split horizon

   ○ **C.** Classless Inter-Domain Routing

   ○ **D.** Poison reverse

7. Which of the following is considered a current updated standard to the WEP protocol?

   ○ **A.** WPA2

   ○ **B.** SMLI

   ○ **C.** PGP

   ○ **D.** POP

8. Which of the following closely resembles a packet-filtering device because it makes decisions on addresses, ports, and protocols?

   ○ **A.** Stateless firewall

   ○ **B.** Circuit-level proxy

   ○ **C.** Application proxy

   ○ **D.** Stateful firewall

9. This protocol is considered a forerunner to Frame Relay and works over POTS lines.

   ○ **A.** SMDS

   ○ **B.** ATM

   ○ **C.** X.25

   ○ **D.** T-carriers

10. RADIUS provides which of the following?

- ○ **A.** Authentication and accountability
- ○ **B.** Authorization and accountability
- ○ **C.** Authentication and authorization
- ○ **D.** Authentication, authorization, and accountability

11. You have been asked to implement a WAN technology for your client. The client is based in a rural area in the southern US. The client does not want to use a circuit-switched technology. Based on this information, which of the following is a cell-switched technology which you could use?

- ○ **A.** DSL
- ○ **B.** T1
- ○ **C.** ISDN
- ○ **D.** ATM

12. Which of the following is considered a third-generation firewall?

- ○ **A.** Packet filter
- ○ **B.** Circuit proxy
- ○ **C.** Application proxy
- ○ **D.** Stateful firewall

13. Identify protocols that work at OSI Layers 2, 6, 3, 4, and 7.

- ○ **A.** ARP, SQL, ICMP, SMB, and SNMP
- ○ **B.** L2TP, SMB, IP, SQL, and HTTP
- ○ **C.** WEP, ASCII, IPX, TCP, and BootP
- ○ **D.** PPP, ZIP, SPX, UDP, and TFTP

14. Which of the following wireless standards has a range of 5.15–5.35 GHz to 5.725–5.825 GHz and a range of approximately 60 feet?

- ○ **A.** 802.11a
- ○ **B.** 802.11b
- ○ **C.** 802.11g
- ○ **D.** 802.11n

15. Which of the following is the BEST description of ISAKMP?

    ○ **A.** Defines procedures and packet formats to establish, negotiate, modify, and delete Security Associations and defines payloads for exchanging key generation and authentication data. Typically utilizes IKE for key exchange, although other methods can be implemented

    ○ **B.** Enables the authentication of the parties involved in a secure transition and contains the certificate issuer's name, valid from-date and valid to-date, the owner of the certificate (the subject), the subject's public key, the time stamp, and the certificate issuer's digital signature.

    ○ **C.** A framework for managing private keys and certificates that provides a standard for key generation, authentication, distribution, and storage, establishes who is responsible for authenticating the identity of the owners of the digital certificates, and follows the X.509 standard.

    ○ **D.** ISAKMP is the standard that defines how to protect keys and establish policies for setting key lifetimes, and sets out essential elements of business continuity and disaster recovery planning.

Answers to Exam Prep Questions

1. **C.** EAP-TLS is one of the most secure but also the most costly as it requires certificates for both the server and the client. Answer A and B is incorrect because both EAP-LEAP and EAP-MD5 are known to be insecure. Answer D is incorrect because EAP-SIM is used for smart phones and mobile devices.

2. **D.** Cell phone hackers scan for electronic serial numbers and mobile identification numbers. These are used to clone phones. Answer A is incorrect because bank card hacking would most likely target a database. Answer B is incorrect because the individuals that target modems are known as war dialers. Answer C is incorrect because PBX hacking is performed by phreakers.

3. **B.** IPsec in tunnel mode provides link encryption, is compatible with IP v6 and can be used to encrypt any traffic supported by IP. It also can be used with L2TP or alone and operates at layer 3 of the OSI model. A is not correct because transport mode encrypts only the IP payload. C is not correct because PPTP does not offer encryption. Answer D is wrong because it works at layer 2 of the OSI model and does not provide data encryption.

4. **D.** NAT allows a single device, such as a router, to act as an agent between the Internet and the internal network. ARP is used for physical address resolution, so answer A is incorrect. DNS is used for IP address resolution, so answer B is incorrect. DHCP is used to assign dynamic addresses, so answer C is incorrect.

5. **B.** Teredo is the correct answer as it an a transition technology that can be used for IPv6-capable hosts that are on the IPv4 Internet that have no native connection to an IPv6 network. Answer A is incorrect as Virtual Router Redundancy Protocol (VRRP) is used for router redundancy. Answer C is incorrect because 802.1AE is a layer 1 OSI technology known as MACSEC. Answer D is incorrect because although 6to4 is an Internet transition mechanism for migrating from IPv4 to IPv6 it is typically used where there is connectivity to an IPv6 network.

6. **D.** Poison reverse sets the number of hops to the unconnected gateway to a number that indicates infinite. All other answers are incorrect. Answer A describes the loop back address which has no relevance to the question. Answer B is incorrect because split horizon is a route advertisement that prevents routing loops in distance-vector routing protocols by prohibiting a router from advertising a route back onto the router interface from which it was discovered. Answer C is incorrect because Classless Inter-Domain Routing was designed to slow the growth of routing tables on routers across the Internet, and to help slow the rapid exhaustion of IPv4 addresses.

7. **A.** WPA2 is the current standard for wireless security. SMLI, answer B, is incorrect because it is a firewall technology. Answer C is incorrect because PGP is an email-protection mechanism, and POP, answer D, is associated with email, so neither of these is correct.

8. **B.** Circuit-level proxies closely resemble packet-filtering devices because they examine addresses, ports, and protocols. Stateless firewalls are packet-filtering devices and application proxies and stateful firewalls examine higher-level content, so answers A, C, and D are incorrect.

9. **C.** X.25 predates Frame Relay. Although it is not fast, it is reliable and works over analog phone lines. SMDS is a high-speed MAN/WAN packet-switched protocol, so answer A is incorrect. ATM is a modern protocol that offers high speed and various classes of service, so answer B is incorrect. T-carriers are circuit-switched technology, so answer D is incorrect.

10. **C.** RADIUS is a client/server protocol used to authenticate dial-in users and authorize access. The other answers are incorrect because they do not meet the specification of RADIUS.

11. **D.** ATM is a cell-switched technology. DSL, T1, and ISDN are not based on cell-switching technology, and therefore are incorrect.

12. **D.** Stateful firewalls are considered intelligent firewalls and are third-generation devices. Circuit and application proxies are second-generation devices and packet filters are first-generation devices, so answers A, B, and C are incorrect.

13. **C.** WEP is found at Layer 2. ASCII is found at Layer 6, IPX is found at Layer 3, TCP is found at Layer 4, and BootP is found at Layer 7.

14. **A.** 802.11a has a range of 5.15–5.35 GHz to 5.725–5.825 GHz and a range of approximately 60 feet.

15. **A.** ISAKMP is Internet Security Association and Key Management Protocol. It defines procedures and packet formats to establish, negotiate, modify, and delete Security Associations, and defines payloads for exchanging key generation and authentication data. It typically utilizes IKE for key exchange, although other methods can be implemented. Answer B and C are both incorrect because they deal specifically with certificate management. Answer D is not correct because it deals with key management.

Need to Know More?

Introduction to TCP/IP: pclt.cis.yale.edu/pclt/COMM/TCPIP.HTM

An introduction to the OSI Model: www.rfdesign.info/doc-desc/15/Introduction-to-OSI-model-and-Networking-Components.html

Encapsulation: www.tcpipguide.com/free/t_IPDatagramEncapsulation.htm

Bluetooth keyboard sniffing: www.gossamer-threads.com/lists/fulldisc/full-disclosure/64769?page=last

Securing OSI: www.infosecwriters.com/text_resources/pdf/KRodriguez_OSI_Model.pdf

Electronic serial numbers: en.wikipedia.org/wiki/Electronic_Serial_Number

Phone phreaking: www.telephonetribute.com/phonephreaking.html

Phone phreaking history: en.wikipedia.org/wiki/John_Draper

The RADIUS authentication protocol: en.wikipedia.org/wiki/RADIUS

Wireless standards: www.wi-fi.org/

CHAPTER 8

Identity and Access Management

Terms you'll need to understand:

▶ Identification and authentication of people and devices

▶ Mandatory access control (MAC)

▶ Discretionary access control (DAC)

▶ Role-based access control (RBAC)

▶ Single sign-on (SSO)

▶ Crossover error rate (CER)

▶ Zephyr chart

Topics you'll need to master:

▶ Identity and Access Management

▶ Understand the methods of authentication for people and devices

▶ Describe the differences between discretionary, mandatory, and role-based access control

▶ Know the advantages of single sign-on technologies

▶ Be able to differentiate authorization types

Introduction

Identity and access management is a key component of security because it helps to keep unauthorized users out and it keeps authorized users honest; it is critical for accountability and auditing. It is part of what is known as the triple-A process of *authentication, authorization,* and *accountability*. Take note—you may see "accountability" and "auditing" used synonymously; they mean the same thing.

Authentication systems based on passwords have been used for many years because they are cheaper and easier to integrate. Today, many more organizations are using tokens and biometrics. Some organizations even enforce two-factor authentication, whereas other entities are moving to federated authentication.

Security administrators have more to worry about than just authentication. Many employees now have multiple accounts to keep up with. Luckily, there is a way to consolidate these accounts: single sign-on solutions. A single sign-on solution allows users the ability to authenticate only once to access all needed resources and systems. Authentication systems can be centralized, decentralized, or hybrid. This chapter introduces each concept.

> **Tip**
>
> *Single Sign-on (SSO)* is NOT the same as *Password Synchronization*. Password Synchronization typically uses a static password that is shared across multiple systems or programs, whereas in an SSO solution a user must authenticate to an authentication server, and the authentication server provides further provisional access control privileges for the user.

Although knowing who to authenticate serves as a basis of access control, there also exists the issue of authorization. *Authorization* defines what access the user has and what abilities are present. Authorization is a core component of access control. Once a user has been authenticated to a domain, server, application, or system, what are they authorized to do?. As an example, administrators are typically authorized to perform many more functions than an average user. Controlling access is the first line of defense in allowing authorized users access while keeping unauthorized users out.

This chapter examines authorization in the context of discretionary, nondiscretionary, and role-based access control. Authorization should be implemented to allow the minimum access required for a user to accomplish his or her task. This approach helps control access, minimizes the damage that a single employee can inflict on the organization, and mitigates the risks associated with access control. The principle that employees should be provided only the amount of control and access that they need to accomplish their job duties, and nothing more is referred to as the principle of least privilege.

If something does go wrong, a method will be required to determine who has done what. That is the process of audit and accountability. In an audit, those individuals tasked with enforcement of network security review records to determine what was done, and by whom. Accountability means that malicious and repetitive mistakes can be tracked and tied to a specific individual, or at least traced to that individual's credentials.

Identification, Authentication, and Authorization of People and Devices

Identification, authentication, and authorization are three of the core concepts of access control. Together, these items determine who gets into the network and what they have access to. When someone thinks of authentication, what might come to mind is who gains access; however, identification comes first. At the point of identification you are a claimant.   This simply means that you may say you are Michael. But how does the system actually know this? That is where authentication comes into play by proving the veracity of a claim. Let's look at some basic concepts and terms before reviewing more in-depth topics:

- ▶ *Identification* is the process of identifying yourself to an authentication service.

- ▶ *Authentication* is the process of proving the veracity of an identity claim; phrased differently, it is used to determine whether a user is who he or she claims to be.

- ▶ *Authorization* is the process of determining whether a user has the right to access a requested resource.

- ▶ *Accountability* is the ability to relate specific actions and operations to a unique individual, system, or process.

- ▶ *Access* is the transfer of information between two entities. When access control is discussed, it is usually in terms of access, subjects, and objects.

- ▶ A *subject* is an active entity that can be a person, application, or process.

▶ An *object* is a passive entity that contains or holds information. An object can be a server, database, information system, etc.

Tip

It is important to note that a person can be a subject or an object. In this domain the person is typically the active entity, or subject. In other domains the application, for example, can be the subject.

Authentication Techniques

In network security, authentication is the process of determining the legitimacy of a user or process. Various authentication schemes have been developed over the years. Some common categories that have been established are as follows:

▶ **Something you know (Type 1)**—Typically an alphanumeric password or PIN number.

▶ **Something you have (Type 2)**—Can include smart cards, tokens, memory cards, or key fobs.

▶ **Something you are (Type 3)**—Items like fingerprints, facial scans, retina scans, or voice recognition.

Tip

Some sources list a fourth type of authentication, which is *somewhere* you are. As an example, consider a callback system that requires you to be in a specific location to receive the call to authenticate. Another example is the use of GPS in a smartphone or tablet to identify where you are.

The authentication process is something that most individuals have performed thousands of times. Consider the log-in prompt at the website of your local bank. You are prompted to enter your username and password, which, if entered correctly, provides you with access. As an example, you might now be able to access your own bank records, but you should not be able to see some-one else's bank balance or access their funds. Your level of authorization as a bank user will be much different from that of a bank manager or loan officer. What is important to understand is that authorization can offer a wide range of access levels from all to nothing.

Organizations require this level of control to enforce effective controls and maintain a secure environment. *Enforcement* also requires audit and accountability. Enforcement means that someone must review employee and user activities. Just as the bank manager has a greater level of access than the average bank user doesn't mean that his or her access is unchecked. Controls are needed to limit what the bank manager can access; furthermore, it is needed to enforce accountability so that fraud can be detected if the manager were to decide to take a small amount of the customers' money each month and stash it away in a Swiss account.

The way in which authentication is handled is changing. As an example, federated authentication allows you to log in once and access multiple resources without having to log in to each unique site or service. The overarching framework is for organizations to share authentication information over the world wide web using Security Association Markup Language (SAML) with HTTPS; therefore, once users have proven their identity, if two organizations trust each other, a user's shopping experience online gets easier and their security token goes with them. For example, if you were to book an airline ticket, you might be presented with a pop-up that asks if you also need to book a hotel room. Clicking **Yes** might take you to a major hotel chain website to which your identity and travel information have already been passed. This saves you the process of logging in a second time to the hotel website.

Such systems are already in use, and one early example was Microsoft Passport. These technologies allow for third-party identity management. As another example, you might go to a shopping site and be asked to log in with your Facebook credentials. These systems function by establishing a trust relationship between the identity provider and the service or application. Also, more organizations are starting to adopt authentication as a service (AaaS). AaaS enables organizations to easily apply strong authentication delivered from the cloud and use it as needed, from anywhere.

Something You Know (Type 1): Passwords and PINs

We begin our discussion of authentication systems by discussing passwords. Of the three types of authentication, passwords are the most widely used. The problem with this method is that passwords are typically weak. Consider the following:

▶ People use passwords that are easy to remember.

▶ Difficult passwords might be written down and left where others can find them.

▶ Most of us are guilty of reusing passwords.

▶ Reputability is a real issue with passwords because it is hard to prove who made a specific transaction or gained access.

▶ Passwords can be cracked, sniffed, observed, replayed, or broken. Common password cracking can use dictionary, hybrid, or exhaustive search (brute force) attacks.

▶ Dictionary attacks use common dictionary words, and hybrid password cracking uses a combination of words as random characters, such as 1password or p@ssw0rd. Brute force attempts all possible variations, which is typically time consuming. Rainbow table attacks use precomputed hash tables to reduce password cracking time and recover the plaintext password.

▶ Many people are predictable and, as such, might use passwords that are easily guessed. Many times passwords are based on birthdays, anniversaries, a child's name, or even a favorite pet. With the massive growth of the Internet and "Big Data" it is easy to use social engineering to find this information.

Tip

In May 2014, news sources reported that eBay had suffered a massive security breach and was advising all users to change their passwords. eBay suggest that about 145 million users change their passwords. See mashable.com/2014/05/21/ebay-breach-ramifications/#9rCZ8zr.euqY for more details.

This makes password security an important topic for anyone studying access control. Many times a password is all that stands between an unauthorized user and account access. If you can't make the change to a more robust form of authentication, you can implement controls to make passwords more robust. A few of these options are as follows:

▶ **Password length**—Short passwords can be broken quickly via brute force attacks.

▶ **Password composition**—Passwords should not be based on personal information or consist of common words or names. If you use cognitive information, you should make this information up during enrollment. Remember, your "real" information can be found on the Internet.

▶ **Password complexity**—A combination of numbers, symbols, upper/lowercase letters, and so on should be used. As an example, a company might use a standard that requires passwords must be at least eight characters, two of which must be numbers and two of which must be uppercase letters. The company might also suggest using a combination of symbols and lowercase letters for the remaining characters.

▶ **Password aging**—Unlike fine wine, passwords do not get better with age. Two items of concern are maximum age and minimum age. Maximum age is the longest amount of time a user can use a password. Minimum age defines the minimum amount of time the user must keep the password.

▶ **Password history**—Authentication systems should track previous passwords so that users cannot reuse previous passwords.

▶ **Password attempts**—Log-on attempts should be limited to a small number of times, such as three successive attempts. Applying this control is also called setting a *clipping* or *threshold* level. The result of a threshold or clipping event can be anything from a locking of the account to a delayed re-enabling of the account

▶ **Password storage**—Use the strongest form of one-way encryption available for storage of passwords, and never store in cleartext.

ExamAlert

You will be expected to understand CISSP terminology before attempting the exam. One such term is *clipping level*. Used in this context, it is simply another term for a log-on limit. Remember that a clipping level is the threshold or limit that must be reached before action is taken. A big part of the exam is understanding the terms that might be used and applying them in the context of the test question.

If all this talk of passwords has left you feeling somewhat vulnerable, you may want to consider a passphrase. A *passphrase* is often a modified sentence or phrase like "Uaremy#1lady4l!fe." After being entered into a computer system, it is converted into a virtual password. Passphrases function by having someone enter the phrase into the computer. Software converts, or *hashes*, that phrase into a stronger virtual password that is harder for an attacker to crack. Using a passphrase adds a second layer of protection and requires the passphrase to be used to access the secret key.

Static and Dynamic Passwords

Another issue to consider when evaluating password-based authentication is what type of password-based system is being used. Is it a static password, dynamic password, or a cognitive password? Static passwords are those that are fixed and do not normally change. As an example, I once set up a Gmail account for email and assigned a password. This password remained in effect until I no longer used the account. *Dynamic passwords* are also known as *single-use passwords* and can be thought of as the facial tissue of the security world: You use them once or for a short period, and then they are discarded. One-time passwords might be provided through a token device that displays the time-limited password on an LCD screen. Finally, there are cognitive passwords, which are discussed next.

> **Tip**
>
> Cracking passwords are just one technique that hackers can attempt. Attacks against access control systems can also include directly targeting the hashes. There are tools to attempt this remotely, or the attacker can attempt this via physical access.

Cognitive Passwords

Cognitive passwords are another interesting password mechanism that has gained popularity. For example, three to five questions like the following might be asked:

▶ What country were you born in?

▶ What department do you work for?

▶ What is your pet's name?

▶ What is the model of your first car?

▶ What is your mother's maiden name?

If you answer all the questions correctly, you are authenticated. Cognitive passwords are widely used during enrollment processes and when individuals call help desks or request other services that require authentication. Cognitive passwords are not without their problems. For example, if your name is Sarah Palin and the cognitive password you're prompted for by Yahoo! Mail is "What's the name of your high school," anyone who knows that fact or that you grew up in Wasilla, Alaska could probably figure out where you went to high school and easily access your account. The most common area that cognitive systems are used is in self-service password reset systems. Should you forget your password, you are prompted with several questions that were answered during registration to verify your authenticity. If you answer correctly, the password is emailed or sent to you to restore access.

ExamAlert

Exam candidates must understand the strengths and weaknesses of passwords and how password-based authentication can be enhanced. Passwords should always be created by means of a one-way process (hashing), should be randomized (salted), and should never be stored in cleartext.

Something You Have (Type 2): Tokens, Cards, and Certificates

Something you have is the second type of authentication we will discuss. Examples of something you have include tokens, smart cards, magnetic stripe cards, and certificates.

One of the most common examples of type 2 authentication is a token. As an example, if you have been to a sports event lately, you most likely had to possess a token to enter the game. In this instance, the token was in the form of a ticket. In the world of network security, a token can be a *synchronous token* or an *asynchronous token* device. Tokens are widely used with *one-time passwords* (OTPs) or single-use passwords. These passwords change every time they are used. Thus, OTPs are often implemented with tokens.

Another great feature of token-based devices is that they can be used for two-factor authentication. Although physical tokens and key fobs can suffer from problems like battery failure and device failure, using tokens offers a much more secure form of authentication than using passwords.

Synchronous Tokens

Synchronous tokens are synchronized to the authentication server. This type of system works by means of a clock or time-based counter. Each individual passcode is valid for only a short period. Even if an attacker were able to intercept a token-based password, it would be valid for only a limited time. After that small window of opportunity, it would have no value to an attacker. As an example, RSA's SecurID changes user passwords every 60 seconds. Figure 8.1 shows an example.

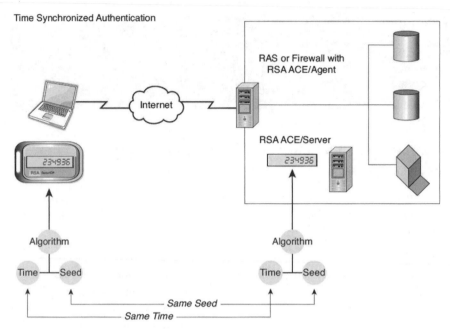

Time Synchronized Authentication

FIGURE 8.1　**RSA token authentication.**

Asynchronous Token Devices

Asynchronous token devices are not synchronized to the authentication server. These devices use a challenge-response mechanism and usually require the user to press a key on the token and on the authentication server. The server sends the user a random value and the user will enter the random value into the device along with a username and password. Together, this authentication method is considered strong authentication as it is actually multifactor authentication (something you know and something you have). Figure 8.2 shows an example.

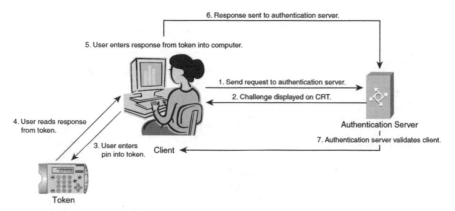

FIGURE 8.2 **Asynchronous token authentication.**

These devices work as follows:

1. The computer generates a value and displays it to the user.

2. The value is entered into the token.

3. The user is prompted to enter a secret passphrase.

4. The token performs a computation on the entered value.

5. The new value is displayed on the LCD screen of the token device.

6. The user enters the displayed value into the computer for authentication.

7. The value is forwarded to an authentication server and compared to the value the authentication server is expecting.

Cards

Card-based authentication can be accomplished by means of a smart card, memory card, or magnetic stripe card. A smart card is an intelligent token with an embedded integrated circuit chip. It provides not only memory capacity, but computational capability because of its built-in microprocessor. The types of smart cards include:

▶ **Contact smart cards**—When inserted into the reader, electrical contacts touch the card in the area of the integrated circuit (IC). These contacts provide power and a data path to the smart card.

▶ **Contactless smart card**—When brought into the proximity of a reader, an embedded antenna provides power to the IC. When the correct PIN is entered into the smart card, processing can begin. Figure 8.3 shows an example of a generic smart card.

FIGURE 8.3 **Generic smart card.**

Memory cards are like smart cards but cannot process information. They must be used in conjunction with readers and systems that can process the data held on the memory card. One of the primary advantages of a memory card is that, unlike passwords, memory cards require the user to possess the card to perform authentication. An older form of a card token is the magnetic stripe card, established as a widely used standard in the 1970s. The magnetic stripe contains information used to authenticate the user. Care must be exercised in the storage of information on the magnetic card. Although cleartext should not be used, some credit cards still hold information in cleartext. Magnetic stripe readers are cheap and easy to use. Anyone possessing such a device and a PC can steal card information anywhere cards are used, such as at a restaurant or store. Memory cards typically hold a PIN that when activated by a computer system will pull authentication information from a database.

Certificates

Some authentication methods, such as Protected Extensible Authentication Protocol (PEAP) and Extensible Authentication Protocol (EAP), can use certificates for authentication of computers and users. Certificates can reside on a smart card or can be used by Internet Protocol Security (IPSec) and Secure Sockets Layer (SSL) for web authentication. These digital certificates provide some basic information to prove the identity of the holder.

Digital certificates typically contain the following critical pieces of information:

▶ Identification information that includes username, serial number, and validity dates of the certificates.

▶ The public key of the certificate holder.

▶ The digital signature of the signature authority. This piece is critical because it validates the entire package.

X.509 is the standard for digital signatures because it specifies information and attributes required for the identification of a person or a computer system. Version 3 is the most current. It is considered a secure process to store digital certificates in tokens.

Something You Are (Type 3): Biometrics

Biometrics is a means of authentication based on personal attributes or behavioral or physiological characteristics that are unique to each individual. Personal attributes are more closely related to identity features such as fingerprints and retina scans, whereas an example of a behavioral trait is the way an individual signs his or her name, referred to as signature dynamics. This is not the same as a digital signature. Biometrics is a very accurate means of authentication, but is typically more expensive than the password systems that were discussed.

Biometric authentication systems have been slow to mature because many individuals are opposed to the technology. Issues like privacy are typically raised. Some individuals see the technology as too much of a Big Brother technology. Individuals who are accustomed to quickly entering usernames and passwords are forced to be much more patient and allow the biometric system to gather multiple sets of biometric data. Issues like sanitization are can be a barrier because users often have to touch authentication devices, including but not limited to placing their face on or near a small device for the retina scan.

During the authentication process, the biometric system might not be able to collect enough data on the first reading to compare to the reference file in the authentication store. This could mean that the user must allow the biometric system to make two or more passes before authentication takes place. These technical barriers further reduce acceptance of the biometric system.

However, the need for greater security has led more companies to look at biometric authentication systems as a way to meet the need for stronger security. Biometric authentication offers the capability of unique authentication of every single person on the planet. Biometric systems work by recording information that is very minute and unique to every person.

When the biometric system is first used, the system must develop a database of information about the user. This is considered the enrollment period. When enrollment is complete, the system is ready for use. If an employee then places his or her hand on the company's new biometric palm scanner, the scanner compares the ridges and creases found on the employee's palm to the one identified as belonging to that individual in the device's database. This process is considered a one-to-one match of the individual's biometric data.

In reality, the user's unique attribute value is converted into a binary value and then hashed before being stored in an authentication server. In organizations that implement strong security, a user may be authenticated with both biometrics and a username/password. This is to ensure if one layer of security fails the system or facility is still protected, following the defense-in-depth approach. Different biometric systems have varying levels of accuracy and sensitivity.

The attributes are measured by the percentage of Type I and Type II errors it produces.

Type I errors, known as the *false rejection rate* (FRR), are a measurement of the percentage of individuals who should have been but were not allowed access. Think of the FRR as the insult rate. It's called that because valid users are insulted that they were denied access even though they are legitimate users.

Type II errors, known as the *false acceptance rate* (FAR), are the percentage of individuals or subjects are a measurement of the percentage who got in but should not have been allowed access. Consider a situation where I, the author of this book and not an employee of your organization, show up at your work site and attempt to authenticate to one of the company's systems. If I were allowed in, that would be an example of a Type II error.

Together these two values can be used to determine the overall accuracy of the system. This is one of the primary ways to evaluate the accuracy of a biometric device. Suppose you have been asked to assess similar biometric devices. In this situation, the crossover error rate (CER) can be used to help guide you into selecting the best system for your organization. This is determined by mapping the point at which Type I errors equal Type II errors. Figure 8.4 depicts the CER. The lower the CER, the more accurate is the biometric system. For example, if system A has a CER of 4 and system B has a CER of 2, system B has the greater accuracy.

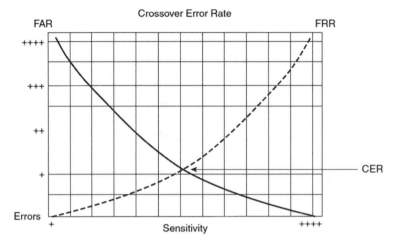

FIGURE 8.4 **Crossover error rate.**

ExamAlert

Before attempting the CISSP exam, make sure you understand the difference between Type I and Type II errors and the CER. Type II values are considered the most critical error rate to examine, whereas the CER is considered to be the best measurement of biometric systems accuracy.

The following are some of the more common biometric authentication systems. These systems are listed in order of best response times and lowest error rates.

1. **Palm scan**—Analyzes characteristics associated with a user's palm, such as the creases and ridges. If a match is found, the individual is allowed access.

2. **Hand geometry**—Another biometric system that uses the unique geometry of a user's shape, length, and width of his or her fingers and hand to determine the user's identity. It is one of the oldest biometric techniques.

3. **Iris recognition**—An eye-recognition system that is considered the most accurate biometric system because it has more than 400 points of reference when matching the irises of an individual's eyes. These systems typically work by taking a picture of the iris and comparing it to one stored in a database.

4. **Retina pattern**—Another ocular-based technology that scans the blood vessels in the back of the eye. It requires users to place their eye close to the reader. Older systems used a cup-and-air technique that some users found invasive as you must put. The cup-and-air technique also raises the possibility of exchange of bodily fluids. Although retina-based biometric system are considered very accurate, drawbacks include the fact that the retina can change due to medical conditions like diabetes. Pregnancy can also cause subtle changes in the blood vessels of the retina. Because of the privacy concerns related to revealed medical conditions, retina scans are not readily accepted by users.

5. **Fingerprint**—Widely used for access control to facilities and items, such as laptops. It works by distinguishing up to 30 to 40 details about the peaks, valleys, ridges, and minutiae of the user's fingerprint. However, many commercial systems limit the number that is matched to around eight to ten.

6. **Facial recognition**—Requires users to place their face in front of a camera. The facial scan device performs a mathematical comparison with the face prints (*eigenfeatures*) it holds in a database to allow or block access.

7. **Voice recognition**—Uses voice analysis for identification and authentication. Its main advantage is that it can be used for telephone applications, but it is vulnerable to replay attacks. Anyone that has seen the movie *Sneakers* might remember the line "Hi, my name is Werner Brandes. My voice is my passport. Verify me."

Regardless of which of the previous methods is used, all biometric systems basically follow a similar usage pattern:

1. **Users must first enroll into the system**—Enrollment is not much more than allowing the system to take multiple samples for analysis and feature extraction. These features will be used later for comparison.

2. **A user requests to be authenticated**—A sample is obtained, analyzed, and features are extracted.

3. **A decision is reached**—A match of multiple features allows the user access, whereas a discrepancy between the sample and the stored features causes the user to be denied access.

Different biometric systems have varying levels of accuracy. For example, fingerprint-scanning systems base their accuracy on fingerprint patterns and minutiae. Fingerprint patterns include arches, loops, and whorls, whereas minutiae include ridge endings, bifurcations, and short ridges. These are found on the fingertips, as seen in Figure 8.5.

Although the number of minutiae varies from finger to finger, the information can be stored electronically in file sizes that are usually from 250 to 1,000 bytes. When a user logs in, the stored file containing the minutiae is compared to the individual's finger being scanned.

FIGURE 8.5 **Fingerprint analysis.**

Other considerations must be made before deploying a biometric system:

▶ **Employee buy-in**—Users might not like or want to interact with the system. If so, the performance of the system will suffer. For example, a retina scan requires individuals to look into a cuplike device, whereas an iris scanner requires only a quick look into a camera.

▶ **Age, gender, or occupation of the user**—Older users might find biometric devices too Big Brotherish; women might not like the idea that the company's new retina scanner can be used to detect whether they are pregnant. Users who perform physical labor or work in an unclean environment might find fingerprint scanners frustrating.

▶ **The physical status of the user**—Users who are physically challenged or disabled might find the eye scanners difficult to reach. Those without use of their hands or fingers will be unable to use fingerprint readers, palm scanners, or hand geometry systems.

▶ **If the user can use the biometric**—Some users may not be able to use the biometric. For example, some people cannot have their fingerprints read. This can be genetic or based on the job the person does. For example, brick layers and bank tellers typically cannot use fingerprint readers because their fingerprints may be worn off.

A final consideration of biometrics is selection. With so many technologies, it takes a significant amount of effort to get the right system that meets user criteria and is technologically feasible. One tool that can aid in this task is the Zephyr chart. The International Biometric Group's Zephyr Analysis provides a means of evaluating different biometric technologies. Two categories are defined as follows:

▶ **User Criteria**—Effort and intrusiveness

▶ **Technology Criteria**—Cost and accuracy

ExamAlert

Exam candidates must understand the different ways in which biometric systems can be evaluated. When comparing like devices, the CER can be used; for unlike devices, a Zephyr chart is the preferred method.

Strong Authentication

To make authentication stronger, you can combine several of the methods discussed previously. This combination is referred to as *multifactor* or *strong authentication*. The most common form of strong authentication is two-factor authentication. Tokens combined with passwords form an effective and strong authentication. If you have a bank card, you are familiar with two-factor authentication. Bank ATMs require two items to successfully access an account: something you have (bank card) and something you know (your PIN).

The decision to use strong authentication depends on your analysis of the value of the assets being protected. What are the dollar values of the assets being protected? What might it cost the organization in dollars, lost profit, potential public embarrassment, or liability if unauthorized access is successful?

ExamAlert

CISSP exam questions are known for their unique style of wording. As such, make sure you can identify two-factor authentication. True two-factor authentication would require items from two of the three categories. As such, a password and a token would be two-factor authentication, whereas a password and a PIN would not.

Identity Management Implementation

Identity management has moved far beyond control of simple usernames and passwords. It involves a lifecycle of access control from account creation to decommissioning, and the management of each process in between. Provisioning is one important aspect. *User provisioning* is the creation, management, and deactivation of services and accounts of user objects. Access control is not an easy task because employees are hired, change roles, are promoted, gain additional duties, and are fired or resign. This constant state of flux requires organizations to develop effective user-provisioning systems.

Managing users is just the start of the process. Another area of concern is password management. Password management has forced organizations to develop different methods to address the access control needs of a complex world. Several techniques include the following:

▶ **Self-Service Password Reset**—This approach allows users to reset their own password. For example, if you cannot access your LinkedIn account, their site allows you to reset your own password.

▶ **Assisted Password Reset**—This method provides helpdesk and other authorized personnel a standardized mechanism to reset passwords. For example, Hitachi Systems makes a web portal product for just this application.

▶ **Password Synchronization**—These systems are used to replicate a user's password so that all systems are synchronized.

Any identity management systems must also consider *account management*. Account management should include the following:

▶ How to establish, manage, and close accounts

▶ Periodic account review

▶ Periodic rescreening for individuals in sensitive positions

Typically, when an account is established a profile is created. *Profile management* is the control of information associated with an individual or group. Profiles can contain information like name, age, date of birth, address, phone number, and so on. Modern corporations have so much data to manage that systems like directory management are used. The idea is to simplify the management of data. One of the primary disadvantages of such systems is the integration of legacy systems. Mainframes, non-networked applications, and applications written in archaic languages like FORTRAN and COBOL make it more difficult to centrally manage users.

Another approach to the management of user access to multiple sites is federation. *Federation* is used in identity management systems to manage identity across multiple platforms and entities. Some of the directory standards used to ease user management are the X.500 standard, Lightweight Directory Access Protocol, and Active Directory.

Today's systems are much more distributed than in the past and have a much greater reliance on the Internet. At the same time, there has been a move toward service-enabled delivery of services. There has also been a move to create web services that have a more abstract architectural style. This style, known as service-oriented architecture (SOA), attempts to bind together disjointed pieces of software. SOA allows for a company with distributed departments using different systems and services in different business domains to access services with security designed into the process. For example, suppose the legal department and the IT department provide different services on different systems and you want to have the legal department programs loaded on IT department systems. With the use of a web portal, the other department can access the service if required by employing Security Association Markup Language using HTTP.

A CISSP should have some knowledge of components of identity management, such as the following:

▶ **Web Services Security**—WS Security is an extension to Simple Object Access Protocol (SOAP) and is designed to add security to web services.

▶ **XML**—Years ago, hypertext markup language (HTML) dominated the web. Today, extensible markup language (XML) is the standard framework. XML is a standard that allows for a common expression of metadata. XML typically follows the SOAP standard.

▶ **SPML**—Service Provisioning Markup Language is an XML-based framework that can be used to exchange access control information between organizations so that a user logged into one entity can have the access rights passed to the other.

Single Sign-On

Single sign-on is an attempt to address a problem that is common for all users and administrators. Various systems within the organization likely require the user to log on multiple times to multiple systems. Each of these systems requires the user to remember a potentially different username and password combination. Most of us become tired of trying to remember all this information and begin to look for shortcuts. The most common shortcut is just to write down the information. Walk around your office, and you might see that many of your co-workers have regrettably implemented this practice. Single sign-on is designed to address this problem by permitting users to authenticate once to a single authentication authority and then access all other protected resources without being required to authenticate again.

Before you run out and decide to implement single sign-on at your organization, you should be aware that it is expensive, and if an attacker can authenticate, that attacker then has access to everything. Kerberos, SESAME, KryptoKnight (by IBM), NetSP (a KryptoKnight derivative), thin clients, directory services, and scripted access are all examples of authentication systems with operational modes that can implement single sign-on.

> **Caution**
>
> *Thin clients* can be considered a type of single sign-on system because the thin client holds no data. All information is stored in a centralized server. Thus, after a user is logged in, there is no reason for that user to authenticate again.

Kerberos

Kerberos, created by the Massachusetts Institute of Technology (MIT), is a network authentication protocol that uses secret-key cryptography. Kerberos has three parts: a client, server, and a trusted third party called the Key Distribution Center (KDC) to mediate between them. Clients obtain tickets from the KDC, and they present these tickets to servers when connections are established. Kerberos tickets represent the client's credentials. Kerberos relies on symmetric key cryptography (shared or *secret* key cryptography). Version 5 of Kerberos was implemented with Data Encryption Standard (DES). However, the Advanced Encryption Standard, which supersedes DES, is supported in later versions of Kerberos and operating systems like Microsoft Windows 7, 8, 10, Server 2012 and others. Kerberos communicates through an application programming interface (API) known as Generic Security Services (GSS-API). Common Kerberos terms include:

▶ **Ticket**—Generated by the KDC and given to a principal for use in authenticating to another principal.

▶ **Realm**—A domain consisting of all the principals for which the KDC provides security services; used to logically group resources and users.

▶ **Credentials**—A ticket and a service key.

▶ **Principal**—Can be a user, a process, or an application. Kerberos systems authenticate one principal to another.

The KDC is a service that runs on a physically secure server. The KDC consists of two components:

▶ **Authentication service**—The authentication service issues ticket-granting tickets (TGTs) that are good for admission to the ticket-granting service (TGS). Before network clients can get tickets for services, they must obtain a TGT from the authentication service.

▶ **Ticket-granting service**—Clients receive tickets to specific target services.

> **Note**
>
> Keep in mind that the TGT is an encrypted identification file with a limited validity window. The TGT is temporarily stored on the requesting principal's system and is used so that the principal does not have to type in credentials multiple times to access a resource.

The basic operation of Kerberos, as depicted in Figure 8.6, is as follows:

1. The client asks the KDC for a ticket, making use of the authentication service.

2. The client receives the encrypted ticket and the session key.

3. The client sends the encrypted TGT to the TGS and requests a ticket for access to the application server. This ticket has two copies of the session key: One copy is encrypted with the client key, and the other copy is encrypted with the application server key.

4. The TGS decrypts the TGT using its own private key and returns the ticket to the client, granting it access to the application server.

5. The client sends this ticket, along with an authenticator, to the application server.

6. The application server sends confirmation of its identity to the client.

> **Note**
>
> Kerberos authenticates only authentication traffic; subsequent communications is not protected. If the supplicant uses an insecure protocol like File Transfer Protocol (FTP), the network traffic would be in the clear.

Although Kerberos can provide authentication, integrity, and confidentiality, it's not without its weaknesses. One weakness is that Kerberos cannot guarantee availability. Some other weaknesses are as follows:

▶ Kerberos is time-sensitive; therefore, it requires all system clocks to be closely synchronized.

▶ The tickets used by Kerberos, which are authentication tokens, can be sniffed and potentially cracked.

▶ If an attacker targets the Kerberos server, it can prevent anyone in the realm from logging in. It is important to note that the Kerberos server can be a single point of failure.

▶ Secret keys are temporarily stored and decrypted on user workstations, making them vulnerable to an intruder who gets access to the workstation.

▶ Kerberos is vulnerable to brute force attacks.

▶ Kerberos may not be well-suited for large environments that have many systems, applications, users, and simultaneous requests.

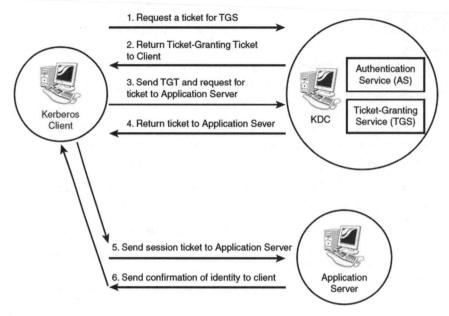

FIGURE 8.6 **Kerberos operation.**

Sesame

Kerberos is the most widely used SSO solution, but there are other options. One such option is the *Secure European System and Applications in a Multivendor Environment* (SESAME) project that was developed to address one of the biggest weaknesses in Kerberos: the plaintext storage of symmetric keys. SESAME uses both symmetric and asymmetric encryption, whereas Kerberos uses only symmetric encryption. Another difference is that SESAME incorporates MD5 and CRC32 hashing and uses two certificates. One of these certificates is used to provide authentication, as in Kerberos, and the second certificate is used to control the access privileges assigned to a client.

SESAME uses Privilege Attribute Certificates (PACs). PACs contain the requesting subject's identity, access capabilities of the subject, and life span of the subject requiring access. KryptoKnight by IBM and NetSP, a KryptoKnight derivative, are also SSO technologies, but are not widely deployed. Although you are unlikely to see these systems, you should know their names and that they are used for SSO if they happen to show up on the exam.

Authorization and Access Control Techniques

With a user identified and authenticated, the next step to consider is authorization. After the user is logged in, what can they access and what types of rights and privileges do they have? At the core of this discussion is how subjects access objects and what they can do with these resources after access is established. The three primary types of access control are as follows:

- Discretionary access control (DAC)

- Mandatory access control (MAC)

- Role-based access control (RBAC)

These might not be concepts that you are used to thinking about; however, in reality these types of decisions are made early on in the design of an operating system. Consider the design of early Microsoft Windows products where the design of the operating system was peer-to-peer—this is much different from SUSE Linux 12.0. Let's look at each model to further describe their differences.

Discretionary Access Control

The DAC model is so titled because access control is left to the owner's discretion. It can be thought of as similar to a peer-to-peer computer network. Each user is left to control their own system and resources. The owner is authorized to determine whether other users have access to files and resources. One significant problem of DAC is that its effectiveness is limited by the user's skill and ability. A user who is inexperienced or simply doesn't care can easily grant full access to files or objects under his or her control.

These are the two primary components of a DAC:

- **File and data ownership**—All objects within a system must have an owner. Objects without an owner will be left unprotected.

- **Access rights and permissions**—These control the access rights of an individual. Variations exist, but a basic *access control list* (ACL) checks read, write, or execute privileges.

The ACL identifies users who have authorization to specific information. This is a dynamic model that allows data to be easily shared. As an example,

I might inform my son that he may not download any more music from the Internet onto his computer upstairs. From my computer in the den, my son might simply deny me access to the folder he has been downloading music into to prevent me from accessing it to monitor his activities. This case demonstrates that DAC is much like a peer-to-peer network in that users are in charge of their own resources and data.

Table 8.1 shows a sample ACL, with columns defining access to objects. A subject's capabilities refers to a row within the matrix, and describe what actions can be taken on which objects. A subject's capabilities refer to a row within the matrix and reference what action can be taken.

TABLE 8.1 **Sample Access Control List**

Subject	Object 1	Object 2	Object 3	Object 4
Jeff	Full control	Full control	Full control	Full control
Michael	Read	Read	Read write	No access
Christine	Read	Read write	No access	No access

You can think of capabilities as the actions that a specific user can perform within the access matrix. DAC controls are based upon this matrix, and you can think of it as a means to establish access permission of a subject to an object.

Although the data owner can create an ACL to determine who has access to a specific object, mistakes can lead to a loss of confidentiality, and no central oversight exists as in other more restrictive models.

Mandatory Access Control

A MAC model is static and based on a predetermined list of access privileges; therefore, in a MAC-based system, access is determined by the system rather than the user. To do this, a MAC system uses labels and clearances. Figure 8.7 shows the differences between DAC and MAC.

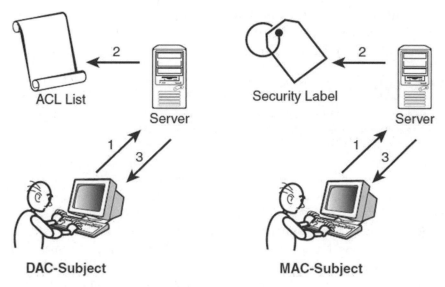

ACL List
Server

Security Label
Server

DAC-Subject
MAC-Subject

FIGURE 8.7   **Differences between DAC and MAC.**

The MAC model is typically used by organizations that handle highly sensitive data, such as the Department of Defense, NSA, CIA, and FBI. Examples of MAC systems include SELinux, among others. Systems based on the MAC model use clearance on subjects, and mark objects by sensitivity label. For example, the military uses the clearances of top secret, secret, confidential, sensitive but unclassified (SBU), and unclassified. (See Chapter 2, "Logical Asset Security," for a more in-depth discussion of government data classification.) Terms that you will need to know to understand this model include:

▶ **Objects**—Passive entities that provide data or information to subjects.

▶ **Subjects**—Active entities that can be a user, system, program, or file.

When a subject attempts to access an object, the object's label is examined for a match to the subject's level of clearance. If no match is found, access is denied. This model excels at supporting the need-to-know concept. Here is an example: Jeff wants to access a top secret file. The file is labeled "top secret, Joints Chiefs of Staff (JCS)." Although Jeff has top secret clearance, he is not JCS; therefore, access is denied. In reality, it is a little more complicated than the previous example details, but remember that the CISSP exam is considered a mile wide and an inch deep.

▶ **Clearance**—Determines the type of information a user can access.

▶ **Category**—Applied to objects and used to silo information.

▶ **Sensitivity Labels**—Used to classify information. As previously mentioned, the U.S. military uses the labels of Top Secret, Secret, Confidential, Sensitive but Unclassified (SBU), and Unclassified.

> **Caution**
>
> Any time you see the term *sensitivity label*, you should start thinking MAC because this system is most closely associated with this term.

For the exam, you should know that MAC systems can be hierarchical, compartmentalized, or hybrid. *Hierarchical designs* work by means of classification levels. Each level of the hierarchy includes the lower levels as well. As an example, in a hierarchical system, Dwayne might be cleared for "top secret" and as such can also view "secret" and "confidential" information because those are less sensitive. If Dwayne was authorized to access only "confidential" data, however, he would not be able to read up to higher levels like "secret." Compartmentalized objects require clearance from a specific domain or group like the Department of Homeland Security.

In a *compartmentalized system*, there is the ability to separate data into separate categories. As an example, Dwayne, who works for the Department of Defense, would not be able to read documents cleared for the State Department; therefore, Dwayne has a Top Secret - Sensitive Compartmented Information Clearance (TS-SCI). The military would be exercising a MAC system with least privileges to ensure that because Dwayne has TS, he has only the necessary access required to complete his job.

A *hybrid design* combines elements of both hierarchical and compartmentalized.

Important items to know about the MAC model include:

▶ It's considered a need-to-know system.

▶ It has more overhead than DAC.

▶ All users and resources are assigned a security label.

> **Caution**
>
> Although MAC uses a security label system, DAC systems allow users to set and control access to files and resources.

Role-Based Access Control

RBAC, also known as nondiscretionary access control, enables a user to have certain pre-established rights to objects. These rights are assigned to users based on their roles in the organization. The roles almost always map to the organization's structure. Many organizations are moving to this type of model because it eases access management. As an example, if you are the IT administrator of a bank, there are some clearly defined roles, such as bank manager, loan officer, and teller. RBAC allows you to define specific rights and privileges to each group. The users are then placed into the groups and inherit the privileges assigned to the group. If Joan is a teller and gets promoted to loan officer, all the administrator must do is move her from the teller group to the loan officer group. Many modern OS designs use the RBAC model.

RBAC is well-suited to organizations that have a high turnover rate. Assigning access rights and privileges to a group rather than an individual reduces the burden on administration. How RBAC is implemented is up to the individuals designing the operating system. For RBAC to work, roles within the organization must be clearly defined by policy.

Your organization might decide to use *static separation of duty* (SSD). SSD dictates that the member of one group cannot be the member of another group. Let's say Mike is a member of the network administrators group. If that is true, Mike cannot also be a member of the security administrators group or the audit group. For SSD to work, roles must clearly be defined to see where conflicts exist within the organization.

Another design is *dynamic separation of duties* (DSD). DSD dictates that a user cannot combine duties during any active session. Let's say Mike is a member of the audit group and audit management group. If Mike logs on to perform an audit test, he does not have management rights. If Mike logs on under the audit management group, he cannot perform an audit test.

An example of separation of duties is shown in Table 8.2.

TABLE 8.2 **Separation of Duties**

Role	Example of Allowed Access
User	Web browsing, approved applications, changes to desktop appearance
Auditor	Review of firewall logs, server logs, application logs
Security Admin	Firewall admin, ACL updates, server patching

Finally, there is task-based access control (TBAC). TBAC is similar to RBAC but instead of being based on roles it uses tasks. TBAC is based on tasks so that the allowed duties are based around the types of tasks a specific individual would perform. A good example of this can be seen when you access a Windows Server 2012. In the user administration group, you will see some predefined profiles, such as print manager, backup manager, and power user. The access assigned to each of these is based on the types of tasks that individual would perform.

Other Types of Access Controls

Other types of access control techniques include rule-based access control. Rule-based access control is based on a specific set of rules, much like a router ACL. Rule-based access control is considered a variation of the DAC model. Rule-based access control is accomplished by

1. Intercepting each request

2. Comparing it to the level of authorization

3. Making a decision

For instance, a router may use a rule-based ACL that might have permissions set to allow web traffic on port 80 and deny Telnet traffic on port 23. These two basic rules define the ACL. ACLs are tied to objects. Permissions can be assigned in three different ways: explicitly, implicitly, or inherited. ACLs have an implicit deny all statement that is the last item processed. A sample Cisco-formatted ACL is shown here with both allow (permit) and deny statements:

```
no access-list 111
access-list 111 permit tcp 192.168.13.0 0.0.0.255 any eq www
access-list 111 deny tcp any any eq telnet
access-list 111 deny icmp any any
interface ethernet0
ip access-group 111 in
```

> **ExamAlert**
>
> Although some people interchange the terms *access control list* and *capability table*, they are not the same. Capability tables are bound to subjects; ACLs are bound to objects.

Content-dependent access control (CDAC) is based on the content of the resource. CDAC is primarily used to protect databases that contain potentially sensitive data. CDAC is also used to filter out unauthorized traffic and is typically used by proxies or the firewall. As an example, you may be able to log in to the company SharePoint page and see the number of days you will be expected to travel next month, yet you are unable to see when or where the CEO will be traveling during the same period.

Finally, there is lattice-based access control (LBAC). This MAC-based model derivative functions by defining the least upper and greatest lower bound The upper bound is called a *join*, and a lower bound is called a *meet*. This information flow model deals with access in complex situations. The lattice model allows access only if the subject's capability is greater than or equal to that of the object being accessed. For example, Figure 8.7 demonstrates these boundaries. If you were cleared for secret access, you could read the level below, which is confidential.

> ### ExamAlert
>
> Don't sweat the terms. As you might have noticed, both role-based access control (RBAC) and rule-based access control (RBAC) have the same abbreviation. The CISSP exam will spell out these terms and most others. You are not expected to memorize these; you are expected to know the concepts.

Access Control Models

Access control models can be divided into two distinct types: *centralized* and *decentralized*. Depending on the organization's environment and requirements, one methodology typically works better than the other.

Centralized Access Control

Centralized access control systems maintain user IDs, rights, and permissions in one central location. Remote Authentication Dial-In User Service (RADIUS), Terminal Access Controller Access Control System (TACACS), and Diameter are all examples of centralized access control systems. Characteristics of centralized systems include:

▶ One entity makes all access decisions.

▶ Owners decide what users can access, and the administration supports these directives.

Consider old-school dialup. CNET reports that as of 2015 up to 2 million people still pay for it. There is most likely a certain amount of churn each month. The ISP might have many users sign up or leave each billing cycle. Centralized access control gives the ISP an easy way to manage this task. Users who do not pay can be denied access from one centralized point and those users who are paid up can be authenticated and allowed access to the Internet. Users are typically authenticated with one of the following authentication protocols:

▶ **Password Authentication Protocol (PAP)**—Uses a two-way handshake to authenticate a peer to a server when a link is initially established, but is considered weak because it transmits passwords in cleartext. PAP also offers no protection from replay or brute force attacks.

▶ **Challenge Handshake Authentication Protocol (CHAP)**—Uses a one-way hash function and a handshake to authenticate the client and the server. This process is performed when a link is initially established and may be repeated at defined intervals throughout the session. Although better than PAP, it is susceptible to replay attacks.

▶ **MS-CHAPv2**—An authentication method that has been extended to authenticate both the client and the server. MS-CHAPv2 also uses stronger encryption keys than CHAP and MS-CHAP.

▶ **Extensible Authentication Protocol (EAP)**—A framework that allows for more than just your standard username and password authentication by implementing various authentication mechanisms, such as MD5-challenge, token cards, and digital certificates.

RADIUS

RADIUS is an open protocol UDP-client/server protocol defined in RFCs 2058 and 2059. RADIUS provides three services: authentication, authorization, and accountability. RADIUS facilitates centralized user administration and keeps all user profiles in one location that all remote services share. When a RADIUS client begins the communication process with a RADIUS server, it uses attribute-value pairs (AVPs). These are really just a set of defined fields that will accept certain values. RADIUS was originally designed to provide protection from attack over dialup connections. It has been used by ISPs for years and has become a standard in many other ways. RADIUS can be used by mobile employees and integrates with lightweight directory access protocol (LDAP). RADIUS is considered a triple "AAA" protocol (authentication, authorization, and accountability), and all these services are performed together. It is important to note that RADIUS only encrypts the user's password as it travels from the client to the server, and that other information is sent in cleartext.

> **Note**
>
> The LDAP protocol can be used by a cluster of hosts to allow centralized security authentication as well as access to user and group information.

RADIUS is also used for wireless LAN authentication. The IEEE designed EAP to easily integrate with RADIUS to authenticate wireless users. The wireless user takes on the role of the supplicant, and the access point serves as the client. RADIUS uses the following UDP ports.

▶ UDP port 1812 for authentication and authorization services

▶ UDP port 1813 for accounting of RADIUS services

If the organization has an existing RADIUS server that's being used for remote users, it can be put to use authenticating wireless users, too.

RADIUS functions are as follows (see Figure 8.8):

1. The user connects to the RADIUS client.

2. The RADIUS client requests credentials from the user.

3. The user enters credentials.

4. The RADIUS client encrypts the credentials and passes them to the RADIUS server.

5. The RADIUS server then accepts, rejects, or challenges the credentials.

6. If the authentication was successful, the user is authenticated to the network.

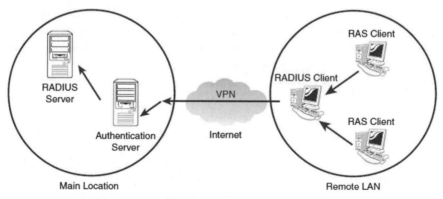

FIGURE 8.8   **RADIUS authentication.**

TACACS

Terminal Access Controller Access Control System is available in three variations: TACACS, XTACACS (Extended TACACS), and TACACS+. TACACS allows authentication, authorization, and auditing functions to be split up which gives the administrator more control over its deployment; conversely, RADIUS does not split these up. TACACS is highly Cisco- and MS-centric, and is considered proprietary. XTACACS separates the authentication, authorization, and accountability processes, and TACACS+ features two-factor authentication and security tokens. TACACS+ is a completely new and revised protocol that is incompatible with other versions of TACACS. TACACS has failed to gain the popularity of RADIUS; it is now considered a somewhat dated protocol.

There are some major differences between RADIUS and TACACS+. Where RADIUS only encrypts the password sent between the client and the server, TACACS+ encrypts all the information. TACACS+ also allows for more administration and has more AVPs because it can split up the AAA protocols. Where RADIUS uses UPD, TACACS+ uses TCP.

Diameter

You can never say the creators of Diameter didn't have a sense of humor. Diameter's name is a pun because the "diameter is twice the RADIUS." Actually, Diameter is enhanced RADIUS in that was designed to do much more than provide services to dialup users. A single Diameter peer can support over a million concurrent Diameter sessions and Diameter can even do peer-to-peer authentication. Diameter is detailed in RFC 3588 and can use TCP, UDP, or Stream Control Transport Protocol (SCTP). Diameter can support protocols and devices not even envisioned when RADIUS and TACACS were created, such as VoIP (Voice over IP), Ethernet over PPP, and mobile IP. VoIP is the routing of voice communication over data networks and mobile IP is the ability of a user to keep the same IP. Consider the example of Mike taking his IP-based phone from his provider's network to an overseas location. In such a situation, he needs a home IP address and also a "care of" address. Although Mike is normally a T-Mobile customer, his data needs to be routed to him while in Jamaica and using the AT&T network. Diameter provides this capability and is considered a very secure solution because cryptographic support of IPSec or TLS is mandatory.

Diameter is designed to use two protocols. The first is the base protocol that is used to provide secure communication between Diameter devices, and enables various types of information to be transmitted, such as headers, security options, commands, and AVPs.

The second protocol is really a set of extensions. Extensions are built on top of the base protocol to allow various technologies to use Diameter for authentication. This component is what interacts with other services, such as VoIP, wireless, and cell phone authentication. In a world of the Internet of Things, Internet of Everywhere, and System of Systems, where organizations are subscribing to "BYOD," and all the intelligence is at the edge of the network and growing, Diameter creates the way forward for authentication of these devices into the organization's network. It provides granular access and authorization beyond what an active directory domain controller can do.

Finally, Diameter is not fully backward-compatible with RADIUS, but there are several options for upgrading RADIUS component communication paths.

Decentralized Access Control

Decentralized access control systems store user IDs, rights, and permissions in different locations throughout the network. As an example, domains can be thought of as a form of decentralized access control. Large organizations typically establish multiple domains along organizational boundaries, such as manufacturing, engineering, marketing, sales, or R&D; or by geographical boundaries, like New York, Atlanta, San Jose, and Houston. When more than one domain exists, there has to be some type of trust between them. A trust is simply a separate link between domains that is necessary to resolve their different security policies and security databases. Trusts can be one-way or two-way. The important concept here is that although all of a domain's authentication is centralized on domain controllers, a domain's access control is distributed throughout the domain's members. Access to resources is assigned and defined on the resource wherever it might reside in the domain.

Characteristics of a decentralized system include the following:

▶ Gives control to individuals closer to the resource, such as department managers and occasionally users

▶ Maintains multiple domains and trusts

▶ Does not use one centralized entity to process access requests

▶ Used in database-management systems (DBMS)

▶ Peer-to-peer in design

▶ Lacks standardization and overlapping rights, and might include security holes

Audit and Monitoring

Regardless of what method of authorization is used and what types of controls are enforced, individuals must be held accountable. For auditing to be effective, administrative controls are needed in the form of policies to ensure that audit data is reviewed on a periodic basis and not just when something goes wrong. Technical controls are needed so that user activity can be tracked within a network. Physical and technical controls are needed to protect audit data from being tampered with.

Although auditing is used only after the fact, it can help detect suspicious activity or identify whether a security breach has taken place. For example, security administrators often review logs for failed log-on attempts only, whereas successful log-ons hurt most and can show you who is in the network but should not be. One example might be if Mike, who works Monday through Friday, 9 to 5, in Houston has been logging in Sundays from 12 to 9 p.m. from San Jose. Maybe Mike is on vacation but there is also the possibility someone is using his account. Since he has a valid user account, it does not raise an alarm.

Monitoring Access and Usage

Computer resources are a limited commodity provided by a company to help meet its overall goals. Although many employees would never dream of placing all their long distance phone calls on a company phone, some of those same individuals have no problem using computer resources for their own personal use. Consider these statistics from Personal Computer World. According to information on its site, one-third of time spent online at work is not work-related, and more than 75% of streaming radio downloads occur between 5 a.m. and 5 p.m.

Accountability must be maintained for network access, software usage, and data access. In a high-security environment, the level of accountability should be substantial, and users should be held responsible by logging and auditing their activities.

Good practice dictates that audit logs are transmitted to a remote centralized site. Centralized logging makes it easier for the person assigned the task to review the data. Exporting the logs to a remote site also makes it harder for hackers to erase or cover their activity. If there is a downside to all this logging, it is that all the information must be recorded and reviewed. A balance must be found between collecting audit data and maintaining a manageable log size. Reviewing it can be expedited by using *audit reduction tools*. These tools parse the data and eliminate unneeded information. Another useful tool is a variance detection tool. These tools look for trends that fall outside the realm of normal activity. As an example, if an employee normally enters the building around 7 a.m. and leaves about 4 p.m. but is seen entering at 3 a.m., a variance detection tool would detect this abnormality.

Intrusion Detection Systems

Intrusion detection systems play a critical role in the protection of the IT infrastructure. *Intrusion detection* involves monitoring network traffic, detecting attempts to gain unauthorized access to a system or resource, and notifying the appropriate individuals so that counteractions can be taken. An IDS is designed to function as an access control monitor. Intrusion detection is a relatively new technology. It was really born in the 1980s when James Anderson put forth the concept in a paper titled *Computer Security Threat Monitoring and Surveillance* (csrc.nist.gov/publications/history/ande80.pdf).

An IDS can be configured to scan for attacks, track a hacker's movements, alert an administrator to ongoing attacks, and highlight possible vulnerabilities that need to be addressed. The key to what type of activity the IDS will detect is dependent on where the intrusion sensors are placed. This requires some consideration because, after all, a sensor in the DMZ will work well at detecting misuse there but will prove useless against attackers inside the network. Even when you have determined where to place sensors, they still require specific tuning. Without specific tuning, the sensor will generate alerts for all traffic that matches given criteria, regardless of whether the traffic is indeed something that should generate an alert. An IDS must be trained to look for suspicious activity. That is why I typically tell people that an IDS is like a 3-year-old. They require constant care and nurturing, and don't do well if left alone.

> **Note**
>
> Although the exam will examine these systems in a very basic way, modern systems are a mix of intrusion detection and intrusion prevention. These systems are referred to as intrusion detection and prevention (IDP) systems and are designed to identify potential incidents, log information, attempt to stop the event, and report the event. Many organizations even use IDP systems for activities like identifying problems with security policies, documenting threats, and deterring malicious activity that violates security policies. NIST 800-94 is a good resource to learn more (csrc.nist.gov/publications/nistpubs/800-94/SP800-94.pdf).

A huge problem with intrusion detection systems is that they are after-the-fact devices—the attack has already taken place. Other problems with IDS are false positives and false negatives. *False positives* refer to when the IDS has triggered an alarm for normal traffic. For example, if you go to your local mall parking lot, you're likely to hear some car alarms going off due to reasons other than car theft. These car alarms are experiencing false positives. False positives are a big problem because they desensitize the administrator. *False negatives* are even worse. A false negative occurs when a real attack occurs; however, the IDS does not pick it up.

> ### ExamAlert
>
> A false negative is the worst type of event because it means an attack occurred, but the IDS failed to detect it.

IDS systems can be divided into two basic types: *network-based intrusion detection systems* (NIDS) and *host-based intrusion detection systems* (HIDS).

Network-Based Intrusion Detection Systems

Much like a protocol analyzer operating in promiscuous mode, NIDS capture and analyze network traffic. These devices diligently inspect each packet as it passes by. When they detect suspect traffic, the action taken depends on the particular NIDS. Alarms could be triggered, sessions could be reset, or traffic could be blocked. Among the advantages are that they are unobtrusive, they have the capability to monitor the entire network, and they provide an extra layer of defense between the firewall and the host. Their disadvantages include the fact that attackers can send high volumes of traffic to attempt to overload them, they cannot decrypt or analyze encrypted traffic, and they can be vulnerable to attacks. Conversely, attackers will send low levels of traffic to avoid tripping the IDS threshold alarms. Tools like NMAP have the ability to vary timing to avoid detection. Things to remember about NIDS include the following:

▶ They monitor network traffic in real time.

▶ They analyze protocols and other relevant packet information.

▶ They integrate with a firewall and define new rules as needed.

▶ When used in a switched environment, they require the user to perform port spanning and/or port mirroring.

▶ They send alerts or terminate an offending connection.

▶ When encryption is used, a NIDS will not be able to analyze the traffic.

Host-Based Intrusion-Detection Systems

HIDS are more closely related to a virus scanner in their function and design because they are application-based programs that reside on the host computer. Running quietly in the background, they monitor traffic and attempt to detect suspect activity. Suspect activity can range from attempted system file modification to unsafe activation of ActiveX commands. Although they are effective in a fully switched environment and can analyze network-encrypted traffic, they can take a lot of maintenance, cannot monitor network traffic, and rely on the underlying operating system because they do not control core services. HIDS are best served on high-value targets that require protection. Things to remember about HIDS include the following:

▶ HIDS consume some of the host's resources.

▶ HIDS analyze encrypted traffic.

▶ HIDS send alerts when unusual events are discovered.

▶ HIDS are in some ways just another application running on the local host that is subject to attack.

Signature-Based, Anomaly-Based, and Rule-Based IDS Engines

Signature-based, *anomaly-based*, and *rule-based IDS systems* are the three primary types of analysis methods used by IDS systems. These types take different approaches to detecting intrusions.

Signature-based engines rely on a database of known attacks and attack patterns. This system examines data to check for malicious content, which could include fragmented IP packets, streams of SYN packets (DoS), or malformed Internet Control Message Protocol (ICMP) packets. Any time data is found that matches one of these known signatures, it can be flagged to initiate further action. This might include an alarm, an alert, or a change to the firewall configuration. Although signature-based systems work well, their shortcoming is that they are only as effective as their most current update. Any time there is a new or varied attack, the IDS will be unaware of it and will ignore the traffic. The two subcategories of signature-based systems include the following:

▶ **Pattern-based**—Looks at specific signatures that packets are compared to. The open-source IDS Snort started as a pattern-matching IDS.

▶ **State-based**—A more advanced design that has the capability to track the state of the traffic and data as it moves between host and target.

A behavioral-based IDS observes traffic and develops a baseline of normal operations. Intrusions are detected by identifying activity outside the normal range of activities. As an example, if Mike typically tries to log on only between the hours of 8 a.m. and 5 p.m., and now he's trying to log on 5,000 times at 2 a.m., the IDS can trigger an alert that something is wrong. The big disadvantage of a behavior-based IDS system is that an activity taught over time is not seen as an attack, but merely as normal behavior. These systems also tend to have a high number of false positives.

The three subcategories of anomaly-based systems include the following:

▶ **Statistical-based**—Compares normal to abnormal activity.

▶ **Traffic-based**—Triggers on abnormal packets and data traffic.

▶ **Protocol-based**—Possesses the capability to reassemble packets and look at higher-layer activity. If the IDS knows the normal activity of the protocol, it can pick out abnormal activity. Protocol-decoding intrusion detection requires the IDS to maintain state information. As an example, DNS is a two-step process; therefore, if a protocol-matching IDS sees a number of DNS responses that occur without a DNS request having ever taken place, the system can flag that activity as cache poisoning.

An anomaly-based IDS often compares the behavior of a protocol against what the RFC states. For example, it will look at how the flags in a TCP packet are set at the beginning start up session—the SYN flag should be set to 1. In contrast, a *behavioral*-based IDS will look at system or environment performance that would be considered normal, such as "Mike typically tries to log on only between the hours of 8 a.m. and 5 p.m., and now he's trying to log on 5,000 times at 2 a.m." This required the IDS to go through a learning phase to catch this anomaly. The military has been using this for years to monitor their employees.

A rule-based IDS involves rules and pattern descriptors that observe traffic and develop a baseline of normal operations. Intrusions are detected by identifying activity outside the normal range. This expert system follows a four-phase analysis process:

1. Preprocessing

2. Analysis

3. Response

4. Refinement

All IDS systems share some basic components:

▶ **Sensors or Agents**—Detect and send data to the system. Place the sensor where you want to monitor traffic. On a HIDS, there can be many agents that report back to a server in a large environment.

▶ **Central monitoring system**—Processes and analyzes data sent from sensors.

▶ **Report analysis**—Offers information about how to counteract a specific event.

▶ **Database and storage components**—Perform trend analysis and store the IP address and information about the attacker.

▶ **Response box**—Inputs information from the previously listed components and forms an appropriate response.

ExamAlert

Carefully read any questions that discuss IDS. Remember that several variables can change the outcome or potential answer. Take the time to underline such words as *network*, *host*, *signature*, and *behavior* to help clarify the question.

Sensor Placement

Your organization's security policy should detail the placement of your IDS system and sensors. The placement of IDS sensors requires some consideration. IDS sensors can be placed externally, in the DMZ, or inside the network. Your decision to place a sensor in any one or more of these locations will require specific tuning. Without it, the sensor will generate alerts for all traffic that matches a given criteria, regardless of whether the traffic is indeed something that should generate an alert. The placement of your sensors is dynamic and must constantly change as your environment changes. Sensors should not have an IP address associated with them or potentially be deployed via a one-way networking cable so that it is harder for the hacker to scanner and find them.

ExamAlert

Although an anomaly-based IDS can detect zero day attacks, signature-based and rule-based IDS cannot.

Intrusion Prevention Systems

Intrusion prevention systems (IPS's) build on the foundation of IDS and attempt to take the technology a step further. IPS's can react automatically and actually prevent a security occurrence from happening, preferably without user intervention. IPS is considered the next generation of IDS and can block attacks in real time. The National Institute of Standards and Technology (NIST) now uses the term IDP (Intrusion Detection and Prevention) to define modern devices that maintain the functionality of both IDS and IPS devices. These devices typically perform deep inspection and can be applied to devices that support OSI Layer 3 to OSI Layer 7 inspection.

Two Great Tools Combined as One

SIEM is the combination of the two separate services Security Information Management (SIM) and Security Event Management (SEM). SIM is used to process and handle the long-term storage of audit and event data, whereas SEM is used for real-time reporting of events. Combining these two technologies provides users with the ability to alert, capture, aggregate, and review log information from many different systems and sources. Vendors that offer SIEM tools include Network Intelligence, e-Security, ArcSight, and others.

Although technologies like SIEM are a great addition to the security professional's toolkit, keep in mind that you should strive for defense in depth. For example, combining an IDS/IPS with SIEM provides much greater protection than either technology by itself.

Network Access Control

IDS and IDP can be seen as just the start of access control and security. The next step in this area is *Network Access Control* (NAC) or IEEE 802.1x. NAC has grown out of the trusted computer movement and has the goal of unified security. NAC offers administrators a way to verify that devices meet certain health standards before allowing them to connect to the network. Laptops, desktop computers, or any device that doesn't comply with predefined requirements can be prevented from joining the network or can even be relegated to a controlled network where access is restricted until the device is brought up to the required security standards. Currently, there are several different incarnations of NAC available, which include the following:

▶ **Infrastructure-based NAC**—Requires an organization to upgrade its hardware and/or operating systems.

▶ **Endpoint-based NAC**—Requires the installation of software agents on each network client. These devices are then managed by a centralized management console.

▶ **Hardware-based NAC**—Requires the installation of a network appliance. The appliance monitors for specific behavior and can limit device connectivity should noncompliant activity be detected.

Keystroke Monitoring

Keystroke monitoring can be accomplished with hardware or software devices and is used to monitor activity. These devices can be used for both legal and illegal activity. As a compliance tool, keystroke monitoring allows management to monitor a user's activity and verify compliance. The primary issue of concern is the user's expectation of privacy. Policies and procedures should be in place to inform the user that such technologies can be used to monitor compliance. In 1993, the department of justice requested that NIST publish guidance on keystroke monitoring. This guidance can be found in NIST bulletin 93-03 (csrc.nist.gov/publications/nistbul/csl93-03.txt). A sample acceptable use policy is shown here:

> This acceptable use policy defines the boundaries of the acceptable use of this organization's systems and resources. Access to any company system or resources is a privilege that may be wholly or partially restricted without prior notice and without consent of the user. In cases of suspected violations or during the process of periodic review, employees can have activities monitored. Monitoring may involve a complete keystroke log of an entire session or sessions as needed to vary compliance to company polices and usage agreements.

Unfortunately, key logging is not just for the good guys. Hackers can use the same tools to monitor and record an individual's activities. Although an outsider to a company might have some trouble getting one of these devices installed, an insider is in a prime position to plant a keystroke logger. Keystroke loggers come in two basic types:

▶ **Hardware keystroke loggers** are usually installed while users are away from their desks and are completely undetectable, except for their physical presence. Just take a moment to consider when you last looked at the back of your computer. Even if you see it, a hardware keystroke loggers can be overlooked because it resembles a balun or dongle. These devices are even available in wireless versions that can communicate via

802.11b/g/n/ac and Bluetooth. You can see one example at www.wirelesskeylogger.com/products.php.

▶ **Software keystroke loggers** sit between the operating system and the keyboard. Most of these software programs are simple, but some are more complex and can even email the logged keystrokes back to a pre-configured address. What they all have in common is that they operate in stealth mode and can grab all the text, mouse clicks, and even all the URLs that a user enters.

Exam Prep Questions

1. Christine works for a government agency that is very concerned about the confidentiality of information. The government agency has strong controls for the process of identification, authentication, and authorization. Before Christine, the subject, can access her information the security label on objects and clearance on subjects are verified. What is this an example of what?

   ○ **A.** DAC

   ○ **B.** LBAC

   ○ **C.** RBAC

   ○ **D.** MAC

2. Which of the following biometric systems would be considered the most accurate?

   ○ **A.** Retina scan CER 3

   ○ **B.** Fingerprint CER 4

   ○ **C.** Keyboard dynamics CER 5

   ○ **D.** Voice recognition CER 6

3. What are the two primary components of a DAC?

   ○ **A.** Access rights and permissions, and security labels

   ○ **B.** File and data ownership, and access rights and permissions

   ○ **C.** Security labels and discretionary access lists

   ○ **D.** File and data ownership, and security labels

4. You have been hired as a contractor for a government agency. You have been cleared for secret access based on your need to know. Authentication, authorization, and accountability are also enforced. At the end of each week, the government security officer for whom you work is tasked with the review of security logs to ensure only authorized users have logged into the network and have not attempted to access unauthorized data. The process of ensuring accountability for access to an information system included four phases. What is this an example of?

   ○ **A.** Identification

   ○ **B.** Accountability

   ○ **C.** Authorization

   ○ **D.** Authentication

5. When registering for a new service, you were asked the following questions: "What country were you born in? What's your pet's name? What is your mother's maiden name?" What type of password system is being used?

   ○ **A.** Cognitive

   ○ **B.** One-time

   ○ **C.** Virtual

   ○ **D.** Complex

6. Mark has just completed his new peer-to-peer network for the small insurance office he owns. Although he will allow Internet access, he does not want users to log in remotely. Which of the following models most closely match his design?

   ○ **A.** TACACS+

   ○ **B.** MAC

   ○ **C.** RADIUS

   ○ **D.** DAC

7. Which of the following is the best answer: TACACS+ features what?

   ○ **A.** One-factor authentication

   ○ **B.** Decentralized access control

   ○ **C.** Two-factor authentication

   ○ **D.** Accountability

8. A newly hired junior security administrator will assume your position temporarily while you are on vacation. You're trying to explain the basics of access control and the functionality of rule-based access control mechanisms like ACL. Which of the following best describes the order in which an ACL operates?

   ○ **A.** ACLs apply all deny statements before allow statements.

   ○ **B.** Rule-based access control and role-based access control is basically the same thing.

   ○ **C.** ACLs end with an implicit deny all statement.

   ○ **D.** ACLs are processed from the bottom up.

9. RADIUS provides which of the following?

   ○ **A.** Authorization and accountability

   ○ **B.** Authentication

   ○ **C.** Authentication, authorization, and accountability

   ○ **D.** Authentication and authorization

10. Which of the following is the best description of a situation where a user can sign up for a social media account such as Facebook, and then use their credentials to log in and access another organization's sites, such as Yahoo?

○ **A.** Transitive trust

○ **B.** Federated ID

○ **C.** Non-transitive trust

○ **D.** Single sign-on

11. What type of attack targets pronounceable passwords?

○ **A.** Brute-force attacks

○ **B.** Dictionary attacks

○ **C.** Hybrid attacks

○ **D.** Rainbow tables

12. Which of the following represents the best method of password storage?

○ **A.** A cleartext file

○ **B.** Symmetric encryption

○ **C.** A one-way encryption process

○ **D.** An XOR process

13. Which access control model makes use of a join and a meet?

○ **A.** Rule-based access control

○ **B.** MAC

○ **C.** DAC

○ **D.** Lattice

14. Which of the following access control models is commonly used with firewall and edge devices?

○ **A.** Rule-based access control

○ **B.** MAC

○ **C.** DAC

○ **D.** Lattice

15. Because of recent highly publicized hacking news reports, senior management has become more concerned about security. As the senior security administrator, you are asked to suggest changes that should be implemented. Which of the following access methods should you recommend if the method is to be one that is primarily based on pre-established access, can't be changed by users and works well in situations where there is high turnover?

   ○ **A.** Discretionary access control

   ○ **B.** Mandatory access control

   ○ **C.** Rule-based access control

   ○ **D.** Role-based access control

Answers to Exam Prep Questions

1. **D.** MAC is correct because it uses security labels and clearances. A is not correct because DAC is uses ACLs; B is not correct because LBAC is lattice-based access control, which uses upper and lower limits; C is incorrect because RBAC uses roles or tasks in an organization based on the organization's security policy.

2. **A.** The lower the CER, the better; retina scan CER 3 (answer A) is correct. Fingerprint CER 4 (answer B), keyboard dynamics CER 5 (answer C), and voice recognition CER 6 (answer D) are incorrect because they have higher CERs. The CER is determined by combining Type I and Type II errors.

3. **B.** The two primary components of a DAC are file and data ownership, and access rights and permissions. With file and data ownership, all objects within a system must have an owner. Objects without an owner will be left unprotected. Access rights and permissions control the access rights of an individual. Variation exists, but a basic access control list checks read, write, and execute privileges. Answers A, C, and D are incorrect.

4. **B.** The four key areas of identity and access management are identification, authentication, authorization, and accountability. The fact that the security officer is reviewing the logs for accuracy is a form of accountability. Therefore, answers A, C, and D are incorrect.

5. **A.** Cognitive passwords are widely used during enrollment processes, when individuals call help desks, or when individuals request other services that require authentication. All other answers are incorrect: One-time passwords (answer B) are associated with tokens, virtual passwords (answer C) are a form of passphrase, and the question does not describe a complex password (answer D).

6. **D.** The discretionary access control (DAC) model is so named because access control is left to the owner's discretion. This can be thought of as being similar to a peer-to-peer computer network. All other answers are incorrect: A MAC model (answer B) is static and based on a predetermined list of access privileges, and both TACACS+ (answer A) and RADIUS (answer C) are used for remote access and do not properly address the question.

7. **C.** TACACS+ features two-factor authentication. All other answers are incorrect: TACACS+ offers more than one-factor authentication (answer A); it is a centralized, not decentralized, access control system (answer B); and although it offers accountability (answer D), it also offers authorization.

8. **C.** ACLs have an implicit deny all statement. As an example, if the ACL only had the one statement "Deny ICMP any, any," ICMP would be denied; however, the implicit "deny all" would block all other traffic. Answers A and D are incorrect as ACLs are processed from top to bottom. Answer B is incorrect because rule-based access control and role-based access control are not the same thing.

9. **C.** RADIUS provides three services: authentication, authorization, and accountability. RADIUS facilitates centralized user administration and keeps all user profiles in one location that all remote services share. Answers A, B, and D are incorrect because they do not fully answer the question.

10. **B.** Federation is an arrangement that can be made among multiple enterprises (such as Facebook and Yahoo) that lets subscribers of one service use the same identification/authentication credentials to gain access to the second organization's resources. It differs from single sign-on (SSO) in that SSO is used within a single organization. Examples of SSO include Kerberos and SESAME. Answers A and C are incorrect as a transitive trust is a two-way relationship automatically created between parent and child domains, and a non-transitive trust is a trust that will not extend past the domains it was created with. Both of these terms are directly associated with Microsoft operating systems.

11. **B.** Dictionary attacks target pronounceable passwords. Brute-force attacks (answer A), hybrid attacks (answer C), and rainbow tables (answer D) are all used to target any password combination for A–Z, 0–9, special characters, or any combination.

12. **C.** The best way to store passwords is by means of a one-way process. This one-way process is also known as hashing, and is used by operating systems like Microsoft Windows and Linux. A cleartext file (answer A) can be easily exposed. Symmetric encryption (answer B) would allow the process to be easily reversed by anyone with a key. An XOR process (answer D) would only obscure the password and not provide any real protection.

13. **D.** The lattice model makes use of a join and a meet. The lattice-based access control model (LBAC) is considered a complex model used to manage the interaction between subjects and objects. Answers A, B, and C are incorrect as they do not use these terms.

14. **A.** Rule-based access control is used with firewalls and routers. RBAC is based on a specific set of rules, much like a router ACL. Answer B, MAC, makes use of labels and is well suited for high-security environments. Answer C, DAC, describes discretionary control, and answer D, lattice, is a complex model that makes use of upper and lower bounds.

15. **D.** Role-based access control (RBAC) allows specific people to be assigned to specific roles with specific privileges. It allows access to be assigned to groups and works well where there are high levels of turnover. Answers A, B, and C do not meet that description.

Suggesting Reading and Resources

Zephyr Charts: www.cse.unr.edu/~bebis/CS790Q/Lect/Chapter_8.ppt

Honeypot resources: www.honeypots.net

Getting a grip on access control:
www.owasp.org/index.php/Access_Control_Cheat_Sheet

Performance metrics for biometrics: www.biometric-solutions.com/index.php?story=performance_biometrics

Federated Identity: msdn.microsoft.com/en-us/library/aa479079.aspx

Differences between Kerberos and SESAME:
cadse.cs.fiu.edu/corba/corbasec/faq/multi-page/node148.html

Comparison of Biometric Methods: mms.ecs.soton.ac.uk/2011/papers/4.pdf

RADIUS best practices: msdn.microsoft.com/en-us/library/bb742489.aspx

CHAPTER 9

Security Assessment and Testing

Terms you'll need to understand:

▶ Audit

▶ Vulnerability assessment

▶ Penetration testing

▶ Trojans

▶ Malware

▶ Rootkits

▶ Logic bombs

▶ Forensics

▶ Chain of custody

▶ Password cracking

▶ Social engineering

▶ Viruses

Topics you'll need to master:

▶ Security assessment and testing

▶ Assessment and test strategies

▶ Identifying attack methodologies

▶ Automated and manual testing techniques

▶ Example penetration test methodology

▶ Crime investigation techniques

▶ Understanding evidence types

▶ Performing security assessments and penetration tests

▶ Honeypot use and deployment

▶ Incident response techniques

Introduction

Readers preparing for the ISC^2 Certified Information Systems Security Professional exam and those reviewing the security assessment and testing domain must know which resources should be protected, types of tests that can be used for security control testing, and the threats that a CISSP has to be aware of.

This chapter examines audits, vulnerability assessments, and penetration tests. Each has a role to play in securing the organization. Penetration tests are carried out by organizations to see what the criminal hacker can access, how such access can be used, and what risk or impact such access might have. Keep in mind that security violations aren't always malicious; sometimes things break or accidents happen. Therefore, security testing must also be prepared to deal with these accidents.

This chapter also discusses how the threat landscape has changed. The risks are many; it's not just viruses and worms anymore. Attackers have many different tools available to them to hack, target, and attack organizations. There will need to be an incident response plan in place that has been tested and approved. Potential evidence will need to be handled in a legal manner and forensics may need to be performed. These are just a few of the topics this chapter will cover, along with investigations and legal proceedings.

Security Assessments and Penetration Test Strategies

The world of information security continually evolves. There are more tools available to attackers and defenders than ever before. This makes it imperative that organizations periodically review the organization's security. This section will review several techniques for remediation and review that can be used to meet this challenge, including policy reviews (audits), vulnerability scanning, and penetration testing. Each of these techniques is useful in identifying and resolving security architecture vulnerabilities.

Audits

Policy reviews or audits are used as a means to review the presence and strength of operation (management), technical, and physical controls, and report their capability to protect the organization. Most organizations want to do the right thing and are interested in proper controls, but might just be overwhelmed by the day-to-day demands of business. This is why it is so important for auditors to verify compliance and demonstrate due diligence.

An audit is a planned, independent, and documented assessment to determine whether agreed-upon requirements and standards of operations are being met. Basically, it is a review of the operation and activities of an organization. An auditor uses the company's standards and procedures to guide the audit. One of the most widely used frameworks for auditing is the Control Objectives for Information and related Technology (COBIT). COBIT is a system of best practices.

Although audits can help verify that controls have been developed and are being implemented, an audit is just one piece of the puzzle in ensuring operational security. Any time problems are found, an organization needs to have procedures to perform root cause analysis to discover the cause of the problem. Root cause analysis can be described as a structured approach to identifying problems, assessing their magnitude, and determining what actions need to be taken to prevent the recurrence of similar situations.

Vulnerability Assessments

The term vulnerability assessment generally refers to a software package used to scan for known vulnerabilities. Vulnerability assessments are used to identify all potential vulnerabilities that could be exploited in an environment. Much has changed in the way the IT industry views vulnerability assessments since the first software program was created for this purpose in the early 1990s. At that time, two well-known security professionals, Dan Farmer and Wietse Venema, wrote a landmark paper titled "Improving the Security of Your Site by Breaking Into it." They went on to develop SATAN (System Administrator Tool for Analyzing Networks), the first vulnerability assessment program used to scan for problems. Sun Microsystems actually fired Dan Farmer for releasing the program. At the time the tool was seen as something that could be dual-use—for good and bad—and some people were also uncomfortable with the name.

Today, vulnerability assessment tools are used by companies around the world to scan their networks for software problems, misconfigurations, and security vulnerabilities. A vulnerability scanner can be run against a single address or a range of addresses, and can also test the effectiveness of layered security measures.

Many vulnerability assessment tools are now available. Vulnerability assessment software can be used to scan systems, compiled software, or even source code. Nessus is a good example of a system level vulnerability scanner. Even though vulnerability assessment software tools are another control that can be used to increase security, they are not a perfect solution. Vulnerability scanners cannot test for every conceivable vulnerability, and might cause a system to crash. What this really means is that vulnerability assessment tools are simply one of many items that help provide for defense in depth. As an example, you will want to layer vulnerability assessment software along with audits, penetration testing, and anti-virus to get true security. Table 9.1 provides some sample intervals for common security review functions.

TABLE 9.1 **Security Review Intervals**

Technique	Daily	Weekly	Monthly	Bi-Yearly	Yearly
Antivirus	✓				
Log reviews	✓	✓	✓		
Audits				✓	
Vulnerability assessments	✓				
Penetration testing					✓

Vulnerability assessment software is not a substitute for more thorough tests and examinations, a gap that penetration testing can help fill.

Penetration Testing

Penetration testing is the process of evaluating the organization's security controls. These tests can be performed in a number of ways, including whitebox testing, blackbox testing, and graybox testing. *Whitebox testing* occurs when the test team knows everything about the network. The team of testers has been provided network maps, diagrams, and documents specifying all details of the organization's network. *Blackbox testing* occurs when the test team has no details of the organization's network. As an example, last year my company did a blackbox test for an organization and was provided only the IP address range. The client wanted us to ascertain all other details during the penetration test. *Graybox testing* is used to examine what is possible with insider access.

Although you might have seen these terms used to describe application testing, they are also used by penetration testers. Penetration testing can be performed by a manual process or via automated software packages, such as Core Impact and Metasploit. The target of the penetration test can be

▶ **Outsider testing**—A common type of penetration test that examines what hackers or other outsiders can access or do.

▶ **Physical security testing**—This form of penetration test refers to techniques using physical access to see what can be accomplished. Some might argue that if physical barriers can be bypassed, there is no security at all.

▶ **Wireless network testing**—This form of testing is done to verify the organization's wireless access policies and to ensure that no misconfigured devices have been introduced that may cause additional security exposures. Such tests might include Bluetooth and RFID testing of devices on premises.

▶ **Application security testing**—Many organizations offer access to core business functionality through web-based applications. This can give attackers a big potential target. Application security testing verifies that the controls over the application and its process flow are adequately designed.

▶ **Denial-of-service (DoS) testing**—The goal of DoS testing is to evaluate the network's susceptibility to DoS attacks.

▶ **War dialing**—War dialing is an attempt to systematically call a range of telephone numbers and identify modems, remote access devices, and maintenance connections of computers that could exist on an organization's network.

▶ **Social engineering testing**—This form of penetration test refers to using social interaction techniques involving the organization's employees, suppliers, and contractors to gather information and penetrate the organization's systems.

> **Caution**
>
> Penetration testing can be performed with the full knowledge of the security staff, as a blind test, or as a double-blind test. A blind test is one in which only publicly available information is used. A double-blind test is one in which only publicly available information is used and the security staff is not notified of the event. A double-blind test allows the organization to observe the reactions of the security staff.

Determining the mode of the test is just one piece of a penetration test. The network infrastructure also plays an important role. The design of the network should be such that there are layers of security. Figure 9.1 demonstrates an example of this concept.

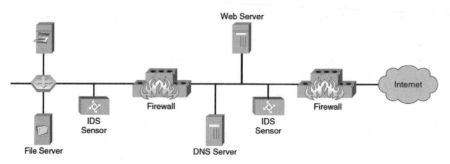

FIGURE 9.1   **Network infrastructure.**

Security tests of any type are a large undertaking. The organization will need a team to carry out these duties. This team is responsible for determining the weaknesses, technical flaws, and vulnerabilities of the organization. This team is known as a penetration test team or, informally, a red team, and the individuals on it are known as ethical hackers. Ethical hackers perform the same activities as malicious hackers, but they do so with the approval of the organization and without causing damage. The goal is to test the network in much the same fashion as a malicious hacker would. Because of the global nature of the Internet and the increased emphasis on networking, these types of activities have gained increased prominence in the last several years.

Regardless of what is known about the network, the penetration test team typically starts with basic user access. Its goal is to advance to root access or administrator access and to try to control the network. The most critical step distinguishing malicious hacking from ethical hacking is obtaining corporate approval. Without a signed consent of the company's owner, the penetration test team could very well be breaking the law. A generic model of a penetration test is as follows:

1. **Discovery or reconnaissance**—Identify and document information about the targeted organization.

2. **Enumeration**—Use intrusive methods and techniques to gain more information about the targeted organization; for example, using software tools to scan for live machines.

3. **Mapping the attack surface**—Vulnerability mapping is used to discover the correlation between the findings from enumeration to known and potential vulnerabilities that could be used to gain access.

4. **Exploitation**—Attempt to gain user and privileged access by launching attacks against known vulnerabilities.

5. **Report to management**—Prepare a report of the findings of the penetration test, and detail the issues that need to be addressed, along with their priority.

Documents beyond basic penetration tests are available that offer guidance on performing tests and identifying key areas of concern. The Open Source Security Testing Methodology Manual (OSSTMM) (www.isecom.org) is a good example of a structured test guide. The Open Web Application Security Project (www.owasp.org) is another source for testing methodologies and tips. The National Institute of Standards and Technology (NIST) also has documents that are helpful for organizations planning security assessments. NIST-800-115 has areas that address:

► Risk analysis

► Certification

► Accreditation

► Policy development

NIST 800-115 includes recommendations for tools intended for self-evaluation. NIST divides penetration testing into four primary stages:

1. **Planning**—As the saying goes, success is 90% preparation and 10% perspiration. What's the point? Good planning is the key to success. Know where you are going, what your goals are, what the time frame is, and what the limits and boundaries are.

2. **Discovery**—This stage consists of two distinct phases: passive and active.

   ► **Passive**—During this stage, information is gathered in a very covert manner. Examples of passive information gathering include surfing the organization's website to mine valuable information and review job openings to gain a better understanding of the technologies and equipment used by the organization. This stage is deemed passive because the penetration test team is not port scanning or launching attack tools, only information gathering from available data sources.

   ► **Active**—This phase of the test is split between network scanning and host scanning. As individual networks are enumerated, they are further probed to discover all hosts, determine their open ports, and attempt to pinpoint their OS. Nmap or Zenmap (a GUI) are popular scanning programs.

3. **Attack**—At this point, the ethical hacker attempts to gain access, escalate privilege, browse the system, and finally, expand influence.

4. **Reporting**—This is the final step listed, but it is not the least in importance. Reporting and documentation should be conducted throughout each step of the process. This documentation should be used to compile the final report. The report should serve as the basis for corrective action. Corrective action can range from nothing more than enforcing existing policies to closing unneeded ports and adding patches and service packs.

NIST 800-115 recommends that organizations make network security a routine event and that you should always use caution when testing. Things can go wrong! It is also important that the employees be trained in security testing, so that when negative events do occur the organization has people that are already trained.

Although these are good guidelines, it's also important to understand the limitations of security-testing activities. Penetration testing is not the cure to every conceivable problem. You still need to patch and update systems regularly, have good policies, and train employees. At the completion of the test, the results are delivered in a comprehensive report to management. Security of the report is an important issue, as is distribution and storage.

Test Techniques and Methods

There is a variety of test techniques and methods that can be used to test software, systems, and networks. The best way to start is to build security into the product. That is what the security software development lifecycle model (SSDLC) was designed for. Every step of the SSDLC model stresses the importance of incorporating security into the process. These steps are shown here:

▶ Requirements Gathering

  1. Security Requirements

  2. Assessment of Risk

▶ Design

  1. Design requirements identification from security perspective

  2. Design & architecture reviews

  3. Threat modeling

▶ Coding

  1. Coding best practices

  2. Static analysis review

► Testing

  1. Vulnerability assessment

  2. Fuzzing

► Deployment

  1. Server, network, and platform configuration review

Securing software takes a lot of time because software is very different from hardware. Most problems associated with software can be traced back to codes or errors in coding. This is the primary reason that security software development should be performed as part of system design. As an example, code review and testing might focus on which programming language was used and which functions were implemented. The C language, for instance, has some functions that can be exploited (because they do not check for proper buffer size), including `strcat()`, `strcpy()`, `sprintf()`, `vsprintf()`, `bcopy()`, `scanf()`, and `gets()`.

You might also use *misuse case testing*. Think of this as a negative scenario. You are testing for things that should not happen. As an example, if you enter a negative quantity in a field that requires a positive value, will the web application actually accept it? It shouldn't! Another example is testing for an *integer overflow*. This occurs when a program or application attempts to store a number in a variable that is larger than that variable's type can handle. Consider the situation where an allocated buffer can hold a value up to 65,535. If someone can exceed this value and tries to store a value in an unsigned integer type that is larger than the maximum value, only the modulus might remain—for example, 65535 + 1 might become 0. A good example of this can be seen in Figure 9.2.

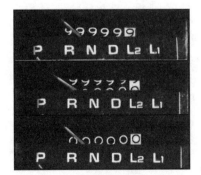

FIGURE 9.2 **Integer overflow.**
Source: https://en.wikipedia.org/wiki/Integer_overflow#/media/File:Odometer_rollover.jpg

Yet another test technique is *synthetic transactions*. These are real-time transactions that are performed on monitored objects. Synthetic transactions can be used to measure the performance of a monitored object and to see how it reacts when it is stressed. As an example, you configure a synthetic transaction on a web server that simulates a user browsing website pages and perform common activities. Synthetic transactions can be used to see whether your monitoring settings, such as alerts and notifications, perform as expected.

It's not just about input and output data. It is also about how an application passes data from system to system, subsystem to subsystem, or variable to variable. That is where interface testing is used. Its purpose is to verify whether all the interactions between various modules and components are working properly, and whether errors are handled properly.

Once the application and/or system is deployed it still must be monitored. Security professionals should periodically monitor system logs to make sure that no problems are occurring. Some of the logs that should be reviewed include the following:

▶ **System logs**—Should be exported to a central location and have someone assigned to periodically review. System logs should be backed up and have a hash/timestamp applied to verify that no tampering has occurred.

▶ **Event logs**—Designed to record system occurrences related to memory, process, system performance, uptime, or hardware issues. While the event log is not focused on security concerns, it is still something that should be reviewed.

▶ **Audit logs**—Monitor and record user activity. Audit logs are a concern of security professionals as they can be used to track compliance with security policy.

▶ **Security logs**—Track events that correlate directly or indirectly with security. Security logs record information, such as user access, user-privileged operations, firewall issues, IDS/IPS alerts, and so on.

▶ **Access logs**—Record information pertaining to access activity. Access logs should be copied to centralized servers and protected from unauthorized access and modification.

> **Note**
>
> Why is testing so important? Attackers are always trying to tamper with data. One example is data diddling. This type of attack works by changing data as it is keyed in or processed by a computer. It can include canceling debts without proper authority or assigning a large hourly pay increase to your salary. Trying to track down the problem is difficult, and it could be months before the attack is uncovered.

Security Threats and Vulnerabilities

Now that we have examined some of the types of tests that an organization can perform, let's turn our attention to some of the threats and vulnerabilities. By reviewing the types of threats the organization might face, we can start to build controls to address these specific issues. It is much cheaper to be proactive and build in good controls than it is to be reactive and figure out how you are going to respond after an attack has occurred.

Threat Actors

Who are the people you have to worry about? Well, generally, they can be divided into two groups:

- **Insiders**—These are individuals who either currently work for the organization, or have been fired or quit yet still have access. These insiders could be disgruntled employees or current or former contractors.

- **Outsiders**—These individuals have never worked for you and you are probably lucky they haven't. Overall, outsiders can be segregated into several subgroups:

  - **Script kiddies**—These individuals cause harm with scripts, tools, and rootkits written by other, more skilled individuals. Often they don't understand how the exploits that they are using work.

  - **Hacktivists**—These hackers have an agenda in that their attacks are driven by the need to protest or make a statement. Groups like LulzSec and Anonymous can be seen as examples. They might use DDoS tools or search for and publish private or identifying information about a target; this is known as *doxing*.

  - **Corporate spies**—These individuals work for rival firms. Their goal is to steal your proprietary information.

▶ **Skilled hackers**—Although they're not driven by corporate greed or the desire to advance agendas like hacktivists, these individuals do have motives. Maybe they are looking for ways to proclaim their advanced hacking skills, or they might be at odds with a stand or position your organization has taken.

▶ **Hacker researchers**—These individuals may accidentally (or intentionally) discover vulnerabilities in a product or infrastructure and then attempt to communicate the issue to the responsible parties.

▶ **Organized crime members**—The primary motivation of organized crime is to make money. Their activities might include creating and renting botnets, monetizing PII, and generating revenue from crimeware kits and ransomware.

▶ **Foreign government agents**—These individuals seek ways to advance the interests of their country. Your data might be the target. Their techniques include highly customized attacks and they may spend months or years to achieve their objectives.

> **Note**
>
> Being a hacker researcher is not without risk. A hacker known as Weev was part of a group that exposed a flaw in AT&T security which allowed the e-mail addresses of 114,000 iPad users, including those of celebrities, to be revealed. Weev was charged and found guilty of identity fraud and conspiracy to access a computer without authorization. While the original conviction was later overturned, Weev did serve more than a year of his original sentence.

So, which group represents the biggest threat? The distinction between insiders and outsiders isn't always useful. We should not really trust anyone. Insiders typically have the means and the opportunity to commit a crime. All they lack is a motive. Outsiders, on the other hand, are not trusted with access and being outside the organization's structure could present them with little opportunity or means to launch an attack. Yet outsiders can be driven by motivations like money, prestige, or national interests. Figure 9.3 shows example threat actors and sample attacks.

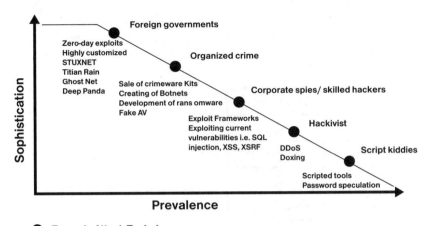

FIGURE 9.3 **Threat actors.**

Attack Methodologies

Attacks typically target one or more items that are tied to the security triad: confidentiality, integrity, or availability. Whereas confidentiality and integrity attacks actually give the attacker access to your data, availability attacks do not. Availability attacks usually result in denial of service (DoS).

DDoS Attacks in Real Life

In December 2010, websites including Visa and MasterCard were shut down due to persistent DDoS attacks. The attacks were coordinated via Twitter by the group Anonymous. They rallied users to download a DDoS tool known as Low Orbit Ion Cannon (LOIC) to join a voluntary botnet. The attack was to protest the fact that financial firms had cut ties with WikiLeaks over its planned publication of U.S. Defense Department documents.

Hackers target a variety of devices but their modus operandi remain fairly constant. Their methodology of attack generally proceeds as follows (see Figure 9.4):

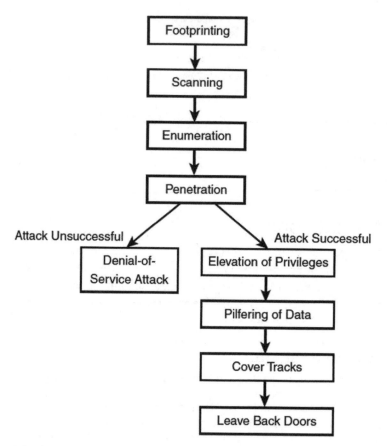

FIGURE 9.4 **Attack methodology.**

1. **Footprinting**—The attackers identify potential targets, looking for information in such places as the organization's website, public databases, WHOIS, NSLOOKUP, Google groups, and EDGAR financial records.

2. **Scanning**—This moves beyond passive information gathering. During this step of the assault, the attackers use a variety of tools to scan for open ports and processes.

3. **Enumeration**—Somewhat similar to scanning, this step involves obtaining more detailed information about target devices, such as OS identification. Poorly protected network shares and weak passwords are two items that are probed for at this step of the assault.

4. **Penetration**—What makes this step different from the previous one is that the hacker is attacking the network with the goal of gaining access. If access is not possible, the attacker might decide to launch a DoS attack.

5. **Escalation**—Many times the initial level of access gained by an attacker is not root or administrator. Under these circumstances, the hacker attempts to escalate privilege, pilfer data, and gain access to restricted information.

6. **Covering tracks**—After they're in control of the system, most hackers seek to destroy evidence of their activities. Most likely, they will attempt to plant tools and rootkits on the compromised system to further extend their stay. Rootkits typically serve the purpose of leaving back doors so that the attackers can come and go as they please.

> **Note**
>
> Escalation of privilege is required because some computer operations require special privileges to complete their tasks or can only be run from root or administrative accounts. Horizontal privilege escalation is where an attacker moves from one user account to another user account that has the same level of access. Vertical privilege escalation occurs when an attacker moves from a lower privilege to higher privileged account. Many processes can only be executed as administrator, system, or root.

Network Security Threats and Attack Techniques

Many threats to network security exist. Many attackers are opportunistic and typically take the path of least resistance. This means they choose the most convenient route and exploit the most well-known flaw. Others, such as government spies and corporate hackers, might go to great lengths to gain access to the data or information they desire. In these instances the attackers or advanced persistent threats (APTs) may spend large amounts of time and money to gain access to resources they covet. Threats to network security can include denial-of-service attacks, sniffing, session hijacking, and botnets.

Session Hijacking

This attack allows an attacker to take over an existing connection between two hosts communicating. It is an effective attack because most TCP services perform authentication only at the beginning of the session. So, in this case, the attacker simply waits until authentication is complete and then jumps in and takes control of the session. Session hijacking can be performed at the host-to-host layer or the application layer. Applications like FTP and Telnet can be targeted by prediction of sequence and acknowledgement numbers, whereas others can be targeted at the application layer. Notice how some sites may log you in as HTTPS; however, the site will continue with the HTTP connection. In such situations the session ID and variable will be passed via a cleartext cookie over port 80 instead of port 433.

Preventive measures include limiting incoming connections and the use of encryption provided by tools like Kerberos or IPsec. Cleartext protocols like FTP and Telnet are very vulnerable to session hijacking because all communication is sent in cleartext. Secure Shell (SSH) is a good alternative. SSH establishes an encrypted channel between the local and remote host. Detection can be improved by using IDS or IPS systems. The use of switches, protocols like SSH, and the design of software that uses more random initial sequence numbers (ISN's) make session hijacking more difficult.

Sniffing

A *sniffer* is a packet-capturing program that captures network traffic and can decode the captured frames. Sniffers work by placing the hosting system's network card into promiscuous mode. A network card in *promiscuous mode* can receive all the data it can see, not just packets addressed to it.

Sniffing performed on a hub is known as *passive sniffing*. When sniffing is performed on a switched network, it is known as *active sniffing*. Switches are smarter than traditional network hubs and know which particular switch port to send all addressed network packets to, and to block all the rest. (There can be exceptions to this rule because some switches can have one port configured to receive copies of all the packets in the broadcast domain.) Attackers might not have physical access to the switch, and as a result might use techniques like Address Resolutions Protocol (ARP) poisoning and Media Access Control (MAC) address flooding to bypass the functionality of a switch.

Sniffers operate at the data link layer 2 of the OSI model. Sniffers can intercept whatever they see on the wire and record it for later review. They allow the user or attacker to see all the data contained in the packet, even information that should remain hidden. Although sniffing is a danger, it is not quite as powerful as it once was because most organizations have replaced their hubs with switches. For sniffers to be successfully used by an attacker, the attacker must be on your local network or on a prominent intermediary point, such as a border router through which traffic passes.

Cleartext protocols are particularly at risk. An example of a cleartext FTP session is shown in Figure 9.5. To further reduce the threat of sniffing, protocols like IPSec, SSL, and Secure Shell (SSHv2) should be used to pass user names, passwords, and data.

```
Response: 220 W2K-STU-01 Microsoft FTP Service (Version 5.0).
Request: USER testuser
Response: 331 Password required for testuser.
Request: PASS plaintext
Response: 230-This FTP Site is for authorized users only! Violators will be towed.
Response: 230 User testuser logged in.
Request: PORT 172,16,30,2,7,234
Response: 200 PORT command successful.
Request: LIST
Response: 150 Opening ASCII mode data connection for /bin/ls.
Response: 226 Transfer complete.
Request: PORT 172,16,30,2,7,235
Response: 200 PORT command successful.
Request: RETR textfile1.txt
Response: 150 Opening ASCII mode data connection for textfile1.txt(22 bytes).
Response: 226 Transfer complete.
Request: QUIT
Response: 221 See ya later
```

FIGURE 9.5 **Sniffing cleartext passwords.**

Wiretapping

Wiretapping traditionally involves connecting to telephone wires but now it could include network sniffing, VoIP sniffing, and radio frequency sniffing (for 802.11 networking, cellular traffic, Bluetooth, and so on). If an organization does not encrypt communications before transmission takes place over public networks, it can be passively or actively eavesdropped on. In the United States, Communications Assistance for Law Enforcement Act (CALEA) requires that all telecommunication providers, regardless of the technologies involved, must make it possible to eavesdrop on all forms of communications so that law enforcement can collect information when a proper search warrant is issued. Some of the techniques used to intercept traffic include intercept access points, mediation devices, and programs installed at the ISP that perform the collection function. Although you might not be too concerned about the government intercepting data, what you should be concerned about is the fact that an attacker could also attempt to use techniques like these to intercept your sensitive and private information.

DoS Attacks

Denial-of-service attacks seek to destroy the availability of information or information systems. Such attacks can be a last-ditch effort by malicious users to bring down a network, extort money, or hold the network hostage. The attitude could be summarized as "If I can't get in, I'll make sure no one else does either." Traditionally, a DoS attack might be launched simply to get attention from peers or to see whether it will really work. Look no farther than the case of MafiaBoy. In 2000, this 16-year-old teenager launched DoS attacks against websites Amazon, Dell, eBay, and others with the goal of saying "look what I can do!" Today these attacks are usually focused on a hostage-type ransom approach and are designed to make money for the attacker. Botnets are used to facilitate DoS attacks and generate revenue for those that control the army of bots. Some common DoS attacks include the following:

▶ **Ping of death**—An oversize packet is illegal but possible when fragmentation is used. When the fragments are reassembled at the other end into a complete packet, it can cause a buffer overflow or fill up the data pipe on the receiving system.

▶ **Smurf**—Uses a spoofed ping packet addressed to the broadcast address, with the source address listed as the victim. It floods the victim with ping responses.

▶ **Teardrop**—Sends packets that are malformed, with the fragmentation offset value tweaked so that the receiving packets overlap. These overlapping fragments crash or lock up the receiving system, thereby causing a denial of service.

▶ **Land**—Sends a packet with the same source and destination port and IP address. The receiving system typically does not know how to handle these malformed packets, so the system freezes or locks up, thereby causing a denial of service.

▶ **SYN flood**—A SYN flood disrupts Transmission Control Protocol (TCP) by sending a large number of fake packets with the SYN flag set. This large number of half-open TCP connections fills the buffer on the victim's system and prevents it from accepting legitimate connections. Systems connected to the Internet that provide services like HTTP or SMTP are particularly vulnerable. Because the source IP address is spoofed in a SYN attack, it is very hard to identify the attacker.

▶ **Fraggle**—Similar to a Smurf attack in that its goal is to use up bandwidth. Whereas Smurf uses ICMP for the attack, Fraggle uses UDP packets. Packets are sent to the UDP port 7. It's a popular target because it's the echo port and will generate additional traffic. Even if port 7 is closed, the victim will still be blasted with a large amount of ICMP unreachable messages. If enough traffic is generated, the network bandwidth will be used up and communication might come to a halt.

Distributed Denial of Service

A DDoS attack is an amplified DoS attack. The DDoS attack started to become more popular around the year 2000, when botnets started gaining ground. A DDoS attack is similar to DoS in that the goal is a disruption of service. However, it is more powerful in that it uses a large number of previously compromised systems to direct a coordinated attack against the target. These systems, known as zombies, wait until the attacker signals the attack. A DDoS attack can be devastating because of the tremendous amount of traffic generated. Historic DDoS command and control attack tools include the following:

▶ Trinoo

▶ Shaft

▶ Tribal Flood Network

▶ TFN 2K

▶ Stacheldraht

> **Note**
>
> 2007 was the first year that a large-scale DDoS attack was launched against a nation. This attack against Estonia caused severe outages and was blamed on Russia.

> **Note**
>
> Today hackers use booters for DDoS. Booters are websites that offer DDoS services. These are operated by cyber crime groups that provide paying customers with DDoS attack capabilities on demand. These services can hide behind multiple layers of IP addresses and be very difficult to take down.

Botnets

This trend of launching DoS/DDoS attacks has changed. Attackers are no longer content with just making a name for themselves. Today's attacks are about making money. These attackers might be out-of-work Eastern European and Russian computer engineers or others working from all over the globe.

Attacks might be performed for extortion or to generate revenue. *Botnets* fulfill this need for the attacker. Botnets, which were first seen around the year 2001, are a massive collection of computers that have been compromised or infected with dormant bots or zombies. Botnets are used to distribute spam, steal passwords used at banking and shopping websites, launch denial-of-service attacks for extortion, and spread infections to other computer systems. An example of a botnet is shown in Figure 9.6.

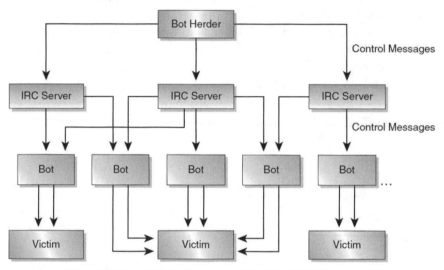

Used for bogus e-mails, SPAM, pump and dump, and DoS

FIGURE 9.6 **Botnets.**

> **Note**
>
> The year 2010 is notable because it was one of the first times a large group of hacktivists was able to organize a large-scale opt-in botnet attack. The attack was organized by the group Anonymous and targeted sites like MasterCard and Visa. These attacks used Low Orbit Ion Cannon (LOIC) to flood these sites and disrupt communication. Hacktivism is a combination of the words "hack" and "activism". Hacktivists like to refer to themselves as protesters in cyberspace.

Botnet attacks start when the controller (called a *bot herder*) seeks to bypass the access control of third-party computers. These computers can be broadband users, home users, or even poorly configured corporate systems. To get an idea how big the problem is, Rick Wesson, CEO of Support Intelligence, stated in *USA Today* (www.usatoday.com/tech/news/

computersecurity/2008-03-16-computer-botnets_N.htm) that on a typical day in 2008, about 40% of the 800 million computers connected to the Internet were infected with bots.

Bot herders can use a variety of techniques to avoid detection. For example, a fast-flux botnet has numerous IP addresses mapped to one domain name. This allows the attacker to swap out IP addresses at an extremely high frequency to hide phishing and malware delivery sites behind an ever-changing network of compromised hosts that act as proxies. Figure 9.7 shows an example.

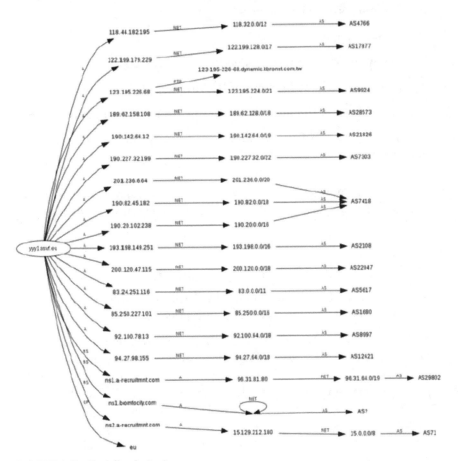

FIGURE 9.7 **Fast-flux botnet.**

The evolution of botnets has now progressed to the point that they are packaged into *crimeware kits*. These prepackaged botnets offer attackers everything they need and typically include detailed instructions.

> **Note**
>
> Botnets have evolved into a multi-million-dollar industry. You can read an analysis of the Zeus crimeware kit at www.techrepublic.com/whitepapers/on-the-analysis-of-the-zeus-botnet-crimeware-toolkit/3895727.

Botnets pose a real threat to computer operations and therefore require multiple layers of defense to counter this threat. Defenses include:

▶ Patched and hardened computers

▶ Web security appliances

▶ Updated anti-virus software to identify known threats

▶ Firewalled networks and the use of IDP to monitor traffic

▶ Routers configured to block spoofed traffic from within a network

▶ User training to guard against advanced persistent threats and to adopt safer computing practices

Although these techniques might not prevent all attacks, they are a good starting point. Organizations must develop better security practices to deal with this threat.

Other Network Attack Techniques

There is no shortage of attack techniques that hackers can use to attempt to violate network security. Some basic attack techniques are listed here:

▶ **ARP poisoning**—This attack usually is done to redirect traffic on a switch during the address resolution from IP to MAC. Because switches do not send all traffic to all ports, as a hub does, attackers must use ARP poisoning, which places the attacker in the middle of a data exchange. When this has been achieved, the attacker can attempt a series of attacks, including sniffing, session hijacking and interception of confidential information. Many tools, such as Ettercap and Hunt, are available to help the attacker perform ARP poisoning.

▶ **Database attacks**—These attacks target an organization's databases. SQL injection is one common attack vector. Although the techniques vary, the results are the same: Malicious users can run their code on the victim's database server or steal information from the server. This can be a serious threat to the integrity or confidentiality of the organization.

▶ **DNS spoofing**—Much like ARP poisoning, this attack attempts to poison the DNS process while addresses are being resolved from FQDN to IP. Individuals who succeed have their fake DNS entry placed into the victim's DNS cache or anywhere else the address resolution is taking place, such as on a cooperating DNS server. Victims then can be redirected to the wrong Internet sites, or to a rogue server filled with malware, sitting in someone's basement and collecting your private information.

▶ **Mail bombing**—Used to target a victim with a large amount of bogus email. Mail bombing attempts to send so much email that the user's email account is completely full.

▶ **Pharming attack**—Pharming exploits are another type of attack that misuses the DNS protocol. Normally DNS is responsible for translating web addresses into IP addresses. Pharming attacks hijack the DNS and force it to redirect your browser to another site, allowing fake software updates used to install malware.

▶ **Traffic analysis**—The sniffing of encrypted traffic to deduce information. As an example, even if the data is encrypted, frequent communications can signal planning is occurring.

▶ **War dialing**—This old-school attack is based on the premise that if the attacker can successfully connect to the victim's modem, he might be able to launch an attack. War-dialing programs work by dialing a predetermined range of phone numbers in hopes of finding one connected to an open modem. The threat of war dialing is that the compromised host acts as a gateway between the network and the Internet. War dialing is resurging because of VoIP's low cost and ability to easily spoof the source of the attack.

▶ **War driving**—The practice of war driving, flying, boating, or walking around an area is to find wireless access points. Many individuals that perform this activity look specifically for unsecured wireless networks to exploit. The primary threat is that these individuals might then have a direct connection to your internal network or unrestricted Internet access. This access can then be used to conduct attacks on other Internet sites, send spam, promote pump-and-dump financial schemes, sell counterfeit goods, and so on.

▶ **Zero-day exploits**—A zero-day exploit can target corruption, modification, release, or interruption of data. This attack takes advantage of an exploit that might not be known to the vendor and that has no patch available.

Access Control Threats and Attack Techniques

Access control is probably one of the most targeted security mechanisms. After all, its job is to keep out unauthorized individuals. To try to bypass or subvert access control, attackers can use a variety of tools and techniques, such as unauthorized access, access aggregation, password attacks, spoofing/masquerading, sniffers, eavesdropping, shoulder surfing, and even wiretapping to capture passwords.

Unauthorized Access

Information needs to be properly protected from unauthorized access, modification, disclosure, and destruction. Part of protecting data requires the selection of the best method of authentication. One important step to help determine what authentication should be used is to perform an asset valuation. Asset valuation can be used to assign the correct dollar and non-dollar value of an asset. After the value of the asset is known, you can then start to examine the appropriate access controls to prevent unauthorized access.

> **Caution**
>
> You can use threat modeling to examine the security risks of an application, including the problem of unauthorized access. A threat model details potential attacks, targets, and any vulnerabilities of an application. In part, threat modeling can help determine the types of access control mechanisms that are needed to prevent an attack.
>
> To learn more about threat modeling, review Microsoft's Threat Modeling tool at www.microsoft.com/security/sdl/adopt/threatmodeling.aspx.

Access Aggregation

Access aggregation, or privilege creep, is the collection of access permissions in one or more systems. For example, Betsy starts on the help desk and in six months moves to tech support. She now gains access to the rights and permissions of a technical support representative while maintaining help desk rights and privileges. Access aggregation is a common problem and one way that allows employees to potentially end up with a greater level of access than they should have. This is a big problem for many organizations. It violates the security principle of least privileges. I have witnessed this at almost every organization I have worked at, but it can be managed with regular user audits and a good principle of least privileges policy.

Password Attacks

Do you think your passwords are secure? In 2014, a security breach at eBay required that about 145 million users change their password. Many individuals don't practice good password security. That is a real problem because a majority of organizations and individuals still use passwords. Attackers are well aware of this and seek out passwords to attempt to gain unauthorized access. There are many ways passwords can be obtained. Listed here are some of the more common methods of attack:

▶ **Password guessing**—Passwords are problematic. Most of us lack the cognitive ability to create several unique, unrelated passwords. A Gartner study performed in 2000 reported that 90% of respondents reported having passwords that were dictionary words or names, whereas only 9% used cryptographically strong passwords. During penetration testing, it's a common technique to use local sports teams' names, landmarks, personalized license plates from a drive-by of the target parking lot, and so on.

▶ **Password sharing**—As discussed earlier, passwords have a real problem with repudiation. Passwords can be shared both directly and indirectly. For example, maybe a co-worker mentions how she uses a pet's name as an easy-to-remember password. In some places, sharing passwords is a common occurrence and often happens unknowingly, especially in situations where workstations are unlocked and no timeout is enforced. Other areas might have a common shared password, such as computers in hospital wards. Doctors and nurses resist having timeouts and having to log into a system while a patient requires immediate action.

▶ **Physical access**—If the attacker can physically access the system, there are many tools that can be used to extract passwords. Although the passwords will most likely be encrypted, password-cracking tools can be used to attempt recovery.

▶ **Sniffing password hashes**—Even without direct physical access, the attacker can attempt to sniff network communication. There are many tools designed specifically for this task. Although the CISSP exam will not expect you to know the names of such tools, several are listed here for the simple purpose of helping you understand the real threat. Pass the Hash from www.coresecurity.com is one such tool that can, among other actions, passively monitor the wire and capture passwords to the screen or to a file. The Dsniff suite also contains a strong SSH attack tool that is effective against SSHv1 (see www.hackinglinuxexposed. com/articles/20020430.html).

▶ **Cracking**—Attackers typically use one of several methods to crack passwords: a dictionary crack or a brute-force crack.

Dictionary Crack

A dictionary crack uses a predefined dictionary to look for a match between the encrypted password and the encrypted dictionary word. Many dictionary files are available, ranging from Klingon to popular movies, sports, and the NFL. Many times, these cracks can be performed in just a few minutes because individuals tend to use easily remembered passwords. If passwords are well known, dictionary-based words, dictionary tools will crack them quickly.

Just how do cracking programs recover passwords? Passwords are commonly stored in a hashed format, so most password-cracking programs use a technique called *comparative analysis* (see Figure 9.8):

1. The hashed password must be recovered.

2. The recovered password is loaded into the cracking program and the dictionary list is loaded.

3. Each potential password found in a dictionary list is hashed and compared to the encrypted password.

4. If a match is obtained, the password has been discovered. If not, the program continues to the next word, computes its hashed value, and compares that to the hashed password.

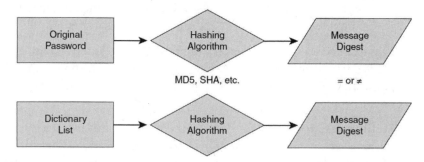

FIGURE 9.8 **Password cracking.**

These programs are comparatively smart because they can manipulate a word and use its variations. For example, take the word "password". A dictionary-cracking program would process this one word as "Password", "password", "PASSWORD", "PassWord", "PaSSword", and so on. All common permutations of a word are attempted.

> **Caution**
>
> Never store passwords as cleartext. Passwords should always be created and stored by means of a one-way hashing process.

If a dictionary attack does not recover the password, the attacker can also try simple modifications of each dictionary word. Those modifications might include adding common prefixes, suffixes, and extended characters to try to crack the password. This is called a *hybrid attack*. Using the previous example, these attempts would look like "123password", "abcpassword", "drowssap", "p@ssword", "pa44w0rd", and so on. These various approaches increase the odds of successfully cracking an ordinary word or any common variation of it.

> **Caution**
>
> Never allow passwords to be indexed or listed on the Internet in any form. The www.hackersforcharity.org/ghdb/ website has listings of this to help identify the problem. A sample search you can perform through Google is shown here for you to see how big this problem is. Just enter the following into Google: **filetype:htpasswd htpasswd**.

Brute-Force Crack

If attackers have not recovered a valid password, don't expect them to give up. A *brute-force crack* is a type of password assault (usually associated with encryption, but it doesn't have to be) and can take hours, days, months, or years, depending on the complexity of the password and the key combinations used. This type of password crack depends on the speed of the CPU's power because the attacker attempts every combination of letters, numbers, and characters. With enough time, recovery is possible. As an example, password crackers have been developed to recover passwords of 14 or fewer characters in under a week for many common operating systems. There are also many online sites that can be used for cracking or to test password strengths.

Rainbow Tables

What if you do not have a week to crack passwords? An alternative to traditional brute-force password cracking is to use a rainbow table. Whereas traditional password cracking encrypts each potential password and looks for a match, the rainbow table technique precomputes all possible passwords in advance and stores them in a table. This is considered a time/space/memory trade-off technique. Precomputing the hashes requires the creation of massive databases of hashed values for every potential password, from single characters on up, using all keyboard characters. A character set that includes *ABCDEF-GHIJKLMNOPQRSTUVWXYZ0123456789!@#$%^&* ()-_+=~'[]{}| \:;"'<>,.?/* would require about 64GB and a considerable amount of time to create. When this process is complete, the passwords and their corresponding encrypted values are stored in a file called a *rainbow table*. An encrypted password can be quickly compared to the values stored in the table and cracked within a few seconds. For those that do not have the time or want to build their own, rainbow tables are available via BitTorrent, or available online with web front ends offered via free or for-pay service.

> **Caution**
>
> Rainbow tables currently exist for Windows LM (LAN Manager) passwords up to 14 characters in length. These precomputed hashes have been demonstrated to attack and crack passwords with a 99% success rate in less than three hours. This means that if an attacker can recover a basic LM password, the encrypted password can most likely be cracked!

To protect yourself from these password attacks, seek to implement two-factor authentication, examine lockout thresholds, monitor access to electronic password files, and enforce a strong password policy using as many different types of characters as possible, including lowercase, uppercase, numbers, and symbols. Change your password frequently, never reuse a previous password, and never use the same password for more than one account.

> **Caution**
>
> Some organizations and government agencies require passwords to be longer than 15 characters. Having a longer password makes cracking it via brute force more difficult, and requires the hacker to use additional time and resources to discover the password. However, hackers constantly adjust and many are now using the cloud services offered by Amazon and others to use large numbers of virtual machines to crack passwords.

Spoofing

Spoofing can best be described as the act of pretending to be something other than what you are on a network, and can take place at different layers of the OSI model by spoofing different protocols, processes, services, and humans up and down the OSI. *User spoofing* occurs when one user pretends to be another user. User spoofing can occur by changing user names, IP addresses, or even MAC addresses. *Process spoofing* occurs when a process pretends to be a valid process when in fact it is not. An example of process spoofing is a fake login screen. This could occur inside an organization or on the web. When the victim attempts to log in, the first attempt to the fake login screen might be unsuccessful and the user information is cached. At this point, the user is redirected to the real login page for a second attempt. The victim might think they simply mistyped the password the first time.

Eavesdropping and Shoulder Surfing

Securing voice communication is a critical component of good security. There are plenty of opportunities to eavesdrop on phone calls and conversations, or intercept communication. Has anyone else noticed how people typically talk louder on a cell phone? During a recent trip, I had an interesting breakfast at the hotel because the person a few tables away gave out their username and password to someone on the phone needing assistance. *Eavesdropping* is the act of overhearing sensitive information or data, either on purpose or by accident. This can be by telephone, network traffic, email, or instant messaging. *Shoulder surfing* is a related activity in which someone glances over your shoulder while you enter a password or username. Employees should be provided security training to help them be more aware of such potential problems. Some users even use monitor mirrors to see who is behind them or looking over their shoulder (see www.thinkgeek.com/computing/accessories/2940/).

Identity Theft

Identity theft has become a big problem and can be described as the process of obtaining key pieces of information about an individual. The goal of identity theft is typically monetary. Most attacks of the past were launched for notoriety and fame. Today's attackers seek money and access to valuable resources. Identity theft can happen when attackers dig through the trash looking for information, or attempt to trick users out of the information they need.

Current and past United States military veterans came close to learning the cost of theft of personal identification when it was revealed that the personal details of as many as 26.5 million veterans had been potentially compromised because of a stolen laptop. Although the laptop and data were eventually recovered, the possibility existed that all the data on the laptop had been copied while in possession of unauthorized persons; moreover, the recovery did not negate the breach of confidentiality or the fact that stronger security controls had not been used.

Social-based Threats and Attack Techniques

Social engineering attacks use a variety of techniques and can be launched in person, remotely via phone, or via a computer. The target of the attack can be known or unknown. Think of *phishing* as throwing out a broad net to all users, like the email you get from a person in Nigeria offering to give you one million dollars. Some phishing scams work by sending the victim an email from what appears to be an official site, such as a bank or credit card company. The email will usually contain a link that promises to take the user to the real website to update, change, or modify that person's account. The real purpose of the email and link is to steal the victim's username, PIN, account number, or password. Employees should be trained to always be wary of links obtained in emails, be alert to messages that request passwords be verified or reset, be skeptical of emails requesting information, and to always verify that the correct URL is listed in the address bar. PayPal has lots of information on phishing (see tinyurl.com/3cy86a).

Spear phishing is targeted phishing. As an example, a phishing email may be sent only to people that use a particular service. *Whaling* is a term used to denote the attempt to capture an important user, such as an executive or even a CEO. Some social engineering attacks make use of the SMS messaging service used over mobile phone devices; that's known as *smishing*.

Another social engineering attack vector is pretexting. *Pretexting* is the practice of obtaining personal information about an individual under false pretenses. Pretexting is usually done when an individual wants more information about a certain individual in order to investigate their activities, so as to sue them, to steal their assets, or to obtain credit in their name. Pretexters use a variety of techniques, but these are all simple variations of social engineering techniques. Pretexters might call your cell phone provider and ask for a reprint of a bill. They also might call back and say they lost their checkbook, or even contact your credit card provider. In most cases, pretexting is illegal and there are laws against pretending to be someone else to gain personal information.

Regardless of how the victim is targeted, social engineering attacks are designed to lure victims into disclosing confidential information, passwords, or other sensitive data. Social engineering is nothing new and predates the computer era. Social engineering is much like an old-fashioned con game in that the attacker uses the art of manipulation to trick a victim. What's interesting is that many times social engineering attacks are combined with technical attacks. As an example, you find a thumb drive in the parking lot that is labeled "spring break photos". Unknown to you is that the photos are actually wrapped remote control software, such as Trojans, designed to infect your computer. Table 9.2 lists some well-known examples of social engineering techniques.

TABLE 9.2 **A Social Engineering Techniques**

Name	Example
Impersonation	Pretending to be someone or something else
Spoofing	Taking someone else's IP address, domain name, MAC address, etc.
Shoulder surfing	Looking over someone's shoulder to view sensitive information
Virus hoax	Not a real virus but pretends to be one to elicit a specific response
Tailgating and mantraps	Driving or following someone through a checkpoint
Dumpster diving	Digging through the trash to look for items of value, such as passwords, manuals, account names, etc.

The best defense against social engineering is to educate your users and staff never to give out passwords and user IDs over the phone, via email, or to anyone who isn't positively identified. Users should be leery of links and login pages that don't look right. Training can go a long way toward teaching employees how to spot social engineering.

> **Note**
>
> Fake login screens are a common social engineering technique that are used to trick users into attempting to login and are usually associated with phishing. The login information is then saved so the attacker can use it at a later time. Users might be given an error or be redirected to the authentic login screen for subsequent attempts.

Malicious Software Threats and Attack Techniques

During the 1970s when mainframes were prominent, the phrase *computer virus* did not even exist. Fred Cowen is credited with coining the term in 1983. Early computer crimes included malware, such as the Brain (1986). The Brain was written by two Pakistani brothers that said they were just out to make a name for themselves. Even the 1988 Morris Worm was said to have been an accident. Today's malicious software is much more advanced than the simple viruses and worms from years ago. Next we will examine the evolution of this threat.

Viruses

Virus propagation requires human activity, such as booting a computer or opening an email attachment. Some basic techniques that viruses propagate throughout the computer world include:

▶ **Master boot record infection**—This is the original method of attack. It works by attacking the master boot record of floppy disks or the hard drive. This was effective in the days when everyone passed around floppy disks.

▶ **File infection**—This slightly newer form of virus relies on the user to execute the file. Extensions like .com and .exe are typically used. Usually, some form of social engineering is used to get the user to execute the program. Techniques include renaming the program, or renaming the .exe extension to make the file appear to be a graphic or document.

▶ **Macro infection**—The most modern type of virus began appearing in the 1990s. Macro viruses exploit scripting services installed on your computer. Most of you probably remember the I Love You virus, a prime example of a macro infector. Macro viruses infect applications like Word or Excel by attaching themselves to the application's initialization sequence or automated tasks within the application. These tasks run without user intervention, and when the application is started, the virus's instructions execute before control is given to the application. Then the virus replicates itself, infecting additional parts of the computer.

For example, some government and/or military agencies require the use of specific formats for their memorandums. Rather than recreate new documents every time and have to look up format rules, users just use templates. These templates can carry malicious code, while appearing to do nothing more than what the users expect.

As the antivirus companies have developed better ways to detect viruses, virus writers have fought back by trying to develop viruses that are harder to detect. One such technique is to make a multipartite virus. A *multipartite virus* can be in more than one area of the system at once. It can infect boot sectors and program files at the same time. The idea is that this would give the virus added survivability if one part is killed by antivirus software. Another technique that virus developers have attempted is to make the virus polymorphic (from Greek "poly", meaning "many", and Greek "morph", meaning "shape"). *Polymorphic viruses* can make copies of themselves and change their signature every time they replicate and infect a new file. This technique makes it much harder for the antivirus program to detect the virus.

Worms

Worms are unlike viruses in that they can self-replicate, while viruses require user interaction. True worms require no intervention and are hard to create. Worms do not attach to a host file, but are self-contained and propagate across networks automatically. The first worm to be released on the Internet was the 1988 Morris worm. It was developed by Robert Tappan Morris and meant to be only a proof of concept. It targeted aspects of sendmail, finger, and weak passwords. The small program disabled roughly 6,000 computers connected to the Internet. Its accidental release was a rude awakening to the fact that worms can do massive damage to the Internet. The cost of the damage from the worm was estimated to be between $10 million and $100 million.

While this was the first, many other worms have been created since then. Probably the most well-known worm in the last 10 years was Stuxnet.

Worms, like viruses, are currently in a state of decline; they are becoming less commonplace as malware creators focus their time on something that will generate revenue. Keep in mind for the CISSP exam that today's malware is much more sophisticated and can actually perform the tasks of both viruses and worms.

> **Note**
>
> Spam is one of the techniques used to spread viruses and worms. While much of the spam of the past was simply junk mail, more and more of it today is malicious in nature.

Logic Bombs

Logic bombs are somewhat different from viruses and worms as they are hidden in the code itself. The logic bomb gets its name as the malicious programming code is placed in the application's code so that it will execute under given circumstances, such as the lapse of a certain amount of time or the completion of a specific event.

> **Note**
>
> Logic bombs and other kinds of malware can be used to launch salami attacks. This financial crime works by taking small amounts of money from accounts over an extended period. For the attackers to be successful, they must remove an amount so small that it will go unnoticed. The movie Office Space offers a good example of this type of attack.

Backdoors and Trojans

Trojans get their name from Homer's epic tale *The Iliad*. To defeat their enemy, the Greeks built a giant wooden horse with a hollow belly. The Greeks tricked the Trojans into bringing a large wooden horse into the fortified city of Troy. Unbeknown to the Trojans, and under the cover of darkness, the Greeks crawled out of the wooden horse, opened the city's gate, and allowed the waiting Greek soldiers in, which led to the complete fall and destruction of the city.

Trojans are programs that seem to do something you want but actually perform another, malicious, act. Before a Trojan program can act, it must trick the user into downloading it or performing some type of action.

Consider the home user who sees nothing wrong with downloading a movie illegally from the Internet. After it has been downloaded, however, the user realizes the movie will not play. The user receives a message about a missing driver or codec and is prompted to go to a site that has a movie player with the right codec installed. The user does as instructed and downloads the movie player and, sure enough, everything works. Seems like a movie without any cost. Well, not quite, because at the time the user installed the movie player, he also installed a remote access Trojan (RAT). The Trojan was actually part of the player.

The Trojan may be configured to do many things, such as log keystrokes, add the user's system to a *botnet*, or even give the attacker full access to the victim's computer. A user might think that a Word doc, PDF, image, or file looks harmless and is safe to run but, once executed, it delivers its malicious payload.

Even instant messaging (IM) and Internet Relay Chat (IRC) can be used to spread Trojans. These applications were not designed with security controls in mind. You never know the real contents of a file or program that someone has sent you. IM users are at great risk of becoming a target for Trojans and other types of malware. IRC is full of individuals ready to attack the newbies who are enticed into downloading a free program or application.

You might be wondering at this point how users get Trojans. Often, the infection results from a scenario similar to the one described in the preceding section: they download one from a web site. Just consider that you get an email that appears to be from HR but is actually spoofed and has an attachment named "pending fall layoffs." Might you be tempted to open it? Social engineering plays a big part in the infection process; after all, we all want to see the attachments that are important or which we believe is sent by a friend or coworker.

The effects of Trojans can range from benign to the extreme. Some users who become infected may not know they are infected, whereas others may experience complete system failure. More often than not, the victim may just notice that something is not right. Sometimes programs will open up by themselves, or the web browser might open pages that weren't requested. If the hacker wants, he can read your email, browse your files, capture your keystrokes, and upload/download files.

Packers, Crypters, and Wrappers

Distributing Trojans is no easy task. Users are more alert, less willing to click email attachments, and more likely to be running antivirus or other antimalware tools than in the past. Years ago, it used to be enough for the hacker to just add more space between the filename and executable extension, like *important_message_text.txt.exe*, or the hacker could simply choose program suffixes or names from programs that would normally be installed and running on the victim's machine, such as notepad.exe.

Today, it is not uncommon for attackers to use multiple layers of techniques to obfuscate code—that is, make hostile code undetectable by anti-virus programs, and to employ techniques to prevent others from examining the code. These techniques improve the attacker's chances of controlling a computer infected by a Trojan, and using it for many types of illegal purposes. Techniques to be aware of are packers, crypters, and wrappers.

Wrappers offer hackers a method to slip past a user's normal defenses. A wrapper is a program used to combine two or more executables into a single packaged program, essentially creating a new executable file. Some wrappers only allow two programs to be joined; others allow the binding together of three, four, five, or more programs. Basically, these programs perform like installation builders and setup programs. Wrappers also add additional layers of obfuscation and encryption around the target file.

Packers work much like programs such as WinZip, Rar, and Tar, in that they compress the file. While compression programs do this to save space, packers do this to obfuscate the activity of the malware. The idea is to prevent anyone from viewing the malware's code until it is placed in memory. Packers serve a second valuable goal to the attacker in that they work to bypass network security protection mechanisms, such as HIDS and NIDS intrusion detection systems. It is not until the malware packer decompresses the program in memory that the program's original code is revealed.

Crypters function to encrypt or obscure the code. Some crypters obscure the contents of the Trojan by applying an encryption algorithm. Crypters can use any encryption scheme, from AES or RSA to Blowfish, or they might use more basic obfuscation techniques, such as XOR obfuscation, Base64 encoding, or ROT 13. Again, these techniques are used to conceal the contents of the executable program, making it undetectable by antivirus software and resistant to reverse-engineering efforts. A quick search on the Internet will show you how many different types of these tools are readily available. An example is shown in Figure 9.9.

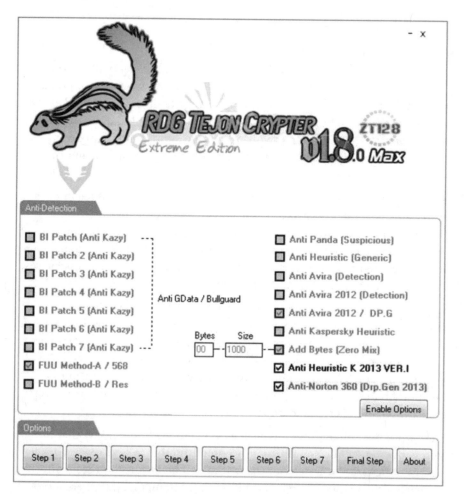

FIGURE 9.9   Tejon Crypter.

Rootkits

Rootkits are a collection of tools that allow an attacker to take control of a system. *Rootkits* can be divided into several different types. These include application, kernel module, hardware, firmware, and bootloader. As an example, a loadable kernel module (LKM) rootkit is loaded as a driver or kernel extension. Because LKM rootkits corrupt the kernel they can do almost anything, and are by far the most dangerous. Rootkits can also avoid detection by many software methods, but there are means to detect them. Tools like MD5sum, Tripwire, and GMER can be a big help in uncovering some types of rootkits. Although the use of rootkits is very widespread, many security professionals still don't know much about them.

Once installed, a rootkit can be used to hide evidence of an attacker's presence and give them backdoor access to the system. Rootkits can contain log cleaners that attempt to remove all traces of the attacker's presence from the log files. Even if you can detect and clean a system with a rootkit, the fact is that a majority of individuals who attack systems go unpunished. Even though you may find evidence of an attack, that doesn't mean the individual will be brought to justice.

Crimeware Kits

Crimeware kits offer someone with no or little programming experience the ability to create, customize, and distribute malware. A large portion of these kits are sold by hackers from eastern Europe and Russia. In fact, roughly 70 percent of crimeware and exploit kits released in the fourth quarter of 2012 came from Russia, according to a study by Solutionary (news.softpedia .com/news/Solutionary-Q4-2012-Report-70-of-Exploit-Kits-Originated-in -Russia-323487.shtml).

A well-known example of crimeware is Citadel. It became popular around 2014 in part because of its ease of use. Citadel allows individuals to create their own tailored Trojan botnets and was a popular crimeware kit for entry-level criminals to get involved in cybercrime.

Some crimeware also offers bulletproof hosting. Bulletproof hosting refers to the practice of protecting malware-infected websites from being shut down by their service providers. In the U.S., for instance, when a website is found to contain malware, there are legal recourses to take the site offline and prevent it from being used to infect other websites. That is not always the case in Russia—these infected websites are sometimes protected from takedowns, allowing cybercriminals to thrive by having a safe platform to host their malware for infecting U.S. consumers and businesses.

Advanced Persistent Threats

Advanced persistent threats (APTs) refer to a group, government, or organization that has the capability to target an organization for an extended period of time. Such attackers might use sophisticated malware and techniques to exploit vulnerabilities in targeted systems. The Stuxnet worm is an example of an APT.

Ransomware

Imagine this: you come in-to work one day, boot up your laptop and find a warning message on your screen like the one shown in Figure 9.10. Sometimes the messages claim to be from the FBI, an international law enforcement agency, or it may accuse users of illegal activity, perhaps visiting illegal or inappropriate websites. What they all have in common is one thing: a hacker has taken over your computer and wants money before he or she will give it back. What I have just described is ransomware. Ransomware is a type of malware that hackers use to install on your computer so they can lock it from a remote location and then demand money.

Experts estimate that as many of 3% of victims actually pay the ransom, meaning that criminals are making money from the scheme. One recent ransomware scheme netted the criminals approximately $30,000 a day, according to Symantec (www.symantec.com/content/dam/symantec/docs/reports/istr-21-2016-en.pdf).

Your computer has been locked due to suspicion of illegal content downloading and distribution.
Mentioned illegal content (414 Mb of video files) was automatically classified as child pornographic materials. Such actions, in whole or in part, violate following U.S. Federal Laws:
   18 U.S.C. § 2251- Sexual Exploitation of Children (Production of child pornography)
   18 U.S.C. § 2252- Certain activities relating to material involving the sexual exploitation of minors (Possession, distribution and receipt of child pornography)
   18 U.S.C. § 2252A- certain activities relating to material constituting or containing child pornography

Any individual who violates, or attempts to violate, or conspires to violate mentioned laws shall be sentenced to a mandatory term of imprisonment from 4 to 30 years and shall be fined up to $250,000.

   Technical details:
   Involved IP address:
   Involved host name:
   Source:

All suspicious files from your computer were transmitted to a special server and shall be used as evidences. Don't try to corrupt any data or unblock your account in an unauthorized way.

Your case can be classified as occasional\unmotivated, according to title 17 (U. S. Code) § 512. Thus it may be closed without prosecution. Your computer will be unblocked automatically.

In order to resolve the situation in an above-mentioned way you should pay a fine of $300.

HOW TO UNLOCK YOUR COMPUTER:

1 $ Take your cash to one of this retail locations:
Walmart   K   [logo]   [logo]
CVS pharmacy   Walgreens

2 MoneyPak Get a MoneyPak and purchase it with cash at the register

3 [lock icon] Come back and enter your MoneyPak code to unlock your computer (5 attempts available)

Code: [_____]   Submit

1	2	3
4	5	6
7	8	9
Delete	0	Enter

FIGURE 9.10   **Ransomware.**

Another important item to keep in mind is that if your computer gets infected with ransomware, it may difficult or impossible to open your files. This is why it's so important to constantly back up your data and encrypt it yourself; then, when it is stolen, you can tell the bad guys to keep your encrypted data because it is useless to them, and you can just restore your backup. There are many ways to back up either locally or to cloud-based providers. You need to be prepared for a disaster like this because you may not get a second chance to recover your data.

Caution

Closely related to ransomware is rogue security software. It is fake antivirus software that attempts to convince users their computer is infected, and manipulates them into buying and downloading the fake software. Don't click the link and download this software—this is a link that infects your computer.

How Computer Crime Has Changed

Computer crime has changed much since the early days of computing. During these early years, computer criminals were typically seeking fame and publicity. Just consider the following:

▶ **The Melissa virus**—Written to impress a girl.

▶ **I Love You virus**—Written because the creator was bored with school.

Early threats were very one dimensional in that they came on strong, caused widespread damage, and hit the Internet like tsunamis. These attacks used large amounts of network traffic and required significant amounts of time to repair. Security professionals quickly turned to products like antivirus and intrusion detection to counter this threat. Somewhere around the year 2000, computer organizations and individuals began to face new threats. Traditional countermeasures started losing their effectiveness. Initially, these threats came in the form of spam and spyware.

Criminals are no longer working alone and are typically much more focused on financial gain. Today they might be financed by organized crime, businesses, or even governments. The attack vectors available to such criminals has also multiplied as rising market share of laptops, portable devices, mobile technologies, USB drives, and Wi-Fi–enabled devices offer attackers new targets. To get an idea of how big this problem is, go to your favorite web search engine and enter "stolen laptops and identity theft."

2007 became the first year that a large-scale DDoS attack was launched against a nation state. This attack against Estonia caused severe outages and was blamed on Russia, according to www.virusbtn.com/news/2007/05_17_virus .xml. The last several years has also shown an increase in firms and countries accusing other nations of launching attacks and engaging in cybercrime. These types of crimes are difficult to prove. In 2014, the U.S. Department of Justice announced that a federal grand jury had returned an indictment of five Chinese nationals on charges of theft of confidential business information and intellectual property from U.S. commercial firms, and of planting malware on their computers. It is believed these hackers had direct ties to the Chinese government.

In 2015, www.krebsonsecurity reported that several Israeli citizens were indicted and accused of hacking into JPMorgan Chase in 2014, stealing the names, addresses, phone numbers, and email addresses of the holders of some

83 million accounts at the financial institution. The Justice Department has dubbed this breach the "largest theft of customer data from a U.S. financial institution in history."

New technologies will be required for the security professional to deal effectively with these threats, such as Intrusion Detection and Prevention (IDP), Network Access Control (NAC), and other technologies to detect advanced persistent threats (APTs). These issues make it important for the security professional to understand ethics, computer crime, laws, incident response, and forensics.

Well-Known Computer Crimes and Criminals

The well-known hackers of today grew out of the phone-phreaking activities of the 1960s. In 1969, "The Midnight Skulker," Mark Bernay, wrote a computer program that allowed him to read everyone else's IDs and passwords at the organization where he worked. Although he was eventually fired, no charges were ever filed because computer crime was so new; there were no laws against it. Some well-known computer hackers and crackers include the following:

- ▶ **John Draper**—Dubbed "Captain Crunch" for finding that a toy whistle in a box of Cap'n Crunch® cereal had the same frequency as the trunking signal of AT&T—2600 Hz. This discovery was made with the help of Joe Engressia. Although Joe was blind, he could whistle into a phone and produce a perfect 2600 Hz frequency.

- ▶ **Robert Morris Jr.**—The son of a chief scientist at the NSA, Morris accidentally released the "Morris Worm" from a Cornell lab in 1988. This is now widely seen as the first release of a worm onto the Internet.

- ▶ **Kevin Mitnick**—Known as Condor, Mitnick was the first hacker to hit the FBI's Most Wanted list. Mitnick was known for his social engineering attacks. One such attack targeted Motorola. He was arrested in 1994, but has now been released and works as a legitimate security consultant.

- ▶ **LulzSec**—A Black Hat hacker group that claimed responsibility for hacking into the CIA, FBI, and Sony. Other high-profile hacks include hacking into a News Corporations account and placing a false report that Rupert Murdoch had passed away and planting another fake news story on PBS that Tupac was alive and living in New Zealand.

▶ **Hector Monsegur**—Known as Subu, this hacker served as one of the leaders of LulzSec. After being arrested by the FBI, he turned informant.

▶ **Albert Gonzalez**—Known for his SQL injection attacks against sites like TJ Maxx, Gonzalez was charged with stealing and reselling more than 170 million credit card and ATM numbers. In March of 2010, he was sentenced to 20 years in federal prison.

> **Tip**
>
> Can a 75-cent error lead to the discovery of foreign government hackers? It did for Clifford Stoll. He used the accounting error to track down and find KGB hackers. Being trained in astrophysics didn't deter him, nor did initial resistance from the FBI in taking him seriously. You can read more about it in his book *The Cuckoo's Egg* (Doubleday, 1989).

Investigating Computer Crime

Security incidents can come in many forms. It could be an honest mistake by an employee who thought he was helping or it could be the result of an intentional attack by an insider or outsider. One of the basic tests to help identify or eliminate the proper suspect is *Means, Opportunity, and Motive* (MOM), as illustrated in Figure 9.11. This is also known as *the crime triangle* and demonstrates why insiders pose a greater threat to security than outsiders. Insiders possess the means and opportunity to launch an attack whereas outsiders might have only a motive.

FIGURE 9.11 **Crime triangle.**

Whatever the motive or reason, the response should always be the same. Security breaches should be investigated in a structured, methodical manner. Most companies would not operate a business without training their employees how to respond to fires, but many companies do not build good incident response and investigation procedures for cybercrime.

Computer Crime Jurisdiction

The unpleasant truth is that tracking and prosecuting hackers can be a difficult job because international law is often ill-suited to deal with these problems. Unlike conventional crimes that occur in one location, hacking crimes might originate in India, use a compromised computer network located in Singapore, and target a computer network located in Canada. Each country's conflicting views on what constitutes cybercrime, and disagreements on how, or even if, the hackers should be punished can cause a legal nightmare. It is hard to apply national borders to a medium like the Internet that is essentially borderless. The United States has proposed legislation that will claim jurisdiction over any criminal activity that travels through a U.S.-controlled portion of the Internet, regardless of the starting or destination country.

Incident Response

The Defense Advanced Research Projects Agency (DARPA) formed an early Emergency Response Team in 1988. Many people attribute the founding of the Computer Emergency Response Team (CERT) to the Morris Worm, which occurred earlier that year. The "Information Superhighway" was little more than a dirt road in 1988, so the delayed response wasn't fatal. Few of us today have the same luxury with regard to waiting until after an attack to form an incident response plan. To reduce the amount of damage that these individuals can cause, organizations need to have incident response and handling policies in place. These policies should dictate how the organization handles various types of incidents. Most companies set up a *Computer Security Incident Response Team* (CSIRT) or *Computer Incident Response Team* (CIRT) because CERT is now a registered trademark of Carnegie Mellon University. The CIRT's function is

- ▶ Analysis of an event notification

- ▶ Response to an incident if the analysis warrants it

- ▶ Escalation path procedures

- ▶ Resolution, post-incident follow-up, and reporting to the appropriate individuals

- ▶ Deter future attacks

The first step is the analysis of the event. An *event* is a noticeable occurrence. As an example, an IDS alert was tripped. This requires an investigation because it must be determined whether the event was an incident. An *incident* is an adverse event or series of events that violates law, policy, or procedure. The individuals investigating the incident need a variety of skills, including

▶ Recognition skills and abilities

▶ Technical skills and abilities

▶ Investigative and response skills

The individuals in charge of the incident must be able to recognize that something has happened. In the example of the IDS alert, recognition is not enough because those responsible must also have the ability to look at logs, event records, and perform incident analysis. Skills are also needed to properly investigate the incident. This requires understanding concepts like chain of custody. Let's look now at who should be involved in this process as the incident response team.

Incident Response Team

Incident response team members need to have diverse skill sets. Internal teams should include representation from various departments:

▶ Information security

▶ Legal

▶ Human resources

▶ Public relations

▶ Physical security

▶ Network and system administration

▶ Internal auditors

▶ Information Technology Helpdesk

There will be many people involved in the incident if the attack came from the inside. Legal, HR, and others must determine what will be done. Incidents traced to the outside of organizations must also have many groups involved. Will management want to involve the police? If so, someone will need to act as a company spokesperson. Roles must be clearly defined, as must the process for escalating incidents to the proper authority. With the team in place, let's turn our attention to the specific steps of the incident response process.

Incident Response Process

Incident response requires organizations to define the specific steps that will be carried out when an incident takes place. Good incident response procedures give the organization an effective and efficient means of dealing with the incident in a manner that reduces the potential impact. These procedures should also provide management with sufficient information to decide on an appropriate course of action. By having these procedures in place, the organization can maintain or restore business continuity, defend against future attacks, and prosecute violators to deter attacks.

The primary goal of incident response is to contain the damage, find out what happened, recover from the incident, get systems back online, and prevent it from reoccurring. This list identifies the basic steps of incident response (see Figure 9.12):

1. **Planning and preparation**—The organization must establish policies and procedures to address the potential of security incidents.

2. **Identification and evaluation**—The detection of the event. Automated systems should be used to determine whether an event occurred. There must be a means to verify that the event was real and not a false positive. The tools used for identification include IDS, IPS firewalls, audits, logging, and observation.

> **Caution**
>
> Is it an event or an incident? An event is a noticeable occurrence, whereas an incident is a violation of policy or law.

3. **Containment and mitigation**—Preplanning, training, and the use of predeveloped procedures are key to this step in the process. The incident response plan should dictate what action is required to be taken. The incident response team requires training to the desired level of proficiency to properly handle the response. This team will also need to know how to contain the damage and determine how to proceed.

> **Note**
>
> Management needs to make the decision as to whether law enforcement should be called in during a security breach. There are reasons both pro and con as to why they may or may not be notified.

4. **Eradication and recovery**—Containing the problem is not enough. It must also be removed and steps need to be taken to return to normal business processes.

5. **Investigate and closure**—What happened? When the investigation is complete, a report, either formal or informal, must be prepared. This will be needed to evaluate any needed changes to the incident response policies.

6. **Lessons learned**—At this final step, all those involved will need to review what happened and why. Most importantly, what changes must be put in place to prevent future problems? Learning from what happened is the only way to prevent it from happening again.

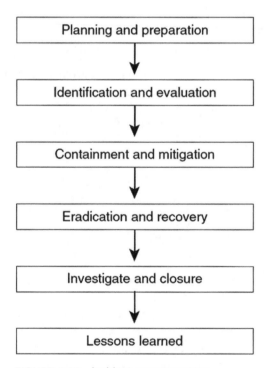

FIGURE 9.12   Incident response steps.

Incident Response and Results

Incident response procedures must be of such detail that specific types of incidents are documented and advice given as to what the proper response would be. Documentation to address each of these potential incidents is critical because investigating computer crime is complex and involved.

Missteps can render evidence useless and unusable in a court of law. This means that team members must be knowledgeable of the proper procedures and have had training on how to secure and isolate the scene to prevent contamination. Table 9.3 outlines some sample response strategies.

TABLE 9.3 **Sample Incident Response Strategies**

Incident	Response Strategy
Possible data theft	Contact legal department, make forensic image, secure evidence
External hacker attack	Capture logs, monitor activities, gather evidence, contact management
Unauthorized use of computer resources	Gather evidence, make forensic image, analyze data, review corporate policy

In the end, incident response is about learning. The results of your findings should be fed back into the system to make changes or improve the environment so that the same incident isn't repeated. Tasks you might end up doing because of an attack include the following:

▶ Figuring out how the attack occurred and looking for ways to prevent it from happening again.

▶ Upgrading tools or software in response to finding out what the team lacked that prevented effective response to the incident.

▶ Finding things that went wrong and making changes to the incident response plan to improve operations during the next incident.

Although no one ever wants to end up in court or to take incident response to the next level, this is not always how it works out. All incident response must be handled meticulously to be prepared for whatever unfolds in an investigation. Sometimes, the forensic skill level required will mandate that the forensic analysis be handed off to a more skilled forensics lab. The next section discusses what happens in forensic labs.

> **Caution**
>
> Ultimately, incident response is about learning. What happened, how did it happen, can we prevent it from happening again, how can we better prepare and respond for the next time, and what did we learn? These are the questions that should be answered.

Forensics

Although government, military, and law enforcement have practiced forensics for many years, it's a much younger science for private industry. Its growth can be tied to the increased role of computers in the workplace and the type of information and access these computers maintain. There are four types of digital forensics:

▶ **Software forensics**—Includes the analysis of malware and other types of malicious code, such as bots, viruses, worms, and Trojans. Companies like McAfee and Symantec perform such duties. Tools like decompilers and disassemblers are used.

▶ **Network forensics**—Includes the review of network traffic and communication. Tools used include sniffers like Wireshark and Snort.

▶ **Computer forensics**—Includes the review of hard drives, solid state drives, and computer media, such as CDs, DVDs, USB thumb drives and so on. Tools used include hex editors, Encase, and FTK.

▶ **Hardware/embedded device forensics**—Includes the review of smart phones, tablets, routers, and other hardware devices.

> **Tip**
>
> Hardware forensics continues to grow in importance as our reliance on electronic devices increases. One report for a former Pentagon analyst alleges that a large amount of foreign-made Telco gear has built-in back doors. See www.zdnet.com/former-pentagon-analyst-china-has-backdoors-to-80-of-telecoms-7000000908/ for more details.

As a foray into forensics, computer forensics will be examined. This branch of forensics is a complex field and includes the following:

1. Plan and prepare by means of procedures, policies, and training.

2. Secure and isolate the scene to prevent contamination.

3. Record the scene by taking photographs and recording data in an investigator's notebook.

4. Interview suspects and witnesses.

5. Systematically search for other physical evidence.

6. Collect or seize the suspect system or media.

7. Package and transport evidence.

8. Submit evidence to the lab for analysis.

Before discussing the basic steps of computer forensics, let's examine the overall concepts and targets of forensic activities. *Computer forensics* defines a precise methodology to preserve, identify, recover, and document computer or electronic data. Growth in this field is directly related to the ever-growing popularity of electronics.

Computers are one of the most targeted items of examination, but they are not the only devices subject to forensic analysis. Smartphones, PDAs, tablets, digital cameras, iPods, USB drives, and just about any electronic device can also be analyzed. Attempted hacking attacks and allegations of employee computer misuse have added to the organization's need to examine and analyze electronic devices. Mishandling concerns can cost companies millions. Companies must handle each event in a legal and defensible manner. Computer forensics follows a distinct and measurable process that has been standardized.

Standardization of Forensic Procedures

In March 1998, the International Organization on Computer Evidence (IOCE) was appointed to draw up international principles for the procedures relating to digital evidence. The goal was to harmonize methods and practices among nations and guarantee the capability for using digital evidence collected by one country in the courts of another country. The IOCE (www.ioec.org) has established the following six principles to govern these activities:

▶ When dealing with digital evidence, all generally accepted forensic and procedural principles must be applied.

▶ Upon seizing digital evidence, actions taken should not change that evidence.

▶ When it is necessary for a person to access original digital evidence, that person should be trained in the techniques to be used.

▶ All activity relating to the seizure, access, storage, or transfer of digital evidence must be fully documented, preserved, and available for review.

▶ An individual is responsible for all actions taken with respect to digital evidence while the digital evidence is in his or her possession.

▶ Any agency that is responsible for seizing, accessing, storing, or transferring digital evidence is responsible for compliance with these principles.

Computer Forensics

Computer forensics can be subdivided into the following stages:

1. **Acquire**—This is usually performed by means of a *bit-level copy*. A bit-level copy is an exact duplicate of the original data using a write blocker, allowing the examiner to scrutinize the copy while leaving the original copy intact.

2. **Authenticate**—This process requires an investigator to show that the original data is unchanged and has not been tampered with, and that the bit-level copy is an exact copy. Authentication can be accomplished through the use of checksums and hashes, such as MD5 and SHA.

> **Tip**
>
> Message digests, such as MD5 and SHA, are used to ensure the integrity of files and data and to ensure that no changes have occurred.

3. **Analyze**—The investigator must be careful while examining the data and ensure that all actions are thoroughly documented. The investigator recovers evidence by examining files, state information, drive slack space, file slack space, free space, hidden files, swap data, Internet cache, and other locations, such as the Recycle Bin. Copies of the original disks, drives, or data are usually examined to protect the original evidence.

Is it real or fake?

While many of us have seen or heard of fake designed watches and purses, the market for fake goods extends far beyond consumer items. One such item is networking gear. In one example, the FBI discovered about 400 routers that had been delivered to the Pentagon that were fake. These fake devices could facilitate foreign espionage, have built-in back doors, logic bombs, or even cause accidents. Identifying this gear is not always easy and can potentially require the skills of a hardware forensic analysts.

The methods used to handle, recover, and document evidence often determines whether the best evidence is admissible as credible and relevant. Let's start by reviewing the acquisition process in more detail.

Acquire

To acquire is to assume possession of evidence or contracting to assume possession. In many instances, the forensic analyst is asked to acquire hard drives, computer, media, or other items on site. Just as with any investigation, the analyst should make careful notes as to what physical evidence is recovered, and include a chain of custody of all evidence acquired. Physical evidence and computer forensics can help build a relationship between the incident scene, victim, and suspect. Figure 9.13 illustrates this relationship.

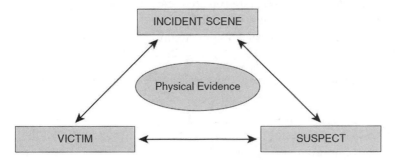

FIGURE 9.13   **Relationship of evidence to suspect.**

Acquisition includes the following items:

▶ Documenting and collecting the evidence

▶ Protecting chain of custody

▶ Identification, transportation, and storage

▶ Approved duplication and copy

During collection and handling of evidence, it is important to record everything. A digital camera can be used to record the layout of the scene. Document the condition of the computer systems, attachments, cables, physical layout, and all electronic media. The camera can even be used to take pictures of any screen settings visible on a running system. You will also want to document internal storage devices and hardware configuration, to include hard drive make, model, size, jumper settings, location, and drive interface as well as internal components such as sound card, video card, and network card. The goal is for the forensic analyst to keep adequate records and begin to build a proper chain of custody. Although the chain of custody is something that those in law enforcement are familiar with, it might be new to many IT professionals but will surely be called into question for all digital evidence in the court of law as well. *Chain of custody* is used to address the reliability and creditability of evidence. Chain of custody should be able to answer the following the questions:

▶ Who collected the evidence?

▶ Where was the evidence collected?

▶ When was possession of the evidence taken?

▶ How was the evidence stored and protected, meaning which software tool was used? Is this tool a best practice used by the industry? Is the professional trained on the tool? How many times has the professional used the tool?

▶ If the was evidence removed from storage, why, by whom, and for how long?

Chain of custody is the process of documenting the journey of any and all evidence while keeping it under control.

Caution

Computer evidence is very volatile; as such it is of utmost importance to protect the chain of custody throughout the entire evidence lifecycle.

Even though many forensic investigations might not lead to a court case or legal showdown, you must always maintain the integrity of the evidence in case it does. After collecting and recording the evidence, it is likely that you have now reached the point at which you might need hard drives or fixed disks for duplication. Any analysis will need to be performed on a copy of the original evidence so that the original can remain safely stored away. The objective of disk imaging is to preserve the original copy in a pristine state and to provide the analyst with a copy to use for investigation. This process usually consists of three steps, which are:

1. Remove the drive from the suspect's computer.

2. Connect the suspect's drive to a write blocker and fingerprint it using a message digest.

3. Use a clean wiped drive to make a copy of the suspect's computer, or copy to an image file.

The copy must be an exact copy of the original. This is known as a bit-level copy, or *physical copy*. A bit-level copy copies everything, including all files, file slack, and drive slack or free space. A logical copy will not perform this type of copy.

Caution

Investigators must use caution when seizing computer systems because the equipment might be booby-trapped. That is, the device may be set up to act as a dead man's switch that will activate when a network connection is broken or when a computer case is opened. In this situation, the switch can wipe all the information on a device, encrypt files, turn off a self-encrypted drive, or take other actions which will make the data inaccessible.

It's critical that the hard drive used to receive a copy of the evidence not have any files, data, or information stored on it. Common practice is to wipe the drive before using it to receive the copy. *Drive wiping* is the process of overwriting all addressable locations on the disk. The Department of Defense (DoD) drive-wiping standard #5220-22M states, "All addressable locations must be overwritten with a character, its complement, then a random character and verify." Drive wiping is useful for forensic purposes, organizations that want to dispose of hard drives, and criminals who want to dispose of evidence. By making up to seven passes over the media, an organization can further decrease the possibility of data recovery.

Authenticate

Having an exact copy is just a start. It must also be shown that the copy and the original are exactly the same. This verification can be accomplished by means of hashing or other integrity algorithms that fingerprint the original drive and the forensically produced copy. Integrity checks ensure the veracity of the information, and allow users of that information to have confidence in its correctness. There are many ways that data can become distorted, either accidentally or intentionally. A forensic analyst must protect against both.

Integrity

Integrity can apply to paper documents as well as electronic ones. Forgers can copy and create fake paper documents, but it is not a skill easily learned. Integrity in electronic documents and data is much more difficult to protect. Forensic duplication and verification requires cryptographic algorithms. These routines use one-way hashing algorithms. Rules of evidence generally require that when a duplicate of the original data is admitted as evidence, it must be an exact duplicate of the original. The hash values must match and be of sufficient strength to overcome the argument of tampering. Not every investigation you become involved in will go to court, but ethics and good practice require that evidence be authenticated as unchanged, from the moment of discovery to the point of disposal. Now let's look at the third step, analysis.

> **Tip**
>
> A primary image is the original image. It should be held in storage and kept unchanged. The working image is the one used for analysis purposes. Forensics examiners should work on the copy only.

Analysis

Analysis is the process of examining the evidence. Forensic analysts typically make two copies of the original drive and work with one of the copies. Some common items of investigation include

▶ Word documents, ZIP files, images

▶ Deleted items

▶ Files created/accessed/modified on suspect dates

▶ Email files (.PST and the like)

▶ Files stored in NTFS streams

In real life, forensic investigators use many different programs to review the evidence. We have been discussing *dead analysis*, where a machine is turned off and the drive analyzed. Sometimes, a machine must be analyzed without turning it off, which is a *live analysis*. In this case, it is critical that evidence be examined from most the volatile to least volatile. Please note that no single program will do everything you need to perform during an investigation. Some software tools are available only for law enforcement, whereas others, such as hex editors, are publicly available. Hex editors can be used to examine slack space and deleted items.

> **Tip**
>
> The handling of evidence is of special importance to the forensic investigator. This is addressed through the *chain of custody*, a process that helps protect the integrity and reliability of the evidence by providing an evidence log that shows every access to evidence, from collection to appearance in court.

How Forensics Was Used to Catch the Creator of the Melissa Virus

When the Melissa virus was released, it quickly slowed the Internet. By disguising itself as email from friends or colleagues, it spread quickly and took down networks. As the manhunt intensified to find the creator, computer forensics was put to the test. David Smith was tracked down and apprehended in about one week.

Many were surprised by how quickly the FBI found the perpetrator. Much of this success was linked to the FBI's capability to use software to sniff newsgroups to determine where the virus was originally posted and then by examining and tracking a globally unique identifier (GUID). A GUID is a unique number embedded in a Word file that shows which computer the file was created on. David Smith was fined $5,000 and sentenced to 20 months in prison. The Melissa virus is believed to have caused more than $80 million in damages.

Investigations

Investigations are another important part of this domain. An investigation is typically a probe or inquiry into questionable activities and can occur after an incident response or in conjunction with forensic activities. Our limits as IT professionals are much different from law enforcement professionals. Some areas of concern are reviewed in the sections that follow.

Search, Seizure, and Surveillance

In the workplace, surveillance can be broken down into two categories:

▶ **Physical**—Closed-circuit television (CCTV) cameras, observation, and security guards

▶ **Logical**—System monitoring, keystroke logging, and network sniffers

Caution

Before you attempt any type of monitoring, be sure to check with your organization's legal department. Most states and federal law require that each user operating the computer be notified of such activities. Otherwise, you could be breaking federal or state laws.

Interviews and Interrogations

At some time during the investigation, it might be determined that interviews and interrogations need to be conducted. If so, areas of concern include the possibility that disclosing the investigation might tip the suspect to halt his or her activities. The suspect might also flee to avoid prosecution. Some suspects might even try to deceive the investigator to prevent further action. Many individuals will lie or misrepresent the truth to avoid being fired or face legal action.

Investigators must be properly trained to carry out interviews and interrogations. As an example, investigators must understand the difference between enticement and entrapment. *Enticement* is legal and ethical, whereas entrapment is illegal. This is an issue with honeypots, which are discussed next.

Honeypots and Honeynets

Honeypots and honeynets are much like an IDS in that they are tools for detecting intrusion attempts. A *honeypot* is really a tool of deception. Its purpose is to fool an intruder into believing that the honeypot is a vulnerable computer. Honeypots contain files, services, and databases that have no real value to an organization if compromised, but are generally attractive to the hacker. Honeypots are effective because they can appear attractive without risking sensitive information. For these lures to be effective, they must adequately persuade hackers that a real system has been discovered. Some honeypot vendors sell products that can simulate an entire network, including routers and hosts, that are actually located on a single workstation—these are called *honeynets*. The honeynet can be deployed in such a manner that it is a separate server not being used by production.

Real servers can generate tons of traffic, which can make it hard to detect malicious activity. Because nothing is running on the honeypot or honeynet, any activity can be easily detected as potential intrusions.

Honeypots can be configured as low interaction or high interaction. Low-interaction honeypots simulate only some parts of the service. As an example, using a tool like netcat as a low-interaction honeypot, you can set a listener on a common port:

```
nc -v -n -l -p 80
```

This would show the port as open but would not return a banner; however, a high-interaction honeypot would not only show the port as open but could also return the proper banner:

```
HTTP/1.1 400 Bad Request

Server: Microsoft-IIS/5.0

Date: Wed, 18 Jul 2012 18:08:25 GMT

Content-Type: text/html

Content-Length: 87
```

Honeypots can be configured in such a way that administrators will be alerted to their use and will have time to plan a defense or guard of the real network. However, the downside of honeypots includes the fact that, just like any other security system on the network, they require time and configuration. And, in fact, they are attracting a malicious element into your domain. Administrators must spend a certain amount of time monitoring these systems. In addition, if an attacker can successfully compromise the honeypot, he now has a base of attack from which to launch further attacks.

Honeypots were originally designed to research attack styles and enable improved architectures and antimalware. More and more agencies are deploying honeypots as ways of acting as a decoy and diverting away from the real system attacks, and to act as early warning systems. It is considered legal to entice someone, but not to entrap. The fuzzy distinction can lead to interesting court cases. A good site to learn more about honeypots is www.honeynet.org.

Evidence Types

The gathering, control, storage, and preservation of evidence are extremely critical in any legal investigation. Evidence can be computer generated, oral, or written. Because computer evidence is easily altered, special care must be taken when handling it. Different types of evidence have different levels of validity in court. For evidence to be accepted in court, it must meet certain standards:

▶ Relevant

▶ Legally obtained and legally permissible

▶ Reliable

▶ Identifiable

▶ Properly preserved and documented

There are also various types of evidence, different ways in which the evidence can be gathered, and legal and illegal ways in which those who break the law can be prosecuted:

▶ **Best evidence**—Best evidence is considered the most reliable form of evidence. Original documents are an example of best evidence.

▶ **Secondary evidence**—Although not as reliable or as strong as best evidence, secondary evidence can still be used in court. A copy of evidence and an oral description of its contents are examples of secondary evidence.

▶ **Hearsay evidence**—Hearsay is generally not admissible in court because it is considered secondhand information. Some computer-generated records and other business records fall under this category.

▶ **Direct evidence**—This form of evidence either proves or disproves a specific act through oral testimony. It is based on information gathered through the witness's five senses.

▶ **Enticement and entrapment**—*Enticement* is the legal activity of luring an individual to perform a questionable activity. Using a honeypot to observe and monitor individuals attempting to attack your network could be seen as an act of enticement. *Entrapment* occurs when individuals illegally induce or trick a person into committing a crime that he had not previously considered.

▶ **Trace evidence**—Whenever two objects come into contact, a transfer of material will occur. This is known as the *Locard's Exchange Principle* and is almost universally accepted by all forensic analysts. No matter how hard someone tries, some evidence always remains. Although criminals can make recovery harder by deleting files and caches, some trace evidence always remains.

Trial

Basically two types of trials occur: one heard by a judge and the other heard by a jury. Most jury panels are composed of ordinary citizens from the court's surrounding geographical area, referred to in most jurisdiction as a jury of one's peers. In many cases the jury might or might not be technically savvy. Computer crimes are difficult to prosecute in court because the advancement of technology is fast, whereas change in the legal system is slow. Trials also require a prosecutor with experience in computer crime. Even when cases are successful, computer criminals sometimes receive lighter sentences because this is considered a white-collar crime.

> **Tip**
>
> *Negligence* is the failure to meet the required standards in protecting information.

The Evidence Life-Cycle

Evidence follows a set life cycle-that begins when the evidence is seized and ends when it is destroyed or returned to the victim/suspect. The evidence lifecycle has the following five stages:

1. Identified and collected
2. Analyzed
3. Preserved, stored, and transported securely
4. Presented in court case or legal venue
5. Returned to suspect or victim

At the end of a trial or legal proceeding, whatever evidence the court is holding will typically be returned to the owner. Some items, such as drugs, counterfeit items, or illegal items, will not be returned. Also, some items might require that the owner to petition the court to fight for their return. As an example, if someone is arrested on drug charges and they possess a large amount of cash, it might be assumed the money is from proceeds of the drug trade and require the owner to prove otherwise to obtain the return of the funds. This may also be the case for information systems that were confiscated and child pornography was discovered on them. If a computer was used as a tool to commit a crime, there is no guarantee it will be return to the owner. Computer crime is increasing, and being seen through the same lens as traditional crimes. For example, in some states in America, if a motor vehicle is used in drug trafficking, that vehicle is often confiscated, never returned, and further used by the police departments for their patrol duties.

Exam Prep Questions

1. IP spoofing is commonly used for which of the following types of attacks?

   ○ **A.** Salami

   ○ **B.** Keystroke logging

   ○ **C.** DoS

   ○ **D.** Data diddling

2. Which of the following best describes session hijacking?

   ○ **A.** Session hijacking works by first subverting the DNS process. If this is successful, an attacker can use an already established TCP connection.

   ○ **B.** Session hijacking subverts the UDP protocol. It allows an attacker to use an already established connection.

   ○ **C.** Session hijacking targets the TCP connection between a client and a server. If the attacker learns the initial sequence, he might be able to hijack a connection.

   ○ **D.** Session hijacking works by first subverting the DNS process. If this is successful, an attacker can use an already established UDP connection.

3. Several of your company's employees have been hit with email scams over the last several weeks. One of these attacks successfully tricked an employee into revealing his username and password. Management has asked you to look for possible solutions to these attacks. Which of the following represents the best answer?

   ○ **A.** Implement a new, more robust password policy that requires complex passwords.

   ○ **B.** Start a training and awareness program.

   ○ **C.** Increase the organization's email-filtering ability.

   ○ **D.** Develop a policy that restricts email to official use only.

4. In part, the ISC² Code of Ethics states which of the following?

   ○ **A.** Thou shalt not use a computer to harm other people.

   ○ **B.** Compromising the privacy of users is unethical.

   ○ **C.** All information should be free.

   ○ **D.** Act honorably, honestly, justly, responsibly, and legally.

5. Which of the following groups presents the largest threat to your organization?

    O   **A.** Insiders

    O   **B.** Corporate spies

    O   **C.** Government spies

    O   **D.** Script kiddies

6. Locard's Exchange Principle states which of the following?

    O   **A.** The chain of custody should never be broken.

    O   **B.** There is always some trace evidence.

    O   **C.** Three things are required for a crime: means, motive, and opportunity.

    O   **D.** Checksums should be used to authenticate evidence.

7. Which of the following international organizations was established to standardize the handling of forensic evidence?

    O   **A.** The International Organization on Forensic Analysis

    O   **B.** The EU Policy Council of Criminal Evidence

    O   **C.** The United Nations Organization on Computer Evidence

    O   **D.** The International Organization on Computer Evidence

8. For evidence to be used in court, it must *not* be which of the following?

    O   **A.** Relevant

    O   **B.** Properly preserved

    O   **C.** Identifiable

    O   **D.** Justifiable

9. Which of the following best defines hearsay evidence?

    O   **A.** Can be used in civil cases

    O   **B.** Is not admissible in court

    O   **C.** Is considered third-hand information

    O   **D.** Can be used to verify what has been presented through best evidence

10. Ethical hackers are different from hackers in which of the following ways?

    O   **A.** They have permission to destroy a network.

    O   **B.** Their goal is to do no harm.

    O   **C.** They cannot be held liable for any damage.

    O   **D.** They cannot be prosecuted or jailed.

11. When dealing with computer forensics, which item should be addressed first?

- ○ **A.** Hard drive(s)
- ○ **B.** DVDs
- ○ **C.** Contents of RAM
- ○ **D.** Computer printouts

12. Which of the following best describes SATAN?

- ○ **A.** It is used for password cracking.
- ○ **B.** It is used for reviewing audit logs.
- ○ **C.** It is used to exploit systems.
- ○ **D.** It is used to find vulnerabilities.

13. The computer forensic investigator should do what during duplication?

- ○ **A.** Make a direct copy
- ○ **B.** Make a bit level copy
- ○ **C.** Make a logical copy
- ○ **D.** Format the target drive to clear any contents before copying

14. What type of penetration test examines what insiders can access?

- ○ **A.** Whitebox
- ○ **B.** Graybox
- ○ **C.** Blackbox
- ○ **D.** Bluebox

15. These individuals are known for their attacks on PBX and telecommunication systems.

- ○ **A.** Script kiddies
- ○ **B.** Phreakers
- ○ **C.** Crackers
- ○ **D.** Hackers

Answers to Exam Prep Questions

1. **C.** IP spoofing is a common practice when DoS tools are used to help the attacker mask his identity. Salami attacks, data diddling, and keystroke logging do not typically spoof IP addresses, so answers A, B, and D are incorrect.

2. **C.** This more advanced spoof attack works by subverting the TCP connection between a client and a server. If successful, the attacker has a valid connection to the victim's network and is authenticated with his credentials. This attack is very hard to do with modern operating systems but is trivial with older operating systems. Answer A is incorrect because session hijacking does not involve DNS; it functions by manipulating the TCP sequence number. Answer B is incorrect because session hijacking does not use the UDP protocol. UDP is used for stateless connections. Answer D is incorrect because, again, session hijacking is not based on DNS and UDP. These two technologies are unrelated to TCP sequence numbers.

3. **B.** The best defense against social engineering is to educate your users and staff. Training can go a long way toward teaching employees how to spot these scams. Although the other answers are not bad ideas, they will not prevent social engineering, so answers A, C, and D are incorrect.

4. **D.** It's a requirement for CISSP candidates to subscribe to the ISC^2 Code of Ethics, which, in part, states, "Act honorably, honestly, justly, responsibly, and legally." All other answers are incorrect.

5. **A.** Insiders represent the biggest threat to the organization because they possess two of the three things needed to attempt malicious activity: means and opportunity. Answers B, C, and D are incorrect because although outsiders might have a motive, they typically lack the means or opportunity to attack your organization.

6. **B.** There is always some trace evidence. Locard's Exchange Principle states that whenever two objects come into contact, a transfer of material will occur. Answers A, C, and D are incorrect because they do not describe Locard's Exchange Principle.5

7. **D.** The International Organization on Computer Evidence (IOCE) was appointed to draw up international principles for the procedures relating to digital evidence. The goal was to harmonize methods and practices among nations and guarantee the capability to use digital evidence collected by one state in the courts of another state. Answer A, B, and C are incorrect because the these are not the correct name of the forensic that was established to standardize the handling of forensic evidence.

8. **D.** For evidence to be accepted in court, it must meet certain standards: It must be relevant (answer A), legally permissible, reliable, identifiable (answer C), and properly preserved (answer B) and documented. Because the question asked which is *not* applicable, the only possible answer is D, justifiable.

9. **B.** Hearsay is generally not admissible in court because it is considered secondhand information. Answer A is incorrect because hearsay evidence cannot be used in civil cases. Answer C is incorrect because hearsay evidence is considered secondhand information. Answer D is incorrect because hearsay evidence cannot be used to verify what has been presented through best evidence.

10. **B.** Ethical hackers use the same methods as crackers and black-hat hackers, but they report the problems they find instead of taking advantage of them. Ethical hacking has other names, such as *penetration testing*, *intrusion testing*, and *red-teaming*. Answer A is incorrect because ethical hackers do not have permission to destroy networks. Answer C is incorrect because ethical hackers can be held liable. Answer D is incorrect because ethical hackers can be jailed if they break the law or exceed the terms of their contract.

11. **C.** Contents of RAM should be examined first because the process should always move from most volatile to least volatile. The contents of RAM will be lost when the system is powered down. Hard drives, DVDs, printouts, and other such items can be examined later, so answers A, B, and D are incorrect.

12. **D.** SATAN was the first vulnerability assessment program and was designed to find vulnerabilities in a network. Programs like Retina and Nessus are also used for vulnerability assessments. SATAN is not used for password cracking (answer A), auditing logs (answer B), and is not used to exploit systems (answer C).

13. **B.** Make a bit-level copy. Bit-level copies are exact copies and include file slack, drive slack, and all contents of the drive being duplicated. Making a direct copy (answer A) would not be performed because the drive must be protected with a write blocker to prevent changes to the suspect's drive. Logical copies (answer C) copy only files, not slack. Formatting the drive (answer D) would not effectively clean the disk—a drive wipe would be the approved method of preparation.

14. **B.** Graybox testing looks to determine what type of activities can be performed. Answer A is incorrect because whitebox testing is where everything is known about the network, answer C is incorrect because blackbox testing is where nothing is known about the network, and answer D is incorrect because blueboxing is a term used by phreakers to make free phone calls via a mechanical device.

15. **B.** Phreakers are individuals that are known for their attacks on PBX and telecommunications equipment. Answers C and D are incorrect because hackers and crackers both identify computer criminals. Answer A is incorrect because script kiddies are defined as junior hackers that rely on the work of others through predefined processes and programs to attack computers.

Need to Know More?

RFC 1087: www.faqs.org/rfcs/rfc1087.html

Computer Emergency Response Team: www.cert.org/

DOJ site on cybercrime: www.cybercrime.gov/

2600: The Hacker Quarterly: www.2600.com/

Underground Hacking Event: www.defcon.org/

40 years of hacking: https://trinity-hackers.wikispaces.com/ CNN+40+Years+of+Hacking

ISC² Code of Ethics: https://www.isc2.org/ethics/default.aspx

Forensic procedure information: www.forensicmag.com/articles/2007/10/documenting-computer-forensic-procedures

EU privacy laws: en.wikipedia.org/wiki/Data_Protection_Directive

Rules of evidence: www.law.cornell.edu/rules/fre/

Identity theft information: www.idtheftcenter.org/index

Honeypots and honeynet white papers: www.honeynet.org

Forensic Best practices: www.us-cert.gov/reading_room/forensics.pdf

CHAPTER 10

Security Operations

Terms you'll need to understand:

- ▶ Redundant array of inexpensive disks
- ▶ Clustering
- ▶ Distributed computing
- ▶ Cloud computing
- ▶ Media management
- ▶ Least privilege
- ▶ Mandatory vacations
- ▶ Due care / due diligence
- ▶ Privileged entities
- ▶ Trusted recovery
- ▶ Clipping level
- ▶ Resource protection

Topics you'll need to master:

- ▶ Understanding disaster recovery processes and plans
- ▶ Understanding foundational security concepts
- ▶ Defining different types of RAID
- ▶ Understanding backup and recovery
- ▶ Describing different types of anti-malware tools
- ▶ Implement disaster recovery processes
- ▶ Auditing and monitoring

Introduction

Readers preparing for the ISC^2 Certified Information Systems Security Professional exam and those reviewing the security operations domain must know resources that should be protected: principles of best practices, methods to restrict access, protect resources, and monitor activity, and response to incidents.

This domain covers a wide range of topics involving operational security best practices. Security professionals apply operational controls to daily activities to keep systems running smoothly and facilities secure. This domain reviews these controls, and shows how their application to day-to-day activities can prevent or mitigate attacks.

The process starts before an employee is hired. Employers should perform background checks, reference checks, criminal history reports, and educational verification. Among many on-boarding tasks, after someone is hired, the new employee must be trained on corporate policies.

Additional controls need to be put in place to limit the ability and access the employee has. Access is a major control that should be limited to just what is needed to complete required tasks; this kind of limit is referred to as *least privileges*. Job rotation, dual control, and mandatory vacations are some more examples of these types of controls.

Controls are not just about people. Many of the controls discussed in this chapter are technical in nature. These controls include intrusion prevention, network access control, anti-virus, RAID and security information, and event management. Each is used in a unique way so that we can seek to prevent, detect, and recover from security incidents and exposures. Keep in mind that violations to operational security aren't always malicious; sometimes things break or accidents happen. Therefore, operational security must also be prepared to deal with these unintended occurrences by building in system resilience and fault tolerance.

Foundational Security Operations Concepts

Ask any seasoned security professional what it takes to secure its networks, systems, applications, and data, and the answer will most likely involve a combination of operational, technical, and physical controls. This process starts before you ever hire your first employee. Employees need to know what is expected of them. Accounts need to be configured, users need to have the appropriate level of access approved, and monitoring must be implemented. These are the topics that will be discussed in the first section.

Managing Users and Accounts

One foundational control to increase accountability is to enforce specific roles and responsibilities within an organization. Most organizations have clearly defined controls that specify what each job role is responsible for. Some common roles within organizations are:

- ▶ **Librarian**—Responsible for all types of media, including CDs, DVDs, USB thumb drives, solid state hard drives, and so on. Librarians must track, store, and recall media as needed. They also must document whether the media is encrypted, when the media was stored, when it was retrieved, and who accessed it. If media moves offsite, librarians track when it was sent and when it arrived. They might also be asked to assist in an audit to verify what type of media is still being held at a vendor's site.

- ▶ **Data entry specialist**—Although most data entry activities are now outsourced, in the not-too-distant past, these activities were performed in-house at an information processing facility. During that time, a full-time data entry specialist was assigned the task of entering all data. (Bar codes, scanning, and web entry forms have also reduced the demand for these services.)

- ▶ **Systems administrator**—Responsible for the operation and maintenance of the LAN and associated components, such as Windows Server 2012 R2, Linux, or even mainframes. Although small organizations might have only one systems administrator, larger organizations might have many.

- ▶ **Quality assurance specialist**—Can fill either of two roles: quality assurance or quality control. Quality assurance employees make sure programs and documentation adhere to standards; quality control employees perform tests at various stages of product development to make sure the products are free of defects.

- ▶ **Database administrator**—Responsible for the organization's data and maintains the data structure. The database administrator has control over all the data; therefore, detective controls and supervision of duties must be closely observed. This role is usually filled by a senior information systems employee because these employees have control over the physical data database, implementation of data definition controls, and definition and initiation of backup and recovery.

▶ **Systems analyst**—Involved in the system development life cycle (SDLC) process responsible for determining the needs of users and developing the requirements and specifications for the design of needed software.

▶ **Network administrator**—Responsible for maintenance and configuration of network equipment, such as routers, switches, firewalls, wireless access points, and so on.

▶ **Security architect**—Responsible for examining the security infrastructure of the organization's network.

Job titles can be confusing because different organizations tend to use different titles for identical positions and in smaller organization they tend to combine duties under one position or title. For example, some network architects are called network *engineers*. The critical concept for a security professional is to understand that, to avoid conflicts of interest, certain roles should not be combined. Table 10.1 lists some examples of role combinations and whether it's okay to combine them.

TABLE 10.1 **Separation of Duties**

First Job Role	Can Be Combined With?	Second Job Role
Systems analyst	No	Security administrator
Application programmer	Yes	Systems analyst
Help desk	No	Network administrator
Data entry	Yes	Quality assurance
Computer operator	No	Systems programmer
Database administrator	Yes	Systems analyst
System administrator	No	Database administrator
Security administrator	No	Application programmer
Systems programmer	No	Security administrator

The titles and descriptions in Table 10.1 are just examples and many companies might describe these differently or assign more or less responsibility to any one job role. To better understand the effect of role combinations that can conflict, consider a small company that employs one person as both the network administrator and the security administrator. This represents a real weakness because of the conflict of interest in the range of duties that a security administrator and a network administrator must perform.

This conflict arises because a network administrator is tasked with keeping the system up and running, keeping services available, while a security administrator is tasked with turning services off, blocking them, and denying users access. A CISSP should be aware of such incompatibilities and be concerned about the risks that can arise when certain roles are combined. Finally, any employee of the organization who has elevated access requires careful supervision. These individuals should be considered privileged entities.

Privileged Entities

A *privileged entity* is anyone that has a higher level of access than the normal user. Privileged entities can include mainframe operators, security administrators, network administrators, power users, or anyone with higher than normal levels of access. It important that sufficient controls be placed on these entities so that misuse of their access is deterred or, if their access is misused, it can be detected and corrected.

Controlling Access

Before hiring employees, you must make sure that you have the right person for the right job. Items such as background checks, reference checks, education/certification checks, or even Internet or social media checks might be run before new-hire orientation ever occurs. New employees might be asked to sign *nondisclosure agreements* (NDAs), agree to good security practices, and agree to *acceptable use policies* (AUPs).

When employees are on-boarded there are a number of controls that can be used to control access and privilege. First there is s*eparation of duties.* It describes the process of dividing duties so that more than one person is required to complete a task. Job rotation can be used to maintain redundancy, back up key personnel, and even help identify fraudulent activities. The principle of *least privilege* is another important concept that can go a long way toward an organization achieving its operational security goals. Least privilege means that individuals should have only enough resources to accomplish their required tasks.

Even activities such as mandatory vacations provide time for audits and to examine user activity for illicit activities. Each of these items will need to be backed up by policies, procedures, and training. Keep in mind that organizations benefit when each employee actively participates in the security of the organization.

Clipping Levels

No one has the time to investigate every event or anomaly that might occur but there must still be systems in place to log and monitor activities. One such technique is a clipping level. A *clipping level* is set to identify an acceptable threshold for the normal mistakes a user might commit. Events that occur with a frequency in excess of the clipping level lead to administrative notification and investigation.

The clipping level allows the user to make an occasional mistake, but if the established level is exceeded, violations are recorded or some type of response occurs. The network administrator might allow users to attempt to log in three times with an incorrect password. If the user can't get it right on the third try, the account is locked and he or she is forced to call the help desk for support. If an administrator or help desk staffer is contacted to reset a password, a second type of authentication should be required to protect against a social engineering attack. Chapter 9, "Security Assessment and Testing," covers social engineering in more detail.

> **Tip**
>
> To prevent social engineering attacks, individuals who need to have their password reset by automated means should be required to provide strong authentication such as user ID, PIN, or two or more cognitive passwords. For systems with higher security, physical retrieval or in-person verification should be used for password recovery.

Resource Protection

When you think of resource protection you might think of servers or other tangible assets. But resources can be both tangible and intangible. Tangible assets include equipment and buildings, whereas intangible assets can include such things as patents, trademarks, copyrights, and even brand recognition. Loss of a trade secret to a competitor can be just as, or more, devastating than an employee stealing a laptop. This means the organization must take reasonable care to protect all items of value.

Due Care and Due Diligence

Due care is focused on taking reasonable ongoing care to protect the assets of an organization. Due diligence is the background research. As an example, before accepting credit cards you might want to research the laws that govern their use, storage, and handling. Therefore, due diligence would be associated with reviewing the controls highlighted within PCI-DSS. Actually, due diligence was first used as a result of the United States Securities Act of 1933.

Organizations and their senior management are increasingly being held to higher levels of due care and due diligence. Depending on the law, senior management can be held responsible for criminal and/or financial damages if they are found negligent. The Sarbanes-Oxley Act of 2002 and the Federal Information Security Management Act have increased an organization's liability for maintaining industry compliance. As an example, United States federal sentencing guidelines allow for fines in excess of $200 million dollars.

A legal challenge to an organization's due diligence often results in the court system looking at what a "prudent person" would have done, and this is in fact referred to as the *reasonably prudent person rule*. For example, a prudent person would implement PCI-DSS controls for credit card transactions for a retail store using a point of sale (POS) device with over 80,000 transactions a year. The reasonably prudent person is a legal abstraction; in the context of cyber-security, it would be a professional, well trained, certified, educated individual with common sense in cyber-defense.

> **Note**
>
> While PCI is a major standard for control of financial information, the Group of Eight (G8) started as a forum for the governments of eight of the world's largest economies to discuss issues related to commerce. Today, it has grown to 20 members.

Asset Management

Asset management is the process of identifying all the hardware and software assets within an organization, including the organization's employees. There is no way to assess risk, or to consider what proper operational controls are, without good asset management. Asset management not only helps an organization gain control of its software and hardware assets, but also increases an organization's accountability. Consider the process of hardening, patching, and updating. This process cannot be effectively managed without knowing what operating systems and/or software a company owns, and on what systems those products are installed.

System Hardening

Once we know what assets we have, *system hardening* is used to eliminate all applications, processes, and services that are not required for the business to function. When attackers attempt to gain access to a system, they typically look for systems that are highly vulnerable or that have "low-hanging fruit." This phrase describes services and applications that are easily exploitable, often because they are unnecessary and unmanaged. The purpose of system hardening is to reduce the attack surface by removing anything that is not needed, or at least to isolate vulnerable services away from sensitive systems. After a system has been reduced to its bare essentials, there are fewer avenues for a potential attacker to exploit.

System hardening applies to all platforms. But consider for a moment the Nimda attack of 2001. Nimda focused on Microsoft web servers, and it used TFTP to upload the malware to the web server. Simply removing the TFTP service would have gone a long way toward protecting these vulnerable web servers. While most everyone does this now, little thought was given to this process then. Commonly removed services nowadays include FTP, Telnet, file and print sharing, NetBIOS, DNS, and SNMP.

Hardening should also be considered from a hardware perspective. Hardware components such as CD drives, DVD drives, and USB ports should be disabled or removed. Also, hardening can be extended to the physical premise itself. Wiring closets should be locked, data centers should have limited access, and network equipment such as switches, routers, and wireless access points should be physically secured.

> **Note**
>
> After performing many security assessments, one of the first things I now look for when I enter a facility is the lack of physical controls; this includes wireless access points, telecommunication equipment, servers, and riser rooms. If an asset is physically accessible to an intruder, it is insecure.

Once a system has been hardened and approved for release a baseline needs to be approved. *Baselining* is simply capturing a configuration or image at a point in time and understanding the current system security configuration. All our work up to this point would do little good if the systems are not maintained in a secure state. This is where change management comes into play.

Change and Configuration Management

Companies put a lot of effort into securing assets and hardening systems. To manage required system changes, controls must be put in place to make sure all changes are documented and approved. This is accomplished with the *change management* process. Any time a change is to be made, it is important to verify what is being requested, how it will affect the systems, and what unexpected actions might occur. Most companies will not directly deploy patches without first testing them to see what changes will occur after the patch has been installed. It is important to ensure that changes do not somehow diminish or reduce the security of the system. Configuration management should also provide a means to roll back or undo any applied changes should negative effects occur because of the change. Although change management processes can be implemented slightly differently in various organizations, a generic process can be defined:

1. Request a change.

2. Approve the change.

3. Catalog the change.

4. Schedule the change.

5. Prepare a means to roll back the change if needed.

6. Implement the change.

7. Test or confirm the change.

8. Report the completion of the change to the appropriate individuals/groups.

> **Tip**
>
> While some might question the need to have a rollback plan, things can go wrong. A good example of this can be seen in 2010 when a McAfee Antivirus update caused Windows XP systems to blue screen. See www.eweek.com/c/a/Security/Buggy-McAfee-Security-Update-Takes-Down-Windows-XP-Machines-827503/.

Despite the fact that each organization might implement change management differently, there can be no argument over the value of using comprehensive change management. The primary benefits of change management include:

▶ Verification that change is implemented in an orderly manner through formalized testing

▶ Verification that the user base is informed of impending/completed changes

▶ Review of the effects of changes on the system after implementation

▶ Mitigation of any adverse impact that changes might have had on services, systems, or resources

Trusted Computer System Evaluation Criteria (TCSEC), frequently referred to as the *Orange Book*, specifies that change management is a requirement at the A1, B3, and B2 levels (see Table 10.2). The *Orange Book* defines operational assurance in terms of a system's architecture, its capability to provide system integrity, its resistance to known attacks (such as covert channels), its provision of facility management, and its capability to provide trusted recovery. Although it's safe to say the measurement of assurance has progressed way beyond the Orange Book, TCSEC does provide a basis for discussing assurance through the use of operational controls.

TABLE 10.2 **TCSEC Levels and Ratings**

TCSEC Rating	Description
A1	Verified Protection
B3	Security Domains
B2	Structured Protection
B1	Labeled Security Protection
C2	Controlled Access Protection
C1	Discretionary Security Protection
D	Minimal Protection

Take a moment to review Chapter 5, "Security Engineering," to review more about Orange Book levels and their meaning, and about more current specifications like Common Criteria. Change management can also be used to demonstrate due care and due diligence.

Trusted Recovery

Trusted recovery is one of the assurance requirements found in the Orange Book. Administrators of B3-A1 systems must be able to restore the systems to a secure state whenever a failure occurs. Failures can occur in all types of operating systems. Many older readers may remember Windows NT and the blue screen of death (BSOD) that administrators were tasked with dealing with. These system failures usually required a reboot to recover. Administrators that experienced these issues had to understand what caused the failure and how to recover the system to a usable state. Luckily, the BSOD is encountered much less frequently now than in those early years. A system failure can be categorized as a system reboot, an emergency system restart, or a system cold start. The Orange Book describes these as follows:

▶ **System reboot**—Performed after shutting down the system in a controlled manner in response to a trusted computer base (TCB) failure. For example, when the TCB detects the exhaustion of space in some of its critical tables or finds inconsistent object data structures, it closes all objects, aborts all active user processes, and restarts with no user process in execution.

▶ **Emergency system restart**—Occurs after a system fails in an uncontrolled manner in response to a TCB or media failure. In such cases, the TCB and user objects on nonvolatile storage belonging to processes active at the time of the TCB or media failure may be left in an inconsistent state.

▶ **System cold start**—Occurs when unexpected TCB or media failures take place. The recovery procedures cannot bring the system to a consistent state, so intervention by administrative personnel is required to bring the system to a consistent state from maintenance mode.

> **Tip**
>
> Whereas modern client/server systems use the term *reboot*, mainframes use the term *initial program load* (IPL). Historically, when a mainframe had to have a configuration change, it was said to be re-IPL'd.

Any failure that endangers the security of a system must be understood and investigated. It is critical that the environment be protected during recovery. Consider a Windows 2008 or 2012 Server. Did you ever notice that when you shut down a Windows Server, you are asked why? This screen is an example of an operational control.

To protect the environment during the reboot/restart process, access to the server must be limited. This prevents anyone from having an opportunity to disrupt the process. Some example recovery limits include:

▶ Prevent system from being booted from network, CD/DVD, or USB

▶ Log restarts so that auditing can be performed

▶ Block complementary metal-oxide semiconductor (CMOS) changes to prevent tampering

▶ Deny forced shutdowns

Remote Access

As transportation, utilities, and other associated costs associated with traditional 9-to-5 employees continue to rise, more and more companies are permitting employees to telecommute, access resources remotely, and use cloud computing. Companies might also have sales reps and others that need remote access. These requirements lead companies to enable remote access to their networks.

Remote access also offers an attacker a potential means of gaining access to the protected network. Therefore, companies need to implement good remote access practices to mitigate risk. Some basic remote access controls include the following:

▶ Implementing caller ID

▶ Using a callback system

▶ Disabling unused authentication protocols

▶ Using strong authentication

▶ Implementing remote and centralized logging

▶ Using VPNs and encryption

Media Management, Retention, and Destruction

Resource protection techniques do not just include when the resource is being used. It also includes disposal. If the media is held on hard drives, magnetic media, or thumb drives, it must eventually be sanitized. *Sanitization* is the process of clearing all identified content, such that no data remnants can be recovered. When sanitization is performed, none of the original information can be recovered. Some of the methods used for sanitization include drive wiping, zeroization, degaussing, and physical destruction:

▶ *Drive wiping* is the act of overwriting all information on the drive. It allows the drive to be reused.

▶ *Zeroization* involves overwriting the data with zeros. Zeroization is defined as a standard in ANSI X9.17.

▶ *Degaussing* is used to permanently destroy the contents of the hard drive or magnetic media. Degaussing works by means of a powerful magnet that uses its field strength to penetrate the media and polarize the magnetic particles on the tape or hard disk platters. After media has been degaussed, it cannot be reused.

▶ *Physical destruction* may be required to sanitize newer solid-state drives.

Telecommunication Controls

Guglielmo Marconi probably had no idea that his contributions to the field of radio would lead to all the telecommunications systems available today. Even though a CISSP is not going to be tasked with building the first ship-to-shore radio system like Marconi did, he/she must be aware of current telecommunication systems and understand their usage and potential vulnerabilities. These systems include items such as cloud computing, email systems, facsimile (fax) machines, public branch exchanges (PBXs), whitelisting, sandboxing, and anti-malware.

Cloud Computing

Cloud computing uses Internet-based systems to perform on-demand computing. Users only have to pay for the services and computing resources they require. They can increase usage when more computing resources are needed or reduce usage when the services are not needed. Some of the most common types of cloud computing are:

▶ Monitoring as a Service (MaaS)—Allows IT and other organizations to remotely monitor and manage networks, applications, and services.

▶ Communication as a Service (CaaS)—The service provider seamlessly integrates multiple communication devices or channels for voice, video, IM, and email as a single solution.

▶ Infrastructure as a Service (IaaS)—Enables organizations to rent storage and computing resources, such as servers, networking technology storage, and data center space.

▶ Platform as a Service (PaaS)—Provides access to platforms that let organizations develop, test, and deploy applications. It is a cloud computing service delivery model that delivers a set of software. In PaaS, the user's application resides entirely on the cloud from its development to delivery.

▶ Software as a Service (SaaS)—Allows the use of applications running on the service provider's environment. It is a cloud service model that delivers prebuilt applications over the Internet on an on-demand basis. If an organization wants to use the software for a short duration, SaaS delivers a single application to multiple customers within the organization using a multi-tenant architecture.

Cloud computing models generally fall into one of the categories shown here:

▶ Private—All of the cloud and its components are managed by a single organization.

▶ Community—Cloud components are shared by multiple organizations and managed by one of them, or by a third party.

▶ Public—Open for any organization or user to use, public in nature, and managed by third-party providers.

▶ Hybrid—This service model has components of more than one of the private, community, and public service models.

> **ExamAlert**
>
> For the exam you will need to know not just cloud computing types like SaaS and MaaS but also their various categories.

Email

Email provides individuals the ability to communicate electronically through the Internet or a data communications network. Email is the most used Internet application. Just take a look around the office and see how many people use a BlackBerry or another device that provides email services. Email is not a new Internet technology and, as such, it comes with some security concerns. Email was designed in a different era and, by default, sends information via cleartext. Anyone able to sniff such traffic can read it. Email can be easily spoofed so that the true identity of the sender is masked. Email is also a major conduit for spam, phishing, and viruses.

Email functions by means of several underlying services, which can include the following:

▶ **SMTP**—Used to send mail and to relay mail to other SMTP mail servers. SMTP uses TCP port 25. Messages sent through SMTP have two parts: an address header and message text. All types of computers can exchange messages with SMTP.

▶ **POP**—Currently at version 3. POP3 is the one of the protocols that can be used to retrieve messages from a mail server. POP3 performs authentication in cleartext on TCP port 110. An alternative to POP3 is IMAP.

▶ **IMAP**—Used as a replacement for POP, operates on TCP port 143, and is designed to retrieve messages from an SMTP server. IMAP4 is the current version and offers several advantages over POP. IMAP has the capability to work with email remotely. Many of today's email users might need to access email from different locations and devices, such as PDAs, laptops, and desktops. IMAP provides this functionality so that multiple clients can access the email server and leave the email there until it's deleted.

> **Tip**
>
> An updated version of POP that provides authentication is known as Authenticated Post Office Protocol (APOP).

Basic email operation consists of the SMTP service being used to send messages to the email server. To retrieve email, the client application, such as Outlook, might use POP or IMAP, as seen in Figure 10.1.

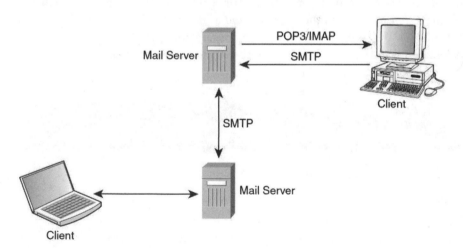

FIGURE 10.1 **Email configuration.**

In sum, anyone who uses email needs to be aware of the security risks. Spam is an ongoing problem, and techniques like graylisting can be used to deal with it. The sending of sensitive information by cleartext email is another area of concern. If an organization has policies that allow email to be used for sensitive information, encryption should be mandatory. This will require an evaluation of the needs of the business. Several solutions exist to meet this need.

One is Pretty Good Privacy (PGP). Other options include link encryption or secure email standards like Secure Multipurpose Internet Mail Extensions (S/MIME) or Privacy Enhanced Mail (PEM).

Whitelisting, Blacklisting, and Graylisting

Other good technical controls are whitelisting, blacklisting, and graylisting. A whitelist is used to determine what is allowed access or can be performed. Anything that is not included on the whitelist is prohibited.

Blacklists operate in the opposite way. Blacklisting consists of banning or denying. As a real-world example, just about anyone is allowed in a casino to gamble. However, some individuals may be specifically prohibited (this happened to actor Ben Affleck in 2014: nypost.com/2014/05/02/ben-affleck-banned-for-life-from-vegas-casino/). In the network sense, the prohibition might be against a list of users, access, or resources. The problem with blacklisting is that as the list continues to grow it requires more ongoing maintenance and oversight.

Finally, there are graylists. Graylists are used by many email administrators as a technique to deal with spam. When a graylist is implemented it will reject any email sender that is unknown. If the mail is from a legitimate email server it will be retransmitted after a period of time. This moves the graylisted email off the graylist and on to the whitelist, and at that time places the email in the inbox of the receiving account. The email is not necessarily blacklisted or deleted until the user evaluates the decision and makes a human decision to reject or accept the sender.

> **ExamAlert**
>
> Exam candidates should understand blacklists, graylists, and whitelists.

Fax

Fax machines can present some security problems if they are being used to transmit sensitive information. These vulnerabilities reside throughout the faxing process and include the following:

▶ When the user feeds the document into the fax machine for transmission, wrongdoers have the opportunity to intercept and decode the information while in transit.

▶ When the document arrives at its destination, it is typically printed and deposited into a fax tray. Anyone can retrieve the printed document and review its contents.

▶ Many fax machine use ribbons. Anyone with access to the trash can retrieve the ribbons and use them as virtual carbon copies of the original documents.

▶ Fax machines can also allow unauthorized connections using dial-up. As an example, a contractor could attempt to use a fax phone port to access personal accounts or bypass firewalls.

Fax systems can be secured by one or more of the following techniques:

▶ **Fax servers**—Can send and receive faxes and then hold the fax in electronic memory. At the recipient's request, the fax can be forwarded to the recipient's email account or can be printed.

▶ **Fax encryption**—Provides fax machines the capability to encrypt communications. Fax encryption requires that both the transmitting and receiving device support a common protocol.

▶ **Fax activity logs**—Implement activity logs and review exception reports to detect any anomalies.

Caution

Although fax servers have solved many security problems, they have their own challenges. Many use hard drives where companies store a large amount of commonly used administrative documents and forms. Others allow HTTP and/or FTP access to the print queue, where someone can capture the files. These issues must be addressed before effective security can be achieved.

PBX

PBX systems are used by private companies and permit users to connect to a public switched telephone network (PSTN). The PBX can be used to assign extensions, provide voice mail, and special services for internal users and customers. The issue with PBXs is that, like other organizational resources, a PBX can be a potential target. Some PBX issues are:

▶ PBX without the default password changed

▶ PBX used by attackers to call in to public address lines and make announcements that might be inappropriate

▶ PBX allowing callers to call out and make free long distance phone calls that are charged to the company

PBX hacking is not as prevalent as in the past, but a PBX can still pose a threat to operational security. If criminals can crack the security of the PBX system, it's possible for them to sell the victim's phone time. These charges are usually discovered after 30 to 60 days, but this window of opportunity allows the criminal to run up thousands of dollars in phone charges. Any attack will require time, money, and effort to repair. Individuals that target PBX and phone systems are known as *phreakers*.

FEMA Learns About Phreakers

Although it is easy to think of PBX hacking as something of the past, the United States Federal Emergency Management Administration (FEMA) found out otherwise in August of 2008.

According to ABC News, phone phreakers broke into the FEMA PBX system on the weekend of August 16, 2008 and used the phone system to place more than $12,000 worth of calls in two days.

Most of the calls were only a few minutes long and were placed to locations such as India, Yemen, and Afghanistan. It is believed that the attackers gained access through an unsecured PBX access line. More charges were prevented when the volume of calls flagged the attention of the telecommunications provider.

Phreakers

Long before modern-day hacking existed, phreakers were practicing their trade. *Phreaking* is the art of hacking phone systems. Although this might sound like a rather complicated affair, back in the early 1970s it was discovered that free phone calls could be made by playing a 2600Hz tone into a phone. The 2600Hz tone allowed the phreaker to bypass the normal billing process. The first device tailored to this purpose was known as a *blue box*. Some of the other box devices used by phreakers were:

▶ **Red box**—Duplicates tones of coins being dropped into pay phone.

▶ **Gold box**—Connects to two lines so that one is called into, while the other is used for outbound communication. Such devices were designed to prevent line tracing.

▶ **Orange box**—Spoofs caller ID information on the called party's phone.

Most of these boxes were invented in the 1970s and used until the early 1990s. Most won't work on modern telephone systems. New telephone system networks use out-of-band (OOB) signaling, in which one channel is used for the voice conversation and a separate channel is used for signaling. With OOB, it is no longer possible to just play tones into the mouthpiece to signal equipment within the network. Although these tools are primarily historical, phreakers can still carry out activities like caller ID spoofing, or might even target VoIP phone systems for DoS attacks or sniffing attacks.

Two other techniques attackers can use are *slamming* and *cramming*; both terms are used with telephony. Slamming refers to switching users' long-distance phone carriers without their knowledge. Cramming relates to unauthorized phone charges. One cramming technique is to send a fake SMS message that, when clicked on, authorizes the attacker to bill the victim for a small amount each month. Sometimes these charges can seem incidental, but multiplied by hundreds or thousands of users can add up to a great deal of money.

Anti-malware

Malware is a problem that computer users are faced with on a daily basis. Training users in safe computing practices is a good start, but anti-malware tools are still needed to protect the organization's computers. When you find suspected malware there are generally two ways to examine it: static analysis and active analysis. While static analysis requires you to decompile or disassemble the code, active analysis requires the suspected malware to be executed. Because executing malware on a live, production environment can be dangerous, it is typically done on a stand-alone system or virtual machine, referred to as a sandbox. The sandbox allows you to safely view or execute the suspected malware or any untrusted code while keeping it contained. Keep in mind that even when malware is run in a sandbox, there is always some possibility that it may escape and infect other systems.

Along with testing malware you will want to try and prevent malware from ever executing on your systems. This is where anti-malware software comes in. Anti-malware software should be installed on servers, workstations, and even portable devices. It can use one or more techniques to check files and applications for viruses and other types of common malware. These techniques include:

▶ **Signature scanning**—In a similar fashion to IDS pattern-matching systems, signature scanning looks at the beginning and end of executable files for known virus signatures. Virus creators attempt to circumvent the signature scanning process by making viruses polymorphic.

▶ **Heuristic scanning**—Heuristic scanning examines computer files for irregular or unusual instructions. As an example, think of your word processing program. It probably creates, opens, and updates text files.

If the word processor attempts to format the C drive, this is something that a heuristics scanner would quickly identify as unusual activity for a word processor. In reality, antivirus vendors must strike a balance with heuristic scanning because they do not want to produce too many false positives or false negatives. Many antivirus vendors use a scoring technique that evaluates many types of behaviors. Only when the score exceeds a threshold (also called a clipping level) will the antivirus program actually flag an alert.

▶ **Integrity checking**—Integrity checkers work by building a database of checksums or hashed values. Periodically, new scans are performed and the results are compared to the stored results. Although it is not always effective for data files, this technique is useful for executables because their contents rarely change. For example, the MD5sum of the Linux bootable OS Kali Linux 5.0 is a66bf35409f4458ee7f35a77891951eb. Any change to the Kali.iso would change this hashed value, which would easily be detected by an integrity checker.

▶ **Activity blockers**—An activity blocker intercepts a virus when it starts to execute and blocks it from infecting other programs or data. Activity blockers are usually designed to start at boot up and continue until the computer shuts down.

Honeypots and Honeynets

A honeypot can be used to trap, jail, or even examine a hackers' activities. A honeypot is really nothing more than a fake system. A honeynet is an entire network of fake systems. One of the primary uses of a honeypot is to deflect an attack. The idea is that the hacker is drawn to the honeypot while the real system avoids attack.

Honeypots can also be used to gather research about hackers' activities. You can see a good example of this at old.honeynet.org/papers/forensics/index. html. There is more information on honeypots in Chapter 9.

Caution

Honeypots are used for diversion and analysis of an attacker's tactics, tools, and methods. Honeypots are simply fake systems or networks. A key issue is to avoid entrapment because entrapment can itself be illegal. Warning banners can help avoid claims of entrapment by clearly noting that those who use or abuse the system will be monitored and potentially prosecuted.

Patch Management

Patch management is important in helping to identify problems and getting them updated in an expedient manner to reduce overall risk of a system compromise. Patch management is key to keeping applications and operating systems secure. The organization should have a well developed patch management testing and deployment system in place. The most recent security patches should be tested and then installed on host systems as soon as possible. The only exception is when an immediate installation would interfere with business requirements.

Before a patch can be tested and deployed it must first be verified. Typical forms of verification include digital signatures, digital certificates, or some form of checksum and/or integrity verification. This is a critical step that must be performed before testing and deployment to make sure that it has not been maliciously or accidentally altered. Once testing is complete deployment can begin. Change management protocols should be followed throughout this process.

System Resilience, Fault Tolerance, and Recovery Controls

Plan to fail because things will surely go wrong; it is just a matter of when. Therefore, understanding how to react and recover from errors and failures is an important part of operational security.

Good operational security practices require security planners to perform contingency planning. Contingency planning requires that you develop plans and procedures that can be implemented when things go wrong. Although covered in detail in Chapter 12, "Business Continuity Planning," this subject is mentioned here because it is closely tied to operations security. Contingency planning should occur after you've identified operational risks and performed a risk analysis to determine the extent of the impact of the possible adverse events. Backup, fault tolerance, and recovery controls are discussed in the sections that follow.

Backups

Three types of backup methods exist: full, incremental, and differential. The method your organization chooses depends on several factors:

▶ How much data needs to be backed up?

▶ How often should the backup occur?

▶ Where will the backups be stored?

▶ How much time do you have to perform each backup?

Each backup method has benefits and drawbacks. Full backups are the most comprehensive, but take the longest time to create. So, even though it might seem best to do a full backup every day, it might not be possible due to the time and expense.

> **Tip**
>
> Two basic methods can be used to back up data: automated and on-demand. Automated backups are scheduled to occur at a predetermined time. On-demand backups can be scheduled at any time.

Full Backups

During a full backup, all data is backed up, and no files are skipped or bypassed; you simply designate which server to back up. A full backup takes the longest to perform and the least time to restore because only one backup dataset is required.

Differential Backups

Using differential backup, a full backup is typically done once a week and a differential backup, which backs up all files that have changed since the last full backup, is done more frequently, typically daily. If you need to restore, you need the last full backup and the most recent differential backup.

Differential backups make use of files' *archive bit*. The archive bit indicates that the file is ready for archiving, or backup. A full backup clears the archive bit for each backed up file. Then if anyone makes changes to one of these files, its archive bit is toggled on. During a differential backup, all the files that have the archive bit on are backed up, but the archive bit is not cleared until the next full backup. Because more files will likely be modified during the week, the differential backup time will increase each day until another full backup is performed; still, this method takes less time than a daily full backup. The value of a differential backup is that only two backup datasets are required; the full and the differential.

Incremental Backups

With this backup strategy, a full backup is scheduled for once a week (typically) and only files that have changed since the previous full backup *or* previous incremental backup are backed up more frequently (usually daily).

Unlike a differential backup, in an incremental backup the archive bit is cleared on backed up files; therefore, incremental backups back up only changes made since the last incremental backup. This is the fastest backup option, but it takes the longest to restore, because the full backup must be restored, then all the incremental backups, in order.

Tape Rotation Schemes

Tapes and other media used for backup will eventually fail. It is important to periodically test backup media to verify its functionality. Some tape rotation methods include Tower of Hanoi and grandfather-father-son (GFS). This scheme performs a full backup once a week, known as the father. The daily backups, which can be differential or incremental, are known as the son. The last full backup of the month is retained for a year and is known as the grandfather.

Fault Tolerance

Fault tolerance requires a redundant system so that in the event of a failure, a backup system can take its place. Some common devices used for fault tolerance include tape and hard drives. Tape-based systems are an example of a *sequential access storage device* (SASD). Should you need information from a portion of the tape, the tape drive must be traversed to the required position for the information to be accessed. Hard drives are an example of a *direct access storage device* (DASD). The advantage of a DASD is that information can be accessed much more quickly. One option that can be used to speed up the sequential process when large amounts of data need to be backed up is a *redundant array of independent tapes* (RAIT). RAIT is efficient for instances where large numbers of write operations are needed for massive amounts of data. RAIT stripes the data across multiple tapes much like a RAID array and can function with or without parity.

A technology similar to RAIT is *massive array of inactive hard drives* (MAID). This technology uses hard drives instead of tape drives and could be useful in situations where the hard drives are inactive for the majority of time and powered up only when the transfer of data is needed. Although the controller stays active, the drives are inactive most of the time. Because the drives are inactive, power consumption is reduced and life expectancy is increased.

Storing and managing all this data can become a massive task for many organizations. Companies might have tape drives, MAID, RAID, optical jukeboxes, and other storage solutions to manage. To control all these systems, many companies now use *storage area networks* (SANs). Although SANs are not common in small companies, large organizations with massive amounts of data can use them to provide redundancy, fault tolerance, and backups. The beauty of the system is that the end user does not have to know the location of the information—the user must only make the request for the data and the SAN will retrieve and recover it.

It is not just data that can be made fault tolerant. Computer systems can also benefit. Redundant servers can be used and the computing process can be distributed to utilize the power of many computers. Two such concepts are:

▶ **Clustering**—A means of grouping computers and moving to a greater level of usability over redundant servers. Whereas a redundant server waits until it's needed, a clustered server is actively participating in responding to the server's load. Should one of the clustered servers fail, the remaining servers can pick up the slack. An example of a clustered system can be seen at www.beowulf.org.

> **Note**
>
> When is a cluster not a cluster? When it is referred to as a *server farm*. A server farm can be used as a cluster of computers. Such clusters can be used for complex tasks or in instances where supercomputers might have been used in the past.

▶ **Distributed computing**—This technique is similar to clustering except there is no central control. *Distributed computing*, also known as *grid computing*, can be used for processes that require massive amounts of computer power. Because grid computing is not under a centralized control, processes that require high security should not be considered. Distributed computing also differs from clustering in that distributed computers can add or remove themselves as they please.

> **Note**
>
> An example of distributed computing can be seen in projects such as www.distributed.net. This project asks that users download a small application that makes use of their computers' spare processing power. This project was able to crack the RC4 encryption algorithm by brute force in July, 2002, after 1,757 days.

RAID

Redundant Array of Inexpensive Disks (RAID) is one critical piece. RAID offers capacity benefits and can be used for fault tolerance and for performance improvements. Another important part of contingency planning, backup, and recovery is some type of data backup system. All hard drives and data storage systems fail. It's not a matter of if, but when. Although there are many types of RAID, Table 10.3 lists and describes the nine most common types.

TABLE 10.3 **RAID Levels and Services**

Level	Title	Description
Level 0	Striped Disk without Fault Tolerance	Provides data striping but no fault tolerance. If one drive fails, all data in the array is lost.
Level 1	Mirroring and Duplexing	Provides disk mirroring. Level 1 provides twice the read transaction rate of single disks and the same write transaction rate as single disks.
Level 2	Error-Correcting	Stripes data at the bit level rather than the block level. This is rarely used.
Level 3	Bit-Interleaved Parity	Offers byte-level striping with a dedicated parity disk.
Level 4	Dedicated Parity Drive	Provides block-level striping. If a data disk fails, the parity data is used to create a replacement disk.
Level 5	Block Interleaved Distributed Parity	Provides data striping at the byte level, good performance, and good fault tolerance. It is also one of the most popular.
Level 6	Independent Data Disks with Double Parity	Provides block-level striping with parity across all disks.
Level 10	A Stripe of Mirrors	Creates mirrors and a RAID 0 stripe. This is not one of the original RAID levels. Sometimes referred to as 0+1.
Level 15	Mirrors and Parity	Creates mirrors RAID 1 and RAID 5 distributed parity. This is not one of the original RAID levels.

It is worth mentioning that RAID Level 0 is for performance only, not for redundancy. The most expensive RAID solution to implement is RAID Level 1 because all the data on disk A is mirrored to disk B. Mirroring also has another disadvantage; if data on disk A is corrupted, data on disk B will also become corrupted. The most common form of RAID is RAID 5. What makes RAID 5 striping so useful is that it offers a balance of performance and usability. RAID 5 stripes both data and parity information across three or more drives, whereas RAID 3 uses a dedicated parity drive.

Striping the data and parity across all drives removes the drive stress that the dedicated parity drive inflicts. Fault tolerance is provided by ensuring that, should any one drive die, the other drives maintain adequate information to allow for continued operation and eventual rebuilding of the failed drive (once replaced).

When is RAID not RAID? When it is *Just a Bunch of Disks* (JBOD). JBOD is somewhat like a poor man's RAID, but it is really not RAID at all. JBOD can use existing hard drives of various sizes. These are combined together into one massive logical disk. There is no fault tolerance and no increase in speed. The only benefit of JBOD is that you can use existing disks and if one drive fails, you lose the data on only that drive. Both of these advantages are minimal, so don't expect to see too many organizations actually use this technique. To better understand how these technologies map to each other, take a moment to review Figure 10.2.

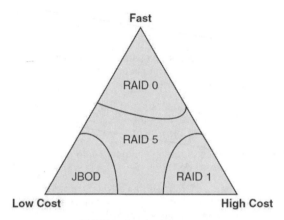

FIGURE 10.2   **RAID technologies.**

ExamAlert

Fault tolerance and RAID are important controls. For the exam, you should be able to define RAID and describe specific levels and each level's attributes. For example, RAID 1 has the highest cost per byte; RAID 5 is the most widely used.

Recovery Controls

Recovery controls are those applied after the fact. They are administrative in nature and are useful for contingency planning and disaster recovery. Most of us know *contingency planning*. As an example, while writing this book, I had a hard drive failure. Although I was lucky to have backed up the data, I still needed to finish the chapter and get it emailed by the deadline. My contingency plan was to use my laptop until I could get the desktop system back up and running. Even though most major organizations have much more detailed contingency plans than this, it is important to have some plan in place. The process of *recovery* is to have a mechanism to restore lost services after a disruptive event. Some of the issues that need to be considered to make sure recovery goes smoothly include elimination of single points of failure, mean time between failures (MTBF), and mean time to repair (MTTR).

A single point of failure is never a good thing. Single points of failure can be found everywhere from power supplies, hard drives, servers, telecommunication lines, firewalls, and even facility power. As an example, to keep power flowing, a company might use power leads from two substations and also have a backup generator on site. The idea is to try to avoid any single point of failure.

MTBF is a product's average time until failure. Engineers will often discuss MTBF in terms of the bathtub curve (see Figure 10.3). This graphic example of average time before failure looks at the average rate of failure of a population of devices. Whereas some devices will fail early, most will last until the end of service.

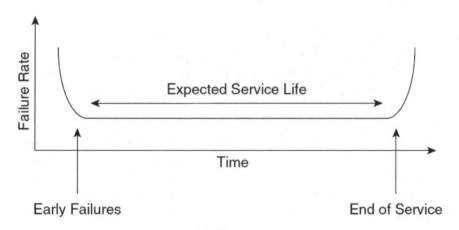

FIGURE 10.3 **MTBF and the bathtub curve.**

Devices that survive until their end of life will start to fail at an increasing rate as they wear out. Good operational control practices dictate that companies should have some idea how long a device is calculated to last. This helps the organization plan for replacement before outages occur and services are disrupted.

For those items that fail before the expected end of service, a second important variable is MTTR. The MTTR is the amount of time it will take to get the item repaired. As an example, a product that can be repaired in-house will typically have a much lower MTTR than a product that needs to be shipped back to its manufacturer in China. One way companies deal with such unknowns is to use service-level agreements (SLAs).

Monitoring and Auditing Controls

Computer resources are a limited commodity provided by the company to help meet its overall goals. Although many employees would never dream of placing all their long-distance phone calls on a company phone, some of those same individuals have no problem using computer resources for their own personal use. Consider these statistics from Personal Computer World: according to information on its site, one-third of time spent online at work is not work-related, and more than 75% of streaming radio downloads occur between 5 a.m. and 5 p.m.

Accountability must be maintained for network access, software usage, and data access. In a high-security environment, the level of accountability should be substantial, and users should be held responsible by logging and auditing their activities.

Good practice dictates that audit logs be transmitted to a remote centralized site. Centralized logging makes it easier for the person assigned the auditing task to review the data. Exporting the logs to a remote site also makes it harder for hackers to erase or cover their activity. If there is a downside to all this logging, it is that all the information must be recorded and reviewed. A balance must be found between collecting audit data and maintaining a manageable log size. Reviewing it can be expedited by using *audit reduction and correlation tools*, such as SIEM. These tools parse the data and eliminate unneeded information. Another useful tool is a variance detection tool. These tools look for trends that fall outside the realm of normal activity. As an example, if an employee normally enters the building around 7 a.m. and leaves about 4 p.m. but is seen entering at 3 a.m., a variance detection tool would detect this abnormality.

Auditing and monitoring require *accountability* because if you don't have accountability, you cannot perform an effective audit. True security relies on the capability to verify that individual users perform specific actions. Without the capability to hold individuals accountable, organizations can't enforce security policies. Some of the primary ways to establish accountability are as follows:

▶ Auditing user activity

▶ Monitoring application controls

▶ Security information and event management

▶ Emanations

▶ Network access control

▶ Tracking the movement of individuals throughout the organization's physical premises

Auditing User Activity

Auditing produces audit trails. These trails can be used to re-create events and verify whether security policies have been violated. The biggest disadvantage of the audit process is that it is detective in nature and that audit trails are usually examined after an event. Some might think of audit trails only as something that corresponds to logical access, but auditing can also be applied to physical access. Audit tools can be used to monitor who entered a facility and what time certain areas were accessed. The security professional has plenty of tools available that can help isolate activities of individual users.

Many organizations monitor network traffic to look for suspicious activity and anomalies. Some monitoring tools enable administrators to examine just packet headers, whereas others can capture all network traffic. Snort, Wireshark, and TCPdump are several such tools. Regardless of the tools used to capture and analyze traffic, administrators need to make sure that policies are in place detailing how such uncovered activities will be handled. Warning banners and AUPs go a long way in making sure that users are adequately informed of what to expect when using company resources.

ExamAlert

Exam candidates should understand the importance of monitoring employees and that tools that examine activity are detective in nature.

Tip

A *warning banner* is the verbiage a user sees at the point of entry into a system. Its purpose is to identify the expectations that users accessing those systems will be subjected to. The banners also aid in any attempt to prosecute those who violate the AUPs. A sample AUP is shown here:

WARNING: Unauthorized access to this system is forbidden and will be prosecuted by law. By accessing this system, you agree that your actions may be monitored if unauthorized use is suspected.

Monitoring Application Transactions

Good security is about more than people. A big part of a security professional's day is monitoring controls to ensure that people are working according to policy. With so much of today's computing activity occurring on servers that are connected to the Internet, these systems must be monitored.

In the modern world it is very possible that the output of one system might be the input of another. In such situations, data must be checked to verify the information from both the sending and receiving applications. Input controls can be automated or manual. Consider the last time you were at your local discount store. If there was an item that did not ring up as the correct price, you might have had to wait for the clerk to signal a supervisor to correct the error. Before the correction could occur, the supervisor had to enter a second-level password to authorize the price correction. This is an example of a *manual authorization input control*.

Process controls are another item that should be monitored. Process controls should be designed to detect problems and initiate corrective action. If procedures are in place to override these controls, their use should be logged and periodically reviewed. Individuals who have the ability to override these controls should not be the same ones responsible for reviewing the log; this is an example of separation of duties.

Output controls are designed to provide assurance of the results of data that has completed processing. Output controls should be designed to ensure that processing executed correctly and the data is distributed and archived in a secure manner. Sensitive data should have sufficient controls to monitor access and usage. These controls will vary, depending on whether the information is centrally stored or distributed to end-user workstations.

All input, processed, and output data should be monitored. Inputs must be validated. Consider the example of a dishonest individual browsing an e-commerce website and entering a quantity of −1 for an expensive item worth $2,450.99. Hopefully, the application has been written in such a way as to not accept a negative quantity for any items advertised. Otherwise, the merchant could end up crediting money back to the dishonest customer. Figure 10.4 shows an example of an application that lacks this control.

The Solution Firm - Demo Application Entry Form			
DESCRIPTION	QTY	Unit Price	Total Price
SNR142 1 Carat Diamond Ring Color: Gold Select Ring Size Review Item	1	($2450.99)	($2450.99)
Total			($2450.99)
Coupon [ ] View coupon status		0.00	($2450.99)
Shipping [UPS Ground ▼] Calculate my shipping			
Gift Certificate [ ] View gift certificate status			
Grand Total			$-2450.99
To remove an item, change the Qty to Zero, then click "Recalculate"			
[Continue Shopping] [Recalculate] [Clear Cart] [Check Out Now (Step 1 of 3)]			

FIGURE 10.4   **Shopping cart.**

> **Note**
>
> One good example of an output control can be seen in many modern printer configurations. For example, some employee evaluation reviews might be configured so that they can be printed only to the supervisor's printer. Another example can be seen in products such as Adobe's Acrobat, which can limit printing of PDFs or embed password controls to limit who can open or edit PDFs.

Security Information and Event Management (SIEM)

Security information and event management (SIEM) is a relatively new technology that seeks to collect and analyze auditable events. SIEM allows for centralized logging and log analysis, and can work with a variety of log data, such as Netflow, Sflow, Jflow, and syslog. Most SIEM products support controls for confidentiality, integrity, and availability of log data. While SIEM can be used to spot attacks and security incidents, it can also be used for the day-to-day operational concerns of a network. SIEM can be used to detect misconfigured systems, unresponsive servers, malfunctioning controls, and failed applications. SIEM can also handle the storage of log data by disregarding data fields that are not significant to computer security, thereby reducing network bandwidth and data storage. Most SIEM products support two ways of collecting logs from log generators:

▶ **Agentless**—The SIEM server receives data from the hosts without needing to have any special software (agents) installed on those hosts.

▶ **Agent Based**—An agent program is installed on the hosts and may be used to generic log input such as Syslog and SNMP.

Two Great Tools Combined as One

SIEM is the combination of the two separate services Security Information Management (SIM) and Security Event Management (SEM). SIM is used to process and handle the long-term storage of audit and event data, whereas SEM is used for real-time reporting of events. Combining these two technologies provides users with the ability to alert, capture, aggregate, and review log information from many different systems and sources. Vendors that offer SIEM tools include Network Intelligence, e-Security, ArcSight, and others.

Although technologies such as SIEM are a great addition to the security professional's toolkit, keep in mind that you should strive for defense in depth. For example, combining an IDS/IPS with SIEM provides much greater protection than either technology by itself.

Network Access Control

IDS and IDP can be seen as just the start of access control and security. The next step in this area is *Network Access Control* (NAC). NAC has grown out of the trusted computer movement and has the goal of unified security. NAC offers administrators a way to verify that devices meet certain health standards before allowing them to connect to the network. Laptops, desktop computers, or any device that doesn't comply with predefined requirements can be prevented from joining the network or can even be relegated to a controlled network where access is restricted until the device is brought up to the required security standards. Currently, there are several different incarnations of NAC available, which include the following:

▶ **Infrastructure-based NAC**—Requires an organization to upgrade its hardware and/or operating systems.

▶ **Endpoint-based NAC**—Requires the installation of software agents on each network client. These devices are then managed by a centralized management console.

▶ **Hardware-based NAC**—Requires the installation of a network appliance. The appliance monitors for specific behavior and can limit device connectivity should noncompliant activity be detected.

Keystroke Monitoring

Keystroke monitoring can be accomplished with hardware or software devices and is used to monitor activity. These devices can be used for both legal and illegal activity. As a compliance tool, keystroke monitoring allows management to monitor a user's activity and verify compliance. The primary issue of concern is the user's expectation of privacy. Policies and procedures should be in place to inform the user that such technologies can be used to monitor compliance. A sample AUP is shown here:

> This acceptable use policy defines the boundaries of the acceptable use of this organization's systems and resources. Access to any company system or resources is a privilege that may be wholly or partially restricted without prior notice and without consent of the user. In cases of suspected violations or during the process of periodic review, employees can have activities monitored. Monitoring may involve a complete keystroke log of an entire session or sessions as needed to vary compliance with company polices and usage agreements.

Unfortunately, key logging is not just for the good guys. Hackers can use the same tools to monitor and record an individual's activities. Although an outsider to a company might have some trouble getting one of these devices installed, an insider is in a prime position to plant a keystroke logger. Keystroke loggers come in two basic types:

▶ **Hardware keystroke loggers** are usually installed while users are away from their desks and are completely undetectable, except for their physical presence. Just take a moment to consider when you last looked at the back of your computer. Even if you see it, a hardware keystroke logger can be overlooked because it resembles a dongle or extension. These devices are even available in wireless versions that can communicate via 802.11b/g and Bluetooth, or that can be built into the keyboard. You can see one example of a Bluetooth keystroke logger at www.wirelesskeylogger.com/products.php.

▶ **Software keystroke loggers** sit between the operating system and the keyboard. Most of these software programs are simple, but some are more complex and can even email the logged keystrokes back to a preconfigured address. What they all have in common is that they operate in stealth mode and can grab all the text, mouse clicks, and even all the URLs that a user enters.

Keystroke Logging and the Law

The United States Department of Justice has noted that administrators should protect themselves by giving notice to users if keystroke monitoring has been implemented. This notification can be by means of company policy or a warning banner. Administrators who fail to implement operational policies that specify how keystroke monitoring will be used could be subjected to criminal and civil liabilities.

Emanation Security

The United States government was concerned enough about the possibility of emanations that the Department of Defense started a program to study it. Research actually began in the 1950s with the result being TEMPEST technology. The fear was that attackers might try to sniff the stray electrical signals that emanate from electronic devices. Devices that have been built to TEMPEST standards, such as cathode ray tube (CRT) monitors, have had TEMPEST-grade copper mesh, known as a *Faraday cage*, embedded in the case to prevent signal leakage. This costly technology is found only in very high-security environments.

TEMPEST is now considered somewhat dated; newer technologies such as white noise and control zones are now used to control emanation security. White noise uses special devices that send out a stream of frequencies that make it impossible for an attacker to distinguish the real information. *Control zones* are facilities, walls, floors, and ceilings designed to block electrical signals from leaving the zone. Eavesdropping on the contents of a CRT by emanation leakage is referred to as *Van Eck phreaking*.

Controlling Physical Access

No monitoring plan is complete without implementing controls that monitor physical access. Some common facility access controls include:

▶ Watching CCTV to monitor who enters or leaves the facility and correlating these logs with logical access and for the access control polices for systems and faculties for the company security policy.

▶ Installing card readers or biometric sensors on server room doors to maintain a log of who accesses the area.

▶ Mounting alarm sensors on doors and windows to detect possible security breaches.

▶ Using mantraps and gates to control traffic and log entry to secured areas. Remember that mantraps are double doors used to control the flow of employees and block unauthorized individuals.

ExamAlert

Make sure you know the difference between audit and accountability for the exam. Audit controls are detective controls, which are utilized after the fact, and are usually implemented to detect fraud or other illegal activities. Accountability is the capability to track actions, transactions, changes, and resource usage to a specific user within the system. This is accomplished in part by having unique identification for each user, using strong authentication mechanisms and logging events.

Intrusion Detection Systems

Intrusion detection systems play a critical role in the protection of the IT infrastructure. *Intrusion detection* involves monitoring network traffic, detecting attempts to gain unauthorized access to a system or resource, and notifying the appropriate individuals so that counteractions can be taken. An IDS is designed to function as an access control monitor. Intrusion detection is a relativity new technology and was really born in the 1980s when James Anderson put forth the concept in a paper titled "Computer Security Threat Monitoring and Surveillance."

An IDS can be configured to scan for attacks, track a hacker's movements, alert an administrator to ongoing attacks, and highlight possible vulnerabilities that need to be addressed. The key to what type of activity the IDS will detect is dependent on where the intrusion sensors are placed. This requires some consideration because, after all, a sensor in the DMZ will work well at detecting misuse there but will prove useless against attackers inside the network. Even when you have determined where to place sensors, they still require specific tuning. Without specific tuning, the sensor will generate alerts for all traffic that matches some given criteria, regardless of whether the traffic is indeed something that should generate an alert. An IDS must be trained to look for suspicious activity. That is why I typically tell people that an IDS is like a 3-year-old. They require constant care and nurturing, and don't do well if left alone.

> **Note**
>
> Although the exam will examine these systems in a very basic way, modern systems are a mix of intrusion detection and intrusion prevention, so they are referred to as intrusion detection and prevention (IDP) systems. IDP systems are designed to identify potential incidents, log information, attempt to stop the event, and report the event. Many organizations even use IDP systems for activities such as identifying problems with security policies, documenting threats, and deterring malicious activity that violates security policies. NIST 800-94 is a good resource to learn more (csrc.nist.gov/publications/nistpubs/800-94/SP800-94.pdf).

A huge problem with an IDS is that it is an after-the-fact device—the attack has already taken place. Other problems with IDS are false positives and false negatives. *False positives* refer to when the IDS has triggered an alarm for normal traffic. For example, if you go to your local mall parking lot, you're likely to hear some car alarms going off that are experiencing false positives. False positives are a big problem because they desensitize the administrator. *False negatives* are even worse. A false negative occurs when a real attack occurs but the IDS does not pick it up.

> **ExamAlert**
>
> A false negative is the worst type of event because it means an attack occurred, but the IDS failed to detect it.

IDS systems can be divided into two basic types: *network-based intrusion detection systems* (NIDS) and *host-based intrusion detection systems* (HIDS).

▶ **Network based (NIDS)**—These devices attach to the LAN and sniff for traffic that has been flagged to be anomalous.

▶ **Host based (HIDS)**—This form of IDS resides on the host device and examines only the traffic going to or coming from the host computer.

Network-Based Intrusion Detection Systems

Much like a protocol analyzer operating in promiscuous mode, NIDSs capture and analyze network traffic. These devices diligently inspect each packet as it passes by. When they detect suspect traffic, the action taken depends on the particular NIDS. Alarms could be triggered, sessions could be reset, or traffic could be blocked. Among their advantages are that they are unobtrusive, they have the capability to monitor the entire network, and they provide an extra layer of defense between the firewall and the host. Their disadvantages include the fact that attackers can send high volumes of traffic to attempt to overload them, they cannot decrypt or analyze encrypted traffic, and they can be vulnerable to attacks. (Sometimes attackers will send low levels of traffic to avoid tripping the IDS threshold alarms.) Tools like NMAP have this capability built-in. Things to remember about NIDS include the following:

▶ They monitor network traffic in real time.

▶ They analyze protocols and other relevant packet information.

▶ They integrate with a firewall and define new rules as needed.

▶ When used in a switched environment, they require the user to perform port spanning.

▶ They send alerts or terminate an offending connection.

▶ When encryption is used, a NIDS will not be able to analyze the data traffic.

Host-Based Intrusion-Detection Systems

HIDS are more closely related to a virus scanner in their function and design because they are applications that reside on the host computer. Running quietly in the background, they monitor traffic and attempt to detect suspicious activity. Suspicious activity can range from attempted system file modification to unsafe activation of ActiveX commands. Although they are effective in a fully switched environment and can analyze network-encrypted traffic, they can take a lot of maintenance, cannot monitor network traffic, and rely on the underlying operating system because they do not control core services. Things to remember about HIDS include the following:

▶ HIDS consume some of the host's resources.

▶ HIDS analyze encrypted traffic.

▶ HIDS send alerts when unusual events are discovered.

▶ HIDS are in some ways just applications running on the local host, which is subject to attack.

Signature-Based, Anomaly-Based, and Rule-Based IDS Engines

Signature-based, *anomaly-based*, and *rule-based IDS systems* are the three primary types of analysis methods used by IDS systems. These types take different approaches to detecting intrusions.

Signature-based engines rely on a database of known attacks and attack patterns. This system examines data to check for malicious content, which could include fragmented IP packets, streams of SYN packets (DoS), or malformed Internet Control Message Protocol (ICMP) packets. Anytime data is found that matches one of these known signatures, it can be flagged to initiate further action. This might include an alarm, an alert, or a change to the firewall configuration. Although signature-based systems work well, their shortcoming is due to the fact that they are only as effective as their most current update. Anytime there is a new or varied attack, the IDS will be unaware of it and will ignore the traffic. The two subcategories of signature-based systems are:

▶ **Pattern-based**—Looks at specific signatures that packets are compared to. Snort started as a pattern-matching IDS.

▶ **State-based**—A more advanced design that has the capability to track the state of the traffic and data as it moves between host and target.

An anomaly-based IDS observes traffic and develops a baseline of normal operations. Intrusions are detected by identifying activity outside the normal range of activities. As an example, if Mike typically tries to log on only between the hours of 8 a.m. to 5 p.m., and now he's trying to log on 5,000 times at 2 a.m., the IDS can trigger an alert that something is wrong. The big disadvantage of a behavior-based IDS system is that an activity taught over time is not seen as an attack, but merely as normal behavior. These systems also tend to have a high number of false positives. The three subcategories of anomaly-based systems are:

▶ **Statistical-based**—Compares normal to abnormal activity.

▶ **Traffic-based or Signature-based**—Triggers on abnormal packets and data traffic or by comparing to a database of well known attack signatures.

▶ **Protocol-based**—Possesses the capability to reassemble packets and look at higher layer activity. If the IDS knows the normal activity of the protocol according to the RFC, it can pick out abnormal activity. Protocol-decoding intrusion detection requires the IDS to maintain state information. As an example, DNS is a two-step process; therefore, if a protocol-matching IDS sees a number of DNS responses that occur without a DNS request having ever taken place, the system can flag that activity as cache poisoning.

A rule-based (also called *behavior-based*) IDS involves rules and pattern descriptors that observe traffic and develop a baseline of normal operations.

Intrusions are detected by identifying activity outside the normal range. This expert system follows a four-phase analysis process:

1. Preprocessing

2. Analysis

3. Response

4. Refinement

All IDS systems share some basic components:

▶ **Sensors**—Detect and send data to the system.

▶ **Central monitoring system**—Processes and analyzes data sent from sensors.

▶ **Report analysis**—Offers information about how to counteract a specific event.

▶ **Database and storage components**—Perform trend analysis and store the IP address and information about the attacker.

▶ **Response box**—Inputs information from the previously listed components and forms an appropriate response.

ExamAlert

Carefully read any questions that discuss IDS. Remember that several variables can change the outcome or potential answer. Take the time to underline such words as *network*, *host*, *signature*, and *behavior* to help clarify the question.

Sensor Placement

Your organization's security policy should detail the placement of your IDS system and sensors. The placement of IDS sensors requires some consideration. IDS sensors can be placed externally, in the DMZ, or inside the network. A sensor in any of these locations will require specific tuning. Without it, the sensor will generate alerts for all traffic that matches a given criterion, regardless of whether the traffic is indeed something that should generate an alert.

ExamAlert

Although an anomaly-based IDS can detect new attacks, signature-based and rule-based IDS cannot.

Intrusion Prevention Systems

Intrusion prevention systems (IPSs) build on the foundation of IDS and attempt to take the technology a step further. IPSs can react automatically and actually prevent a security event from happening, preferably without user intervention. IPS is considered the next generation of IDS and can block attacks in real time. The National Institute of Standards and Technology (NIST) now uses the term IDP (intrusion detection and prevention) to define modern devices that maintain the functionality of both IDS and IPS devices. These devices typically perform deep inspection and can be applied to devices that support OSI Layer 3 to OSI Layer 7 inspection.

Responding to Operational Security Incidents

There can be many different types of incidents, from unauthorized disclosure, to theft of property, to outage by DoS, to the detection of an intrusion. What all of these activities have in common is that they should be driven by a preexisting procedure and policy. You will need to have created a team to deal with the investigation. The team will need to understand how to properly handle the crime scene. As an example, does the team understand how to protect evidence and maintain it in the proper chain of custody? You will also need to have established specific roles and responsibilities within the team, including a team lead to be in charge of the response to any incident.

You must establish contacts within the organization. As an example, if an employee is discovered to have been hacking, the supervisor may want to fire the employee, but must first discuss the issue with Human Resources and the legal department. Even when an incident has been contained and is in the recovery phase you will need to think about what lessons can be learned and how you will report and document your findings. What all this points to is a specific incident response policy.

Incident Response

The most important thing to understand when it come to incident response is that every company needs to have a plan before something unfortunate occurs. This methodology is shown here:

▶ Preparation—Create an incident response team to address incidents.

▶ Identification—Determine what has occurred.

▶ Mitigation and containment—Halt the effect of the incident and prevent it from spreading further.

▶ Investigation—Determine what the problem is and who is responsible.

▶ Eradication—Eliminate the problem.

▶ Recovery—Clean up any residual effects.

▶ Follow-up and resolution—Improve security measures to prevent or reduce the impact of future occurrences.

Both incident response and forensics are very similar, except that incident response is more focused on finding the problem and returning to normal activities, whereas forensics is more focused on the legal aspects and potentially prosecuting the accused. Also, only some companies can justify forensic investigation due to the potential cost. Both incident response and forensics are discussed in detail in Chapter 9. Outsourcing forensic investigation is quite common.

The Disaster Recovery Life Cycle

Closely related to incident response is disaster recovery. Disaster recovery's purpose is to get a damaged organization restarted so that critical business functions can resume. When a disaster occurs, the process of progressing from the disaster back to normal operations includes:

▶ Crisis management

▶ Recovery

▶ Reconstitution

▶ Resumption

When disasters occur, the organization must be ready to respond. Federal and state government entities typically use a Continuity of Operations (COOP) site. The COOP is designed to take on operational capabilities when the primary site is not functioning. The length of time that the COOP site is active, and the criteria in which the COOP site is enabled, depend upon the business continuity and disaster recovery plans. Both governmental and non-governmental entities typically make use of a checklist to manage continuity of operations. Table 10.4 shows a sample disaster recovery checklist.

TABLE 10.4 **Disaster Recovery Checklist**

Time	Activity
When disaster occurs	Notify disaster recovery manager and recovery coordinator
Within 2 hours	Assess damage, notify senior management, and determine immediate course of action
Within 4 hours	Contact offsite facility, recover backups, and replace equipment as needed
Within 8 hours	Provide management with updated assessment and begin recovery at updated site
Within 36 hours	Re-establish full processing at alternate site and determine timeline for return to primary facility

---

ExamAlert

The disaster recovery manager should direct short-term recovery actions immediately following a disaster.

Individuals responsible for emergency management will need to assess damage and perform triage. Areas impacted the most will need attention first. Protection of life is a priority while working to mitigate damage. Recovery from a disaster will entail sending personnel to the recovery site. When employees and materials are at the recovery site, interim functions can resume operations. This might entail installing software and hardware. Backups might need to be loaded and systems might require configuration.

Each step might not occur in series. As an example, while the recovery process is taking place, teams will also be dispatched to the disaster site to start the cleanup, salvage, and repair process. When those processes are complete, normal operations can resume.

When operations are moved from the alternate operations site back to the restored site, the efficiency of the restored site must be tested. In other words, processes should be sequentially returned, from least critical to most critical. In the event that a few glitches need to be worked out in the restored facility, you can be confident that your most critical processes are still in full operation at the alternate site.

Flat Tires Are a Fact of Life

When teaching this domain in the classroom, one of the things I always try to impress on students is that this is something that, in reality, they already really know. Consider this: While driving home from the airport, I had a flat tire. Here is what transpired step-by-step:

▶ **Crisis management**—On realizing I had a flat, I pulled safely off the freeway.

▶ **Recovery**—Working quickly, I jacked up the car and replaced the flat tire with the emergency spare that GM generously provides.

▶ **Reconstitution**—Back on the freeway, I was able to limp along with my 50-miles-per-hour-rated spare until I could reach a tire repair shop.

▶ **Resumption**—As expected, the technician confirmed that the tire could not be fixed. But for only $149 plus a few fees, he could get me back on the road. I headed home with the new tire on the car and my wallet a little emptier.

Consider this story when you are trying to conceptualize disaster recovery and, hopefully, it will make the task a little easier.

Teams and Responsibilities

Individuals involved in disaster recovery must deal with many things; when called to action, their activities center on emergency response, assessing the damage, recovery operations, and restoration. Figure 10.5 illustrates an example of disaster recovery activities.

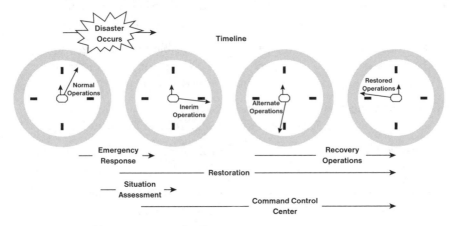

FIGURE 10.5 **Disaster recovery timeline.**

The salvage team is responsible for the reconstruction of damaged facilities. This includes cleanup, recovery of assets, creation of documentation for filing insurance or legal actions, and restoration of paper documents and electronic media. The recovery team has the necessary authority and responsibility to get the alternate site up and running. This site will be used as a stand-in for the original site until full operations can be restored. Although the CISSP exam will not require an in-depth understanding of all the teams and their responsibilities in a real disaster, a few additional teams and their roles are as follows:

▶ **Emergency response team**—The first responders for the organization. They are tasked with evacuating personnel and saving lives.

▶ **Emergency management team**—Executives and line managers that are financially and legally responsible. They must also handle the media and public relations.

▶ **Damage assessment team**—These individuals are the estimators. They must determine the damage and estimate the recovery time.

▶ **Communications team**—Responsible for installing communications (data, voice, phone, fax, radio, video) at the recovery site.

▶ **Security team**—Manages the security of the organization during the time of crisis. They must maintain order after a disaster.

▶ **Emergency operations team**—These individuals reside at the alternative site and manage systems operations. They are primarily operators and supervisors that are familiar with system operations.

▶ **Incident response team**—This team responds to incidents and acts as a central clearinghouse for information.

▶ **Transportation team**—This team is responsible for notifying employees that a disaster has occurred, and is also in charge of providing transportation, scheduling, and lodging for those needed at the alternate site.

▶ **Coordination team**—This team is tasked with managing operations at different remote sites and coordinating the recovery efforts.

▶ **Finance team**—Provides budget control for recovery and provides accurate accounting of costs.

▶ **Administrative support team**—Provides administrative support and might also handle payroll functions and accounting.

▶ **Supplies team**—Coordinates with key vendors to maintain needed supplies.

Caution

Physical security is always of great importance after a disaster. Precautions such as guards, temporary fencing, and barriers should be deployed to prevent looting and vandalism.

Exam Prep Questions

1. You have been given an attachment that was sent to the head of payroll and was flagged as malicious. You have been asked to examine the malware. You have decided to execute the malware inside a virtual environment. What is the best description of this environment?

   ○ **A.** Honeypot

   ○ **B.** Hyperjacking

   ○ **C.** Sandbox

   ○ **D.** Decompiler

2. Which of the following is not a security or operational reason to use mandatory vacations?

   ○ **A.** It allows the organization the opportunity to audit employee work.

   ○ **B.** It ensures that the employee is well rested.

   ○ **C.** It keeps one person from easily being able to carry out covert activities.

   ○ **D.** It ensures that employees will know that illicit activities could be uncovered.

3. What type of control is an audit trail?

   ○ **A.** Application

   ○ **B.** Administrative

   ○ **C.** Preventative

   ○ **D.** Detective

4. Which of the following is *not* a benefit of RAID?

   ○ **A.** Capacity benefits

   ○ **B.** Increased recovery time

   ○ **C.** Performance improvements

   ○ **D.** Fault tolerance

5. Separation of duties is related to which of the following?

   ○ **A.** Dual controls

   ○ **B.** Principle of least privilege

   ○ **C.** Job rotation

   ○ **D.** Principle of privilege

6. Phreakers target which of the following resources?

- ○ **A.** Mainframes
- ○ **B.** Networks
- ○ **C.** PBX systems
- ○ **D.** Wireless networks

7. You recently emailed a colleague you worked with years ago. You noticed that the email you sent him was rejected and you have been asked to resend it. What has happened with the message transfer agent?

- ○ **A.** Whitelist.
- ○ **B.** Graylist.
- ○ **C.** Blacklist
- ○ **D.** Black hole

8. Your organization has experienced a huge disruption. In this type of situation which of the following is designed to take on operational capabilities when the primary site is not functioning?

- ○ **A.** BCP
- ○ **B.** Audit
- ○ **C.** Incident response
- ○ **D.** COOP

9. Which RAID type provides data striping but no redundancy?

- ○ **A.** RAID 0
- ○ **B.** RAID 1
- ○ **C.** RAID 3
- ○ **D.** RAID 4

10. Which of the following is the fastest backup option but takes the longest to restore?

- ○ **A.** Incremental
- ○ **B.** Differential
- ○ **C.** Full
- ○ **D.** Grandfathered

11. Which of the following types of intrusion detection systems could be best described as one that compares normal to abnormal activity?

   ○ **A.** Pattern-based.

   ○ **B.** Statistical-based.

   ○ **C.** Traffic-based.

   ○ **D.** Protocol-based.

12. Which of the following processes involves overwriting the data with zeros?

   ○ **A.** Formatting

   ○ **B.** Drive-wiping

   ○ **C.** Zeroization

   ○ **D.** Degaussing

13. What type of RAID provides a stripe of mirrors?

   ○ **A.** RAID 1

   ○ **B.** RAID 5

   ○ **C.** RAID 10

   ○ **D.** RAID 15

14. Which of the following is the name of a multidisk technique that offers no advantage in speed and does not mirror, although it does allow drives of various sizes to be used and can be used on two or more drives?

   ○ **A.** RAID 0

   ○ **B.** RAID 1

   ○ **C.** RAID 5

   ○ **D.** JBOD

15. You have been assigned to a secret project that requires a massive amount of processing power. Which of the following techniques is best suited for your needs?

   ○ **A.** Redundant servers

   ○ **B.** Clustering

   ○ **C.** Distributed computing

   ○ **D.** Cloud computing

Answers to Exam Prep Questions

1. **C.** A virtual environment where you can safely execute suspected malware is called a sandbox. Answer A is incorrect because a honeypot is a fake vulnerable system deployed to be attacked. Answer B is incorrect because hyperjacking is a type of attack against a virtual system. Answer D is incorrect because a decompiler is used to disassemble an application.

2. **B.** Mandatory vacations are not primarily for employee benefit, but to better secure the organization's assets. Answers A, C, and D are incorrect. As answer A states, this gives the organization the opportunity to audit employee work. In answer C, it keeps one person from easily being able to carry out covert activities. In answer D, it ensures that employees will know that illicit activities could be uncovered. Each is a valid reason to use mandatory vacations.

3. **D.** Audit trails are considered a detective type of control. Answers A, B, and C are incorrect because audit trails are not an application, administrative, or preventive control.

4. **B.** RAID provides capacity benefits, performance improvements, and fault tolerance; therefore, answers A, C, and D are incorrect. Although RAID might reduce recovery time, it certainly won't increase it.

5. **B.** Separation of duties is closely tied to the principle of least privilege. Separation of duties is the process of dividing duties so that more than one person is required to complete a task, and each person has only the minimum resources needed to complete the task. Answer A is incorrect because dual controls are implemented to require more than one person to complete an important task. Answer C is incorrect because job rotation is used to prevent collusion. Answer D is incorrect because the principle of privilege would be the opposite of what is required.

6. **C.** Phreakers target phone and voice systems (PBX). Answer A is incorrect because mainframes are typically not a target of phreakers. Answer B is incorrect because networks might be a target of hackers, but phreakers target phone systems. Answer D is incorrect because wireless networks are targeted by war drivers or hackers, not phreakers.

7. **B.** When graylisting is implemented it will reject any email sender that is unknown. Mail from a legitimate email server will be retransmitted after a period of time. This moves the graylisted email off the hold list and on to the whitelist and at that time places the email in the inbox of the receiving account. Whitelisting only approves what is on an allowed list whereas blacklisting blocks specific items. Black holes silently discard or drop traffic without informing the source.

8. **D.** COOP is designed to take on operational capabilities when the primary site is not functioning. Business continuity plans generally focus on the continuation of business services in the event of any type of interruptions. Therefore, answers A, B, and C are incorrect.

9. **A.** RAID 0 provides data striping but no redundancy. Answers B, C, and D are incorrect because RAID 1 provides disk mirroring, RAID 3 provides byte-level striping with a dedicated parity disk, and RAID 4 is considered a dedicated parity drive.

10. **A.** Incremental backup is the fastest backup option, but takes the longest to restore. Answers B, C, and D are incorrect: A grandfathered backup is not a valid answer, a differential backup takes less time overall but longer to restore, and a full backup takes the longest to perform, though it's the fastest to restore.

11. **B.** Statistical-based IDS compares normal to abnormal activity. Pattern-, traffic-, and protocol-based IDS do not; therefore, answers A, C, and D are incorrect.

12. **C.** Zeroization overwrites the data with all zeros. Answer A is incorrect because formatting does not remove any data on the file allocation table (FAT). Answer B is incorrect because drive-wiping writes patterns of ones and zeros. Answer D is incorrect because degaussing works by means of a magnetic field.

13. **C.** RAID 10 provides a stripe of mirrors. RAID 1 offers only striping. RAID 5 is seen as a combination of good, cheap, and fast because it provides data strip-ing at the byte level, good performance, and good fault tolerance. RAID 15 is the combination of RAID 1 and RAID 5.

14. **D.** JBOD can use existing hard drives of various sizes. These are combined together into one massive logical disk. There is no fault tolerance and no increase in speed. The only benefit of JBOD is that you can use existing disks and if one drive fails, you lose the data on only that drive. Answers A, B, and C are incorrect because RAID 0, 1, and 5 do not match the description provided.

15. **B.** Clustering is a means of grouping computers and moving to a greater level of usability. Answer A is incorrect because a redundant server waits until it's needed before being used. Answer C is incorrect because distributed computing is not centrally controlled and, as such, should not be used for sensitive or classified work. Answer D is incorrect because placing sensitive information in the cloud could be a real security concern.

Need to Know More?

Snort IDS: www.it.uu.se/edu/course/homepage/sakdat/ht05/assignments/pm/programme/Introduction_to_snort.pdf

Understanding TCSEC: www.fas.org/irp/nsa/rainbow/tg022.htm

The Open Source Security Testing Methodology Manual: to www.isecom.org/

Employee fraud controls: www.cricpa.com/CRI_Anti-Fraud%20Controls.pdf

Remote access best practices: technet.microsoft.com/en-us/library/cc780755.aspx

Clustering: arxiv.org/abs/cs/0004014

Antivirus techniques: searchsecurity.techtarget.com/tip/How-antivirus-software-works-Virus-detection-techniques

Keystroke-monitoring ethics and laws: www.privacyrights.org/fs/fs7-work.htm

Historical keystroke-monitoring recommendations: csrc.nist.gov/publications/nistbul/csl93-03.txt

Cloud computing security issues: www.infoworld.com/article/2613560/cloud-security/cloud-security-9-top-threats-to-cloud-computing-security.html

CHAPTER 11

Software Development Security

Terms you'll need to understand:

▶ Acceptance testing

▶ Cohesion and coupling

▶ Tuple

▶ Polyinstantiation

▶ Inference

▶ Fuzzing

▶ Bytecode

▶ Database

▶ Buffer overflow

Topics you'll need to master:

▶ Identifying security in the software development lifecycle and system development life-cycle

▶ Understanding database design

▶ Knowing the capability maturity model

▶ Stating the steps of the development life-cycle

▶ Determining software security effectiveness

▶ Recognizing acquired software security impact

▶ Describing different types of application design techniques

▶ Understanding the role of change management

▶ Recognizing the primary types of databases

Introduction

Software plays a key role in the productivity of most organizations, yet our acceptance of it is different from everything else we tend to deal with. For example, if you were to buy a defective car that exploded in minor accidents, the manufacturer would be forced to recall the car. However, if a user buys a buggy piece of software, the buyer has little recourse. The buyer could wait for a patch, buy an upgrade, or maybe just buy another vendor's product. Well-written applications are essential for good security. As such, this chapter focuses on information the CISSP must know to apply security in the context of the CIA triad to the software development lifecycle, including programming languages, application design methodologies, and change management. A CISSP must not only understand the software development lifecycle, but also how databases are designed.

Databases contain some of the most critical assets of an organization, and are a favorite target of hackers. The CISSP must understand design, security issues, control mechanisms, and common vulnerabilities of databases. In addition to protecting the corporation's database from attacks, the security professional must be sensitive to the interconnectivity of databases and the rise of large online cloud databases.

Software Development

A CISSP is not expected to be an expert programmer or understand the inner workings of a Java program. What the CISSP must know is the overall environment in which software and systems are developed. The CISSP must also understand the development process, and be able to recognize whether adequate controls have been developed and implemented. Know that it's always cheaper to build in security up-front than it is to add it later. Organizations accomplish this by using a structured approach, so that:

▶ Risk is minimized.

▶ Return on investment from using said software is maximized.

▶ Security controls are established so that the risk associated with using software is mitigated.

New systems are created when new opportunities are discovered; organizations take advantage of these technologies to solve existing problems and accelerate business processes and improve productivity. Although it's easy to see the need to incorporate security from the beginning of the process, the historical reality of design and development has been deficient in this regard. Most organizations are understaffed and duties are not properly separated. Too often, inadequate consideration is given to the implementation of access-limiting controls from within a program's code.

As a result, this has caused excessive exposure points and has led to a parade of vulnerabilities following the defective code's release. New technologies and developments such as cloud computing and the Internet of Things (IoT) have made a structured, secure development process even more imperative. It is critical that development teams enforce a structured software development life-cycle that has checks and balances where security is thought through from start to finish.

Avoiding System Failure

No matter how hard we plan, systems will still fail. Organizations must prepare for these events with the proper placement of compensating controls. These controls help limit the damage. Some examples of compensating controls are checks and application controls, and fail-safe procedures.

Checks and Application Controls

The easiest way to minimize problems in the processing of data is to ensure that only accurate, complete, and timely inputs can occur. Even poorly written applications can be made more robust by adding controls that check limits, data formats, and data lengths; this is all referred to as *data input validation*. Controls that verify data is only processed through authorized routines should be in place. These application controls should be designed to detect any problems and to initiate corrective action. If there are mechanisms in place that permit the override of these security controls, their use should be logged and reviewed. Table 11.1 shows some common types of controls.

TABLE 11.1 **Checks and Controls**

Check or Application Control	Purpose
Sequence check	Verifies that all sequence numbers fall within a specific series. For example, checks are numbered sequentially. If the day's first-issued check is number 120, and the last check is number 144, all checks issued that day should fall between those numbers, and none should be missing.
Limit check	Ensures that data to be processed does not exceed a predetermined limit. For example, if a sale item is limited to five per customer, sales over that amount should trigger an alert.

(Continued)

TABLE 11.1 *Continued*

Check or Application Control	Purpose
Range check	Ensures that data is within a predetermined range. For example, a date range check might verify that any date input is after 01/01/2016 and before 01/01/2025.
Validity check	Looks at the logical appropriateness of data. For example, orders to be processed today should be dated with the current date.
Table lookups	Verifies that data matches one from a set of values entered into a lookup table.
Existence check	Verifies that all required data is entered and appropriate.
Completeness check	Ensures that all required data has been added and that no fields contain null values.
Duplicate check	Ensures that a transaction is not a duplicate. For example, before a payment on invoice 833 for $1,612 is made, accounts payable should verify that invoice number 833 has not already been paid.
Logic check	Verifies logic between data fields. For example, if Michael lives in Houston, his ZIP code cannot be the Dallas ZIP code 76450.

Failure States

Knowing that all applications can fail, it is important that developers create mechanisms for a safe failure, thereby containing damage. Well-coded applications have built-in recovery procedures that are triggered if a failure is detected; the system is protected from compromise by terminating the service or disabling the system until the cause of failure can be investigated.

> **Tip**
>
> Systems that recover into a fail-open state can allow an attacker to easily compromise the system. Systems that fail open are typically undesirable because of the security risk. However, some IDS/IPSs (intrusion detection systems/intrusion prevention systems) will go into fail-open state to prevent the disruption of traffic.

The System Development Lifecycle

The utilization of a framework for system development can facilitate and structure the development process. As an example, The National Institute of Standards and Technology (NIST) defines the System Development Lifecycle (SDLC) in NIST SP 800-34 as "the scope of activities associated with a system, encompassing the system's initiation, development and acquisition, implementation, operation and maintenance, and ultimately its disposal that instigates another system initiation." Many other framework models exist, such as Microsoft's Security Development Lifecycle (SDL). It consists of Training, Requirements, Design, Implementation, Verification, Release, and Response. Regardless of the model, the overall goal is the same: to control the development process and add security at each level or stage within the process. The System Development Lifecycle we will review has been separated into seven distinct steps:

1. Project initiation

2. Functional requirements and planning

3. Software design specifications

4. Software development and build

5. Acceptance testing and implementation

6. Operational/maintenance

7. Disposal

ExamAlert

Read all test questions carefully to make sure you understand the context in which SDL, SDLC, or other terms are being used.

Regardless of the titles that a given framework might assign to each step, the SDLC's purpose is to provide security in the software development lifecycle. The failure to adopt a structured development model increases a product's risk of failure because it is likely that the final product will not meet the customer's needs. Table 11.2 describes each step of development and the corresponding activities of that phase.

TABLE 11.2 **SDLC Stages and Activities**

Step	Description	Activities
1	Project initiation	Project feasibility, cost, and benefit analysis
		Payback analysis
		Establish project preliminary timeline
		Risk analysis
2	Functional requirements and planning	Define the need for the solution
		Identify the requirements
		Review proposed security controls
3	Software design specifications	Develop detailed design specifications
		Review support documentation
		Examine adequacy of security controls
4	Software development and build	Programmers develop code
		Check modules
5	Acceptance testing and implementation	Enforce separation of duties
		Perform testing
6	Operational/maintenance	Release into production
		Perform certification and accreditation
7	Disposal	End of life, remove data from system or application first, then remove from production
		Define necessary level of sanitization and destruction of unneeded data, appropriate for classification

Project Initiation

This initial step usually includes meeting with everyone involved with the project to answer the big questions like what are we doing? why are we doing it? and who is our customer? At this meeting, the feasibility of the project is considered. The cost of the project must be discussed, as well as the potential benefits that the product is expected to bring to the system's users. A *payback analysis* should be performed to determine how long the project would take to pay for itself. In other words, the payback analysis determines how much time will lapse before accrued benefits overtake accrued and continuing costs.

Should it be determined that the project will move forward, the team will want to develop a preliminary timeline. Discussions should be held to determine the level of risk involved with handling data, and to establish the ramifications of accidental exposure. This activity clarifies the precise type and nature of information that will be processed, and its level of sensitivity. This is the first look at security. This analysis must be completed before the functional requirements and planning stage begins.

> **ExamAlert**
>
> For the exam you should understand that users should be brought into the process as early as possible. You are building something for them and must make sure that the designed system/product meets their needs.

Functional Requirements and Planning

This phase is responsible for fully defining the need for the solution, and mapping how the proposed solution meets the need. This stage requires the participation of management as well as users. Users need to identify requirements and desires they have regarding the design of the application. Security representatives must verify the identified security requirements, and determine whether adequate security controls are being defined.

An *entity relationship diagram* (ERD) is often used to help map the identified and verified requirements to the needs being met. ERDs define the relationship between the many elements of a project. ERDs are a type of database, grouping together like data elements. Each entity has a specific attribute, called the *primary key*, which is drawn as a rectangular box containing an identifying name. Relationships, drawn as diamonds, describe how the various entities are related to each other.

ERDs can be used to help define a data dictionary. After the data dictionary is designed, the database schema is developed. This schema further defines tables and fields, and the relationships between them. Figure 11.1 shows the basic design of an ERD. The completed ERD becomes the blueprint for the design, and is referred to during the design phase.

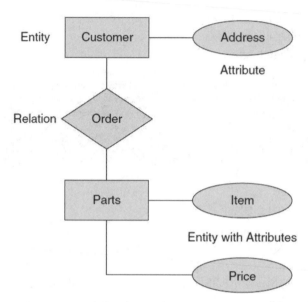

FIGURE 11.1 **Entity Relationship Diagram.**

Software Design Specifications

Detailed design specifications are generated during this stage, either for a program that will be created or in support of the acquisition of an existing program. All functions and operations are described. Programmers design screen layouts and chart process diagrams. Supporting documentation will also be generated. The output of the software design specification stage is a set of specifications that delineate the new system as a collection of modules and subsystems.

Scope creep most often occurs here, and is simply the expansion of the scope of the project. Small changes in the design can add up over time. Although little changes might not appear to have a big cost or impact on the schedule of a project, these changes have a cumulative effect and increase both length and cost of a project.

Proper detail at this stage plays a large role in the overall security of the final product. Security should be the focus here as controls are developed to ensure input, output, audit mechanisms, and file protection. Sample input controls include dollar counts, transaction counts, error detection, and correction. Sample output controls include validity checking and authorization controls.

Software Development and Build

During the software development and build phase, programmers work to develop the application code specified in the previous stage, as illustrated in Figure 11.2.

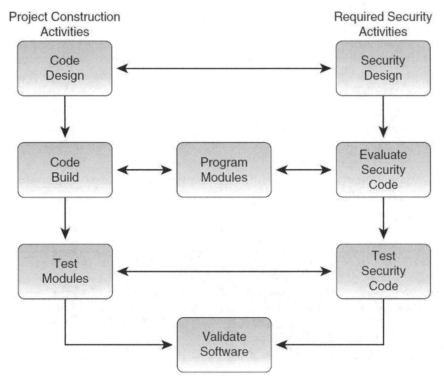

FIGURE 11.2 **Development and Build Activities.**

Programmers should strive to develop modules that have high cohesion and low coupling. *Cohesion* addresses the fact that a module can perform a single task with low input from other modules. *Coupling* is the measurement of the amount of interconnections or dependencies between modules. Low coupling means that a change to one module should not affect another and the module has high cohesion.

> **Tip**
>
> Sometimes you may not actually build the software and find that purchasing a previously developed product is easier. In these situations security cannot be forgotten. You will need to fully test the acquired software to verify its security impact. In these situations the source code may not always be available and you may need to perform other types of testing.

This stage includes testing of the individual modules developed, and accurate results have a direct impact on the next stage: integrated testing with the main program. *Maintenance hooks* are sometimes used at this point in the process to allow programmers to test modules separately without using normal access control procedures. It is important that these maintenance hooks, also referred to as backdoors, be removed before the software code goes to production. Programmers might use online programming facilities to access the code directly from their workstations. Although this typically increases productivity, it also increases the risk that someone will gain unauthorized access to the program library.

> **ExamAlert**
>
> For the exam you should understand that separation of duties is of critical importance during the SDLC process. Activities such as development, testing, and production should be properly separated and their duties should not overlap. As an example, programmers should not have direct access to production (or released) code or have the ability to change production or released code.

> **Caution**
>
> Maintenance hooks or trapdoors are software mechanisms that are installed to bypass the system's security protections during the development and build stage. To prevent a potential security breach, these hooks must be removed before the product is released into production. You can find an example of a maintenance hook at www.securityfocus.com/bid/7673/discuss. This alert discusses a weakness in the TextPortal application and covers how an attacker can obtain unauthorized access. The issue exists due to an undocumented password of "god2" that can be used for the default administrative user account.

Controls are built into the program during this stage. These controls should include preventive, detective, and corrective mechanisms. Preventive controls include user authentication and data encryption. Detective controls provide audit trails and logging mechanisms. Corrective controls add fault tolerance and data integrity mechanisms. Unit testing occurs here, but acceptance testing takes place in the next stage. Test classifications are broken down into general categories:

▶ **Unit testing**—Examines an individual program or module.

▶ **Interface testing**—Examines hardware or software to evaluate how well data can be passed from one entity to another.

▶ **System testing**—A series of tests that starts in this phase, and continues into the acceptance testing phase, and includes recovery testing, security testing, stress testing, volume testing, and performance testing.

Caution

Reverse engineering can be used to reduce development time. This is somewhat controversial because reverse engineering can be used to bypass normal access control mechanisms or disassemble another company's program illegally. Most software licenses make it illegal to reverse engineer the associated code. Laws such as DMCA can also prohibit the reverse engineering of code.

Acceptance Testing and Implementation

This stage occurs when the application coding is complete, and should not be performed by the programmers. Instead, testing should be performed by test experts or quality assurance engineers. The important concept here is separation of duties. If the code is built and verified by the same individuals, errors can be overlooked and security functions can be bypassed. Models vary greatly on specifically what tests should be completed and how much if any iteration is necessary within that testing. With that said, Table 11.3 lists some common types of acceptance and verification tests of which you should be aware.

TABLE 11.3 **Test Types**

Test	Description
Alpha test	The first and earliest version of a completed application, expected to be followed with a beta test. Both of these versions are considered prereleases of the application.
Pilot test	Used to evaluate and verify the functionality of an application (sometimes referred to as beta testing) with limited users on limited production systems.

(Continued)

TABLE 11.3 *Continued*

Test	Description
Whitebox test	Verifies inner program logic; can be cost prohibitive for large applications or systems.
Blackbox test	Integrity-based testing; looks at inputs and outputs, but does not care about the inner workings.
Function test	Validates the application against a checklist of requirements.
Regression test	Used after a change to verify that inputs and outputs are correct, and that interconnected systems show no abnormalities in how subsystems and processes are affected by the change.
Parallel test	Used to verify a new or changed application by feeding data into the new application and simultaneously into the old, unchanged application, and comparing the results.
Sociability test	Verifies that the application can operate in its targeted environment.
Final test	Usually performed after the project staff is satisfied with all other tests, just before the application is ready to be deployed.

When all pertinent issues and concerns have been worked out between the QA engineers, the security professionals, and the programmers, the application is ready for deployment.

ExamAlert

For the exam you should understand that fuzzing is a form of blackbox testing technique that enters malformed data inputs and monitors the application's response. This is commonly referred to as "garbage in, garbage out" testing because it throws "garbage" at the application to see what it can handle.

Operations and Maintenance

The application is prepared for release into its intended environment during the implementation phase. This is the stage where final user acceptance is performed, and any required certification and/or accreditation is achieved. This stage is the final step, wherein management accepts the application and agrees that it is ready for use.

Certification requires a technical review of the system or application to ensure that it does what is supposed to do. Certification testing often includes an audit of security controls, a risk assessment, and/or a security evaluation. *Accreditation* is management's formal acceptance of the system or application. Typically, the results of the certification testing are compiled into a report that becomes the basis for the acceptance from management referred to as accreditation. Management might request additional testing, ask questions about the certification report, or simply accept the results. When the system or application is accepted, a formal acceptance statement is usually issued.

> **Tip**
>
> *Certification* is a technical evaluation and analysis of the security features and safeguards of a system to establish the extent to which the security requirements are satisfied and vendor claims are verified.
>
> *Accreditation* is the formal process of management's official approval of the certification.

Operations management begins when the application is rolled out. Maintenance, support, and technical response must be addressed. Data conversion might also need to be considered. If an existing application is being replaced, data from the old application might need to be migrated to the new one. The rollout of the application might occur all at once or in a phased process over time. Changeover techniques include:

▶ **Parallel operation**—Both the old and new applications are run simultaneously with all the same inputs and the results between the two applications compared. Fine-tuning can also be performed on the new application as needed. As confidence in the new application improves, the old application can be shut down. The primary disadvantage of this method is that both applications must be maintained for a period of time.

▶ **Phased changeover**—If the application is large, a phased changeover might be possible. With this method, applications are upgraded one piece at a time.

▶ **Hard changeover**—This method establishes a data at which users are forced to change over. The advantage of the hard changeover is that it forces all users to change at once. However, this does introduce a level of risk into the environment because things can go wrong.

Disposal

This step of the process is reached when the application is no longer needed. Those involved in this step of the process must consider how to dispose of the application, archive any information or data that might be needed in the future, perform disk sanitization (to ensure confidentiality), and dispose of equipment. This is an important step that is sometimes overlooked.

Disposal Is a Big Problem

Computer forensics investigators at the University of Glamorgan in England examined more than 100 drives purchased at random on eBay. Only two of the drives contained no data. All the remaining drives contained various amounts of residual information. One contained psychological reports on school children, and several others contained additional confidential information.

If hard drives are not destroyed, they should be wiped and sanitized. One standard is Department of Defense standard 5220.22-M. It recommends overwriting all addressable locations with a character, its complement, and then a random character to verify that the residual data has been cleared and sanitized.

Development Methods

So, what is the most important concept of system development? Finding a good framework and adhering to the process it entails. The sections that follow explain several proven software-development processes. These models share a common element in that they all have a predictive life-cycle. Each has strengths and weaknesses. Some work well when a time-sensitive or high-quality product is needed, whereas others offer greater quality control and can scale to very large projects.

The Waterfall Model

Probably the most well known software development process is the *waterfall model*. This model was developed by Winston Royce in 1970, and operates as the name suggests, progressing from one level down to the next. The original model prevented developers from returning to stages once they were complete; therefore, the process flowed logically from one stage to the next. Modified versions of the model add a feedback loop so that the process can move in both directions. An advantage of the waterfall method is that it provides a sense of order and is easily documented. The primary disadvantage is that it does not work for large and complex projects because it does not allow for much revision.

The Spiral Model

This model was developed in 1988 by Barry Boehm. Each phase of the spiral model starts with a design goal and ends with the client review. The client can be either internal or external, and is responsible for reviewing progress.

Analysis and engineering efforts are applied at each phase of the project. An advantage of the spiral model is that it takes risk much more seriously. Each phase of the project contains its own risk assessment. Each time a risk assessment is performed, the schedules and estimated cost to complete are reviewed and a decision is made to continue or cancel the project. The spiral model works well for large projects. The disadvantage of this method is that it is much slower and takes longer to complete. Figure 11.3 illustrates an example of this model.

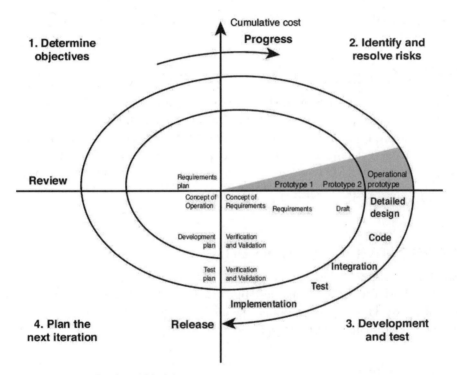

FIGURE 11.3 **The Spiral Model.**

Joint Application Development

Joint Application Development (JAD) is a process developed at IBM in 1977. Its purpose is to accelerate the design of information technology solutions. An advantage of JAD is that it helps developers work effectively with the users who will be using the applications developed. A disadvantage is that it requires users, expert developers, and technical experts to work closely together throughout the entire process. Projects that are good candidates for JAD have some of the following characteristics:

▶ Involve a group of users whose responsibilities cross department or division boundaries

▶ Considered critical to the future success of the organization

▶ Involve users who are willing to participate

▶ Developed in a workshop environment

▶ Use a facilitator who has no vested interest in the outcome

Rapid Application Development

Rapid Application Development (RAD) is a fast application development process, created to deliver speedy results. RAD is not suitable for all projects, but it works well for projects that are on strict time limits. However, this can also be a disadvantage if the quick decisions lead to poor design and product. This is why you won't see RAD used for critical applications, such as shuttle launches. Two of the most popular RAD tools for Microsoft Windows are Delphi and Visual Basic.

Incremental Development

Incremental development defines an approach for a staged development of systems. Work is defined so that development is completed one step at a time. A minimal working application might be deployed while subsequent releases enhance functionality and/or scope.

Prototyping

Prototyping frameworks aim to reduce the time required to deploy applications. These frameworks use high-level code to quickly turn design requirements into application screens and reports that the users can review. User feedback is used to fine-tune the application and improve it. Top-down testing works best with this development construct. Although prototyping clarifies user requirements, it also leads to a quick skeleton of a product with no guts surrounding it. Seeing complete forms and menus can confuse users and clients and lead to overly optimistic project timelines. Also, because change happens quickly, changes might not be properly documented and scope creep might occur. Prototyping is often used where the product is being designed for a specific customer and is proprietary in nature.

ExamAlert

Prototyping is the process of building a proof-of-concept model that can be used to test various aspects of a design and verify its marketability. Prototyping is widely used during the development process.

Modified Prototype Model (MPM)

MPM was designed to be used for web development. MPM focuses on quickly deploying basic functionality and then using user feedback to expand that functionality. MPM is especially useful when the final nature of the product is unknown.

Computer-Aided Software Engineering

Computer-Aided Software Engineering (CASE) enhances the software development life-cycle by using software tools and automation to perform systematic analysis, design, development, and implementation of software products. The tools are useful for large, complex projects that involve multiple software components and lots of people. Its disadvantages are that it requires building and maintaining software tools, and training developers to understand how to use the tools effectively. CASE can be used for

▶ Modeling real-world processes and data flows through applications

▶ Developing data models to better understand process

▶ Developing process and functional descriptions of the model

▶ Producing databases and database management procedures

▶ Debugging and testing the code

Agile Development Methods

Agile software development allows teams of programmers and business experts to work closely together.

According to the agile manifesto at agilemanifesto.org/, "We are uncovering better ways of developing software by doing it and helping others do it. Through this work, we have come to value:

▶ Individuals and interactions over processes and tools.

▶ Working software over comprehensive documentation.

▶ Customer collaboration over contract negotiation.

▶ Responding to change over following a plan."

Agile project requirements are developed using an iterative approach, and the project is mission-driven and component-based. The project manager becomes much more of a facilitator in these situations. Popular agile development models include the following:

▶ **Extreme programming (XP)**—The XP development model requires that teams include business managers, programmers, and end users. These teams are responsible for developing usable applications in short periods. Issues with XP are that teams are responsible not only for coding but also for writing the tests used to verify the code. There is minimal focus on structured documentation, which can be a concern. XP does not scale well for large projects.

▶ **Scrum**—Scrum is an iterative development method in which repetitions are referred to as sprints and typically last thirty days. Scrum is typically used with object-oriented technology, and requires strong leadership and a team that can meet at least briefly each day. The planning and direction of tasks passes from the project manager to the team. The project manager's main task is to work on removing any obstacles from the team's path. The scrum development method owes its name to the team dynamic structure of rugby.

Capability Maturity Model

The *Capability Maturity Model* (CMM) was designed as a framework for software developers to improve the software development process. It allows software developers to progress from an anything-goes type of development to a highly structured, repeatable process. As software developers grow and mature, their productivity will increase and the quality of their software products will become more robust. There are five maturity levels to the CMM, as shown in Table 11.4.

TABLE 11.4 **Capability Maturity Model**

Maturity Level	Description
Initial	Ad hoc process with no assurance of repeatability.
Repeatable	Change control and quality assurance are in place and controlled by management, although formal processes are not defined.
Defined	Defined process and procedures are in place and used. Qualitative process improvement is in place.
Managed	Qualitative data is collected and analyzed. A process improvement program is used.
Optimized	Continuous process improvement is in place and has been budgeted for.

Although there might be questions on the exam about the CMM, it is important to note that the model was replaced in December 2007 with the Capability Maturity Model Integration (CMMI), in part due to the standardization activities of ISO 15504.

ExamAlert

Read any questions regarding CMM or CMMI carefully to make sure you understand which model the question is referencing.

The steps for CMMI include: (1) Initial, (2) Managed, (3) Defined, (4) Quantitatively Managed, and (5) Defined, Optimizing. These steps are shown in Figure 11.4. CMMI has similarities with agile development methods, such as XP and Scrum. The CMMI model contains process areas and goals, and each goal comprises practices.

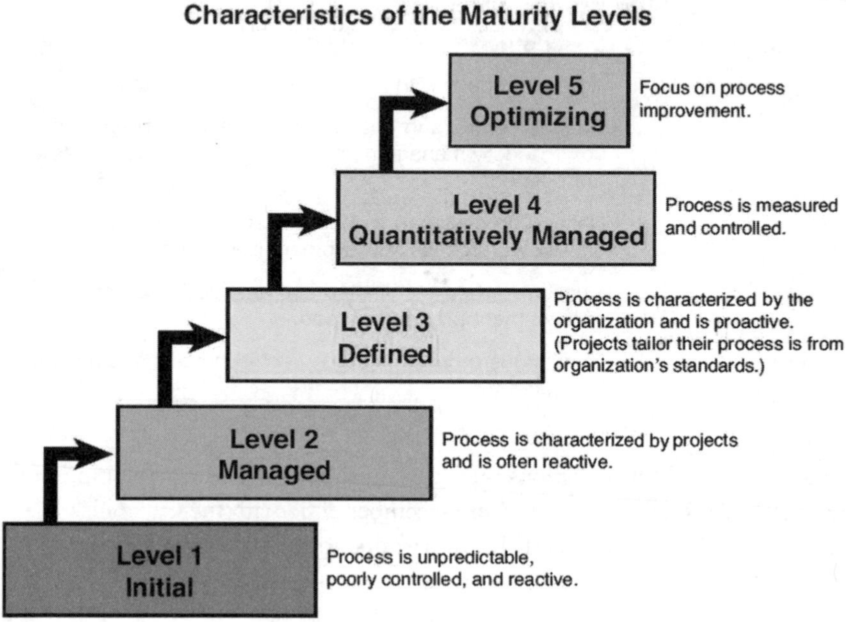

Characteristics of the Maturity Levels

FIGURE 11.4 **The CMMI Model.**

Scheduling

Scheduling involves linking individual tasks. The link relationships are based on earliest start date or latest expected finish date. Gantt charts provide a way to display these relationships.

The *Gantt chart* was developed in the early 1900s as a tool to assist the scheduling and monitoring of activities and progress. Gantt charts show the start and finish dates of each element of a project. Gantt charts also show the relationships between activities in a calendar-like format. They have become one of the primary tools used to communicate project schedule information. Their baselines illustrate what will happen if a task is finished early or late.

Program Evaluation and Review Technique (PERT) is the preferred tool for estimating time when a degree of uncertainty exists. PERT uses a critical path method that applies a weighted average duration estimate.

Probabilistic time estimates are used by PERT to create a three-point time estimate of best, worst, and most likely time evolution of activities. The PERT weighted average is calculated as follows:

PERT Weighted Average = Optimistic Time + 4 × Most Likely Time + Pessimistic Time / 6

Every task branches out to three estimates:

▶ **One**—The most optimistic time in which the task can be completed.

▶ **Two**—The most likely time in which the task will be completed.

▶ **Three**—The worst-case scenario or longest time in which the task might be completed.

Change Management

Change management is a formalized process for controlling modifications made to systems and programs: analyze the request, examine its feasibility and impact, and develop a timeline for implementing the approved changes. The change management process provides all concerned parties with an opportunity to voice their opinions and concerns before changes are made. Although types of changes vary, change control follows a predictable process. The steps for a change control process are as follows:

1. Request the change.
2. Approve the change request.
3. Document the change request.
4. Test the proposed change.
5. Present the results to the change control board.
6. Implement the change if approved.
7. Document the new configuration.
8. Report the final status to management.

> **Tip**
>
> One important piece of change management that is sometimes overlooked is a way to back out of the change. Sometimes things can go wrong and the change needs to be undone.

Documentation is the key to a good change control process. All system documents should be updated to indicate any changes that have been made to the system or environment. The system maintenance staff of the department requesting the change should keep a copy of that change's approval. Without a change control process in place, there is a significant potential for security breaches. Indicators of poor change control include

▶ No formal change control process is in place.

▶ Changes are implemented directly by the software vendors or others without internal control, which can indicate a lack of separation of duties.

▶ Programmers place code in an application that is not tested or validated.

▶ The change review board did not authorize the change.

▶ The programmer has access to both the object code and the production library; this situation presents a threat because the programmer might be able to make unauthorized changes to production code.

▶ No version control.

Finally, this does not mean that there will never be a situation where a change occurs without going through the change control process, because situations might arise in which emergency changes must be made. These emergencies typically are in response to situations that endanger production or could halt a critical process. If programmers are to be given special access or provided with an increased level of control, the security professional with oversight should make sure that checks are in place to track those programmers' access and record any changes made.

Programming Languages

Programming languages permit the creation of instructions using instruction sets that a computer can understand. The types of tasks that get programmed, and the instructions or code used to create the programs, depend on the nature of the organization. If, for example, the company has used FORTRAN for engineering projects for the last 25 years, it might make sense to use it again for the current project. Programming has evolved through five generations of languages (GLs), as illustrated in Figure 11.5 and described in the list that follows.

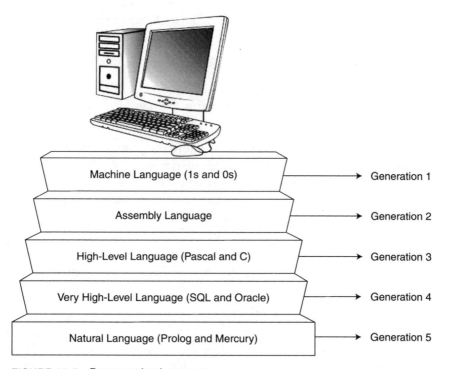

FIGURE 11.5 **Programming Languages.**

1. **Generation 1**—Machine language, the native language of a computer consisting of binary ones and zeros.

2. **Generation 2**—Assembly language, human-readable notation that translates easily into machine language.

3. **Generation 3**—High-level programming languages. The 1960s through the 1980s saw an emergence and growth of many third-generation programming languages, such as FORTRAN, COBOL, C+, and Pascal.

4. **Generation 4**—Very high-level language. This generation of languages grew from the 1970s through the early 1990s. 4GLs are typically those used to access databases. SQL is an example of a fourth-generation language.

5. **Generation 5**—Natural language. These took off strong in the 1990s and were considered the wave of the future. 5GLs are categorized by their use of inference engines and natural language processing. Mercury and Prolog are two examples of fifth-generation languages.

After the code is written, it must be translated into a format that the computer will understand. These are the three most common methods:

▶ **Assembler**—A program translates assembly language into machine language.

▶ **Compiler**—A compiler translates a high-level language into machine language.

▶ **Interpreter**—Instead of compiling the entire program, an interpreter translates the program line by line. Interpreters have a fetch-and-execute cycle. An interpreted language is much slower to execute than a compiled or assembled program, but does not need a separate compilation or assembly step.

Hundreds of different programming languages exist. Many have been written to fill a specific niche or market demand. Examples of common programming languages include the following:

▶ **ActiveX**—This language forms a foundation for higher-level software services, such as transferring and sharing information among applications. ActiveX controls are a Component Object Model (COM) technology. COM is designed to hide the details of an individual object and focus on the object's capabilities. An extension to COM is COM+.

▶ **COBOL**—Common Business Oriented Language is a third-generation programming language used for business finance and administration.

▶ **C, C+, C++, C#**—The C programming language replaced B and was designed by Dennis Ritchie. C was originally designed for UNIX and is very popular and widely used. From a security perspective some C functions are known for issues related to buffer overflows.

▶ **FORTRAN**—This language features an optimized compiler that is widely used by scientists for writing numerically intensive programs.

▶ **HTML**—Hypertext Markup Language is a markup language that is used to create web pages.

▶ **Java**—This is a general-purpose computer programming language, developed in 1995 by Sun Microsystems.

▶ **Visual Basic**—This programming language was designed to be used by anyone, and enables rapid development of practical programs.

▶ **Ruby**—An object-oriented programming language that was developed in the 1990s and designed for general-purpose usage. It has been used in the development of such projects as Metasploit.

▶ **Scripting languages**—A form of programming language that is usually interpreted rather than compiled and allows some control over a software application. Perl, Python, and Java are examples of scripting languages.

▶ **XML**—Extensible Markup Language (XML) is a markup language that specifies rules for encoding documents. XML is widely used on the Internet.

Object-Oriented Programming

Multiple development frameworks have been created to assist in defining, grouping, and reusing both code and data. Methods include data-oriented system programming, component-based programming, web-based applications, and object-oriented programming. Of these, the most commonly deployed is *object-oriented programming* (OOP), an object technology resulting from modular programming. OOP allows code to be reused and interchanged between programs in modular fashion without starting over from scratch. It has been widely embraced because it is more efficient and results in lower programming costs. And because it makes use of modules, a programmer can easily modify an existing program.

In OOP, objects are grouped into classes; all objects in a given group share a particular structure and behavior. Characteristics from one class can be passed down to another through the process of inheritance. Java and C++ are two examples of OOP languages.

Some of the attributes of OOP include:

▶ **Encapsulation**—This is the act of hiding the functionality of an object inside that object or, for a process, hiding the functionality inside that process's class. Encapsulation permits a developer to keep information disjointed; that is, to separate distinct elements so that there is no direct unnecessary sharing or interaction between the various parts.

▶ **Polymorphism**—Technically this means that one thing has the capability to take on many appearances. In OOP, it is used to invoke a method on a class without needing to care about how the invocation is accomplished. Likewise, the specific results of the invocation can vary because objects will have different variables that will respond differently.

▶ **Polyinstantiation**—Technically, this means that multiple instances of information are being generated. This is a tool used in many settings. For example, polyinstantiation is used to display different results to different individuals who pose identical queries on identical databases, due to those individuals possessing different security levels. This deployment is widely used by the government and military to unify information bases, while protecting sensitive or classified information. Without polyinstantiation, an attacker might be able to aggregate information for various sources to do what is referred to as an inference attack to determine secret information. Initially, a piece of information by itself appears useless like a piece to a puzzle, but when put with together with several other pieces of the puzzle you have an accurate picture.

During programming, object-oriented design (OOD) is used to bridge the gap between a real-world problem and the software solution. OOD modularizes data and procedures. This provides for a detailed description as to how a system is to be built. OOA and OOD are sometimes combined as object-oriented analysis and design (OOAD).

CORBA

Functionality that exists in a different environment from your code can be accessed and shared using vendor-independent middleware known as *Common Object Request Broker Architecture* (CORBA). CORBA's purpose is to allow different vendor products, such as computer languages, to work seamlessly across distributed networks of diversified computers. The heart of the CORBA system is the *Object Request Broker* (ORB). The ORB simplifies the client's process of requesting server objects. The ORB locates the requested object, transparently activates it as necessary, and then delivers the requested object back to the client.

Database Management

Databases are important to business, government, and individuals because they provide a way to catalog, index, and retrieve related pieces of information and facts. These repositories of data are widely used. If you have booked a reservation on a plane, looked up the history of a used car you were thinking about buying, or researched the ancestry of your family, you have most likely used a database during your quest. The database itself can be centralized or distributed, depending on the database management system (DBMS) that has been implemented. The DBMS allows the database administrator to control all aspects of the database, including design, functionality, and security. There are several popular types of databases, although the majority of modern databases are relational. Database types include:

▶ **Hierarchical database management system**—This form of database links structures into a tree structure. Each record can have only one owner. Because of this, a hierarchical database often can't be used to relate to structures in the real world.

▶ **Network database management system**—This type of database system was developed to be more flexible than the hierarchical database. The network database model is referred to as a *lattice structure* because each record can have multiple parent and child records.

▶ **Relational database management system**—This database consists of a collection of tables linked to each other by their primary keys. Many organizations use this model. Most relational databases use SQL as their query language. The RDBMS is a collection based on set theory and relational calculations. This type of database groups data into ordered pairs of relationships (a row and column) known as a tuple.

▶ **Object-relational database system**—This type of database system is similar to a relational database but is written in an object-oriented programming language. This allows it to support extensions to the data model and to be a middle ground between relational databases and object-oriented databases.

Database Terms

If you are not familiar with the world of databases, you might benefit from a review of some of the other common terms. Figure 11.6 illustrates several of the following terms, which security professionals should be familiar with:

▶ **Aggregation**—The process of combining several low-sensitivity items, and drawing medium- or high-sensitivity conclusions.

▶ **Inference**—The process of deducing privileged information from available unprivileged sources.

▶ **Attribute**—A characteristic about a piece of information. Where a row in a database table represents a database object, each column in that row represents an attribute of that object.

▶ **Field**—The smallest unit of data within a database.

▶ **Foreign key**—An attribute in one table that cross-references to an existing value that is the primary key in another table.

▶ **Granularity**—Refers to the level of control the program has over the view of the data that someone can access. Highly granular databases have the capability to restrict views, according to the user's clearance, at the field or row level.

▶ **Relation**—Defined interrelationship between the data elements in a collection of tables.

▶ **Tuple**—Used to represent a relationship among a set of values. In an RDBMS, a tuple identifies a column and a row.

▶ **Schema**—The totality of the defined tables and interrelationships for an entire database. It defines how the database is structured.

▶ **Primary key**—Uniquely identifies each row and assists with indexing the table.

▶ **View**—The database construct that an end user can see or access.

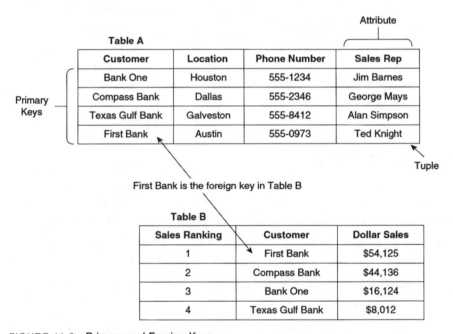

FIGURE 11.6 **Primary and Foreign Keys.**

An Example of Aggregation and Inference

Many students struggle with the concepts of aggregation and inference. The following are the two examples I use in the classroom to explain these concepts.

Aggregation refers to adding together available information. An aggregation attack is possible when pieces of information are combined from different sources to included different data classification levels to result in a composite view of data that exceeds the user's access. As an example, when Mike was a teenager, he would tell his parents he was spending the night at his friend's house Friday night. His friend would tell his own parents that he was spending the night at Mike's house. This enabled Mike and his friend to stay out late until one parent called the other, and both were able to verify that Mike and his friend were at neither house.

Inference results from someone's ability to fill in gaps in what information is provided. Inference is possible when retrieved, authorized information can be used to deduce new information. As an example, consider a situation in HR, where an employee is authorized to see payroll as department totals only, but not to see individual salaries. In fact, this employee might still be able to infer what someone is paid. If the employee can look at payroll totals the month before the new individual starts, and then look at the total the month after the individual is hired, the difference provides an inference to be drawn about the new individual's salary.

Integrity

The integrity of data refers to its accuracy. To protect the semantic and referential integrity of the data within a database, specialized controls are used, including rollbacks, checkpoints, commits, and savepoints.

▶ **Semantic integrity**—Assures that the data in any field is of the appropriate type. Controls that check for the logic of data and operations affect semantic integrity.

▶ **Referential integrity**—Assures the accuracy of cross references between tables. Controls that ensure that foreign keys only reference existing primary keys affect referential integrity.

Transaction Processing

Transaction management is critical in assuring integrity. Without proper locking mechanisms, multiple users could be altering the same record simultaneously, and there would be no way to ensure that transactions were valid and complete. This is especially important with online systems that respond in real time. These systems, known as *online transaction processing* (OLTP) are used in many industries, including banking, airlines, mail order, supermarkets, and manufacturing. Programmers involved in database management use the ACID test when discussing whether a database management system has been properly designed to handle OLTP:

▶ **Atomicity**—Results of a transaction are either all or nothing.

▶ **Consistency**—Transactions are processed only if they meet system-defined integrity constraints.

▶ **Isolation**—The results of a transaction are invisible to all other transactions until the original transaction is complete.

▶ **Durability**—Once complete, the results of the transaction are permanent.

Artificial Intelligence and Expert Systems

An *expert system* is a computer program that contains a knowledge base, a set of rules, and an inference engine. At the heart of these systems is the *knowledge base*—the repository of information that the rules are applied against.

Expert systems are typically designed for a specific purpose and have the capability to infer. For example, a hospital might have a knowledge base that contains various types of medical information; if a doctor enters the symptoms of weight loss, emotional disturbances, impaired sensory perception, pain in the limbs, and periods of irregular heart rate, the expert system can scan the knowledge base and diagnose the patient as suffering from beriberi.

> **Tip**
>
> How advanced are these expert systems? A computer named Watson, created by IBM, routinely wins at Jeopardy and beats human opponents by looking for the answers in unstructured data using a natural query software language. www-03.ibm.com/ibm/history/ibm100/us/en/icons/watson/.

The challenge in the creation of knowledge bases is to ensure that their data is accurate, that access controls are in place, that the proper level of expertise was used in developing the system, and that the knowledge base is secured. *Neural networks* are ones capable of learning new information. An example is shown in Figure 11.7. Artificial intelligence (AI) = expert systems + neural networks. Neural networks make use of nodes. There are typically multiple levels of nodes that are used to filter data and apply a weight. Eventually, an output is triggered and the fuzzy solution is provided. It's called a fuzzy solution as it can lack exactness.

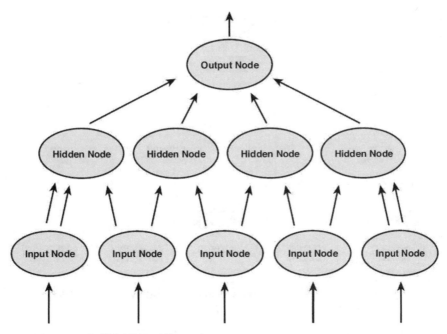

FIGURE 11.7 **Artificial Neural Network.**

Security of the Software Environment

The security of software is a critical concern. Protection of the confidentiality, integrity, and availability of data and program variables is one of the CISSP top concerns. During the design phase you should consider what type of data the application will be processing. As an example, if the application will deal with order quantities, these numbers should be positive—you would not order negative 17 of an item. Sanitizing inputs and outputs to just allow qualified values reduces the *attack surface*. Think of the attack surface as all of the potential ways in which an attacker can attack the application.

Threat modeling is one technique that can be used to reduce the attack surface of an application. Threat modeling details the potential attacks, targets, and any vulnerabilities of an application. It can also help determine the types of controls that are needed to prevent an attack; as an example, when you enter an incorrect username or password do you get a generic response, or does the application respond with too much data, as shown in Figure 11.8? Just keep in mind that the best practice from a security standpoint is to not identify which entry was invalid, and have a generic answer.

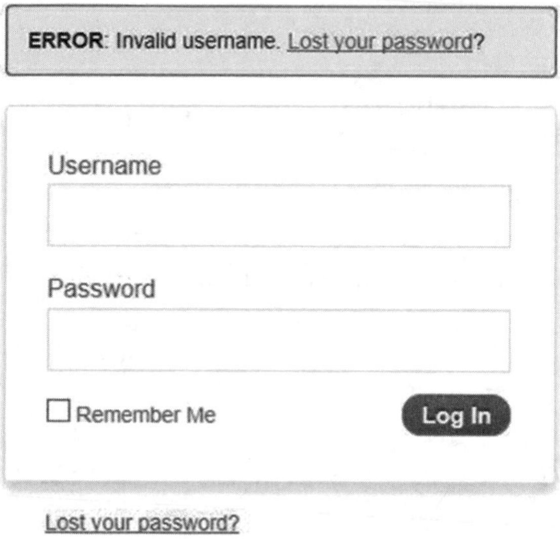

FIGURE 11.8 **Non-generic Response that Should be Flagged by Threat Modeling.**

Security doesn't stop after the software development process. The longer a program has been in use, the more vulnerable it becomes as attackers have had more time to probe and explore methods to exploit the application. Attackers might even analyze patches to see what they are trying to fix and how such vulnerabilities might be exploited.

This means that CISSPs need to take security into account by including proper planning for timely patch and update deployment. A *patch* is a fix to a particular problem in software or operating system code that does not create a security risk but does create problems with the application. A *hot fix* is quick but lacks full integration and testing, and addresses a specific issue. A *service pack* is a collection of all patches to date; it is considered critical and should be installed as soon as possible.

The CISSP will also want to consider:

▶ What is the software environment?—Where will the software be used? Is it on a mainframe, or maybe a publicly available website? Is the software run on a server, or is it downloaded and executed on the client (mobile code)?

▶ What programming language and toolset was used?—While programming languages have evolved, some languages, such as C, are known to be vulnerable to buffer overflows.

> **Note**
>
> Java is estimated to be installed on more than 850 million computers, 3 billion phones, and millions of TVs, but it was not until August of 2014 that the company changed its update software to remove older, vulnerable versions of Java during the installation process.

▶ What are the security issues in the source code?—Depending on how the code is processed it may or may not be easy to identify problems. As an example, a compiler translates a high-level language into machine language, whereas an interpreter translates the program line by line. Also, can the attacker change input, process, or output data? Will the program flag on these errors?

▶ How do you identify malware and defend against it?—At a minimum, malware protection (antivirus) software needs to be deployed and methods to detect unauthorized changes need to be implemented.

Mobile Code

Mobile code refers to software that will be downloaded from a remote system and run on the computer performing the download; it is widely used on the web. The security issue with mobile code is that it is executed locally. Many times the user might not even know that the code is executing. Examples of mobile code include scripts, VBScript, applets, Flash, Java, and ActiveX controls. The downloaded program will run with the access rights of the logged-in user.

Java is the dominant programming language of mobile code. Java:

▶ Is a compiled high-level language

▶ Can be used on any type of computer

▶ Employs a sandbox security scheme (virtual machine)

Java is extremely portable, since the output of the Java compiler is not executable code, but bytecode. *Bytecode* is a type of instruction set designed for efficient execution by a software interpreter to be executed by the Java run-time system, which is called the Java Virtual Machine (JVM).

A Java *applet* is a specific type of Java program that is designed to be transmitted over the Internet and automatically executed by a Java-compatible web browser, such as Edge, Internet Explorer, Firefox, Chrome, or Safari. The security issue with applets is that they are downloaded on demand, without further interaction with the user.

Buffer Overflow

A *buffer* is a temporary data storage area whose length and type is defined in the program code that creates it, or by the operating system. *Buffer overflows* occur when programmers use unsecured functions or don't enforce limits on buffers—basically, when programmers do not practice good coding techniques. For example, a program should check for and prevent any attempt to stuff 32 letters into a buffer intended for 24 digits.

However, this type of error checking does not always occur, and buffer overflows are commonly used by attackers to gain access to systems and/or for privilege escalation. Attackers can use unprotected buffers to attempt to inject and run malicious code. Worse, if the original code executed has administrator or root level rights, those privileges are granted to the attacker as well. The result is that, many times, the attacker gains access to a privileged command shell on the system under attack. When this occurs, the attacker has complete control.

Because buffer overflows are such a huge problem, you can see that any hacker, ethical or not, is going to search for them. The best way to prevent them is to have perfect programs. Because that is not possible, there are compensating controls:

- ▶ **Audit the code**—Nothing works better than a good manual audit. The individuals that write the code should not be the ones auditing the code. Audits should be performed by a different group of individuals trained to look for poorly written code and potential security problems. Although effective, this can be an expensive and time-consuming process with large, complex programs.

- ▶ **Use safer functions**—There are programming languages that offer more support against buffer overflows than C. If C is going to be used, ensure that safer C library support is used.

- ▶ **Improved compiler techniques**—Compilers such as Java automatically check whether a memory array index is working within the proper bounds.

- ▶ **Harden the stack**—Buffer overflows lead to overwrites of code and pointers in the program's stack space, which holds the code and predefined variables. This overwriting is called "smashing the stack."

A good paper on this topic is at insecure.org/stf/smashstack.html. However, products such as StackGuard and Visual Basic have evolved special guard buffers called *canaries* that are compiled into code. A *canary* is a protected zone that is added between chunks of stack code. The code's execution is immediately halted if a canary is breached in a stack smashing attempt. Such techniques are not 100% effective and might still be vulnerable to heap overflows.

Financial Attacks

A large number of the attacks that occur today are for financial reasons. One example is a rounding-down attack. Rounding down skims off small amounts of money by rounding down the last few digits. Let's say a bank account has $8,239,128.45 and the amount is rounded down to $8,239,128.40. A *salami* attack is similar; it involves slicing off small amounts of money so that the last few digits are truncated. As an example, $8,239,128.45 becomes $8,239,128.00. Both rounding and salami attacks work under the concept that small amounts will not be missed and that over time the pennies will add up to big profits for the attacker. When you take a break from studying, check out the movie "Office Space" to see a good example of an attempted salami attack.

The attacker might even plant code with the thought of waiting until a later date to have it execute. This is called a *logic bomb*, and while it is not just for financial attacks, it can cause a great deal of damage. The logic bomb can be designed to detonate on some predetermined action or trigger. Because they are buried so deep in the code, logic bombs are difficult to discover or detect before they become active. Fired employees might do this to strike back at their former employer.

Change Detection

Hashing is one of the ways in which malicious code can be detected. Hash-based application verification ensures that an application has not been modified or corrupted, by comparing the file's hash value to a previously calculated value. If these values match, the file is presumed to be unmodified.

Change detection is another useful technique. Tripwire is an example of this type of software. Change detection software detects changes to system and configuration files. Most of these programs work by storing a hashed value of the original file in a database. Periodically, the file is rechecked and the hashed values are compared. If the two values do not match, the program can trigger an alert to signal that there might have been a compromise.

Hashed values are the most widely used mechanisms for detecting changes in files. Most software vendors provide a web-accessible summary that lists the fingerprints of all files included in their products. This gives users a way to ensure they have the authentic file.

Viruses

Computer *viruses* are nothing new; they have been around since the dawn of the computer era. What has changed through the years is the way in which viruses infect systems. Some of the ways in which viruses can spread include the following:

▶ **Master boot record infection**—This is the oldest form of malicious attack. The technique involves the placement of malicious code on the master boot record. This attack was very effective in the days when everyone passed around floppy disks.

▶ **File infection**—A slightly newer form of virus, file infectors rely on the user to execute the infected file to cause the damage. These viruses attach to files based on their extensions, such as .com and .exe. Some form of social engineering is normally used to get the user to execute the program.

▶ **Macro infection**—This modern style of virus began appearing in the 1990s. Macro viruses exploit scripting services installed on your computer. Most of you probably remember the I Love You virus, a prime example of a macro infector. Macro infections are tied to Microsoft Office scripting capabilities.

▶ **Polymorphic**—This style of virus has the capability to adapt and change so that it can attempt to evade signature-based antivirus tools (see below). Such viruses might even use encryption to avoid detection.

▶ **Multipartite**—This style of virus can use more than one propagation method and targets both the boot sector and program files. One example is the NATAS ("Satan" spelled backwards) virus.

▶ **Meme**—While not a true virus, it spreads like one and is basically a chain letter or email message that is continually forwarded. It is sometimes referred to as a cultural virus.

Viruses can use many techniques to avoid detection. Some viruses might spread fast, whereas others spread slowly. *Fast infection* viruses infect any file that they are capable of infecting. Others, known as *sparse infectors*, limit their rates of spread. Some viruses forego a life of living exclusively in files and load themselves into RAM. These viruses are known as *RAM-resident*.

Antivirus software is the best defense against these types of malware. Most detection software contains a library of signatures that it uses to detect viruses. A *signature* identifies a pattern of bytes found in the virus code. Here is an example of a virus signature:

> X5O!P%@AP[4\PZX54(P^)7CC)7$EICAR-STANDARD-ANTIVIRUS-TEST-FILE!$H+H*

If you were to copy this code into a text file and rename the extension so that the file is recognized as an executable, your antivirus software should flag the file as a virus. This file is actually harmless, but contains a signature found within a classic virus. This particular sequence was developed by the European Institute of Computer Anti-virus Research (EICER) as a means of testing the functionality of antivirus software.

> **Tip**
>
> Many antivirus programs work by means of signatures. Signature programs examine boot sectors, files, and sections of program code known to be vulnerable to viral programs. Although the programs are efficient, they are only as good as their latest signature lists. They must be updated regularly to detect the most recent type of computer viruses. Even then there are a variety of tools that attackers can use to try to make virus payloads harder to detect. One such tool is Tejon Cryptor.

Worms

Worms, unlike viruses, require no interaction on the user's part to replicate and spread. One of the first worms to be released on the Internet was the RTM worm. It was developed by Robert Morris Jr. back in 1988 and was meant only to be a proof of concept. Its accidental release brought home the fact that this type of code can do massive damage to the Internet.

Today, the biggest changes to worms are:

- ▶ The mechanism by which worms spread.

- ▶ The new methods of how they attack.

- ▶ The new types of payloads might do nothing more than display a message on your screen at a certain data and time, whereas others could encrypt your hard drive until you pay a ransom.

▶ The goals of worms and even malware in general now tend to be much more specific. As an example, Stuxnet was developed to target programmable logic controllers (PLCs), which control the automation of centrifuges used for separating nuclear material.

Sality: A Classic Example of Modern Malware

Sality has been around since 2003, yet is still widely used to exploit systems today. Sality has a wide range of capabilities and has its roots in such malware as Nimda and Conficker. It's considered polymorphic as it has the ability to change to thwart detection. Once a system becomes infected with this malware it quickly goes to work. Sality disables antivirus software and prevents access to antivirus and security websites. It also adds itself to the registry and then attempts to further hide itself by avoiding files protected by System File Checker or any executable that might raise the suspicion of an end user.

Sality prevents infected systems from booting into safe mode, and then starts to spread to the root of any discoverable drives, network shares, or USB drives. Once installed and hidden, Sality "phones home" via its own P2P network. This allows it to accept commands, check for updates, and act as a malware dropper to install additional malware. Sality's payload is typically executed in the context of other processes, which allows it to bypass firewalls and makes cleaning difficult. Depending on the version it can:

▶ Steal cached passwords.

▶ Access the Microsoft Outlook address book to send spam.

▶ Install a key logger to capture passwords and credit card numbers.

▶ Attempt to download and install pay-per-install executables.

▶ Try to access the local router with default usernames and passwords, in an attempt to alter DNS settings.

Exam Prep Questions

1. A CISSP must understand the different types of application updates. All updates should be obtained from the manufacturer only, and deployed into production only once tested on non-production systems. As such, what is the **best** answer that describes updates, patches, hot fixes, and service packs?

   ○ **A.** A hot fix has undergone full integration testing, has been released to address vulnerability, and addresses a specific issue; in most cases a hot fix is not appropriate for all systems. A security patch lacks full integration and testing, has been released to address a vulnerability, and is mandatory. A service pack is a collection of patches that are critical, and should be installed quickly.

   ○ **B.** A hot fix is quick, lacks full integration and testing, and addresses a specific issue; in most cases a hot fix is not appropriate for all systems. A security patch is a collection of patches that are critical and has been released to address a vulnerability. A service pack is a collection of patches and is considered critical.

   ○ **C.** A hot fix is a quick collection of critical, install ASAP patches that address a specific issue; in most cases a hot fix is not appropriate for all systems. A security patch has undergone full integration testing, and has been released to address a vulnerability. A service pack is a collection of patches.

   ○ **D.** A hot fix is slow and has full integration and testing, and addresses a broad set of problems; in most cases a hot fix is appropriate for all systems. A security patch is a collection of patches that are not critical. A service pack is a collection of patches and is not considered critical.

2. Which is the correct solution that describes the CIA triad when applied to software security?

   ○ **A.** Confidentiality prevents unauthorized access, integrity prevents unauthorized modification, and availability deals with countermeasures to prevent denial of service to authorized users.

   ○ **B.** Confidentiality prevents unauthorized modification, integrity prevents unauthorized access, and availability deals with countermeasures to prevent denial of service to authorized users.

   ○ **C.** Confidentiality prevents unauthorized access, integrity prevents unauthorized modification, and availability deals with countermeasures to prevent unauthorized access.

   ○ **D.** Confidentiality deals with countermeasures to prevent denial of service to authorized users, integrity prevents unauthorized modification, and availability prevents unauthorized access.

3. Which of the following tools can be used for change detection?

- ○ **A.** DES
- ○ **B.** Checksums
- ○ **C.** MD5sum
- ○ **D.** Parity bits

4. Bob has noticed that when he inputs too much data into his new Internet application, it momentarily locks up the computer and then halts the program. Which of the following best describes this situation?

- ○ **A.** Fail-safe
- ○ **B.** Buffer overflow
- ○ **C.** Fail-open
- ○ **D.** Fail-soft

5. Which of the following types of database is considered a lattice structure, with each record having multiple parent and child records?

- ○ **A.** Hierarchical database management system
- ○ **B.** Network database management system
- ○ **C.** Object-oriented database management system
- ○ **D.** Relational database management system

6. Which database term refers to the capability to restrict certain fields or rows from unauthorized individuals?

- ○ **A.** Low granularity
- ○ **B.** High resolution
- ○ **C.** High granularity
- ○ **D.** Low resolution

7. Which of the following types of testing involves entering malformed, random data?

- ○ **A.** XSS
- ○ **B.** Buffer overflow
- ○ **C.** Fuzzing
- ○ **D.** Whitebox testing

8. OmniTec's new programmer has left several entry points in its new e-commerce shopping cart program for testing and development. Which of the following terms best describes what the programmer has done?

   ○ **A.** Back door

   ○ **B.** Security flaw

   ○ **C.** SQL injection

   ○ **D.** Trapdoor

9. Generation 2 programming languages are considered what?

   ○ **A.** Assembly

   ○ **B.** Machine

   ○ **C.** High-level

   ○ **D.** Natural

10. Which of the following is considered middleware?

   ○ **A.** Atomicity

   ○ **B.** OLE

   ○ **C.** CORBA

   ○ **D.** Object-oriented programming

11. After Debbie became the programmer for the new payroll application, she placed some extra code in the application that would cause it to halt if she was fired and her name removed from payroll. What type of attack has she launched?

   ○ **A.** Rounding down

   ○ **B.** Logic bomb

   ○ **C.** Salami

   ○ **D.** Buffer overflow

12. While working on a penetration test assignment, you just discovered that the company's database-driven e-commerce site will let you place a negative quantity into an order field so that the system will credit you money. What best describes this failure?

   ○ **A.** Referential integrity error

   ○ **B.** Buffer overflow

   ○ **C.** Semantic integrity error

   ○ **D.** Rounding down

13. Which of the following best describes bytecode?

- ○ **A.** Is processor-specific
- ○ **B.** Is used with ActiveX
- ○ **C.** Is not processor-specific
- ○ **D.** Is used with COM and DCOM

14. One of the best approaches to deal with attacks like SQL, LDAP, and XML injection is what?

- ○ **A.** Using type-safe languages
- ○ **B.** Manual review of code
- ○ **C.** Using emanations
- ○ **D.** Adequate parameter validation

15. Which of the following program techniques would this phrase most closely be associated with? *Two objects may not know how the other object works and each is hidden from the other.*

- ○ **A.** Data modeling
- ○ **B.** Network database management system
- ○ **C.** Object-oriented programming
- ○ **D.** Relational database management system

Answers to Exam Prep Questions

1. **B.** A hot fix is quick, lacks full integration and testing, and addresses a specific issue; in most cases a hot fix is not appropriate for all systems. A security patch is a collection of patches that are critical and has been released to address a vulnerability. A service pack is a collection of patches and is considered critical. Answers A, C, and D are all incorrect because the definitions are swapped and connected to the wrong solution. Software updates are optional, and usually functionality-, not security-, related. Firmware releases are produced to address security issues with hardware.

2. **A.** Answers B, C, and D are incorrect and are just scrambled definitions that look similar to confuse the test-taker. Confidentiality prevents unauthorized access, integrity prevents unauthorized modification, and availability deals with countermeasures to prevent denial of service to authorized users.

3. **C.** One of the ways in which malicious code can be detected is through the use of change-detection software. This software has the capability to detect changes to system and configuration files. Popular programs that perform this function include Tripwire and MD5sum. Answer A is incorrect because DES is an asymmetric algorithm. Answers B and D are incorrect because both checksums and parity bits can be easily changed and, therefore, do not protect the software from change.

4. **D.** A fail-soft occurs when a detected failure terminates the application while the system continues to function. Answers A and C are incorrect because a fail-safe terminates the program and disables the system, while a fail-open is the worst of events because it allows attackers to bypass security controls and easily compromise the system. Answer B is incorrect because although a buffer overflow could be the root cause of the problem, the question asks why the application is halting in the manner described.

5. **B.** Network database management systems are designed for flexibility. The network database model is considered a lattice structure because each record can have multiple parent and child records. Answer A is incorrect because hierarchical database management systems are structured like a tree: each record can have only one owner, and because of this restriction, hierarchical databases often can't be used to relate to structures in the real world. Answer C is incorrect because object-oriented database management systems are not lattice-based and don't use a high-level language like SQL. Answer D is incorrect because relational database management systems are considered collections of tables that are linked by their primary keys.

6. **C.** Granularity refers to control over the view someone has of the database. Highly granular databases have the capability to restrict certain fields or rows from unauthorized individuals. Answer A is incorrect because low granularity gives the database manager little control. Answers B and D are incorrect because high resolution and low resolution do not apply to the question.

7. **C.** Fuzzing is a form of blackbox testing that enters random input and monitors for flaws or a system crash. The idea is to look for problems in the application. Answers A, B, and D are incorrect: this is not an example of white-box testing, a buffer overflow, or XSS.

8. **D.** A trapdoor is a technique used by programmers as a secret entry point into a program. Programmers find these useful during application development; however, they should be removed before the code is finalized. All other answers are incorrect: answer B is also a security flaw, but is not as specific as trapdoor; back doors (answer A) are malicious in nature; SQL injection (answer C) is targeted against databases.

9. **A.** Programming languages are categorized as follows: Generation 1 is machine language, Generation 2 is assembly language, Generation 3 is high-level language, Generation 4 is very high-level language, and Generation 5 is natural language.

10. **C.** Common Object Request Broker Architecture (CORBA) is vendor-independent middleware. Its purpose is to tie together different vendor products so that they can seamlessly work together over distributed networks. Answer B is incorrect because Object Linking and Embedding (OLE) is a proprietary system developed by Microsoft to allow applications to transfer and share information. Answer A is incorrect because atomicity deals with the validity of database transactions. Answer D is incorrect because object-oriented programming is a modular form of programming.

11. **B.** A logic bomb is designed to detonate sometime later when the perpetrator leaves; it is usually buried deep in the code. Answers A, C, and D are incorrect: rounding down skims off small amounts of money by rounding down the last few digits; a salami attack involves slicing off small amounts of money so that the last few digits are truncated; a buffer overflow is storing more information in a buffer than it is intended to hold.

12. **C.** Semantic integrity controls logical values, data, and operations that could affect them, such as placing a negative number in an order quantity field. Answers A, B, and D are incorrect: referential integrity ensures that foreign keys only reference existing primary keys; buffer overflow is storing more information in a buffer than it is intended to hold; rounding down skims off small amounts of money by rounding down the last few digits.

13. **C.** Bytecode is not processor-specific and is a form of intermediate code used by Java. Answers A, B, and D are incorrect: bytecode is not processor-specific and can run on many systems; bytecode is not associated with ActiveX; COM / DCOM are technologies associated with ActiveX.

14. **D.** Adequate parameter validation is seen as the best approach to dealing with input problems. All data, when input, when processed, and when output, must be checked for validity. Answers A, B, and C are incorrect: moving to a type-safe language will not prevent buffer overflows; although manual review of code may find some problems, this might not always be possible; switching to mobile code is also something that is not seen as feasible in all situations.

15. **C.** Object-oriented development allows an object to hide the way an object works from other objects. Answers A, B, and D are incorrect: data modeling considers data independently; network database management systems are designed for flexibility; relational database management systems are considered collections of tables that are linked by their primary keys.

Need to Know More?

Building security software: www.owasp.org/index.php/
OWASP_Guide_Project

Microsoft SDL: www.microsoft.com/en-us/sdl/

Six steps to change management: www.techrepublic.com/article/
implement-change-management-with-these-six-steps/5074869

Object-oriented programming: encyclopedia2.thefreedictionary.com/
Object-oriented+programming

Meme virus: asocial.narod.ru/en/articles/memes.htm

Java exploits: heimdalsecurity.com/blog/java-biggest-security-
hole-your-computer/

Buffer overflows: insecure.org/stf/smashstack.html

How Trojan horse programs work: computer.howstuffworks.com/
trojan-horse.htm

The history of SQL injection attacks: motherboard.vice.com/read/
the-history-of-sql-injection-the-hack-that-will-never-go-away

SQL injection and database manipulation: www.securiteam.com/
securityreviews/5DP0N1P76E.html

CORBA FAQ: www.omg.org/gettingstarted/corbafaq.htm

CHAPTER 12

Business Continuity Planning

Terms you'll need to understand:

▶ Business continuity

▶ Hot site

▶ Warm site

▶ Cold site

▶ Criticality prioritization

▶ Maximum tolerable downtime (MTD)

▶ Remote journaling

▶ Electronic vaulting

▶ Qualitative assessment

▶ Quantitative assessment

▶ Database shadowing

Topics you'll need to master:

▶ Development and processing of contingency plans

▶ Completing business impact analyses

▶ Creation of backup strategies

▶ Integrating management responsibilities

▶ Steering team responsibilities

▶ Testing emergency plans

▶ Notifying employees of procedures

▶ Testing issues and concerns

Introduction

Most of this book has focused on ways in which security incidents can be prevented. This chapter addresses the need to prepare for, and how to respond to, disasters that could put your company out of business. Notable recent events, such as tsunamis in Japan and Southeast Asia, 9/11 in New York, Pennsylvania, and Washington, D.C., Hurricane Katrina in New Orleans, earthquakes in China, and Hurricane Ike in Houston, continue to highlight the need for organizations to be adequately prepared. Even after these calamitous events, Disaster Recovery Institute (DRI) reports that most United States companies still spend, on average, only 3.7% of their IT budget on disaster recovery planning, whereas best practice calls for 6%.

For a company to be successful under duress of hardship or catastrophe, it must plan how to protected time sensitive business operations and the IT assets that support these business operations in the face of these major disruptions. A business continuity plan (BCP) identifies how a business would respond and recover in the wake of serious damage, and evolves only as the result of a risk assessment that identifies potentials for serious damage. It is an unfortunate reality that this critical planning for disasters and disruptions is an often-overlooked area of IT security.

> **ExamAlert**
>
> Note: ISC² covers business continuity (BC) in the Security Operations domain, but there is a lot to cover, so I have placed BC into this chapter. Remember that for the exam you will be given 250 questions from the 8 domains. You will not be asked or need to know which domain they are based on.

Some key elements of this chapter include project management and planning, business impact analysis (BIA), continuity planning design and development, and BCP testing and training.

Threats to Business Operations

A disaster is something that many of us would prefer not to think about. Many might see it as an unpleasant exercise or something that is safe to ignore. Sadly, disasters and incidents are something that we all will find occasion to deal with, and the threats they pose vary. For example, mainframes face a different set of threats than distributed systems, just as computers connected to modems face a different set of threats than do wireless-connected computers. This means that planning must be dynamic: able to change with time and circumstance.

Threats can be man-made or natural, accidental or intentional; however, regardless of the cause, threats have the potential to cause an incident with the same end result. Incidents and disruptions come in many forms. Those foolish enough not to prepare could witness the death of their business. Categories of threats that should be provided for include:

▶ **Man-made/political**—Disgruntled employees, riots, vandalism, accidents, theft, crime, protesters, and political unrest

▶ **Technical**—Outages, malicious code, worms, hackers, electrical power problems, equipment outages, utility problems, and water shortages

▶ **Natural**—Earthquakes, storms, fires, floods, hurricanes, tornados, and tidal waves

Each of these can cause an interruption in operations and should be defined in your company disaster recovery plan (DRP). The DRP should address the impact of a disaster or disruption on time-sensitive business processes and on critical services and resources that support those business processes. Each company will be different. Disruption of services can be categorized as follows:

▶ **Minor**—Operations are disrupted for several hours to less than a day.

▶ **Intermediate**—Operations are disrupted for a day or longer. The organization might need a secondary site to continue operations.

▶ **Major**—The entire facility is unusable. Ancillary sites will be required while the original site is rebuilt or a new facility is found or built.

Business Continuity Planning (BCP)

There are many different approaches to BCP. Some companies address these processes separately, whereas others focus on a continuous process that interweaves the plans. The National Institute of Standards and Technology (NIST) (www.csrc.nist.gov) offers a good example of the contingency process in Special Publication 800-34: Continuity Planning Guide for Information Technology Systems. In NIST SP 800-34, the BCP/DRP process is defined as:

1. Develop the contingency planning policy statement.

2. Conduct the BIA (business impact analysis).

3. Identify preventive controls.

4. Develop recovery strategies.

5. Develop an IT contingency plan.

6. Test the plan, train employees, and hold exercises.

7. Maintain the plan.

Before we go further, let's define the terms *disaster* and *business continuity*. A disaster is any sudden, unplanned calamitous event that brings about great damage or loss. Entire communities have concerns following a disaster; however, businesses face special challenges because they have responsibilities to protect the lives and livelihoods of their employees, and to guard company assets on behalf of shareholders. In the business realm, a disaster can be seen as any event that prevents the continuance of critical business functions for a predetermined period of time. In other words, the estimated outage might force the declaration of a disaster.

> **ExamAlert**
>
> For the exam keep in mind that human safety always comes first and has priority over all other concerns.

Business continuity is the process of sustaining operation of a critical business function (CBF) to keep the company in business for the long term. (A DRP is part of a BCP, but deals with more with technology and short-term issues: "What do we do right now to stop the bleeding and get critical systems and services running?" The overall BCP, by contrast, lays out what a company does to stay in business and return to normal operations. The CISSP candidate must know the difference for the exam.) The goal of business continuity is to reduce or prevent outage time and optimize operations. The Business Continuity Institute (www.thebci.org), a professional body for business continuity management, defines it as a holistic management process that identifies potential impacts that threaten an organization, provides a framework for building resilience, ensures an effective response, and safeguards its reputation, brand, value, and the interests of its key stakeholders.

Although there are competing methodologies that can be used to complete the BCP/DRP process, this chapter will follow steps that most closely align with reference documentation recommended by ISC[2]. Figure 12.1 illustrates an overview of the process, the steps for which are as follows:

1. Project initiation

2. Business impact analysis (BIA)

3. Recovery strategy

4. Plan design and development

5. Implementation

6. Testing

7. Monitoring and maintenance

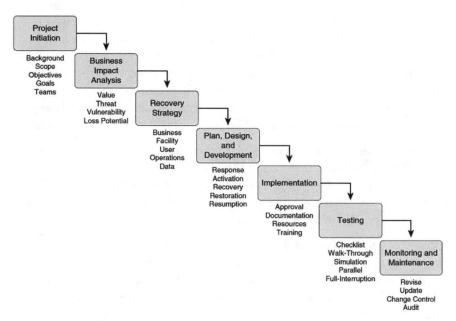

FIGURE 12.1 **BCP/DRP Process.**

We will discuss each of these steps individually.

Project Management and Initiation

Before the BCP process can begin, it is essential to have the support of senior management, because they are responsible for:

▶ Setting the budget

▶ Determining the team leader

▶ Starting the BCP process

Without senior management support, you will not have funds to successfully complete the project, and resulting efforts will be marginally successful, if at all. One way to gain their support this is to prepare and present a seminar for them that overviews the risks the organization faces, identifies basic threats, and documents the costs of potential outages. This is a good time to remind them that, ultimately, they are legally responsible. Customers, shareholders, stockholders, or anyone else could bring civil suits against senior management if they feel the company has not practiced due care.

Senior management must choose a team leader. This individual must have enough credibility with senior management to influence them in regard to BCP results and recommendations. After the team leader is appointed, an action plan can be established and the team can be assembled. Members of the team should include representatives from management, legal staff, recovery team leaders, the information security team, various business units, the networking team, and the physical security team. It is important to include asset owners and the individuals that would be responsible for executing the plan.

Next, determine the project scope. A properly defined scope is of tremendous help in maximizing the effectiveness of the BCP plan. You cannot protect everything and you really do not need to, either. For example if you are planning for a company that has offices in California, Florida, New York, and Montana you would not have contingency plans for hurricanes for all offices.

Be sensitive to interoffice politics, which, if it gets out of control, can derail the entire planning process. Another problem to avoid is *project creep*, which occurs when more and more items that were not part of the original project plan are added to it. This can delay completion of the project or cause it to run over budget.

The BCP benefits from adherence to traditional project plan phases. Issues such as resources (personnel and financial), time schedules, budget estimates, and any critical success factors must be managed. Schedule an initial meeting to kick off the process.

Finally, the team is ready to get to work. The team can expect a host of duties and responsibilities:

▶ Identifying regulatory and legal requirements that must be complied with

▶ Identifying all possible threats and risks

▶ Estimating the probability of these threats and correctly identifying their loss potential

▶ Performing a BIA

▶ Outlining the priority in which departments, systems, and processes must be up and running

▶ Developing the procedures and steps to resume business functions following a disaster

▶ Assigning crisis situation tasks to employee roles or individuals

▶ Documenting plans, communicating plans to employees, and performing necessary training and drills

It's important for everyone on the team to realize that the BCP is the most important corrective control the organization will have, and to use the planning period as an opportunity to shape it. The BCP is more than just corrective controls; the BCP is also about preventive and detective controls. These three elements are:

▶ **Preventive**—Including controls to identify critical assets and prevent outages

▶ **Detective**—Including controls to alert the organization quickly in case of outages or problems

▶ **Corrective**—Including controls to restore normal operations as quickly as possible

Business Impact Analysis

The next task is to create the BIA, the role of which is to measure the impact each type of disaster could have on critical or time-sensitive business functions. It is necessary to evaluate time as a metric, just as you would the importance of the function. For example, paying employees is not critical from the perspective of business activities, but if you don't pay them on time, your company will still go out of business because it will lose its employees.

The BIA is an important step in the process because it considers all threats and the implications of those threats. As an example, the city of Galveston, Texas is on an island known to be prone to hurricanes. Although it might be winter in Galveston and the possibility of a hurricane is extremely low, it doesn't mean that planning can't take place to reduce the potential negative impact if and when a hurricane arrives. The steps for accomplishing this require trying to think through all possible disasters, assess the risk of those disasters, quantify the impact, determine the loss, and identify and prioritize operations that would require disaster recovery planning in the event of those disasters.

The BIA is tasked with answering three vital questions:

▶ **What is most critical?**—The prioritization must be developed to address what processes are most critical to the organization.

▶ **How long an outage can the company endure?**—The downtime estimation is performed to determine which processes must resume first, second, third, and so on, and to determine which systems must be kept up and running.

▶ **What resources are required?**—Resource requirements must be identified and require correlation of system assets to business processes. As an example, a generator can provide backup power, but requires fuel to operate.

> **Note**
>
> Criticality prioritization is something that companies do all the time. Consider the last time you phoned your favorite computer vendor to order new equipment. How long were you placed on hold? Most likely, your call was answered within a few minutes. Contrast that event with the last time you phoned the same company to speak to the help desk. How long was the wait? Most likely, much longer.

The development of multiple scenarios should provide a clear picture of what is needed to continue operations in the event of a disaster. The team creating the BIA will need to look at the organization from many different angles and use information from a variety of sources. Different tools can be used to help gather data. Strohl Systems' BIA Professional and SunGard's Paragon software can automate portions of the data input and collection process. Although the CISSP exam will not require that you know the names of various tools, it is important to understand how the BIA process works, and it helps to know tools that are available.

Whether the BIA process is completed manually or with the assistance of tools, its completion will take some time. Any time individuals are studying processes, techniques, and procedures they are not familiar with, a learning curve will be involved.

As you might be starting to realize, creation of a BIA is no easy task. It requires not only the knowledge of business processes but also a thorough understanding of the organization itself, including IT resources, individual business units, and the interrelationships of each. This task will require the support of senior management and the cooperation of IT personnel, business unit managers, and end users. The general steps within the BIA are:

1. Determine data-gathering techniques.

2. Gather business impact analysis data.

3. Identify critical business functions and resources that support these functions.

4. Verify completeness of data.

5. Establish recovery time for operations.

6. Define recovery alternatives and costs.

> ### Note
>
> A vulnerability assessment is often included in a BIA. Although the assessment is somewhat similar to the risk-assessment process discussed in Chapter 9, "Security Assessment and Testing," this assessment focuses on providing information specifically for the business continuity plan.

Assessing Potential Loss

There are different approaches to assessing potential loss. One of the most popular methods is the use of a questionnaire. This approach requires the development of a questionnaire distributed to senior management and end users. The objective of the questionnaire is to maximize the identification of potential loss by the people engaged in business processes that would be jeopardized by a disaster. This questionnaire might be distributed and independently completed or filled out during an interactive interview process. Figure 12.2 shows a sample questionnaire.

BIA Questionnaire

Item	Description	Conclusions
Introduction		
Unit Name		
Date of Interview		
Contact		
Description of Business Unit Function		
Financial Impacts		
Revenue Loss Impact		
Expense Impact		
Operational Impact		
Business Interruption Impact		
Loss of Confidence		
Loss of Customers		
Loss of Market Share		
Technology Dependence		
System Function		
System Interdependencies		
Existing BCP Controls		
Other BIA Issues		

FIGURE 12.2 **BIA Questionnaire.**

The questionnaire can also be completed in a round table setting. In fact, this sort of group completion can add synergy to the process, as long as the dynamics of the group allow for open communication and the required key individuals can all schedule and meet to discuss the impact specific types of disruptions would have on the organization. The importance of the inclusion of all key individuals must be emphasized because management might not be aware of critical key tasks for which they do not have direct oversight.

A questionnaire is a qualitative technique for assessing risk. Qualitative assessments are scenario-driven and do not attempt to assign dollar values to anticipated loss. A qualitative assessment ranks the seriousness of an impact using grades or classes, such as low, medium, high, or critical. As an example:

▶ **Low**—Minor inconvenience that customers might not notice. Outages could last for up to 30 days without any real inconvenience.

▶ **Medium**—Loss of service would impact the organization after a few days to a week. Longer outages could affect the company's bottom line or result in the loss of customers.

▶ **High**—Only short-term outages of a few minutes to hours could be endured. Longer outages would have a severe financial impact. Negative press might also reduce outlook for future products and services.

▶ **Critical**—Outage of any duration cannot be endured. Systems and controls must be in place or be developed to ensure redundancy so that no outage occurs.

This sort of grading process enables a quicker progress in the identification of risks, and provides a means of classifying processes that might not easily equate to a dollar value. This will also help you to understand the appropriate recovery techniques or technologies based on the level of criticality. Table 12.1 provides an example of this.

TABLE 12.1 **Example of Qualitative Ranking**

Asset or Resource	Availability	Integrity	Confidentiality
Application server	High	Medium	Critical
Firewall	High	Low	Low
Web server	Medium	High	Low
HR database	High	High	Critical

The BIA can also be undertaken using a quantitative approach. This method of analysis attempts to assign a monetary value to all assets, exposures, and processes identified during the risk assessment. These values are used to calculate the material impact of a potential disaster, including both loss of income and expenses. A quantitative approach requires:

1. Estimation of potential losses and determination of single loss expectancy (SLE)

2. Completion of a threat frequency analysis and calculation of the annual rate of occurrence (ARO)

3. Determination of the annual loss expectancy (ALE)

The process of performing a quantitative assessment is covered in much more detail in Chapter 4, "Security and Risk Management". It is important that a quantitative study include all associated costs resulting from a disaster, such as:

▶ Lost productivity

▶ Delayed or canceled orders

▶ Cost of repair

▶ The value of the damaged equipment or lost data

▶ The cost of rental equipment

▶ The cost of emergency services

▶ The cost to replace equipment or reload data

Both quantitative and qualitative assessment techniques require the BIA team to examine how the loss of service or data would affect the company. Each method is seeking to reduce risk and plan for contingencies, as shown in Figure 12.3.

FIGURE 12.3 **Risk Reduction Process.**

The severity of an outage is generally measured by considering the *maximum tolerable downtime* (MTD) that the organization can survive without that resource, function, or service.

Tip

Know terms like MTD and understand their meaning for the exam.

Will there be a loss of revenue or operational capital, or will the organization be held legally liable? Although the team might be focused on what the immediate effect of an outage would be, costs are not necessarily immediate. Many organizations are under regulatory requirements; the result of an outage could be a legal penalty or fine. Or an organization's reputation could be tarnished.

> **Caution**
>
> MTD is a measurement of the longest time that an organization can survive without a specific business function.

Reputation Has Its Value

Although some organizations might focus solely on dollar amounts when working through a BIA, reputation also needs to be considered. A quote from Benjamin Franklin states, "It takes many good deeds to build a good reputation, and only one bad one to lose it." To illustrate this point, consider the following brand names and their business reputations:

- ▶ **Cisco**—An industry leader of quality networking equipment.
- ▶ **Ruth's Chris Steak House**—An upscale eatery known for serving high-quality steaks seared at 1800° Fahrenheit.
- ▶ **Rolls-Royce**—Known for high-quality luxury automobiles.
- ▶ **Enron**—A symbol of corporate fraud and corruption.
- ▶ **Yugo**—A low-quality car released in the United States in the mid-1980s.
- ▶ **Volkswagen**—A well-known auto maker that was scarred by a public relations thrashing over its "Dieselgate" scandal.

Perhaps your vision of the companies listed is different than what was documented. The intent of the listing is to demonstrate that well-known corporate names do generate visions when people hear and read them. Companies work hard for years to gain a level of respect and positive reputation. Catastrophes don't just happen. Most occur because of human error or as the result of a series of overlooked mistakes. Will a mistake be fatal to your organization? Reputations can be easily damaged. That is why disaster recovery is so important. The very future of your organization may rest on it.

Recovery Strategy

A recovery strategy involves planning for failure by using methods of resiliency. Developing a successful recovery strategy requires senior management's support. To judge the best strategy to recover from a given interruption, the team must evaluate and complete:

1. Detailed documentation of all costs associated with each possible alternative.

2. Quoted cost estimates for any outside services that might be needed.

3. Written agreements with chosen vendors for all outside services.

4. Possible resumption strategies in case there is a complete loss of the facility.

5. Documentation of findings and conclusions as a report to management of chosen recovery strategy for feedback and approval.

This information is used to determine the best course of action based on the analysis of data from the BIA. With so much to consider, it is helpful to divide the organization's recovery into specific areas, functions, or categories:

▶ Business process recovery

▶ Facility and supply recovery

▶ User recovery

▶ Operations recovery

▶ Data and information recovery

Business Process Recovery

Business processes can be interrupted due to the loss of personnel, critical equipment, supplies, or office space; or from uprisings, such as strikes. As an example, in 2005 after Katrina, New Orleans had a huge influx of workers in the city rebuilding homes, offices, and damaged buildings. Fast food restaurants were eager to meet the demand these workers had for burgers, fries, tacos, and fried chicken. However, there was insufficient low-cost housing for the fast food industry's employees. The resulting shortage forced fast food restaurants to pay bonuses of up to $6,000 to entice potential employees to the area. It is worth noting that even if the facility is intact after a disaster, people are still required and are an important part of the business process recovery.

Workflow diagrams and documents can assist business process recovery by mapping relationships between critical functions to evaluate interdependencies. Often, a critical process cannot be done because a related process was left out of the workflow. For example, you bring in the hardware, software, electric supply, and a system engineer to restore a computerized business process; however, you do not have any network cables to connect the equipment. Now all the vendors are closed because of the storm; therefore, no five-dollar networking cables are available! A process flow can identify what needs to be done and what parts and components are needed. The process order for a widget illustrates a sample flow:

1. Is the widget in stock?

2. Which warehouse has the widget?

3. When can the widget be shipped?

4. Confirm capability to fulfill order with customer and provide total.

5. Process credit card information.

6. Verify funds were deposited in the bank.

7. Ship item to customer.

8. Restock widget for subsequent sales.

A more detailed listing would be appropriate for industrial use, but you get the idea. Building these types of flowcharts allows organizations to examine the resources required for each step and the functions that are critical for continued business operations.

Facility and Supply Recovery

Facility and supply interruptions can be caused by fire, loss of inventory, transportation or telecommunications problems, or even heating, ventilating, and air conditioning (HVAC) problems. An emergency operations center (EOC) must be established and redundant services enabled for rapid recovery from interruptions. Many options are available, from a dedicated offsite facility, to agreements with other organizations for shared space, to the option of building a prefab building and leaving it empty as a type of cold backup site. The following sections examine some of these options.

Subscription Services

Building and running data-processing facilities is expensive. Organizations might opt instead to contract their EOC facility needs to a subscription service. The CISSP exam categorizes these subscription services as hot, warm, and cold sites.

A *hot site* is ready to be brought online quickly. It is fully configured and is equipped with the same systems as the regular production site. It can be made operational within just a few hours. A hot site will need staff, data, and procedural documentation. Hot sites are a high-cost recovery option, but can be justified when a short recovery time is required. As a subscription service, a range of associated fees exist, including monthly cost, subscription fees, testing costs, and usage or activation fees. Contracts for hot sites need to be closely examined because some charge extremely high activation fees to discourage subscribers from utilizing the facility for anything less than a true disaster. To get an idea of the types of costs involved, www.drj.com reports that subscriptions for hot sites average 52 months in duration and costs can be as high as $120,000 per month.

> **Caution**
>
> Is one backup site enough? It's possible that during a disaster, the backup site might not be available. That is why many organizations use a backup to the backup site. Such a site is known as a tertiary site.

Regardless of what fees are involved, the hot site needs to be periodically tested. These tests should evaluate processing abilities as well as security. The physical security of the hot site should be at the same level or greater than the primary site. Finally, it is important to remember that the hot site is intended for short-term usage only. As a subscriber-based service, there might be others in line for the same resource once your contract ends. The organization should have a plan to recover primary services quickly or move to a secondary location.

> **Caution**
>
> Hot sites should not be externally identifiable, as this will increase their risk of sabotage and other potential disruptions.

For those companies lacking the funds to spend on a hot site or in situations where a short-term outage is acceptable, a *warm site* might be acceptable. A warm site has data equipment and cables, and is partially configured. It could be made operational within a few hours to a few days. The assumption with a warm site is that necessary computer equipment and software can be procured in spite of the disaster. Although the warm site might have some computer equipment installed, it is typically of lower processing power than the primary site. The costs associated with a warm site are slightly lower than those of a hot site. The warm site is a popular subscription alternative, as shown in Figure 12.4.

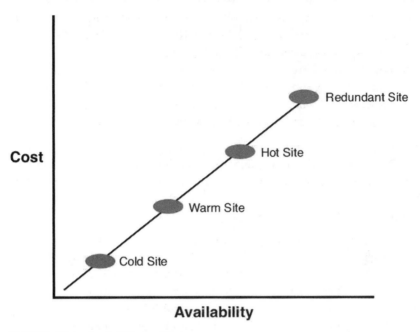

FIGURE 12.4   Availability vs. Cost.

In situations where even longer outages are acceptable, a cold site might be the right choice. A cold site is basically an empty room with only rudimentary electrical power and computing capability. Although it might have a raised floor and some racks, it is nowhere near ready for use. It might take several weeks to a month to get the site operational. Cold sites offer the least preparedness when compared to hot and warm subscription services discussed. Associated costs are also much lower than for hot or warm sites, averaging between $500 and $2,000 per month.

> ### Tip
> Cold sites are a good choice for the recovery of non-critical services.

Redundant Sites

The CISSP exam considers redundant sites to be sites owned by the company. Although these might be either partially or totally configured, the CISSP exam does not typically expect you to know that level of detail. A redundant site is capable of handling all operations if another site fails. Although there is an increased cost, it offers the company fault tolerance and this is necessary if you cannot withstand the downtime. If the redundant sites are geographically dispersed, the possibility of more than one being damaged is reduced. For low- to medium-priority services, a distance of 10 to 20 miles from the primary site is considered acceptable. If the loss of services, for even a very short time, could cost the organization millions of dollars, the redundant site should be farther away. Therefore, redundant sites that are meant to support highly critical services should not be in the same geographical region or subject to the same types of natural disasters as the primary site.

For organizations that have multiple sites dispersed in different regions of the world, multiple processing centers might be an option. Multiple processing centers allow a branch in one area to act as backup for a branch in another area.

Mobile Sites

Mobile sites are another processing alternative. *Mobile sites* are usually tractor-trailer rigs that have been converted into data-processing centers. These sites contain all the necessary equipment and are mobile, permitting transport to any business location quickly. Rigs can also be chained together to provide space for data processing and provide communication capabilities. Mobile units are a good choice for areas where no recovery facilities exist and are commonly used by the military, large insurance agencies, and others for immediate response during a disaster. They work well in getting critical services up and running, and commonly provide tactical satellite services, but are not a long-term solution.

> **Note**
>
> Mobile sites are a non-mainstream alternative to traditional recovery options. Mobile sites typically consist of fully contained tractor-trailer rigs that come with all the facilities needed for a data center. Units can be quickly moved to any site and are perfect for storms, whose boundaries are hard to predict.

Whatever recovery method is chosen, regular testing is important to verify that the redundant site meets the organization's needs, and that the team can handle the workload to meet minimum processing requirements.

Reciprocal Agreement

The reciprocal agreement option requires two organizations to pledge assistance to one another in case of disaster. The support requires sharing space, computer facilities, and technology resources. On paper, this appears to be a cost-effective approach, but it has its drawbacks. Each party to this agreement must place its trust in the other organization to provide aid in case of a disaster. However, people who are not victims may become hesitant to follow through when a disaster actually occurs.

Also, confidentiality requires special consideration. This is because the damaged organization is placed in a vulnerable position while needing to trust the other party's housing of the victim's confidential information. Legal liability can also be a concern; for example, one company agrees to help the other and as a result is hacked. Finally, if the two parties of the agreement are geographically near one another, there is the danger that disaster could strike both, thereby rendering the agreement useless.

The biggest drawbacks to reciprocal agreements are that they are hard to enforce and that, many times, incompatibilities in company hardware, software, and even cultures are not discovered until after a disaster strikes.

User Recovery

User recovery is primarily about what employees need so that they can do their jobs. Requirements include:

▶ Procedures, documents, and manuals

▶ Communication system

▶ Means of mobility and transportation to and from work

▶ Workspace and equipment

▶ Alternate site facilities

▶ Basic human requirements like food and water, sanitation facilities, rest, money, and morale

At issue here is the fact that a company might be able to get employees to a backup facility after a disaster, but if there are no phones, desks, or computers, the employees' ability to work will be severely limited.

User recovery can even include food. As an example, my brother-in-law works for a large chemical company on the Texas Gulf Coast. During storms, hurricanes, or other disasters, he is required to stay at work as part of the emergency operations team. His job is to stay at the facility regardless of time; the disaster might last two days or two weeks. During a simulation test several years ago, it was discovered that someone had forgotten to order food for the facility where the employees were to remain for the duration of the drill. Luckily, the 40 or so hungry employees were not really in a disaster, and were able to order pizza and have it delivered. Had it been a real disaster, no takeout would have been available.

Operations Recovery

Operations recovery addresses interruptions caused by the loss of capability due to equipment failure. Redundancy solves this potential loss of availability, such as redundant equipment, Redundant Array of Inexpensive Disks (RAID), backup power supplies (BPS), and other redundant services.

Hardware failures are one of the most common disruptions that can occur. Preventing this disruption is critical to operations. The best place to start planning hardware redundancy is when equipment is purchased. At purchase time, there are two important numbers that the buyer must investigate:

▶ **Mean time between failure (MTBF)**—Used to calculate the expected lifetime of a device. A higher MTBF means the equipment should last longer.

▶ **Mean time to repair (MTTR)**—Used to estimate how long it would take to repair the equipment and get it back into production. Lower MTTR numbers mean the equipment requires less repair time and can be returned to service sooner.

A formula for calculating availability is

MTBF / (MTBF + MTTR) = Availability

To maximize availability of critical equipment, an organization can consider obtaining a *service level agreement* (SLA). There are all kinds of SLAs. In this situation, the SLA is a contract between a company and a hardware vendor, in which the vendor promises to provide a certain level of protection and support. For a fee, the vendor agrees to repair or replace the covered equipment within the contracted time.

Fault tolerance can be used at the server or drive level. For servers, there is *clustering*, which is technology that allows for high availability; it groups multiple servers together, so that they are viewed logically as a single server. Users see the cluster as one unit. The advantage is that if one server in the cluster fails, the remaining active servers pick up the load and continue operation.

Fault tolerance on the drive level is achieved primarily with RAID, which provides hardware fault tolerance and/or performance improvements. This is accomplished by breaking up the data and writing it across one or more disks. To applications and other devices, RAID appears as a single drive. Most RAID systems have hot-swappable disks. This means that faulty drives can be removed and replaced without turning off the entire computer system. If the RAID system uses parity and is fault tolerant, the parity data can be used to reconstruct the newly replaced drive. The technique for writing the data across multiple drives is called *striping*. Although write performance remains almost constant, read performance is drastically increased. RAID has humble beginnings that date back to the 1980s at the University of California. RAID is discussed in depth in Chapter 10, "Security Operations."

Although operations can be disrupted because of the failure of equipment, the loss of communications can also disrupt critical processes. Protecting communication with fault tolerance can be achieved through redundant WAN links, diverse routing, and alternate routing. Whatever method is chosen, the organization should verify capacity requirements and acceptable outage times. The primary methods for network protection include:

▶ **Diverse routing**—This is the practice of routing traffic through different cable facilities. Organizations can obtain both diverse routing and alternate routing, but the cost is not low. Many telecommunications companies use buried facilities. These systems usually enter a building through the basement and can sometimes share space with other mechanical equipment. Recognize that this sharing adds to the risk of potential failure. Also, many cities have aging infrastructures, which is another potential point of failure.

▶ **Alternate routing**—Also called redundant routing, this provides use of another transmission line if the regular line is busy or unavailable. This can include using a dialup connection instead of a dedicated connection, cell phone instead of a landline, or microwave communication instead of a fiber connection.

▶ **Last mile protection**—This is a good choice for recovery facilities; it provides a second local loop connection, and is even more redundantly capable if an alternate carrier is used.

▶ **Voice communication recovery**—Many organizations are highly dependent on voice communications, and some have started making the switch to Voice over IP (VoIP) for both voice and fax communication because of the cost savings. But some landlines should always be maintained to provide backup capability; they are still the most reliable form of voice communication.

Networks are susceptible to the same types of outages as equipment. If operations recovery concerns are not addressed, these outages can be a real problem for companies that rely heavily on networks to deliver data when needed.

> **Note**
>
> *Free Space Optics* (FSO) is an emerging technology that can be used to obtain high bandwidth, short haul, redundant links. FSO uses LED and/or laser light to transmit data between two points and is inexpensive, easy to install, and works great on campus WANs (see en.wikipedia.org/wiki/Free_Space_Optics).

Data and Information Recovery

The focus here is on recovering the data. Solutions to data interruptions include backups, offsite storage, and/or remote journaling. Because data processing is essential to most organizations, the data and information recovery plan is critical. The objective of the plan is to back up critical software and data, which permits quick restores with minimum loss of content. Policy should dictate when backups are performed, where the media is stored, who has access to the media, and what the reuse or rotation policy will be. Types of backup media include tape reels, tape cartridges, removable hard drives, solid state storage, disks, and cassettes.

Tape and optical systems still have the majority of market share for backup systems. Common types of media include:

▶ 8mm tape

▶ CDR/W media (recommended for temporary storage only)

▶ Digital Audio Tape (DAT)

▶ Digital Linear Tape (DLT)

▶ Quarter Inch Tape (QIC)

▶ Write Once Read Many (WORM)

Another technology worth mentioning is MAID (massive array of inactive disks). *MAID* offers a distributed hardware storage option for the storage for data and applications. It was designed to reduce the operational costs and improve long-term reliability of disk-based archives and backups. MAID is similar to RAID except that it provides power management and advanced disk monitoring. MAID might or might not stripe data and/or supply redundancy. The MAID system powers down inactive drives, reduces heat output, reduces electrical consumption, and increases the disk drive's life expectancy.

In addition to defining the media type, the organization must determine how often and what type of backups should be performed. Answers will vary depending on the cost of the media, the speed of the restoration needed, and the time allocated for backups. Backup methods include:

▶ **Full backup**—During a *full backup*, all data is backed up. No data files are skipped or bypassed. All items are copied to one tape, set of tapes, or backup media. If a restoration is required, only data set is needed. A full backup resets the archive bit on all files.

▶ **Differential backup**—A *differential backup* is a partial backup performed in conjunction with a full backup. Any restoration requires the last full backup and the most recent differential backup. This method takes less time than a full backup per each backup, but increases the restoration time because both the full and differential backups will be needed. A differential backup does not reset the archive bit on files.

▶ **Incremental backup**—An *incremental backup* is faster yet to perform. It backs up only those files that have been modified since the previous incremental (or full) backup. A restoration requires the last full backup and all incremental backups since the last full backup. An incremental backup resets the archive bit on files.

▶ **Continuous backup**—Some backup applications perform *continuous backups*, and keep a database of backup information. These systems are useful when a restoration is needed because the application can provide a full restore, point-in-time restore, or restore based on a selected list of files such as file synchronization programs from a source to a target that can be on any schedule.

ExamAlert

Test questions regarding different backup types can be quite tricky. Make sure you clearly know the difference before the exam. Backups can also be associated with DRP planning metrics such as RPO, RTP, and MTTR.

Backup and Restoration

Backups need to be stored somewhere and backups are needed quickly when it's time to restore not just the data, but applications and configurations settings as well. Where the backup media is stored can have a real impact on how quickly data can be restored and brought back online. The media should be stored in more than one physical location so that the possibility of loss is reduced. These remote sites should be managed by a media librarian. It is this individual's job to maintain the site, control access, rotate media, and protect this valuable asset. Unauthorized access to the media is a huge risk because it could impact the organization's capability to provide uninterrupted service. Who transports the media to and from the remote site is also an important concern. Important backup and restoration considerations include:

▶ Maintenance of secure transportation to and from the site

▶ Use of bonded delivery vehicles

▶ Appropriate handling, loading, and unloading of backup media

▶ Use of drivers trained on proper procedures to pick up, handle, and deliver backup media

▶ Legal obligations for data, such as encrypted media, and separation of sensitive data sets, such as credit card numbers and CVCs

▶ 24/7 access to the backup facility in case of an emergency

It is recommended that companies contract their offsite storage needs with a known firm that demonstrates control of their facility and is responsible for its maintenance. Physical and environmental controls at offsite storage locations should be equal to or better than the organization's own facility. A letter of agreement should specify who has access to the media and who is authorized to drop it off or pick it up. There should also be agreement on response times that will be met in case of disaster. Onsite storage should maintain copies of recent backups to ensure the capability to recover critical files quickly.

Backup media should be securely maintained in an environmentally controlled facility with physical control appropriate for critical assets. The area should be fireproof, and anyone depositing or removing media should have a record of their access logged by a media librarian.

Table 12.2 shows some sample functions and their recovery times.

TABLE 12.2 **Organization Functions and Example Recovery Times**

Process	Recovery Time	Recovery Strategy
Database	Minutes to hours	Database shadowing (covered in the later section, "Other Data Backup Methods")
Help desk	7 to 14 days	Warm site
Research and development	Several weeks to a month	Cold site
Purchasing	1 to 2 days	Hot site
Payroll	1 to 5 days	Multiple site

Software itself can be vulnerable, even when good backup policies are followed, because sometimes software vendors go out of business or no longer support needed applications. In these instances, *escrow agreements* can help.

> ### Caution
>
> Escrow agreements are one possible software-protection mechanism. Escrow agreements allow an organization to obtain access to the source code of business-critical software if the software vendor goes bankrupt or otherwise fails to perform as required. Given the myriad of compilers and operating systems, escrow is now requiring everything required to build the product including operating systems, all tools, compilers, and so on.

Data Replication Techniques

Data replication can be handled by two basic techniques, each of which provides various capabilities:

▶ **Synchronous replication**—This technique uses as an atomic write operation. An atomic write operation will either complete on both sides, or will be abandoned. Its strength is that it guarantees no data loss.

▶ **Asynchronous replication**—This technique updates as allowed, but may have small performance degradation. Its downside is that the remote storage facility may not have the most recent copy of data; therefore, some data may be lost in case of an outage.

Media-Rotation Strategies

Although most backup media is rather robust, no backup media can last forever. This means that media rotation is another important part of backup and restoration. Additionally, backup media needs to be periodically tested. Backups will be of little use if you find out during a disaster that they have malfunctioned and no longer work.

These media-rotation strategies are most often applied to tape backups:

▶ **Simple**—A simple tape-rotation scheme uses one tape for every day of the week and then repeats the pattern the following week. One tape can be for Monday, one for Tuesday, and so on. You add a set of new tapes each month and then archive the previous month's set. After a predetermined number of months, you put the oldest tapes back into use.

▶ **Grandfather-father-son (GFS)**—This scheme typically uses one tape for monthly backups, four tapes for weekly backups, and four tapes for daily backups (assuming you are using a five-day work week). It is called *grandfather-father-son* because the scheme establishes a kind of hierarchy. The grandfather is the single monthly backup, the fathers are the four weekly backups, and the sons are the four daily backups.

▶ **Tower of Hanoi**—This tape-rotation scheme is named after a mathematical puzzle. It involves using five sets of tapes, each set labeled A through E. Set A is used every other day; set B is used on the first non-A backup day and is used every 4th day; set C is used on the first non-A or non-B backup day and is used every 8th day; set D is used on the first non-A, non-B, or non-C day and is used every 16th day; and set E alternates with set D.

Other Data Backup Methods

Other alternatives that exist for further enhancing a company's resiliency and redundancy are listed below. Some organizations use these techniques by themselves; others combine these techniques with other backup methods.

▶ **Database shadowing**—Databases are a high-value asset for most organizations. File-based incremental backups can read only entire database tables and are considered too slow. A database shadowing system uses two physical disks to write the data to. It creates good redundancy by duplicating the database sets to mirrored servers. Therefore, this is an excellent way to provide fault tolerance and redundancy. Shadowing mirrors changes to the database as they occur.

▶ **Electronic vaulting**—Electronic vaulting makes a copy of database changes to a secure backup location. This is a batch-process operation copying all current records, transactions, and/or files to the offsite location. To implement vaulting, an organization typically loads a software agent onto the systems to be backed up, and then, periodically, the vaulting service accesses the software agent on these systems to copy changed data.

▶ **Remote journaling**—Remote journaling is similar to electronic vaulting, except that information is duplicated to the remote site as it is committed on the primary system. By performing live data transfers, this mechanism allows alternate sites to be fully synchronized and fault tolerant at all times. Depending on configuration, it is possible to configure remote journaling to record only the occurrence of transactions and not the actual content of the transactions. Remote journaling can provide a very high level of redundancy.

▶ **Storage area network (SAN)**—SAN supports disk mirroring, backup and restore, archiving, and retrieval of archived data in addition to data migration from one storage device to another. A SAN can be implemented locally or use storage at a redundant facility.

▶ **Cloud computing backup**—This can offer a cost-savings alternative to traditional backup techniques. These should be carefully evaluated, as there are many concerns when using cloud-based services. Cloud backups can be deployed in a variety of configurations, as an on-site private cloud or an off-site public or private cloud.

> **Caution**
>
> Remember that if using off-site public cloud storage, you should look at encrypting the backup.

Choosing the Right Backup Method

It is not easy to choose the right backup method. To start the process, the team must consider how long an outage the organization can endure and how current the restored information must be. These two recovery requirements are technically called:

▶ **Recovery point objective (RPO)**—Defines how much data an organization can afford to lose. The greater the RPO, the more tolerant the process is to interruption.

▶ **Recovery time objective (RTO)**—Specifies the maximum acceptable time to recover the data. This same metric would be used to evaluate the application that stores the data or the time it would take to transfer the data to the alternate site. The goal for DRP would be to determine the time it would take to get the data up and running, regardless of whether it was at the primary or alternate site. The greater the RTO, the longer the recovery process can take and the more tolerant the organization is to interruption. Figure 12.5 illustrates how the RTO can be used to determine acceptable downtime.

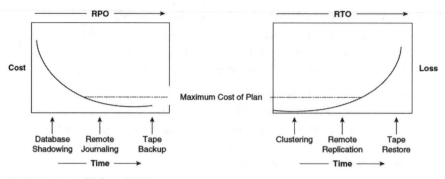

FIGURE 12.5   **RPO and RTO.**

> **Tip**
>
> For the exam you must know the terms RPO and RTO.

The RPO and RTO metrics are very important. What you should realize about them both is that the lower the time requirements are, the higher the maintenance cost will be to provide for reduced restoration capabilities. For example, most banks have a very small RPO because they cannot afford to lose any processed information. Think of the recovery strategy calculations as being designed to meet the required recovery time frames. We can write this as MTD = RTO + WRT, where MTD is the maximum tolerable downtime, and WRT is the work recovery time, which is simply the remainder of the MTD used to restore all business operations. This is shown in Figure 12.6.

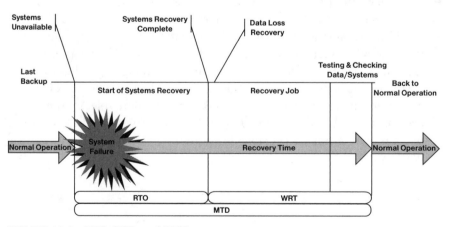

FIGURE 12.6   **MTD, RTO, and WRT.**

> **Tip**
>
> The work recovery time (WRT) is the remainder of the MTD used to restore all business operations.

Plan Design and Development

The BCP process is now ready for its next phase—plan design and development. In this phase, the team designs and develops a detailed plan for the recovery of critical business systems. The plan should be directed toward major catastrophes. Worst-case scenarios are planned for on the assumption that the entire facility has been destroyed. If the organization can handle these types of events, less severe events that render the facility unusable only for a time, can be readily dealt with.

The BCP should be a guide for implementation. The plan should include information on both long-term and short-term goals and objectives:

1. Identify time-sensitive critical functions and priorities for restoration.

2. Identify support systems needed by time-sensitive critical functions.

3. Estimate potential outages and calculate the minimum resources needed to recover from the catastrophe.

4. Select recovery strategies and determine which vital personnel, systems, and equipment will be needed to accomplish the recovery. There must be a team for the primary site and the alternate site.

5. Determine who will manage the restoration and testing process.

6. Determine what type of funding and fiscal management is needed to accomplish these goals.

The plan should also detail how the organization will contact and mobilize employees, provide for ongoing communication between employees, interface with external groups and the media, and provide employee services. Each of these items is discussed next.

Personnel Mobilization

The process for contacting employees in case of an emergency needs to be worked out before a disaster. The process chosen depends on the nature and frequency of the emergency. *Outbound dialing systems* and *call trees* are widely used.

An outbound dialing system stores the numbers to be called in an emergency. These systems can provide various services, such as:

▶ **Call rollover**—If one number gets no response, the next is called.

▶ **Leave a recorded message**—If an answering machine answers, a message can be left for the individual.

▶ **Request a call back**—Even if a message is left, the system will continue to call back until the user calls in to the predefined phone number.

A call tree is a communication system in which the person in charge of the tree calls a lead person on every "branch", who in turn calls all the "leaves" on that branch. If call trees are used, the team will want to verify that there is a feedback mechanism built in. As an example, the last person on any branch of the tree calls and confirms that he or she got the message. This can help ensure that everyone has been contacted. Call trees can be automated with VoIP and public switched telephone networks (PSTNs) and online services.

Personnel mobilization can also be triggered by emails to tablets, smartphones, and so on. Such systems require the email server to be functioning.

It is also important to plan for executive succession planning. The company needs to be able to continue even if key personnel are not available. The company should have measures in place that account for the potential loss of key individuals. If there is no executive succession planning, the loss of key individuals could mean the organization may not be able to continue.

Interface with External Groups

A public affairs officer (PAO) typically will decide how to interact with external groups. This can affect the long-term reputation of your business. Damaging rumors can easily start, and it is important to have protocols in place for dealing with incidents, accidents, and catastrophes. The organization must decide how to deal with response teams, the fire department, the police department, ambulance, and other emergency response personnel. If you do not tell the pubic what you want them to know, the media will decide for you. In a world of social media, your employees or former employees may even contribute to this cause; therefore, have a policy and a canned statement for your PAO.

A media spokesperson should be identified to deal with the media. Negative public opinion can be costly. It is important to have a properly trained spokesperson to speak and represent the organization. The media spokesperson must be in the communication path to have the facts before speaking or meeting with the press. He or she should engage with senior management and legal counsel prior to making any public statement.

Meeting with the media during a crisis is not something that should be done without preparation. The corporate plan should include generic communiqués that address each possible incident. The spokesperson will also need to know how to handle tough questions. Liability should never be assumed; the spokesperson should simply state that an investigation has begun. Tackling these tough issues up front will allow the company to have a preapproved framework should a real disaster occur.

Employee Services

Companies have an inherent responsibility to employees and to their families. This means that paychecks must continue and that employees need to be taken care of. Employees must be trained in what to do in case of emergencies and in what they can expect from the company. Insurance and other necessary services must continue.

> ### Caution
>
> The number-one priority of any BCP or DRP plan is to protect the safety of employees.

Before a disaster, senior management must determine who is in charge during a disaster to avoid chaos and confusion. Employees must know what is expected of them and who is in charge. You don't want the CFO telling the person in charge what to do, so make the decision now, in policy. Tragically, people die during a disaster, so it's important to have a succession of command.

Furthermore, someone must have the authority to allocate emergency funding as needed. After Hurricane Katrina, the U.S. Congress passed 48 C.F.R. § 13.201(b) (2005), which increased the limit on FEMA-issued credit cards to $250,000. The idea was to allow government employees to acquire needed items quickly and without delay. Of course, although funding is important, controls must also be in place to ensure that funds are not misappropriated.

Insurance

Insurance is one option that companies can consider to remove a portion of the risk the team has uncovered during the BIA. Just as protection insurance can be purchased by individuals for a host of reasons, companies can purchase protection insurance for such things as:

▶ Outages

▶ Data centers

▶ Hacker or cyber insurance (which might include potential penalties and fines)

▶ Software recovery

▶ Business interruption

▶ Documents, records, and important papers

▶ Errors and omissions

▶ Media transportation

Insurance is not without its drawbacks, such as high premiums, delayed claim payout, denied claims, and problems proving real financial loss. Also, most insurance policies pay for only a percentage of any actual loss and do not pay for lost income, increased operating expenses, or consequential loss. It is also important to note that many insurance companies will not ensure companies who have not exercised due care with the implementation of a DRP and BCP.

Implementation

The BCP team is now nearing the end of the plan's development process, and is ready to submit a completed plan for implementation. The plan is the result of all information gathered during the project initiation, the BIA, and the recovery strategies phase. A final checklist for completeness ensures the plan addresses all relevant factors, such as:

▶ Calculating what type of funding and fiscal management is needed to accomplish the stated goals

▶ Determining the procedures for declaring a disaster and under what circumstances this will occur

▶ Evaluating potential disasters and calculating the minimum resources needed to recover from the catastrophe

▶ Determining critical functions and priorities for restoration

▶ Identifying what recovery strategy and equipment will be needed to accomplish the recovery

▶ Identifying individuals that are responsible for each function in the plan

▶ Determining who will manage the restoration and testing process

The completed plan should be presented to senior management for approval. References for the plan should be cited in all related documents so that the plan is maintained and updated whenever there is a change or update to the infrastructure. When senior management approves the plan, it must be released and disseminated to employees. Awareness training with the individuals who would be responsible for carrying out the plan is critical and will help make sure that everyone understands what their tasks and responsibilities are when an emergency occurs.

Awareness and Training

The goal of awareness and training is to make sure all employees are included and internal and external personnel that are involved in the plan, including contractors and consultants, are involved to ensure they know what to do in case of an emergency. It is certain that you will require support from external agencies, such as law enforcement, and they will likely not have time to participate in your training; however, having a face-to-face meeting with them and getting to know them prior to a disaster is a good idea, so you understand their resources and capabilities.

If employees are untrained, they might simply stop what they're doing and run for the door anytime there's an emergency. Even worse, they might not leave when an alarm has sounded, even though the plan requires that they leave because of possible danger. Instructions should be written in easy-to-understand language that uses common terminology. The organization should design and develop training programs to make sure each employee knows what to do and how to do it. Employees assigned to specific tasks should be trained to carry them out. If possible, plan for cross-training of teams so that team members are familiar with a variety of recovery roles and responsibilities.

> **Caution**
>
> Although some companies might feel that the BCP development job is done once the plan is complete, it is important to remember that no demonstrated recovery exists until the plan has been tested.

Testing

This final phase of the process is to test and maintain the BCP. Training and awareness programs are also developed during this phase. The test of the disaster-recovery plan is critical. Without performing a test, there is no way to know whether the plan will work. Testing transforms theoretical plans into reality. Testing should be repeated at least once a year.

Tests should start with the easiest parts of the plan and then build to more complex items. The initial tests should focus on items that support core processing, and they should be scheduled during a time that causes minimal disruption to normal business operations. As a CISSP candidate, you should be aware of the five different types of BCP tests:

▶ **Checklist**—Although this is not considered a replacement for a live test, a checklist is a good first test. A checklist test is performed by sending copies of the plan to different department managers and business unit managers for review. Each recipient reviews the plan to make sure nothing was overlooked.

▶ **Structured walkthrough**—This test, also known as a tabletop test, is performed by having the members of the emergency management team and business unit managers meet in a conference to discuss the plan. The plan then is "walked through" line by line. This gives all attendees a chance to see how an actual emergency would be handled and to discover discrepancies. By reviewing the plan in this way, errors and omissions might become apparent.

Tip

The primary advantage of the structured walkthrough is to discover discrepancies between different departments.

▶ **Simulation**—This is a drill involving members of the response team acting in the same way they would if there had been an actual emergency. This test proceeds to the point of recovery or to relocation to the alternate site. The primary purpose of this test is to verify that members of the response team can perform the required duties with only the tools they would have available in a real disaster.

▶ **Parallel**—A parallel test is similar to a structured walkthrough but actually invokes operations at the alternate site. Operations at the new and old sites are run in parallel.

▶ **Full interruption**—This plan is the most detailed, time-consuming, and disruptive to your business. A full interruption test mimics a real disaster, and all steps are performed to complete backup operations. It includes all the individuals who would be involved in a real emergency, both internal and external to the organization. Although a full interruption test is the most thorough, it is also the scariest because it can be so disruptive as to create its own disaster.

ExamAlert

The CISSP exam will require you to know the differences of each test type. You should also note the advantages and disadvantages of each.

The final step of the BCP process is to combine all this information into the BCP plan and inter-reference it with the organization's other emergency plans. Although the organization will want to keep a copy of the plan onsite, there should be another copy offsite. If a disaster occurs, rapid access to the plan will be critical.

Caution

Access to the plan should be restricted so that only those with a need to know can access the entire plan. This is because access to the plan could become a playbook for an attack.

Monitoring and Maintenance

When the testing process is complete, a few additional items still need to be considered. This is important because some might falsely believe that the plan is completed once tested. That's not true. All the hard work that has gone into developing the plan can be lost if controls are not put into place to maintain the current level of business continuity and disaster recovery. Life is not static and neither should the organization's BCP plans be. The BCP should be a living document, subject to constant change.

To ensure the plan is maintained, first build in responsibility for the plan. This can be done by

▶ **Job descriptions**—Individuals responsible for the plan should have this responsibility detailed in their job description. Management should work with HR to have this information added to the appropriate documents. The best way to enforce a plan is to have someone to hold accountable.

▶ **Performance reviews**—The accomplishment (or lack of accomplishment) of appropriate plan maintenance tasks should be discussed in the responsible individual's periodic evaluations.

▶ **Audits**—The audit team should review the plan and make sure that it is current and appropriate. The audit team will also want to inspect the off-site storage facility and review its security, policies, and configuration.

Table 12.3 lists the individuals responsible for specific parts of the BCP process.

TABLE 12.3 **BCP Process Responsibilities**

Person or Department	Responsibility
Senior management	Project initiation, ultimate responsibility, overall approval, and support
Middle management or business	Identification and prioritization of critical systems unit managers
BCP committee and team members	Planning, day-to-day management, implementation, and testing of the plan
Functional business units	Plan implementation, incorporation, and testing

Disaster recovery implications for monitoring, maintaining, and recovery should be made a part of any discussions for procuring new equipment, modifying current equipment, new employment of key personnel, or for making changes to the infrastructure. The best method to accomplish this is to add BCP review into all change management procedures. If changes are required to the approved plans, they must also be documented and structured using change management, and the plan should be updated and distributed if even 10% of the plan, employees, or company are affected by the change. A change control document should be kept with the plan at all times, using good version control. A centralized command and control structure eases this burden.

> **Tip**
>
> Senior management is ultimately responsible for the BCP. This includes funding, project initiation, overall approval, and support.

Exam Prep Questions

1. You are an information assurance manager for a large company that wants to develop a BCP. You would like have your team thoroughly test the plan to ensure that when the company faces a natural disaster, it will survive. The company relies heavily on e-commerce and must ensure that in the event a server fails, customers will still be able to complete financial transactions online. You have already implemented redundancy for the web application servers, and you have deployed a database activity monitor and a web application firewall. Your concern is that backup systems come on if the primary system fails. You would like to test these systems but do not want to take primary systems offline. What *best* explains the type of test you are recommending?

   ○ **A.** Tabletop/walkthrough

   ○ **B.** Simulation

   ○ **C.** Parallel

   ○ **D.** Full interruption

2. Which of the following groups is responsible for project initiation?

   ○ **A.** Functional business units

   ○ **B.** Senior management

   ○ **C.** BCP team members

   ○ **D.** Middle management

3. When an organization starts to plan for business continuity and disaster recovery it will likely be a very large, complex, and multi-disciplinary project that would bring key associates within the organization together. What *best* describes the role of senior management?

   ○ **A.** They will plan for money for the DR project manager, technology experts, process experts, or other financial requirements from various departments within the organization

   ○ **B.** To be willing to make the discussion to make DRP a priority, commit and allow staff the time, and set hard dates for completion.

   ○ **C.** To manage the multi-disciplinary people to keep them all on the same page

   ○ **D.** To be experts and understand specific processes that require a special skill set

4. Which of the following is not considered an advantage of a mutual aid agreement?

   ○ **A.** Low cost

   ○ **B.** Enforcement

   ○ **C.** Documentation

   ○ **D.** Testing

5. Which of the following uses batch processing?

   ○ **A.** Remote journaling

   ○ **B.** Hierarchical storage management

   ○ **C.** Electronic vaulting

   ○ **D.** Static management

6. Which of the following BCP tests carries the most risk?

   ○ **A.** Full interruption

   ○ **B.** Parallel

   ○ **C.** Walkthrough

   ○ **D.** Checklist

7. Which of the following is the best definition of a software escrow agreement?

   ○ **A.** Provides the vendor with additional assurances that the software will be used per licensing agreements

   ○ **B.** Specifies how much a vendor can charge for updates

   ○ **C.** Gives the company access to the source code under certain conditions

   ○ **D.** Provides the vendor access to the organization's code if there are questions of compatibility

8. Which of the following will a business impact analysis provide?

   ○ **A.** Determining the maximum outage time before the company is permanently damaged

   ○ **B.** Detailing how training and awareness will be performed and how the plan will be updated

   ○ **C.** Establishing the need for BCP

   ○ **D.** Selecting recovery strategies

9. Mike had a server crash on Thursday morning. Bob performed a backup in which he used the complete backup from Sunday and several other tapes from Monday, Tuesday, and Wednesday. Which tape-backup method was used?

   ○ **A.** Full restore

   ○ **B.** Structured restore

   ○ **C.** Differential restore

   ○ **D.** Incremental restore

10. Which of the following tape-rotation schemes involves using five sets of tapes, with each set labeled A through E?

    ○ **A.** Tower of Hanoi

    ○ **B.** Son-father-grandfather

    ○ **C.** Complex

    ○ **D.** Grandfather-father-son

11. If the recovery point objective (RPO) is low, which of the following techniques would be the most appropriate solution?

    ○ **A.** Clustering

    ○ **B.** Database shadowing

    ○ **C.** Remote journaling

    ○ **D.** Tape backup

12. You have been assigned to the BCP team responsible for backup options and offsite storage. Your company is considering the purchase of software from a small startup operation that has a proven record for unique software solutions. To mitigate the potential for loss, which of the following should you recommend?

    ○ **A.** Clustering

    ○ **B.** Software escrow

    ○ **C.** Insurance

    ○ **D.** Continuous backup

13. Which of the following is one of the most important steps that is required before developing a business continuity plan?

    ○ **A.** Perform a BIA

    ○ **B.** Perform quantitative and qualitative risk assessment

    ○ **C.** Get senior management buy-in

    ○ **D.** Determine membership of the BCP team

14. When developing a business continuity plan, what should be the number-one priority?

○ **A.** Minimizing outage times

○ **B.** Mitigating damage

○ **C.** Documenting every conceivable threat

○ **D.** Protection of human safety

15. Which of the following could be used to determine MTD for a vital function?

○ **A.** Payroll

○ **B.** Product support

○ **C.** Purchasing

○ **D.** Research and development

Answers to Exam Prep Questions

1. **C.** The correct answer is C, because a parallel test sets up recovery servers and runs select or limited transactions to see if the servers work while keeping primary servers up and running. Answer A is incorrect because a tabletop/walkthrough test would consist of a group of experts meeting in person to step through recovery procedures and discuss issues along the away. Answer B is incorrect because a simulation is a group of experts that go through a disaster script scenario to observe how the procedures work. Answer D is incorrect because a full interruption test is a when the recovery team brings down the primary servers and brings up the backup servers so that a business processes can continue.

2. **B.** Although the other groups listed have responsibilities in the BCP process, senior management is responsible for project initiation, overall approval, support, and is ultimately responsible and held liable. Answer A is incorrect because the functional business units are responsible for implementation, incorporation, and testing. Answer C is incorrect because the BCP team members are responsible for planning, day-to-day management, and implementation and testing of the plan. Answer D is incorrect because middle management is responsible for the identification and prioritization of critical systems.

3. **B.** The *best* answer is B. If senior management does not get behind the DRP and fully support it, the DRP will more than likely fail. Answer A is not the best answer because this describes the roles of a budget manager or budget department. Answer C is not the best answer because this describes the roles of a project manager. Answer D is not the best answer as it describes the roles of a subject matter expert.

4. **B.** The parties to this agreement must place their trust in the reciprocating organization to provide aid in the event of a disaster. However, the non-victim might be hesitant to follow through if such a disaster occurred. None of the other answers represents a disadvantage because this is a low-cost alternative, it can be documented, and some tests to verify that it would work can be performed.

5. **C.** Electronic vaulting makes a copy of data to a backup location. This is a batch-process operation that functions to keep a copy of all current records, transactions, or files at an offsite location. Remote journaling is similar to electronic vaulting, except that information is processed continuously in parallel, so answer A is incorrect. Hierarchical storage management provides continuous online backup, so answer B is incorrect. Static management is a distractor and is not a valid choice, so answer D is incorrect.

6. **A.** A full interruption is the test most likely to cause its own disaster. All the other answers listed are not as disruptive, so answers B, C, and D are incorrect.

7. **C.** A software escrow agreement allows an organization to obtain access to the source code of business-critical software if the software vendor goes bankrupt or otherwise fails to perform as required. Answer A is incorrect because an escrow agreement does not provide the vendor with additional assurances that the software will be used per licensing agreements. Answer B is incorrect because an escrow agreement does not specify how much a vendor can charge for updates. Answer D is incorrect because an escrow agreement does not address compatibility issues; it grants access to the source code only under certain conditions.

8. **A.** A BIA is a process used to help business units understand the impact of a disruptive event. Part of that process is determining the maximum outage time before the company is permanently crippled. The other answers are part of the BCP process but are not specifically part of the BIA portion, so answers B, C, and D are incorrect.

9. **D.** Incremental backups take longer to restore. Answer A is incorrect because a full backup backs up everything and, therefore, takes the longest time to create. Answer B is incorrect because the term *structured* addresses how a backup is carried out, not the method used. Answer C is incorrect because a differential backup does not reset the archive bit. It takes increasingly longer each night, but would require a shorter period to restore because only two restores would be needed: the last full and the last differential.

10. **A.** The Tower of Hanoi involves using five sets of tapes, with each set labeled A through E. Set A is used every other day. Set B is used on the first non-A backup day and is used every 4th day. Set C is used on the first non-A or non-B backup day and is used every 8th day. Set D is used on the first non-A, non-B, or non-C day and is used every 16th day. Set E alternates with set D. Answer B is incorrect because son-father-grandfather is a distractor. Answer C is incorrect because complex does not refer to a specific backup type. Answer D is incorrect because grandfather-father-son includes four tapes for weekly backups, one tape for monthly backups, and four tapes for daily backups; this does not match the description in the question.

11. **D.** The RPO is the earliest point at which recovery can occur. If the company has a low RPO, tape backup is acceptable because there is a low need to capture the most current data. If the backup occurs at midnight and the failure is at noon the next day, 12 hours of data has been lost. Answers A, B, and C are incorrect because each of these would be used when a higher RPO, or more current data, is required.

12. **B.** The core issue here is that the software provider is a small startup that may not be around in a few years. If this were to happen, your company must protect itself so that it has access to the source code. Escrow agreements allow an organization to obtain access to the source code of business-critical software if the software vendor goes bankrupt or otherwise fails to perform as required. Answers A, C, and D are incorrect because clustering and continuous backup do nothing to provide the company access to the source code should they cease to exist, and, while insurance is an option, the expense is not necessary if the organization has rights and access to the code should something occur.

13. **C.** Before the BCP/DRP process can begin, you must get senior management buy-in. Answers A, B, and D are important but activities like developing the team occur after management buy-in, and the risk assessment process is performed during the BIA.

14. **D.** The protection of human safety is always the number-one priority of a CISSP. Answers A, B, and C are incorrect. Minimizing outages is important but not number one. Preventing damage is also important, but protection of human safety is number one. It not possible to identify and place a dollar amount on every conceivable threat.

15. **A.** Payroll is typically considered a vital process. While most employees may come to work for a while without a check, this would most likely not continue for very long. Answers B, C, and D are incorrect because while product support could be vital, it is not for many companies. Also, many companies may be able to survive without purchasing for a short period of time, and R&D looks to long-term revenues.

Need to Know More?

Business Continuity Institute: thebci.org/

Cloud backup strategies: searchdatabackup.techtarget.com/tip/ The-pros-and-cons-of-cloud-backup-technologies

Recovery point objective: www.disaster-resource.com/articles/03p_068.shtml

Disaster recovery best practices: www.pcmag.com/ article2/0,2817,2288745,00.asp

Availability in relation to MTBF: www.barringer1.com/ar.htm

Electronic vaulting: www.disaster-resource.com/articles/ electric_vault_rapid_lindeman.shtml

Free space optics: www.lightpointe.com/free-space-optics-technology-overview.html

Common disaster recovery terms and concepts: defaultreasoning. com/2013/12/10/rpo-rto-wrt-mtdwth/

Recovery strategies: www.disaster-recovery-guide.com/

Disaster recovery planning: www.utoronto.ca/security/documentation/ business_continuity/dis_rec_plan.htm

Practice Exam I

You will have 90 minutes to complete this exam, which consists of 60 questions. The actual exam requires a minimum passing score of 700 out of 1,000. Ensure you read each question, looking for details that would rule out any of the answers. Many times there will be two or more correct answers; however, there is only one **best** answer that can be selected. This is a reflection of the real world, where the CISSP often has several options to secure his/her network but one best option. Such is the case when choosing the best encryption to secure data or wireless networks.

Remember that the CISSP exam asks many conceptual questions that may not have a perfect answer. In that case, choose the most correct answer. Leaving a question blank will count against you, so you are always better off taking your best guess. The exam may present you with drag-and-drop questions, or scenarios, or offer figures or diagrams. Examine each question carefully. It's best to work through the entire test once, answering the questions that you can easily answer. On the second pass, work on the more difficult questions. Others that you have already answered could help you answer the remaining questions.

Practice Exam Questions

1. What type of access control features security labels?
   - ○ **A.** Restricted access control
   - ○ **B.** Discretionary access control
   - ○ **C.** Mandatory access control
   - ○ **D.** Role-based access control

2. Information security models bridge the gap between access control concepts and implementation of the concepts through the operating system. Place the following models into the category that best describes their design. Some categories may or may not be used.
   - ○ **A.** Biba
   - ○ **B.** Clark-Wilson
   - ○ **C.** Bell-LaPadula
   - ○ **D.** Brewer-Nash

Integrity (1)	Confidentiality (2)	Conflict of Interest (3)

3. What form of biometric system analyzes the features that exist in the colored tissue surrounding the pupil to validate access?
   - ○ **A.** Retina
   - ○ **B.** Cornea
   - ○ **C.** Iris
   - ○ **D.** Optic nerve

4. What is the most important item to consider when examining biometric systems?
   - ○ **A.** The crossover acceptance rate—the lower the number, the better the biometric system
   - ○ **B.** The crossover error rate—the higher the number, the better the biometric system
   - ○ **C.** The crossover acceptance rate—the lower the number, the better the biometric system
   - ○ **D.** The crossover error rate—the lower the number, the better the biometric system

5. You have been asked to help with an authentication problem that was reported after moving to biometric authentication. One of your company's employees enrolled with a fingerprint reader and was able to authenticate for several weeks using the new system. Then, one day, the employee complained that after cutting his finger he could no longer authenticate and received a "Type 1" error. What is most likely the problem?

- ○ **A.** The system does not examine enough information to determine the user.
- ○ **B.** Fingerprint readers are not very good at handling type 1 errors by nature, since these are very dynamic.
- ○ **C.** Fingerprint readers are not very good at handling type 1 errors by nature, since they have high cross-over error rates.
- ○ **D.** The system examines too much information and needs to be configured to be less sensitive.

6. What height of fence will deter only casual trespassers?

- ○ **A.** 2–3 feet
- ○ **B.** 3–4 feet
- ○ **C.** 4–5 feet
- ○ **D.** 5–7 feet

7. When discussing policies and procedures, who is strictly responsible for the protection of the company's assets and data?

- ○ **A.** User
- ○ **B.** Data owner
- ○ **C.** Data custodian
- ○ **D.** Security auditor

8. Which of the following is considered a flaw, loophole, oversight, or error that makes the organization susceptible to attack or damage?

- ○ **A.** Risk
- ○ **B.** Vulnerability
- ○ **C.** Exposure
- ○ **D.** Threat

9. Which of the following are the correct steps involved in determining the single loss expectancy?

- ○ **A.** Single loss expectancy = Asset value / Exposure factor
- ○ **B.** Single loss expectancy = Asset value × Exposure factor
- ○ **C.** Single loss expectancy = Risk / Exposure factor
- ○ **D.** Single loss expectancy = Vulnerability × Exposure factor

10. Estimating potential loss is an important task of CISSP-certified professionals. In order, which of the following are the steps used to perform a quantitative assessment?

○ **A.** Estimate potential losses, perform a vulnerability assessment, and determine annual loss expectancy.

○ **B.** Estimate potential losses, conduct a threat analysis, and rank losses as high, medium, or low.

○ **C.** Assemble a team, prepare a matrix of critical systems and services, and rank losses as high, medium, or low.

○ **D.** Estimate potential losses, conduct a threat analysis, and determine annual loss expectancy.

11. What is the Delphi Technique an example of?

○ **A.** A BCP analysis technique

○ **B.** A quantitative assessment technique

○ **C.** A DRP analysis technique

○ **D.** A qualitative assessment technique

12. What is the formula for total risk?

○ **A.** (Threat − Countermeasure) / Asset value = Total risk

○ **B.** (Threat − Countermeasure) × Asset value = Total risk

○ **C.** Threat × Vulnerability × Asset value = Total risk

○ **D.** Threat × Vulnerability / Asset value = Total risk

13. What method of dealing with risk occurs when individuals do a cost-benefit analysis and determine that the cost of the benefits outweigh the cost of the potential loss?

○ **A.** Risk reduction

○ **B.** Risk rejection

○ **C.** Risk transference

○ **D.** Risk acceptance

14. The security kernel is found at what protection ring level?

○ **A.** Ring 0

○ **B.** Ring 1

○ **C.** Ring 2

○ **D.** Ring 4

15. You have been brought in as a consultant for a small local startup firm. They have provided you the diagram shown below. Initially they want to connect to remote sites but would like to plan for remote user access in the future. With this in mind how do you advise them as to which VPN method is less likely to work through NAT?

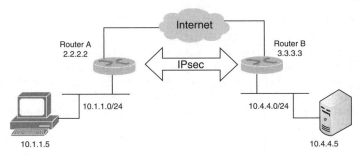

NAT Tunnel

- ○ **A.** IPsec transport mode
- ○ **B.** IPsec tunnel with AH
- ○ **C.** IPsec tunnel with ESP
- ○ **D.** Suggest they use PPTP

16. Which of the following are considered temporary storage units within the CPU?

- ○ **A.** I/O buffer
- ○ **B.** Registers
- ○ **C.** Control circuitry
- ○ **D.** ALU

17. Confidentiality and integrity are important concepts when discussing security models. Which of the following was one the first models developed to address only one goal of integrity?

- ○ **A.** Biba
- ○ **B.** Clark-Wilson
- ○ **C.** Brewer and Nash
- ○ **D.** Chinese Wall

18. Which of the following is considered the first security model to be based on confidentiality?

- ○ **A.** Biba
- ○ **B.** Bell-LaPadula
- ○ **C.** Graham-Denning
- ○ **D.** Clark-Wilson

19. What country-specific standard was developed to evaluate integrity of individual systems and is broken into four categories?

- ○ **A.** ITSEC
- ○ **B.** TCSEC
- ○ **C.** Common Criteria
- ○ **D.** CTCPEC

20. You are a consultant for a contractor that is doing work for an individual government agency; the government requires that all people must have a clearance for most restricted information in the information systems, and a valid need to know. All people do not have to have a clearance for all information in the information system. What mode of security do you recommend for the GSA contractor?

- ○ **A.** Dedicated security mode
- ○ **B.** System high security mode
- ○ **C.** Compartmented security mode
- ○ **D.** Multi-level security mode

21. When using PKI there are two methods by which you can handle revocation of certificates, as shown in the following diagram. When using Online Certificate Status Protocol (OCSP), messages are encoded and typically transmitted over HTTP. When compared to certificate revocation lists (CRLs), which of the following is not true?

CRL vs OCSP Server

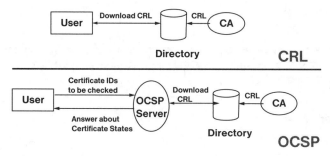

PKI

- ○ **A.** Does not mandate encryption
- ○ **B.** Contains more information than a typical CRL
- ○ **C.** Discloses that a particular network host used a particular certificate at a particular time
- ○ **D.** Places less burden on client resources

22. You have been asked to examine a database to evaluate referential integrity. Which of the following should you review?

- ○ **A.** Field
- ○ **B.** Aggregation
- ○ **C.** Composite key
- ○ **D.** Foreign key

23. Which of the following wireless standards uses frequency-hopping spread spectrum (FHSS) by default?

- ○ **A.** Bluetooth
- ○ **B.** 802.11a
- ○ **C.** 802.11b
- ○ **D.** 802.11g

24. Which of the following is the original technique used to digitize voice with 8 bits of sampling 8,000 times per second, which yields 64Kbps for one voice channel?

- ○ **A.** DAT
- ○ **B.** CDMA
- ○ **C.** PCM
- ○ **D.** GSM

25. How many DS0 channels are bundled to make a T1?

- ○ **A.** 18
- ○ **B.** 21
- ○ **C.** 24
- ○ **D.** 32

26. Which of the following protocols was developed in the mid-1970s for use in Systems Network Architecture (SNA) environments?

- ○ **A.** SDLC
- ○ **B.** ISDN
- ○ **C.** LAP-B
- ○ **D.** X.25

27. Which of the following best defines transaction persistence?

   ○ **A.** Database transactions should be all or nothing to protect the integrity of the database.

   ○ **B.** The database should be in a consistent state, and there should not be a risk of integrity problems.

   ○ **C.** The database should be the same before and after a transaction has occurred.

   ○ **D.** Databases should be available to multiple users at the same time without endangering the integrity of the data.

28. What is the capability to combine data from separate sources to gain information?

   ○ **A.** Metadata

   ○ **B.** Inference

   ○ **C.** Aggregation

   ○ **D.** Deadlocking

29. Ted considers himself a skillful hacker. He has devised a way to replace the existing startup programs between the moment that the system boots yet before the system actually executes these programs. He believes that if he can perfect his attack, he can gain control of the system. What type of attack is described here?

   ○ **A.** Synchronous attack

   ○ **B.** TOC/TOU attack

   ○ **C.** DCOM attack

   ○ **D.** Smurf attack

30. Which of the following is evidence that is not based on personal knowledge but that was told to the witness?

   ○ **A.** Best evidence

   ○ **B.** Secondary evidence

   ○ **C.** Conclusive evidence

   ○ **D.** Hearsay evidence

31. Which mode of DES functions by means of taking each block of cipher text and XORing it with the next plain text block to be encrypted, with the result being a dependency on all the previous blocks?

   ○ **A.** ECB

   ○ **B.** CBC

   ○ **C.** CFB

   ○ **D.** OFB

32. What mode of DES is susceptible to a meet-in-the-middle attack?

　　○　**A.** DES

　　○　**B.** 2DES

　　○　**C.** 3DES

　　○　**D.** 3DES EDE2

33. Which asymmetric cryptosystem is used for digital signatures?

　　○　**A.** DES

　　○　**B.** SHA1

　　○　**C.** Diffie-Hellman

　　○　**D.** ECC

34. When developing the organization's contingency plan, which of the following should *not* be included in the process?

　　○　**A.** Damage-assessment team

　　○　**B.** Legal counsel

　　○　**C.** Salvage team

　　○　**D.** Red team

35. Which of the following is a valid form of attack against ARP?

　　○　**A.** Flooding

　　○　**B.** Spanning tree attack

　　○　**C.** Name server poisoning

　　○　**D.** Reverse lookups

36. Which of the following is considered an authentication type that can use smart cards and certificates?

　　○　**A.** CHAP

　　○　**B.** EAP

　　○　**C.** MS-CHAP

　　○　**D.** PAP

37. Which of the following address ranges is *not* listed in RFC 1918?

　　○　**A.** 10.0.0.0 to 10.255.255.255

　　○　**B.** 172.16.0.0 to 172.31.255.255

　　○　**C.** 172.16.0.0 to 172.63.255.255

　　○　**D.** 192.168.0.0 to 192.168.255.255

38. Which of the following is **not** a reason why email should be protected?

   ○ **A.** Encryption is a difficult, time-consuming process.

   ○ **B.** Faking email is easy.

   ○ **C.** Sniffing email is easy.

   ○ **D.** Stealing email is difficult.

39. Which of the following statements about instant messaging is incorrect?

   ○ **A.** No capability for scripting

   ○ **B.** Can bypass corporate firewalls

   ○ **C.** Lack of encryption

   ○ **D.** Insecure password management

40. ActiveX is used by which of the following technologies?

   ○ **A.** Java

   ○ **B.** CORBA

   ○ **C.** EJB

   ○ **D.** DCOM

41. Which of the following protocols is said to use "a web of trust"?

   ○ **A.** PKI

   ○ **B.** IGMP

   ○ **C.** PGP

   ○ **D.** PEM

42. Which of the following is considered the act of encouraging or inducing a person to commit a crime in order to bring criminal charges against him?

   ○ **A.** Inducement

   ○ **B.** Entrapment

   ○ **C.** Honeypotting

   ○ **D.** Enticement

43. Which of the following terms describes the coalition of nations that have been meeting since the 1970s to solve the world's economic problems?

   ○ **A.** G8

   ○ **B.** MLAT

   ○ **C.** SWAT

   ○ **D.** UN Resolution 1154

44. Which of the following is *not* one of the main BCP testing strategies?

    ○ **A.** Partial interruption

    ○ **B.** Structured walk-through

    ○ **C.** Parallel

    ○ **D.** Full interruption

45. When discussing the BCP, critical resources are usually divided into five primary categories. The categories are which of the following groups?

    ○ **A.** Business, administrative, user, technical, and data

    ○ **B.** Administrative, policy, user, technical, and data

    ○ **C.** Business, facility and supply, user, technical, and nontechnical

    ○ **D.** Business, facility and supply, user, technical, and data

46. Which of the following is *not* one of the three layers used by the Java interpreter?

    ○ **A.** Java language

    ○ **B.** Java script

    ○ **C.** Java libraries

    ○ **D.** Java interpreter

47. Which of the following protocols is used for router multicasting?

    ○ **A.** ICMP

    ○ **B.** RIPv1

    ○ **C.** 224.0.0.1

    ○ **D.** IGMP

48. VoIP uses which of the following because network congestion can be such a critical problem?

    ○ **A.** Time-division multiplexing

    ○ **B.** TCP protocol

    ○ **C.** VLANs technology

    ○ **D.** Isochronous design

49. Which of the following is considered a network technology based on transferring data in cells or packets of a fixed size?

    ○ **A.** ATM

    ○ **B.** ISDN

    ○ **C.** SMDS

    ○ **D.** Frame Relay

50. WEP has vulnerabilities. Which of the following is not a reason why it is vulnerable?

- ○ **A.** Shared WEP keys among all clients
- ○ **B.** An RC4 engine not properly initialized
- ○ **C.** 20-bit initialization vector
- ○ **D.** 40-bit WEP keys

51. You are an advisory board member for a local charity. The charity has been given a new server, and members plan to use it to connect their 24 client computers to the Internet for email access. Currently, none of these computers has antivirus software installed. Your research indicates that there is a 95% chance these systems will become infected after email is in use. A local vendor has offered to sell 25 copies of antivirus software to the nonprofit organization for $400. Even though the nonprofit's 10 paid employees make only about $9 an hour, there's a good chance that a virus could bring down the network for an entire day. They would like you to tell them what the ALE for this proposed change would be. How will you answer them?

- ○ **A.** $423
- ○ **B.** $950
- ○ **C.** $720
- ○ **D.** $684

52. A Common Criteria rating of "structurally tested" means the design meets what level of verification?

- ○ **A.** EAL 1
- ○ **B.** EAL 2
- ○ **C.** EAL 4
- ○ **D.** EAL 5

53. Which of the following is not a valid Red Book rating?

- ○ **A.** A1
- ○ **B.** B2
- ○ **C.** C1
- ○ **D.** C2

54. What Bell-LaPadula model rule states that someone at one security level cannot write information to a lower security level?

- ○ **A.** Star * property
- ○ **B.** Simple security rule
- ○ **C.** Simple integrity property
- ○ **D.** Strong star rule

55. You are an advisory board member for a organization that has decided to go forward with a proposed Internet and email connectivity project. Here are the projected details:

24 computers connected to the Internet

95% probability of virus infection

10 paid employees who make $9 an hour

A successful virus outage could bring down the network for an entire day

25 copies of antivirus software will cost the nonprofit $399

The CEO would like to know how much money, if any, will be saved through the purchase of antivirus software. How much money will be saved?

- ○ **A.** $218
- ○ **B.** $285
- ○ **C.** $380
- ○ **D.** $490

56. Which of the following is considered the first line of defense against human attack?

- ○ **A.** Cryptography
- ○ **B.** Physical security
- ○ **C.** Business continuity planning
- ○ **D.** Policies

57. HVAC should provide which of the following?

- ○ **A.** HVAC should be a closed-loop system with negative pressurization.
- ○ **B.** HVAC should be an open-loop system with positive pressurization.
- ○ **C.** HVAC should be an open-loop system with negative pressurization.
- ○ **D.** HVAC should be a closed-loop system with positive pressurization.

58. Which of the following types of fire detectors uses rate-of-rise sensors?

- ○ **A.** Flame-activated
- ○ **B.** Heat-activated
- ○ **C.** Smoke-activated
- ○ **D.** Ion-activated

59. A fire caused by electrical equipment is considered which class of fire?

- ○ **A.** D
- ○ **B.** C
- ○ **C.** B
- ○ **D.** A

60. While Jim was examining the clapper valve of a failed fire suppression system on the loading dock, he started to wonder whether he installed the right fire suppression system. The facility is unheated and located in a major city in the northeastern United States. Based on this information, which system would you recommend to Jim?

  ○ **A.** Deluge

  ○ **B.** Wet pipe

  ○ **C.** Preaction

  ○ **D.** Dry pipe

Answers to Practice Exam I

1. C	23. A	48. D
2. A 1	24. C	49. A
2. B 1	25. C	50. C
2. C 2	26. A	51. D
2. D 3	27. B	52. B
3. C	28. C	53. A
4. D	29. B	54. A
5. D	30. D	55. B
6. B	31. B	56. B
7. B	32. B	57. D
8. B	33. D	58. B
9. B	34. D	59. B
10. D	35. A	60. D
11. D	36. B	
12. C	37. C	
13. D	38. D	
14. A	39. A	
15. B	40. D	
16. B	41. C	
17. A	42. B	
18. B	43. A	
19. B	44. A	
20. C	45. D	
21. B	46. B	
22. D	47. D	

Question 1

The correct answer is C. A mandatory access control (MAC) model is static and based on clearances on subjects and labels on objects. Therefore, in a MAC-based system, access is determined by the system rather than the user. One feature of this model is security labels. Answer A is incorrect because there is no access control model known as restricted access control. Answer B is incorrect because discretionary access control (DAC) leaves access control up to the owner's discretion. Answer D is incorrect because role-based access control models are used extensively by banks and other organizations that have very defined roles. Chapter 8

Question 2

The correct answer is shown in the table below. Information security models are a key topic that you can expect to be questioned on. While there are more than the four shown in this question, these are some of the most commonly tested. Both Biba and Clark-Wilson are integrity models (note they both have an "i" in their name.) Bell-LaPadula is an example of a confidentiality model whereas the primary purpose of Brewer-Nash is to prevent conflicts of interest. Chapter 5

Integrity (1)	Confidentiality (2)	Conflict of Interest(3)
Biba	Bell-LaPadula	Brewer-Nash
Clark-Wilson		

Question 3

The correct answer is C. Iris recognition functions by analyzing the features that exist in the colored tissue surrounding the pupil to confirm a match. These systems can analyze more than 200 points for comparison. Answer A is incorrect because retina scanning analyzes the layer of blood vessels in the eye. The retina is also more prone to change than the iris. Answer B is incorrect because there is no cornea scan. Answer D is incorrect because there is no optic nerve scan. Chapter 8

Question 4

The correct answer is D. The crossover error rate is defined as a percentage in which a lower number indicates a better biometric system. It is the most important measurement when attempting to determine the accuracy of the system. Answer A is incorrect because there is no crossover acceptance rate. Answer B is incorrect because higher numbers are less accurate. Answer C is incorrect because, again, there is no crossover acceptance rate. Chapter 8

Question 5

The correct answer is D. A biometric system cannot examine all the detail in an object, or it will be prone to false rejection type I errors. Answer A, B, and C are incorrect as Type I errors occur when legitimate users are improperly denied access. If they, however, do not examine enough information about an object they are prone to false accepts type II errors. Type II errors occur when unauthorized individuals are granted access to resources and devices they should not have. Fingerprints are fairly static metrics and some systems are very accurate. Exam candidates should know the difference between Type I and Type II errors and how CER is used. Chapter 8

Question 6

The correct answer is B. A 3- to 4-foot fence will deter only casual trespassers. Answers A, C, and D do not correctly address the question: Fences 2 to 3 feet high can be easily crossed and would not be considered a deterrent. Fences that are 5–7 feet high are considered more difficult to climb than a shorter fence. Fences that are 8 feet high should be used to deter a determined intruder. Chapter 3

Question 7

The correct answer is B. The data owner, who is typically a member of senior management, is responsible for protecting company assets and data. Answer A is incorrect because the user is the individual who uses the documentation. Answer C is incorrect because the data custodian is responsible for maintaining and protecting the company's assets and data. Answer D is incorrect because the auditor makes periodic reviews of the documentation, verifies that it is complete, and ensures that users are following its guidelines. Chapter 10

Question 8

The correct answer is B. A vulnerability is a flaw, loophole, oversight, or error that makes the organization susceptible to attack or damage. Answer A is incorrect because a risk is the potential harm that can arise from an event. Answer C is incorrect because exposure is the amount of damage that could result from the vulnerability. Answer D is incorrect because a threat is a natural or manmade event that could have some type of negative impact on the organization. Chapter 4

Question 9

The correct answer is B. The correct formula to determine single loss expectancy is Single loss expectancy = Asset value × Exposure factor. Answers A, C, and D are incorrect because none is the correct formula. Items to consider when calculating the SLE include the physical destruction or theft of assets, the loss of data, the theft of information, and threats that might cause a delay in processing. Chapter 4

Question 10

The correct answer is D. Quantitative assessment deals with numbers and dollar amounts. It attempts to assign a cost (monetary value) to the elements of risk assessment and to the assets and threats of a risk analysis. To complete the assessment, first estimate potential losses, then conduct a threat analysis, and finally determine annual loss expectancy. Answers A, B, and C do not detail the steps needed to perform a quantitative assessment. Chapter 4

Question 11

The correct answer is D. The Delphi Technique is an example of a qualitative assessment technique. It is not used for quantitative assessment, DRP, or BCP; therefore, answers A, B, and C are incorrect. Chapter 4

Question 12

The correct answer is C. It properly defines the formula for total risk. Total risk is calculated by Threat × Vulnerability × Asset value. Answers A, B, and D are incorrect because they do not properly define the formula. Chapter 4

Question 13

The correct answer is D. Risk acceptance means that the risk has been analyzed and the individuals responsible have decided that they will accept such risk. Answer A is incorrect because risk reduction occurs when a countermeasure is implemented to alter or reduce the risk. Answer B is incorrect because risk rejection means that the responsible party has decided to ignore the risk. Answer C is incorrect because risk transference transfers the risk to a third party. Chapter 4

Question 14

The correct answer is A. Ring 0 is the most trusted ring. The security kernel resides at ring 0, and protection rings support the security of the system. Answers B, C, and D are incorrect because the security kernel is not located at the respective rings. Chapter 5

Question 15

The correct answer is B. Answers A, C, and D would all work; the question asks which would *not* work. Authentication Header (AH) checks the integrity of an IP address and is intrinsically incompatible with Network Address Translation (NAT). Chapter 7

Question 16

The correct answer is B. Registers are considered the temporary storage units within the CPU. CPUs consist of registers, arithmetic/logic unit (ALU), and control circuitry. Answers A, C, and D are incorrect because the I/O buffers, control circuitry, and the ALU are not considered temporary storage units in the CPU. Chapter 5

Question 17

The correct answer is A. The Biba model, which was published in 1977, was the first model developed to address the concerns of integrity. It looks at preventing unauthorized users from making changes to the system and addresses only one goal of integrity (outsiders). Answer B is incorrect because although the Clark-Wilson model is based on integrity, it was not the first model. Answer C is incorrect because the Brewer-Nash model is based on confidentiality. Answer D is incorrect because the Chinese Wall is another name for the Brewer-Nash model. Chapter 5

Question 18

The correct answer is B. Bell-LaPadula was the first model to address the concerns of confidentiality. It was developed in the 1970s and was considered groundbreaking because it supported multilevel security. Although it is well suited for the DoD and government, it is not well suited for modern commercial entities. Answer A is incorrect because the Biba model is an integrity model. Answer C is incorrect because the Graham-Denning model was not the first model to be developed on integrity. Answer D is incorrect because the Clark-Wilson model is another example of an integrity model. Chapter 5

Question 19

The correct answer is B. TCSEC (or the Orange Book) was developed to evaluate the integrity of standalone systems. Answer A is incorrect because the ITSEC is an international standard developed in Europe. Answer C is incorrect because Common Criteria is a global standard that built on TCSEC, ITSEC, and the CTCPEC. Answer D is incorrect because the CTCPEC is the Canadian version of the Orange Book. Chapter 5

Question 20

The correct answer is C. Compartment security mode requires all subjects to have a clearance for most restricted information and a valid need to know. A is not correct because a dedicated security mode would require a clearance for *all* information; this question requires a security clearance for most, not all, information. B is not correct because a system high security mode must have a clearance for all information and a valid need to know for some information. This scenario requires a clearance for most restricted information and a valid need to know. D is not correct because with a multi-level mode some subjects do not have clearance for all information and each subject has a need to know for all information they will access. CISSP candidates must know the four different security modes of operation. Chapter 5

Question 21

The correct answer is B. During the actual exam expect to see some enhanced questions that feature figures or diagrams. There are two methods by which PKI revocation can be handled. The first is a CRL. A CRL is generated and published periodically or after a certificate has been revoked. The second method is the OCSP. OCSP does not mandate encryption, discloses that a particular network host used a specific certificate, and generally places less of a burden on client resources. It does not contain more information. Chapter 6

Question 22

The correct answer is D. The foreign key is correct because it refers to an attribute in one table whose value matches the primary key in another table. Answer A is incorrect because the field refers to the smallest unit of data within a database. Answer B is incorrect because aggregation refers to the process of combining several low-sensitivity items, with the result that these items produce a higher-sensitivity data item. Answer C is incorrect because a composite key is two or more columns that are together designated as the computer's primary key. Chapter 11

Question 23

The correct answer is A. Bluetooth uses frequency-hopping spread spectrum (FHSS). FHSS functions by modulating the data with a narrowband carrier signal that hops in a random but predictable sequence from frequency to frequency. Bluetooth can be susceptible to bluejacking and other forms of attack. Answer B is incorrect because 802.11a uses orthogonal frequency-division multiplexing. Answer C is incorrect because 802.11b uses direct sequence spread spectrum (DSSS) technology. Answer D is incorrect because 802.11g also uses orthogonal frequency-division multiplexing. Chapter 7

Question 24

The correct answer is C. Pulse code modulation (PCM) is the original technique used to digitize voice with 8 bits of sampling 8,000 times per second, which yields 64Kbps for one voice channel. Answer A is incorrect because DAT is digital audio tape and is an analog voice-transmission method. Answers B and D are incorrect because CDMA and GSM are methods for cellular phone transmission. Chapter 7

Question 25

The correct answer is C. Twenty-four DS0 lines are bundled to make one T1. A T1 line has a composite rate of 1.544Mb. Answers A, B, and D are incorrect because 18, 21, and 32 DS0 line bundles do not exist. Chapter 7

Question 26

The correct answer is A. The Synchronous Data Link Control (SDLC) protocol was developed in the mid-1970s for use in Systems Network Architecture (SNA) environments. SDLC is unique in that it was the first synchronous, link layer, bit-oriented protocol. The ISO modified SDLC to create the High-Level Data Link Control (HDLC) protocol and release it as a standard. Answer B is incorrect because ISDN is an end-to-end telephone service that is digital in nature. Answer C is incorrect because Link Access Procedure-Balanced (LAP-B) is a subset of HDLC and is not used by SNA. Answer D is incorrect because X.25 is an efficient protocol developed in the 1970s for packet-switched networks. Chapter 7

Question 27

The correct answer is B. Transaction persistence means that the state of the database security is the same after a transaction has occurred. In addition, there is no risk of integrity problems. Answer A is incorrect because it does not define transaction persistence. Answer C is wrong because transaction persistence does not state that the database should be the same before and after a transaction. Answer D is incorrect because even though databases should be available to multiple users at the same time without endangering the integrity of the data, that fact is not a definition of transaction persistence. Chapter 11

Question 28

The correct answer is C. Aggregation is the capability to combine data from separate sources to gain information. Answer A is incorrect because metadata is data about data. Answer B is incorrect because inference attacks occur when authorized users infer information by analyzing the data they have access to. Answer D is incorrect because deadlocking is a database stalemate. Chapter 11

Question 29

The correct answer is B. A TOC/TOU attack can occur when the contents of a file have changed between the time the system security functions checked the contents of the variables, and the time the variables are actually used or accessed. This is a form of asynchronous attack. Answer A is incorrect because the description describes an asynchronous attack. Answer C is incorrect because the example does not describe a DCOM attack. Answer D is incorrect because although the network might be vulnerable to a Smurf attack, the subsequent lock would not change the status of such an attack. Chapter 5

Question 30

The correct answer is D. Hearsay evidence is not based on personal knowledge, but is information that was told to a witness by another person. It is inadmissible in a court of law. Answer A is incorrect because best evidence is the preferred type of evidence. Answer B is incorrect because secondary evidence is admissible and is usually a copy of original evidence. Answer C is incorrect because conclusive evidence is also admissible. Chapter 9

Question 31

The correct answer is B. Cipher block chaining (CBC) builds a dependency between the blocks of data. To find the plain text of a particular block, you need to know the cipher text, the key, and the cipher text for the previous block. This feature makes CBC unique. Answer A is incorrect because Electronic Code Book is fast but not chained or secure. Answer C is incorrect because cipher feedback (CFB) can be used to emulate a stream cipher and features a feedback function. Answer D is incorrect because output feedback (OFB) can also emulate a stream cipher and can pregenerate the key stream independent of the data. Chapter 6

Question 32

The correct answer is B. 2DES or double DES is no more secure than single DES and is susceptible to a meet-in-the-middle attack. Answers A, C, and D are incorrect because none is susceptible to a meet-in-the-middle attack. Chapter 6

Question 33

The correct answer is D. Elliptic curve cryptosystems (ECC) is an asymmetric cryptosystem created in the 1980s to create and store digital signatures in a small amount of memory. Answer A is incorrect because DES is a symmetric algorithm. Answer B is incorrect because SHA1 is a hashing algorithm. Answer C is incorrect because Diffie-Hellman is used for key exchange. Chapter 6

Question 34

The correct answer is D. The red team's purpose is to penetrate security. Red teams are sometimes called tiger teams or penetration testers. Answers A, B, and C are incorrect because individuals from all those groups should be involved in the contingency-planning process. Chapter 12

Question 35

The correct answer is A. Attackers can attack ARP by flooding the switch and other devices with bogus MAC addresses or by ARP poisoning. Answer B is incorrect because although spanning tree is a valid attack, it is typically used for DoS. Answer C is incorrect because name server poisoning is another type of DNS attack. Answer D is incorrect because a reverse lookup is a term associated with DNS, not ARP. Chapter 7

Question 36

The correct answer is B. EAP is a strong form of authentication that uses more advanced methods of authentication besides passwords. Answers A, C, and D are incorrect because none of these methods use more advanced forms of authentication, such as digital certificates. Chapter 8

Question 37

The correct answer is C. RFC 1918 specifies the addresses that are to be used for private address schemes. Addresses 172.16.0.0 to 172.63.255.255 are not part of the specified range; therefore, answer C is the correct choice. Answers A, B, and D are incorrect because RFC 1918 specifies 10.0.0.0 to 10.255.255.255, 172.16.0.0 to 172.31.255.255, and 192.168.0.0 to 192.168.255.255. Chapter 7

Question 38

The correct answer is D. Stealing email is not difficult because it is clear text and easily sniffed. Email is one of the most popular Internet applications and deserves protection. Although answers B and C are incorrect, they all outline potential vulnerabilities in standard email. Answer A is incorrect as encryption is not difficult. Chapter 10

Question 39

The correct answer is A. Instant messaging (IM) has the capability for scripting, which is one reason it is dangerous for the organization. Answers B, C, and D do not properly answer the question because they are all reasons why IM is vulnerable. IM can bypass corporate firewalls, most versions lack encryption, and IM uses insecure password management. Chapter 10

Question 40

The correct answer is D. The Distributed Object Component Model (DCOM) allows applications to be divided into pieces and objects to be run remotely over the network. Potential vulnerabilities exist because of the way ActiveX is

integrated with DCOM. Answers A and B are incorrect because CORBA is a set of standards that addresses the need for interoperability between hardware and software. Answer C is incorrect because Enterprise JavaBeans (EJB) is designed for enterprise networks. Chapter 11

Question 41

The correct answer is C. Pretty Good Privacy (PGP) uses a web-like model because there are no certificate authorities; there are only end users. Anyone who uses PGP must determine whom they trust: Without a certificate authority, there is no centralized or governing agency to control and validate other users. Answer A is incorrect because PKI does not use a web of trust. Answer B is incorrect because IGMP is used for multicast router group management. Answer D is incorrect because Privacy Enhanced Email (PEM) is an email-security protocol. Chapter 7

Question 42

The correct answer is B. Entrapment is considered the act of tricking a person to commit a crime in order to bring criminal charges against him or her. Although entrapment might be seen as illegal behavior, enticement usually is not. Answer A is incorrect because inducement is the act of bringing about the desired result. Answer C is incorrect because a honeypot is a trap set to detect or slow attempts at unauthorized use of information systems. Answer D is incorrect because enticement is the act of influencing by exciting hope or desire. Chapter 9

Question 43

The correct answer is A. The G8 is a group of economically advanced nations that have agreed to work together to work to solve economic problems. The G8 has now grown to 20 members and is also known as the G20. Answer B is incorrect because Mutual Legal Assistance Treaties (MLATs) are agreements that United States law-enforcement agencies have with law-enforcement agencies in other nations to fight computer crime and terrorism. MLATs are relatively recent developments created to improve the effectiveness of judicial assistance and to regularize and facilitate cooperation. Answer C is incorrect because SWAT is a term used for Special Weapons and Tactics police teams. Answer D is incorrect because UN Resolution 1154 deals with weapons inspections in Iraq. Chapter 10

Question 44

The correct answer is A. The five main types of BCP testing strategies include checklist, structured walk-through, simulation, parallel, and full interruption. Therefore, answers B, C, and D are incorrect because the question asked which is not a valid type. Answer A describes a partial interruption, which is not one of the five valid types. Chapter 12

Question 45

The correct answer is D. Business, facility and supply, user, technical, and data are the five primary categories. Answers A, B, and C are incorrect because they do not describe the five categories. Chapter 12

Question 46

The correct answer is B. The Java script is used by the Java interpreter and is not one of the three layers. Answers A, C, and D do not successfully answer the question, but they do make up the three layers used by the Java interpreter. These include the Java language, which interprets code downloaded from a website; Java libraries, which prevent undesired access to resources and help implement a security policy; and the Java interpreter, which converts the code into native machine code. Chapter 11

Question 47

The correct answer is D. Internet Group Management Protocol (IGMP) is used by hosts to report multicast group memberships to neighboring multicast routers. Security problems exist with IGMP because anyone can start a multicast group or join an existing one. Answer A is incorrect because ICMP is used for logical errors and diagnostics. Answer B is incorrect because the Routing Information Protocol (RIP) is a broadcast-based routing protocol. Answer C is incorrect because although 224.0.0.1 is a multicast address, it is not a protocol used for multicast management. Chapter 7

Question 48

The correct answer is D. VoIP is very time sensitive and, as such, should be based on an isochronous design. This means that the entire system must be engineered to deliver output with exactly the same timing as the input. FireWire is another example of a device that contains an isochronous interface.

Answer A is incorrect because VoIP does not use time-division multiplexing. Answer B is incorrect because VoIP uses UDP for the voice portion of the call, not TCP. Some implementations of VoIP can use TCP for setup and call control. Answer C is incorrect because VLANs are not used for timing and delay problems, but are used to separate the VoIP from general traffic to make it more secure from sniffing. Chapter 7

Question 49

The correct answer is A. ATM creates a fixed channel, or route, between two points whenever data transfer begins, and packages the data into 53-byte fixed-length cells. ATM can be used in LANs, WANs, and MANs. It supports high-bandwidth data needs. Answer B is incorrect because ISDN provides a completely end-to-end digital connection. Answer C is incorrect because Switched Multimegabit Data Service (SMDS) is a low-market-share service used to interconnect LANs. Answer D is incorrect because Frame Relay does not package data into 53-byte fixed-length cells. Chapter 7

Question 50

The correct answer is C. One issue with WEP is the initialization vector (IV); it is 24 bits, not 20. Answers A, B, and D detail some of the vulnerabilities of WEP. For example, WEP uses a single shared key among all clients, which means that you are authenticating groups, not devices or single users. Also, RC4 is the correct encryption type and can be implemented in 40- or 104-bit configuration, but WEP does not properly initialize it. This means that the key values roll over and are predictable. Finally, a 24-bit IV vector is too short, and a 40-bit key is weak. Chapter 7

Question 51

The correct answer is D. The formula for the annual loss expectancy is:

ALE × ARO = SLE, or 0.95 × 720 = $684

Annual rate of occurrence is 95%, or 0.95

Single loss expectancy is ($9 per hour × 8 hours per employee) × 10 employees = $720

Therefore, the nonprofit could expect to lose $684 by not using antivirus software. Chapter 4

Question 52

The correct answer is B. An evaluation that is carried out and meets an evaluation assurance level (EAL) 2 specifies that the design has been structurally tested. Answers A, C, and D are incorrect because EAL 1 = functionally tested; EAL 4 = methodically designed, tested, and reviewed; and EAL 5 = semi-formally designed and tested. Chapter 5

Question 53

The correct answer is A. The Red Book lists the following ratings: B2 Good, C2 Fair, C1 Minimum, and None. Therefore, answers B, C, and D are incorrect because the question asked which is not a valid rating. Chapter 5

Question 54

The correct answer is A. The star * property rule states that someone at one security level cannot write information to a lower security level. Answer B is incorrect because the simple security rule states that someone cannot read information at a higher security level. Answer C is incorrect because the simple integrity property deals with the Biba model, not Bell-LaPadula. Answer D is incorrect because it states that read and write privileges are valid only at the level at which the user resides. Chapter 5

Question 55

The correct answer is B. Annual loss expectancy is calculated this way:

ALE = ARO × SLE or 0.95 × 720 = $684

The annual savings is the ALE minus the cost of the deterrent, or $684 − $399 = $285. Therefore, answers A, C, and D are incorrect Chapter 4

Question 56

The correct answer is B. Physical security is considered the first line of defense against human behavior. Items such as gates, guards, locks, and cameras can be used for physical defense. Answer A is incorrect because cryptography is best used to protect the integrity and confidentiality of data. Answer C is incorrect because business continuity planning should be used to prevent critical outages. Answer D is incorrect because policies are an administrative control. Chapter 3

Question 57

The correct answer is D. HVAC should be a closed-loop system with positive pressurization. Closed loop means that the air inside the building is filtered and continually reused. Positive pressurization should be used to ensure that inside air is pushed out. This is a big safety feature in case the building catches fire. Answers A, B, and C are incorrect because they do not contain both closed-loop systems and positive pressurization. Chapter 3

Question 58

The correct answer is B. Heat-activated sensors can be either rate-of-rise or fixed-temperature sensors. Answer A is incorrect because flame-activated sensors respond to the infrared energy that emanates from a fire. Answer C is incorrect because smoke-activated sensors use a photoelectric device. Answer D is incorrect because there is no category of fire detector known as ion-activated. Chapter 3

Question 59

The correct answer is B. Electrical fires are considered Class C fires. All other answers are incorrect because Class A fires consist of wood and paper products, Class B fires consist of liquids such as petroleum, and Class D fires result from combustible metals. Chapter 3

Question 60

The correct answer is D. A dry pipe system is the preferred fire suppression method for locations that are unheated or subject to freezing. Dry pipe systems are unique in that they use pressurized air or nitrogen. In the event of a fire, the sprinkler head opens and releases the pressurized air. Although these systems do typically use a clapper valve, the term is used here because it might be unfamiliar to many readers. The exam might also use terms that you are not familiar with. All other answers are incorrect because deluge systems release a large amount of water in a very short period of time, wet pipe systems hold water in the pipe, and preaction systems release water into the pipe only when a specified temperature or separate detection device triggers its release. Chapter 3

Practice Exam II

You will have 90 minutes to complete this exam, which consists of 60 questions. You will need to get at least 42 correct. Ensure you read each question and look for details that would rule out any of the answers. Many times there will be two or more correct answers; however, there is only one *best* answer that can be selected. This is a reflection of the real world, where the CISSP often has several options to secure his/her network but one best option. Such is the case when choosing the best encryption to secure data or wireless networks.

Leaving a question blank will count against you, so you are always better off taking your best guess. It's best to work through the entire test once, answering the questions that you can easily answer. On the second pass, work on the more difficult questions. Others you have already answered could help you answer the remaining questions.

Practice Exam Questions

1. What height of fence is required to prevent a determined intruder?

    ○ **A.** 4-foot

    ○ **B.** 6-foot

    ○ **C.** 8-foot

    ○ **D.** None of these is correct.

2. A fire caused by combustible metals would be considered which class of fire?

    ○ **A.** A

    ○ **B.** B

    ○ **C.** C

    ○ **D.** D

3. Controls should work in a layered approach. Review the following diagram; which order does the diagram most closely represent?

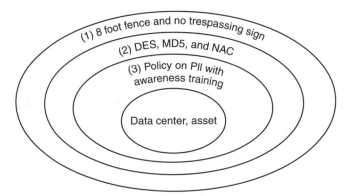

(1) 8 foot fence and no trespassing sign

(2) DES, MD5, and NAC

(3) Policy on PII with awareness training

Data center, asset

Layered defense

    ○ **A.** (1) Physical/preventative, (2) administrative/preventative, (3) technical/ deterrent control layered approach

    ○ **B.** (1) Physical/preventative/deterrent, (2) technical /preventative/detective/, (3) administrative/preventative layered approach

    ○ **C.** (1)Deterrent/preventative, (2) administrative/ detective (3) preventative training

    ○ **D.** (1) Physical/preventative/deterrent, (2) hardware/software preventative (3) administrative/preventative layered approach

4. Which of the following types of card keys contains rows of copper strips?

- ○ **A.** Magnetic strip
- ○ **B.** Electronic circuit
- ○ **C.** Magnetic stripe
- ○ **D.** Active electronic

5. Tony's company manufactures proprietary tractor-trailer tracking devices. Now that employees will be issued laptops, Tony is concerned about the loss of confidential information if an employee's laptop is stolen. Which of the following represents the best defensive method?

- ○ **A.** Use integrity programs such as MD5 and SHA to verify the validity of installed programs.
- ○ **B.** Place labels on the laptops offering a reward for stolen or missing units.
- ○ **C.** Issue laptop users locking cables to secure the units and prevent their theft.
- ○ **D.** Encrypt the hard drives.

6. Under what conditions can halon be expected to degrade into toxic compounds?

- ○ **A.** At temperatures greater than 500° F
- ○ **B.** At temperatures greater than 900° F and concentrations greater than 10%
- ○ **C.** At temperatures greater than 900° F
- ○ **D.** At temperatures greater than 500° F and concentrations greater than 7%

7. According to NIST perimeter lighting standards, critical areas should be illuminated to what measurement?

- ○ **A.** 10 feet in height, with 2 foot-candles of illuminance
- ○ **B.** 12 feet in height, with 4 foot-candles of illuminance
- ○ **C.** 8 feet in height, with 2 foot-candles of illuminance
- ○ **D.** 8 feet in height, with 4 foot-candles of illuminance

8. What type of biometric error signifies that an authorized user has been denied legitimate access?

- ○ **A.** Type I
- ○ **B.** Type II
- ○ **C.** Type III
- ○ **D.** Type IV

9. In biometrics, the point at which the FAR equals the FRR is known as which of the following?

   ○ **A.** Crossover error rate

   ○ **B.** Error acceptance rate

   ○ **C.** Crossover acceptance rate

   ○ **D.** Failure acceptance rate

10. RSA's SecurID is an example of which of the following?

   ○ **A.** SSO system

   ○ **B.** Synchronous authentication

   ○ **C.** Token authentication

   ○ **D.** Asynchronous authentication

11. Which of the following is a weak implementation of EAP?

   ○ **A.** EAP-FAST

   ○ **B.** LEAP

   ○ **C.** PEAP

   ○ **D.** EAP-TLS

12. When discussing the security of SSO systems, which of the following is considered a disadvantage?

   ○ **A.** Single sign-on requires much more maintenance and overhead because all systems are tied together.

   ○ **B.** The biggest disadvantage to single sign-on is that system time on all systems must be held to very tight standards; if deviated from, this can cause serious access problems.

   ○ **C.** There are no real disadvantages to single sign-on.

   ○ **D.** If single sign-on is breached, it offers the intruder access to all systems tied to the SSO implementation.

13. Snort started as what type of system?

   ○ **A.** Behavior-based IPS system

   ○ **B.** Signature-based IDS system

   ○ **C.** Behavior-based IDS system

   ○ **D.** Signature-based IPS system

14. What type of attack is also known as a race condition?

   ○ **A.** Synchronous attack

   ○ **B.** Buffer overflow

   ○ **C.** Asynchronous attack

   ○ **D.** Scanlog attack

15. I/O drivers and utilities are typically found at what protected ring level?

   ○ **A.** Ring 1

   ○ **B.** Ring 2

   ○ **C.** Ring 3

   ○ **D.** Ring 0

16. What type of CPU can interleave two or more programs for execution at any one time?

   ○ **A.** Multiprogramming

   ○ **B.** Multitasking

   ○ **C.** Multiapp

   ○ **D.** Multiprocessor

17. This portion of the CPU performs arithmetic and logical operations on the binary data.

   ○ **A.** I/O buffer

   ○ **B.** Registers

   ○ **C.** Control circuit

   ○ **D.** ALU

18. You are a security consultant for a contracting agency; the agency chief wants to ensure he prevents subjects from writing information to a higher level than the subject's security clearance. He also wants to ensure subjects from a higher level clearance cannot read information at a lower level. They require some type of access control models for their information systems to protect the integrity of their data. What is your best recommendation for a model to use?

   ○ **A.** Bell LaPadula

   ○ **B.** Biba

   ○ **C.** State Machine

   ○ **D.** Clark Wilson

19. What piece of documentation was developed to evaluate stand-alone systems and is a basis of measurement for confidentiality?

   ○ **A.** The Red Book

   ○ **B.** The Orange Book

   ○ **C.** Common Criteria

   ○ **D.** CTCPEC

20. Which level of Orange Book protection is considered mandatory protection and is the first level in which labels are required?

- ○ **A.** B3
- ○ **B.** C2
- ○ **C.** B1
- ○ **D.** A1

21. Which of the following is considered the totality of protection mechanisms within a computer system and is responsible for enforcing security?

- ○ **A.** Rings of protection
- ○ **B.** The security kernel
- ○ **C.** TCB
- ○ **D.** Resource isolation

22. Johnny is worried that someone might be able to intercept and decrypt his VoIP phone calls. Which of the following protocols is most closely associated with VoIP?

- ○ **A.** SKYP
- ○ **B.** SLIP
- ○ **C.** S/MIME
- ○ **D.** SIP

23. Which of the following wireless standards uses direct sequence spread spectrum (DSSS) by default?

- ○ **A.** Bluetooth
- ○ **B.** 802.11a
- ○ **C.** 802.11b
- ○ **D.** 802.11ac

24. What is a rogue AP?

- ○ **A.** An individual connected to an unauthorized modem
- ○ **B.** An unauthorized AP attached to the corporate network
- ○ **C.** An unauthorized modem attached to the network
- ○ **D.** An individual intercepting wireless traffic from inside or outside the organization

25. Pulse code modulation (PCM) is used to digitize a voice with 8 bits of sampling for transmission on a DS0 line. What is the maximum rate of encoding for one of these voice channels?

- ○ **A.** 28.8Kbps
- ○ **B.** 56Kbps

○ **C.** 64Kbps

○ **D.** 128Kbps

26. A T1 uses which of the following to multiplex DS0s into a composite T1?

○ **A.** Channel division

○ **B.** Frequency-hopping spread spectrum

○ **C.** Frequency division

○ **D.** Time division

27. Which of the following focuses on how to repair and restore the data center and information at an original or new primary site?

○ **A.** BCP

○ **B.** BCM

○ **C.** DRP

○ **D.** BIA

28. This type of service is used to provide protection for source code in case the manufacturer declares bankruptcy or goes broke.

○ **A.** Government access to keys

○ **B.** MAD

○ **C.** Electronic vaulting

○ **D.** Software escrow

29. Which of the following describes the cooperative effort between the United States and Europe to exchange information about European citizens between European firms and North American parent corporations?

○ **A.** SB 168

○ **B.** Demar Act

○ **C.** Safe Harbor

○ **D.** Safety Shield

30. Which of the following best describes an approved type of forensic duplication?

○ **A.** Logical copy

○ **B.** Bit copy

○ **C.** Microsoft backup

○ **D.** Xcopy

31. Which of the following best describes the SET protocol?

   ○ **A.** Originated by Victor Miller and Neal Koblitz for use as a digital signature cryptosystem. It is useful in applications for which memory, bandwidth, or computational power is limited.

   ○ **B.** Originated by MasterCard and Visa to be used on the Internet for credit card transactions. It uses digital signatures.

   ○ **C.** Originated by Victor Miller and Neal Koblitz for use as a key exchange cryptosystem. It is useful in applications for which memory, bandwidth, or computational power is limited.

   ○ **D.** Originated by MasterCard and Visa to be used on the Internet for credit card transactions. It uses the SSL protocol.

32. Which of the following information-management systems uses artificial intelligence?

   ○ **A.** Polyinstantiation

   ○ **B.** Known signature scanning

   ○ **C.** Application programming interface

   ○ **D.** Knowledge discovery in databases

33. DNS lookups that are less than 512 bytes are typically performed on which of the following protocols and ports?

   ○ **A.** UDP 53

   ○ **B.** UDP 69

   ○ **C.** TCP 53

   ○ **D.** UDP 161

34. Bob is worried that the program someone gave him at DEFCON has been altered from the original. Which of the following is a valid technique that Bob can use to verify its authenticity?

   ○ **A.** Run AES against the program.

   ○ **B.** Compare the size and date with the version found on the developer's website.

   ○ **C.** Run an MD5sum and check against the MD5sum from developer sites.

   ○ **D.** Calculate a digital signature.

35. Which of the following is not an email encryption security standard?

   ○ **A.** IMAP

   ○ **B.** MOSS

   ○ **C.** PGP

   ○ **D.** PEM

36. Which of the following best describes link encryption?

- ○ **A.** Data is encrypted at the point of origin and is decrypted at the point of destination.
- ○ **B.** The message is decrypted and re-encrypted as it passes through each successive node using a key common to the two nodes.
- ○ **C.** The KDC shares a user-unique key with each user.
- ○ **D.** It requires a session key that the KDC shares between the originator and the final destination.

37. Diameter uses which of the following as a base?

- ○ **A.** TACACS
- ○ **B.** TACACS+
- ○ **C.** RADIUS
- ○ **D.** Kerberos

38. The ACID test is used to describe what?

- ○ **A.** Behavior-based intrusion detection
- ○ **B.** Database transactions
- ○ **C.** Signature-based intrusion detection
- ○ **D.** The strength of a cryptographic function

39. Which fault-tolerant-like system can back up media in much the same way as disk striping?

- ○ **A.** RAID
- ○ **B.** RAIT
- ○ **C.** JBOD
- ○ **D.** MAID

40. Which of the following is a stream cipher?

- ○ **A.** DES
- ○ **B.** Skipjack
- ○ **C.** RC4
- ○ **D.** Twofish

41. Which of the following is considered the weakest mode of DES?

- ○ **A.** Electronic Code Book
- ○ **B.** Cipher Block Chaining
- ○ **C.** Cipher Feedback
- ○ **D.** Output Feedback

42. Which ethical standard states that "access and use of the Internet is a privilege and should be treated as such by all users"?

○ **A.** RFC 1087

○ **B.** ISC^2 Code of Ethics

○ **C.** The Ten Commandments of Computer Ethics

○ **D.** RFC 1109

43. Which of the following would be considered the oldest and most well-known software development method?

○ **A.** Spiral

○ **B.** Clean room

○ **C.** Waterfall

○ **D.** Prototyping

44. Which of the following types of viruses can infect both boot sectors and program files?

○ **A.** File infector

○ **B.** Multipartite

○ **C.** Polymorphic

○ **D.** System infector

45. HTTPS uses TCP and which of the following ports?

○ **A.** 80

○ **B.** 110

○ **C.** 111

○ **D.** 443

46. Which of the following is considered the oldest type of database system?

○ **A.** Hierarchical

○ **B.** Network

○ **C.** Relational

○ **D.** Object-oriented

47. The IEEE separates the OSI data link layer into two sublayers. What are they?

○ **A.** Media MAC Control and Media Access Control

○ **B.** Logical Link Control and Media Access Control

○ **C.** High-Level Data Link Control and Media MAC Control

○ **D.** Data Link Control and Media MAC Control

Questions 48 and 49 refer to the table below

User and Object List

Dwayne	Object 1	Object 2	Object 3
Mike	Write	Read	Read/write
Christine	No access	Read	Read
Betsy	Read/write	Read	Read

48. What does the model shown in the table represent?

- ○ **A.** MAC
- ○ **B.** RBAC
- ○ **C.** LBAC
- ○ **D.** Access Control Matrix

49. Using the model shown in the table, Mike, Christine, Dwayne and Betsy are _____ and Object 1, Object 2, and Object 3 are _____?

- ○ **A.** Objects and subjects
- ○ **B.** Subject and Objects
- ○ **C.** Names of users and resources the users access
- ○ **D.** Names of the users and objects the users access

50. 802.11 networks are identified by which of the following?

- ○ **A.** Security identifier (SID)
- ○ **B.** Broadcast name
- ○ **C.** Kismet
- ○ **D.** Service set identifier (SSID)

51. ISO 17799 evolved from what regional standard?

- ○ **A.** British standard 7799
- ○ **B.** Canadian Trusted Computer Product Evaluation Criteria (CTCPEC)
- ○ **C.** Information Technology Security Evaluation Criteria (ITSEC)
- ○ **D.** Trusted Computer System Evaluation Criteria (TCSEC)

52. A Common Criteria rating of "Functionally Tested" means the design meets what level of verification?

- ○ **A.** EAL 1
- ○ **B.** EAL 2
- ○ **C.** EAL 4
- ○ **D.** EAL 5

53. Which of the following is *not* addressed by the Clark-Wilson security model?

    ○ **A.** Blocks unauthorized individuals from making changes to data

    ○ **B.** Maintains internal and external consistency

    ○ **C.** Protects the confidentiality of the information

    ○ **D.** Blocks authorized individuals from making unauthorized changes to data

54. Which of the following individuals' roles and responsibilities would include the responsibility for maintaining and protecting the company's assets and data?

    ○ **A.** User

    ○ **B.** Data owner

    ○ **C.** Data custodian

    ○ **D.** Security auditor

55. Which of the following is the proper formula used to calculate ALE?

    ○ **A.** Single loss expectancy (SLE) × Annualized rate of occurrence (ARO)

    ○ **B.** Asset value × Annualized rate of occurrence (ARO)

    ○ **C.** Single loss expectancy (SLE) × Annualized rate of occurrence (ARO)

    ○ **D.** Asset value / Annualized rate of occurrence (ARO)

56. Which of the following best describes a qualitative assessment?

    ○ **A.** A qualitative assessment deals with real numbers and seeks to place dollar values on losses. These dollar amounts are then used to determine where to apply risk controls.

    ○ **B.** A qualitative assessment assigns ratings to each risk.

    ○ **C.** A qualitative assessment is performed by experts or external consultants who seek to place dollar values on losses.

    ○ **D.** A qualitative assessment is performed by experts or external consultants, is based on risk scenarios, and assigns non-dollar values to risks.

57. The facilitated risk assessment process is an example of what?

    ○ **A.** A BCP analysis technique

    ○ **B.** A quantitative assessment technique

    ○ **C.** A DRP analysis technique

    ○ **D.** A qualitative assessment technique

58. Classification levels like *confidential* and *secret* are tied to which data classification scheme?

- ○ **A.** ISO 17799
- ○ **B.** U.S. Department of Defense (DoD)
- ○ **C.** RFC 2196 Site Security Guidelines
- ○ **D.** Commercial Data Classification Standard (CDCS)

59. Which of the following methods of dealing with risk is considered the least prudent course of action?

- ○ **A.** Risk reduction
- ○ **B.** Risk rejection
- ○ **C.** Risk transference
- ○ **D.** Risk acceptance

60. Your employer is pleased that you have become CISSP-certified and would now like you to evaluate your company's security policy. Your boss believes that encryption should be used for all network traffic and that a $50,000 encrypted database should replace the current customer database. Based on what you know about risk management, upon what should your decision to use encryption and purchase the new database be based? Choose the most correct answer.

- ○ **A.** If an analysis shows that there is potential risk, the cost of protecting the network and database should be weighed against the cost of the deterrent.
- ○ **B.** If an analysis shows that the company's network is truly vulnerable, systems should be implemented to protect the network data and the customer database.
- ○ **C.** If the network is vulnerable, systems should be implemented to protect the network and the database, regardless of the price.
- ○ **D.** Because it is only a customer database and the company is not well known, the probability of attack is not as great; therefore, the risk should be accepted or transferred through the use of insurance.

Answers to Practice Exam II

1. D	26. D	51. A
2. D	27. C	52. A
3. B	28. D	53. C
4. A	29. C	54. C
5. D	30. B	55. C
6. B	31. B	56. D
7. C	32. D	57. D
8. A	33. A	58. B
9. A	34. C	59. B
10. B	35. A	60. A
11. B	36. B	
12. D	37. C	
13. B	38. B	
14. C	39. B	
15. B	40. C	
16. A	41. A	
17. D	42. A	
18. B	43. C	
19. B	44. B	
20. C	45. D	
21. C	46. A	
22. D	47. B	
23. C	48. D	
24. B	49. B	
25. C	50. D	

Question 1

The correct answer is D. A fence will not prevent a determined intruder. Although fences can deter an intruder, a determined individual could drive through the fence, cut the fence, blow up the fence, and so on. The best design to deter a determined intruder is 8 feet high with three strands of barbed/razor wire. Chapter 3

Question 2

The correct answer is D. Class D fires result from combustible metals. All other answers are incorrect: Class A fires consist of wood and paper products, Class B fires consist of liquids such as petroleum, and Class C fires are electrical fires. Chapter 3

Question 3

The correct answer is B. Defense in depth can be presented in many ways. It can be layers of the same control or different controls. The outer layer is physical/preventative/deterrent, the second layer is technical/preventative/ detective, the third layer is administrative/preventative. When facing this type of question, always identify which type of control you are dealing with: physical, administrative, or technical. Then determine the purpose of the control: detective, preventive, corrective, etc. Chapter 4

Question 4

The correct answer is A. Magnetic strip card keys contain rows of copper strips. Answers B, C, and D are incorrect: electronic circuit card keys have embedded electronic circuits, magnetic stripe card keys have a stripe of magnetic material, and active electronic cards can transmit data. Chapter 8

Question 5

The correct answer is D. Hard-drive encryption offers the best defense against the loss of confidentiality. Answer A is incorrect because integrity programs validate the integrity of installed software but do not validate its confidentiality. Answer B is incorrect; reward labels might or might not encourage someone to return equipment but, again, will not protect its confidentiality. Answer C is incorrect because locking cables might prevent someone from removing a laptop but won't prevent someone from accessing data on the device. Chapter 2

Question 6

The correct answer is B. If halon is deployed in concentrations of greater than 10% and in temperatures of 900° F or more, it degrades into hydrogen fluoride, hydrogen bromide, and bromine. This toxic brew can be deadly. Answers A, C, and D are incorrect because concentrations must be 10% or greater and temperatures must reach 900° F. Chapter 3

Question 7

The correct answer is C. The NIST standard for perimeter protection using lighting is that critical areas should be illuminated with 2 candle-feet of illuminance at a height of 8 feet. Answers A, B, and D do not match the NIST standards. Chapter 3

Question 8

The correct answer is A. A Type I error occurs when a biometric system denies an authorized individual access. Answer B is incorrect because a Type II error occurs when an unauthorized individual is granted access. Answers C and D are incorrect because Type III and IV errors do not exist. Chapter 8

Question 9

The correct answer is A. When comparing biometric systems, the most important item to consider is the crossover error rate (CER). The CER is the point at which the false acceptance rate meets the false rejection rate. The CER relates to the accuracy of the biometric system. Answers B, C, and D are not correct because there are no biometric measurements known as error acceptance rate, crossover acceptance rate, or failure acceptance rate. Chapter 8

Question 10

The correct answer is B. RSA's SecurID is an example of synchronous authentication. RSA SecureID devices or tokens use a one-time password that uses a clock that synchronizes the authenticator to the authentication server during the authentication process. Each individual passcode is valid for only a very short period, normally 60 seconds or less and is used with a user name and password for two-factor authentication. Answer A is incorrect because RSA's SecurID might be part of an SSO system, but this is not an accurate answer. Answer C is incorrect because although the RSA's SecurID fob itself might be considered a token, it is not the *best* answer available out of the four to choose from. Answer D is incorrect because asynchronous authentication devices are not *synchronized* to the authentication server. These devices use a challenge-response mechanism. Chapter 8

Question 11

The correct answer is B. LEAP is considered a weak version of EAP. It makes use if a modified version of CHAP and as such does not adequately protect the authentication process. Answers A, C, and D would all be examples of strong versions of EAP. These stronger options include EAP-FAST, PEAP, or EAP-TLS. Chapter 7

Question 12

The correct answer is D. Single sign-on (SSO) offers the attacker potential access to many systems tied to SSO when authenticated only once. Answer A is incorrect because it is can be breached and offers the intruder access to all systems. SSO does not require much more maintenance and overhead. Answer B is incorrect because although SSO systems such as Kerberos do require clock synchronization, this is not the overriding security issue. Answer C is incorrect because all systems have some type of flaw or drawback. Chapter 8

Question 13

The correct answer is B. Snort started as a signature-based IDS system. Today, Snort has grown to include behavior-based features. A signature-based system examines data to check for malicious content. When data is found that matches one of these known signatures, it can be flagged to initiate further action. Answer A is incorrect because Snort is not a behavior-based IPS system. Answer C is incorrect because Snort is not a behavior-based IDS system. Answer D is incorrect because although Snort is signature-based, it is considered an IDS system, not an IPS system. IPS systems are unlike IDS systems in that IPS systems have much greater response capabilities and allow administrators to initiate action upon being alerted. Chapter 8

Question 14

The correct answer is C. Asynchronous attacks are sometimes called race conditions because the attacker is racing to make a change to the object after it has been changed but before it has been used by the system. Asynchronous attacks typically target timing. The objective is to exploit the delay between the time of check (TOC) and the time of use (TOU). Answers A, B, and D are incorrect because they do not adequately describe a race condition. Chapter 5

Question 15

The correct answer is B. Rings of protection run from ring 0 to ring 3. Ring 2 is the location of I/O drivers and utilities. Answers A, C, and D are incorrect because ring 1 contains parts of the OS that do not reside in the kernel, ring 3 contains applications and programs, and ring 0 is the location of the security kernel. Chapter 5

Question 16

The correct answer is A. Multiprogramming CPUs can interleave two or more programs for execution at any one time. Answer B is incorrect because multitasking CPUs have the capability to perform one or more tasks or subtasks at a time. Answer C is incorrect because there is no type of processor known as multiapp. Answer D is incorrect because the term *multiprocessor* refers to systems that have the capability to support more than one CPU. Chapter 5

Question 17

The correct answer is D. The ALU portion of the CPU performs arithmetic and logical operations on the binary data. Answers A, B, and C are incorrect because I/O buffers, registers, and the control circuits do not perform arithmetic and logical operations. Chapter 5

Question 18

The correct answer is B. The Biba model is integrity-based and will not allow a subject to write to a higher security level or read from a lower security level. Answer A is the Bell-LaPadula model and is based on confidentiality. Answer C, the State Machine model, seeks to see if one state is valid before moving to another. Answer D, the Clark-Wilson model, is an integrity model and is designed to address all goals of integrity. Chapter 5

Question 19

The correct answer is B. The Orange Book's official name is the Trusted Computer System Evaluation Criteria (TCSEC). It was developed to evaluate standalone systems for confidentiality. Answer A is incorrect because the Red Book was developed to evaluate integrity and availability. It is also known as Trusted Network Interpretation (TNI). Answer C is incorrect because Common Criteria is a combined version of TCSEC, ITSEC, and the CTCPEC. Answer D is incorrect because the Canadian Trusted Computer

Product Evaluation Criteria (CTCPEC) is the Canadian version of the Orange Book. Chapter 5

Question 20

The correct answer is C. The Orange Book rates systems as one of four categories. Category A is verified protection, B is mandatory protection, C is discretionary protection, and D is minimal protection. B1 is the first level in which labels are required. Therefore, answers A, B, and D are incorrect. Chapter 5

Question 21

The correct answer is C. The Trusted Computer Base (TCB) is the totality of protection mechanisms within a computer system. This includes hardware, firmware, software, processes, and some inter-process communications. These items are responsible for enforcing security. Answer A is incorrect because rings of protection are designed to protect the operating system. Answer B is incorrect because the security kernel is the most trusted portion of the operating system. Answer D is incorrect because although resource isolation is an important part of implementing security, it is not the totality of protection mechanisms. Chapter 5

Question 22

The correct answer is D. Session Initiation Protocol (SIP) is an application-layer request-response protocol used for VoIP. SIP is transported by UDP, makes use of TCP, and is vulnerable to sniffing attacks. More details can be found in RFC 2543. Answer A is incorrect because there is no protocol SKYP; the proprietary protocol named Skype offers encryption and is used for a peer-to-peer Internet phone service. Answer B is incorrect because SLIP is used by ISPs for dialup connections. Answer C is incorrect because S/MIME is used to secure email. Chapter 7

Question 23

The correct answer is C. 802.11b uses direct sequence spread spectrum (DSSS) technology. DSSS is a transmission method that transmits the data along with a chipping bit to increase the signal's resistance to interference. Answer A is incorrect because Bluetooth uses frequency-hopping spread spectrum. Answer B is incorrect because 802.11a uses orthogonal frequency-division multiplexing. Answer D is incorrect because 802.11ac uses MIMO-OFDM. Chapter 7

Question 24

The correct answer is B. A rogue AP is an unauthorized AP attached to the corporate network. These unauthorized APs represent one of the biggest threats to any secure network. Answer A is incorrect because a connection to an unauthorized modem is not a valid answer. Answer C is incorrect because attaching a modem is not the definition of a rogue AP. Answer D is incorrect because connecting to an unsecured network is not a rogue AP but might be considered an act of war driving. Chapter 7

Question 25

The correct answer is C. Pulse code modulation (PCM) is used to digitize voice with 8 bits of sampling 8,000 times per second, which yields 64Kbps for one DS0 channel. Answers A, B, and D are incorrect because 28.8Kbps, 56Kbps, and 128Kbps are not the rates of transmission for one DS0 channel. Chapter 7

Question 26

The correct answer is D. T1s use time division to break the individual DS0s into 24 separate channels. Time division is the allotment of available bandwidth based on time. It allows the T1 to carry both voice and data at the same time. Answer A is incorrect because there is no system known as channel division. Answer B is incorrect because FHSS is used by mobile devices. Answer C is incorrect because T1s do not use frequency division. Chapter 7

Question 27

The correct answer is C. The disaster recovery plan (DRP) focuses on how to repair and restore the data center and information at an original or new primary site. Answer A is incorrect because the business continuity plan (BCP) is focused on the continuation of critical services. Answer B is incorrect because business continuity management (BCM) is about building a framework for a capable response. Answer D is incorrect because a business impact analysis (BIA) is the functional analysis used to identify the potential impact if an outage occurred. Chapter 12

Question 28

The correct answer is D. Software escrow agreements are used to provide protection for source code in case the manufacturer declares bankruptcy or goes broke. The three items that are most critical in this agreement are where the code will be deposited, under what conditions the code will be released, and the terms of use of the source code upon its release to the user. Answer A is incorrect because government access to keys deals with the government's desire to maintain cryptographic keys used by industry. Answer B is incorrect because mutually assured destruction (MAD) is a term not associated with software protection. Answer C is incorrect because electronic vaulting is a term that describes the bulk transfer of data. Chapter 12

Question 29

The correct answer is C. The Safe Harbor Act describes the cooperative effort between the United States and Europe to exchange information about European citizens between European firms and North American parent corporations. It was enacted because of the large numbers of individuals who have been victims of identity theft and because of the increase of misuses of personal information laws and agreements. Answer A is incorrect because although SB 168 deals with privacy, it is a state law that took effect in 2002, preventing businesses from using California residents' Social Security numbers as unique identifiers. Answer B is incorrect because there is no law known as the Demar Act. Answer D is incorrect because the name of the act is not Safety Shield. Chapter 4

Question 30

The correct answer is B. A bit copy, or physical copy, captures all the data on the copied medium and reproduces an exact copy that includes hidden and residual data, slack space, swap contents, deleted files, and other data remnants. This allows the examiner to perform an analysis of the copy and store the original. Answer A is incorrect because a logical copy will not completely duplicate the structure of the original media. Answer C is incorrect because Microsoft backup is not an approved product for forensic analysis. Answer D is incorrect because although Xcopy can duplicate files, it does not provide a bit-level copy of the original medium. Chapter 9

Question 31

The correct answer is B. Secure Electronic Transaction (SET) was developed by MasterCard and Visa to be used on the Internet for credit card transactions. It uses digital signatures. Answer A is incorrect because SET is not used for digital signatures. Answer C is incorrect because SET is not used for key exchange, and Victor Miller and Neal Koblitz are the creators of ECC. Answer D is incorrect because SET does not use SSL. Chapter 6

Question 32

The correct answer is D. Knowledge Discovery in Databases (KDD) is an artificial intelligence method used to identify useful patterns in data; as such, it provides a type of automatic analysis. Answer A is incorrect because polyinstantiation is a technique used to prevent inference violations. Answer B is incorrect because known signature scanning is a method used to detect computer viruses. Answer C is incorrect because the application programming interface (API) is in no way associated with artificial intelligence. Chapter 11

Question 33

The correct answer is A. Although RFC 1035 does allow DNS lookups over TCP this service is provided for only when lookups are greater than 512 bytes; typically UDP 53 is used. Answers B, C, and D are incorrect because UDP 69 is used for TFTP, TCP 53 is used for zone transfers, and UDP 161 is used for SNMP. Chapter 7

Question 34

The correct answer is C. Running an MD5sum would be the best way for Bob to verify the program. MD5sum is a hashing algorithm. Answer A is incorrect because AES is a symmetric algorithm and will not help Bob verify the program. Answer B is incorrect because the size and date might match the information found on the developer's website, but the program might have still been altered. Answer D is incorrect because a digital signature will not verify the integrity of the program. Chapter 6

Question 35

The correct answer is A. IMAP is associated with email, but it is not an email security standard, it is a protocol to receive email and excels over POP3 when working with mail on multiple devices/clients \ it also leaves a copy on the server. Although answers B, C, and D are all incorrect, they do specify valid email security standards: MIME Object Security Services (MOSS), Pretty Good Privacy (PGP), and Privacy Enhanced Email (PEM). Chapter 6

Question 36

The correct answer is B. With link encryption, the message is decrypted and re-encrypted as it passes through each successive node using a key common to the two nodes. Answers A, C, and D are incorrect because they all describe end-to-end encryption. Chapter 6

Question 37

The correct answer is C. Diameter uses RADIUS as a base and is considered the next generation of authentication, authorization, and accounting services for the Internet with over 16 million attribute variable pair (AVP) tags for negotiation. Answer A is incorrect because TACACS is not considered a base for Diameter. Answer B is incorrect because TACACS+ is a Cisco protocol but is widely used. Answer D is incorrect because Kerberos is not associated with Diameter but is considered a single sign-on technology. Chapter 8

Question 38

The correct answer is B. Programmers involved in database management talk about the ACID test when discussing whether a database management system has been properly designed to handle transactions. The ACID test addresses atomicity, consistency, isolation, and durability. Answer A is incorrect because the ACID test does not deal with behavior-based IDS systems. Answer C is incorrect because ACID is not related to signature-based IDS systems. Answer D is incorrect because the ACID test is not related to the strength of a cryptographic function. Chapter 11

Question 39

The correct answer is B. Redundant Array of Inexpensive Tape (RAIT) is used to back up systems by means of a tape array that stripes the data across the tape. Answer A is incorrect because RAID is not typically used for backup. Answer C is incorrect because JBOD (Just a Bunch of Disks) offers no backup or fault tolerance. Answer D is incorrect because MAID (Massive Array of Inactive Disks) is not a type of tape backup. Chapter 10

Question 40

The correct answer is C. RC4 is a stream cipher. It has been implemented in products such as SSL and WEP. Answer A is incorrect because DES is a block cipher with a 56-bit key size. Answer B is incorrect because Skipjack is a block cipher with a default 80-bit key size. Answer D is incorrect because Twofish is a 256-bit key size block cipher. Chapter 6

Question 41

The correct answer is A. Electronic Code Book (ECB) is fast and simple but is also the weakest mode of DES. Answer B is incorrect because Cipher Block Chaining (CBC) is not the weakest mode of DES. Answer C is incorrect because Cipher Feedback (CFB) is more secure than ECB and OFB. Answer D is incorrect because Output Feedback (OFB) is not the weakest, but it can't detect integrity errors as well as CFB. Chapter 6

Question 42

The correct answer is A. The statement "access and use of the Internet is a privilege and should be treated as such by all users" is part of RFC 1087, which is titled "Ethics and the Internet". Answer B is incorrect because the statement is not part of the ISC^2 Code of Ethics. Answer C is incorrect because the statement is not part of the Ten Commandments of Computer Ethics. Answer D is incorrect because RFC 1109 addresses network management, not ethics. Chapter 4

Question 43

The correct answer is C. The waterfall method is the oldest and one of the most well-known methods for developing software systems. It was developed in the 1970s and is divided into phases. Each phase contains a list of activities that must be performed before the next phase can begin. Answer A is incorrect because the spiral model is a combination of the waterfall and prototyping methods. Answer B is incorrect because the clean room software development method focuses on ways to prevent defects rather than ways to remove them. Answer D is incorrect because prototyping was developed in the 1980s to overcome weaknesses in the waterfall method. It is a four-step process: develop an initial concept, design and implement an initial prototype, refine the prototype until it is acceptable, and then complete and release the final version of the software. Chapter 11

Question 44

The correct answer is B. A multipartite virus can infect both boot sectors and program files. Answer A is incorrect because file infector viruses infect files. Answer C is incorrect because a polymorphic virus is one that has the capability to change. Answer D is incorrect because system infector viruses infect system files. Chapter 9

Question 45

The correct answer is D. HTTPS uses TCP and port 443. Answer A is incorrect because port 80 is used for HTTP, answer B is incorrect because port 110 is used for POP3, and answer C is incorrect because port 111 is for network file service. Chapter 7

Question 46

The correct answer is A. Hierarchical databases link records in a tree structure so that each record type has only one owner. Hierarchical databases date from the information management systems of the 1950s and 1960s. Answer B is incorrect because network databases were not the first. Answer C is incorrect because although relational databases are the most widely used, they were not the first. Answer D is incorrect because they were not the first but were designed to overcome some of the limitations of relational databases. Chapter 11

Question 47

The correct answer is B. IEEE divides the OSI data link layer into sublayers. The upper half is the Logical Link Control (LLC) layer and the lower half is the Media Access Control (MAC) layer. The LLC is based on HDLC; the MAC is where 802.3 addressing is performed. Answers A, C, and D are incorrect because none of these terms matches the proper definition of the sublayers of the data link layer. Chapter 7

Question 48

The correct answer is D. An access control matrix is used to associate the relationship and rights of subjects and objects. A is not the correct answer because MAC uses security labels on objects and clearances for subjects. Answer B is incorrect because RBAC would be based on roles and containers, not users. C is incorrect as LBAC is based on the interaction between any combination of objects and subjects. LBAC provides upper and lower limits for a user. Chapter 8

Question 49

The correct answer is B. Subjects are the active entity, objects are the passive entity. A subject does not have to be a person; it can be an application. However, in this scenario the subject—the active entity—is the list of names. A C, and D are not the correct answers because these are not the definition of a subject and object. It's important that anyone preparing for the exam become intimately familiar with the CBK terminology. Chapter 8

Question 50

The correct answer is D. A service set ID (SSID) is used to identify 802.11 networks. The SSID is a 32-bit character string that acts as a shared identifier and that some describe as a very weak password. The SSID is used to differentiate one WLAN from another. Answer A is incorrect because a security ID (SID) is an identifier used in conjunction with Microsoft domains. Answer B is incorrect because a broadcast name is not the means of identifying a WLAN. Answer C is incorrect because Kismet is a Linux software program used to sniff wireless traffic. Chapter 7

Question 51

The correct answer is A. British standard 7799 formed the underpinnings of the later-developed ISO 17799. This document is considered the code of practice for information security management. Answers B, C, and D are incorrect because the Canadian Trusted Computer Product Evaluation Criteria, Information Technology Security Evaluation Criteria, and Trusted Computer System Evaluation Criteria did not form the underpinnings of the later-developed ISO 17799. Chapter 5

Question 52

The correct answer is A. An evaluation that is carried out and meets an evaluation assurance level (EAL) of 1 specifies that the design has been functionally tested. Answers B, C, and D are incorrect because EAL 2 = structurally tested; EAL 4 = methodically designed, tested, and reviewed; and EAL 5 = semi-formally designed and tested. Chapter 5

Question 53

The correct answer is C. Clark-Wilson does not provide for the confidentiality of the information; Clark-Wilson deals with all three goals of integrity. Answers A, B, and D are all incorrect because the question asks which aspect Clark-Wilson does not address. Chapter 5

Question 54

The correct answer is C. The data custodian is responsible for maintaining and protecting the company's assets and data on a macro level. Answer A is incorrect because the user is the individual who uses the documentation. Answer B is incorrect because the data owner is responsible for protecting the data. Answer D is incorrect because the auditor makes periodic reviews of the documentation and verifies that it is complete and that users are following its guidelines. Chapter 2

Question 55

The correct answer is C. Single loss expectancy (SLE) × Annualized rate of occurrence (ARO) is the formula used to determine ALE. Answers A, B, and D are incorrect because they are not the formulas used to calculate ALE. Chapter 4

Question 56

The correct answer is D. A qualitative assessment ranks the seriousness of threats and sensitivity of assets into grades or classes, such as low, medium, and high. It is performed by experts or external consultants and is based on risk scenarios. Although purely quantitative risk assessment is not possible, purely qualitative risk analysis is. Answers A, B, and C are incorrect because they do not adequately describe qualitative risk assessment. Chapter 4

Question 57

The correct answer is D. The facilitated risk-assessment process (FRAP) is an example of a qualitative assessment technique. It is not used for BCP, quantitative assessment, or DRP; therefore, answers A, B, and C are incorrect. Chapter 4

Question 58

The correct answer is B. The U.S. Department of Defense data classification standard classifies data as unclassified, sensitive, confidential, secret, and top secret. Answer A is incorrect because ISO 17799 is an international security standard policy. Answer C is incorrect because RFC 2196 is the site security handbook and does not address data-classification standards. Answer D is incorrect because there is no CDCS standard. Chapter 2

Question 59

The correct answer is B. Risk rejection is the least acceptable course of action because individuals have decided that risk does not exist and are ignoring it. Answer A is incorrect because risk reduction occurs when a countermeasure is implemented to alter or reduce the risk. Answer C is incorrect because risk transference transfers the risk to a third party. Answer D is incorrect because risk acceptance means that the risk is analyzed, but the individuals responsible have decided that they will accept such risk. Chapter 4

Question 60

The correct answer is A. Risk management requires that vulnerabilities be examined, that loss expectancy be calculated, that a probability of occurrence be determined, and that the costs of countermeasures be estimated. Only then can it be determined whether the value of the asset outweighs the cost of protection. It is possible that the cost of protection outweighs the value of the asset. Whereas some risk assessments use dollar amounts (quantitative) to value the assets, others use ratings (qualitative) based on breaches of confidentiality, integrity, and availability to measure value. Chapter 4

Index

Numbers

A

C

N

S

X-Y

Z